READER'S DIGEST

EXPLORING
THE
SECRETS
OF
NATURE

READER'S DIGEST

EXPLORING THE SECRETS OF NATURE

Published by The Reader's Digest Association Limited
LONDON · NEW YORK · SYDNEY · CAPE TOWN · MONTREAL

Contributors

CONSULTANT EDITOR
Michael Bright, BSc

TECHNICAL EDITOR
Chris Catton, MA

EDITOR John Palmer
ART EDITOR Neal Martin

EXPLORING THE SECRETS OF NATURE
was edited and designed by The Reader's
Digest Association Limited, London.

First Edition Copyright © 1994
The Reader's Digest Association Limited,
Berkeley Square House, Berkeley Square,
London W1X 6AB.
Copyright © 1994 Reader's Digest
Association Far East Limited.
Philippines Copyright © 1994 Reader's Digest
Association Far East Limited.

Printed in Belgium

ISBN 0 276 42107 8

The typefaces used in this book are:
ITC Century light condensed; ITC Cerigo;
Trade Gothic condensed.

AUTHORS
Tim Birkhead, BSc, DPhil, DSc
Robin Dunbar, BA, PhD
Peter Evans, BA
Anne Gatti
David Helton
Conor Jameson, BA
Sanjida O'Connell, BSc

CONSULTANTS
Clair Brunton, BSc, DPhil
John A Burton
Phil Chapman, BSc, MSc
Barry Clark, PhD
Roland Emson, BSc, PhD
Jim Flegg, BSc, PhD
Christopher O'Toole
Geoffrey Potts, BSc, PhD
Ian Redmond, BSc, CBiol
Robert Stebbings, PhD, FI Biol
Martin Wells, MA, ScD

ARTISTS
Richard Bonson
Andrew DaVolls
Sarah Fox-Davies
Malcolm McGregor
Gill Tomblin

Inset, spine *What appears to be the head of a small viper about to strike is actually the tail of a harmless caterpillar. The bold eye markings and and snake-like appearance were evolved by a Costa Rican moth as a defence against hungry birds.*

Cover and contents page *A clownfish peers out from the embrace of an anemone's tentacles. To most small fish, the stings on these appendages are deadly – the anemone's method of providing itself with a meal. But to the clownfish they form a haven against predators. Its immunity may be due to its slimy covering, and it repays the anemone's hospitality by cleaning up food particles.*

Half title page *A pair of black-browed albatrosses may remain faithful to each other from their first attempt at breeding until the death of one partner perhaps 20 years later. Males of other species may mate with 30 or 40 females in a single season. Why animals adopt such different breeding strategies is one of the secrets of courtship and mating.*

Title page *A herd of oryx flees. By staying together rather than scattering, as they twist and turn to escape from danger, the members of the herd make it difficult for a predator to select a target.*

Opposite *The orang-utan was once thought to be man's closest relative, and its eyes seem to express an almost human intelligence. Though not the smartest of the apes, it maintains an elaborate mental map of which trees in the forest will be fruiting at what time of year, and has a sense of 'self' and 'others'.*

Contents

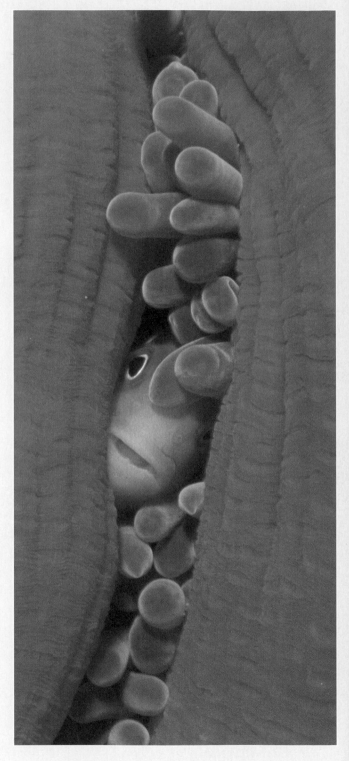

Introduction

Many long-held beliefs about animal behaviour
have been challenged by the discoveries made by
a new generation of naturalists aided by such
modern devices as video cameras, tape recorders
and radio-tracking transmitters.

For many years it was asserted that animals acted
almost entirely by instinct, and that intelligence
played only the smallest role in their behaviour.
Meticulous observation, however, now suggests
that many animals are in fact rational creatures,
capable of making choices and decisions in matters
that affect their lives – in building their homes,
for instance, in finding food or in avoiding
predators. Moreover, it now appears that animals
can learn from one another and pass on their
wisdom to others of their species.

It is in the light of these new theories and exciting
discoveries about the animal world that *Exploring
the Secrets of Nature* has been prepared.

CONSULTANT EDITOR

LAUNCHING INTO LIFE

'THE INFANT, AS SOON AS NATURE WITH GREAT PANGS OF TRAVAIL
HATH SET IT FORTH FROM THE WOMB OF ITS MOTHER INTO THE
REGIONS OF LIGHT, LIES, LIKE A SAILOR CAST OUT FROM THE WAVES
NAKED UPON THE EARTH IN UTTER WANT AND HELPLESSNESS.'
≈ FRANCIS BACON, *COGITATIONES DE NATURA RERUM*, 1604.

The moment of birth is a major milestone. For weeks or months, or perhaps even years, the mother animal has been directing all her energies towards this moment. Now a new life has begun, to carry her genetic make-up into the next generation.

Animals will go to incredible lengths to make sure their family line continues. Some animal parents invest all their energies in producing vast numbers of eggs and then leave them to take their chances. Others produce fewer offspring but put more effort into nurturing them. Whichever strategy the animal adopts, the moment eventually arrives when a new individual opens its eyes on the world for the first time. For the parents, this is nothing less than a major success. But for the newborn, it is the first step along a road fraught with danger – a road which, with luck, will lead to maturity and a family of its own.

Sexual selection
In summer, water fleas give birth to live young that are all females and are identical copies of their mothers. In autumn, they produce males. Then males and females mate and lay eggs that can survive drought and cold.

Safe on father's feet
Emperor penguin chicks hatch in the Antarctic winter. While the father incubates the egg, the mother remains at sea, returning with food for the chick soon after it hatches.

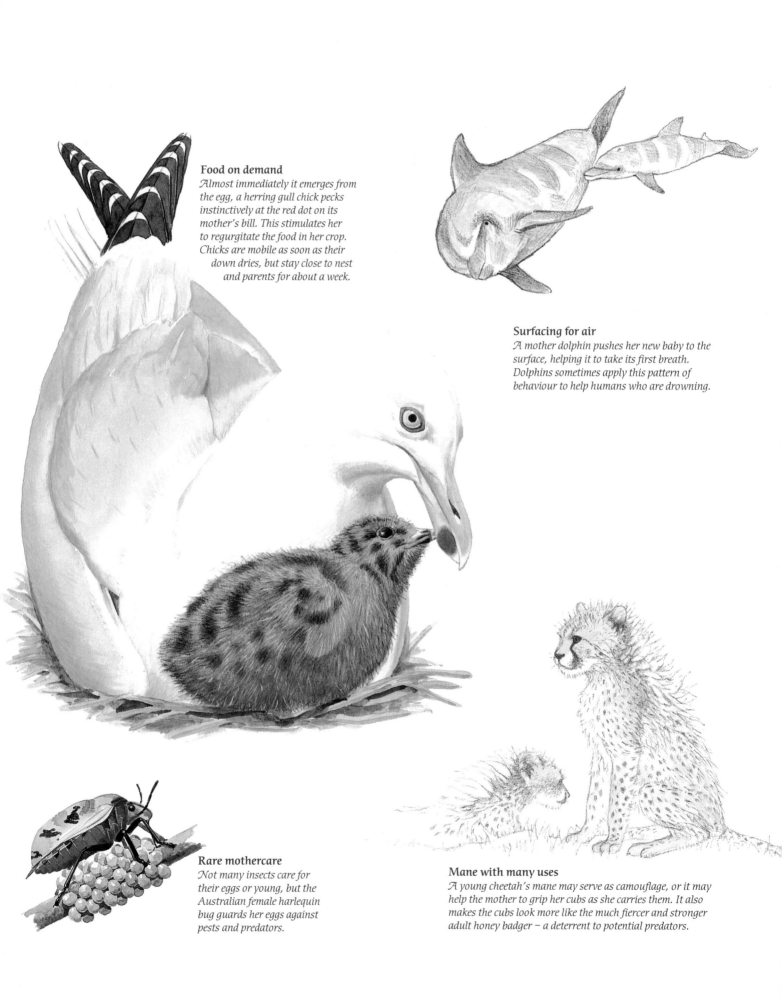

Food on demand
Almost immediately it emerges from the egg, a herring gull chick pecks instinctively at the red dot on its mother's bill. This stimulates her to regurgitate the food in her crop. Chicks are mobile as soon as their down dries, but stay close to nest and parents for about a week.

Surfacing for air
A mother dolphin pushes her new baby to the surface, helping it to take its first breath. Dolphins sometimes apply this pattern of behaviour to help humans who are drowning.

Rare mothercare
Not many insects care for their eggs or young, but the Australian female harlequin bug guards her eggs against pests and predators.

Mane with many uses
A young cheetah's mane may serve as camouflage, or it may help the mother to grip her cubs as she carries them. It also makes the cubs look more like the much fiercer and stronger adult honey badger – a deterrent to potential predators.

THE SOCKEYE SALMON'S EPIC JOURNEY

Each summer, a generation of sockeye salmon comes in from the wide Pacific and travels up to the headwaters of the North American rivers that gave it birth. It is coming home to breed and die.

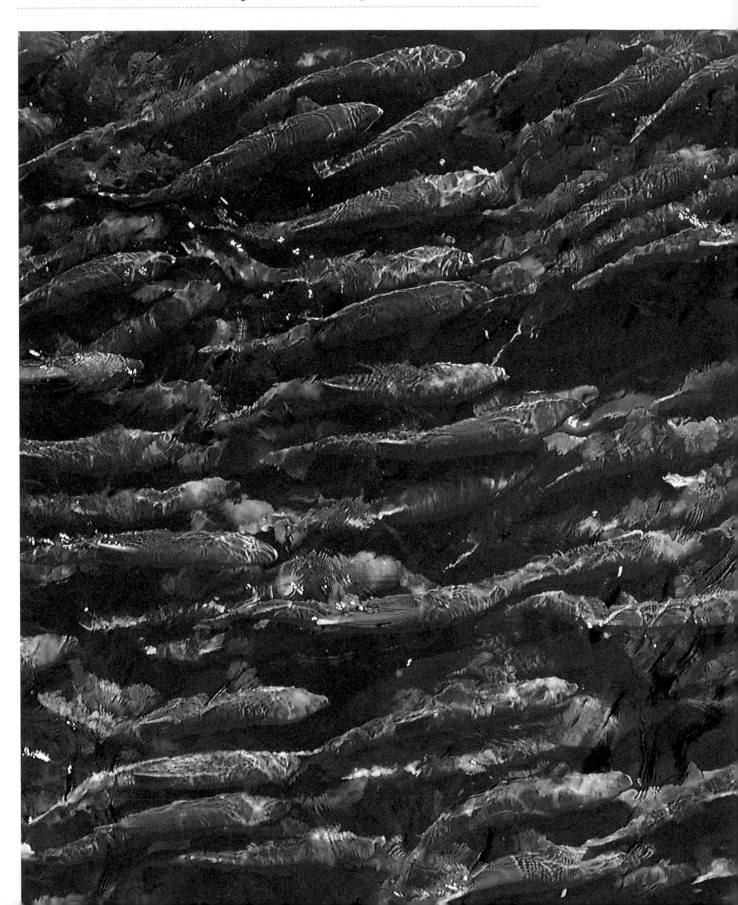

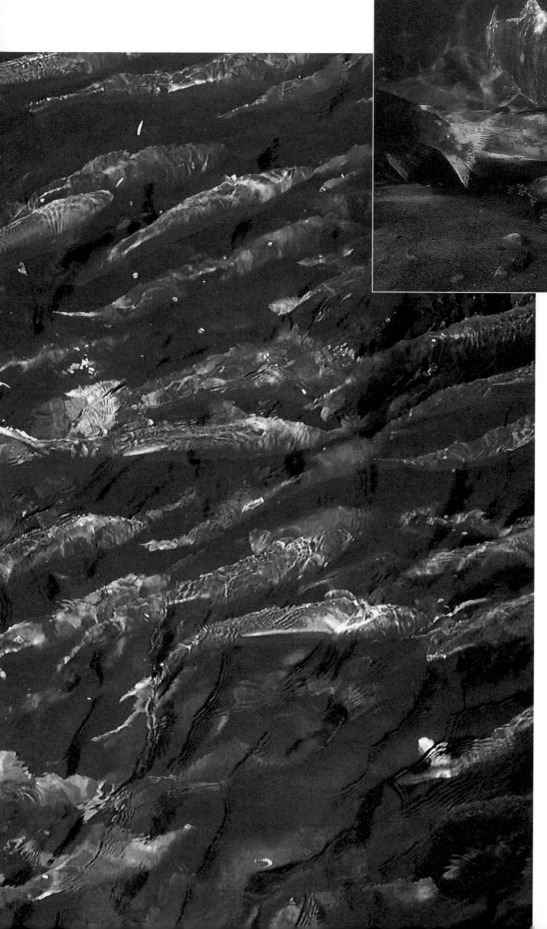

Pacific salmon make a final run upriver

In spring or early summer, the sockeye salmon living in the far distances of the Pacific set out on the journey of a lifetime. They were born six years earlier in the headwaters of North American rivers. Now it is time to return, responding to a long-remembered scent. From the coast, the salmon surge upriver to their birthplace, a trek of maybe another 1500 miles (2400 km).

When waterfalls block the way, the salmon leap them, thrashing their powerful tails until they have climbed the wall of water. Once they reach their goal, the fish mate, scooping shallow nests in the gravel and laying thousands of eggs. Then they die in hosts, their energy spent. But many of their offspring will survive, the inheritors and recipients of ancestral genes and ancestral urges.

Predestined ordeal *Following the same routes as a million forebears, Pacific sockeye salmon return to the river of their birth. After mating many die exhausted (inset), but in years to come their offspring will make the same journey from ocean to river, beckoned by the well-remembered scent of their home water. Each section of river has its distinctive smell, concocted of the soil and vegetation of the land it drains.*

11

RISKING DEATH TO REPRODUCE

The tideline where land and sea meet has an ancestral pull for many creatures. Some answer it still, many at their peril.

The fish that breed on a Californian beach

Every March, when the moon is full, the beaches along the Pacific coast of southern California are silvered by the shiny bodies of grunion in their millions. These small fish strand themselves in a ribbon stretching along the water's edge as far as the eye can see and, as each wave breaks over the sand, it brings in a fresh cargo to lie writhing on the shore.

The females wriggle themselves swiftly into the sand by thrashing their tails until they are wedged upright with only their heads sticking out. Each male grunion selects a partner and bends himself about her to deposit his sperm, or milt, as she lays her eggs. The next wave washes the pair back into the sea.

If the grunion get their timing right and the females lay their eggs at exactly the right spot, the fertilised eggs remain undisturbed in the damp sand during the ensuing two weeks, out of reach of any sea predators, until the gravitational pull of moon and sun combine to raise the highest tide of the month. As the waves thunder across the sands of the spawning ground, their vibrations trigger the hatching of the eggs.

The grunion's breeding method seems hazardous and inevitably a many are left stranded above the waterline to provide an easy meal for gulls – a fate that also awaits many of the eggs and hatchlings. Present-day grunion have inherited their dangerous practice from a myriad of earlier generations, but why they should have adopted it in the first place remains a mystery. Perhaps long ago there were fewer predators on the shoreline, so the eggs were safer on the beach than at sea. If so, then at that time, the risk was worth taking.

Annual stranding *Each year, grunion risk death to mate on Californian beaches, for they soon suffocate out of the water. A male curves round a female (inset) to fertilise her eggs, which stay buried in the sand for two weeks and hatch at the next high tide.*

Prisoners of a past before the dinosaurs

Horseshoe crabs are not really crabs at all. They are distant relatives of scorpions and spiders. Their smooth shells give them an oddly alien air, but in fact they are among the oldest of the Earth's inhabitants, and their appearance has changed very little in almost 200 million years.

In early summer, horseshoe crabs drag themselves from the sea to lay their eggs along the sandy beaches of the eastern United States, much as their ancestors did before the days of the dinosaurs. The females scrape a shallow nest in the sand in which each lays up to 80 000 eggs. As they do so the males cling to them with their forelegs, preparing to fertilise the eggs as soon as they are laid.

Tough, horseshoe-shaped shells protect the crabs from predators, but their small, greenish eggs provide a feast for birds that flock to the beaches to gorge. Some birds making their annual migration from South America to their Arctic breeding grounds may well time their journey to coincide with the peak bounty of eggs.

With such a large array of hungry mouths waiting to seize the eggs it is difficult to understand why the crabs lay them in the sand rather than at sea. To some extent they are prisoners of a pattern developed in the remote past. Yet in the modern world too they are perfectly successful. Not even the armies of their predators can consume all the eggs, and the survivors ensure the continuance of the species.

Crabs bounty *In May thousands of horseshoe crabs emerge from the sea to breed on the eastern US coast. Each female lays some 80 000 eggs in a nest in the sand. Laughing gulls are among the many species that gorge on the eggs.*

Red crabs make annual pilgrimage to the shore

Christmas Island lies in the Indian Ocean some 200 miles (320 km) south of Java. Tropical rain forest covers most of it, forming a habitat for 120 million red land crabs that feed on flowers and fruit on the forest floor, and occur nowhere else on Earth.

The crabs have little competition, because few other terrestrial creatures have found their way to the island. Although their distant ancestors came from the sea, the crabs are now creatures of the land since they breathe air and cannot swim. But despite the success of their colonisation, their larvae can still develop only in the sea.

Each year millions of crabs leave their forest burrows and head for the coast to breed. Many die on the way and those that arrive are at some risk of drowning. Mating takes place on the

Red tide *On Christmas Island, hundreds of thousands of red land crabs swarm out of the rain forest in November and march down to the coast to breed.*

shore, and each female carries thousands of eggs in the brood pouch under her tail down to the tide line. There she shakes them into the waves. Some females are swept away, but many survive and return to the forest. The eggs hatch in the sea and the larvae develop there, struggling ashore as miniature crabs after 25 days.

Eight-week navigational feat by green turtles

Every two or three years, in November, numbers of green turtles strike out from their home near the Brazilian coast to begin an epic journey of over 1250 miles (2000 km). Their goal is Ascension Island, a land fragment of only 34 sq miles (88 km²) in the middle of the South Atlantic. They reach land about eight weeks later, having swum 30 miles (50 km) or so a day, and mate offshore.

Under cover of darkness, the female turtles drag themselves up the island's beaches. There, each laboriously digs a hole in the sand in which she lays around 140 eggs.

The slow dance of the continents around the globe may partly explain the turtles' extraordinary journey. About 120 million years ago, the African and American continents began to move apart and the Atlantic was born. As volcanic islands appeared in the ocean, the ancestors of some Brazilian turtles nested on them in order to escape mainland predators.

Adult turtles usually return to the beach of their birth to breed, but the pounding of the Atlantic has reclaimed most of the islands, leaving only Ascension above the waves. Time has compounded the turtles' problem, ever-lengthening their journey as South America moves steadily farther from the turtles' breeding island.

Journey's end *A beach on Ascension Island is the goal of a female green turtle's long swim. She drags herself across the sand and, with her flippers, digs a nest to receive her eggs. It may take several attempts before the job is finished – built for movement in the water, she is weighed down by her inflexible shell and finds breathing difficult.*

PLOYS FOR PRESERVING EGGS

Many different methods are used to keep eggs safe in a dangerous world, and to give them the conditions they need for development.

Tree frogs hang their eggs from branches

In southern Africa, the grey tree frog has evolved an original means of protecting its eggs from predators and keeping them moist at the same time. The frog spends most of its life in trees, and at egg-laying time, in the rainy season, the female carries her smaller mate to a tree branch overhanging a short-lived pond or puddle. Here the pair may be joined by several more males, and together they begin to build a nest from a liquid excreted by the female.

In the cool of the night, the males beat the liquid into a foam with their hind legs, rather in the way that cooks beat egg whites. The female then lays her eggs, which are fertilised by her mate as they emerge, into this foamy nest.

The morning sun turns the nest into a half-baked meringue, with a hard-crusted outer surface round a moist interior. The eggs develop inside, safe from the drying sun and birds, until the tadpoles are ready to emerge and slip into the water below.

A similar device is used by grey sea slugs, which live on rocky shores between high and low tide marks. They surround their tiny, white eggs with a layer of jelly that keeps them all moist while the tide is out.

Eggs in jelly *A grey sea slug lays as many as 30 000 small white eggs in an intricate spiral within a layer of jelly.*

Frog spawn with a difference *To keep their eggs moist, grey tree frogs in the arid, tree-scattered plains of southern Africa lay them into a lather of foam (below). The foam nest hangs from a tree branch until the tadpoles are ready to emerge. Then their determined wriggling churns up the damp interior and wets the outer crust. The nest crumbles, launching them into a puddle (left).*

Marines safeguard young turtles' nests

It was the misfortune of the Pacific olive ridley turtle that it became the basis of a large commercial enterprise in Mexico. Its flesh, skin, oil and shell were all eagerly sought after, endangering the creature's very existence. At one time, thousands of olive ridley turtles might haul themselves out onto beaches together to dig nests in the sand. Most turtle species nest at night, but olive ridley turtles, like the Kemp's ridley turtles of the Atlantic, come ashore to nest during the day.

Ancestrally, mass breeding may have been a means of ensuring their survival. By coordinating the laying of their eggs, turtles overwhelm predators with numbers. Sea birds and vultures await the swarms of hatchlings that emerge simultaneously from the sand and dash toward the ocean. Inevitably many hatchlings are eaten, but there are far too many of them for the predators to catch them all.

However, this defence proved inadequate against the demands of industry. Fortunately, however, the Mexican government decided to safeguard the turtles, and even put marine guards over the nesting sites. Many eggs, too, are now hatched in the safety of government incubators.

Mass invasion *An army of Pacific olive ridley turtles swims shorewards to a Costa Rican beach to dig nests and to lay their eggs in the warm sand.*

Tough eggs for some tough customers

Beachcombers everywhere are certain to be familiar with the mermaid's purse – a tough, rectangular pouch, 2 in (50 mm) long, with a long trailing tendril at each corner. This seashore curiosity is actually an egg case of a skate or a dogfish, or one of the other smaller members of the shark family. Quite

Shaped to survive *Once it is laid, a horned shark's corkscrew-shaped egg may work its way into the soft seabed as water currents wash around it.*

unlike any other fish egg, it is a yolk-filled sac protected by a hardy outer coating, whose long tendrils anchor it to seaweed.

Even more remarkable is the egg of the horned shark – a corkscrew shape that, aided by the movement of currents and tides, may well enable the egg to bury itself in the sandy sea floor. It may also be a device for anchoring the egg to the seabed at the moment of laying. This is to some extent backed by reports of female horned sharks picking their eggs up in their mouths and wedging them into rock crevices, to prevent them being washed away.

Precarious perches for fairy tern eggs

Fairy terns exercise some of the most alarming nesting habits in the avian world. They balance their eggs on the bare branches of trees, or on stark rock ledges which are hardly bigger than the egg itself.

These terns seem the very spirit of the tropical and subtropical seas in which they spend most of their lives. So delicate is their soapsud-white plumage that it appears almost transparent in flight. The birds may breed in almost any month on almost any rock or island that takes their fancy, making no effort to collect nesting material. Perhaps this is because some of their chosen coral or volcanic sites are more or less bare of vegetation.

Precision placement

Some of this seeming carelessness is compensated by the precision of the fairy tern's egg-laying technique. The female tern selects the place with the exactness of a darts player, placing the egg upon it with an audible click. And there, without budging, it stays. Vitally so, for if an egg laid on a bare branch can move by as little as ³⁄₈ in (10 mm), it will probably fall and smash.

Both parent terns sit on their egg in turn, one on duty while the other feeds at sea. When the chick hatches, it stays stock still, never moving from the spot until it is ready to fly, about five weeks later.

Balancing act *The fairy tern's black eyes and black bill (right) stand out strongly against the dazzling white of its plumage. At breeding time the terns lay eggs lodged in places such as a knot in a bare tree branch (above).*

Its extra long claws give it a grip on its inhospitable perch, and its parents feed it on such oceanic fare as fish and shrimps.

However precarious their nesting site may be, once they have selected it, fairy tern pairs return to it regularly in a breeding cycle of nine or ten months. It is almost as though their security of habit compensates for the insecurity of the nesting place.

Whatever the reason, fairy terns are among the most successful of bird species that breed on oceanic islands. Probably, despite the risk of their eggs falling from the nest site, they are safer from predation than if they had been laid in scrapes in the ground – which is the type of nest preferred by many other tern species, including the Australian fairy terns.

INSTANT MEALS FOR NEWBORN INSECTS

The survival of the young is best assured by laying eggs directly onto food. Some insects have evolved ingenious means of achieving this.

The passion flowers that fight back

There are numerous species of heliconiine butterflies in Central America and like most species of butterfly and moth, they have favoured plants on which they lay their eggs so that their offspring will have food when they hatch. The heliconiine butterflies always lay theirs on passion flowers, the sole diet of their caterpillars.

Because the caterpillar spends all its time on the same plant until it becomes an adult, the female butterfly always makes a close inspection so as to be sure that no other eggs have been laid there first. Too many eggs laid on one plant will result in all the available food being consumed before the caterpillars turn into butterflies. So if a female finds that eggs have already been laid on a plant, she flies off in search of another.

Some passion flowers seem to have evolved a mechanism to take advantage of this. To avoid being eaten by caterpillars, the flowers produce their own fake eggs — lumps of yellow tissue on their tendrils. These look so much like heliconiine butterfly eggs that the females shun them.

Big wasps have little wasps . . .

The larvae of *Rhyssa*, a type of ichneumon wasp, are parasites that feed on the larvae and pupae of wood wasps. This would not appear to be easy, for the larvae of wood wasps eat the wood of fir trees, and lead a sheltered life in tunnels 1 in (25 mm) or more beneath the tree bark. But *Rhyssa* wasps long ago evolved means of overcoming this difficulty.

A *Rhyssa* female must first detect a wood-wasp larva. She does this by searching the bark of likely trees and tapping it with her antennae. Once she picks up the vibrations of a larva, the *Rhyssa* wasp circles round, tapping the bark rapidly and repeatedly. Then she lifts her abdomen high in the air, preparing to insert her ovipositor – the tube through which she will lay her eggs.

This beautifully adapted tube is almost as long as the rest of her body, though no thicker than a horsehair. When not in use it is protected by two stout sheaths, but these are now withdrawn and the ovipositor drills into the wood to seek out the wood-wasp larva. The holes she drills are not always directly above the larva, but once the tip of the wasp's ovipositor touches the larva, a single egg is squeezed down the tube, to be planted next to, or on top of, the doomed host.

When the egg hatches, the *Rhyssa* larva eats the larva of the wood wasp and then pupates – spins a cocoon in which to develop

Egg dish *A chalcid wasp inserts an egg into the egg of a cabbage moth. Once hatched, the wasp larva will feed on the cabbage-moth egg and destroy it.*

into an adult – in the safety of the ready-made tunnel. The following year, the new *Rhyssa* wasp will find its way to the surface of the fir trunk prepared to plague a new generation of wood wasps.

Calling card of the chalcid wasp

Chalcid wasps are minute, and are specialists in appropriating other insects' eggs and larvae; there is one species, in fact, that lays its eggs inside those of 150 different kinds of insects.

The wasps' senses of touch and smell are extremely acute, and both are employed in finding a host. With her antennae, a female searches out suitable eggs, in each of which she places one of her own eggs with her ovipositor. While she is doing so, the wasp also leaves evidence of her handiwork by coating the outside of each of the host's eggs with her own scent. This is to notify other female chalcid wasps that these eggs have been attended to and they should seek alternative hosts elsewhere.

To complicate the issue further, some chalcid wasps put their eggs inside the larvae of other chalcid wasp species. They insert their ovipositors through the hosts' bodies and into those of the wasp larvae.

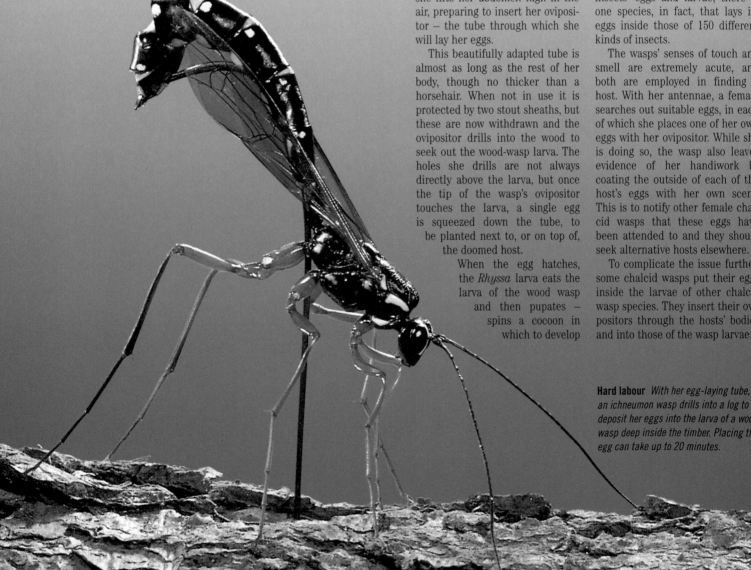

Hard labour *With her egg-laying tube, an ichneumon wasp drills into a log to deposit her eggs into the larva of a wood wasp deep inside the timber. Placing the egg can take up to 20 minutes.*

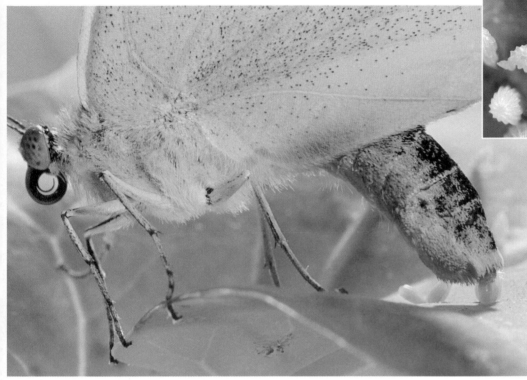

Easy pickings *The caterpillars (above) of the cabbage white butterfly (left) hatch from eggs laid on cabbage leaves. The caterpillars then feed on the leaves until ready to become butterflies.*

Finding offspring a good food supply

Ladybirds have no trouble laying their eggs near food for their young. They eat aphids throughout their lives, so need only take time off from consuming prey to place eggs on the undersides of leaves on which the aphids are feeding. When the ladybird larvae hatch, they have a good chance of getting an instant meal. But for many other species, the process of finding food that suits their young is not quite as simple.

Butterflies generally feed on nectar, but their larvae – caterpillars – eat leaves. A newly hatched caterpillar is too small to look for food, so its mother lays her eggs on a suitable plant. She checks the leaves by 'tasting' them with sensors on her feet and antennae.

Insects whose larvae feed on large mammals have a greater problem, as most mammals have developed ways of removing parasitic eggs from their fur. Grooming, washing and wallowing in mud are all habits that make it difficult for insect eggs to survive for long on a prospective host.

A South American botfly has evolved a roundabout solution to this problem. Instead of laying her eggs directly on a host, the female botfly catches a bloodsucking fly and sticks her eggs along its abdomen. The bloodsucker then carries the eggs with it to its next meal. As it feeds, the eggs hatch instantly and the botfly larvae burrow into the host's skin.

Insects that provide edible protection

Certain insects have made such efficient adaptations that they not only lay their eggs near food, but use the same material to provide shelter as well. Champions among them must be leaf-rolling weevils and the gall wasps.

The female birch-leaf roller makes two neat, S-shaped cuts across a birch leaf, one on each side of the central rib. With her legs, the weevil rolls half the birch leaf into a cone, then wraps the other half round the cone in the other direction. Upon completing the structure, she goes inside and lays a number of eggs in slits on the leaf's inner surface. Finally she tucks a fold over the end of the leaf cone to seal the eggs in safely and provide food and protection for the young when they hatch.

Gall wasps save themselves the trouble of building by getting plants to do it for them. They lay their eggs in plant tissues, often at the tip of a shoot or within a leaf bud. When an egg hatches, the larva begins eating the material around it, stimulating a growth of abnormal tissue.

A home for all

In time, the larvae are surrounded by a mass of large cells – a gall. On its inner surface, the gall produces tissues rich in starch, sugar and protein that the larvae feed upon throughout their growth.

There are also some vegetarian insects that, unable to stimulate host plants into producing galls, have become parasites of the gall wasp, laying their eggs in ready-formed galls – 75 different insect species have been found in oak apple galls, although not all of them at one time.

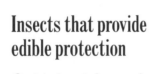

Floral home *The spiky red bloom of a robin's pincushion (above) is the home of a group of gall wasp larvae (right). It provides them with food and shelter until they are ready to become adults. The plant tissue is thought to be stimulated to grow by secretions deposited onto the eggs by the wasp. These cause changes in the dividing plant cells that develop into a gall, or a gathering of large cells.*

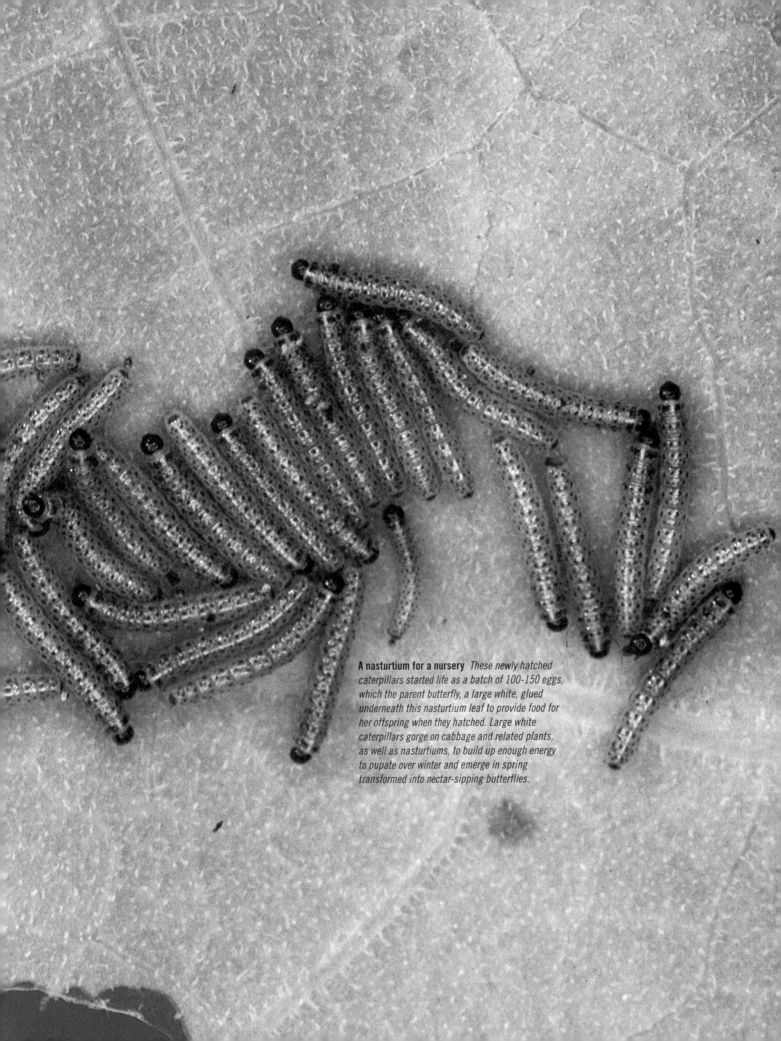

A nasturtium for a nursery *These newly hatched caterpillars started life as a batch of 100-150 eggs, which the parent butterfly, a large white, glued underneath this nasturtium leaf to provide food for her offspring when they hatched. Large white caterpillars gorge on cabbage and related plants, as well as nasturtiums, to build up enough energy to pupate over winter and emerge in spring transformed into nectar-sipping butterflies.*

WHY EGG DESIGN MATTERS

Of all Nature's engineering feats, few are more remarkable than the egg, precision-tailored over ages to suit the needs of each species.

How an egg's shape protects the embryo

Although all birds' eggs are oval, there are significant differences between those laid by various species. The more rounded types, for example, are generally laid by birds that nest in holes, or in deep cups where their rolling will not cause problems. Owls' eggs are rounder than most, and the eggs of swifts and swallows are long and narrow. Birds such as guillemots, which nest on precipitous rock ledges, lay sharply tapered eggs that roll in tight circles, and which have shells that are thickened at the pointed end.

The hard shell of a bird's egg is a defence against predators. An inexperienced predator may be discouraged by the difficulty of picking up an object that is so smooth, hard and round. Turtles' eggs, on the other hand, are soft and have a leathery shell. As they are buried in the sand until they hatch, a hard shell is of no benefit to them.

Insects can lay their eggs almost anywhere, because their eggs have very efficient life-support systems. Most have a surface structured so that it traps a layer of air, enabling the embryo developing within to breathe, no matter where the egg has been laid. Insects can therefore deposit their eggs near a food supply and then abandon them.

This may be the reason why further parental care is so rare in the insect world. Among the least caring of insect parents must be the sepsid fly, which lays its eggs in cowpats. Inside, the atmosphere must be suffocating, but each egg is equipped with a long breathing tube that protrudes through the surface of the dung.

Cliff hanger *Brünnich's guillemots (right) breed on sea-facing cliff ledges and lay a single egg on the bare rock. Their eggs are tapered ovals that roll in a tight circle, so do not fall off the ledge.*

Eggs burden small birds more than big ones

The largest bird's egg ever laid is believed to have been that of the elephant bird of Madagascar, now extinct. This 10 ft (3 m) tall creature produced eggs that tipped the scales at 24 lb (11 kg). Today's largest bird is the African ostrich, whose 6 ft (1.8 m) tall females lay eggs weighing about 3 lb (1.4 kg).

But if egg weight is related to bird size, the performance of some of the smaller birds is even more impressive. Large though it is, an ostrich egg represents only one per cent of the female's body weight. But though the world's smallest bird, the Cuban bee hummingbird, lays eggs that are no bigger than peas, they represent over six per cent of the female's body weight. In other words, were it ostrich-sized, its eggs would be six times heavier than those of the ostrich. Even more remarkable is the fact that the bee hummingbird flies while carrying this weight, whereas the burden of the flightless ostrich requires far less effort.

Usually, the size of a bird's egg is determined by the size of the bird, although differing lifestyles can lead to modifications. Waders and game birds, for instance, lay larger eggs than many birds of similar size because their chicks leave the nest on hatching. The chicks then start to forage for themselves, so need to be well developed. But species whose chicks stay in the nest and are fed for some time by their parents produce smaller eggs.

Heavy burden *The world's largest eggs in relation to body weight are laid by New Zealand's kiwis. Each cream-coloured egg can weigh as much as 25 per cent of the hen's weight; it sustains the embryo chick over an incubation period of 9-12 weeks.*

Why birds' eggs are different in colour

Birds' eggs get their colour from pigments laid on the egg shell while it is within the female. Birds whose eggs are stationary in the oviduct while colours are being deposited have spotted eggs, but those species whose eggs move about have streaked coloration.

Birds that build cup-shaped nests in trees often lay pale blue eggs, and for a long time it was believed that this pale blue colour was designed to imitate spots of sun on the leaves and so confuse predators. Recent studies, however, have disproved this theory; they show that the colour of the egg makes little difference because

predators usually find the nest before they have seen the eggs.

Birds that nest in holes and those that sit tight when danger threatens often have white or unmarked eggs. So do birds like ducks and geese, which hide their eggs beneath their own feathers or cover them with vegetation when they leave the nest to feed.

Egg camouflage is most highly developed among birds such as the lapwing, which try to lead predators away from the nest, and in so

Now you see it, now you don't *Ringed plovers lay eggs (right) that are cleverly camouflaged to blend in with their surroundings. If a predator approaches, the parent tries to draw it away from the nest by feigning a broken wing. Turtles (below) bury their eggs in holes in the sand, so the eggs need no camouflage.*

doing leave the eggs unattended. Their eggs are patterned with spots and blotches in colours that blend with the background, breaking up the outlines and making them very difficult to pick out.

For cuckoos, egg pattern is particularly important because they

have to lay eggs that look like their host's. Though cuckoos produce a range of patterns, an individual female can lay only one pattern of egg. She probably inherits the egg pattern from her mother, and then chooses the right nest by finding the species that raised her.

PROTECTING THE UNBORN

Few times in an animal's life are more hazardous than its beginnings. So various wiles have evolved to ensure that the family line continues.

Mussels act as fishes' foster-parents

Bitterlings are small and silvery fishes found in lakes and slow-moving rivers, and are remarkable for their egg-laying habits. They deposit them inside freshwater mussels. Since mussels snap their tough shells closed at the first hint of danger, they provide excellent protection for the eggs. But first the bitterling has a problem – how to get the eggs inside the mussel?

As the breeding season draws near, a female bitterling grows an egg-laying tube (or ovipositor) so long that the tip reaches past the 2-3 in (50-75 mm) long fish's tail fin and trails behind her. She uses it to insert her eggs into the respiratory tube with which the mussel draws in water, so that they are carried to its gill chamber.

First, however, she must get the mussel to relax so that it will not close its shell while she is laying. She repeatedly nudges it with her mouth until it gets used to the disturbance. As she lays her eggs, the male bitterling swims past and releases its sperm, which are inhaled by the mussel and fertilise the eggs in its gill chamber.

The eggs develop in the safety of the mussel's shell, bathed in the steady stream of oxygen-rich water flowing over the creature's gills. A month after the eggs were laid, the young bitterlings swim out of the breathing tube into the river. The mussel spawns at the same time, and until they are ready to settle, the mussel larvae hitch a ride on the bodies of the young fishes.

Mussel bound *A Japanese female bitterling pushes her egg-laying tube into the inhaling tube of a freshwater mussel preparatory to injecting her eggs. The male hovers close by, ready to release his sperm. It is the male bitterling that selects a territory containing a suitable mussel, and defends it against rivals.*

Lizard nursery in a termite mound

One of many quandaries that occur in Nature is whether an animal is better served by spending energy protecting the young through the first vulnerable period of life, or if instead it should use the energy to seek for food and perhaps to mate and breed again.

Evolution has produced different solutions to this dilemma. Some species produce and abandon huge numbers of young; others produce very few, which they cosset almost into adulthood. A third group has avoided the problem altogether by getting someone else to do the work in their stead. The Australian lace monitor lizard belongs to the third group.

The lizard lives in a landscape of termite mounds. Each mound is air-conditioned by tunnels that give the termites a secure, moist and warm environment – and provide the lace monitor lizard with perfect conditions for incubating its eggs. The female scratches a hole in the mound and there lays her eggs. The termites repair the damage quickly, leaving the lizard eggs safely inside the termite fortress. For the next nine months they are guaranteed almost perfect conditions for incubation. The young lizards hatch to find themselves trapped inside the hard clay walls. And there they would stay were it not for their mother, for somehow she senses when it is time to return and dig them out.

Survival by termite *The lace monitor lizard, 6 ft (2 m) long, has a large territory in which to hunt for birds' eggs and small creatures. The territory must also have termite mounds, for it is in these that the female lizard lays her eggs.*

Flycatchers make use of both thorns and ants

Robin-sized kiskadees, which are yellow-chested flycatchers of Central America, are opportunists that feed on frogs, fish and fruit as well as insects. They also make use of thorny bull-horn acacia trees to protect their ball-shaped nests. Bull-horn acacias have large, hollow, thorns that dissuade grazing animals, and they are also home to aggressive ants of the *Pseudomyrmex* genus. In return for board and lodging, the ants guard the plants from attack by insects and birds.

The kiskadees, however, succeed in making use of the acacia's ant bodyguard. Initially, the ants subject the birds to an onslaught of bites and stings, but gradually they come to tolerate them, even though their resentment of other creatures remains strong. So the kiskadees are able to incubate from two to five eggs and feed the hatchlings in comparative safety.

Some of the 2500 species of stick insect also enlist the aid of ants to protect their eggs from wasps. Many different kinds of

Selling a dummy *All stick insects are masters of disguise. Some species lay eggs so much like seeds that ants carry them off to store in their nests.*

insects are plagued by parasitic wasps, of which some of the most successful are the types that lay their eggs inside the eggs of other species. Stick insects that lay their eggs on the ground encourage ants to collect and bury their eggs where wasps cannot get at them.

Each stick insect's egg has a small bump on the surface that gives it some resemblance to a seed. On a seed the bump is nutritious tissue that is eaten by the ants. Although the bump on the egg is not nutritious, the ants are misled and nevertheless carry the pseudo seeds underground, storing them in the safety of their nests.

Bottom dweller *Sculpins are spiny-finned fishes noted for the care they lavish on their eggs. The dragon sculpin is an exception – it leaves parental care to a sponge.*

Safety in a sponge

Unlike its many spiny finned sculpin relatives, the dragon sculpin fish does not make a nest for its eggs. Instead, it lays them in a sponge, which both protects the eggs from predators and provides an excellent nursery. The female sculpin pushes her stiff egg-laying tube through the soft tissues of the sponge to insert her eggs directly into the canals through which the sponge draws in sea water. Here they lie with water running over them and keeping them supplied with oxygen. The sponge also produces antifungal and antibacterial chemicals that protect both itself and the fish eggs from disease.

PARENTS THAT PROTECT THEIR EGGS WITH THEIR BODIES

Most species that lay eggs are anxious about the safety of their charges. Some solve the problem by carrying them everywhere.

Hunting spiders carry their eggs in a pack

A nursery-web spider is so called because of the web she builds to protect her newly hatched young. Normally she is a roving hunter, relying on speed, agility and excellent vision to catch insects and even small frogs and lizards. This way of life has a drawback, however. Spiders that catch food on webs can keep a constant guard over their eggs. But a mobile hunting spider must either carry her eggs with her or leave them alone and vulnerable to predators.

The nursery-web spider carries her eggs with her in a large silken ball attached to her fangs. While the eggs are developing, she does not hunt because she cannot eat. Nevertheless, she moves around from one sunny spot to another to keep the eggs warm.

When the spiderlings are about to hatch, she cuts a small opening in the tough threads of their prison and builds a nursery tent of silk round the egg sac, which she then straddles until the youngsters have dispersed to fend for themselves.

Wolf spiders also wrap their eggs in silken bundles, but carry them on their backs, attached to the silk-weaving spinnerets on their abdomens. In this way the mother's fangs remain unencumbered while the eggs develop. When the spider senses that her eggs are about to hatch, she cuts through the tough sac enclosing them. The spiderlings clamber out and up her legs, trailing silk draglines that catch on specially adapted hairs on her back. The young ride on their mother's back for several days.

After the eggs hatch the silken sac can be discarded. But in some species the instinct to carry it is so strong that the female drags it around for some time.

A precious load *The female nursery-web spider is weighed down by an ungainly ball of silk that contains hundreds of eggs. When the tiny spiderlings hatch, the mother must free them from their silken prison or they will perish inside it.*

Fish that fast to keep their young safe

It might be thought that a parent's mouth would be a risky place for fish eggs and fry to develop. Yet in the lakes of Africa, several species of cichlid fish look after their eggs and young in just this way.

One cichlid parent – usually the mother – collects up the eggs in its mouth as they are laid and keeps them there until they hatch about ten days later. To make sure that none is swallowed accidentally, the parent eats nothing while brooding its eggs; but accidents can happen. If the brooding fish gets a fright, it may accidentally swallow the eggs it had been trying so hard to protect. Another danger is theft. There is one species of cichlid that forces mouth-brooding parents to cough up their young – and then eats them. On the whole, however, mother's mouth is a safe place, and for as long as a week after they have hatched, the cichlid fry seek protection there, darting into it whenever danger threatens.

A mouthful of fry *A cichlid fish in Africa's Lake Malawi spits one of its newly hatched offspring out into the world. One or the other cichlid parent incubates batches of eggs in its mouth, doing without food to provide the young with the maximum security possible.*

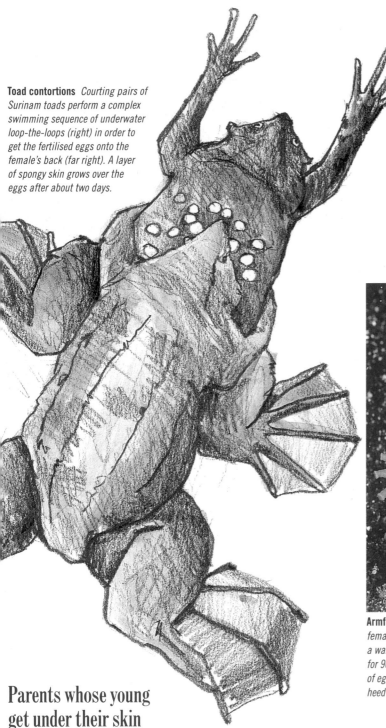

Toad contortions *Courting pairs of Surinam toads perform a complex swimming sequence of underwater loop-the-loops (right) in order to get the fertilised eggs onto the female's back (far right). A layer of spongy skin grows over the eggs after about two days.*

Armfuls of eggs *The colouring of the female southern blue-ringed octopus is a warning of her venomous bite. Though for 90 days she carries a tempting parcel of eggs in her tentacles, most predators heed the signal and leave her alone.*

Parents whose young get under their skin

Many kinds of frogs and toads carry their eggs on their backs. For Surinam toads in equatorial South America, getting the eggs onto the female's back requires elaborate synchronised swimming.

The courting toads swim up to the water surface while mating, and near the surface turn over in an underwater loop-the-loop. At the top of the loop the female lays a few eggs, which the male fertilises, and in repeated loop-the-loop manoeuvres, the pair lay and fertilise a clutch of 100 or so. As the fertilised eggs sink down, they tumble onto the female's back, where a pad of spongy tissue grows over them. Within a day or two they have disappeared, completely embedded in her back. The mother carries the eggs for the next three months or so until they turn into tadpoles, which wriggle out from beneath her skin and swim away.

A female South American marsupial frog also protects her eggs on her back, where a layer of skin forms a pouch that opens in a narrow slit close to her back legs. To get the eggs into her pouch, the female carefully positions herself during mating, with her head down and back legs raised. The male clings to her back and fertilises the eggs as she lays them one by one. They slide down a moist groove on her back into the waiting pouch.

Here the eggs become tadpoles, and stay in the pouch while they develop into froglets. When the youngsters are fully developed, the mother marsupial frog reaches up with her back feet and pulls open the pouch for them to hop out.

The cradling embrace of the blue-ringed octopus

The female blue-ringed octopus keeps her eggs wrapped up safely in her tentacles during the whole of their 90-day incubation. Many predators would gladly feast on the eggs, but few are equipped to tackle this brightly coloured parent's poisonous bite.

The blue rings are a signal that this octopus is venomous, so for her the safest place is in the open ocean where the colours can be clearly seen. This contrasts with most other octopuses, which lay their eggs in rocky nooks and crannies. Even though the females stay close to the eggs to keep a cleansing water flow over them, concealment is the first line of defence.

MALE PARENTAL CARE

In some species, the female deserts her young and leaves the male to bring them up – a challenge that may demand ingenious answers.

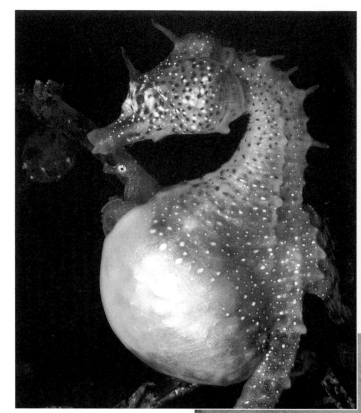

'Pregnant' male sea horses reverse the roles

Few fathers go to greater lengths to protect their young than the sea horse, which broods the eggs in a pouch on his belly.

A female sea horse lays several thousand eggs into a male's pouch, where he fertilises them and protects the embryos until they hatch. The lining of the pouch secretes a nourishing fluid that feeds the growing young. After about two weeks, a brood of miniature sea horses is expelled by a series of contractions of the pouch.

The sea horse is perhaps the best-known example of male 'pregnancy', but similar adaptations have evolved in a number of its relations, including the broad-nosed pipe-fish, which lives among eelgrass off the west coast of Sweden. Biologists studying these fish have discovered that, in this species, the reversal of the normal sex roles is almost complete.

With most animals, the male initiates courtship and mating, the female being choosy about who she mates with. In the instance of the pipefishes there are never enough males to brood all the females' eggs. Consequently, the male is much in demand – and it is the female that does the courting.

Father's farewell *A male sea horse sends his offspring into the world. Sea horses drift with the current, and mate when the female twines about the male and deposits eggs in his brood pouch.*

The responsibilities of one-parent fish families

Only a few fish species look after their young, but when they do it is often the father who does the work. This is because it is generally the father that is left with the eggs. Fish eggs are usually fertilised outside the body – the female lays her eggs and the male fertilises them later, by which time the female has usually left the scene. Sticklebacks exemplify this behaviour. The female lays her eggs in the nest built by the male and abandons them; from then on the male looks after them alone. He fans water over the eggs to make sure that they get enough oxygen, keeps them clean and defends them from predators.

However, the male left in this situation has a choice. He can look after the fertilised eggs or he can go off in search of another female to breed with. If he leaves, he has wasted the time and energy that it took to build the nest and court the female. If he stays, he loses nothing. Other females may still come to lay in his nest – in fact, it seems that female sticklebacks

Father's regard *The male stickleback watches tirelessly over the well-being of his hatchlings. His red coloration is actually a courtship display, but he puts it to good use later, as a warning to intruders to keep well away from the nest and his offspring.*

prefer to mate with males that are already guarding eggs, because these are the partners that are likely to spend more time protecting the young, and less time in courting new females.

Not all males that look after the eggs are model fathers. The Cortez damselfish lives in the Sea of Cortez off the west coast of Mexico and, like the stickleback, the female leaves her eggs in the care of the male. Although he protects the eggs against the dangers of the sea, he also eats some of them. As evolution tends to favour individuals that leave the most progeny, this behaviour is unusual.

What counts for the male damselfish, though, is not how many of one brood survive but how many young he can father in his lifetime. Well-fed males are better able to court and mate again after their eggs hatch, so it may be that by eating a few of his eggs today, a male will keep fit enough to eventually provide more for posterity.

Varying degrees of fatherly attention

Without the benefit of water, a female Darwin's frog lays her eggs directly onto the floor of the beech forests of southern Chile. The male watches over them until the tadpoles start to move within their protective covering of jelly, whereupon he swallows them and carries them about in his vocal sac for some three weeks. There the young go through the tadpole stage and develop into small frogs. Their presence does not stop the father from eating, but they do change the sound of his call. He spits them out once they are big enough and leaves them to fend for themselves.

A rather more attentive father is the newt-like giant salamander, or hellbender, found in North America. The male hides the fertilised eggs under rocks in a fast-flowing stream and then guards them from all comers, including members of his own species. Any intruder that attempts to slip under the rocks covering the salamander's precious eggs is fiercely repelled.

On their own *A male Darwin's frog releases his young from his vocal sac, in which he has carried them from early tadpole stage onwards, not only to keep them safe, but mainly to ensure that they develop in moist conditions.*

Burden of parenthood *Laden with eggs, a male giant water bug engages in the underwater exercises that keep his offspring supplied with oxygen.*

The hazardous life of the giant water bug

In the deserts of Arizona in North America, streams present special problems for the animals that live in them. During the rainy season, flash floods can transform a watercourse containing a few stagnant pools into a raging torrent in a matter of hours.

These streams are the habitat of the giant water bug, an animal that has made several useful adaptations to its hazardous environment. As the streams dry out these bugs gorge themselves on the dying insect life trapped in the temporary pools. And once they have fattened themselves up, the bugs begin to breed. A female may lay more than 100 eggs, which she deposits on the back of her mate.

Without the father's care the eggs cannot survive, for the pools are stagnant and hold very little oxygen, and without oxygen the embryo bugs would quickly die. To prevent this, the male perches on a rock just below the water surface and steadily flexes and extends his back legs. This keeps a constant flow of water passing over the eggs, supplying them with life-giving oxygen.

The fathers pay a high price for the care they give their offspring. The giant water bug is a carnivore, relying on speed, agility and a venomous bite to catch and subdue its prey. The eggs are an awkward load to carry, and while carrying them a male bug is unable to feed efficiently – while they are hatching, he stops feeding completely. A brooding male loaded with eggs also finds it harder to escape from predators. The result is that by the end of the breeding season there are always many more females than males left in the pools.

Because guarding and tending the eggs is so risky, a male water bug needs to be very sure that he is indeed looking after his own offspring. He does this by constantly interrupting the female after every egg she lays in order to mate with her again. In this way, the bug makes it as certain as he can that he really is the father of all the eggs that he may have to give his life to protect.

NEITHER TOO HOT NOR TOO COLD

Some birds have evolved ingenious methods of keeping their eggs as warm – or as cool – as necessary in rigorous conditions.

Incubating eggs in the chill of the Antarctic

Although it is essentially a water bird, the emperor penguin lays its single egg far inland on the Antarctic continent at the start of winter. Courting begins in autumn, and by the time the female lays her egg two months later, the demands of producing it and the rigours of the long journey to the breeding grounds have cost her about 20 per cent of her body weight.

As soon as the egg is laid she rolls it onto her feet with her beak to prevent it from freezing. Almost immediately her mate shuffles up to her and the egg is transferred from her feet to his. She then returns to the sea to feed, leaving the egg in the care of the male. His task is to keep it warm in the face of a winter so severe that the temperature can plummet as low as −60°C (−76°F) and the wind can reach 125 mph (200 km/h).

There is no nest – the male incubates the egg on his feet to keep it from touching the ice, covering it with a fold of skin hanging from his lower belly. The feathers on this patch of skin moult shortly before incubation to create a brood patch. Beneath the skin of the brood patch lies a rich supply of blood vessels, a controlled central heating system that keeps the egg at exactly the right temperature.

The male birds incubate the eggs continuously for two months

Egg warmers *With their eggs hidden beneath a fold in their bellies, male emperor penguins wait out the last days of incubation. Once hatched, a chick will stand on its father's feet until its mother returns from feeding at sea.*

while the females are at sea. They live off their ample supply of body fat and do all they can to keep warm and conserve their energy reserves. During severe weather they huddle in large groups, sometimes 6000 strong, each bird resting its beak on the one in front, and each one constantly shuffling forwards, trying to push through to the warm centre. Usually, the chicks hatch just as their mothers return from the sea to take over parental duties from their mates.

Creating shade *Birds that nest in the open have to provide shade for their eggs, particularly if they live in hot climates. Both the little ringed plover (right), which nests in open patches of gravel among which its eggs are well camouflaged — and the blue-footed booby (below) — which nests on islands off the coast of South America — stand over their eggs, casting a shadow to protect them from the worst of the heat.*

Keeping eggs cool in the heat of the tropics

Most eggs can survive for a short time if their temperature drops from the normal 37°C (98°F) to as low as 25°C (77°F). But a slight rise in their temperature to 39°C (102°F) for the same length of time is fatal. For birds nesting in the tropics, keeping their eggs cool is a continual battle, and they have developed a variety of tricks to prevent them from overheating.

The blacksmith plover of the grassy, tree-scattered plains of East Africa — whose nest is no more than a small depression in the ground (often the imprint made by an animal hoof) — stands over its eggs with wings spread to shade them from the sun. Some tropical herons even coat their eggs with their droppings to maintain their temperature. This acts like a cool bag — the outside may get hot, but the contents stay cool.

By using such ingenious tactics to protect the eggs from the scorching sun, birds can nest in unlikely places such as the middle of an open desert or on bare tree-

tops — places where the eggs and nestlings are less likely to be at the mercy of predators.

Shading works well enough if the eggs are exposed only to direct sunlight, but if the air temperature around them is too high, a different tactic is necessary. The Australian black-necked, or jabiru, stork carries water in its beak to spray over its eggs. The Egyptian plover, however, cannot carry very

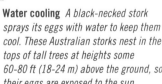

Water cooling *A black-necked stork sprays its eggs with water to keep them cool. These Australian storks nest in the tops of tall trees at heights some 60-80 ft (18-24 m) above the ground, so their eggs are exposed to the sun.*

much water in its small beak, so it covers its eggs with sand, then soaks its breast feathers in the nearest water and dashes back to the nest to shake water droplets over the sand-covered eggs.

KEEPING EGGS WARM

For cold-blooded reptiles, maintaining incubation temperature calls for special measures. And some birds have problems, too.

When egg temperature determines sex

The American alligator, like all reptiles, is cold-blooded, so the female is poorly equipped to incubate her eggs. Instead, she builds an incubator, using her immensely strong tail to scrape together a mound of vegetation in which she buries her eggs. Just like a garden compost heap, the pile begins to decay and warms up as it does so to something approaching the ideal incubation temperature of 37°C (98°F).

This is a useful solution to the problem of incubation. But it is not entirely satisfactory. The temperature within the heap varies by only a few degrees, but even a small change can have a major impact on the size and vitality of the newborn. Eggs that incubate at lower than ideal temperatures will take longer to develop, and more of the food content will be used up by the embryo in keeping itself alive. So when they hatch, the young are smaller than those incubated at the ideal temperature.

In a shrewd evolutionary development, the alligator has adapted to this unpredictability. The size of a female alligator is relatively unimportant. A small female produces proportionately fewer eggs than a large one, but at least she will produce some. However, for males, size is crucial. Large

males win the ferocious fights that happen at the start of the mating season, and gain the most females. Small males may never mate at all.

To ensure her young get the best chance to breed successfully, and so pass on her genes, a mother alligator needs her large offspring to be male, and her smaller offspring to be female. In fact, sex is determined by the temperature at which an egg is incubated. Eggs that develop in ideal incubation conditions produce large males, but those that are inadvertently kept cooler will turn out smaller females. For every male produced, there are five females.

As with alligators, the sex of tortoises is determined by egg temperature. However, the tortoise differs entirely from the alligator in that tortoise eggs developing at the right temperature produce large females, and those incubated at lower temperatures produce smaller males.

For male tortoises there is little advantage in being large, since tortoise fights are relatively rare and most males have a chance to mate. For females, however, there are definite advantages in being big. The number of eggs that a female can carry inside her is strictly limited by the size of her shell. Large females lay more eggs than small

ones. Again, the determination of sex by temperature ensures that females produce young with the best prospects of continuing the species. Another nursery gardener,

the Australian mallee fowl, incubates its eggs by burying them in a heap of vegetation or compost. It builds a mound up to 3 ft (1 m) high and about 16 ft (5 m) wide, collecting together some 4 tons of leaves and soil. The female lays up to 30 eggs in its centre, then she departs and the male covers

Parental protection *A female ostrich (left) sits on her own eggs having thrown out those of her rivals to distract the attention of predators. The male (above) takes the night watch; most animals are wary of his powerful kick.*

How the 'major hen' protects her own

The ostrich, the largest living bird, is unable to fly and must therefore make its nest in a scrape on the ground. Ostrich eggs weigh about 3 lb (1.5 kg) each, and make a meal not to be despised by even such large predators as jackals, hyenas and the occasional lion. Major hazards to survival call for special measures to combat them. The ostrich's response has been to evolve a highly unusual pattern of breeding and incubating.

A male ostrich forms a pair-bond with only one bird, the 'major hen', although he will also mate with as many other females as he can. These 'secondary females' are allowed to lay their eggs into the nest, but take no part in incubating them. This task the male shares with his major hen. He sits on the eggs during the night when the danger is greater, and she takes over in the day.

It is rare for an animal to look after the offspring of others, since helping them will decrease the food and other resources available for its own. And the major hen is no more unselfish than any other female bird.

When the nest is full and she can no longer effectively incubate all the eggs, she pushes out some of those that do not belong to her. These make a circle of discarded eggs round the nest.

Lying neglected in the sun, these discarded eggs will never hatch, but they are the first eggs that any predator will find, and may well be sufficient to satisfy its hunger. They will at any rate divert attention from the major hen's eggs, which remain in relative security beneath the parent in the centre of the nest.

The warm maternal embrace of the python

Parental solicitude is unusual in snakes. Most are satisfied with burying their eggs in a safe place, then abandoning them to take their chances. However, there are some pythons that not only protect their eggs, but incubate them too.

After laying a clutch of about 100 eggs, the female python coils herself round them. She then begins to shiver, making rhythmic contractions of her muscles that can raise her body temperature by as much as 7°C (13°F) above that of her surroundings. She can also gently shuffle the eggs in and out of the sun.

Because they are cold-blooded (they have to bask in the sun to warm their bodies) snakes cannot use body heat to incubate their eggs. Although several other species of snake guard their eggs, so far as is known only the python incubates them. This may well be because other species lack the massive muscle power required to generate the required warmth.

For reptiles, the ideal environment is a warm climate whose

the eggs and takes up his vigil. The male constantly probes the nest with his beak to gauge the temperature, which must be about 33°C (92°F). The eggs take only seven weeks to develop and hatch, but the whole process keeps the male mallee fowl busily occupied for 11 months of the year.

Alligator patrol *For a female alligator of the Florida Everglades, nest-building is a simple matter of raising a pile of mud and swamp vegetation with a few sweeps of her powerful tail. Having buried her eggs within, she patrols the area to deter raccoons. But despite her early care, once the young are hatched, they are on their own.*

Shivering with heat *Like other pythons, the green tree python is able to raise its temperature and incubate its eggs by shivering. The hatching young are reddish in colour (they turn green later), and can catch and eat tree frogs almost at once.*

even temperatures permit the eggs to hatch unaided. But reptiles are also found in places ranging from tropical rain forest to chilly moorland. In some of these a number of species have found different solutions to the problem of incubating eggs. The European grass snake, for example, lays its eggs in piles of rotting vegetation. The heat generated by the chemical breakdown of the plant material is just right for the eggs.

But there are dangers, too, in such an environment. Fungi and bacteria abound, and some protection from them is essential if the developing young are to survive It is provided by the tough, leathery, shell of the grass snake's eggs.

GETTING THE TIMING RIGHT

Being born in optimum conditions can greatly enhance an animal's chances of survival. So some delay development or their emergence into the world.

Tuatara offspring take their time

The tuatara is the only remaining member of an ancient reptile family – its relations died out more than 65 million years ago. Today the lizard-like survivors live only on New Zealand's North Island and some small islands to its south.

Tuataras take their time with most things. There have been reports of their not breathing for an hour or more, and falling asleep while chewing food. Reproduction is no exception – the female takes three or four years to build up enough energy to produce a clutch of 6-15 small, oval eggs. Mating takes place in summer, but a female stores the sperm in her body for about ten months before fertilising her eggs, which she lays the following spring. At first, the embryos develop quickly, but slow down almost to a halt during the winter. The offspring finally hatch in summer – some 15 months after being laid – the longest incubation period of any reptile.

Slow but sure *Tuatara lifestyle is leisurely – the young take 20 years to reach sexual maturity and 37 months elapse between mating and hatching. These lizard-like creatures do not stop growing until they are 60 years old, and are thought to live for about 100 years.*

Brine shrimps can wait years for their moment

Lake Eyre lies deep in the desert heart of Australia. Usually this shallow depression is dry and covered in a salty crust that sparkles under a glaring blue sky. But once in a decade or so, heavy rains fall on distant mountains and the rivers that feed the lake flow again. The salt pavement is transformed into a vast pool, and the water brings a brief bloom of life.

Even when it is flooded Lake Eyre is extremely salty, and few creatures can survive in such a difficult environment. But brine shrimps do, and throughout the world make salt lakes their homes.

The shrimps' survival depends on their eggs hatching during the floods. Within hours of the water's arrival, tiny brine shrimp eggs begin to hatch. The eggs were laid years before and have remained dormant ever since. But now the shrimps seize their opportunity and cram their lives into the time before the water evaporates. They probably have only a few days in which to hatch, grow and breed.

Seizing the day *The secret of the brine shrimps' survival is to be patient then act fast. Lake Eyre fills with water about once every ten years, but the shrimp eggs, baked into the salty crust by the sun, may have to wait as long as 25 years before the distant rains send water to the lake, triggering them to hatch.*

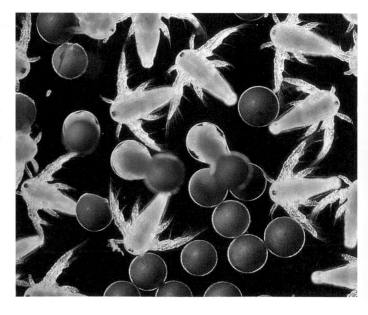

Batch laying for reproductive success

Like many other birds, the hen pheasant does not lay all her eggs at once. Instead she gradually builds up to her complete clutch. Pheasants lay up to 20 eggs – one every day or so. But not until she has laid the full complement does the hen start incubating. This is because the survival of the chicks depends on them all hatching at about the same time. Only a day or two after they hatch, their mother leads them away from the nest to look for food. Any too weak to follow her will die.

Experiments have shown that if a clutch of pheasant eggs is put under a broody hen, and another clutch added 12 hours later, all the chicks still hatch at the same time. Developing chicks can be heard peeping and tapping inside their shells. These may well be signals to ensure that all hatch together.

Such behaviour helps to secure the survival of a single brood. But each brood is only a small part of one hen pheasant's reproductive effort. These birds start breeding at one year old, and will probably produce some 60 eggs divided between yearly batches during their breeding life. One of the many benefits bestowed by this yearly interval between broods is that more of the hatchlings will survive to maturity than if all 60 were produced at once.

Not so with many insects, which live only long enough to produce one large batch of eggs. Drought or some other disaster could wipe out the whole batch in one go. Even so, some Australian stick insects manage to spread the risk. Geared to their harsh and unpredictable environment, they lay batches of eggs that develop equally unpredictably. Some hatch within days, others may take weeks, months or even years to do so. This increases the chances of at least some offspring hatching at a favourable time for them to survive.

Safety first *A hen pheasant rolls her eggs over, a measure that prevents the membranes from sticking to the shells.*

The right weather for coming out of a shell

Billabongs, or stagnant pools, are the home of the pig-nosed turtles of Australia. In the dry season, the female turtles emerge to dig holes in the sandy banks, high above the water line, and in its hole each lays a dozen or so eggs. These develop safely in the warm sand until ready to hatch, about ten weeks later. If the rainy season has begun and the sand is wet, the young turtles break out of their leathery shells immediately and slip down into the water below. Otherwise they wait patiently for the rains to arrive, lapsing into a torpor in which they need no food and hardly any air.

Another freshwater turtle, the painted turtle, also delays its arrival into the active world. These turtles survive the cold of southern Canada in the same way as many of its mammals – by hibernating.

Female painted turtles nest in midsummer in south-facing banks. There they lay their eggs, and 12 weeks later the youngsters hatch. But by this time winter is approaching, so the young turtles stay where they are until spring.

During the winter they, too, go into a torpor, eating nothing and barely moving. Their bodies contain a natural antifreeze that enables them to survive for long periods when the temperature in the nest drops below freezing.

Turtle timing *Painted turtles hatch from their leathery eggs in autumn. Before emerging into the world they will spend their first winter in the nest (above). The intricate yellow and red markings, which earn them their name, are visible even at this early stage of life. A tiny pig-nosed turtle in Australia (right) makes its way down a sandy bank to the backwater where it will spend the rest of its life. The first rains have washed out a nest of pig-nosed turtles and stimulated their hatching. Another egg, about the size and shape of a table-tennis ball, still contains its patient occupant.*

HOLDING BACK THE TIME OF BIRTH

Delays between mating and implantation in the womb ensure that the young are born when food is plentiful and the weather kind.

Storing winter's sperm for a summer's day

A Javan wart snake that died after scientists had kept it in isolation for seven years was found to be pregnant. Most likely, the snake fertilised her own eggs from sperm received in matings many years before. Reptiles hold most records for the length of the delay between copulation and birth.

Other animals also delay giving birth, to ensure that the young are born at the best time of year for survival. Turkeys hold the record for the bird world, with a lapse of 117 days between mating and hatching. Reptiles and birds can delay birth by storing sperm from mating, then fertilising their eggs later. Most mammals cannot do this because their sperm rarely live for more than a day or two. Human sperm can stay active for five days, but this is unusual. So mammals that delay birth usually halt the embryo's growth by delaying the moment of its implantation in the mother's womb, rather than by delaying fertilisation.

Bats are the exception to the mammal rule. Female European pipistrelles store sperm from their autumn mating for up to seven months, during the period of their winter hibernation. In spring the bats use the stored sperm to fertilise the eggs in their ovaries, so as to give birth in summer when food is most abundant.

Snake sperm store
A female Javan wart snake, also known as an elephant-trunk snake, can store sperm in her body for years before she uses it to fertilise her eggs.

Prolonged pregnancy saves lives on the floes

Each year, pregnant grey seals haul themselves out of freezing northern waters onto ice floes or beaches to give birth. Within days of producing her pup each mother is fertile again, and so mates with one of the males gathered around the pupping sites.

A pup takes only seven or eight months to develop in the womb but, by delaying the onset of development, the mother seal can carry her young for a year. Soon after mating the fertilised egg begins to divide and grow inside the female, but once a hollow ball of cells has formed there is a break in development. The embryo lies dormant in its mother's womb for about four months until she has stopped suckling her previous pup.

There is a sound reason for mother seals carrying their babies for longer than seems necessary. Though they are superbly adapted to life in the sea, the seals must still come ashore to mate and give birth. Lissom and graceful creatures in the water, they are heavy and clumsy on land. Their awkwardness at this time is well

known to the Arctic's most deadly predator, the polar bear.

By prolonging their pregnancies, female seals eliminate the risk of coming ashore twice a year – once to mate and again seven months later to give birth. With these two events occurring one after the other, the danger is considerably reduced. The same technique is used by the common long-nosed armadillo – the fertilised egg floats free and dormant for 14 weeks. But before it implants in the wall of the womb to complete its development, the egg splits into four. An armadillo female, therefore, always gives birth to quadruplets.

Mother and pup *Grey seals come ashore once a year to give birth and to mate. By delaying the development of the young in her womb, a female seal manages to fit in the two events within a short while of each other, so reducing the length of time she must face danger on land. In all, the mother seal carries her pup for a year – although the youngster needs only seven months to grow and develop.*

Young stoats conceive before being weaned

Stoats and weasels do not give birth until some ten months after mating. This is an unusually long time for such small creatures.

Male and female stoats avoid each other for most of the year, but during the breeding season, which is between February and July, the male stoats vigorously defend those territories where there are females to be found.

Mating is an aggressive business. The male grabs the female by the scruff of her neck and drags her around roughly before finally mating with her – sometimes for up to an hour. The act of mating is thought to encourage the female to release her eggs to be fertilised. The eggs then float free in the female's womb for as long as ten months before they implant in the wall and continue to develop.

Only the female cares for the young when they are born. And because of the delay in implantation, a new male often takes over both the territory and the female before her young have been weaned, taking further advantage of the situation by mating with her female offspring as well. This means that the young females, having conceived as nurslings, manage to produce an extra litter during their lifetimes.

All in the family *Stoats make caring, protective mothers, but if the nursling being carried is a female, then both this youngster and her sisters will be made pregnant by their mother's latest mate before they are weaned.*

Mother grizzly is her cubs' winter larder

The life of a grizzly bear is one of feast and famine. In summer and autumn there are fish and carrion, ripe fruit, nuts and berries to gorge on; but for at least three months of winter the bears must fast in their dens. During this time the female grizzly also nurses her young cubs, which are born blind and naked soon after she moves into her winter quarters. This nursing takes its toll, and by the time the female emerges again in the spring, she has lost about a quarter of her body weight.

Grizzly bears mate during late spring or early summer, and the fertilised egg starts to grow almost immediately. The embryo stops developing, however, when it is no more than a tiny ball of cells. This hollow ball floats free in the female grizzly's reproductive tract for as long as five months, and does not begin to grow again until she is getting ready to hibernate in October or November.

It would seem easier for the grizzlies to mate in spring and give birth in summer – when food is plentiful. Or for them to mate in the autumn and avoid the complication of delaying the birth. They do not do this because the autumn glut of food is short-lived and, in order to store enough fat to survive the winter, the bears need to eat as much of whatever is on offer as they can. For a female to mate, or to be nursing a young family in autumn, would take up precious time needed for eating.

By mating early in the year, and delaying the development and birth of her young until she is in her winter den, the female grizzly makes certain she can eat as much as possible in the autumn. This ensures that she builds up the fat stores that give her and her cubs the best possible chance of surviving the lean winter months.

Mother and triplets *In spring a mother grizzly and her three cubs emerge from the den in which they sheltered from the winter cold. The cubs were born in the den and the entire family lived off the food stored in the mother's fat.*

SHUNNING PARENTHOOD'S CHORES

Some birds avoid nest building and feeding the young by foisting their eggs on to others. But the policy is not without its hazards.

The most determined confidence trickster

The things that everyone knows about the cuckoo are its familiar call in spring, and its breeding behaviour – behaviour that has given rise to the word 'cuckold', the derisory term for a man whose wife has been unfaithful to him. As a result of this, he may raise children who are not his own.

The European cuckoo is fussy as to whose nests she lays her eggs in. Among her favourites are those of warblers, dunnocks and pipits. Since it is crucial that her egg is added before, or soon after, the potential host has finished laying its clutch, the cuckoo spends several days in studying the situation.

Having selected a victim, she waits until the parents are away foraging for food, then flies to the nest, removes an egg, and replaces it with one of her own. Sometimes she carries the egg away first and then returns to lay. There is no time to settle so the egg is laid without care, often as she perches upon the edge of the nest. Marvellously, the replacement egg is patterned to match those already in the nest and, though it is often larger, the new foster parents are usually taken in by it.

To aid her in choosing the right moment to make the switch, the

Hijack in the hedgerow *A cuckoo about to foist its offspring on others steals an egg while the parents, such as the reed warblers (above) are absent and then lays its own in its place. When the cuckoo chick hatches, it swiftly grows to fill the nest (right) and the foster parents spend all their waking hours feeding it. But sometimes the intended dupe, like the warbler (below) spots the replacement and gives it short shrift.*

female cuckoo has the ability to hold an egg in her reproductive tract for up to 24 hours after it is ready to lay. Cuckoo eggs generally hatch before those of the host, but this extra day of incubation within the natural mother gives them an additional start. As the cuckoo egg hatches, the chick starts to shove

the other eggs over the edge of the nest to break on the ground. And – exceptionally among birds that are nest parasites – it attempts to shoulder out any of its stepbrothers and stepsisters that have hatched, by hunching its back, spreading its stubby wings and pushing backwards towards the

edge of the nest. In this way, the cornered and helpless chicks are forced out. Free of competition, the interloper eats everything its foster parents provide.

Proceeding by stealth

The cuckoo's ploy is not invariably successful, however. Stealth is essential if the bird is to succeed in her deception. Foster parents may become aware that a strange egg has appeared in the nest, and different species react in different ways. Reed warblers, for example, may simply abandon the whole nest and start again, often building a new nest on top of the old one.

Elbow room *From its earliest days, the cuckoo chick is genetically geared to remove all competition from its immediate living area. Here, scarcely hatched itself, a young cuckoo elbows a meadow pipit's egg out and over the edge of the nest to destruction.*

Japanese cuckoos were losing this particular battle, a new group of innocents appeared on the scene. About 30 years ago, azure-winged magpies moved into the cuckoos' breeding areas. Cuckoos rapidly switched to these new and naive hosts, and ten years later almost three-quarters of the magpies were raising cuckoos rather than their own offspring. But recently the magpies have begun to fight back, learning to attack cuckoos and eject their eggs from the nests.

Deceit and destruction

Since some species seem to recognise and counter cuckoo invasions eventually, the bird's continuance is something of a puzzle. The answer seems to be that its deception is good enough to create uncertainty. If a host that suspects one of its eggs to be an intruder's discards the egg, it could be destroying one of its own kin. A host that accepts the foisted package risks losing its whole brood.

When there are large numbers of cuckoos dropping their eggs in an area, birds that push out suspect eggs hold the advantage because they have saved their own brood. But if cuckoos move on, the birds with the best defences suffer most because they may be pushing out their own eggs by mistake.

Other birds may destroy the cuckoo's egg by puncturing it with their bills. Some birds build nests that are largely enclosed, and it may be that they have evolved this strategy to deter cuckoos and other nest predators. But female cuckoos have developed the return gambit of dropping an egg through the entrance hole, relying on its tough shell to protect it when it hits the bottom.

In Japan, one of the cuckoo's most frequent hosts is the Siberian meadow bunting. But many of these birds can identify cuckoo eggs and push them from the nest. Just when it seemed that the

Neighbourly acts in the outback

Cuckoos are not the only birds that lays eggs in nests not their own. Many birds deposit eggs in the nests of others of the same species, thus saving themselves the trouble of raising their young. Since the eggs match the originals almost perfectly, there is little chance of them being detected.

In zebra finch colonies in the Australian outback, it has recently been discovered that a third of the nests contain one or more eggs that have been laid by a female other than the occupier. Apart from avoiding the responsibilities of the nursery, this female gains another advantage – by laying eggs in other nests she can produce more offspring than she could rear in her own nest. However, she must move quickly and discreetly if the legitimate tenant is not to

Nest invader *The zebra finch palms eggs onto others of its own kind.*

detect her egg and destroy it. As it happens, no zebra finches have ever been observed laying in another's nest, although DNA tests on the finches' eggs prove without a doubt that clandestine laying is taking place. It would seem, therefore, that for zebra finches rearing their own brood of chicks, laying a few more in a neighbour's nest is the equivalent of adding some icing to the genetic cake.

Uninvited guest saves infant chicks' lives

Desirable residence *Whole villages of stocking-like nests are woven by female oropendolas, which lay their eggs in the stocking 'feet'. Although the nests seem secure, cowbirds, after watching the oropendolas' progress in nest-building and egg-laying, brashly push their way in and lay their eggs beside the host's.*

Another bird that palms off its offspring on others is the Central American cowbird. Its favourite target is the chestnut-headed oropendola, which builds beautifully woven hanging nests in the tree tops. The cowbird, however, unlike the secretive cuckoo, is quite blatant about its activities, and will even push the intended foster parent from its nest in order to lay.

This is tolerated because it is in the oropendola's own interest to permit the cowbird's invasion. Its chicks are often plagued by botflies – their larvae burrow beneath the youngsters' skins to feed on the tissues. Although a chick can withstand a few of these parasites, it is weakened by them, and a large infestation will kill it.

But a cowbird chick is a much tougher prospect. A newly hatched oropendola chick is helpless, but a cowbird chick emerges from the egg in a relatively advanced state. It gulps down female botflies that enter the nest, destroying them before they can lay. In this way it protects the oropendola chicks, and enables more young to survive than would otherwise be the case.

LEAVING SOMEONE ELSE TO BRING UP THE FAMILY

Instead of nurturing their own progeny, some parents provide them with the best of care by proxy – in some other creature's nest.

Fish that deposit their eggs on neighbours

Cuckoos, which lay their eggs in the nests of other birds, are not the only creatures to get most of the advantages of parenthood with minimum effort. Some species of fish have recently been discovered to practise similar ploys.

One species of minnow takes advantage of the vigilant nesting habits of the Japanese freshwater perch by laying its eggs in the perch's nest. The perch eggs are stuck to the bottom sections of reed stems, and the male guards them aggressively. To evade the defending male perch, the minnows make mass spawning runs in schools of up to 20 fish. They lay their eggs beside the perch and abandon them there for him to look after. In the same way as the cuckoo, the minnows choose their moment carefully. The perch stops guarding the eggs as soon as his own hatch, so the minnows pick a host guarding recently laid eggs. They know these by their colour, because the eggs darken as the embryo inside them grows.

Lake Tanganyika in Africa has more than 160 species of fish that carry their young in their mouths. Two species of the lake fish take advantage of such parental care. One of these is itself a cichlid in which the eggs and hatchlings normally shelter in their mother's mouth. The father usually helps to look after them once they are large enough to swim on their own. If one parent deserts, the other cannot look after all the youngsters alone, so farms them out. Taking a few of them in its mouth at a time, it swims to the territory of another breeding pair and releases them. The young mingle with the hatchlings of the unwitting foster parents, who care for them all.

The other cuckoo is a catfish that makes no attempt to look after its own young but leaves the job entirely to a mouth-brooding cichlid. Quite how the catfish gets her eggs into the host's mouth is a mystery. She may lay them at the same time as the cichlid, and somehow succeed in mixing them together so that the cichlid picks up the catfish eggs as well as her own. Once in the cichlid's mouth, the catfish eggs are protected as well as the cichlid's. And when the catfish hatch, they feed on the unsuspecting young cichlids.

Caring and sharing *A mouth-brooding cichlid fish (top) swims near its young. The brood may include hatchlings that another parent has farmed out. The cuckoo catfish (bottom) slips her eggs in with a cichlid's batch.*

Fooled into feeding the offspring of others

Ants and alpine gentians are both essential to the European rebeli blue butterfly. Like the large blue butterfly, the rebeli (a local variant of the alcon blue) is one of a group of butterflies that exploits ants. The caterpillars of the large blue are 'adopted' by worker ants, and feed on the ants' larvae. The rebeli blue, however, has a more subtle approach – its caterpillars are fed by the ants on the same food as their own larvae.

The female rebeli lays her eggs on a single species of alpine gentian, and the caterpillars eat the gentian flowers for the first few weeks of their life. When this stage of their feeding and growth is done, the caterpillars moult and drop to the ground, where the lucky ones are found by foraging ants, who carry them to their nest.

Generally, the caterpillars drop from flowers in the late afternoon. This is the time when the right kind of red ant is most likely to be abroad and they stand the best chance of being picked up.

Instead of tearing the caterpillar into pieces and feeding it to their larvae, the ants tend it as if it were one of their own. Not only do they feed it, but if it wanders off they drag it back to the brood chamber. What makes the caterpillar so attractive to ants is the substance it secretes from a special gland. Worker ants eat the sugary treat, which may have a scent like that of the ant brood. If so, the ants may be persuaded that the caterpillar, despite its looks, is an ant larva.

Ant hospitality *Because it secretes a sugary substance that probably smells like their own larvae, red ants take a caterpillar of the rebeli blue butterfly home to their nest and feed it. Only one kind of red ant does this – other species with different scents apparently know the caterpillar is a stranger and kill it.*

Cruel guests *A ruby-tailed wasp (left) leaves a solitary wasp's nest after laying a 'cuckoo' egg. A bomber-fly (below) emerges from its pupal skin to begin a life of bombing bees' nests with its eggs.*

Intruders that feed on their nursery mates

With insects as with fish, it is the species that provide the best parental care whose broods are the most vulnerable to parasites. And the best parents of the insect world are bees, wasps and ants.

Most insect brood parasites behave in much the same way as cuckoos, and lay their eggs in other insects' nests. The European ruby-tailed wasp, for instance, chooses solitary wasps to bring up its young. While the owner is away gathering food, it crawls into the wasp's nest and lays a single egg. But the invader's larva delays its development until the host's larvae have eaten all their stored food. Then it starts to eat its adopted brothers and sisters. Not surprisingly, if a solitary wasp returns to its nest to find a cuckoo wasp inside, there is a vicious fight.

Bomber-flies are another group of insect cuckoos. They leave their eggs with ground-nesting bees, but avoid any conflict with the host by laying their eggs without entering the nest. The bees' nests have vertical entrance tunnels, and the bomber-fly hovers over an entrance and bombards it with eggs.

The accuracy of the bomber's aim is astonishing. Its eggs bounce down the tunnel and come to rest close to the mass of pollen that the bee has painstakingly collected to feed its own larvae. The bee larvae eat the pollen, and then, in turn, the bomber-fly youngsters feed on the fattened bee larvae.

THE TRIALS OF A HATCHLING

Emerging from the egg can be a dangerous experience for young reptiles that must fend for themselves from the moment they hatch.

Race to the sea *Young green turtles emerge from their nest in the sand (top right) before making a dash towards the ocean (above and right). All the eggs from one nest hatch at the same time, so the young can dig their way out together, gaining some protection from their large numbers.*

Green turtles break out of the nursery

A green turtle heaves herself up a Costa Rican beach to dig a pit some 3 ft (1 m) deep. In this, she lays about 100 eggs which she covers with sand before returning to the sea, leaving the young to develop and hatch alone.

The task of escaping from this nursery is a formidable one and a single individual would probably be unable to dig itself free. Sheer numbers are essential if the nest is not to become a grave. To escape from their interment the hatchlings must work together. The first ones to hatch do not try to dig themselves out of the sand immediately, but wait until some of their nest-mates have also emerged.

Eventually, about 100 miniature turtles, all working together, raise the entire nest chamber like a lift, rising through the sand. The turtles at the top dig upwards and those underneath aid the effort by compressing the sand beneath them. This lower crowd of turtles

appears to act as a stimulus for those that are digging, spurring them to work harder.

Although a female green turtle lays her eggs deep in the sand, many of them have been lost to predators by the time the others begin to hatch. Most eggs hatch at night when the sand is cooler. But should the hatchlings at the top of the nest start to dig upwards too soon, and find the heat at the surface is too great, they slow down their efforts and become almost torpid. Then, when the temperature has dropped enough, the upward movement continues.

Young turtles that do hatch out in daylight run two risks on their way to the sea: dying from heat exhaustion on the burning sand or being attacked by birds and crabs.

Black vultures gather beside the nests, picking off the young as soon as they appear. And frigate birds hover above, ready to swoop down and pluck the turtles from the beach as they scuttle to the sea.

Easy pickings *On a Costa Rican beach, a ghost crab grasps a Pacific ridley turtle hatchling in its claws. Young turtles are vulnerable when they emerge from the nest, particularly so as they run the gauntlet across the beach to the sea.*

Newborn iguanas with the guts to survive

Evolution dictates that a mother will give her offspring as good a start as she can. In this manner, species thrive and continue. The degree of help mothers award their offspring, however, varies greatly from one species to another.

For some animals, mothers provide full protection and food until the young can look after themselves. Others, like turtles, have no maternal care at all and have only their large numbers at hatching to ensure that some will survive. Iguanas have a difficult time when they hatch out since they, too, must venture into the world without parental protection.

Natives of South and Central America, common iguanas, like many other herbivores, rely on bacteria and other microbes in their gut to digest plants. This process has two stages. First, nematode worms in an iguana's gut break down the plant food. Then single-celled protozoans and bacteria break down the cellular walls of the plant. This releases nutrients which are absorbed by the iguana.

Newly born iguanas have none of these digestive aids, because the eggs and spores are incorporated in adult droppings. So the mother deposits droppings near the nest, where her offspring are likely to eat them as their first meal. Then, suitably prepared, they can move on to their proper diet.

High life An adult common iguana balances in the branches of a tree in the Llanos wetlands of Venezuela. Female iguanas lay their eggs in ground nests, burying them in sandy soil and abandoning them. Hatchlings then climb up into the forest canopy.

Snakes that saw their way out of the shells

Snake eggs have a tough leathery shell, and getting out of this protective fortress is not easy. To cut their way out of the eggshell, snake embryos are supplied with a special implement, an egg tooth, that in most snake species curves forwards from the centre of the upper lip. The egg tooth is usually flat and very sharp; the infant snake uses it like a saw, waving its head from side to side until it cuts a slit in the shell. Once the young snake is out of its nursery, the egg tooth soon falls off.

Unlike snakes, crocodile and turtle embryos do not have an egg tooth, though they do develop a horny thickening of skin at the tip of their snouts. They use this to break out of the egg in a similar way. Like the egg tooth, the thick skin is shed shortly after hatching.

Cutting edge A young python emerges from its egg after slicing through the hard shell with its egg tooth. The egg tooth projects from the upper lip just before hatching, and is discarded once the snake has emerged from its shell.

BIG OR SMALL, WET OR TALL

An animal's size, surroundings and way of life can sometimes present problems when the time comes for the mother to give birth.

Attending an elephant's birthday

Largest of all the land mammals, the elephant also undergoes the longest of all mammal pregnancies, 22 months. The dramatic moment of birth for a 250 lb (115 kg) elephant calf is usually witnessed by one or two other females from the herd, often its older sisters, who act as 'midwives' and companions to the mother during the birth. The role of these female attendants may be to stand guard against lions, but they have also been seen trying to help with the birth, pulling gently at the youngster with their trunks. Quite often it is one of the midwives that lifts the newborn to its feet and helps to free it from the foetal membranes. But this is not the most important contribution the midwives make. Probably their main function is to reassure the mother in her time of stress. During the birth, which takes about 15 minutes, one attendant or another gently touches the mother with her trunk.

When the time is ripe for a female elephant to give birth, she and her daughters or other female companions move away from the main herd into the privacy of some shady thicket or woodland near water. When they emerge to rejoin the herd an hour or two later, the newborn calf is tottering between them, supported and protected.

To give birth, the mother stands on all fours and the calf drops headfirst to the ground. The drop ruptures the umbilical cord that, while the calf was developing within the mother, supplied all its nutrients from her bloodstream and took away its waste products. The elephant calf will be suckled for the next three years or more.

Large litter *Unusually among bats, the North American red bat gives birth to twins or triplets. Most species of bat bear only one offspring at a time.*

Topsy-turvey problems of a bat mother

The female bat is possessed of a unique problem – that of flying while burdened by the additional weight of the developing foetus. Birds, by laying eggs, have to carry extra weight only briefly. But the bat carries it for the six weeks or so that elapse between the implantation of the egg in the uterus and the young bat's birth. Although, in temperate climates, bats mate before or during hibernation, the female stores the sperm and fertilisation may be delayed until spring. In one or two species the fertilised egg divides but does not implant until weeks or months later.

Female bats have a second problem. Since they roost hanging by their feet, they must give birth upside-down. A few species turn head uppermost to give birth, and hang by claws on the front of their wings, but most of them do it in the reversed position. The mother catches her newborn offspring, naked and blind, in the folds of her wings. It clings to her fur with its strong claws, and then crawls down to take its first draught of milk from a teat in one of her armpits. Only occasionally does the mother leave the young, and that is to feed herself.

Enter an elephant *After nearly two years in the womb, an elephant calf is launched into the world (top). The mother or her companion 'midwives' gently remove the foetal sac (left) and carefully hoist the youngster to its feet (below). They direct it to the mother's nipples where it takes a first drink, using its mouth, not its trunk.*

The dangerous birth of a humpback whale

Humpback whales, unlike highly sociable sperm whales, live in loose and ever-changing groups of about four to ten. However, the stablest and longest-lasting relationships are between a mother and her calf. They keep close to each other for up to a year.

Usually a humpback whale gives birth to a single calf, launched tail first. The short umbilical cord breaks as it is pulled taut, and instinctively the newborn calf swims towards the surface to take its first breath. The mother urges the youngster up, pushing with her snout or one of her flippers. These first seconds are crucial for the calf, because until it has filled its lungs with air, its body is heavier than water and it is in danger of sinking and drowning.

Birth beneath the waves *Born into a watery world, a young humpback whale must breathe within the first few seconds or it will die. Its 40 ft (12 m) long mother helps the 14 ft (4.3 m) calf to the surface for its first breath. The youngster will be suckled by its mother for 6-10 months and stay close beside her for about a year. Gradually it becomes more independent and then leaves her.*

The tiny difficulties of giant panda parents

It may seem surprising that the young of the rare giant panda are proportionately the smallest of all the placental mammals (those nourished within the uterus via an umbilical cord). The mother is almost a thousand times heavier than her mouse-sized cub which, at its birth, weighs no more than 3-4½ oz (90-130 g).

As the cub is utterly helpless, the large mother has to feed and warm a tiny cub that is blind and naked apart from some thin, white hair. At this early stage the baby cannot even defecate unless the mother stimulates it by constant licking. She rarely leaves it during its first three weeks.

Giant pandas often give birth to twins, but the demands of the tiny offspring are so great that mothers rarely succeed in raising both. When twins are born in captivity the mother always rejects one instantly. In the wild, giant pandas have occasionally been seen with two well-grown cubs of the same age, but only one case of twins being raised to maturity is known.

Newborn grazers 'hit the ground running'

The ability to run from virtually the moment of birth is nowhere more important than it is among the grazing animals on the African plains, for nothing is at greater risk than a newborn calf.

Big cats, wild dogs and hyenas are all skilled hunters that can quickly spot a weak or vulnerable animal among a herd. So for many species of grazer, prolonged development in the mother's uterus allows a young animal to gain the physical abilities needed to escape danger from the hour of its birth.

A newborn giraffe, for example, emerges fully developed after its 15-month gestation period inside its mother. Although it is unsteady on its legs at first, within 20 minutes of taking its first breath the calf can keep up with the herd. Within an hour it is taking milk.

Born fleet of foot *Although a young giraffe is as tall as a man at birth, it has a long drop to the ground, for its 15 ft (4.6 m) mother gives birth standing. At first the calf has difficulty controlling its long neck, but it can run within an hour.*

CRAWLING FROM WOMB TO CRADLE

Pouched mammals are born at a very early stage of development, so their mothers carry the youngsters with them in a built-in cradle.

The perilous journey of a baby kangaroo

The moment it is born, the young kangaroo, or joey, undertakes the most hazardous journey of its life – the climb from its mother's genital opening to her pouch. A baby eastern grey kangaroo, less than ½ in (13mm) long, is 12 000 times lighter than its 4 ft (1.2 m) tall mother. After only about five weeks in the womb, the baby has to crawl 6-8 in (15-20 cm) to find one of the four nipples in her pouch – its lifeline for the next 18 months or so. It struggles through a forest of fur, pulling itself forwards by its forelegs, which are no more than short stumps.

Pocket cradle

Pouched mammals such as the kangaroo are called marsupials. They give birth to young that are immature and that complete their development inside the mother's pouch. Female marsupials do not produce a placenta – an encompassing membrane that provides nutrients for the foetus. Unborn marsupial babies absorb what nutrients they can through the wall of the uterus. Before she gives birth, a female kangaroo cleans the inside of her pouch and her genital area for several hours with her tongue, smoothing the way for her offspring. Because of the baby's diminutive size, the birth itself takes little effort.

Exactly how the embryonic kangaroo manages to find its mother's nipple is a mystery. At this stage the joey is completely blind, so it probably relies on smell. Most youngsters succeed in finding the way. Once the joey arrives at its goal, it clamps its mouth over the nipple, which swells to fix it firmly in place. Not until the infant is a month old are its jaws sufficiently developed for it to be able to release itself.

At this time the joey begins to move around in the pouch, testing its muscles. But it does not emerge until it is seven months old, and only when it is about 11 months old does the youngster vacate the pouch for good. By then a new joey is ready for its first journey.

A waterproof pouch for a yapok's young

South America's fish-eating water opossum, or yapok, is the only marsupial well adapted for life in the water. It has dense, oily, water-repellent fur and webbed hind feet and the female carries her ten or so babies in a waterproof pouch.

When she is submerged, she closes her rear-opening pouch with strong sphincter muscles, trapping air inside, which allows the youngsters to breathe. Long hairs lining the lips of the pouch and fatty secretions create a watertight seal.

Water opossum *A yapok is striped, furry and rat-like with a hairless tail. It feeds on fish and other water life. Females swim with babies in the pouch.*

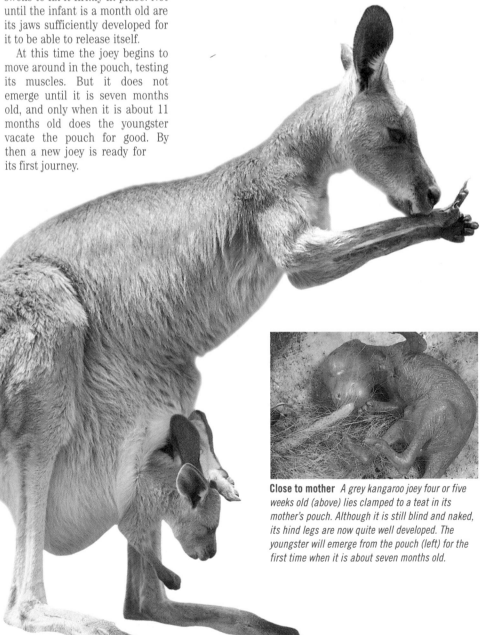

Close to mother *A grey kangaroo joey four or five weeks old (above) lies clamped to a teat in its mother's pouch. Although it is still blind and naked, its hind legs are now quite well developed. The youngster will emerge from the pouch (left) for the first time when it is about seven months old.*

Mammals that lay eggs and suckle their young

That mammals have evolved from reptile ancestors is evident from the reproductive behaviour of the Australian echidna, or spiny anteater. It is one of just a handful of mammals, called monotremes, that still have the reptilian habit of laying soft-shelled eggs.

To lay her single egg in the pouch on her abdomen, a female lies on her back and extends her genital area. The egg shell is covered in sticky slime, and this may help hold it in the pouch as the mother moves it around. After about ten days the young echidna cuts its way out of the shell with its egg tooth and a horny patch on the end of its snout. Although the mother has no nipples, the baby feeds on milk that seeps into her

fur from patches on her abdomen. Not until it is seven weeks old do the infant's spines begin to develop. At this stage it leaves the pouch, but is suckled for several months more and stays with its mother until about a year old.

Apart from the echidnas – of which there are two species, the Australian short-beaked echidna and the long-nosed echidna of New Guinea – the only other mammal that lays eggs is the Australian duckbilled platypus. The platypus, unlike the echidnas, has no pouch.

Hatched in a burrow

A month after mating the female lays two or three eggs in a waterside burrow and curls her body round the eggs to incubate them. They hatch after about ten days. Between mating and laying, the mother's milk glands swell until they cover her belly. Now milk flows from under her skin and the ½ in (13 mm) long babies suck it from her fur – she has no teats.

The young platypuses stay in the burrow, relying entirely on their mother's milk, for three months. Each time she leaves them to hunt for food, she plugs the burrow entrance with soil to keep out predators such as snakes.

After leaving the burrow the youngsters take milk for about two weeks more, until they are weaned onto a diet of bottom-living water creatures such as shrimps.

Spiny anteater *A short-beaked echidna (above), rabbit-sized and rather like a porcupine in appearance, shuffles about in search of ants and termites, which it digs out with its long, sharp claws and licks up with its long tongue. A female echidna carries her baby in the pouch (right) for a few weeks until its spines begin to prick her. Then she keeps it in a burrow. It takes milk for six months or so.*

Young bandicoots have a lifeline to the pouch

Bandicoot babies spend less time in their mother's womb than any other mammal – a mere 12-13 days. One reason for this brief stay may be that, as pouched mammals have no way of switching off their natural defences against foreign bodies, there is nothing to prevent the mother's body from rejecting them. The babies within the womb are, unlike those of other pouched mammals, in a placenta-like sac linked to the uterus wall.

Each baby of the litter of up to seven ¼ in (10 mm) long babies is anchored to the mother's womb by

a stalk-like cord. As the offspring crawl towards the rear-opening pouch, the cords act like climbing ropes, so that if a baby falls from its mother's fur it still has a chance of reaching a nipple.

After being suckled for seven weeks, they leave the pouch, and about ten days later are weaned. Where food is plentiful, they may be mature at three months old. Bandicoots feed mainly at night on insects, plants and small creatures such as earthworms, which they dig up with their front claws.

Growing up *A day-old barred bandicoot (left) has crawled into its mother's pouch to find a teat after less than two weeks in the womb. Two northern brown bandicoots about two months old (above) sit behind their rabbit-sized mother in the grasslands of northern Australia.*

45

LIVE BIRTH VERSUS EGG LAYING

Less than 3 per cent of animals give birth to live young. And even among that small number there are some surprises.

The link that joins a shark and a guppy

Even though water is a dangerous environment, most fish lay their eggs to develop in it. They do so in spite of the fact that there would seem to be greater advantage in being born live after developing within the safety of the mother's body. Among the few fishes that have taken the live-birth route are some species of shark. They are able to hunt within hours of being launched into the world.

Young sand tiger sharks do not even wait for birth. While still in the oviduct the strongest embryo eats its mother's unfertilised eggs and then consumes its brothers and sisters. Only this one survives to be born, but as sand tiger sharks are equipped with two oviducts, a female usually gives birth to two young at a time. Already aggressive and well-nourished after eating their batch-mates, both can fend for themselves at birth.

Not all fish that bear live young are voracious hunters. Guppies, popular attractions in tropical fish tanks, also produce live young. Their eggs hatch within the oviduct and the developing fry float free inside their mother, nourished by the egg yolks, which are later supplemented by secretions from the oviduct lining.

Rather than floating free, lemon shark embryos are attached to the mother's oviduct by a long cord. Gila topminnows show a further adaption in that the embryos feed through blood vessels connecting them to the oviduct wall, rather like the placenta in mammals. Neither does the female waste any unused sperm. She stores it for fertilising later egg batches. This allows her to carry two broods of different ages at the same time.

Caring and carrying mothers *A mother guppy swells visibly while she is carrying her young (right). The inoffensive guppy shares with the rapacious sand tiger shark (above) the trait, unusual in fish, of giving birth to live young. Guppy babies hatch from eggs contained inside the mother's body and emerge into the world fully formed, 25 at a time. Young sand tiger sharks hatch from eggs inside their mother's two oviducts. In each, the dominant youngster eats all its brothers and sisters during its year's stay, and emerges already a third of the length of its 10 ft (3 m) long mother. It is born headfirst so that its sharp scales do not damage its mother's soft tissues.*

Snakes in a cold climate give birth to live young

Largely creatures of the warmish climes, snakes generally reproduce by laying eggs. Even with snakes that give birth to live offspring, the young develop in eggs that hatch within the mother's body. The common garter snake of North America, however, is one of the very few species in which the developing youngsters are actually nourished by their mother's body.

Garter snakes range from southern Canada to Texas, USA. Even in summer, temperatures in southern Canada can fall to 15°C (59°F),

which is not warm enough for incubating eggs laid in the open. Birds incubate their eggs with their body heat, but snakes are cold-blooded and regulate their body temperatures to around 25°C (77°F) mainly by moving between sunshine and shade. Few can produce enough heat to incubate eggs unless they are inside the body.

Young garter snakes developing inside their mother's body are covered by paper-thin membranes that are meshed with the wall of her reproductive tract and pass oxygen and food to the embryos. After about three months, the female gives birth to as many as 80 young. But once born, they are

Snake mother *A common garter snake in southern Canada gives birth to her young at the end of summer. They break out of the thin membrane encasing them (inset). These snakes hibernate for up to nine months to escape the harsh Canadian winter, with temperatures as low as -40 °C(-40 °F).*

on their own; no snake species is known to look after its offspring.

A few species of lizard bear live young, including the European common lizard. So do the blue-tongued lizard and the shingleback skink of Australian deserts. This may be because youngsters within their mother's body are better protected from cold, drought or flood than eggs in a nest would be.

Bulky birth *A female tsetse fly gives birth to its huge larva.*

The African fly that suckles its young

Tsetse flies are bloodsucking flies of Africa that transmit sleeping sickness. Massive efforts to eradicate them have so far been unsuccessful, yet each female raises just one larva at a time, and only a dozen or so in her six-month life. She lavishes so much care on each larva – a creature almost as big as herself – that most of her offspring survive, and she has no need to produce large numbers of them.

A larva begins as a fertilised egg inside its mother's pouch, nourished by a special fluid oozing from a nipple on the wall. The growing larva breathes through a pair of tubes projecting from the mother's genital opening, and by the time it is born it is ready to pupate (transform from larva to adult) at once.

The violent delivery of the female fish louse

To bring her young into the world, a female fish louse spectacularly sacrifices her own life. Ant-sized relatives of the crab, fish lice play out an annual drama of birth and almost instant death in the tidal creeks of Britain's salt marshes.

Each blind female spends the first part of her year-long life feeding on fish blood. On reaching her second larval stage in April, she

sets off in search of males, which hole up in burrows in the banks of creeks. From the mouth of his burrow, each male squirts a steady stream of alluring scent to draw females to him. When one swims close enough, he grabs her in his jaws and drags her into the burrow to join his harem.

As each female louse moults to become an adult, the male quickly fertilises her. Up to 100 offspring begin to grow inside the female's body, and to accommodate them she gradually loses all her internal

organs. When the youngsters are fully developed they take up every last corner of her body, peering out through her transparent and tightly stretched skin.

In autumn, each female gives birth, or rather explodes, releasing all her offspring into the rushing waters of the rising tide. The larvae swim off, leaving their mother looking little more than a crumpled pile of tissue. The male then throws her remains out of the nest. He outlives all his mates to father countless offspring.

LARGE FAMILIES OR SMALL?

To ensure the family line keeps going, animal breeding patterns vary from producing millions of eggs to frequent litters or just one offspring in six years.

Testing times for young Virginia opossums

At first, the reproductive habits of the Virginia opossum, a North American marsupial, or pouched mammal, seem wasteful. Although a female may bear as many as 56 offspring at a time, most are doomed because she has only 13 teats, some of which may not produce milk. As with all marsupials, the newborn opossum must, if it is to survive, attach itself firmly to a teat for the first two months or more of its life. Although the teats are spaced in a horseshoe shape to accommodate 13 young, it is rare for more than eight to survive.

An embryonic opossum, born the size of a bee, has to crawl to its mother's pouch to find a teat. On the way it is extremely vulnerable, and if all the teats are occupied, it dies. But if only one embryo finds its way to the pouch it, too, is quite likely to die, as its sucking will not be strong enough to stimulate its mother's milk production.

Survival of the strongest

This overproduction of young and the deaths of solitary embryos may well improve the opossum's breeding success. The tiny youngsters represent only a small investment of their mother's energy resources when they are born, but once she begins to suckle them the demand on her strength is much greater.

The competition to reach a teat ensures that only the strongest youngsters are raised. And if only one embryo is produced and dies, the female is free to mate again and perhaps raise a larger brood.

As the young opossums grow, they hang on their mother's elongated nipples. Sucking stretches the nipples into lifelines that allow the brood to move around while attached to them. But before being weaned, the young often take short breaks to ride on her back.

Growing up *When young Virginia opossums are about 12 weeks old, they detach themselves from their mother's teats and stay in the nest when she goes to forage for fruit, nuts or small animals.*

Going forth to multiply, sometimes in millions

In one year an American oyster sheds 500 million eggs, whereas a female orang-utan, on average, has a single birth once every six years. Between these extremes lies a wide range of family sizes as each species of animal deals with the challenge of reproducing itself in sufficient and surviving numbers to ensure that its line continues.

Damselfish, for example, lay their eggs in clusters of several hundreds in well-constructed nests among the coral and algae of Australia's Great Barrier Reef. The parents defend their nests and watch over their eggs, increasing the chances of their offsprings' survival in this way. Sea hares, on the other hand, leave their hatched larvae to float defenceless in the ocean. So the sea hare lays many millions of eggs in a year, relying on the sheer weight of numbers to ensure that some survive.

Two in a million *The sea hare drapes millions of tiny eggs in ribbons round seaweeds to give them some protection from predators. Luckily, only two larvae need to mature and breed for sea hares to maintain their population numbers.*

The dangers of breeding like rabbits and voles

Rabbits have a reputation as fast breeders. Starting her breeding career at three months old, a female North American cottontail rabbit can produce 30 babies a year. The European rabbit is not quite so prolific, but when it was introduced into Australia, where it had no natural predators, in the mid-19th century, it became a serious pest and numbers reached plague proportions. Hunting and trapping proved inadequate as ways of controlling the rabbits, but the introduction of the virus disease myxomatosis quickly reduced their numbers. The case of the cottontail illustrates the paradox that lies at the heart of mammalian reproduction – in spite of the fact that they invest so much energy in the care of their young, they still manage to increase their numbers at spectacular speeds.

The North American meadow vole produces up to nine offspring at a time, and can have as many as 17 litters in a season. Each of its offspring is ready to reproduce within a few weeks of being born, so in theory a single pair of voles could, between spring and autumn of just one year, end up with millions of direct descendants. The reason why none has ever done this, however, is that, in practice, nothing like this rate of reproduction is ever achieved. Only about two-thirds of the population survives to be two months old. Snakes and weasels eat litters, and owls and hawks prey on adults.

There are many reasons why the death rate is high during the breeding season. At times when the population is numerous, the meadow voles may run out of food in their territories, or the strain on living space may prompt aggressive defence of the territory, which can inhibit mating.

A relative of the meadow vole is the prolific Norwegian lemming, which – when food is plentiful, predators are few and there is a warm covering of snow over the burrows – can produce litters of from five to eight every three or four weeks. In years when such conditions prevail, the average lemming population reaches its peak. This abundance also increases the populations of hunters such as arctic foxes and snowy and short-eared owls, whose chief item of diet they are. However, years of plenty are invariably followed by leaner times when fewer lemming young are born and even foxes must turn to eating berries.

Rabbits at risk *A female cottontail rabbit may have six litters of five youngsters in a year. If all her offspring lived and reproduced, after six years her family would number 11 million rabbits. But the cottontail population is kept under rigorous control by disease and predators.*

Moving on *On becoming pregnant, female meadow voles move from the place where they were born. This gives vole colonies the opportunity to develop in new and better living areas.*

Life as a diet *Lemmings, a basic food for a number of Arctic animals, are prolific breeders when conditions are favourable. But overcrowding brings changes in the pattern. The young take longer to mature, fewer babies are born and males fight for females. Females must also defend their offspring against males that will kill them to mate with the mother.*

GROWING UP AND LEARNING

'*W*HOSO NEGLECTS LEARNING IN HIS YOUTH LOSES
THE PAST AND IS DEAD FOR THE FUTURE.'
≈ EURIPIDES, 485-406 BC, *PHRIXUS*.

Most animals do not have the opportunity to be taught. The vast numbers that make up the plankton of the seas, many insects and most fish, reptiles and amphibians never know their parents. Initially, they rely only on their instincts to survive, gaining experience by trial and error. Without the care and protection of their parents, many of these independent creatures die; but without the heavy burden of caring for their young, those that do survive can reproduce in far greater numbers.

The world is full of dangers for most young animals, but it can be made safer if they learn from parents or relatives how to survive. A young elephant or chimpanzee growing up in its family group can draw on the collected experience of its elders and also experiment with its playmates. Any animal that fails to learn in its youth is more vulnerable as an adult. It may not be 'dead for the future' but it has certainly increased the risk.

Learning to leap
Leaping from the water requires enormous strength. By imitating its mother, a humpback whale calf develops the necessary muscles.

Feeding on fungus
A female fungus beetle shepherds her larvae from one small patch of fungus to another, ensuring a steady food supply for them.

Lessons in shell-opening
Floating among the kelp forest with its mother, a young sea otter watches as she cracks a shell open on a stone she has selected from the seabed. Sea otter pups spend about six months with their mothers – long enough to learn essential food-finding skills.

Singing lessons
Great tits have a repertoire of up to seven songs. Birds from the same area sing similar songs, learning them from neighbours as well as from parents.

Future harem holders
Young male hamadryas baboons hone their fighting skills in play; they will need strength, guile and agility to form their own harems one day.

Boisterous badgers
Although badgers usually forage alone, the cubs stay close to their mother throughout their first summer, learning the best places to search for food. An area round the entrance to the sett may be trampled flat by the youngsters' exuberant games, during which they develop their skills.

CONSOLIDATING FAMILY FEELINGS

Grooming, scent, recognising a pitch and tone of voice, all help to establish one of the most powerful of natural bonds – that between parent and offspring.

Family ties ensure that the offspring survive

The most dangerous time in the life of any young animal lies in the first hours after its birth. Its world is baffling, largely hostile and full of creatures that regard it as a potential meal. But the new-born has one ally ready to defend it against all perils: its mother.

During those first few hours a powerful bond is formed between mother and young. Often it is one that will impel the mother to any sacrifice to ensure that her offspring is fed and protected. Protecting the young is a heavy burden on the mother – one that she will rarely assume for offspring not her own. For both a mother and her young, therefore, early recognition of each other is vital.

Bonding before hatching

The mother-offspring tie often begins even before the infant is hatched. While incubating eggs, female mandarin ducks call to the embryos within the eggs, and the developing chicks respond with a series of cheeps. Already a bond has been formed between mother and young, so that when the chicks hatch, they will respond only to the quacks of the mother.

Other birds, geese among them, have an inbuilt mechanism that bonds them, shortly after hatching, to the first moving object they see – normally a parent, but if these are missing then to anything else, including humans.

Marrying visual bonding to vocal bonding is crucial if chicks are to survive their first ventures out of the nesting area. They instinctively seek the protection of a parent, but if they cannot pick a parent out of a crowd, they may follow an adult of their own species who will reject or even kill them.

Overture and beginners *Ostrich eggs are incubated for about six weeks. At least a week before hatching, the chicks within announce their presence with a loud and musical cheeping. Thus the adults are able to identify their offspring by their cries as soon as the chicks break out of their thick-shelled eggs and begin to move about. More importantly, the prenatal chirruping has aroused their parental instincts, compelling the adults to care for the young (left) and protect them from predators. The chicks for their part recognise and respond to the parents' cries.*

Crowded crèches by the side of the ocean

In a crowded sub-Antarctic fur seal colony, parenthood calls for a special kind of care. On her return to the shore after feeding at sea, each female is faced with the task of finding her own young among a host of others. As she flops up the beach, she calls repeatedly, anxiously listening for the distinctive reply of her pup.

From birth, the female is able to identify her pup by its scent, but she has learned quickly how to tell its cry among hundreds of others. Though she is mobbed by dozens of youngsters on her way up the beach, she unerringly locates her own and, after a quick confirmatory sniff, begins to suckle it.

For an Adélie penguin to pick its own chick out from a crowd of virtually identical fellows requires even greater concentration. Penguins have no sense of smell, and must rely almost entirely on sound to identify their offspring. On emerging from the sea, a parent heads for its nesting place, calling all the way. The chick, huddling against the cold among hundreds of other youngsters, recognises its parent's call and waddles back to the nest to be fed.

Most birds that live in crowded colonies have evolved distinctive recognition calls. Terns, for example, often nest in large numbers on small sandy islands. There, the parents identify their nest and eggs by features in their surroundings. This is fine until the eggs hatch; once they do so, the chicks wander all over the island, taking cover in crannies from the elements and from predators. Relocating their young in such

Mutual warming *Awaiting the return of their parents, young Adélie penguins crowd together for warmth. Parents and chicks will be reunited by mutual cries.*

circumstances could be a problem, so when the parents fly back to the colony, they circle above it, calling loudly until the offspring recognise the call and reply. Then the parent birds land and feed the chicks wherever they happen to be.

The ability to recognise parental calls is found in most bird species – among them ducks, coots, rails and ostriches – whose chicks leave the nest and wander almost as soon as they have hatched.

Dinner call *On returning from sea, Adélie parents summon their young with cries that the chicks recognise, and begin to feed them on regurgitated fish.*

The inseparable bonds woven by scent

Among mammals, it is a common trait for the female to lick her offspring clean immediately after birth. This first act of motherly care helps free the infant from the foetal membranes and clears its nostrils so that it can begin to breathe. It also dries the fur, helping to conserve heat within the tiny body, and disperses odours that might attract predators. But most important of all, it is probably this process that unites the mother to her newborn by its scent.

For goats, this bonding takes about ten minutes, after which the female will suckle her own kid and no other. In the case of sheep, 20 minutes is required for the ewe to be scent-linked with her lamb. For centuries, shepherds have made use of this fact when fostering an orphaned lamb on to a ewe that has lost its own young. If the two are introduced after the live lamb has been rubbed with the wool of the dead one, the foster mother will accept it. But if some hours have elapsed since the birth, then the ewe will accept no substitutes. In some cases, shepherds tie the dead lamb's skin onto the orphan, leaving it on for a few days, until they are sure the bonding process has taken place.

Licked into shape *With little else in common, a lioness and a springbok doe share a similar compulsion to groom their newborn. This process familiarises the parent with the scent of the young and arouses strong protective instincts, and in the young a sense of dependency.*

53

STRENGTHENING RELATIONSHIPS

There must be strong ties between animals living in groups, but bonds between mothers and offspring may be exclusive or all-encompassing.

Why sociable hyenas need time alone

Packs of spotted hyenas on the African plains do almost everything together. Yet the females give birth alone, staying away from their clan for up to a week before moving their litter into the communal puppy den.

For sociable animals this is puzzling behaviour, but it is safer for females to give birth on their own as adult males will eat the pups. Another reason may be that the mother and her youngsters need time alone to get to know each other. For spotted hyenas, a strong bond between a mother and her offspring is crucial. All the females in a pack breed, and the eventual status of the pups depends on their mother's position in the group.

Looking after a family is hard work. Each mother hyena suckles her pups for up to 18 months. To produce the copious amounts of milk needed for the pups she must gorge herself at the pack kills, fighting fiercely for her share, then journey back to her cubs at the communal den. In a year, a nursing female may cover up to 4000 miles (6500 km) as she travels to and from her pups.

Since bringing up a family takes so much energy, a female hyena normally raises two pups at a time. None of the breeding mothers in a pack wants to expend energy feeding another female's cubs, or bestow on them her own hard-won social status. So when a mother goes to feed her cubs she calls them with a 'whoop' that only they recognise, and the cubs run from the den 'whooping' back.

Selective feeding *Bonds between young spotted hyenas and their mothers are strong and exclusive. She alone feeds them for the first 18 months of their lives. If she were to suckle pups indiscriminately, she might end up feeding another's stronger cubs.*

Elephant reunions are touching affairs

A reunion of a family of elephants is a noisy ritual of trumpeting, rumbling, ear flapping and caressing each other with their trunks. Females and young males live in a tightly knit group in which all the animals are usually closely related.

The group breaks into smaller groups from time to time – if the food supply is limited, for example. But usually the separation is brief, so when the elephants get together again greetings are restricted to a few rumbles. Only if the separation has been a long one is there a full greeting ceremony.

Good companions

This strengthening and reaffirmation of bonds is common among animals that spend a lot of time together. Troops of apes and monkeys, for example, practise mutual grooming, which helps to cement relationships between individuals.

In any group of animals, the close contact between older and younger members allows valuable knowledge of the surroundings and food sources to be passed on.

Family greeting *Even after only a few hours apart, elephants of the same group greet each other with caresses and rumbles. After many days of separation, reunions are noisy and emotional, with ear flapping, trumpeting and touching.*

Monkey business *Grooming each other is a common pastime among monkeys. As well as keeping them free of pests it helps to strengthen and maintain the bonds between a family or group, and also provides a way of creating new alliances.*

For some parents, any baby in the nest will do

Some animals cannot identify their own youngsters as individuals, and some youngsters do not recognise their parents. Rats, mice and many birds feed any babies in their nest, even if none is their own. Some birds will also feed chicks of a different species.

Kittiwakes, which are a northern species of gull, breed on high coastal cliffs. Experimenting biologists have exchanged cormorant chicks for kittiwake chicks, and found that the adult birds fed the changelings as if nothing had happened. The biologists also changed the number of chicks in the nest, even doubling it, and the parents still carried on feeding the brood, apparently unaware of any difference. It seems that the kittiwakes simply assumed that any chicks in

their nest must be their own. Kittiwake chicks rarely wander from their cliff-edge nest – any chick that does is likely to fall to its death. As adventurous chicks do not live long enough to breed, natural selection makes it fairly certain that kittiwakes can rely on their chicks staying in one place and therefore being their own.

The cormorant chicks placed in the kittiwake nest took the change of 'mother and father' in their stride. But all chicks, even if they do not specifically know their own parents, have to learn to distinguish between food-bringers and predators, so adults often signal in some way. Night herons, for example, bow to their chicks before feeding them, showing their glossy black crowns and raising the long white neck feathers. If the parent herons fail to greet their chicks correctly, the nestlings treat them as a threat and attack them.

Nestling confusion *Before feeding its chicks, a black-crowned night heron (above) bows to let them know it is friendly. When white pelicans and cormorants nest in overlapping colonies there can be mix-ups. A pelican chick (right) has wandered into the wrong nest, but luckily for it, adult cormorants will feed any youngster in their nest.*

55

MOTHERS THAT CARE

On mountain tops and grassland, even in the hollow of a leaf, devoted mothers provide the protection that ensures the survival of their line.

The maternal anxieties of a bromeliad crab

So far as is known, the bromeliad crab is the only crab that takes care of its young after hatching. Breeding as she does in puddles of rainwater that collect in the large leaves of bromeliad plants, the mother crab lacks the constant water temperature, the levels of oxygen, salinity and acidity that sea-spawning crabs enjoy. So she must create an environment in which her eggs can develop.

The Jamaican mountain forests where the crabs live receive plenty of rain, but if the mother simply laid her eggs in a puddle and left them, they would be unlikely to survive. Spiders and damselfly nymphs would swiftly devour them – or the emerging larvae – if the mother crab did not keep a vigilant watch. She must also clear leaf debris from the puddle nursery; otherwise, as it rots, it will drain away oxygen from the water, turning it into acid tea.

The shells of snails, however, are excepted from this housewifely diligence. These boost the water's calcium content and therefore the health of the developing crab larvae. The shell's calcium carbonate also helps to neutralise acid in the water, making the leaf-puddle a perfect nursery environment.

Even after the crab larvae have become tiny bromeliad crabs, their mother's work continues. For a further three months she protects her tiny offspring by chasing away predatory spiders and lizards from the pool and fetching cockroaches, beetles and similar delicacies for the youngsters to eat.

Small world *The bromeliad crab, so called from its modest habitat in a rain puddle in the hollow of a bromeliad plant leaf (right), leads, for the most part, a solitary life. The males leave their puddles briefly to mate, but the females remain firmly in theirs to raise the young (above). They make brave and indulgent mothers that defend their offspring against predators, and allow them to take food from their mouths.*

Maternal imperative *Care of their young is the principal preoccupation of most mammal mothers. When grazing on steep slopes, female mountain goats (left) always position themselves below their kids to block their fall if they slip. And like the sable antelope (below), they must also eat more than usual to maintain the milk supply for the young.*

Mothers in defence are deadlier than the males

By nature, the female wildebeest is a placid, even timorous, creature, a grazer of Africa's tree-scattered grassland that will generally flee in the face of danger. But in defence of her calf, she becomes a force to be reckoned with – one that will stand her ground against a lion and fight to the death.

Even though the male wildebeest is bigger and better armed, it is almost always the female that fights to protect the young. Male wildebeests mate with more than one female, so diluting what loyalties they have among a number of offspring. Each female, however, has only a single calf to concentrate her protectiveness upon so, as often happens among mammals, it falls to the mothers to take care of the youngsters' well-being.

A female sable antelope does not have to put as much effort into protecting her young as the wildebeest. She relies on her offspring's camouflage and ability to lie still in thick cover to protect it from the attentions of lions or leopards.

Although this allows the female a certain amount of freedom, the young antelope is still a burden upon its mother. It must be fed twice a day, so the mother must constantly return to the hiding place to suckle it. This makes her journey to find food twice as long as it would be if she were not responsible for a calf.

When the calf is older and joins the herd it is actually more vulnerable to predators. Then, like the wildebeest, the mother will defend her young against all comers.

Lacebug mother turns traffic controller

Care for the young among insects is the exception rather than the rule, though there are a few species that make surprisingly attentive parents. Some female shield bugs, for instance, remain with their eggs to guard them, but the most devoted insect mother must surely be a female aubergine lacebug – or at least, some female aubergine lacebugs.

Though no more than the size of a little fingernail, these North American bugs are ferocious in the defence of their eggs and young. Their particular enemies are small parasitic wasps that try to lay their eggs in the lacebug eggs or larvae. When one moves in, the mother lacebug flicks her wings and kicks out with her legs to discourage the intruder.

But not all the eggs that she guards so fiercely are necessarily her own. Many female lacebugs take the contrary view of child care, and if they see another laying eggs they simply dump their own on the unfortunate mother, who then takes care of all the young.

If anything, looking after the mobile young is rather more difficult than looking after the eggs. Once they hatch, the mother shepherds them around the leaves that make up their world and on whose juices they feed. To prevent them wandering off in small groups, the mother positions herself at the point where the leaf joins the plant stem, leaving only one route open, and so makes sure that they all go where she directs. Her traffic controlling ends only when they have all arrived safely on a new leaf.

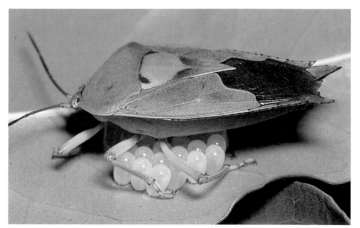

Protective embrace *Many bugs are fierce protectors of their young. Despite her modest size, a female shield bug defends her eggs from predators and parasites.*

57

HOW MOTHERS PROTECT THEIR YOUNG

Females have many ways of giving their young a good start in life, from warming them with their own body heat to fighting off males of their own species.

Cave frogs take their youngsters for a ride

Jamaican robber frog females lay their clutches of about 60 eggs deep within caves, where the temperature stays cool and stable and there is less risk from attackers. Eggs laid on the forest floor or in a pool would be more vulnerable to harsh and unpredictable weather, and also easy prey for birds, fishes and snakes. Unlike most frog species, the eggs hatch as froglets – there is no tadpole stage.

Clutches of the eggs of robber frogs have been found on small crevices and terraces at depths of up to 285 ft (87 m) from the cave mouth. The mother closely guards her eggs until they hatch after 32 days or more. She may even sit on top of them to protect them from creatures such as cave crabs.

It usually takes about 24 hours for the whole of a clutch to hatch. The emerging froglets each have a reserve of white yolk on the abdomen. As each one hatches, it scrambles onto its mother – her back, sides or head. She then carries the whole brood outside to the forest. A mother with newly hatched froglets on her back has been seen to jump as far as 3 ft (1 m) without losing any offspring.

Free ride *A robber frog's eggs (above) are laid deep within a cave, where the female guards her clutch (right). When the froglets hatch, they ride in safety on their mother's back (below) from the cave to their forest feeding grounds.*

Earwigs that make exceptional mothers

Not many insects make attentive mothers, but the giant earwigs of southern Africa and southern Europe are particularly noted for their maternal care. The female lays a batch of up to 50 eggs in a chamber dug out in the moist sand beneath stones and driftwood.

She looks after her eggs for the ten days they take to hatch, turning them over and licking them to stop harmful mould developing. She also protects them from predators such as beetles, spiders and ants, driving them off aggressively.

Once the eggs hatch, the earwig continues caring for her wingless youngsters for a few more days, bringing them petals and other food, which she carries in the pincers at the rear end of her body.

Home guard *A female European earwig closely guards her eggs. While watching over the nest, she licks the eggs to keep them free of mould and bacteria.*

The danger for young monkeys in a harem

Young hanuman monkeys, which live in troops in wooded parts of India, are as much at risk from the males of their own species as they are from natural predators such as tigers and eagles. This is because the males and females of a monkey troop have conflicting interests that determine their behaviour.

Troops are made up of about 20 females and youngsters and one large adult male. He is the harem master, and mates with all the females. But he has to defend his privileged position against regular attacks from bachelor males outside the group. Only a male in his prime can control a harem, and after a few years he is usurped by a younger male. The new male's brief reign over the harem is the only opportunity he has to breed, but it can happen that none of his harem is sexually receptive.

Female langurs do not wean their babies until they are about 20 months old, and while nursing they do not come into season. So if all the females of a troop have youngsters, a new harem master faces the prospect of a long wait before he can mate.

Driven by the desire to produce a family of his own, he tries to kill the young of his newly acquired band of females. If he succeeds, the females will stop producing milk and shortly after, they come into season again, ready to mate with the new harem master. His interests are best served by mating with all his newly acquired females

Mothers' pride *Female hanuman langur monkeys live in groups. If a new male taking over the harem tries to kill their young, the females will get together to protect them.*

as soon as possible. But the male does not always have things his own way because the females often have different interests. They have already made a substantial investment in producing their offspring, and this investment will be lost if these young are killed. So among hanumans, mothercare calls for more than feeding the young – it may involve fighting a male to protect them as well. Some females actually leave their group for a time, balancing the increased risk of living alone against the alternative of losing their offspring.

Male hanuman monkeys are a lot bigger than the females, weighing on average about half as much again. One female alone cannot do very much to protect her offspring from a new harem master. If all the females in a group work together against him, however, his plans can sometimes be frustrated.

Only in recent years have biologists' studies revealed the darker side of male hanuman monkeys' behaviour. Up till then, they had had a good reputation, and have long been revered by Hindus.

Hindu mythology has it that Hanuman, the monkey god, once helped the god Rama to recover his wife, Sita, from the demon Ravana. But Hanuman asked for no reward, happy to have served a good cause. Because of this brave and unselfish act, hanuman monkeys have ever since been considered sacred.

Keeping young rodents warm and comfortable

All rodents, such as rats, gerbils, mice and dormice, show strong maternal instincts. The young of most species are born blind and hairless, so without special protection could easily die of exposure.

To keep her babies warm, a rodent mother builds an insulating nest round them, often using hair plucked from her chest, and curls up beside them. She may lie on top of them to provide extra warmth.

Many young rodents are unable to regulate their own temperatures for the first 10-14 days of life. If a youngster gets cold, it signals to its mother with a high-pitched whistle, above the range of human hearing, and she comes to the rescue by pressing it close to her body. A youngster that falls out of the nest signals in the same way, and is retrieved by the mother and carried to safety.

Rodent mothers regularly lick their young to clean them and also to induce them to urinate and defecate, which at first they do not do spontaneously. A mother ingests the urine to keep the nest clean.

Secure upbringing *A European edible dormouse makes a nest of dry leaves and grass in a sheltered place such as a tree hollow. There she tends a litter of four or five babies for a month or so.*

FATHERCARE IS GOOD BUT RARE

Caring fathers are the exception in the wild, but some males do help to feed their offspring, and a few do most of the work of raising them.

Flying fathers help in their own fashion

Eastern bluebird fathers are very choosy about which chicks of their brood they feed. Among these small North American bluebirds, the gaudy males are more likely to help feed a brood made up largely of daughters, while in any brood a father feeds, he gives a daughter twice as much food as a son. Fortunately, the female bluebird does not discriminate between her sons and daughters.

One reason for the father's favouritism may be that when his daughters grow up they pose less of a threat to him than his sons. Young females eventually leave the area of their birth in search of a mate, but young males settle close by and compete with their father for both territory and mates.

Males of most bird species help their mates to feed the chicks. The males of the Namaqua sandgrouse of southern Africa are particularly devoted fathers. In the harsh dry Namaqualand deserts, sandgrouse feed mainly on seeds and fly long distances to find water. Although chicks can feed themselves, they cannot fly until they are about two months old. So their father carries water back to them – often a round trip of 50 miles (80 km).

Each morning when the adults fly to a pool to drink, a male with chicks dips his belly and soaks water up into modified feathers that act as a sponge. He flies his precious cargo back to the thirsty chicks, who sip it from his feathers. The female sandgrouse is quite capable of carrying water; if the male dies she takes over. But by dividing the work of caring for a family, the parents are more likely to raise their brood successfully.

Favouritism
Bluebird males show a marked preference for feeding their daughters. Perhaps sons pose a future threat.

Thirsty work *Sandgrouse chest feathers can soak up eight times their weight in water (right). Chicks in arid Namaqualand (below) drink the cargo their father has flown so far for.*

Escape chute *An African bullfrog (right) keeps a watchful eye on his offspring. If receding water levels strand his tadpoles, the father uses his hind legs to dig an escape channel back to the main pool (below).*

Baby-sitting bullfrogs protect their tadpoles

Male African bullfrogs look after their eggs and tadpoles in a manner that suggests considerable foresight. The bullfrogs breed and deposit their spawn in temporary pools and puddles created by heavy though sporadic summer rains.

In warm weather these pools quickly shrink, leaving developing tadpoles stranded in tiny puddles round pool rims. If the puddles dry up completely, the tadpoles will die. But the squat, heavily built males, up to 9 in (23 cm) long, appear to be well prepared for this danger. As their broods become isolated by the evaporating water supply, they set to work digging escape channels with their powerful hind legs. In this way they create tiny canals that allow the tadpoles to swim back to the safety of the main pool.

South American arrow-poison frogs are caring fathers, too. These frogs secrete a poison so powerful that Chaco Indians in the rain forests of Ecuador use it to tip their blowpipe darts – the poison stays lethal for up to a year. The adult frogs' brightly coloured, toxic skins put predators off, but the young frogs are brownish black and their skins are not poisonous until they are mature.

A male arrow-poison frog stands guard over the eggs laid by his mate on a leaf or on a patch of ground that has been cleared by them both. Once the tadpoles have hatched, they wriggle onto their father's back. Here they become securely attached by a thick, sticky mucus. The father carries his offspring to a nearby pool, where the mucus dissolves and frees them to complete development.

The female Australian pouched frog lays her eggs on damp leaves or moss and then abandons them. The male, however, returns when the eggs are due to hatch, and by dint of nudging and pushing the tadpoles, stimulates them to wriggle into the pouches on either side of his body. There they develop, well protected beneath his poisonous skin, until they are ready to emerge as froglets.

Taking tadpoles to water *A male arrow-poison frog carries a cluster of his newly hatched tadpoles to water on his back. They are immune to the venom beneath his skin.*

Role reversal works well for lotus birds

Lilytrotter and lotus bird are local names awarded to the comb-crested jacana, which breeds on floating plants in the wetlands of eastern Australia. It walks over plants on its large, long-toed feet.

The male jacana does all the work of raising the family. He alone builds the nest, incubates the eggs and broods the chicks to keep them warm. He feeds the youngsters on insects that settle on nearby plants, and in times of danger calls the brood to shelter under his wings. Then, sweeping his wings close to his sides, he dashes off across the lily pads with the chicks safely tucked away, with only their dangling feet visible.

The female jacana cooperates in the defence of the nest.

She is larger and more brightly coloured than her drab mate, and also more pugnacious and better at driving off water snakes and other predators. Fiercely territorial, she spends much of her time chasing away other females and courting males. Usually she has a harem of up to four males in her territory. If she dies, another female takes over, destroying her predecessor's eggs and mating with the males.

Caring for the chicks seems to give a male jacana his best chance of raising a family. Many of the eggs are taken by predators, and since producing eggs takes more energy than producing sperm, the female is left free to feed and build up energy enough to lay a second clutch if the first eggs are lost.

Watery bed *A comb-crested jacana male watches over his floating nest in an Australian marsh. Females lay eggs in the nest of each male in their territory.*

SHARING PARENTAL CHORES

The commonest task shared by birds is that of feeding their offspring. Some other animals also show a high degree of mutual responsibility.

Gentle giants *A female Nile crocodile (above) uncovers her nest, gently tossing a hatchling into her mouth before carrying it, with its noisy litter mates, to a quiet pool. So small is a newly hatched crocodile, seen here (left) by its mother's claw, that it basks (below) on its mother's head if it tires of insect hunting.*

Nile crocodiles keep in touch with their young

Although seldom celebrated for their sweetness of disposition, it does seem at least that Nile crocodiles are caring parents. Not only do they see to the feeding and well-being of their offspring, they appear to converse with them too.

Both parents watch over the infant crocodiles as they hunt for beetles and small frogs in the water, coming to the rescue whenever they hear the piping alarm call of a youngster that has become separated from its family.

Vocal communication begins just before the female's 90-odd eggs hatch – the youngsters chirp loudly enough within the shells to be heard even through the sand covering the nest. This triggers the mother to begin digging down to the unhatched eggs and hatchling crocodiles. Then, very gently, 20 or so at a time, she carries them in a pouch in her mouth down to the water's edge. She patiently rolls unhatched eggs in her mouth until the hatchlings inside break out.

During the first few weeks, until the young crocodiles learn the basics of hunting and finding food, there is constant calling between parents and offspring and among the young hatchlings themselves. As each new batch of youngsters is brought to the water, those already there greet them with soft calls.

The novice swimmers begin to spread out through the reeds, calling constantly to each other to ensure they keep together. If an eagle or other predator appears, the mother warns the whole brood by vibrating her muscles and creating a tremor that the youngsters feel through the water. They recognise it as a signal to dive and hide. Both parents may leap out of the water at any predatory bird that circles too close. When the danger is past, the female submerges and must signal to them again, for they are all assembled and clinging to her back as she resurfaces.

Male and female birds raise chicks together

Both wandering albatrosses and condors exhaust themselves raising a chick every two years, but they would be quite unable to raise any young at all if the labour was not shared by both parents.

Ninety per cent of birds share the task of parental care, compared with only three per cent of mammals. Part of the reason why male birds help is that they are equally well equipped to do so as females. Young birds eat food that can be collected by either parent, just as either bird can take on the work of nest-building and brooding. Then, too, if the male helps with rearing his young, he might well succeed in raising more offspring than if he takes the riskier option of courting more females.

Lessons for survival

Some birds, such as the wandering albatross, take turns in incubating, allowing one partner to go off and feed. With others, the great hornbill for instance, the male brings food while the female does all the sitting, though she, too, takes on feeding duties when the chicks are half grown. In some other hornbill species, however, the male continues to feed the entire family until the chicks are ready to fly.

But parenthood goes further than just feeding and protection. Tuition is also vital, particularly

Constant care *An Andean condor (right) approaches its nest with food for its young. Parent birds share the care of their single hatchling, which will remain dependent on them for up to six months. They can breed only every second year.*

Maiden journey *Little auk nestlings launch themselves from the cliff tops, urged on by their parents. But parents will stand between their young and the cliff edge if they think they are too young to leave.*

A good provider *A male great hornbill (below) builds the seal that encloses his mate and offspring. Until the chicks are half grown it will be his responsibility alone to ensure constant deliveries of the fruit and insects that make up their diet.*

for fledglings, such as those of the little auk, whose lives are at risk when they leave the safety of the nest. These tiny Arctic sea birds have to glide from their cliff-top nesting ledges to the ocean far below, a hazardous journey for a four-week-old chick. Should it fail to reach the sea it will quickly be snatched up by an arctic fox or other predator. Parents encourage their chicks to make the jump by vigorously calling to them as they launch themselves, repeating their urgings until the chick has landed safely on the water.

Marmosets share the burden of parenthood

Male marmosets – squirrel-sized monkeys living in the canopy of the South American rain forest – do more than just provide food to ensure that the young will survive.

Marmosets are almost entirely vegetarian and are constantly on the move, searching for food. The female cannot raise the young on her own because, within a very short time of birth, they grow too heavy for her to carry through the trees. Although the male makes little contribution towards feeding his offspring, he does do most of the carrying, leaving the female free to collect food and devote her energies to producing milk.

It may not always be the father that carries the young, because marmosets live in extended family groups where usually only one male breeds. All the males, however, help to carry the young. It is only through such division of labour that marmoset parents can successfully rear a family.

Baby minding *Clinging tightly to a male's back, young marmosets are carried through the forest. They are returned to their mothers to be fed, but the family males carry them around until, at two months old, they can travel independently.*

FUEL FOR GROWING UP

In the early stages of life, most creatures need high-energy foods that contain proteins, vitamins, fats and sugars to help them grow quickly.

Fresh food laid on for developing wasp larva

Nectar is the food of adult North American jewel wasps. But their juvenile diet was very different, consisting of high protein cockroaches to give the larvae a good start in life. When she is ready to lay her eggs, a female jewel wasp digs a separate nest for each one, then provisions it with a cockroach as larval food.

But a dead cockroach would soon putrefy in warm weather, and therefore become useless as food. It has to be preserved in some way, and the female wasp resolves the problem by keeping her youngster's meal alive. When she catches a cockroach, she paralyses it with a skilfully delivered sting, and nips off its antennae. Then the victim is dragged into the cool, dark nest where she lays an egg on its body.

Her task complete, the wasp seals the nest with a number of small stones, vibrating each one carefully to fit it into place. Inside, the paralysed cockroach is helpless as the larva hatches and starts to feed on it. Remarkably, it stays alive, because the wasp venom immobilises the wing and leg muscles but has no effect on the heart. By the time the cockroach dies, the larva is ready to pupate and become an adult. Two weeks later it emerges as a jewel wasp.

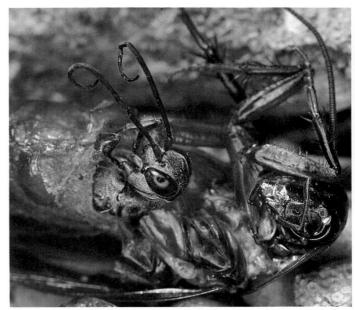

Fresh start *A jewel wasp emerges from the shell of the cockroach on which it fed as a larva. Its mother placed the living but paralysed cockroach in its nest chamber.*

Honeybees prove you are what you eat

The career and prospects of the honeybee are entirely decided by what food it is given when it is a four-day-old larva. The larvae in the hive are fed by young worker bees, and for the first three days all get protein-rich royal jelly, made of pollen and honey, mixed with secretions from glands in the worker's mouthparts.

After this, larvae destined to be worker bees or drones are fed bee bread, which is made mainly of pollen. Ordinary worker bees fed on this diet develop barbed stings and pollen baskets on their legs, essential tools for a life that will be spent protecting and providing food for the hive.

Food for a queen

Most of the larvae of honeybees become workers, but if the queen in a colony begins to fail, or leads a swarm away from an overcrowded colony, the workers prepare several queen cells. The first queen that hatches strips the other cells open and kills her potential rivals, then takes over control of the hive.

The workers construct conical queen cells, which are larger than

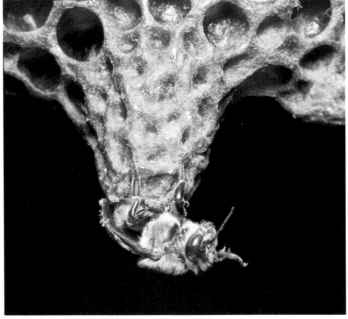

Royal food for a queen *A virgin queen honeybee emerges from her cell, where she has been fed, as a larva, a diet of royal jelly. This food encourages her ovaries to grow.*

the normal six-sided cells that make up the bulk of the honeycomb. Queen cells are attached to the edges of the comb, where they are visited and fed by the workers ten times more often than the cells of other larvae. The larvae within are fed entirely on royal jelly, but it is a richer version containing more sugar and more secretions from the workers' mouth glands. This encourages the larvae to eat more and, in fact, the attendants are so generous with food for them that the future queens literally swim in a sea of royal jelly.

Their rich diet makes the future queens develop large ovaries in place of the pollen baskets and barbed stings of workers.

Mammals get a good start on mother's milk

A mother kangaroo suckling two youngsters of different ages at the same time will produce two different types of milk for them. From one teat, the tiny newborn in her pouch gets slightly diluted milk with very little fat. From the other, a young 'joey' about a year old, which has by now left the pouch for good, gets an increasing amount of fat in its diet.

A complete food

The milk supplied to their young by all mammal mothers is a truly remarkable food. It contains fats and sugars to provide basic energy, essential vitamins and amino acids (the building blocks of proteins) that the youngster cannot make for itself, and water and mineral salts. During the first hours after birth, a mother's milk is also heavily laced with antibodies to protect her young against future infection.

The proportions of the basic ingredients in a mother's milk vary widely from one species to another. Seals and sea lions, for example, produce milk that is rich in fat – a concentrated source of energy for animals in need of protection from extreme cold. By contrast, the milk of a black rhinoceros, for instance, has a high water content, which probably compensates for the dryness of its habitat.

Young mammals lead a very protected life compared with most other creatures. They have to compete for food only with their litter mates, and the ready supply of milk, even while they are being weaned onto adult food, enables them to grow sturdily until they are nearly fully developed. They are defenceless and dependent for longer than most other animals, but have their mother's protection until they are ready for independence.

However, for nearly all other creatures apart from birds, the start in life is more hazardous, because they have to feed themselves from the moment they hatch, and are forced to compete for food not only with litter mates but with other species as well. Although a young alligator, for example, gets parental protection at first, it has to feed itself on

Mother's milk *A Galápagos sea lion calf (below) is suckled by its mother. The pup may be nursed until it is two, though 5-12 months is more usual. A Japanese macaque (right) suckles her young for a year. Mother and daughter bonds last into adulthood, but sons leave the family when they are fully grown.*

water insects as soon as it emerges from the egg, competing for them with adult birds and fish for perhaps several years until it is large and strong enough to take bigger prey, such as fish.

Most insects have to be independent from the moment they hatch as larvae, although the mother usually lays her eggs on or near a food supply. The larvae are often less mobile than their parents – their main function at this stage is to eat and grow. Many insects transform their body shape completely at maturity, after which they eat little or not at all, since they then devote what time and energy they have to the task of reproduction.

Tall order *A giraffe calf grows quickly on its diet of mother's milk. Young males are about 6 ft (1.9 m) high at birth and grow at a rate of roughly 3 in (80 mm) a month, doubling their height by the time they are two years old.*

Well protected *A mother leopard suckles her young on the Masai Mara Reserve in Kenya. The cubs are hidden away until they are six weeks old, and do not leave their mother for another 12-14 months.*

EVER-OPEN MOUTHS

Although only mammals can produce milk, many other animals provide unusual, 'self-prepared' foods for nourishing their young.

Flamingo fish soup and pigeon milk

Only mammals are capable of producing milk to feed their young; however, other creatures can supply nutritious liquids too, including such unusual delicacies as shrimp soup, nectar and even 'crop milk'.

Flamingos feed their young on algae, shrimps or other minute creatures, but when foraging a long way from the nest it would obviously be impractical for them to bring the food back a mouthful at a time. So they swallow it instead and then regurgitate it as a partially digested soup into the beaks of their nestlings.

The female hummingbird carries nectar to the nest in her crop – the throat sac in which birds store food before digesting it. While hovering above the nest, she regurgitates a brew of nectar and insects down her long beak into the throats of her young.

Gulls either carry whole fish back to the nest or regurgitate food for their offspring. The chick pecks at its parent's beak to stimulate the flow of food, then, as the food emerges, grips the parent's bill in its own. Newly hatched chicks will instinctively peck at anything that remotely resembles a beak, but as they grow, they become more discriminating and peck only at a parent's bill.

Pigeons have developed a different adaptation. In place of storing food for their young, they digest and absorb it completely, and feed their offspring on 'crop milk' instead. This secretion, rich in protein and fat, is produced from the lining of the crop. For the first few days after hatching, the squabs – young pigeons – are fed on crop milk, but as they grow, they are 'weaned' on to solid food.

In emergencies, male emperor penguins can also produce crop milk. When the female has finished laying her egg she returns to the sea to feed and recover, leaving incubation to her male partner. As a rule, she returns and relieves the male in time to feed the chick as it hatches. But if she is late the male penguin begins to feed the chick on a form of crop milk, even though he himself has not eaten for almost a month.

Liquid lunches *Greater flamingos (right) solve food haulage problems by feeding their young on semi-digested crustacean soup, while pigeon squabs (below) receive nutrient and fat-rich 'milk' manufactured in the parent's crop.*

Slime and eggs on the nursery menu

Unusual 'milk' producers indeed are the male and female discus fish, both of which secrete a nutritious slime to feed their shoal of youngsters. Deprived of this, the young fish die, even when there is plenty of other food available.

Very few frogs look after their young once they have hatched, but among those that do are the red-and-blue arrow-poison frogs, which feed their tadpoles on infertile eggs that they produce solely for this purpose.

Eggs are also nursery food for ferocious Australian bulldog ants. Normally only queen ants lay eggs but worker bulldog ants lay them too. They give them to the larvae in their care, having first pierced the egg membranes to make feeding easier for their charges.

Fish 'milk' *The myriad young of brown discus fish have few feeding problems since, as with mammals' milk, their parents exude a substance that provides offspring with the nutrition they need.*

Feeding time mayhem among young egrets

As every parent knows, children will fight over almost anything. Seldom, except in myth and legend, do they fight to the death. Not so with egrets, whose parents seem positively to encourage their young to murder.

Great egrets bring fish back to the nest for their chicks, which proceed to squabble over the division of the spoils. If food is scarce, these fights become serious, and often the largest and strongest chick will kill the smaller ones to ensure enough food for itself.

The bullying and eventual slaying of its nestmates by the largest chick results from the way in which the egrets incubate their eggs. Most birds produce an egg each day until they have a full clutch, though do not begin to incubate them until the last egg has been laid. This ensures that all

the chicks hatch at more or less the same time. Egrets, though, commence incubation as soon as the first egg is laid, so giving the first chick a head start on its brothers and sisters.

When the fights begin, the adults make no attempt to intervene. But the parents' seemingly uncaring attitude is actually a device to raise more chicks. In a good year, when there is enough food to go round, there is little fighting and all the chicks survive. In a bad year, battles escalate and the younger chicks are killed. Nevertheless, this at least ensures that the eldest gets sufficient food to survive.

A harsh remedy, but it solves a food problem faced by many birds. In times and places where supplies are variable, one of two things may happen. The birds may be triggered to lay a lot of eggs which, in a year of plenty would give overwhelming reproductive success. The risk of this is that if the year

Survival of the strongest *In times of food shortage, great egret parents ensure that their strongest chick at least survives by permitting it to bully and kill its siblings.*

turns out badly, there will not be enough food to go round – and with so many mouths to feed all the young may starve.

The alternative is that the bird is moved to lay only a single egg.

Even if the season is poor, it will probably be able to feed one chick adequately. But on the other hand, it is unable to take reproductive advantage of any sudden glut of food that might occur.

Lesson for life *Chamois kids are born in spring on secluded, inaccessible Eurasian mountain ledges. Only a few hours after birth, a kid can follow its mother on her return to the herd, learning a harsh lesson in balance and sure-footedness, for it has to skip along precipitous ridges and up steep slopes. One slip can bring death.*

GROWING FAST, GROWING SLOW

Some young are born able to stand on their own feet and fend for themselves. For others, relying on mother is the best way to survive.

From helpless pup to hunter in a fortnight

Harp seal pups, born on Arctic ice floes, are weaned and ready to go to sea and fend for themselves within about 15 days of birth. Their mothers produce copious amounts of exceptionally rich milk, enabling the pups to almost treble their weight in a fortnight. In their brief babyhood, the pups make the most of their mothers' undivided attention before they are abandoned to take their chances alone in the Arctic waters.

Even in comparison with other seals, harp seal pups have a short babyhood. Ringed seal pups, also

born in the Arctic but on fast ice which doesn't break up, are suckled for two months, and southern fur seal pups of the Antarctic area where there are no polar bears, are suckled for about seven months.

Generally, small animals mature faster than large animals, but seals prove that size is not the only determining factor. A harp seal, about 7 ft (2 m) long, is a moderately large creature, yet its pups have one of the shortest suckling times of any mammal.

Exactly why these Arctic seals need to grow up so quickly is uncertain, but it may be that with a longer suckling period, the ice could break up before the

Fast growth *Within a fortnight of birth, a harp seal pup (left) almost trebles in weight from about 26 lb (12 kg) to 70 lb (32 kg). It is born in March as the ice (above) starts to break up and is too unstable for marauding polar bears. It is a race against time for the pup to fatten up before being forced into the water.*

Born to run *Hundreds of eyes watch the birth of wildebeest calves on the African plains – vultures circling overhead, lions lazing in the sun and spotted hyenas nosing round the fringes of the herd. All will make a meal of a newborn wildebeest if they can. To have any chance of survival, calves have to be able to run a minute or so after birth.*

pup had developed a thick enough layer of protective body fat to survive in the icy water. Or maybe the brief but intensive nursing period ensures that seal pups will spend the shortest possible time lying defenceless on the ice.

Harp seals mate not long after giving birth in early March, but they can delay the implantation of the embryo long enough for the pups to be born in the following March, just as the ice begins to break up. This timing protects them from polar bears, which hunt on stable ice earlier in the year.

Other mammals, such as wildebeest and chamois, have young that are born ready to run from predators, but depend on their mother's milk for many weeks.

Growing slowly allows more time to learn

By the time a young oilbird is three months old, it weighs twice as much as its parents, and most of its weight is fat. Oilbirds, gull-sized but more like nightjars in appearance, live in caves in Central America and forage for fruit at night. A chick's thick layer of blubber keeps it warm in a cool cave and frees its parents from the task of brooding, so they can devote themselves to finding food. Even with both parents feeding their two to four chicks, each youngster is often more than four months old before it can fly. It gradually loses its excess weight as its feathers grow.

The oilbird chick's diet, the fruits and berries of palms, laurels and camphor trees, is high in fat but low in protein. It is this shortage of protein that slows down the chick's growth. Many species of seed-eating birds make up for the lack of protein in their diet by feeding their young on protein-rich insects. The beautiful blue-capped

Cave dweller *Oilbirds live in caves and build nests mainly from regurgitated fruit. They feed their chicks on oily palm and camphor fruit for about four months.*

cordon-bleu bird of East Africa, for example, eats only grass seeds but feeds its young solely on termites and other insects.

Youngsters that grow slowly are vulnerable for much longer and need more looking after. But there are benefits, because parents and offspring are together for longer, so the parents may be able to pass on more of their experience. African elephant calves, for instance, are

suckled for two years or more. This gives them time to pick up from their mothers all the subtleties of elephant social behaviour, as well as the chance to learn the best places to eat and drink.

In many cases, it is not so much the quality of the food supply that slows down an infant's growth rate as its need to observe how to survive in places where competition for food and resources is intense.

Competent curlews and helpless songbirds

Curlew chicks hatch with their eyes wide open and a full coat of down. After a few hours spent drying out beneath their mother's wings, they are ready to leave their

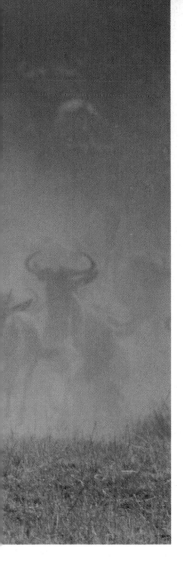

moorland nest and start hunting for insects and worms to eat. Their mother leads her well-camouflaged brood away from the nest – a scrape in the ground – and stands guard over them for the next six weeks until they can fly.

In contrast, a blackbird hatchling emerges from the egg naked

and helpless, able only to open its beak and swallow the food its parents bring it. Each chick's eyes are shut and its legs are too frail to support it. For the first two weeks, the chick stays in its nest, which is well hidden in a thicket of bushes. But by the time it is three weeks old the chick is ready to fly.

Chicks, such as those of blackbirds, which hatch before they are well developed, benefit from early parental care, and can put all their energy into growing and preparing themselves for flight. This is fine as long as they are well hidden.

But chicks such as curlews, which hatch in exposed places, have to be well enough developed to run and hide. They put a lot of energy into looking after themselves, and so take longer to fly.

Foraging family *Curlew parents lead their chicks, commonly four, away from the nest only hours after hatching. Since it is crucial for the chicks to hatch at the same time even though eggs are laid days apart, the hen does not start incubating until the last egg is laid.*

71

WHY DO ANIMALS PLAY?

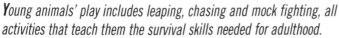

Young animals' play includes leaping, chasing and mock fighting, all activities that teach them the survival skills needed for adulthood.

Practising the skills needed for adult life

Life is an endless game, or rather a series of games, for young lions. A pair of littermates may start their day by playing tag, one bounding after the other and swatting at its legs or grabbing at its rump with a paw.

This game could turn into a wrestling match, with the pair rolling around as they claw and bite at each other. Then there is the pawing game, in which cubs sit or lie down and swipe at each

Water sports *Young grizzly bears play in an Alaskan river. Boisterous games provide good exercise and also teach youngsters the limits of their strength.*

other with a forepaw. More energetic is the hunting game, with one cub stalking the other then rushing at it – a charge that might set off another bout of wrestling. Stalking games do not have to be played with another cub – a grasshopper or the tip of father's tail make equally exciting targets.

Exercise and proficiency

Evolution selects those animals that live their lives as efficiently as possible. So why do so many animals appear to waste energy in playing? Perhaps evolution favours those that play if it helps their young to survive and to reproduce.

Different play activities serve different ends. Most are forms of exercise for growing bodies, but a lone youngster's acrobatic leaping

Provocative behaviour *A lion cub may goad one of its littermates into a mock fight by nuzzling its face (top). This develops both social and defensive skills. Pulling a parent's tail (bottom) is one of the favourite games of lion cubs.*

and twisting may help it to understand and expand the limits of its physical abilities. When youngsters stalk and pounce on grasshoppers, the skill being honed is the coordination of eyes and paws.

Hunting can be dangerous, and by rehearsing in play the skills that will be needed, lion cubs learn the lessons without risking mistakes that could be fatal. But hunting is not the only danger to be faced. At times the cubs may be at risk from other lions. Games with other youngsters in the pride are crucial for learning self-defence.

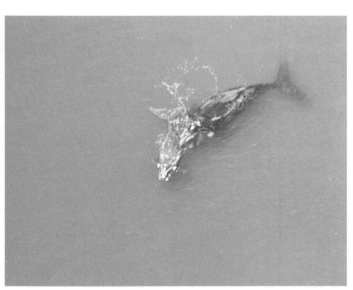

A family affair *A mother southern right whale playfully nudges her calf off the Valdés Peninsula, Argentina, which is a favourite playground for these 50 ft (15 m) whales.*

Youngsters signal mock alarms during play

Acrobatic play can distract whale calves for hours on end. By swimming away from its mother and back to her side in increasingly complex circles and figures of eight, a whale calf develops steadily in strength and ability. At other times it plays by rolling onto its back and floating belly up, or by slapping the surface of the sea with its tail.

As with most play, these actions are specific to an animal species and relate to adult behaviour. The fawn of a red deer – elk in North America – spends the first few days of its life alone with its mother. Then they both return to the rest of the herd, giving the newborn youngster a chance to play with its peers. They never play hunting games as lion cubs do. Because they are prey animals, their play focuses on the behaviour they need for making an escape. They join in chases and make mock alarm signals such as the characteristic high-stepping gait, or they suddenly freeze and stand motionless. This is obviously play behaviour, because there are no predators around to give real cause for alarm. Generally the romping ends as suddenly as it began.

Solitary play like the gambolling of lambs may be a way of exercising growing muscles, and also a means of acquiring the skills needed for such physical feats as climbing steep slopes.

Aggressive games may help in future battles

Red deer fawns frequently play a game that seems much like one that human youngsters play – 'King of the Castle'. One fawn climbs up onto a rock or tree stump, and defends it against all-comers.

The skills perfected in this game of antler-wrestling and pushing are put into practice in later life when males fight in earnest to decide which one of them will win females for his harem.

On alpine mountain slopes, ibex kids clash heads in mock battles similar to the serious battles of older males, and in tropical forests young monkeys play tag or compete to be 'King of the Castle' on a convenient log or termite mound.

For young animals that belong to herds or groups, perhaps the most significant aspect of play is its impact on social behaviour. The 'pecking order' that affects the lives of many social animals is first established during play, when the youngsters learn the limits of self-assertiveness – when to back down and when to take advantage of another's weakness.

Without play, an animal cannot effectively learn to deal with its adult role and may find difficulty in adjusting to adulthood. Rhesus monkeys deprived of playmates, for example, grow up to be antisocial and aggressive. This may explain why it is the social animals that are the most playful, and why it is usually the younger animals in a group that play.

Whatever the reason for play, it is so widespread among animals that human vocabulary is full of references to it – people 'monkey around', for example, indulge in 'horse play', and 'kid' each other.

Gymnastic display *Three young Barbary apes perform acrobatics in a rock pool. Such play exercises growing muscles and teaches youngsters how to behave towards companions.*

Head-on collision *Young Alpine ibex males knock heads in a mock fight. This helps to prepare them for the mating battles they will fight as adults.*

THE SERIOUS SIDE OF A SENSE OF FUN

Since a slap or a tickle might be misinterpreted, animals wishing to frolic are careful to give clear signals of friendly intentions towards prospective playmates.

Gurgles, grunts and grins signal playtime

In playful mood, chimpanzees put on an almost human grin, with eyes wide, lips drawn back and mouth slightly open. No teeth are shown, however, because, as with most monkeys and apes, a chimpanzee that shows its teeth is indicating either fear or aggression.

Dogs, too, 'smile' to solicit play. Although their teeth can be seen, it is through a slight lift of the upper lip – an effect quite different from a snarl, in which the lips are pulled back as though to reveal the size of their canine teeth. The play smile is accompanied by a play bow, in which the dog lowers its forequarters and raises its wagging tail in the air as though eagerly waiting to pounce.

There are many other clues given by an animal with playful intentions. Its step is bouncy, it moves at an angle towards its prospective playfellow rather than in a straight line; often, its head is cocked and its mouth open. But there are other distinctive signals – mongooses whip their tails and polecats make little stiff-legged leaps. Parrots and Steller's sea lions both give a gentle nip to incite play, and douc langur monkeys of Southeast Asia close their eyes to reveal bright blue eyelids.

Play sounds sometimes endorse play movements: gibbons give a grunt-squeal, orang-utans grunt, gorillas chuckle and some mice give little gurgles. However it is expressed, the invitation to play always carries a clear message: 'What follows is not to be taken seriously.' So the bites are half-hearted and never break the skin, and the clawing is restrained.

Grinning for fun *Despite the roughness of the game, the young chimpanzee's 'play face', a grin with no teeth exposed, shows he is not taking it seriously.*

Solitary play develops muscles and skills

A kitten pounces on a drifting leaf or wrestles with a ball of wool; obviously, playing alone or with an inanimate object gives it pleasure. Young monkeys spend happy hours swinging acrobatically or carrying sticks around like a child with a doll. Captive dolphins spontaneously push balls round the pool in solo games of water polo, and bottle-nosed dolphins at sea delight in riding ships' bow waves.

Not all animal play is as easy to identify. When a young bird turns a stick in its beak, for instance, is it playing, or is it manoeuvring the stick to pick insects out of bark?

Making a splash
Young humpback whales frequently put on performances that most humans would interpret as play. Bursting from the sea in a flurry of foam and spray, they twist gracefully in midair before thunderously falling back again, leaving a spout of frothing water to mark their departure. Re-emerging at the surface some minutes later, the whales spiral lazily through the water, smacking the surface with each great flipper in turn.

Then, as a finale, they dive, lifting their great tails out of the water and bringing them down again with a flourish and a crash that can be heard for a long way. Although their behaviour seems no more than a splendid game, the noisy smacking of the surface is thought to be a method of communicating with other whales, or it

Feeling fine Expression and posture announce that, as well as stretching his muscles, this young orang-utan relishes every moment of his treetop flight.

may somehow be connected with the search for food – perhaps to stun or panic a shoal of fish.

It is not always easy to recognise playfulness in another species. Reptiles, fish, insects and wild birds do not seem to play, although crows and ravens often engage in aerobatics in updraughts, apparently for the fun of it. Whether they are playing, or whether this is merely a human interpretation of their behaviour, is difficult to say.

Among mammals, play is confined mainly to carnivores and primates. Even here, play is much rarer among adults than among the young, but it does occur. An adult oriental short-clawed otter, for example, is an adept juggler. Lying on its back, this smallest of all otters – about 3 ft (90 cm) long – tosses a pebble into the air and keeps it airborne by hitting it with alternate paws. Unlike other otters its paws are not webbed, and it is very dexterous – this animal reaches for objects with its forelimbs rather than its mouth.

In another game, it rolls a pebble down a slightly bent forelimb, which it suddenly straightens to flip the pebble back up into its paw. Throwing a stone into the water and diving after it is another otter pastime. In winter, European and North American otters make slides in the snow. At other times of year, and in much warmer climates, they construct muddy slides on steep riverbanks, so that each ride can end with a splash.

Play or plan? A Barbary ape in Morocco (top right) and a young humpback whale off the Newfoundland coast (above) appear to share a common enjoyment of playing in water. Yet their behaviour may have a deeper purpose. The ape, for example, may be ridding itself of parasites, and the whale may be telling other whales where it is.

Rough play teaches a youngster discretion

Although most animal play is characterised by exaggerated movements and restrained 'fights', things do occasionally get out of hand. Older juvenile males of all species invariably play more roughly than very young animals, and the younger ones sometimes get hurt in the free-for-all of a game if boisterous older males are involved. Parents then have to intervene. But a few experiences of this kind at an early stage help to teach a younger animal the limits of its ability.

In primates, for example, the number of very young and juvenile females in a play group is often inversely related to the number of juvenile males present, because the younger animals drop out as the activity gets more frenetic.

Family bonding One of the most important aspects of animal play is that between mother and offspring. Play gives this young chimpanzee confidence, and tighten the ties with its mother.

LEARNING ABOUT LIFE

Although much animal behaviour is determined by inherited genes, some is learnt from parents or by experience and observation.

Learning how to hunt, by trial and error

Sometimes a mother cheetah that has caught a young gazelle for her cubs does not kill it. Instead she releases it in front of them and encourages them to chase the animal and finally bring it down. If the gazelle escapes, the mother may retrieve it and release it again to give her cubs another chance,

although she may let it go instead to teach them a lesson. In this way the cubs can perfect their stalking skills and learn the combination of speed and stealth needed to make a kill successfully.

A cheetah usually hunts alone, but when her cubs are about six weeks old they follow her. At four months old they are weaned, and the mother takes them on practice hunts, giving them a chance to try out the skills they have acquired

while romping with their litter mates in their first few months of life. Now the 'paw slap' they have used endlessly in daily play is used to fell prey. The mother lets her cubs learn from their mistakes, and continues to feed them until they can hunt for themselves.

The ability to learn through trial and error is essential for the survival of many animals. Young badgers get no help from their parents in learning to forage. They enquire

Hunting lessons *Once they are big enough to follow her around, cheetah cubs (top) take great interest in their mother's hunts. When they are half grown (above), the cubs practise their hunting skills on captured prey.*

into everything, and are quick to discover that turning over stones with their snouts produces food such as worms and beetles. They soon learn what tastes good and what does not, and rapidly develop a successful foraging pattern.

Cleaning food *Before eating sweet potatoes, Japanese macaques wash the sand off them in a pool, a technique they have learned from another member of their troop.*

Japanese macaques learn from each other

Biologists working on the Pacific island of Koshima in 1956 began leaving sweet potatoes on a sandy beach to entice a resident troop of Japanese macaque monkeys into the open. One day a year later, one of the troop, a young female named Imo by the biologists, decided to wash a potato before eating it. Until then the monkeys had eaten the potatoes with sand still stuck to them. Imo picked up a potato, wandered over to a pool, dipped the potato in the water and washed it with her other hand.

Having discovered, apparently, that this improved the sweet potato's taste, she kept doing it. A month later, one of her playmates began to imitate her. Four months later her mother began to copy them. Eventually the whole troop learnt to wash sweet potatoes.

Imo's innovations did not stop there. Along with the sweet potatoes the biologists provided grains of rice, which the monkeys picked up from the sand one by one. Collecting this nutritious food was a slow process until Imo came up with a short cut. She began picking up handfuls of sand and grain and flinging them into pools of water. As the sand sank, she skimmed the floating grain from the surface.

Inquisitive, intelligent and playful, Japanese macaques are keen to experiment and quick to learn. Before they are a year old, youngsters have discovered most of the things around them that are good to eat. They catch and taste pieces that fall into their mother's lap as she feeds, and even pick bits out of her mouth with their hands. But infants also learn from their playmates, and it is usually youngsters that are the first to discover a new source of food. Sweets are not part of a macaque's natural diet, but since the monkeys have come into contact with people, they have often been offered this human treat. One troop was watched by biologists as they learned to deal with this new kind of food.

Benefits for all

At first none of the troop recognised the sweets as food, but eventually a particularly adventurous two-year-old tried chewing one. Before long her mother and her playmates had acquired the taste. Within a year most of the troop knew that sweets tasted good.

For the macaques there are great advantages in learning from each other. It helps individuals to respond quickly to changes in their environment, and also allows a whole troop to benefit from the chance discovery by an individual – something that cannot happen among creatures whose behaviour is determined by genes alone.

Mothers teach their young to handle food

In a small pine forest not far from Jerusalem, the local black rats spend almost all their time in the trees, hardly ever descending to the ground. They have effectively taken the place of squirrels, which are not found in this forest. The rats feed almost exclusively on pine seeds, a food that no other rats anywhere in the world have ever been recorded as eating. They have no difficulty in stripping the scales from the pine cones to reach the nutritious kernels inside.

Like the young of a number of other animals – grizzly bears and raccoons, for instance – the rats learn from their mothers how to obtain food. Studies have shown that city-living rats cannot open pine cones, but if their babies are fostered by forest-dwelling mothers they grow up with the skill. On the other hand, if the babies of forest-dwelling rats are fostered by city-living mothers, they never find out how to eat pine seeds.

Learning by example *Grizzly cubs (right) in North America learn to enjoy the taste of fish from their mothers, who take their young ones with them when they go to rivers in summer to catch the salmon as the fish head upstream for their breeding grounds. Young raccoons (below), known as kits, not only learn from their mothers that crayfish are good to eat, they also find out how to hunt by watching her closely and imitating her every movement. At first the kits are too excitable and clumsy to be successful but with time they become efficient hunters.*

PIGGYBACK AND OTHER RIDES

For some mothers, the simplest way to get helpless offspring out of danger is to pick them up and carry them. There are many different ways of doing this.

Mother's pouch is not always a safe haven

A newly born kangaroo is little more than a breathing foetus. As soon as the baked-bean-sized baby is born, it drags itself up its mother's belly to the safety of her pouch and there it fastens onto one of the four teats inside. Then it settles down to do nothing but feed for the next six months or so.

When, at about seven months old, the infant hops out to join the outside world, it has developed into a miniature kangaroo. Until it is almost a year old, the youngster hops back into its mother's pouch whenever any danger threatens. A year-old kangaroo is a heavy load, however, and a mother may sometimes have to jettison her youngster in order to give herself an extra life-saving spurt of speed.

The female brown antechinus or broad-footed marsupial mouse from Australia, has a saucer-shaped 'skirt' of loose skin round the outer limits of her underbelly. It acts as a shield for her litter of up to 12 youngsters, who hang by their mouths from her nipples as she moves. In this way, she carries them about with her for the first month of their lives.

Hanging on *The yearling Western grey kangaroo surveying the world from its mother's pouch (above) will shortly have to vacate it for a tiny brother or sister, but it will still be suckled for another six months or so. The babies of the brown antechinus (left) dangle from their mother's nipples as she forages at night for insects and other small creatures.*

Mother's back is the safest way to travel

Wherever she travels, a mother baboon carries her baby with her. From the moment it is born, the youngster clings to the fur on her chest and sucks from her teats as she moves about. At about five months old the baby transfers to ride on its mother's back so that it can see what is going on, although it may continue to be suckled until it is eight months old.

Scorpions, too, cling to their mother's back for protection. They are born well formed but with soft, white outer casings, and their stings are blunt. Until these vulnerable babies are ready to hunt insects and spiders for themselves, they climb on their mother's back and ride there, protected by the venomous sting in her tail.

In the tropical forests of South America, a female tamandua, or lesser anteater, suckles her single baby for the first six months of its life. Anteaters develop slowly, and a youngster cannot forage on its own until it is nearly two years old. It clings to its mother's back as she forages amid the trees at night, and learns how to tear open ant or termite nests with its curved front claws and then catch the inhabitants on its long, sticky tongue.

Safely in the saddle *Amid Kenyan grassland, a young olive baboon rides on its mother's back while her companion playfully caresses it.*

Sting in the tail *Young scorpions crowd onto their mother's back beneath the shelter of her lethal sting.*

Clinging to mother *A young tamandua anteater clings to its mother's back. It is suckled for six months, but hangs on for a further 18 months until it is independent.*

Line-ahead formation for foraging shrews

Almost as soon as their eyes are open at about three weeks old, young white-toothed shrews begin to supplement their mother's milk with insects they find for themselves. This helps to relieve the physical demands on the mother of suckling six or seven babies.

Adult shrews weigh no more than ½ oz (15 g), but have to eat their own weight in insects every day to stay alive. So for a female shrew, feeding herself is a full-time job, apart from producing milk for a litter. Adult shrews quickly die if they go without food for just a few hours, so the mother has to forage constantly, and she takes her litter with her as soon as they can see.

The shrew family travels in single file, one baby grasping its mother's tail in its teeth, and the others holding the tail of the one in front. The group may split up to forage, but if danger threatens a call from their mother reunites them within seconds, and they reform the chain and hurry to safety.

Nose to tail *African white-toothed shrews file behind their mother, each one hanging on to the one in front so tightly that if she is picked up they dangle like a furry rope.*

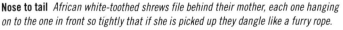

A caring bite on the back of the neck

Lions may be the lords of the African plains, but their cubs, like all cats, are born blind and helpless. Their eyes open when they are six days old. To keep their litters of up to five out of harm's way, the females keep them well hidden in thickets or reed beds.

If marauding hyenas or hunting dogs get too close to the den for comfort, the lionesses move their cubs one by one to a safer place as quickly and silently as possible.

Like all cats, they pick up a cub by the loose skin at the back of its neck, and to avoid bumping it carry it with head held high. The cubs hang still and silent so that they are unobtrusive and easy to carry. Cubs are slightly spotted, but the spots fade around weaning time at about three months old.

Silent move *A lioness chooses her den carefully to keep her cubs hidden. If she feels threatened, she moves them, one by one, quickly and quietly to a new den.*

NURSERIES AND BABY MINDING

Keeping youngsters safe while their parents are finding food or until they are strong enough to fend for themselves can be a family or community undertaking.

Ways and means of minding youngsters

Large flocks of rheas graze amid herds of bush deer on the South American pampas. Relatives of the ostrich, the flightless greater rheas stand up to 5 ft (1.5 m) tall, but many of the flock may be smaller youngsters being shepherded by their father, and they whistle to each other to keep in touch.

A male rhea invites perhaps 12 females to lay in his nest, a scrape on the ground. He alone incubates the combined clutch of 30 or more eggs – instances of 80 eggs have been known. The youngsters hatch after about five weeks and the father watches over them as they forage for grass, insects and small creatures such as mice. Strays may tag along with his flock – chicks wander in all directions, following any adult bird. So a rhea father may be minding a crèche of his own and other fathers' chicks.

Safety on a cliff

Sometimes the terrain offers animals an opportunity to shepherd their young in an unusual way. In the Ein Avdat valley in Israel's Negev desert, ibex kids jostle on a cliffside ledge, bleating for attention. From time to time a female leaves her browsing higher up and descends to the nursery, a journey that ends in a downward leap across a 3 ft (1 m) gap above a sheer drop of some 40 ft (12 m).

Kids gather round, attempting to suck from her teats. Carefully she steps round them searching for her own kid. Only when she is satisfied by the scent that a youngster is hers does the ibex suckle it. Hyenas and other predators cannot reach this cliffside nursery, to which each mother led her kid when it was a few weeks old. Not for several weeks will it be strong enough to make the upward leap necessary to follow her out again.

Looking after the children *On the Chilean pampas, a male lesser rhea (above), a slightly smaller relative of the greater rhea of more northern parts of South America, keeps watch over a flock of highly active chicks. Not all of them are his own. The chicks grow fast; at about five months old they will be as tall as he is.*

Family partnership in bringing up babies

In any pride of lions, the lionesses are almost always relatives, because only in exceptional circumstances does a lioness leave the group into which she was born. So a drowsy lioness stretched out suckling four cubs may be feeding the youngsters of four different mothers. The reason for this altruistic behaviour is probably that, by suckling her young relatives, the female is helping to raise animals that are part of her family line and share some of her genes.

Lionesses are not the only female animals that do not seem to mind caring for youngsters other than their own. Coatis, forest-living relatives of raccoons, for instance,

live in all-female groups in South America and share their maternal duties. Capybaras, or water pigs, which graze on the grasslands of South America from Panama to Paraguay, keep their litters of up to eight babies together in a family crèche. Nursing females suckle any youngsters that demand milk.

A mother elephant often allows her baby to be cared for by other related females of her group. It is often the younger females who take on babysitting duties, maybe because it is a way of learning how to care for a youngster and keep it

out of trouble – experience that will come in useful when they have offspring of their own.

Some birds use babysitters – for example the 25 species of bee-eaters that live in tropical and sub-tropical regions of the Old World. They breed in large colonies, digging nest tunnels into sandbanks. In almost half the nests, chicks are fed by one or more helpers – usually older brothers and sisters that have not yet found mates of their own – as well as by their parents.

Community care *A capybara (right) suckles babies that may not be her own. Any hungry youngster in a family group of perhaps a male and three females is fed on demand. A lioness (below) relaxes with playful cubs – probably some of her own and some belonging to a relative.*

Flying parents create enormous crèches

The world's largest crèche must be in Carlsbad Cavern in New Mexico, in the USA, which is home to over 20 million Mexican free-tailed bats. Each year at breeding time, the female bats fly 800 miles (1300 km) north from Mexico to the southern United States, where they search for a safe and suitable nursery. Ideally this should be a warm and humid cave in an area rich in insects for the mother to feed on at night. As few caves meet these criteria, and because there are huge numbers of bats, suitable sites such as Carlsbad Cavern, one of the biggest caverns in the world, are very crowded.

Each night, the young bats are left hanging from the cave walls while their mothers fly off to feed. On her return, each mother usually succeeds in finding her own offspring among the millions. First, she narrows the odds by returning to the part of the cave that she left. Then she tentatively identifies her youngster from its calls. As she crawls towards it through the swarming mass of young – packed about 2000 to a square yard or metre – each hungry youngster tries desperately to take milk from her, but with wings folded across her teats, the bat fends them off with bites and kicks. When she eventually gets to

her own offspring, she sniffs it for the two smells that will confirm her choice – its own distinctive smell from its large sweat glands, and the odour imparted from her own muzzle gland as she groomed it. Only when she is convinced that the call and the smells match up does she suckle the baby.

Identities are sometimes mistaken, but four times out of five a female ends up nursing her own youngster – an extraordinary tribute to her fine-tuned senses amid such a wealth of odours.

Soda lake crèche

Lake Natron is part of a chain of soda lakes in Africa's Great Rift Valley and has one of the world's most spectacular crèches. Lesser flamingos breed here, building huge colonies of mud nests. When the downy grey chicks are about a week old, their parents usher them to a crèche of up to 30 000 other young flamingos. The young birds are relatively safe from four-footed predators such as hyenas, which are unlikely to venture through the caustic, alkaline sludge round the lake shores, but not from winged predators like fish eagles.

Flamingo parents may have to fly 50 miles (80 km) to forage for food in other lakes, and to find fresh water to drink. On their return they rely on their youngster's call to identify it amid the noise and confusion, for, like most birds, they have no sense of smell. Until they are fledged at about three months old, chicks are fed on regurgitated 'crop milk'.

Overcrowded nursery *In the midst of this shifting and squeaking mass of young free-tailed bats, a returning mother finds her youngster by its unique call and smell.*

HOMEBODIES AND INDEPENDENTS

Some young animals flee the family as soon as possible; others cling as long as they can. Factors swaying choice are many and complex.

Influences that decide who stays and who goes

Prairie dogs are one of the many species for which the advantages of living together outweigh the attractions of a solitary existence. A large group makes watching for predators, defending the common territory and searching for food (when it is plentiful) much easier, safer and more successful. Even so, some of the animals born into such close-knit groups will have to leave home once they are old enough.

Animals have different reasons for departing from home. Black-tailed prairie dogs, for example, live in large colonies in the grasslands of the western United States. Each colony consists of a series of adjacent family groups, each with a single breeding male and three

or four breeding females. Despite close family structures, inbreeding is rare. Young males disperse at adolescence, and adult breeding males – who are more capable of adapting to new surroundings – generally leave the group before their daughters reach maturity.

Dispersal is probably not essential to avoid inbreeding since, like many animals, prairie dogs are able to recognise their close relatives and avoid mating with them. Both the males and the females usually begin breeding in their second year, though if a female's father remains in the burrow she is less likely to come into heat. Even if she does, the father is unlikely to mate with her.

Males, it seems, leave home, not so much to avoid inbreeding as to maximise the number of possible mates. In many species, emigration

coincides with adolescence, and leaving the family certainly reduces the chances of inbreeding. Matings between close relatives can mean the young carry damaging blends of genes, and animals usually improve their reproductive success if they avoid inbreeding.

On the other hand, the young animals that do stay with their natal groups depend largely on the status of their mothers for the quality of their lives. In species as diverse as elk and macaque monkeys, a dominant mother will

Home and away *Young macaque monkeys stay close to their mothers (right), depending on her dominance to assure their place in the group. Young male black-tailed prairie dogs (below), on the other hand, tend to leave the family burrow in adolescence. This maximises their chances of finding a mate while lessening the possibilities of inbreeding.*

intervene on her offspring's behalf and so effectively raise its place in the hierarchy. These privileged young have access to better feeding sites and, when danger threatens, get the safest spots.

The pampered youngsters grow faster and bigger, and suffer far less stress than their less fortunate cousins. Even if their mother dies, they are likely to be in much better condition than their rivals, and so able to maintain their status even when their mother's support has been withdrawn.

Mothers teach their young to be independent

After lavishing months of loving care on her dependent cubs, the day will come when a mother grizzly bear chases her young up a tree, just as she has always done when danger threatens. Only this time, it is different; she walks away and leaves them. Now, she is telling them, they are on their own.

This behaviour, from a mother whose devotion has known no bounds, may seem cruel. But once her cubs can survive on their own, they become a threat. If they stay in their mother's territory, they begin to compete for food and den sites, making it more difficult for her to survive and breed again. Neither she nor they will gain from her further help.

For all solitary-living animals, the time will come when the young must leave their mothers and begin life alone. The mothers will have done all they can to ensure that their offspring enter the world with the best possible chances of continuing the family line. And though leaving mother is a decisive break, it usually follows a period of steadily growing independence.

Gorillas choose to leave
At four months, a young gorilla will almost always be within reach of its mother. If it strays farther off, it will be picked up and carried back. By eight months, however, it plays at rather greater distances and takes itself off for longer periods.

Male gorillas become sexually mature at about 11 years of age. Shortly after this they become peripheral males, spending less time with their families, but staying within sight of the group. Eventually they make a complete break and go off in search of their own territories.

Whether a youngster is chased from home or leaves of its own accord, a lone young adult faces great dangers. It must find food for itself and avoid conflict with its own species as well as with predators of other species. The area that surrounds the mother's territory is most likely to be occupied by the young animal's relations, each trail clearly marked with the off-putting scent of its owner. Youngsters may have to wander a long way before finding a productive, unoccupied territory in which they will be able to establish their own homes.

Driven from home *When a young black bear (above) is about 18 months old and ready to live independently, it will be chased off by its mother. Similarly, mother bobcats encourage their 9-12-month-old kittens to leave home by behaving aggressively towards them. A bobcat kitten (right) is able to hunt alone from the age of about seven months.*

Ganging up provides security for everyone

Young carnivores, driven out to face the world alone, at least have teeth and claws to arm them against life's vicissitudes. Not so young herbivores, though many have learned other measures to improve their chances of survival.

Young male Indian blackbuck, for example, stay with their mothers until they reach maturity, when they are expelled from the herd. Alone, they would stand a poor chance of survival. Instead they form bachelor herds whose combined vigilance gives early warning of predators. This experience of group living also helps a young buck to work out his place in the hierarchy before starting the serious business of competing for a mate. Once the breeding season is over, the bachelors are generally allowed to rejoin the females and fawns to create a mixed herd.

Safety in numbers *On the plains of India young blackbuck males herd together for mutual protection. A sentry's harsh alarm bark warns the group of the presence of a tiger or other predator.*

FINDING A PLACE TO LIVE

'*THE PHOEBE HAD ALREADY COME ONCE MORE AND LOOKED IN AT MY DOOR AND WINDOW, TO SEE IF MY HOUSE WAS CAVERN-LIKE ENOUGH FOR HER, SUSTAINING HERSELF ON HUMMING WINGS WITH CLENCHED TALONS, AS IF SHE HELD THE AIR, WHILE SHE SURVEYED THE PREMISES.*' ≈ HENRY DAVID THOREAU, *WALDEN*, 1854.

The phoebe often chooses a sheltered spot in a house or barn as a nesting site. These cheerful and restless little birds, like humans, choose a place to live that provides security and an agreeable environment which satisfies their needs. For an aphid, this is a single leaf; for a polar bear, a vast area of Arctic wilderness. Like many animals, the polar bear improves the suitability of its home range by creating a shelter that gives protection from the worst of the elements, and a secure base in which the female can raise her young. The cavern that she excavates in the snow for the purpose may even have several chambers, but as a work of animal engineering it is primitive beside the works of nature's home-building specialists. The adobe architecture of termite mounds, the wattle-and-daub construction of ovenbird nests and the hanging baskets of weaverbirds are typically elegant solutions to the problems animals face in building their homes.

Temporary home
A chimpanzee builds itself a nest by bending together branches to make a loosely woven platform. These temporary nesting places are usually built close to where a group finishes its feeding at the end of the day, and are rarely used more than once.

Suited to the terrain
Termite mounds are built in a variety of shapes and sizes, each designed to suit local conditions.

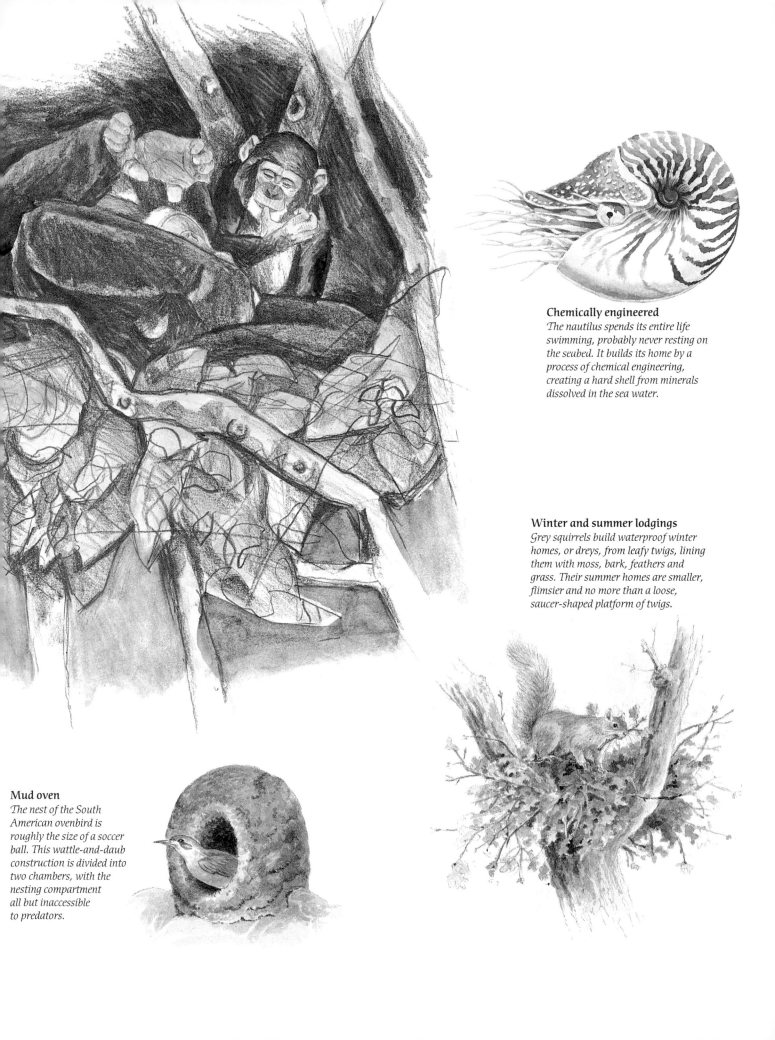

Chemically engineered

The nautilus spends its entire life swimming, probably never resting on the seabed. It builds its home by a process of chemical engineering, creating a hard shell from minerals dissolved in the sea water.

Winter and summer lodgings

Grey squirrels build waterproof winter homes, or dreys, from leafy twigs, lining them with moss, bark, feathers and grass. Their summer homes are smaller, flimsier and no more than a loose, saucer-shaped platform of twigs.

Mud oven

The nest of the South American ovenbird is roughly the size of a soccer ball. This wattle-and-daub construction is divided into two chambers, with the nesting compartment all but inaccessible to predators.

HOW MUCH SPACE IS ENOUGH?

Animals must find the right amount of territory to be able to feed and breed successfully and, having found it, defend it against intruders.

Eating habits dictate territorial needs

Animals are not land hungry. In an ideal world their territories would be precisely geared to the satisfying of their food requirements and no more. It makes no sense to expend energy in defending more territory than one needs. So when an animal occupies a larger territory than is usual for one of its species, it is almost certainly because its dietary requirements in that area are scarce.

Animals living in deserts tend to have larger territories than those living in more fertile regions. But even within the same ecosystem, different species have vastly different spatial requirements. In a typical area of sagebrush desert in the American west, for instance, it has been estimated that a kangaroo rat needs 2½-5 acres (1-2 ha), which is 20 times more than a colony of harvester ants. But an American badger needs around 200 times more space than a kangaroo rat, and a coyote around 130 times more than a badger.

The size of each animal's territory depends on the resident's ability to find the food it requires within it. Harvester ants grow and eat fungus on leaves gathered from their territory, whose boundaries they fiercely hold against invaders.

A single kangaroo rat can survive quite well on the leaves and seeds of the desert bushes within its patch. And if a neighbour shows too much interest in the estate, the landowner repels it by jumping straight up in the air and lashing out with its powerful hind legs.

Badgers and coyotes eat other animals. Since, as in other parts of the world, animals in deserts are far less plentiful than plants, these carnivores require larger territories to provide them with food than do the resident herbivores.

American badgers eat anything from fruit, roots and insects to mammals as large as ground squirrels. Coyotes too are omnivorous, but because they are larger animals than badgers they have mightier appetites that embrace carrion, sheep and even the occasional enfeebled deer.

This is more or less the end of the sagebrush desert food chain. In the desert, a creature the size of a deer needs a big territory to graze in. Consequently its numbers are small, too small to attract many specialist deer hunters, whose territories would have to be larger still. And one reason for the fact that no animal specialises in hunting coyotes, is that it would have to cover a vast area indeed, spending all its time searching for prey.

Desert ranger *Ever watchful for prey, a coyote patrols its territory in southern California's Mohave Desert. It may have to travel a long way to find a meal.*

Homeless birds lie low until the time is right

When two birds stay together, but do not sing, mate or build a nest, the reason could be, quite simply, lack of territory.

Scientists have found that pairs of rufous-collared sparrows in North America live in clearly defined and staunchly defended territories. But not infrequently there is a second pair lurking in the vicinity. These remain as inconspicuous as possible, awaiting some fatality to overtake one if not both of the resident birds. If it does, the 'lurkers' take over their territory. And because animal psychology dictates that any creature already established in a territory has the edge over one coming from farther afield, the 'lurkers' almost always end in possession.

Timing it right
Another way to gain living space is to lie low in another bird's territory and try to breed. Homeless pairs of European tits sometimes wait for a resident pair to go through the territorial rituals – fighting off other birds, singing to announce possession, building the nest, patrolling the boundaries and generally establishing themselves. Once the resident birds become less aggressive and are sitting on their eggs, the deprived birds sneak in, find a discreet spot, swiftly build their nest and start laying and incubating.

If they are caught by the resident male – and they often are – they will be chased away. However, because they have waited so patiently, they do stand some chance of success. On average, the squatters are about half as successful as the residents, raising four fledglings in the season compared with the residents' eight.

Working for a living
Sometimes a bird without territory of its own can earn the right to feed in another bird's territory. The European white wagtail will sometimes waive its fiercely defended territorial rights in a good year when there is enough food in the range for itself and perhaps one other bird. Once an intruder has become a familiar visitor, it is not necessarily chased away but may be kept on as a sort of mercenary. The outsider is allowed to feed in exchange for help with defending the territory – when other birds invade, it takes its turn at seeing them off. But if the situation changes and food becomes short, the hired hand is evicted and has to survive by poaching.

Wagtails will also drop defences when the season becomes harder still and food shortages even more severe. Then all boundaries fall and they become flocking birds, foraging where they can for food.

Pride and vigilance *The proud stance of the red grouse (above) belies its dependence upon territory and status – it loses the will to live when forced out of its area. The female of a resident pair of rufous-collared sparrows (left) guards her youngster in the nest, keeping a sharp lookout for any 'lurkers'.*

Territory not only provides food for an animal – it may help to keep pairs together by compelling birds to stay in their area. Territory may be important also for its sense of security. In adult grouse, for example, homelessness can produce a fatal shock. Ousted from their familiar feeding ground by their developing young, older grouse will stop eating, lose condition and, as the winter sets in, die. This is either because being weaker and more exposed on the wind-swept moor, they fall victim to predators, or as often seems to happen, they simply lose interest in living.

Aphids fight for possession of a leaf

The best size for a territory can be anything from a male Siberian tiger's country-wide estate down through every gradation of size to the most miniscule.

The most desirable territory, to a poplar aphid, for instance, is a whole poplar leaf and nothing less. When another aphid attempts to settle on a leaf-holder's territory, the reaction is immediate and fierce. Eating stops. Reproduction stops. With her hind legs, the resident aphid tries to kick and shove the intruder away and the intruder kicks and shoves back.

The tussle can go on for two or three days, until one or the other prevails. Occasionally the interloper is allowed to stay on some other, less desirable, portion of the leaf. That sharing a leaf is not ideal, and is worth fighting to prevent, has been confirmed by an experiment. This compared the numbers of offspring produced by aphids that had sole occupancy of a leaf with those of aphids that shared a leaf. With two aphids present on a leaf, the insect occupying the prime spot beside the stem had 15 per cent fewer young than an aphid that was monarch of all it surveyed, and the aphid on the inferior spot had 38 per cent fewer.

SHARING A HOME WITH FAMILY, FRIENDS AND STRANGERS

Many animals share their homes with uninvited guests, some of which give little trouble. Other invaders, however, may destroy the nest or kill the hosts.

Basket-weave hotel is the world's biggest nest

A haystack-like object hanging from a tree or telegraph pole is a not uncommon sight in the dry grasslands of southwest Africa. It is in fact an enormous communal nest containing up to 300 woven-grass baskets all clustered under one dome-shaped, thatched roof. It is the communal home of a colony of sociable weaver birds.

The entrance holes are in the 'basement', each one leading to a group of nests. In summer, each cup-shaped nest houses a pair of weavers and their brood, while in winter, it shelters a group of adults huddled together for warmth.

Sociable weaver birds somewhat resemble their close relatives, the European sparrows. They do not migrate, and even when they are not breeding, they occupy the same nests, coming home to sleep in them each evening after feeding on seeds and insects. The work of repairing and adding to the nest is constant, and the birds live for several years. So though a colony may begin with only a small cluster of nests under a communally built thatched roof, in time the home tree's strange fruit may grow into an enormous structure twice the height of a man and four times as long as it is high.

In a land where daytime temperatures of 34°C (93°F) can drop to 16°C (61°F) at night, communal nesting is no bad idea. Inside the nest, the temperature fluctuation is halved by the insulation of the thatched roof and the woven sides.

For security's sake most birds' nests tend to be inconspicuous. Not so the weaver birds', which can be seen from a great distance. These birds rely on safety in numbers and on the fact that few predators are able to reach the entrances without a warning being called by at least one colonist. A problem lies, however, in the weaver birds' own enthusiasm for building. Sometimes a communal nest becomes too heavy, causing the tree to collapse and the work of years to crash to the ground. When that happens, the birds simply start building all over again.

Tree house guests *Sociable weaver birds (above) have nested in a South African kokerboom tree. So spacious are the nests that intruders such as peach-faced love-birds (right) can move into empty chambers and raise their young unchallenged.*

Busy termites thwarted by troublesome tenants

Australian termite mounds are probably the pinnacle of insect architecture. Made from chewed plant matter and coated with clay, these air-conditioned towers rise to about 23 ft (7 m) high, containing within them innumerable chambers and galleries.

Such conspicuous structures are bound to attract creatures that prefer to let someone else do the work of home-building. One of the most determined idlers is the rare golden-shouldered parrot, found only in a small area of northeast Australia. In the breeding season, the female simply tunnels some 14 in (36 cm) into the slab sides of a mound, hollows out a nesting chamber, lays her eggs and sits on them. She does not even try to seal the ends of the termite tunnels she has opened up. The termites do

what they can to discourage the squatter, by working all night to seal its entrance hole. But to no avail. Each morning, the parrot breaks it open again. On rare occasions, the termites manage to entomb a clutch of chicks, but the more usual outcome is that they give up, seal off their own tunnels and ignore the unwanted guests.

However, parrots do not always choose their termite mounds well. Magnetic or compass termites build their tall, blade-shaped towers with the flat sides on a north-south line so they get the most sun in the morning and afternoon and the least at midday. Because the tower thickness is less than 3 ft (1 m), golden-shouldered parrots that try to burrow into one can easily find themselves jabbing at the air on the other side. Thus it is not uncommon to come across rows of magnetic termite mounds looking exactly like enormous, up-ended slices of Swiss cheese.

At worst, golden-shouldered parrots are no more than a nuisance. But termites also suffer from other tenants whose habits may kill a whole colony. They are paradise, or white-tailed, kingfishers. In early November, these beautiful birds migrate from New Guinea to a small area on Australia's north-eastern coast. There, mated pairs make nests in newly built termite mounds that are about knee high.

Sharing a winter home *An Australian golden-shouldered parrot perches on the huge termite mound it has claimed as its winter nesting place. Some older birds will return to the same cosy nesting site, year after year, blithely undoing the termites' painstaking repair work. For the birds, the rain-softened termite mounds are easy to excavate.*

First, the kingfishers create two narrow entrance holes by jabbing at the mound with their beaks. Then, with their feet, they dig out the entire inner chamber for their eggs. The work can take up to a month, and in its course, inflicts more damage than a young termite colony can tolerate. The termites die or abandon the nest, leaving their unfinished home to the king-fishers and their chicks.

Borrowed burrow *A termites' nest in a tree provides a perfect nesting site for an Australasian sacred kingfisher (right). A bat-eared fox and her pups (below) peer out from their home in the 'basement' of a termite mound in Botswana. Hunting at night for grubs, small rodents, birds' eggs, tubers and fruits, they shelter in their shared burrow during the heat of day.*

SQUATTING IN SOMEONE ELSE'S SHELTER

For those animals that do not wish to take the trouble to build their own home there is a simple solution – move in with someone else.

When building a home means gaining a tenant

Some animals are destined to be homemakers for others as well as themselves. Gopher tortoises in eastern North America, for example, dig long-tunnelled burrows using their flattened forefeet to scoop earth aside. Snakes, lizards, raccoons, opossums and foxes may slip into a tortoise's burrow for temporary shelter, and other creatures such as frogs and insects may move in as permanent room-mates.

In addition, long-legged burrowing owls, which are the size of blackbirds, occasionally squat in tortoise tunnels. Usually they dig their own burrows, but do not bother if they can find a tunnel dug by something else. A squatter owl can look very proprietorial, sitting at the tunnel entrance and glaring indignantly as the rightful occupant pushes past.

Shearwaters, prions and petrels, all related birds, dig nesting tunnels on the cliff tops of some of New Zealand's remote offshore islands, and return to them again after several months at sea. Quite often they discover that tuataras,

New Zealand's large, lizard-like reptiles, have taken advantage of their absence and moved in. The sea-bird droppings attract beetles and other insects which tuataras feed upon.

The returning shearwaters have no great objection to their lumbering 2 ft (60 cm) long lodgers, because a tuatara makes a good caretaker, duly keeping the tunnel clean and open. At nesting time the birds lay their eggs in the nesting chamber at the end of the

Standing sentry *A burrowing owl of the North American plains (above) spends much of its time at the burrow entrance surveying its surroundings. Even though the owl is able to dig a burrow of its own, it often squats in one occupied by another creature, often a gopher tortoise.*

Home and shelter *As dusk descends and the temperature, drops, a gopher tortoise (right) emerges from its burrow to search for plants to feed on. Gopher tortoises shelter from the heat of the day in an underground chamber at the end of a long tunnel. Other animals may shelter there too.*

Frog lodgers *Fat-bodied gopher, or crawfish, frogs (above), which have dark markings on their backs and sides, live among the wet meadows and floodplains of eastern North America. They often seek shelter in burrows, where gopher tortoises and crayfish are their hosts.*

tunnel, ignoring the tuatara. They will, however, have to guard the single chick once it has hatched, or the tuatara will eat it. During the breeding season the reptile's main food is shearwater chicks.

Hermit crabs have no shells of their own, so they will take over secondhand, vacated shells of an appropriate size. Usually they look for shells that are a little too large, allowing room for growth. This means there is also room for something else. One large species of hermit crab often has a ragworm for a room-mate. Ragworms, or bristleworms, are small marine creatures with bristles on their many limbs which act as paddles in the water. When a ragworm moves in with the hermit crab, it gets not only a mobile home but meals into the bargain. As the crab forages over the seabed, the ragworm pops out its head and grabs the odd scrap that drops from the crab's scissor-like mouthparts.

Sea anemones make much more welcome guests. Their poisonous tentacles provide a hermit crab with protection from predators. In return, the anemones are able to move around to find food. When the crab changes its shell, it takes the anemones with it, prodding and coaxing them off the old shell and onto the new.

Holed-up penguin *A Magellanic penguin peers cautiously from a rabbit burrow in the Falklands in which it is rearing its chicks. These penguins breed along the southern coastal areas of South America.*

Mounted weapons
Tentacles waving, a sea anemone squats on the shell of a hermit crab. These crabs actively encourage anemones to live on their shells, since the anemone's long, stinging tentacles give it some protection from predators. If it is threatened by an octopus, the crab moves the anemones to the lip of its shell for maximum protection.

Welcome lodger, unwanted intruder *Although the New Zealand tuatara (above) is quite capable of digging its own burrow, it often makes use of the burrows of fairy prions and shearwaters. So many of these birds nest on offshore islands that, where the ground is suitable, there may be three burrows within a space the size of a card table, making it easy for a tuatara to find somewhere to lodge. A North American rattlesnake (right) encounters opposition as it looks for lodgings in a badger's den. Rattlesnakes often move into holes made by other animals to shelter from extreme heat or cold.*

ROOMS TO LET

Birds need a secure place to lay their fragile eggs. Some build their own nests, and others are quite happy to move into the abandoned homes of other birds.

Saguaro sanctuary *Gilded flickers (above and right) nest almost solely in giant cactuses such as the saguaro. Cactus holes make safe nest sites in an area where nesting places are few and far between. Damaged saguaros ooze sap that hardens to form a nest lining.*

Cool nest chambers inside desert plants

Ribbed saguaro cactuses are well known as symbols of the barren American West. For desert birds, these giant, branching plants, that can reach 50 ft (15 m) high and live 200 years, are vital oases.

The soft, spongy interior of a saguaro cactus makes it a living water-storage tank that can swell to twice its normal size during the rainy season. Because the plant's fibrous trunk is considerably softer than that of a tree, it is relatively easy to turn its interior into a cool living space, a fortress home studded with lance-like spikes to deter climbing predators such as snakes.

Commonest of the many saguaro dwellers are the gila woodpecker and the gilded, or northern, flicker. After a season in nest holes pecked into the cactus's trunk, these birds find the accumulation of nest parasites, feathers and food scraps too much for comfort, so move to new premises. This means vacancies for other hole-dwelling birds. The world's smallest owl, the sparrow-sized elf owl, is the usual second tenant. These owls will sometimes share their nests with a thread-like western blind snake that eats lice and other insect parasites.

Forest tenants

In northern conifer forests, the woodpeckers' ability to chip out nest holes in trees means they can move on and build new, cleaner homes at will. So they leave plenty of vacant rooms for other birds, bats or squirrels. A nuthatch often moves into a vacated woodpecker hole. This small insect eater is also known as an upside-down bird because of its rare ability to climb down tree trunks head first. The nuthatch may close part of the entrance hole with mud, but otherwise it leaves it much as it finds it.

Chickadees, or American tits, may take over next. The chickadee may open up an entrance again

Safe shelter *An elf owl (below) peers out at the heat-hazed Arizona desert from the cool haven of an old woodpecker nest in a saguaro cactus. The cactus thorns deter predators. The owl will emerge at dusk to hunt insects and lizards. A cactus wren (left) nests in a hole vacated by an earlier tenant. The 'jug jug' calls of these wrens as they hunt insects are a welcome sign of life in the desert's midday silence.*

Handy hole *A hairy woodpecker (left), named for the feathers round its nostrils, drills out its own nest hole. Many forest birds, including the mountain bluebird (below), readily take over an abandoned woodpecker hole. The nuthatch (below left) has altered an old woodpecker home to suit its own requirements, partly filling in the entrance hole with mud to make it smaller.*

and widen the chamber floor for its bowl-shaped nest. When sanitary conditions force the chickadee out, the next tenant could be a bluebird, followed by a tree swallow.

Starlings, the slum dwellers of the bird world, are usually the final occupants of a nest. They live for years in a rising tide of filth. But even they reach a limit, and the hole eventually ceases to be of use to any of the home-seeking birds.

SECONDHAND HOMES

It is not unusual for one animal to take over another's abandoned home. But sometimes the owners are violently ousted or even eaten.

Borrowed nursery *A queen bumblebee broods her eggs and maintains her own honey pot as she starts up a new colony in an abandoned field mouse nest.*

Finding a suitable place to raise a family

A hollow ball of grass hidden in underbrush makes a desirable residence for a variety of small creatures. Built and deserted by field mice who raised a family in it the previous year, by the following April its next tenant might easily be a house-hunting queen bumblebee. Few secondhand nests would suit her better.

The queen refurbishes it to suit her own needs. She lines the nest with grass and moss then, with wax secreted from her abdomen, constructs a cup. This she supplies with pollen and lays a dozen eggs within it. She seals the cup with wax and builds and stocks a honey container at the nest entrance.

The eggs hatch into larvae and feed on the pollen and honey that the queen pushes through a hole in the cup. The larvae become pupae which, about three weeks after the founding of the colony, emerge as female worker bees. The queen continues to forage and make cups, but as the colony grows, she devotes more and more time to egg-laying. By late summer the mouse's nest contains several hundred bees. At this time the queen lays two special batches of eggs. These will become drones and queens; but of the colony only the young, fertilised queens will survive to start new colonies in the following spring.

Seashell nest

Gobies live in shallow, coastal waters in temperate and tropical seas – there are about 800 species, few more than a finger's length in size. At breeding time the male goby seeks out a discarded shell to use as the roof of his nest. With his mouth he clears the shell of sand, turns it opening down, enters it, and then sweeps sand over the outside with his fins. He has made himself a small chamber beneath a sandy mound on the sea bottom.

With only his head and front fins sticking out of the shell's entrance, he waits for a female goby to pass by. When she appears he darts out, attracts her attention and escorts her to his nest. She turns herself upside-down and lays a batch of sticky eggs on the ceiling of his shell home. The male fertilises the eggs and guards them in the nest until the young fish hatch.

Goby shelter *A male blue-banded goby waits in his shell nest for a female to swim by. He will try to entice her inside to lay her eggs on the roof of the shelter.*

Burrowers that provide lodgings and board too

The American grey fox never digs its own den – it simply moves into another animal's home. If it is lucky, this grizzled fox – the only fox that regularly climbs trees – may find the abandoned earth of a red fox, preferably at the base of a tree. Otherwise, it will make do with a woodchuck's hole, a hollow log or a rocky crevice.

Other opportunist lodgers of the animal world include dwarf mongooses, found in Africa south of the Sahara, that make their homes in abandoned termite nests, and wild dogs on the grassy plains of South Africa, that often use abandoned aardvark burrows in which to rear their pups.

Some animals can lay claim to being the burrow diggers-in-chief of the animal world. On the North American prairies, horsemen must beware of holes dug by black-tailed prairie dogs – holes that are the entrances to an underground maze of burrows up to 10 ft (3 m) deep and extending over an area of about 160 acres (65 ha). These squirrel-sized diggers build whole 'towns', of narrow tunnels and cosy dens for a colony of thousands.

Burrowing owls are happy to adapt prairie dog burrows rather

Problem tenant *A European polecat (right) takes full advantage of rabbits. Not only does it move into their burrows, but it also feeds on its hosts. This slim hunter slinks easily through a tunnel in search of a litter of baby rabbits.*
A disused termite mound (above) makes a comfortable ready-made home for an African dwarf mongoose.

than dig their own, as are ground squirrels, salamanders, mice and snakes. A burrowing owl is not big enough to kill an adult prairie dog, but is not above making a meal of its host's pups. Otherwise the owl lives mainly on the prairie dogs' other lodgers – large insects and small snakes and lizards. But rattlesnake lodgers present far more of a threat. If one moves in, the prairie dogs seal up the section in which it has made its home.

Another unwelcome lodger is North America's rarest mammal, the black-footed ferret. This black-masked hunter nearly died out, but was bred in captivity and re-introduced to the wild in 1991. Not

only do the ferrets live in prairie dog burrows, they also feed entirely on prairie dogs, which they pursue through the labyrinth.

In Europe, the common rabbit, which builds burrows and then abandons them almost as fast as it reproduces, is the major host to other animals. Weasels, stoats and polecats, all of which hunt rabbits,

are among the tenants. They move in and out of rabbit burrows all over a wide home range. A polecat, for example, has a range of about 2½ sq miles (6.5 km²), more than it can cover in a night's hunting. As night ends it retires to the nearest burrow, wherever it happens to be. Only females with young live in one place for long – and that just

for the two months or so that the youngsters spend in the nest.

Manx shearwaters also make use of abandoned rabbit burrows. These gull-sized sea birds breed on isolated cliff tops around most of Europe's coastlines, and lay their eggs in a nest chamber at the end of a burrow. There the chicks stay until they are about ten weeks old.

RAINFALL HOLDS THE KEY

Life depends on water, and where and when an animal will live out the next stage of its life may be determined by a rainstorm.

Breaking out *After years of drought in the Australian desert, when rain falls a burrowing frog emerges from its lengthy sleep in a moisture-holding skin cocoon.*

The big sleep of the burrowing frog

Burrowing frogs in Australia's central desert can be sure of one thing – that the life-giving rains they rely on are few and far between. Years may pass between rains, but the frogs survive without migrating to a wetter place. For they use an amazing survival technique – they bury themselves in a skin cocoon that keeps them from drying out completely.

At the start of a long dry spell, as pools of water are in the last stages of evaporation, a burrowing frog reverses into the mud with a backward swimming motion and finally disappears. At a depth of about 12 in (30 cm), the frog stops and builds a chamber about twice its own size, firming up the walls with its feet. Then it settles down

to a long sleep, slowing breathing and heartbeat until they are just ticking over sufficiently to keep it alive. Next the stout and short-legged frog lowers its head against its chest and tucks its limbs under its body. After about two weeks, the outer layers of the frog's skin loosen up and meld together into a waterproof membrane that, except for two tiny tubes to the nostrils, covers the frog's whole body.

In its moisture-retaining sleeping bag, the frog waits for the next rains. It is said that Aborigines get water from these packaged frogs for, when squeezed, they produce water from their bladders. This is probably why they are also known as water-holding frogs. When the rains finally come, the frog senses the moisture seeping into the soil. It speeds up its heart and lungs, breaks out of its bag and scrabbles its way to the surface, where it

feasts on the myriad insects that have also lain dormant through the dry spell and have just as suddenly sprung to life. The frog eats and drinks until it is bloated.

The puddles, however, last only a few days, and in that time the frog has to complete its entire breeding cycle. Calling for a partner, mating, spawning and the entire egg-to-tadpole development

happen fast. By the time the water has almost gone again, the mud is alive with fully formed burrowing froglets, working their way backwards into the mud in readiness for their long sleep under the Australian desert.

Mosquitoes wait years for the rains to come

Without water mosquitoes cannot reproduce. It stimulates the development of eggs into larvae, and provides the medium in which the larvae swim and feed on algae and organic debris until they are ready to transform into adults. So some mosquitoes lay their eggs in water, and others in places where there will eventually be water.

In central Australia, where rain is very infrequent, *Aedes* mosquitoes (carriers of yellow fever), lay their eggs in pools after a downpour. The pools soon evaporate and the eggs may stay dormant for years until it rains again. Then the mosquito life cycle starts anew as if no time had elapsed.

The eggs of other species of mosquito may not need to wait so long, but they are certainly capable of surviving droughts and similar harsh conditions, such as Arctic winters. With all water frozen, an Arctic winter has the same effect as a drought. But the Arctic *Culex*

Water wait *A female mosquito lurks in a cool crevice until it rains. When it does, she will lay her eggs in a puddle.*

mosquitoes (carriers of viral encephalitis) are some of the most successful breeders. After nine or ten months of suspended animation in ice, their eggs are released in the summer melt-waters. They float on the water in rafts of about a hundred, turn into larvae, then pupate. In a few days, the summer air is thick with adult mosquitoes.

Mosquitoes are the scourge of Arctic animals that are trying to breed during the brief summer. One of the commonest causes of death in newborn mammals and birds is loss of blood from innumerable mosquito bites.

Settling in *Once he takes up his daytime incubation shift, a male superb fruit dove will hide his coloured neck and head and blend in with the greenery.*

Fruit doves are at home where the fruit is ripe

Superb fruit doves live entirely on fruit in eastern Australia's rain forests. In Queensland alone there are more than 50 kinds of edible fruit, all ripening at different times in different areas, depending on the rainfall. So the birds' whereabouts are determined by the current fruit crop. How the fruit doves know where and when there is ripe fruit to be had, nobody knows.

In summer the female lays her one egg in a flimsy nest she builds in the fork of a tree or on a palm leaf. The male does the day shift of sitting on the egg, which hatches after 14-18 days and both birds feed the chick on regurgitated food, called 'pigeon's milk'. The chick flies at two or three weeks, after which the doves travel on once more in search of ripe fruit.

Flying gypsies *These Australian banded stilts lead a nomadic life, appearing in flocks of thousands to feed and breed in temporary lakes and pools that appear after large downpours in desert areas.*

A temporary home for winged wanderers

Maybe only once or twice in a century, Lake Torrens in South Australia's barren wastes – one of Earth's driest places – surges into life. After a heavy rainstorm, this vast salt pan can become a huge shallow lake extending for more than 2000 sq miles (5200 km²). And from nowhere, it seems, the lake is suddenly stocked with wildlife, ranging from algae (minute water plants) to surprisingly large fish that must have been washed in from surrounding creeks.

Literally out of the blue, water birds arrive to breed on the lake in their thousands – Australian pelicans, red avocets, silver gulls, whiskered and gull-billed terns, pied and black cormorants and banded stilts. After the rains of April 1989, at least 100 000 pairs of banded stilts flew in to nest on a sandy island in the middle of the lake. They are long-legged white waders with black wings and a deep chestnut V on the breast, and they feed mainly on brine shrimps. These shrimps hatch from eggs that have lain dormant in the salt pan, saved from drying out completely by their tough skins. The shrimps feed mainly on algae, and can filter minute organisms with tiny hairs on their limbs.

Short-lived colony

How the nomadic stilts knew the lake was there, or where they came from, is still a mystery. They covered the island with their nests, each one a small bowl scraped in the sand and barely a hand's width from its neighbour. In each was a clutch of, usually, four speckled eggs. The flocks of silver gulls that had arrived on the scene wheeled overhead on the lookout for the chance to eat stilt eggs, or the fluffy chicks as they hatched.

After a day or two in the nest, the chicks massed together for safety in thousand-strong crèches. Adult males with no chicks of their own watched over these crèches while most breeding females produced second clutches of eggs. Fathers, meanwhile, fished for food and delivered it to their mates and chicks. Birds appeared to feed only their own chicks, and seemed able to distinguish their cries from the rest in the general cacophony.

By July the lake was rapidly drying out, and would soon become a morass of dazzling white caustic mud. As soon as the second broods of chicks were ready to join the crèches, the banded stilts began shepherding them off the island and over the lake, towards the mainland. In massive downy rafts, the chicks took to the water. Still being fed by their parents – and still being picked off by the gulls – they floated and paddled a journey of some 65 miles (105 km) that for some took six days.

Once safely on the mainland, they stayed a few days longer in their crèches, feeding themselves on the small creatures they dug out of the soft mud of the shoreline with their long bills. Finally the whole flock flew off to an unknown destination – and the lake became a desert salt pan once again.

KEEPING WARM AND STAYING COOL

Some animals have developed ways of regulating the temperature of their burrows or nests, either warming them up or cooling them down.

Cooling stone mounds in the desert heat

In the desert of Pilbara in Western Australia, the temperature often soars as high as 49°C (120°F). No doubt this inspired the pebble-mound mouse to construct a cooling system at its burrow entrance. It is a mound of pebbles, of some 32 sq ft (3 m²), and it works as a dew trap. At night when the pebbles cool, the moisture condenses on them, providing the mouse with its water supply. And as the water evaporates by day, it cools the nest. The mouse spends hours carrying 1 oz (30 g) stones – about half its own weight – to add to the mound.

A pebble mound is also used as a nest platform by the white-crowned black wheatear of North Africa. The male wheatear does the nest-building, gathering small stones, generally flat ones as they

Cooling castle *The energetic pebble-mound mouse (above) adds constantly to its nest. Moisture condensing on the pebbles cools the nest and provides sips of water. A white-crowned black wheatear male (right) prepares a soft bed of grass and feathers on top of the pebbles he has collected to help to keep his eggs cool.*

Moles dig their own ventilation shafts

The common mole rarely needs to leave its burrow, because its food, chiefly earthworms, slugs and insect larvae, come to it through the walls, floors and ceilings of its home. On those occasions that a mole does surface, usually at night, it is likely to fall prey to an owl.

Rare appearance *Common moles are seldom seen above ground, although their tunnels leave ridges across lawns. Their powerful, heavily clawed forepaws clear the soil with a movement rather like a swimmer doing the breast stroke.*

The mole's nesting area is a football-sized chamber lined with grass and dry leaves and dug slightly deeper than the rest of its system of tunnels. Radiating from the chamber are the tunnels that the mole digs during its daily search for food. A burrow system may be about 200 yd (180 m) long. The longest tunnels are in poor soil where food is scarce.

To replace the energy it burns up by digging, the 6 in (15 cm) long mole has to eat prodigiously. As its foraging tunnels are near the surface and not well constructed, they sometimes collapse while new ones are being excavated. The tunnels are the nesting chamber's only ventilation, and create a steady draught of fresh air that is vital to the well-being of the animal. While it is digging, a mole breaks through to the surface every so often, creating a chimney-like shaft that lets in more air. The tunnels seldom cut across each other, so air drawn into a ventilation shaft travels through the living chamber to find another exit. This keeps fresh air circulating throughout the system.

The mole's ventilation system creates piles of earth, or molehills, above ground, each one containing about 2 lb (1 kg) of soil. These can be a nuisance to gardeners and farmers, and tunnelling moles can interfere with plant roots.

The polar bear's warm haven in a frozen land

In November each year, pregnant polar bears begin to construct the dens in which their cubs will be born during the Arctic winter. Although an adult polar bear's thick white coat keeps it warm in even the harshest Arctic weather, the cubs are born blind and with only short, sparse hair, so could not possibly survive in the open.

The best snow for digging out a den is last year's – compacted and dry after several months of settling. With her huge paws, the bear digs an entrance tunnel some 2 yd (1.8 m) long in a snowdrift, then at the end makes a raised threshold and a vaulted chamber. Sometimes she adds other rooms; a den 13 yd (12 m) long and with five chambers has been recorded.

Nursery under the snow

Warmed by the polar bear's body, the den's interior temperature can be 21°C (37°F) higher than the icy -30°C (-22°F) outside. Sometimes dens are ventilated by a hole in the roof, too, although such holes may be made accidentally when a bear scrapes ice off the ceiling to drink.

A polar bear usually gives birth to one or two cubs in December or January and spends the winter in the den. Each cub is about 10 in (25 cm) long and weighs up to 2 lb (1 kg) at birth. Polar bear cubs first

open their eyes at just under five weeks old, and start to walk at about seven weeks. Sometimes the mother suckles them while sitting upright, with a cub in the crook of each foreleg as it sucks at one of her four nipples. She sleeps for much of the time, and the youngsters play together.

The mother bear keeps her den meticulously clean. She herself passes very little urine or faeces during her winter retreat, for although she drinks she does not eat but lives off the body fat built up by eating as much as possible during autumn. The small amounts

Snug billet *For the first three months of its life, a polar bear cub lives under the Arctic snow in the den where it was born. When spring comes, mother and cubs emerge to look for food, and a cub sees the white world outside for the first time.*

of excreta passed by the cubs she covers with snow scraped down from the ceiling.

During March, stimulated by the increasing amount of light coming through the ice ceiling, the ravenously hungry mother bear pushes through the snow and breaks out into the open. Followed by her cubs, she heads for the sea and a long-awaited meal of seal flesh.

---

are easier to carry, from around his chosen nest site until he has a pile of 300-400. Like the pebble-mound mouse, the sparrow-sized bird also carries stones weighing 1 oz (30 g) or so – almost as heavy as himself. The completed platform is about 6 in (15 cm) high and up to 20 in (50 cm) across. On top he builds a cup-shaped nest of plant material lined with feathers and fur.

Platform of success

This wheatear is one of the few bird species that manages to breed in North Africa's hot, dry regions, where the ground temperature can be high enough to fry an egg.

It is thought that the nest may be the key to the bird's success. Perhaps the nest platform keeps the eggs cool as air moves through the loose pile of stones. These are porous, and so retain the morning dew and cool the air passing over. But it is also possible that the platform protects the nest from the desert's flash floods – or perhaps it is simply the male wheatear's way of attracting a female.

SEEKING SHELTER UNDERGROUND

Dens under the snow protect some animals from winter's rigours while others seek safety in earthen burrows at breeding time.

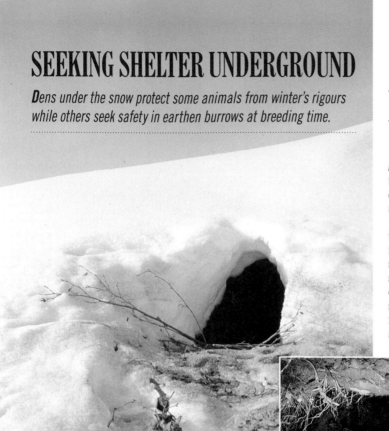

Winter homes for warm-blooded animals

At the first sign of winter, Asian and American black bears find themselves a cave, a hole in a tree or just a good deep pile of leaves and drift off to sleep until spring.

Food is scarce during winter, so the bears eat as much as they can in the summer and autumn and store body fat to enable them to survive the long, cold winter. Bears conserve energy by hibernating. In slumber, their body temperatures may drop by as much as 5°C (9°F) and their metabolic rate by 50 per

Sleeping quarters
Black bears can hibernate in dens for six months in severe Alaskan winters. In more temperate areas, they sleep for two or three months. In Mexico, where food is plentiful, they stay awake all year.

cent. Warm-blooded animals have built-in heating systems that help them to combat cold weather, but many living in cold climates have evolved additional strategies to get them through the coldest periods. Some may continue a more or less normal existence in the 'basement' under the snow, others ignore the winter in sleep.

Arctic lemmings, for example, feed on tundra vegetation in tunnels beneath the snow, which are kept warm by their collective body heat. And when outside temperatures are below zero, the dens of nursing polar bears under the snow are 21°C (37°F) warmer.

North American common poorwills are the only birds known to hibernate, although a number of others can enter into a dormant state for a few days at a time. Ptarmigans, for example, sit out blizzards by settling into a comfortable spot in the snow and dropping their body temperatures to no more than a degree or two above the point of death. They generate little energy and waste none.

Diggers and tunnellers are built for the task

The world's biggest burrowing animal is the wombat of southeast Australia, which is about as heavy as an Old English sheepdog. Massively muscled and with claws like garden forks, the wombat is a powerful digger, and also uses its strong, trowel-like teeth to help burrow through soil – roots, stones and all – at an incredible rate approaching 10 yd (3 m) an hour.

Solitary by nature, wombats are nocturnal foragers for roots, fungi and grass. But they do not share the placid, sociable nature of many herbivores, and occasionally attack other animals, their sharp teeth inflicting deep wounds. They also shun each other. If two wombats are seen together, they are either mating or are a mother and her single youngster, recently emerged into the world from its first six months of life in her pouch.

One advantage of a wombat's solitary life, however, is that when

it finishes its night's foraging it does not have to go home to its mate or offspring. It simply crawls into the nearest empty wombat burrow and goes to sleep.

Another Australian burrower is the duckbilled platypus, which dwells in river banks and hunts in water. The startling appearance of the platypus belies its status as an egg-laying mammal. It has a duck-like bill, brown fur and webbed feet. But its hind feet are only partially webbed, and are mainly used as a rudder while swimming.

Underwater entrance
A female platypus makes a particularly elaborate breeding burrow with an entrance below the waterline, from which a passage rises steeply to the dry living chamber. The tunnel is only just wide enough to admit her, so water is squeezed out of her fur when she returns from the hunt.

In September, the female lays two or three eggs in a lined chamber up to 100 ft (30 m) from the entrance. There the young hatch

and are suckled until they make their first venture into the river at three months.

Badgers, found in Europe and North America, live in extensive burrows or setts, emerging at night to feed on almost anything, ranging from earthworms to young rabbits, grass, roots or berries. Having no natural enemies in their woodland habitat, badgers have little need to make themselves inconspicuous. Their setts make no concession to concealment,

and their nightly forays are lumbering, raucous affairs with much crashing through the undergrowth.

Generally, a badger sett is the work of generations – there is one in England at least 200 years old. Badgers constantly remake and extend their tunnels and chambers until the sett spreads for well over 2000 sq yd (1670 m²) and has as many as 30 entrances and usually

Gone fishing *Leaving its nest in a river bank, a kingfisher sets out on yet another fishing trip. Each parent kingfisher needs to catch at least 50 small fish a day to help feed its six or seven chicks – in addition to the fish it needs to feed itself.*

around 20 inhabitants. This almost constant alteration involves shifting large amounts of soil, and overgrown spoil heaps are a sure sign of a badger sett close by.

Badgers are clean animals. They defecate in well-marked latrines,

Sett for winter *Badgers leave their underground setts at dusk to forage. In winter they become semi-dormant and drowse in bracken-lined bedchambers, waking only briefly to go out and feed.*

and part of their nightly activity is reorganising the bedding. A badger rolls dry vegetation into a ball and holds it between chin and chest as it shuffles backwards into the sett. As it drops more than it carries underground to cushion the chambers, another clue to the presence of a sett is a wide circle of dried grass and ferns scattered round a hole by a hedge, bank or tree root.

Beautiful burrowers make bad housekeepers

For some of the birds that nest in burrows, the benefit may be the protection of the young from the elements. Burrow-nesters are often cliff-top or high altitude species. But for others, the benefit is concealment. An inconspicuous hole behind overhanging foliage might well be missed by predators.

A common kingfisher's nest is usually hard to spot. This is in keeping with the elusiveness of the bird itself, rarely seen as more than a flash of blue and red above a sunlit stream. However, the evil stench from old droppings and fish bones, left after several broods have been raised, may expose the whereabouts of the nest.

At the beginning of the breeding season, both male and female kingfishers spend some two weeks in digging their nest burrow into a river bank. Excavating with their beaks and kicking the soil out backwards with their feet, they make an upward sloping, armlength tunnel with an oval nesting chamber at the end. In this, the female lays a staggered clutch of six or seven eggs.

Even in infancy, each chick needs one small fish every hour, which means that the parents have to catch at least six fish an hour apart from feeding themselves. By the time the chicks are a month old and ready to leave the nest, each chick is eating four fish an hour, requiring an hourly catch

rate of 24-28 fish from both parents. With such a workload there is simply not time for the parent birds to clean the nest, even if they were so inclined. It becomes so fouled with droppings and regurgitated fish bones that after every visit, the parents wash themselves in the stream before they continue to fish, to ensure their feathers do not become clogged and lose their natural waterproofing.

When the chicks are ready to leave home, the male kingfisher teaches them how to fish while the female lays another clutch in the same nest. By the time the second brood is ready to leave, the nest is piled so high with filth that the parents can hardly get in at all.

Breathtaking beauty

The carmine bee-eaters of tropical Africa are a spectacular species of colonial bird. Their brilliant crimson plumage, green or pink throats and long tails make even a single bird a breathtaking sight. Yet in parts of West Africa they can be seen in their thousands, nesting in steep banks riddled with burrow entrances like windows in tower blocks. Bee-eaters form close communities. Young birds set up their homes close beside the parental burrows, so in time the entire cliff is occupied by related birds.

Once paired, bee-eaters pick a suitable spot for excavating and start digging with their beaks, leaning on their wings as they sweep out the dirt with their feet. They dig an upward-sloping tunnel about 3 ft (1 m) long, making a nest chamber at the end and a hump near its entrance to stop the eggs from rolling out. Then they mate. A female lays one egg every two days until she has a clutch of five or so. Nests are unlined, but soon become carpeted with regurgitated pellets of food waste, deep enough to almost bury the eggs.

When the chicks hatch, their parents bring them food such as grasshoppers, beetles, flies and even bees that have had their stings removed. Before long, the nest becomes even more fouled as droppings are trodden into the food debris, which is now alive with beetle larvae, and the entire tunnel reeks of ammonia.

THE CITIES OF ANTS AND TERMITES

Some ant and termite nests are complex communities, capable of processing their own food and making their own heat and water.

Leaf-cutter ants build underground cities

On a human scale, leaf-cutter ants would build nests the size of New York skyscrapers. Long established nests in Central and South American rain forests have been tunnelled into the ground to depths of more than 20 ft (6 m) and measure up to 330 ft (100 m) across. A maze of tunnels and up to 2000 chambers house a highly organised, closely related society.

The heart of the nest is about halfway up the underground 'skyscraper'. Here the large queen sits in the royal chamber, laying eggs – about one every two seconds – for about ten years. She fertilises her eggs with sperm she has stored from a mating that took place before she founded the colony. A swarm of attendants carry off the eggs to nursery chambers where they develop into grub-like larvae.

Gardens of fungi

Beyond the nursery chambers are the fungus gardens that produce the colony's main source of food. Each step of the gardening process is undertaken by a specific group of worker ants.

Scouts and leaf-cutters forage on the forest floor surrounding the nest, bringing back pieces of leaf which they drop at storage areas inside one of many nest entrances. Theirs is the most hazardous task, and they are guarded all the while by fierce soldier ants who are the largest of all the ants in the nest, apart from the queen. They have powerful jaws that are capable of drawing blood.

Slightly smaller porter ants collect the leaves and cut them into tiny fragments. These are taken over by a group of still smaller ants that crush and mould the leaf fragments into tiny pellets which they insert into the existing bed of mulch on which the fungus grows. Even smaller ants propagate the fungus, thinning the denser growth and replanting it on newer mulch surfaces. Then, minute ants, with heads no bigger than a pinhead, crawl about the 'garden', keeping it clean. They pull out small tufts of fungal strands that they carry out and feed to their larger nestmates.

Vegetarian ants *Leaf-cutter ants (above) bring home leaf pieces to their nest (top) in the Central American jungle, to mulch the fungi they cultivate for food. Vegetarian ant species are rare.*

This fungus crop is found only in leaf-cutter colonies. Each queen who founds a colony carries with her a small piece of the fungus mat from her mother-nest, and with it she starts a fungus garden that will eventually feed her own colony of hundreds of thousands of ants.

Wood ants protect their nests with plant litter

Rustlings among the leaves on a Eurasian woodland floor mark the passage of armies of wood ants carrying pine needles, twigs, leaves or moss to pile on their nest. These ¼ in (6 mm) long red ants feed on insects and larvae, caterpillars especially, and build underground nests housing perhaps 300 000.

Over the nest the ants build a mound of plant debris that can be as high as 5 ft (1.5 m) – a covering to keep it warm and keep out predators such as woodpeckers.

Sometimes the mound is supported round a rotting tree stump, as it is easy for the ants to excavate the upper part of the nest in the rotten wood. Tunnels, chambers, nurseries and food stores also extend deep into the soil.

Workers constantly carry material from inside the nest, damp from the breaths of thousands of ants, outside to dry on the surface. On cold days and at night, they block entrance holes with twigs.

Ant hill *Eurasian wood ants pile mounds of plant debris over their underground nests to keep them warm. They nest near trees, where they hunt for caterpillars.*

Insect architecture *Australian compass or magnetic termites build wedge-shaped nests designed to keep them cool in the hot midday sun.*

Master-builders in a self-contained world

Termites, found worldwide in warmer climates, do everything on a grand scale. Termite mounds can be nearly 30 ft (9 m) tall, often extending below ground to a depth of 6-9 ft (2-3 m), and colonies often number millions. In some parts of Africa, termites number as many as 1000 per square foot (10 000 per square metre). In human terms, that is about 60 times as crowded as the Indian city of Delhi.

The world's 2000 or so species of termites have a variety of building styles. Mounds may be tall and chimney-like, umbrella shapes that keep the rain off, or may resemble mountain ranges, pinnacles, slabs or pagodas. Some are tunnelled in tree stumps and some are oval shaped and hang from trees. Most are built of chewed soil, wood, saliva and droppings.

Within these dramatic exteriors, the nests are miracles of design. At the heart of the nest is the central royal chamber, where the queen – up to about 6 in (15 cm) long and about 6000 times heavier than her consort or subjects – lays thousands of eggs each day. She is attended by her consort and busy sterile workers of either or both sexes. The nest also houses warehouses, nurseries and factories. They are kept humid and maintained at an almost constant temperature by a complex air-conditioning system made up of a network of chambers and passages.

Termite art *Mounds sculpted from mud in Nigeria include umbrellas (above) and fungus-growers' towers (right).*

Self-supporting colonies

Giant African fungus-growing termites build mounds from pellets of dried mud. The mounds are up to 25 ft (7.6 m) high and about 10 ft (3 m) across, and are virtually self-supporting, having gardens where the termites cultivate fungi for food. The fungi are grown on a bed of termite droppings mixed with a little dead wood, collected from outside the nest. Food storage vaults are higher up the mound.

Below the garden is the royal chamber and the nurseries, and at the deepest level there is a cellar with a damp floor used as the source of building material. Water vapour, from the breath of millions of termites, condenses and drips down constantly through the floors, keeping the cellar damp. The inner nest is ventilated by a network of passages. Warm air rises to the top of the nest and escapes through tall 'chimneys', drawing in fresh air through the nest walls. The damp cellar cools the constantly circulating air.

Heating control *Compass termites in northwest Australia live in earth mounds 7-10 ft (2-3 m) high that are all aligned with their long sides facing east and west. This layout keeps the temperature at 30 °C (86 °F). During the middle of the day, the sun falls on the narrow sides, which prevents overheating, whereas in the morning and evening, the long sides face the sun and absorb the maximum heat.*

HOMES FOR BEES AND WASPS

Over millions of years, social bees and wasps have perfected architectural styles and building materials that are precisely geared to their way of life.

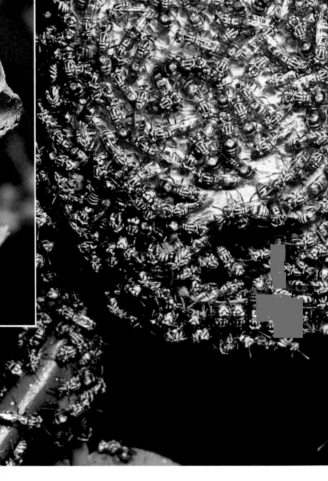

From small beginnings *The founding queen of a paper wasp colony begins by making a pulp structure (above) on which she fashions a single cell. Shortly after, more are added (centre) and eggs laid in them. The queen nurtures the young until they are old enough to emerge as adults. Later offspring complete the multicelled nest (right).*

Intricate architecture fashioned from paper

Though unrelated, bees and wasps have evolved some surprisingly parallel life styles. One group of vespid wasps, for instance, stores honey and pollen as larval food, and a number of South American species produce honey in commercial quantities.

In the same way as bees, social wasps build nests containing cells for their larvae, though the material they use is mud or paper, not wax. Paper-making wasps chew wood into a pulp, which hardens into parchment, providing a much lighter structure than the honeybee's wax. Some wasps arrange cells eccentrically, others vertically with downward openings. Either way, the larvae are wedged into their paper cradles and fed on minced insects. Generally, nests are multistorey, each floor suspended from the one above on stiff paper ropes. Most nests are hung among branches, though some are built in burrows. There, while one worker detail builds cell slabs, another group excavates below, keeping pace with each other as the nest descends into the ground.

Some wasp colonies divide by swarming. In others, one or more queens find and settle a new nest site, though rather in the manner of bumblebees, they have to wait for the first batches of larvae to develop before they can get the building operation fully underway. The progeny start working as soon as they can fly, collecting plant and wood fibres, which are chewed into a pulp that is added to the original modest structure provided by the founding queens.

United artists *The intricate patterning of the paper covering of a wasps' nest is due to the fact that each colour is the work of a different individual. The paper is made from fibres that the wasps obtain from many sources – grass stems, fence posts, cardboard boxes, unpainted planks or dried-out weeds.*

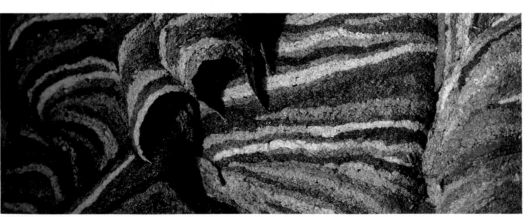

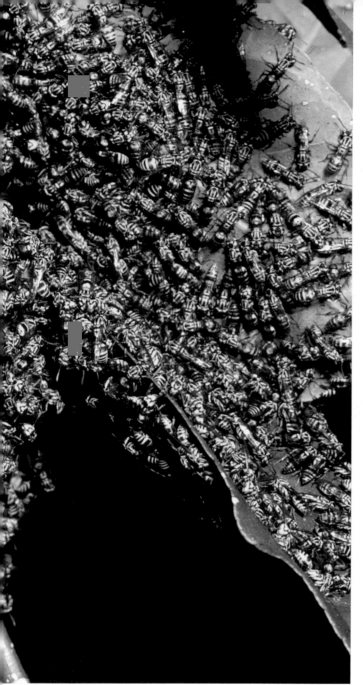

Bee city *An African honeybee's nest has a rough exterior but the interior, which may contain some 80 000 bees, is a model of urban order in which each worker has an allotted task, from feeding the young to nest maintenance.*

A building material that is taken from flowers

In the highly organised world of the honeybee, each worker has its allotted task to perform. This changes as it gets older, but at some time in its short life, it will be one of the team that produces wax, the all-important raw material with which the community builds its tiers of cells, the cradles for the eggs and larvae. The wax producers synthesise the material from collected sugars in nectar; it emerges from glands under the abdomen as thin flakes. The wax producers then pass the flakes to another group of worker bees who chew them. By mixing them with secretions from glands in their mandibles, they change the material from a brittle to a plastic state that can be worked and moulded.

Wax is easiest to mould at a temperature of 35°C (95°F), so a further large team spends its time keeping the hive temperature exactly right. If it is too cold for wax-working, or for the larvae, the bees generate heat by vibrating their flight muscles. If, however, it is too warm, the team fans its wings in unison to cool it through the evaporation of strategically placed water droplets, collected specially for the purpose.

To build the six-sided cells, a worker fashions some wax into three diamond-shaped bases, one at a time, raising the beginnings of walls on each. Then she extends the walls until they are slightly longer than an adult bee, constantly testing to make sure they are of uniform thickness.

Thousands of worker bees toil side by side to build a honeycomb of adjoining hexagonal cells, hanging from the roof of the hive, in the case of domesticated honeybees. In the wild it is a nest, typically of American football shape hanging from a branch or inside a hollow tree. All the cells are tilted upwards so that nothing spills out. In architectural terms, hexagons are excellent forms, as they combine strength with no wasted space where the walls of the cells join.

Not all cells are cradles. Many are honeypots or pollen jars, and have slightly thicker walls than cells for larvae. The larvae are fed with bee-bread, which is a mixture of honey, made by the worker bees by mixing nectar with their own stomach juices and pollen. But a bees' nest is more than just blocks of honeycombs. For instance, there are the cells in which the queen lays her eggs and, away from the centre, there are large bulb-shaped cells for new queens. These begin as basic larval stock, but change when fed upon protein-rich royal jelly, a mixture of honey, pollen and special secretions.

Bumblebees are hardier than honeybees and are able to survive in cooler parts of the world. They live in smaller social groups and, whereas a honeybee queen is solely an egg-layer and starts a new hive aided by a swarm of workers, a bumblebee queen starts out on her own. Because she has to build her own brood cell, lay eggs and sit on them in much the same manner as a bird to hatch out her first brood of workers, an intricate building is out of the question. Her nest has to be ready-made, and is usually built in the abandoned hole of a vole or fieldmouse, or in a grass tussock.

107

THE SOLITARY LIFE

Bees and wasps are widely known for their complex social structures. The majority of both species, however, live successful, solitary lives.

Masons, miners and waspish potters

Working quickly before the mud dries, the female potter wasp builds her nest in much the same way that some of the earliest human craftsmen made pots – with strips of clay formed into circles and laid one on top of the other. Having searched out a patch of wet ground, the wasp gathers a pile of mud, testing its dampness as she works. If the mud is too wet, she leaves it to dry until it is exactly the consistency she wants. If it is too dry, she moistens it by collecting water in her mouth and spitting it into the clay. Then she kneads the material until she has a workable pellet about the size of her head. This she carries to her building site – the underside of a ledge, maybe, or a branch or strip of lifted bark – stretches it into a circle and lays it in place. When it is adjusted to her satisfaction, she flies back to her mud source and repeats the process.

Out of these clay circles she builds up a flask. In this she puts some caterpillars immobilised by her sting. On top of one she lays an egg, then seals the neck with a clay plug, so providing her offspring with a secure refuge.

Some mason bees make their nests from mud, and others use a paste of chewed leaves, petals or animal hairs. A female stocks the nest with bee-bread (a pollen and nectar mix), lays an egg on it and then seals the chamber with a mud plug. Occasionally, fights break out over the possession of old nests from previous seasons.

Nests of clay *Working the mud of the Israeli desert with her legs, feelers and jaws, a potter wasp carefully shapes the lip of her nest (left). When it is finished, the nest lip curves outwards in the same manner as that of the nest of a Costa Rican potter wasp (above).*

Communal nests

Mason bees may sometimes build many-chambered nests that look like small colonies. Although the occupants do not necessarily live in harmony, they fight less than solitary bees. The advantage of communal nests may be that they save work and have thicker walls, so giving added protection from the cuckoo wasps that often break in to lay their own eggs there.

Like colonial mason bees, some mining bees also cluster their nests together to produce many-celled burrows – though probably for constructional reasons rather than for safety. The bees nest in loose, sandy soil, and when a patch is found they all crowd in. Each female bee digs independently, and uses secretions from her abdomen to line her cell and make it waterproof. Then, having laid several eggs, one in each cell, each female finally seals her burrow.

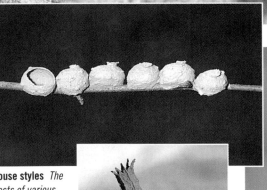

House styles *The nests of various species of potter wasp are found worldwide, from the lone, decorated nest of a Malaysian wasp (right), to the ball-shaped rows of nests made by a North American species (above).*

Fake flower *Some potter wasps build their nests on the leaves of plants. The rounded shape of the nest and the pale clay used to build it, give it a superficial resemblance to a flower or bud. This may help to camouflage it and so protect the egg from predators.*

Leaf-lined home *Clasping a neatly scissored fragment of leaf between her jaws and legs, a leaf-cutter bee heads for her nest hidden in a cactus stem.*

Bees that encase their eggs in leafy bowers

The leaf-cutter bee cushions its nest chamber with the leaves of roses, lilac, willow and laburnum. A female, distinguishable from a honeybee by the pollen sacs on her abdomen, cuts an oval from chosen leaves, folds it with her jaws and carries it between her legs to the nest. This is usually a deep, slim hole in a tree, sometimes one left by tunnelling beetle larvae.

The bee starts to line the nest hole by pushing the rolled-up leaf fragment to the bottom, then goes back to cut out a tiny circle of leaf, which is thrust down to line the base of the nest hole. Then the bee stocks this first cell of her nest with pollen and nectar and lays an egg, fertilising it with sperm retained from mating. Finally the cell is closed with a last leaf disc and cemented with mouth juices.

This done, the bee repeats the whole performance, stacking the next cell on top of the first, and continuing until she has filled 10 or 15 cells. The lowest cells of the nest produce females, but the eggs in the topmost cells, those nearest to the entrance hole, are not fertilised. These develop into males.

FASHIONING HANGING NESTS

Some birds show great skill in constructing enclosed hanging nests, that are often suspended from the tips of branches out of reach of most marauders.

Woven homes *A grass ring (above) is often the basis of a weaverbird's nest. Nest shapes vary with site and species, but most are entered from below, like the layard weaverbird nests (right).*

Master builders of hanging homes

A forked twig is all the support that village weaverbirds need for building their nests. At breeding times, these sparrow-like birds festoon trees in southern Africa with their hanging, woven nests, constructed by the males. Once a male has chosen a site, he collects building materials such as strips of leaves, vines and tall grasses, then knots the strips to his twig using only his beak and feet. In this way he makes a firm grass ring – the foundation of his nest.

Gradually the bird builds up a roof and walls by knotting and threading strips over and under one another with his beak. Next he adds a porch, curving it down over the front of the nest. The final shape is rather like a snail shell

with the entrance underneath. A threshold between the porch and the egg chamber keeps eggs and chicks from rolling out of the nest.

It may take up to a week for the male weaverbird to complete a nest. Once he has finished weaving, he hangs beneath the nest and flutters his wings to attract the attention of a female.

Practice makes perfect

Usually, a young male weaverbird's first attempts at weaving a nest are rather untidy, and he may have to build several nests before he can persuade a female to mate and lay her eggs in one. If he is unlucky he has to start again, sometimes even unravelling his first attempt and utilising the same materials. With

practice, however, his efforts get much neater. Once a female has accepted a nest, she lines the egg chamber with soft grass tips and feathers before laying her clutch of three or four eggs, which she incubates for about two weeks.

An underside entrance makes it difficult for larger birds to get into a weaverbird's nest and steal eggs or chicks. Asian baya weaverbirds and African Cassin's weaverbirds build a sleeve-like entrance tunnel 2 ft (60 cm) long that collapses inwards if a bird of prey attacks it. To enter the nest itself, a weaverbird swoops down at speed to the tunnel entrance and then folds its wings, allowing its momentum to carry it upward through the tunnel without touching the sides.

Come on in *A male masked weaverbird in Botswana hangs beneath his nest and tries to attract a female to mate and lay her eggs in it. Young males may make several nests before achieving success.*

110

Oropendolas hang their nests together

Strips torn from banana leaves and long creepers are among the materials used by crow-sized oropendolas to weave their nests. Tightly woven and waterproof, the drooping, bag-like nests may be up to 7 ft (2 m) long, and they swing in clusters from the tips of tree branches in South and Central America. Each nest is entered from the top of the bag, and the padded nest chamber sits at the bottom.

A female oropendola builds the nest on her own, with no help from the male. He spends much of his time displaying and singing to attract other females. All the mates he attracts build their nests near each other, and his harem of up to 40 nests can festoon a single tree. The advantage of this community is that the females help each other to bring up the chicks.

Although high winds may blow nests down, they provide reasonably good protection for eggs and chicks. Climbing predators such as kinkajous (or honey bears), monkeys and snakes have difficulty reaching them from the thin branch tips, and flying hunters such as hawks are foiled by the tunnel entrances. Some oropendolas build near wasp nests as an added defence. The wasps do not attack the birds, but will attack other animals that disturb them.

Arboreal adornment *A tree in Trinidad is festooned with the closely woven nests of a group of noisy crested oropendolas. Sometimes the birds overload a branch and break it. They feed on fruit, seeds, insects and other small creatures.*

Tailored leaves to fit a tailorbird's needs

The long-tailed tailorbird utilises threads taken from a spider's web to sew its nest together. This sparrow-sized bird makes its home in Indian and Southeast Asian gardens, using large, living leaves as a framework for supporting the nest.

Tailor-made *A female long-tailed tailorbird makes a pouch of living leaves to support her nest. She sews them together using her beak as a needle and cobweb silk for yarn. In the nest she lays a clutch of two or three eggs, which the male bird helps her to incubate.*

The female is the tailor. She pulls together two tree or shrub leaves hanging near each other and pierces holes in adjoining edges with her beak. Then she takes a cobweb strand in her beak, threads it through the holes and knots it. Continuing in this way, she joins the two leaves to form a hanging cradle. This she stuffs with soft vegetable matter.

It takes the tailorbird about four days to complete her nest, as the leaves often tear or the threads break. The living leaves make a stronger nest than dead leaves, and provide almost perfect camouflage for a clutch of eggs, as well as shelter from tropical rains.

HANGING OR HIGH-PLACED HOMES

A home set high above ground not only gives some animals protection from their predators but may also allow them to live close to their source of food.

Harvest mice weave their homes from leaves

There is no obvious entrance to a harvest mouse's round nest, which clings to the stems of reeds, wheat, tall grasses or other stiff-stemmed vegetation.

To weave the tennis-ball-sized breeding nest, the female may use 20 or so leaves. She splits each one lengthways several times with her sharp teeth, then weaves them together without detaching them. As the leaves are still alive, they are elastic enough for the woven walls to stretch apart and then close up again, so the mouse goes in and out where she will. She is so small – only 2½ in (64 mm) long, excluding her tail, and no heavier than a 2p piece – that she moves with ease among the stems, using her long tail as an extra limb.

Harvest home
When she has finished weaving the nest, the russet-coloured mouse lines it with a fine moss-like cushion of chewed grass. Later, she gives birth to up to eight blind, naked babies. She suckles them for just over a week before starting to feed them solid foods such as seeds, grain, new shoots and soft fruit, all close at hand.

After 16 days the grey-brown young harvest mice can fend for themselves. They gradually moult to an adult russet colour, starting at the hindquarters.

Night outing *Nosing her way through the woven grass walls of her nest, a female European harvest mouse, active day and night, sets off in search of food such as seeds or insects. During the breeding season between August and September she may bear up to seven litters, weaving a new nest for each one. Harvest mice build mostly in reed beds, motorway verges or field edges because populations in grain-growing areas have gradually been wiped out.*

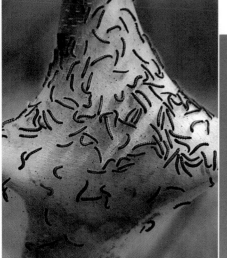

Silken screen *Eastern tent caterpillars (above) spin silken tents slung high on trees such as a cottonwood (right) that they have almost stripped of leaves.*

Caterpillars that pitch tents in the tree tops

White, silken drapes hanging like decorations from tree branches in the eastern USA are in fact the work of caterpillars. Eastern tent caterpillar moths lay masses of eggs in strings round the twigs of trees such as cherry, apple, plum and cottonwood. The 100 or so caterpillars that emerge together on a twig spin a mass of silken threads to form a communal tent that protects them from birds and ants as they eat the leaves.

At first the young black-and-yellow caterpillars spend all their time under the tent, because there are still plenty of discarded egg cases and buds and leaves to eat close by. But as they get larger, the food supply under the tent runs out and the caterpillars have to venture outside and risk the attentions of foraging predators.

But some caterpillars do have a second line of defence. As they eat the leaves, they take in some of the cyanide that the tree produces in tiny quantities in its own defence. Instead of simply expelling the poison, the caterpillars let the cyanide build up in a special gland and regurgitate it in liquid form if a bird, ant or other predator tries to eat them. They leave scent trails to the leaves with the best supply of cyanide. The regurgitated liquid is foul-tasting as well as poisonous, and predators soon learn to leave the caterpillars alone. With this weapon as their daytime protection, caterpillars sometimes strip whole trees of their leaves.

In summer, the tent caterpillars spin cocoons from which they will emerge as moths. These moths lay eggs that overwinter on twigs to hatch in spring as a new generation of tent caterpillars.

Home is inside a leaf for minute tunnellers

Pale squiggles or thin white trails in green leaves are evidence of the work of leaf miners. Some moth caterpillars and the grubs of various beetles, weevils and flies are so minute that they can tunnel inside leaves of all kinds without breaking through either surface. Leaf-mining caterpillars have a flattened, virtually legless, form so that they can fit comfortably within the thickness of a leaf.

Leaf miners feed on the tender cells inside the leaves, and it is the tunnels they create while feeding that appear as pale squiggles. To reach the tender centre of a leaf, the larger leaf-eating animals are forced to eat its tough outer layers, but for the leaf miners these outer layers give the same protection that they give to the inner parts of the leaf itself.

When they are fully grown, some species of leaf-mining caterpillar emerge from the leaves to pupate (change into adults) elsewhere. Other leaf miners pupate inside the leaves and wriggle out.

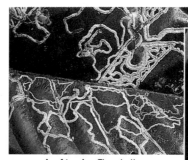

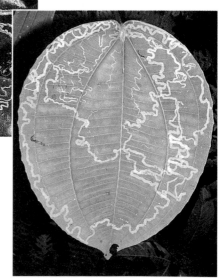

Leaf tracks *The winding, whitish tracks of leaf-mining moth caterpillars can be seen clearly on the leaf of a plant of the melastoma family (right) in the Amazon rain forest, and in closer detail (above) on another rain forest leaf.*

HIGH-RISE HOMES

To protect their eggs and chicks from predators, many birds build their nests high up – on cliffs, trees or even man-made structures.

Cliff nesters *Puffins on Skomer Island (left) off the coast of Wales, like all puffins, either dig their own cliff-top nest tunnels or take over abandoned rabbit burrows. Gannets (below) live in colonies numbering thousands of pairs, and prefer to nest on top of cliffs – for these goose-sized birds need a fair amount of space in order to land easily.*

Cliff-face 'cities' house colonies of sea birds

For millions of sea birds, sea cliffs are ideal places for nesting, especially remote mainland cliffs or those on offshore islands. Here their chicks are safe from land predators such as foxes and stoats, and are near enough to the sea for their parents to fish for food.

In the Northern Hemisphere, many sea birds fly in from the open sea to breed in May and June, and every suitable cliff becomes a noisy and bristling city, with birds lining every available ledge.

Birds of different species seem to prefer different levels. On rocks and in clefts just above the high-tide mark, shags and cormorants build nests of seaweed, grass and driftwood. Higher up, guillemots and razorbills lay their eggs on bare ledges. The guillemots pack together on more open ledges, but razorbills often gather in small groups on less-exposed sites.

Just above these birds are the kittiwakes, which build platforms of mud, seaweed and tufts of grass, that they trample to make a level

Heights of safety *In the Norwegian Arctic, a colony of nesting kittiwakes on Hornoya Island uses these sturdy and well-built cliff-face nests year after year.*

base on a narrow, often sloping, ledge or in seemingly impossible locations. The nest itself is built deep, to guard against eggs being kicked out accidentally, and is fixed firmly to the rock with the birds' droppings.

Near the top of the cliff are the gull-like fulmars, which also nest on bare ledges. They spit a foul-smelling oil at intruders. Gannet colonies are usually in remote spots such as offshore islands, but on crowded cliffs these goose-sized birds with a 6 ft (1.8 m) wingspan prefer to nest on the top, where landing is easier for them. Their nests are made of seaweed bound together with droppings and lined

with feathers and grass. The nests in a gannet colony are usually far enough apart for neighbours to be beyond pecking distance. A returning bird that overshoots its nest and gets too close to another is attacked mercilessly by the sitters it has to pass to get to its nest.

Puffins and shearwaters dig tunnels or take over rabbit burrows in the turf at the cliff top. They may even share an entrance, as puffins fish by day and shearwaters by night – sometimes there are so many burrows that a whole cliff top collapses, destroying the nests.

The cliffs are constantly busy with wheeling birds flying out to sea and returning with fish. Some

birds are away for hours, flying maybe 50 miles (80 km) or more to find a good feeding ground. The other parent stays at the nest to incubate the egg or guard the hatchling from marauders such as skuas and gulls. Because of the time and energy needed to find food, most sea birds produce only one chick in each breeding season.

The advantages of crowding

With almost every available site on a cliff occupied by a nesting pair, some nest spots are much less than a wingspan apart. Guillemots, for example, may be almost shoulder to shoulder. This crowding can have its advantages. Crowded sites

provide good information – birds watch their neighbours returning from fishing expeditions and follow the most successful when they go back to sea.

Crowding has other benefits, too. Each bird is influenced by its neighbour's state of readiness to mate and lay eggs, with the result that a great many eggs are laid at the same time. A host of eggs and hatchlings developing at once provides safety in numbers, because predators simply cannot eat all the food available during the season. So most youngsters have a good chance of reaching adulthood. By late summer, most of them have left the nest and gone to sea.

Nest sites in tree tops, steeples and chimneys

North American bald eagles build some of the biggest tree-top nests, which they re-use year after year, adding new material every time. These big fish-eating eagles often nest in lone trees by rivers or lakes. A bald eagle nest in Ohio that was some 12 ft (3.7 m) deep and 8 ft 6 in (2.6 m) across was estimated to weigh around 2 tons. It crashed to the ground during a storm in its 36th year.

Ospreys, fish hunters that are found worldwide, build huge flat, open nests of sticks in pine tops or on rock pinnacles. They too use nests over and over again – some nest sites have been occupied continuously for more than 40 years.

Old inhabitants

White storks nest high in trees in Europe, Africa and Asia, as well as on chimneys or church spires. In many parts of Europe they are widely regarded as birds of good omen, and many homes have a permanent, protected stork's nest on the roof. Storks return to the same nests year after year and their offspring sometimes take over when the parents die. One nest on a tower in eastern Germany is recorded as first being occupied in 1549, and was still in use in 1930.

Birds incubate their eggs and feed their hatchlings, so building

High living *White storks (right) perch on massive, permanent nests in Greece. A peregrine falcon (above) guards its young in a rudimentary nest on a high, rocky ledge with unrestricted views.*

nests in out-of-reach places keeps eggs and chicks safe from ground-living predators, especially when the parents are away finding food.

For large birds such as eagles and storks, having to build a new nest of sufficient size and strength every year would take a considerable amount of time and energy. Re-using established nests allows these birds to concentrate their efforts on rearing their youngsters.

Northern Europe's most noticeable tree-nesting birds are rooks, which live in colonies that sometimes number hundreds of nests. Their cup-shaped nests, bulky and untidy, are refurbished each year in the tops of tall deciduous trees, long before the leaves appear in spring. Colonies are often near farms and villages, because they provide good pickings for the birds.

WATERFRONT HOMES

Rather like the custodians of moated castles, some creatures put watery defences between their offspring and predators.

Grebes nest snugly in a safe anchorage

It takes a couple of days at least for a pair of western grebes to construct their floating nest platform. The untidy home of these North American birds is made of twigs, reeds and rushes, and the whole thing is anchored to underwater vegetation. What is visible measures only about 12 in (30 cm) across, but this is just the tip of a pyramid which is some three times as wide at its underwater base.

Because the nest is surrounded by water, the eggs and hatchlings are safe from land predators. This allows the parent birds to make lengthy foragings in search of food, having first covered the eggs to conceal them from aerial raiders. The grebes brood their eggs for about 23 days. When the chicks emerge, they immediately climb up on the mother's back. Once all are safely in place, the family sails off and abandons the nest for good.

In the search for a safe place to incubate eggs, many birds build their nests on or over water, using all kinds of methods to keep their eggs dry. Black terns, for instance, also build floating nests that are 2-6 in (50-150 mm) high and made of reeds, sedges and water weeds. The birds anchor them to rushes and lily stems in shallow water. These birds, fairly widespread in North America, Europe and Asia, are usually found in marshy areas or swampy grassland where there is open water to provide feeding.

The nest of the horned coot, which breeds by lakes in the South American Andes, does not float. Instead, the bird raises a cairn of stones – 2-3 ft (60 cm-1 m) high and as much as 13 ft (4 m) across the base – built up from the lake bottom until it protrudes above the surface of the water. It involves considerable labour, since the bird has to lift the quite sizable stones from the lake bottom or the shore to the nest site. When the mound is completed, the coot crowns it with a bed of water plants.

The moorhen, which can be found in watery habitats across the world, builds its large, loosely woven nest of reeds and rushes on the swampy edges of lakes and rivers. The birds always nest in the thick cover provided by plants along the water's edge, well out of the view of predators.

The reed warbler also nests in waterside vegetation, weaving its deep, cup-shaped nest around the stems of reeds in all but the most northerly parts of Europe. The nest is so deep that the female almost vanishes inside it, but the depth does prevent the eggs from falling out as the reeds sway in the wind. The wind often causes problems during building, however, as can be seen from the warbler's struggles as it endeavours to tie the strips of vegetation between the waving reed stems.

Waterborne *Both western grebes (left) and black terns (below) build nests that float. Grebes abandon their nests quite early in the season, after which terns may occasionally take them over.*

Secure lodging *What appears to be an untidy flotsam of branches in the river is in fact a beaver lodge (above). The underwater entrance provides access for the aquatic beavers (right) but denies it to such predators as lynxes and wolves.*

Ingenuity of Nature's hydraulic engineer

The work capacity of the beaver has long invited proverbial comparison. While building its mid-river home, its chisel teeth lop saplings in minutes. Bigger trees take more time, and sometimes more beavers. On a two-animal sized trunk, the pair work at it alternately, gnawing from all sides, until the tree topples over.

Building a home is the first action of a pair of mating beavers. In an ideal world there would be a forest with a broad, slow-flowing river running through it, whose banks were high enough to dig an underwater tunnel in. Such rivers are not plentiful, and as an alternative the beavers dam streams to raise the water level instead.

Having cut down a few trees, they haul them to a shallow place in the river. If the trees grow at some distance from the water's edge, then the beavers dig canals to float their logs down.

Once the logs are at the dam site, the beavers push stout sticks upright into the stream bed and tow the logs athwart them. They weigh the logs down with rocks and pile more logs on top, filling the spaces between with stones, pond weed and mud. At each end of the dam, spillways are constructed to keep the water level constant. Finished, the dam might be more than 100 yd (90 m) long and 10 ft (3 m) high. A dam on the

Jefferson River in the United States stretched 750 yd (690 m), and was strong enough to bear the weight of a man on horseback.

The dam must be maintained constantly, and the beavers open and close the spillways according to the flow of the water supply. In the middle of their created lake, the beavers build their lodge, a huge tangle of branches cemented together with mud, that rises above the surface of the water. The entrance to the lodge is under water, but a passage leads up to a sleeping chamber just above the water line. The entrance, being hidden, defies most predators, and mud packed onto the outside of the lodge in autumn freezes in winter to provide further security.

The beavers inhabit the lodge for the rest of their lives. In winter, they spend all their time in it, except for brief forays under the ice to fetch food. In spring, it is a haven for the kits, which are able to swim at birth, but because of their small size and dense fur – which traps air – are too buoyant to dive for the entrance and leave the safety of the sleeping chamber.

Dubious advantages of a crane's floating home

The rare Siberian crane is rare indeed, for it is believed to nest in only two places, both of them in the tundra of northeast Siberia.

Its plight is not relieved by its building methods. It lays its eggs on rough platforms made of trampled moss about 3 ft (1 m) across, which are built upon the 30-60 ft (9-18 m) wide floating tangles of sedge roots and cotton grass that bump along the shores of the wide, shallow tundra lakes.

These floating islands prove little or no deterrent to predators, since arctic foxes and wolves are able to leap aboard and hunt through the tussocks. But if the eggs survive until the chicks hatch, the nest's proximity to water is an advantage. It enables the youngsters to escape by swimming out into the ice-cold lake – an accomplishment they have almost from hatching – where not even the most determined of predators is likely to follow.

Island home *Standing by its nest on an island of floating turf, a Siberian crane keeps a wary eye out for marauding arctic foxes and wolves.*

SURPRISES ON THE HOME FRONT

Variations on the nesting theme range from hanging nests and leafy tents to stick-built huts on the forest floor and waterside cottages.

Hammocks and huts for unusual nesters

Cobwebs, despite their apparent flimsiness, are used by some Australian birds to anchor their nests. In the northeastern rain forest, frilled monarch flycatchers use cobwebs to sling their cup nests between vines, and among the sandstone hills of the east coast, rock warblers use them to suspend their round, woven-grass nests from cave roofs or rock overhangs. Rock warblers are also known as cave birds and cataract birds – they have a habit of building their nests behind cataracts. However, with human settlements encroaching on their living space, rock warblers nest just about anywhere – even slung under a mattress inside a house.

Another builder of unusual nests is the spine-tailed logrunner

of Australia, which spends most of its time on the forest floor, foraging in and around logs for insects, snails and slugs. Even when startled, the logrunner does not fly off – it just flutters a short distance away before continuing to scuffle about in the leaf litter.

In autumn, an unusual time for nest building, the female logrunner builds her rounded, hut-like nest on the ground against a stone, log, or bank. She makes a platform of sticks, ferns and fibrous leaves, then builds up the walls, leaning them inwards until they touch at the top to form a rounded roof.

Next she furnishes the interior with moss and leaves, and arranges a curtain of greenery across the entrance as an aid to camouflaging the spot. As a finishing touch, she covers the entire edifice with more sticks and leaves. Then, with her home ready for occupation, she lays two white eggs inside.

Precarious perch *In a nest anchored to vines with cobwebs, an Australian male frilled monarch flycatcher takes its turn at incubating the clutch, usually two to four eggs. The bird is named for its courting behaviour of raising its neck feathers to form a frilly white collar.*

Dummy doorways that mislead marauders

To guard their eggs from tree-top predators, penduline tits build their soft, bag-shaped nests hanging from the thinnest twigs – in Europe, the birds often build them over water as well.

Cape penduline tits in southern Africa take their safety strategy even further by building nests that have false entrances. The visible entrance hole near the top of the bag leads to a cul-de-sac – possibly meant to make predators think the nest is empty. Near this hole lies the real entrance – a tiny slit that has to be forced open and closes naturally again behind the bird.

Male penduline tits are the nest builders, using long, tough strands of fibrous plant or animal material ranging from grasses to hair. The bird starts building the framework

Double doors *A Cape penduline tit opens the slit doorway into its felted, rainproof nest. The sham entrance is on the left.*

with a single strand, using his fine beak to tie it fast round a suitable twig. He then adds more and more strands, interweaving them until he has constructed a small hanging basket with a concealed front entrance and a texture resembling felt. Just as carpet-makers knot small strands of wool into coarser fibres, the tits knot short plant fibres into the weave. European penduline tits, for example, use the seed hairs of willows and poplars.

His nest completed, the male tit advertises for a mate who lines the nest with soft fibres, and lays five or six eggs that hatch in about two weeks. Chicks can fly three weeks

later. Parents and fledglings roost together in the nest. These felt-like tits' nests are so strong that children in eastern Europe sometimes wear them as slippers and in Africa, Masai women are known to use them as purses.

Hanging tents and two-storeyed nests

When a bat needs a roost, it most often turns to a ready-made shelter such as an attic, belfry or cave. Bats that build their own roosts are unusual, but some species of American spear-nosed bat and Sphinx's short-faced fruit bat are tent-makers – they roost in tents made from leaves.

Bat tents are very simple constructions. For example, thumb-sized Honduran white bats (which are spear-nosed bats) use the leaves of banana trees or large-leaved heliconias – these are particular favourites. The bats bite a row of perforations along each side of the midrib of a large, broad leaf, causing the sides to fall down as flaps. Small groups of up to a dozen bats roost inside the fold, well protected from rain or sun. They hang head down with hind feet hooked in the bitten holes.

To discourage such predators as snakes, toads and opossums, the bats choose leaves that are about 6 ft 6 in (2 m) above the ground and hanging well away from the main trunk. Any hunter that is light-footed enough to approach

118

A dipper nest behind a curtain of falling water

Dippers build their domed, mossy nests on ledges under bridges or overhanging banks, or behind waterfalls, and then line them with dead leaves or grass. They feed by diving under water in fast-flowing streams and rivers, and then walking along the stream bed to find small water creatures to eat.

Unlike the wren-shaped, thrush-sized European dipper, the Asian brown dipper is a rich brown all over, with no white chin or chest.

Hidden home *A brown dipper returns to its spray-splashed nest behind a Japanese waterfall, where its four or five chicks spend about three or four weeks. The waterside nest is close to the food supply and is difficult for stoats and other predators to reach.*

---

the tent along the leaf will make it vibrate, so alerting the bats and giving them time to escape. Their unusual white colouring probably helps to camouflage them. When the sun shines through the thin leaf roof of their shelter, the bats seem to take on the same colour as the leaf. White bats prefer to circulate among several roosting sites rather than use the same one too often. And although they may use the same sites for up to six weeks or so, they are unlikely to visit the same one two days running.

Nest-building snake
Just as tent-makers are a rarity among bats, so are chambered-nest builders among snakes, yet female king cobras build two-chambered nests in which to lay their eggs. The female uses her head and body as a crook to nudge together a pile of twigs, dead leaves, grass and soil into a suitable heap. Then she shapes a hollow in the heap and lays 20-40 eggs there.

Once the eggs have been laid, the king cobra pushes more vegetation into place to cover them and makes herself a second hollow on top, where she lies ready to defend them if necessary. Humans that come too close may be attacked

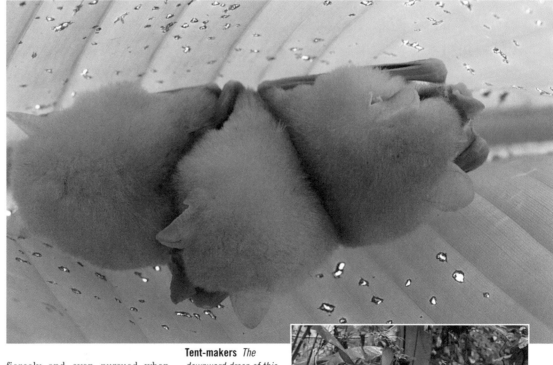

fiercely and even pursued when they run away. Not until the eggs have hatched and the youngsters have gone on their way does the female king cobra leave her nest.

King cobras, or hamadryads, found in Asia, are the world's largest venomous snakes, reaching lengths of around 18 ft (5.5 m).

Tent-makers *The downward droop of this heliconia leaf (right) hints at the presence of three white tent bats (above). They hang by their feet from holes bitten along the leaf's central spine and shelter from the rain.*

MASTERS OF MAKESHIFT

Birds are experts at making the best use of the nesting materials and sites available, and are also good at improvising when needed.

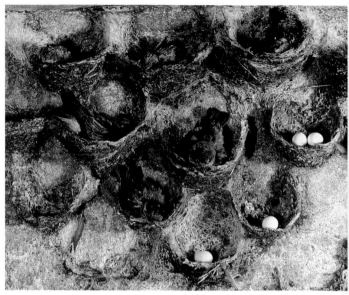

How painstakingly built nests end up in the soup

An industry that brings in millions of dollars in Southeast Asia depends entirely on the breeding activities of tiny birds known as cave swiftlets. Their nests are the main ingredient of bird's-nest soup, highly valued in the Far East for its protein content and flavour.

Swiftlets and swifts spend much of their lives on the wing – they mate, eat and even sleep in the air. These birds have short legs that are adapted for clinging and hanging on to the buildings or rocks in which they nest. Many nest under eaves or in caves, and because they cannot land easily on their short legs, collecting material for nest building is difficult. They tend to use materials they can obtain on the wing. The chimney swift, for example, snaps off twigs as it flies.

Swifts and swiftlets use their saliva as building material. Some use saliva to cement mosses, and others alternate layers of saliva and feathers, giving their nests a striped look. The African palm swift mingles feathers and saliva into a pad and sticks it to the underside of a palm leaf. It glues its egg into the nest and incubates it by clinging to the leaf.

Some cave swiftlets build their nests entirely from saliva, and it is these that are used in making the soup. The swiftlet's salivary glands enlarge as the breeding season approaches so that it can produce the vast amounts of saliva needed. High on the wall of a dark cave, a nesting bird lays the foundations of its nest by flying straight at the wall and touching it briefly with its tongue to deposit a tiny blob of saliva before veering away. In this way the bird gradually builds up a rubbery U-shaped strip, adding to it until it has constructed a pocket of hardened saliva – its nest.

On the wall *From the culinary point of view, the most desirable of swiftlets' nests are those made of pure saliva. But since these are often taken by human gatherers before the birds can lay, they must start again. Lacking sufficient saliva to build entire second nests, the swiftlets mingle the meagre remainder with whatever materials are available.*

Hide cleaners use hairs to build their nests

Oxpeckers provide large grazing animals of the African plains with a valuable cleaning service. They remove blood-sucking ticks and flies from their hides. A zebra, buffalo, rhino, antelope or giraffe placidly puts up with the discomfort of the birds' claws as a dozen or so climb all over it to scissor off the blood-engorged parasites with swift swings of their beaks.

Oxpeckers spend much of their lives on their large hosts, eating, resting, courting and mating. But at breeding time they leave their mobile homes and make nests in high tree holes. A common nest building material is the hair taken from their unwitting host. Groups of up to five oxpeckers help to feed one pair's chicks, and three broods of two or three chicks each may be raised in one season.

Busy cleaners *An oxpecker plucks parasites from the ears of a female kudu on a grassy African plain. In the breeding season, the bird also pulls hairs from its host for use as a building material.*

Nest builders with an eye for the unusual

Magpies in Australia are quite happy to build their basket-shaped nests on power line pylons when trees are scarce. Their traditional building materials are twigs and grass, but the birds also use string, cloth, cardboard, pieces of plastic and shards of glass. Wire offcuts from farm fencing are great favourites and one nest was found to contain 243 pieces of wire, in total about 330 ft (100 m). Many birds are opportunists, and if their nesting materials and sites in the wild disappear, they adapt to using alternatives supplied by humans. Many species nest on buildings – city-living kestrels and peregrines occupy windowsills high on office blocks, for example, as readily as their country relatives make use of tree holes or rocky ledges.

Kittiwakes will nest on ledges on grain silos or warehouses, and gulls settle down on rooftops, spacing their nests just as they would in a colony on a clifftop. Barn owls flourished long before there were barns and house martins nested on cliffs before houses were available.

Possibly some of the world's most durable nests were built in Hereford, England, by several pairs of house martins that fashioned their nests under house eaves, utilising a handy pile of wet cement. House martins usually build nests with mud pellets from ponds and puddles, lining the structures with grass once the mud has hardened and dried.

There are many examples of the nest-building improvisations of birds. European icterine warblers normally build their nests from fine grasses, but one enterprising bird was known to construct a nest from spun glass. A pair of rock doves in the US State of Michigan built a nest close to a factory. It looked like a normal nest of twigs and grass, but was later discovered to be made up mainly with pieces of steel wire. Sadly, wire does not keep a nest warm, and the chick died after three days.

A pair of grebes was once seen with a floating nest made from discarded potato-crisp packets and plastic bottles, an empty gin bottle and a football. A great tit once took over a letterbox in Bristol, and a blackbird once nested in a working car wash. At Biggin Hill airfield, starling populations used to make a nuisance of themselves by nesting in, on or under the aircraft. But no tales of bizarre behaviour can outdo that of the thrush that once began nesting on a piece of toast.

Washday wrens *A Carolina wren in Virginia, USA, feeds her brood of two chicks. The family is comfortably settled in a bag previously used by its human owners for storing clothes pegs.*

Recycling *Spotted flycatchers will make use of any good shelter. This pair raised a brood of five chicks in an old hand mincer that was hung from a nail in a farm shed near Liverpool, England.*

LIFE IN TOTAL DARKNESS

Deep in the world's great cave systems, where light never penetrates, live a variety of animals to whom eyesight has become an irrelevance.

Losing sight *When young, the blind cave characins of Mexico have small but functional eyes. As they grow older, however, these become covered with skin, making the fish blind.*

Pale fish that dwell in the waters of night

Probably it is shortage of food that decrees that the eyeless inhabitants of the cold, dark waters in the world's deep caverns should be tiny. One of the largest is the Kentucky blindfish – just 8 in (20 cm) long. Plants cannot grow in the dark, and the blind crayfish, shrimps and fishes have to rely on other sources of food.

Many cave fish have longer fins and larger heads than their relatives in the outside world, and most have shrunken, useless eyes, if they have eyes at all. To compensate, some cave fish have a highly developed lateral line system – the row of pressure receptors along each side of the body which sense water flow and vibration. Some fish have exposed receptors on the skin of the head, body and tail which increase the animal's sensitivity to pressure changes in the surrounding water. Using these refined sensory systems, cave fish 'feel' their way around, know the extent of their territory and detect prey.

The blind crayfish and shrimps have long, sensitive antennae to find their way around. Needing no colour for courtship display or camouflage, they are generally pure white and more delicate in build than their relatives in the light of the outside world.

A number of amphibians are also found in caves. Frogs and toads visit the underworld to feed on the insects living there, and some species of salamanders are permanent residents. Their ancestors too were once sighted visitors. The first known example of the European cave salamander was recorded in 1680 in southeastern Europe. This unusual species is usually about 12 in (30 cm) long when adult and is pale pink, with feathery red external gills and tiny, vestigial eyes covered with skin. But despite its blindness the animal does appear to be sensitive to light. Small wonder that this odd creature was originally thought to be some kind of dragon.

A similar salamander found in Texan caves has delicate, spindly legs. Its body and rounded snout incorporate nerves sensitive to vibrations, which the salamander relies upon to detect its prey.

The European and Texas blind salamanders never grow out of the larval stage, but similar species found in North America – the Ozark salamander from Missouri, for example – change from stout, dark juveniles with small, rudimentary, functioning eyes into slender, blind, pale-pink adults. The upper and lower eyelids of these salamanders gradually fuse as they grow into adulthood.

Water sculptures *This limestone cavern, the home of blind creatures, was carved over aeons by the stream that wanders through it. Water, too, ornamented the chamber. Charged with calcium as it seeped through the roof over millennia, it created fantastically sculpted stalactites and stalagmites.*

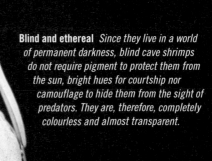

Blind and ethereal *Since they live in a world of permanent darkness, blind cave shrimps do not require pigment to protect them from the sun, bright hues for courtship nor camouflage to hide them from the sight of predators. They are, therefore, completely colourless and almost transparent.*

Feeling their way *The long legs of the cave centipede (left) are its means of navigating the pitch-dark environment of the cave. Cave spiders (below), on the other hand, use their two front legs to check for vibrations in the air. These indicate the presence of the cave crickets that are the spiders' staple diet.*

'Seeing' the way with legs and antennae

A troglobite, or cave dweller, lives all its life in the dark. Unlike the trogloxenes, the cave visitors, such as bats and nesting birds, it never leaves its cave. However, it often relies on visitors to bring in food from outside. Because they live out their lives in complete darkness, troglobites do not require sight. Most have lost the use of their eyes, and some species are without any form of optical structure. Instead, they depend upon highly developed senses of touch, smell and hearing in order to find their way about.

Cave-dwelling spiders, crickets whip scorpions and centipedes generally have long, spindly legs or elongated antennae to extend their sense of touch. The camel cricket, named for its humped upper body, has a pair of immensely long antennae. With these, it feels its way across cave walls and through the dust of the cave floor in its constant search for a meal.

Spiders do not have antennae; however, in the caves of Malaysia, there is a species of blind hunting spider that has evolved a useful substitute. It improvises, by using its front pair of legs, waving them in the air while running about on the other six. Evolution has so modified the front legs that they are now covered in fine, sensory hairs able to detect the minute air disturbances created by the movements of cave crickets – favourite food of the spiders.

Food is particularly difficult to find in this dark environment so cave dwellers have had to adapt.

Home in the dark *Cloaked in perpetual darkness, the cave beetle has no need of sight, strength or speed. Its long legs and feelers bear all the senses it needs to move around its underworld home.*

The troglobites use considerably less energy than their relatives living outside caves. Consequently, they need less food. Many rely on what they happen to come across to provide enough food to survive; though some have developed their sensory organs to increase their chances of tracking down a meal.

Rhadinid beetles – which live in North American caves – have antennae that are particularly sensitive to the scent of cave-dwelling crickets' eggs. The crickets deposit their eggs in the deep silt of the cave floor, and the beetle uses its antennae to 'sniff' them out.

When the rhadinid has found a clutch of eggs, it uses its sharp mandibles to puncture them one by one and devour the contents. If eggs are not readily available, the beetles devour the body wastes of the crickets instead.

Cave-racer snakes make an ally out of darkness

Cave-racer snakes in Borneo are as much at home slithering about on the floors of caves as they are in the undergrowth in the open air. They have adapted to the darkness by creating and following tracks that ribbon through the bat guano plastering the floor and walls of the cave. The snakes' favourite ambush spots are bottlenecks in tunnels, where cave swiftlets and bats crowd into the narrowing spaces while, like the snakes themselves, making their entrances and exits.

Having wound itself about a suitable stalactite or stalagmite, the cave-racer stretches out, awaiting the flurry of birds and bats that greets each dawn and dusk. In the narrow sections of the cavern, cave commuters must fly close to the walls. As a victim nears, the air-pressure waves from its flapping wings trigger the strike, and the snake plucks its prey from midair.

LIVING IN OR ON OTHER CREATURES

*P*arasites of the animal world can either kill their hosts or coexist with them. They may even help to protect them from disease and predators.

Hangers on *Acorn barnacles encrusting the hide of a grey whale (left) fix themselves to its skin with glue-like secretions. Larger barnacles, reaching 5 in (13 cm) across, themselves are home for sea lice (above), which grow to about 1 in (25 mm) long.*

Barnacles hitch a ride and get an easy meal

Barnacles are small shellfish well known for clamping themselves head down to such things as rocks, the bottoms of ships and the legs of oil rigs. Acorn barnacles are the commonest kind, and are themselves often colonised by smaller goose barnacles. Some kinds of barnacle also attach themselves to whales and other sea creatures and collect food more easily than their rock-dwelling relatives, who have to work hard to trap passing organisms with their tentacle-like legs. A whale resident has food brought to it in the flow of water as its host swims along.

Humpback whales have different types of barnacle encrusting different parts of their bodies – one kind lives under the whale's jaw and on its belly, and another is found along the tail, lips and the leading edges of its long white flippers. A third type of barnacle attaches itself not to the whale but to the other barnacles.

Stalked barnacles often attach themselves to the back edge of a blue whale's tail. Some whales seem irritated by their barnacles, and are thought to seek out great river estuaries, such as that of the Zaire, because in fresh water the barnacles die and fall off.

Worms that drive ants to kill themselves

Safe from predators and with food assured, parasites that live inside other creatures can concentrate their energies on reproducing – as long as their host lives.

Worms are the most successful internal parasites. Liver flukes are worms that infest the livers of many kinds of animal. One such worm can even control the actions of one of its hosts. Its life cycle begins when a snail eats fluke eggs contained in the droppings of an infected sheep, deer or rabbit. Inside the snail, the eggs hatch into ball-like cercaria, juvenile flukes, bound together by slimy mucus that eventually leave the snail through its breathing hole. Ants are attracted by the slime and either eat it at once, or take it back to the colony and share it. But if an ant eats a cercaria along with the slime, something very odd happens to it. The maturing fluke takes over, inducing the ant to climb to the tip of a blade of grass and cling to it.

This is virtual suicide, because grazing sheep, deer or rabbits will eat the ant along with the grass. The fluke's life cycle is now almost complete. It finds its way into the grazer's liver, meets another fluke, mates and then produces eggs.

Tapeworms, known to grow to 50 ft (15 m) long, infest animal intestines, attaching themselves by hooks and suckers on their heads. They have no mouths, but absorb food from their hosts through their body walls. A tapeworm may produce 2500 million eggs in its lifetime. One type lives in pigs, and humans who eat contaminated meat may also be infected.

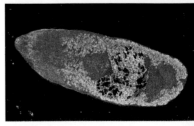

A free lunch *The pupae of a parasitic wasp (above) change to adults on the corpse of the moth caterpillar that provided them with food for growth while they were larvae. A herring gull fluke (right), enters the gull from a fish and spends part of its life cycle inside the bird's gut.*

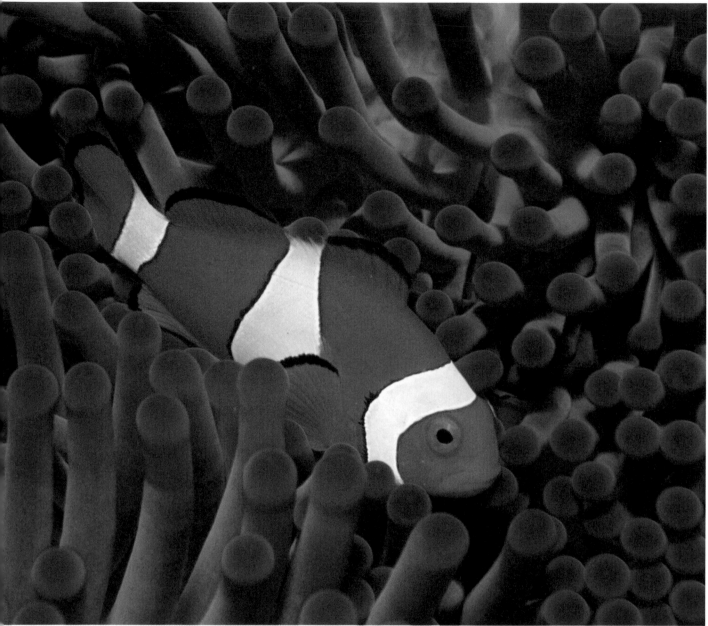

Deadly poison and domestic harmony

Sea anemones sting fish to death in order to feed on them. They attack with rows of tiny barbed, poisonous 'harpoons' on their tentacles. But the colourful anemone clownfish that lives amid coral reefs is immune to the anemone's lethal weapons and lives permanently in its embrace.

The clownfish may get some protection from its coating of thick slime. Also, it may develop immunity by touching the anemone's tentacles then swimming away quickly, returning time and time again until it can tolerate the stings. At night clownfish sleep in pairs inside their deadly bed, safe from enemies as the anemone closes its tentacles round them.

In return the clownfishes chase away some of the sea anemone's predators, such as the butterfly fish that feeds on its tentacles. The clownfishes also help to keep the anemone clean by scavenging particles of leftover fish.

Another mutually advantageous arrangement is that between a Costa Rican mouse and the dozen or so beetles that crawl over its head. The beetles hang on with their large jaws as the mouse scuttles about on the floor of its rain forest home. Nevertheless, they do not draw blood. When the mouse returns to its burrow, the beetles climb off and feast on the fleas in the mouse's nest. The mouse benefits by having fewer fleas, and is the healthier for it.

Unknown guests

Some parasites are so small that their hosts may be quite unaware of them. There are mites so tiny that an entire colony can breed in a tiger moth's ear. The mites seem to limit themselves to only one ear – if they took over both, the moth's balance would be disturbed and it could fall prey to a bat, making the mites part of the meal.

Other mites live on flowers and run up hummingbirds' bills, or climb aboard bumblebees as they

Sea haven *An anemone clownfish, safe among an anemone's tentacles, feeds on minute plants and animals. Although the anemone can live without clownfishes, the fish would not last long on their own.*

probe the heart of a flower for nectar. These mites do not harm their hosts, they just use them as transport to the next plant.

Another type of mite lives on meadow ants. The mite hangs just below an ant's chin and holds on with six hook-like legs. It uses its other two legs, which are much longer than the others, to stroke the antennae of its host in the code used by ants to 'talk' with each other. This persuades the ant to regurgitate a drop of food, providing the mite with a free meal.

IN COMPANY WITH OTHERS

'*T*HE BIRD ITSELF IS A THING OF BEAUTY, SUPREME IN THIS RESPECT AMONG LIVING FORMS, ... THE SYMBOL IN ART OF ALL THAT IS HIGHEST IN THE SPIRITUAL WORLD. NEVERTHELESS WE FIND THAT THE PLEASURE OF SEEING A SINGLE BIRD IS NOTHING COMPARED TO THAT OF SEEING A NUMEROUS COMPANY OF BIRDS.' ≈ W.H. HUDSON, *COLLECTED WORKS*, 1923.

Mysterious gatherings
Why scalloped hammerhead sharks congregate round underwater volcanoes in the Sea of Cortez remains a mystery. Since sharks are solitary hunters, these gatherings are assumed to be associated, in some way, with mating.

Hudson, writing his magnificent essays on natural history, was awed by the spectacle of large flocks of birds, as all lovers of nature are. For those who look closely, a flock of birds is more than just a breathtaking splash of colour and movement: the birds are in constant social interaction, squabbling over food, punishing others lower in the pecking order, maintaining pair bonds and attending to the minutiae of avian social life. As biologists and naturalists develop a better understanding of their society, and appreciate its subtleties and complexities, so the fascination grows. Like birds, most wild creatures reveal many interesting aspects of their behaviour when they associate in large groups. Their reasons for congregating or not may vary from species to species, but whether animals are sociable or solitary generally depends on the type of food they eat and the predators they are likely to encounter.

The nose has it
Clear signs of social status can save group-living animals time and energy and prevent unnecessary fighting and injury. The male proboscis monkey, a leaf-eating inhabitant of Borneo, sports a bizarre swollen nose that probably provides the others in his group with an indication of his rank.

Only top dogs mate
As other members of the pack squabble over food, a low-ranking African wild dog exhibits submission by rolling onto her back. There are usually more males than females in a group, and each sex establishes its own hierarchy. The dominant animals then breed with each other, and their young are cared for by the whole group.

Sound links
A female southern ground hornbill gives an insect to one of the males in her group. These birds live cooperatively in small groups of up to eight, and use booming calls and a wide variety of gestures and displays to communicate with one another.

Mud, blood and thunder
The yawning threat display of a dominant male hippo is often sufficient to remind other group members of his status. Serious fights over territory are usually avoided since they are very dangerous – the animals stand side by side and drive their canines into each other's haunches, flanks and shoulders.

A PLACE AND A TASK FOR EVERYONE

Some animal societies run with seemingly effortless efficiency and remarkable cooperation. Others are so close-knit that they appear to be a single organism.

Coiled killers *Inside the tentacles of a Portuguese man-of-war, venom-carrying threads lie like the turned-in fingers of a rubber glove, ready to shoot out and sting prey or predator.*

All for one and one for all in a superorganism

A deadly scourge of warm tropical and warm temperate seas is how most people regard the Portuguese man-of-war. They usually think of it as a single organism – a 'jellyfish'. But in fact a Portuguese man-of-war is made up of a complex colony of individuals.

The core of the colony is an animal in the form of a floating gas-filled balloon. Trailing from it are tentacles up to 70 ft (21 m) long, each an individual animal known as a zooid. Other specialist zooids produce only eggs and sperm for reproduction.

Every tentacle is armed with powerful stinging cells known as nematocysts, whose function is solely to capture prey. The tentacles then retract, hauling the prey up to the digestion cells below the float. The food is ingested there and is diffused through the body walls of every individual zooid of the colony, and all get their share.

Automatic weapons *Floating in the Atlantic Ocean on a gas-filled balloon up to 12 in (30 cm) long, a Portuguese man-of-war is about to encounter a meal and shoot out its barbs to paralyse the fish with deadly venom.*

The amazing thing about the man-of-war colony, with its well-defined division of labour, is that it all develops from a single fertilised egg. All colony members are therefore genetically identical, even though they differ in appearance and role. A fertilised egg develops into a single larval polyp, and the polyp produces the float. Other types of zooid then bud off from the base of the float, remaining joined together to form a remarkably coordinated superorganism.

Size brings status for naked mole rats

Pink, wrinkled and with no fur, a mouse-sized naked mole rat is not at all attractive to the human eye. Colonies of up to 100 of these creatures are known to inhabit extensive burrows below deserts and arid grasslands in East Africa. Their colonies are well organised, with a sophisticated social system unparalleled in the animal kingdom except by some insects.

A large queen mole rat, usually the largest colony member, rules the roost. Two or three of the largest males are her mates. The rest of the colony is made up of non-breeding male and female workers. Only the queen bears and suckles litters, but the workers help to clean and feed the babies once they are weaned.

Size determines the division of labour, with the youngest and smallest workers collecting food such as plant roots. As mole rats get bigger, they spend more time digging tunnels with their large, sabre-like front teeth to open new foraging areas. The largest non-breeding mole rats are a soldier class whose job it is to defend the colony against trespassing mole

128

Busy bee *A queen honeybee (left) spends her days laying eggs, and cannot perform any other function. She relies on smaller worker bees to feed her and to clean and prepare cells for her eggs.*

The functions and fates of honeybees in a hive

In a honeybee colony there are three castes – queens, drones (or males) and workers. Drones and queens are much larger than workers, all of which are sterile females. A bee's caste depends on whether it develops from a fertilised egg, the food it gets while it is a larva and how much space it is given in its cell.

Each hive has only one fertile queen. She mates with drones, which develop from unfertilised eggs, and once mated spends much of her time laying eggs – maybe 2000 a day during summer.

The brief lives of workers
Most of the eggs become workers, of which there can be up to 60 000 in a colony. They develop from fertilised eggs, and emerge after 21 days in the cell. At first they do nothing but beg for food from older workers. But within a few days they start cleaning empty brood cells and preparing them for new eggs. At five or six days old, glands mature in their mouths, enabling them to feed the queen and the newly hatched larvae in the cells with protein-rich 'royal jelly'. After the fourth day, drone and worker larvae are fed pollen, but potential queens, which may start new colonies or replace the existing queen if she dies, are given larger cells and raised only on royal jelly.

At about 12 days old, a worker's wax-producing glands begin functioning and she starts building new cells and capping cells containing developing larvae. To produce wax she gorges upon honey, and the wax then forms in small flakes in the eight pockets in the underside of her abdomen. She chews the flakes to soften them and then fits them into place. She also spends time processing nectar into honey.

Workers 18-20 days old serve as guards within the hive. At three weeks old they venture outside to forage for nectar, directing others to good foraging areas as they return. Most worker honeybees die at about six weeks old, but a queen may live for four or five years.

Comb life *The eggs inside a honeycomb (above) are tended by the young hive workers. A newly emerged worker (left), tied to the nest and sometimes called a house bee, begs for nectar from an older worker that has returned from foraging with a full honey-stomach.*

rats and predators such as snakes. If a snake such as a cobra enters the burrow, the soldiers dig furiously to seal off the tunnel with an earthen barrier before the snake reaches the breeding chamber.

The queen patrols the tunnel network, pushing and shoving the workers and checking the breeding state of females. All mole rats in a colony are able to breed, but the queen controls their behaviour with a cocktail of chemical agents called pheromones, which repress their normal reproductive development and instincts.

When the queen dies, several females grow rapidly, but only one eventually intimidates the others and becomes the new queen. Her teats swell and her body lengthens, enabling her to be pregnant without being too broad to proceed along the tunnels.

Underground society
Naked mole rats, or sand puppies, live in a society in which only one dominant female breeds four or five times a year.

WARRIORS AND WORKERS – BUILT FOR THE TASK

The world of social insects is one of specialisation. Each caste, from queen to worker, has its role and is equipped with ingenious adaptations to carry it out.

Chemical warfare in the termite mound

Termites evolved and cultivated their communal manner of life at some time in the early morning of the world, and have never been faced with adequate reason to change it since. All members of their millions-strong communities are the offspring of a single queen, and all are interdependent.

The termite workers that endlessly labour to bring in food are blind and sterile, and the soldiers that guard them and the nest have developed jaws that are too massive for foraging – as a result they have to be fed by the workers. Nevertheless, the soldiers' jaws are highly efficient. Some species have sharp mandibles that can shear off the head of an intruding insect, others flick one mandible against the other to inflict a powerful blow and others have no particular weapon, but bring their large heads together to block off the nest galleries against invaders.

Among the most developed weapons are those employed by the soldier castes of the long-nosed tree-nesting nasute termites. Instead of bearing scimitar-like jaws, their heads are fronted by a hollow snout through which they can discharge an acid chemical spray. This becomes sticky when exposed to air, creating a lethal trap for invading insects.

Despite their similar modes of living, termites and ants are totally unrelated. But some ant species, notably the driver ants of Africa and the army ants of tropical America, also have soldier castes that protect large raiding parties of worker ants. With their scissor-like jaws, the workers attack and dismember anything animal in their path and then carry it back in pieces to feed the community.

On the defensive *A nasute soldier termite (above), squirt gun at the ready, confronts an enemy. By contracting its jaw muscles, the termite ejects a sticky chemical secretion over a distance of about a hand's breadth. The termite's role is defensive, like that of the driver ant soldier (below) that guards the worker ants when they are out hunting.*

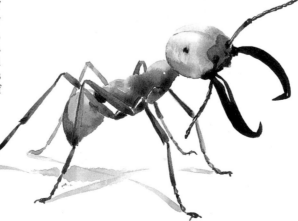

On guard *Although soldier termites are often blind, they are very well equipped to work in the darkness of the nest. Their sense of smell and ability to detect vibrations is acute, and they are armed with weapons to suit different roles. With pincers raised, a group guards a gallery entrance.*

the fungus eaters for the damage they inflict on foliage in tropical America are the leaf-cutter ants of the genus Atta. These, as their name suggests, cut up leaves to make a rich compost on which to grow their food. The workers' jaws are assymetrical and curved, operating like tailors' shears as they slice the leaves into manageable D-shaped pieces for transport. They carry the fragments, each as big as themselves, back to the nest, holding them vertically in their jaws.

The leaf-cutter workers are of medium size, but they are accompanied on their forays by smaller workers, or minims. The minims' task is to protect the working leaf-cutters from the parasitic flies that attempt to lay eggs on them. This they accomplish with snapping jaws and fencing feet as they ride back to the nest on the leaf fragments borne by the workers.

Back at the nest, other specialist workers chew the leaves into pinhead-sized pieces and moisten them to speed decay before adding them to the compost in the fungus garden. The fungi produce small bulbs at their growing points that the ants harvest and eat.

Assembly line *Leaf-cutter ants run a well-organised business, from the cutting operation (left) to the transport department (above). Their activities beat a trail between forest and nest, the flanks guarded by soldier ants. Protection from parasite flies is provided by guards that ride on top of the cut leaves to the nest.*

Gardeners, tailors and tiny tough fighters

Ants eat a wide range of foods. Some prey on other insects, some eat seeds and others collect honeydew from aphids. But some 200 species grow fungus for food, cultivating it in well-tended gardens in the nest. Notorious among

Wings that are meant for one flight only

It happens only once during the termite year. On one warm, still summer evening, breaches appear in the towering earthen mound of an African termite nest. From the holes, fluttering a little inexpertly

on gauzy wings, emerge hundreds, or sometimes thousands, of plump termites. The swarm consists of both males and females of the royal, or reproductive, caste – the only termites to grow wings. Their flight is of short duration. Though they climb some 200 ft (60 m) into the air, they travel no more than 300 yd (275 m) from their home

mound. Like paratroops ridding themselves of their 'chutes, as soon as they land the termites pivot on their wings and break them off, for they are no longer needed. Both sexes search excitedly for a mate, then run off in tandem, the males hard on the females' heels. At this point they are in extreme danger, for even creatures that would not

normally eat termites – spiders, shrews, lizards, birds, even local tribesmen – close in on this insect feast. Very few of the couples survive, but those that do seek a nest site in the ground or in a decaying log, and burrow in, excavating a mating chamber. It is lined with chewed wood mixed with saliva and droppings, and once it is complete, they seal themselves in.

From now on the queen, with her consort beside her, will do nothing but lay eggs, creating a colony that over years may amount to millions. Most of her offspring will become workers, sterile males and females. They forage for food – plant and wood fibres – and build and repair the nest mound, which may eventually reach a height of 30 ft (9 m). Their tasks include feeding and grooming the royal pair, as well as the soldier caste that guards the nest.

Pomp and circumstance *A queen termite, massively swollen by eggs, lies prone surrounded by her worker courtiers. These groom and feed both the queen and her small consort, poised to the left of the queen's head (below).*

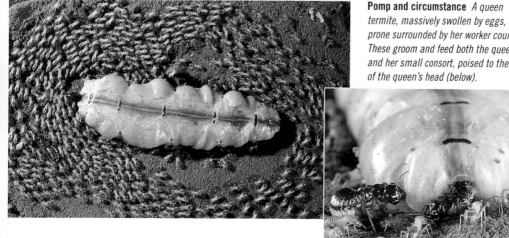

BATTLING TO STAY ON TOP

Most animals use physical superiority to hold their dominant position within a group – but some find that it pays to be small and helpless.

Flying hooves and bared teeth in zebra battles

One of the few times that zebras fight is when the males battle for harems at the beginning of the mating season. Two challenging stallions stamp the dusty grass of the African plain. At first they just shove one another, but as the contest warms up they start to do damage with flying rear hooves and bites to the neck.

Two zebra species, plains and mountain zebras, live in permanent herds consisting of a stallion and eight or nine mares, and a herd's home range may overlap those of other herds. Grevy's zebra, a third zebra species, forms herds for short periods only.

In permanent herds, the mares cement relationships by grooming each other. Occasionally, a herd has two stallions. One is dominant and fathers most of the foals, and the other has the role of protector. If a strange stallion intrudes, the dominant stallion rounds up the mares of the herd while his subordinate chases off the intruder. It is not clear why subordinate stallions accept this role – perhaps they hope to inherit the mares.

Wisdom outweighs strength
Bachelor stallions form all-male groups. Sometimes one may steal a mare from a stallion with a harem. Usually, the harem stallion simply drives his mares out of the way, and fights only if forced to by a determined challenger. A bachelor may manage to steal some mares while his fellow bachelors are distracting the harem stallion.

With both stallions and mares, status depends largely on age and how long they have been in the group, rather than on size. This is perhaps because dominance is dependent more on agility than on strength. A dominant zebra mare always drinks first at a waterhole, and takes the best grazing without being challenged.

Champion challenged *As tension flares at the beginning of the mating season, a male mountain zebra goes for the throat of an established stallion, making a determined bid to take over his harem.*

In a grey wolf pack, only the strongest breed

As the mating season approaches, tension builds up within North America's grey wolf packs. In deer country, a pack may number about seven individuals, all part of an extended family. In moose country, however, there may be as many as 20 animals in one pack. In either case, generally only the dominant pair of wolves mate.

Usually, the dominant male and female maintain their positions by peaceful means – actual fighting is rare. They reinforce their status by looking subordinate wolves in the eye and holding their heads high and their tails and ears erect. Other males and females vie for status among each other, but usually cringe with ears flattened and tails down before the pack leaders. As mating time draws near, the dominant female wolf harasses the younger females – her worrying disrupts their reproductive hormones and stops them from breeding. And the dominant male snaps aggressively at the other males to keep them away from his mate.

Once mating has taken place at the end of winter, peace reigns again and the pack members all help the breeding pair to protect the new litter of five or six cubs and bring them food. But if the dominant male dies, there is fierce fighting among the other males of the pack to fill the vacancy.

Top dog *A North American grey wolf exposes its fangs menacingly at another pack member. Dominant animals maintain their status by their confident stance and growled warnings.*

The power of the puny amongst macaques

Family tiff *A young female Indian rhesus macaque seeks comfort from her mother and an older sister after a squabble over food with another older sister.*

It is the younger female members of the family that often have the highest social standing in a group of rhesus macaques – monkeys that inhabit many parts of Asia.

By the time a young female has reached maturity at four or five years old, she may rank higher in the pecking order than her older sisters, although still lower in status than her mother. This is because whenever two sisters are involved in a dispute – over food, usually – the mother and older sisters invariably go to the defence of the younger of the pair, probably because she is smaller and less able to defend herself.

This protection buffers younger females from the normal rules of dominance, as brute strength, the usual determining factor, no longer applies. So a young female has the edge over her older sisters – until, of course, she is in dispute with an even younger sister.

Colour commands in male prawn clashes

Blue claws are such a powerful status symbol in blue-clawed prawn society that the owner takes precedence over all other prawns. As with most shellfish, these giant freshwater prawns, which live in the Indo-Pacific region undergo a series of moults as they grow.

At first a male is small and has tiny, delicate claws. After the first moult his claws are larger in proportion to his body, and bright orange. At the final growth stage he is up to 10 in (25 cm) long and has blue claws that are larger still and are covered in spines.

Dominance among prawns is related to the size and colour of claws – blue-clawed males are dominant over the other two types, and orange-clawed males possess ascendancy over the small males.

In fights, which are impressive trials of strength, prawns use their claws as weapons, and a dominant male is assured of access to food and shelter. So the colour of a prawn's claws is a badge of status reflecting his fighting ability.

Occasionally, different growth rates of individuals result in some orange-clawed males being bigger and having larger claws than blue-clawed males. A blue-clawed male still takes precedence, however.

Claws make the prawn *Waving its large and imposing blue claws in front of it, a male blue-clawed prawn demonstrates its ability to fight. The size and colour of a prawn's claws establishes its place in the prawn social hierarchy.*

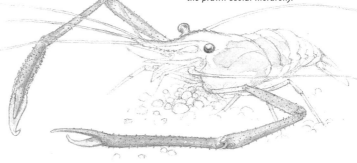

JOSTLING FOR POSITION

*Competition for food and mating is the dominant theme of animal life.
The winners are the wily, the strong and the downright aggressive.*

Brotherly support gains a place in the pride

The only way for young male lions to acquire breeding status is to take over an already established pride. To do this, they must expel the incumbent male or males, a daunting task that is best achieved by coalitions, usually formed by three or four brothers or other close kin. Even so, the resident males will fight hard to retain their breeding rights, partly because, if successful, the incomers will kill all the small cubs, in order to bring their newly acquired females into heat again.

In addition, males that have been ousted from a pride are thereafter genetically dead – it is most unlikely that they will have any further opportunities to breed.

Having gained control of a pride, the triumphant incomers will live harmoniously together. They do not compete for females. Rather, the first male to encounter a female in heat is accepted by the others as being dominant. Because of their close relationship, no aggression will be triggered if one brother mates ahead of another; the family genes will still be passed on to the next generation.

Pride of place *There is little doubt who commands in this dignified family portrait. Not that the dominant male's crown always sits easily. Young outsiders constantly strive to usurp him, and (top) occasionally he must fight to survive.*

Another reason why pride males do not fight amongst themselves is that they will need to cooperate in fending off an attack when another group of males, in turn, puts in its bid for control of their pride.

134

Lifestyles *With only one resident adult male, mountain gorilla family life (above) is relatively peaceful, though its silverback leader will occasionally have to drive hopeful intruders away from his females. For the dominant male olive baboon, however, competition comes from within the troop (right), in which younger males are constantly threatening to usurp his monopoly of fathering all the offspring in the group.*

Scavengers' pecking order sorted by size

Anyone who has a bird table in the garden will know that the species visiting it adopt a certain hierarchy. Blue tits invariably yield place to larger great tits, which in turn are often displaced at the table by nuthatches.

Different species of scavenging birds closing in on carrion are also aware of their place in the scheme of things. A deer carcass rotting in a dried-out riverbed in southern Spain will attract red and black kites, Egyptian vultures and griffon vultures, magpies and other carrion eaters. Each species feeds on a different part of the carcass, but even so they constantly squabble,

Points of attack *The Rüppell's griffon vulture is a soft flesh eater whose pugnacious threat display is usually sufficient to drive competitors away from its chosen portion. Scavenger birds combine aggression with specialisation to ensure their share of the carcass.*

struggling to displace each other from prime feeding areas, jostling endlessly for position.

The vultures are the largest and therefore dominant species, while the smallest, the magpies, are the most submissive. It is body size that determines how the various species interact. A griffon vulture need only make the smallest movement to signal its intention, and a magpie will move out of the way. For magpies to have an effect on a vulture, however, they would need to launch an all-out mob attack.

Gorilla display belies a protective disposition

Once the raw material of all kinds of fearsome travellers' tales, gorillas are now generally acknowleged as gentle creatures. Aggression among them is rare, aroused only when the leader of a troop encounters another male. Even then, he will try to avoid actual combat. By beating his chest, hooting, roaring, tearing up vegetation and making a succession of short sideways charges, he attempts instead to awe his opponent into submission.

Pugnacity is important in the breeding success of male gorillas, since the female's choice of mate is influenced by his ability to protect both herself and her offspring from predators and other males.

A group of gorillas is usually made up of one adult male or silverback, and three or four females and their offspring. Since female gorillas mate with one male at a time, the competition from solitary males is intense. Not only do non-breeding males attempt to take over harems; they also try to kill the young, presumably in anticipation of mating with the females.

Resident silverbacks therefore have their hands full protecting their females and offspring, and it is probably for this reason that

male gorillas are so much bigger than females. Unusually for social mammals, female gorillas within a group are unrelated. Hence the social structure is entirely that formed between the females and the silverback.

Baboon one-upmanship

To the male olive baboon, life is a constant struggle for status, since within his troop it is the dominant males that have a virtual monopoly in breeding opportunities.

A young male rises in the troop's hierarchy by displacing his seniors. This he does by fighting and by means of yawning displays that show off his fearsome canines. As he gets older and stronger his status increases, until he peaks in early middle age. From then on, his strength wanes, and he begins to lose status.

However, young baboons are not entirely bereft. Generally, male baboons of any status may copulate without let or hindrance, but it is when there are opportunities to father young that the advantages of rank are seen. When a female first becomes receptive, the dominant male is happy to allow any other male to copulate with her. But once she begins to ovulate, he guards her closely, ensuring that he alone can mate with her, and that, consequently, he alone will be the father of her offspring.

FORMING FRIENDSHIPS

*Animals are not always 'red in tooth and claw' – touching, grooming
and caring for each other help to keep families and groups together.*

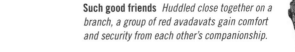

Such good friends *Huddled close together on a
branch, a group of red avadavats gain comfort
and security from each other's companionship.*

Red avadavats huddle together for comfort

For much of the time, the tiny red avadavats of Southeast Asia and India crowd together in clumps on branches. So firmly do these red-and-black finches press up to each other that the outside birds have to prop themselves up with a wing.

Lovebirds are small African parrots that also huddle together in groups or pairs when at rest. These brightly coloured birds are popular as domestic pets, partly because of their apparent attachment for each other. Caged lovebirds perch close to each other for hours. They appear to get a sense of security from this, and if one of a pair dies, the other may pine and die of grief.

Red avadavats nest in wet grasslands and marshes and feed on ripe grass seeds. While they huddle together, they frequently preen the feathers on one another's heads and necks. Mutual preening, which is known as allopreening, is seen as the bird world's equivalent of cuddling. It may have evolved from practical needs, such as cleaning parasites from the parts a bird cannot reach itself.

But allopreening is not only a method of cleaning an animal's inaccessible areas; it also reduces aggression. An avadavat frequently offers its head, with its feathers ruffled, to a bird of another species – this is a sign of goodwill.

Helping hands *Picking out dirt and bugs
from each other's fur is how black-faced
vervet monkeys form the friendships that
keep their societies stable.*

Mutual grooming gains new friends and allies

Among apes and monkeys, the practice of grooming each other is more than simply a method of keeping clean – it is an essential part of promoting friendships.

These animals live together in groups with elaborate hierarchies. A high-ranking animal maintains its place in the group by behaving aggressively to animals of lower status, but within both groups, mutual grooming – cleaning each other's fur and removing flakes of dead skin or the odd parasite – helps to cement friendly relations.

Vervet monkeys, which live in large groups amid the tree-scattered grasslands of Africa, usually groom only their relatives. Sometimes monkeys who are not related groom each other and become friends, and may help each other out in time of need.

A female vervet harassed by a young male, for example, can call for the help of a relative or friend. Relatives normally help each other whatever the circumstances, but an unrelated individual will assist only if the soliciting monkey has recently groomed it.

The harmonious lives of the hyraxes

Hyraxes are furry and rabbit-sized with blunt heads and small ears, and are found in Africa and the Middle East. They live in large family groups numbering up to 20 animals, with females outnumbering males by as many as two to one. There are rock hyraxes, bush hyraxes and tree hyraxes, and on the rocky and densely vegetated hillocks of Africa's Serengeti plain, rock and bush hyraxes live side by side in close accord.

Both types of hyrax sleep in the same holes and huddle together for warmth, and also make many similar calls. Newborn hyraxes are sniffed intensively by animals of both species, and the young ones play together. This relationship is one of the closest known between two species of mammal. Only some apes and monkeys – species of guenon monkeys, for example – have a similar close association.

The two species of hyrax can coexist because they do not compete for food. Bush hyraxes eat leaves and rock hyraxes feed mainly on grass. Yet despite their similarity and closeness, the two species do not interbreed. Mating behaviour is different, and their sexual anatomy is incompatible.

Family group *Rock hyraxes live among rocks where there are plenty of holes to hide in. When they go out to feed on grass, the adult male of the family keeps watch and calls an alarm if danger, such as an eagle, threatens.*

Dolphins like to live in tight-knit groups

The sight of whales helping their injured companions to the surface to breathe suggests that the relationships between individuals are at least as caring and highly developed as those among some land mammals.

Little is known of the social habits of whales and dolphins in the oceans, or how individual whales and dolphins relate to each other – their lives under water are difficult to study. Research has shown, however, that species such as the bottle-nosed dolphin and the orca, or killer whale, do live in closely knit groups.

A school of dolphins varies in size, with maybe only two animals or as many as a thousand. School sizes constantly change as different groups either join or leave for various reasons, such as the amount of food available, the distance offshore and how much need there is for protection from predators such as sharks. The smaller groups within a school are the stable units of society, the most important relationship being that of a mother and her calf, which is suckled for about 18 months.

Orcas live in groups, or pods, which can contain as many as 50 individuals. The pods are made up of an adult male and dominant adult females and their young. Orca pods do join up with others, but only if they belong to the same community – a group of pods that share the same range.

Studies have shown that the cohesion of orca communities is connected to a common 'language' of calls and sounds, with each pod having its own dialect.

Staying in schools *Spotted dolphins can be found in groups of several hundred. But the Atlantic spotted dolphin (below) usually lives in permanent schools of no more than about ten. They are often located in deep, clear, offshore waters.*

FRIENDS AND FAMILIES

Being part of a family or group helps animals to find food and living space and raise offspring. Good relationships cement group stability.

Lonely horses look for amicable partners

In both their wild and domestic states, horses have a deep need for companionship. Horse friends play together, call to each other and stand close to one another when grazing. Lonely domestic horses befriend cows, donkeys and even people.

Although brothers and sisters are often close, and youngsters of the same age often strike up relationships, there is no fixed pattern for friendships among horses. Nor is there an obvious reason why they should be so keen to make friends. But it is likely that friendships help to forge a feeling of group identity among wild horses.

Licking, playing and nuzzling are all signs of friendly behaviour, but mutual grooming, in which each horse scratches or nibbles the other's mane, rump or withers, indicates a special bond.

A domestic horse often tries to reproduce this behaviour by using its teeth to scratch the back of the person brushing it. A horse that has been reprimanded for doing this – it may have been thought that the horse was trying to bite – will still react to being brushed with lip and jaw movements.

Among wild horses, one of a pair of friends is usually the leader – the bolder of the two, or the older of two relatives. Where the leader goes, the other horse follows. This is not a show of dominance but rather a sign of the horses' desire for safety and their need to be with others. The resulting web of relationships can influence the movements of a whole group of horses.

Good fellowship *Among both North American white-tailed deer (below) and the wild horses of the French Carmargue (right), gently nibbling and cleaning each other is the sign of special friendship. In wild horses, affection encourages harmony. Conflict is more likely among groups of domestic horses that cannot choose their friends.*

Home range *Young male cheetahs often band together in small groups in order to defend a home territory from other males. Eventually they may be pushed out by another group or by one, determined, adult male. Some male cheetahs from the same litter stay together for life.*

Young male cheetahs band together

When young male cheetahs are about 18 months old, they leave their mother's home range. Some wander alone until they are strong enough to win a territory, but many live in groups of up to four with brothers from their litter, or with other young males.

It is likely that the young male cheetahs live and hunt together because it is easier for a group of males together to establish and defend a territory than it is for a solitary male. These groups usually defend quite small territories, whose size probably depends on the availability of game. On East Africa's Serengeti plain, the group territories held by young cheetahs cover about 12 sq miles (30 km²).

There are often fierce conflicts between nomadic males and those holding a group territory. On the Serengeti, observers studying a group territory held by three young males once witnessed an invasion by three roving males. One of the intruders was chased and caught by the three territory holders, who attacked him and eventually killed him with one bite to the neck.

The territorial cheetahs then turned their attention to the other two intruders. After a brief fight, one of them broke and ran, and was chased by one of the group for nearly a mile (1.6 km). Then all three of the home band fought with the last intruder, injuring him before finally leaving him alone.

Thus the intruders were routed and the defenders remained in possession of their territory, having suffered only minor injuries.

It is normal for male and female cheetahs to live apart. Females are nomadic, ranging over areas of about 310 sq miles (800 km²) in their search for prey and a safe place in which to rear their cubs. They lead solitary lives, rarely interacting with other females.

Family ties *Related female baboons, like these yellow baboons of Kenya, live together in close-knit groups. Before males are admitted to the family group and allowed to choose mates, they have to prove to the females that they are good friends.*

Females rule the roost in baboon families

Baboon society is held together by the enduring friendships between the females, as well as the females' relationships with their offspring and with adult males. A baboon troop consists of groups of female relatives. The oldest female has the highest rank, and it is round her that the others gather to rest, groom one another and sleep.

Although female baboons stay in the groups they were born into, they mix and play with females from other groups, and often also form close relationships with them.

Male entry into this society is accomplished only through a good deal of hard work. This is because adult males looking for a mate have to break into the strong, close network of female relatives and friends. This protracted business starts with a male slowly and carefully cultivating a friendship with just one female member of a troop. He sits close to her and makes friendly gestures and, after months of patient persistence, finally gets close enough to groom her.

Passport to partnership
Once the male baboon has established a bond with this female, it serves as a passport to friendships with her relations, and this may eventually result in him mating with one or more of them.

Females that are pregnant or nursing usually form special relationships with up to three adult males, keeping close to them while foraging, and huddling together with them while resting by day or sleeping at night. Sometimes the males defend the female or her young from other troop members.

HELPING AROUND THE HOME

When circumstances make it impossible for animals to raise their own offspring, they further their kind by helping to raise others of their kin.

Unlucky bee-eaters assist their relatives

Flashes of cinnamon, gold and blue sparkle in the sunlight as birds of a colony of bee-eaters flit about their nests in a warm, wooded area of southern Europe.

Bee-eaters use their feet and beaks to dig their nests in banks soon after arriving in Europe from southern and eastern Africa in summer. At the start of the breeding season the birds pair up, but as snakes and weasels take their toll of eggs and chicks, many pairs are left with no brood.

Occasionally the bee-eaters that have failed to breed or that have lost their brood help out a relative with a family to feed. As older birds tend to be more successful at breeding, it is normally young birds that help their parents.

Colourful companions *Bee-eaters perch near their nest burrows on a southern European site, sunning themselves and watching for bees and other insects.*

Warblers in waiting become home helps

In 1968, the only place where the Seychelles brush warbler could be found was on the tiny, remote Cousin Island in the Indian Ocean, where the population had been reduced to 30 birds. So the International Council for Bird Preservation turned the island into a nature reserve. By 1980, about 400 birds occupied the island. However, young birds ready for their first year of mating were unable to find territories, so they stayed as helpers to their parents.

Quantity and quality

Seychelles brush warblers build cup nests in thick scrub, and they forage amid the surrounding vegetation for insects and caterpillars. Not all parts of Cousin Island are suitable for breeding. Where territories are rich in insects, the warblers' breeding success is five times as high as in poor territories.

Although lack of breeding space prevents many young birds from mating, not all necessarily compete for a territory that becomes vacant. A brush warbler moves to a vacant territory to breed only if it is likely to be able to rear more chicks itself than could be reared by its parents with its assistance. So if the vacant territory is a poor one, a helper in a good territory stays where it is and a bird from a poor territory takes over. But if a good territory becomes vacant, competition is intense. It usually goes to stronger, better-fed birds from good territories.

When, as part of a conservation effort, some brush warblers were taken from Cousin Island to the unoccupied island of Aride, it became clear that it is certainly lack of breeding space that causes brush warblers to become helpers.

The first birds taken to Aride paired for life and bred without any helpers, as did their offspring once they became old enough to mate. But as numbers increased to the point where space for territories was limited, young birds once more began to act as helpers.

Baby-sitting birds *Young Seychelles brush warblers help their parents to feed and look after the offspring from later broods. This improves the chances of survival for the newly hatched chicks.*

Red foxes lose their lonesome reputation

Red foxes are elusive and hunt mostly at night, and for a long time they were thought to be mainly solitary. However, scientists using radio-tracking and night-vision equipment have discovered that foxes are sociable creatures.

Although in some areas a male and female pair may breed on their own, in others a dominant dog fox may live with up to five vixens. The younger females in the group are usually offspring from previous seasons. Young males emigrate. Instead of breeding, some young vixens may help with feeding the weaned cubs and protecting them from predators such as wolves.

As yet, little is known about the effect of helpers on the red foxes' breeding success. But with silverback jackals, relatives of the fox, family helpers certainly improve the survival chances of the pups. Young jackals in their first year stay with their parents and hunt in family packs. Working together, they catch more food than they can when hunting singly.

Homeward bound *An Alaskan red fox vixen returns to its den with a ground squirrel and a ptarmigan in its jaws. It will share the meal with its family.*

Male wrens make the best of all situations

Its brilliant blue colouring gives the splendid fairy wren its name – it is also called the splendid blue wren and the banded wren. Males in full breeding plumage are among Australia's most dazzling birds, perhaps because they have to compete more strongly than most birds to find a mate.

Females, dull compared with their mates, are often in short supply, because for reasons yet unknown they have a higher death rate than males. When there are equal numbers of each sex, virtually all birds find a partner and breed. But when female numbers are low, many young males fail to find partners. So they do the next best thing; stay at home and help to raise young brothers and sisters.

But in fact the new chicks in the nest may not be such close relatives. Analyses of the wrens' genes have revealed that the breeding male in a group is rarely the father of the chicks he helps to rear. He is, however, often the father of the youngsters next door. It seems that once a male wren has plenty of helpers to do the work, he puts little effort into rearing chicks. He goes off in search of extramarital matings, so is quite often cuckolded while he is out cuckolding.

Family chores *Both the parents and older offspring help to protect and feed splendid fairy wren chicks. Despite this extra attention, only about 20 per cent survive their first year.*

141

HERDING PREY TOGETHER

Humpback whales have developed a remarkable method of hunting in a group – they release thousands of bubbles to form a fishing 'net'.

Blowing bubbles *Migrating humpback whales gather off the coast of Alaska every summer to feed on the large stocks of herring. The technique used by the whales for catching these fish is to trap them within a cylinder of bubbles (above and above top), which they produce by forcing out air through the blowhole. The bubble barrier acts like a net, containing the fish and forcing them towards the surface in a dense shoal.*

Herring huddle *Caught within the spiral bubble 'net', herrings splash and leap at the surface (left). A massive humpback, 40 ft (12 m) long, lunges up through the middle of the gathering of fish (above), jaws wide open as it gulps a mouthful of fish and sea water. Although a lone whale sometimes starts the hunt, its comrades are attracted to its activities, or maybe it calls to them to join it. A group of up to two dozen of the huge whales often work together to herd fish into the concentrated mass that makes them much easier to catch. The whales*

Dining together *After cooperating to herd herrings into their bubble trap, a group of humpback whales (above and below) lunge upwards to fill their jaws full of fish and water in a frenzy of feeding. Humpback whales in the northern oceans feed mainly on fish such as herring, sand eel, capelin, anchovy, cod and mackerel.*

dive down some 50 ft (15 m) to release bubbles round the shoal. They can alter the size of the bubbles according to the size of their prey, just as fishermen choose a net with a mesh of suitable size for the fish they want to catch. Humpbacks have pleats in the skin of the throat, chest and belly to accommodate their mighty mouthfuls of fish-laden water. When they expel the sea water, the fish are held fast behind a fringe of baleen, or whalebone, that hangs inside the top jaw and serves as a sieve through which the water is pushed.

COOPERATING TO HUNT DOWN FOOD

Working in a team may mean smaller shares of food for each hunter, but it has the advantage of protecting the kill from hungry thieves.

Ambush of the unwary on the African plains

Crouching low in the grass, with every muscle tense, the lioness watches as others in her pride drive a panicked zebra towards her. By cooperating in this and other ways, the lionesses are able to lay effective ambushes and they

may even succeed in killing two animals in one ambush. It has been known for a single group of lionesses to bring down as many as seven wildebeest in one attack. In a pride of lions, it is usually the females that do the hunting; generally, the males watch from a distance and join in the feast later.

The hunter's role is by no means devoid of risk. When the prey animal's situation is hopeless, it usually seems to give in. But until then, many will put up a desperate

Stealth and strength *Members of the pride have different roles in the hunt. One lioness (right), panics a zebra herd into stampeding. As she does so, she watches for some laggard that will make an easier catch and drives it towards her co-hunters (left) waiting in ambush. These drag the prey down by sheer weight, and it is finally dispatched by a throttling bite to its windpipe (below).*

fight. A huge African buffalo, for instance, might inflict fearsome injuries upon a single assailant. A group attack however, overwhelms the prey by sheer weight of numbers, cuts down the duration of the fight and, possibly, lessens the risk of injury to individuals.

Lions are the most sociable of all the big cats, and enhanced hunting success was once believed to be the motive for this sociability. It was thought that the greater the number of lions in a pride, the greater share of food to each individual. But recent observations suggest that the reverse is true – as the size of the pride increases,

the smaller the ration for each lion. The real advantage of hunting in a group lies in the ability to hold on to the meal after the kill is made. On the open, grassy plains, a kill can be seen quite clearly from a distance. Even if it were out of sight, the vultures circling overhead would give away its position. As a result, a kill can attract lions from other prides, and hyenas.

Competition for food is always intense, and a pack of hungry hyenas can frighten a single lion away from its kill, whereas a large pride of feasting lions will deter competitors from trying to steal the hard-won meal.

Dolphins cooperate to trap anchovy shoals

Dusky dolphins off the coast of Argentina hunt down anchovies with all the coordination of well-drilled troops. On summer mornings, groups of up to 15 dolphins move into deep water areas, each using its highly developed organs of echolocation to track down vast shoals of the small, silvery fish.

On the hunt, the dolphins swim in line abreast. Once a shoal has been found, an advance party breaks from the line to hem the potential victims in by swimming around them in ever-decreasing circles. When the frightened fish rise to the surface, all the dolphins close in to feed. But they are not alone – sea birds are attracted by the tumult and swoop down to join the feast, attacking the trapped fish from above as the dolphins gulp down mouthfuls from below.

The birds, in turn, serve as a marker, indicating the site of the feast to other dolphins several miles away. The cordon round the fish draws tighter, and containment becomes more complete, as more dolphins arrive to draw out the feeding frenzy even longer.

The ocean is also hunted by well-organised packs of orcas, or killer whales – the largest and fastest of the dolphin family. The key to their success is the strong bond between the ten or so members of the family, or pod. Their tight cohesion and familiarity with one another help them to coordinate their hunting movements with an efficiency that appears almost choreographed, whether the prey is a shoal of salmon, a sea lion or a humpback whale.

When hunting salmon, orcas frighten the fish by slapping their flippers on the water's surface, and then herd the salmon into a group. When the shoal is surrounded, one orca sounds a bizarre call, perhaps best described as a wheezy whistle interrupted by a honk. This is the attack signal, and the orcas close in to snap up the trapped salmon like so many minnows in a pond harried by a pike.

Fishing fleet *Common dolphins (above) swim side by side at the start of a fish-herding operation. A dusky dolphin (right) closes in on a meal that it has helped to round up. The dolphins' fast reactions and awareness of each other account for their effectiveness as cooperative hunters.*

Giant otters fish the Amazon in teams

Giant otters have been reliably observed making successful attacks upon anacondas, the large constrictor snakes of the Amazon. They also hunt caymans – South American crocodiles – and will even frighten off a jaguar if it is threatening one of their pups. Much of their success is due to the fact that, unlike most otters, this rare species employs teamwork.

A giant otter adult is about 6 ft (1.8 m) long and weighs as much as 70 lb (32 kg) – easily the largest of all otters. Living and hunting in permanent groups of up to 20 individuals, giant otters hunt the waters of the Amazon's flooded forests by day. They often dive in unison to chase fish, and may swim submerged in a group for 10-20 seconds. Although they are unable to see one another or the fish they are pursuing through the murky water, the long, sensitive whiskers about their faces help them to detect movement. Fish, each with an otter in close pursuit, jump clear of the water and dive again to be seized below the surface.

Giant otters have appetites to match their size. Adults devour up to 9 lb (4 kg) of fish a day, tearing off the fishes' heads

Close-knit group *When they are not hunting, giant otters doze, play with their pups or groom one another – reinforcing the close social bonds that make the animals' teamwork so efficient.*

with teeth like those of wolves, ripping and relishing every morsel. A cayman as large as 5 ft (1.5 m) long is dealt with by the whole group. The unfortunate reptile is set upon from every direction at once, is swiftly overcome, then disembowelled and eaten.

Slash of colour *Flamingos by the million create a delicate pink 'Milky Way' across the surface of Kenya's alkaline Lake Nakuru. Flocking synchronises the birds' breeding habits, and the safety of numbers helps to protect them from predators as they feed on the plants and small creatures that give them their pink colouring.*

SCHOOLING, FLOCKING AND HERDING

When there are more eyes to watch for predators, individuals have a better chance of survival. So animals of numerous species seek the safety of the crowd.

Profusion of pink *Lesser flamingos feed in vast flocks on African soda lakes, afterwards washing their plumage in freshwater lakes. They are the most numerous of the five flamingo species.*

Birds and fish find safety in numbers

Gathered in vast flocks that sometimes number hundreds of thousands, flamingos carpet the soda lakes of Africa's Great Rift Valley with a delicate pink glow.

Few other large animals can tolerate the harsh alkaline waters, which are rich in floating algae (minute water plants) and small organisms in the bottom mud. Lesser and greater flamingos feed there side by side; the lesser flamingos filter algae through their beaks, and the less numerous greater flamingos filter out creatures from the mud.

Because of the caustic alkaline shores, the lakes offer some protection from hunters on the ground, and the flamingos nest there in huge colonies. Every day, the adults fly off to find more food and fresh water, too, for drinking and washing. The flock rises in a mass, each bird benefiting from the updraught of the one in front.

Many birds fly in flocks, relying on safety in numbers. When a flock of starlings spots a bird of prey, the birds bunch tightly together, because predators usually try to single out stragglers. Fish act in

Mutual protection *Many coral reef fish swim in schools for safety. Both large-mouthed blue-and-yellow snappers (above) and long, slim jacks (right) move in tight groups as they search for food.*

the same way. For instance, herrings form shoals for their mutual protection against bigger fish, sea birds and sea mammals such as seals. Tightly bunched herrings, continually on the move in search of tiny water plants and animals, are difficult to identify individually so each herring has less chance of being eaten if it stays in a crowd.

A shoal moves as one, each fish reacting quickly to its neighbour's movements. Reaction time is forever honed by natural selection. Hunters take laggards, so only the nimble survive to reproduce.

Ostrich sentinels also guard herds of grazers

Its large size prevents the ostrich from taking to the air as a means of escape. Not only do male birds stand some 8 ft (2.4 m) tall and weigh up to 330 lb (150 kg), but their splendid black and white feathers are hardly designed for camouflage. The slightly smaller females though, have much duller plumage. Therefore ostriches rely on their keen eyesight and great speed – about 45 mph (72 km/h) – to keep them out of danger.

Many eyes mean better warnings
Ostriches feed on the leaves, flowers and seeds of various plants, so a feeding ostrich needs to have its head close to the ground. This makes it impossible to eat and keep a look out for hungry lions at the same time. Ostriches tend to feed in small groups, with one or two birds looking about as the others feed. In this way, each one can spend more time eating and less watching for predators.

With one bird or another always on watch, a group is safer than a bird feeding alone – a lone ostrich might look up every two minutes or so, giving a hunter a chance to approach, but with each bird in the group raising and lowering its head at intervals it is more difficult for a prowler to go unnoticed.

Ostriches sometimes mingle with herds of wildebeest and zebra, for whom herding has the same advantages. The bigger the herd, the greater an individual's chance of survival. Hunters usually take the old, sick or young, so a healthy adult has the best chance of life.

Look out *Head erect, an ostrich stands sentry while the rest of the flock feeds. In East Africa, ostriches may mingle with wildebeest and zebra. An alarm call from any animal alerts the whole group to the presence of a lurking hunter.*

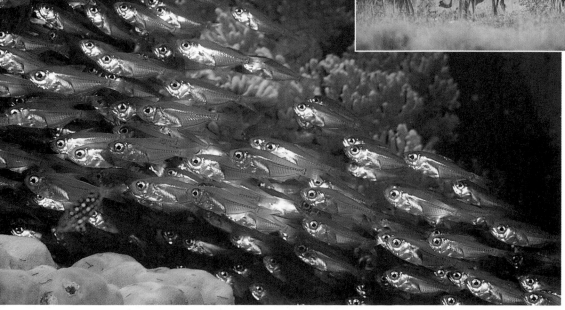

Schooled reactions *Moving together as though they were one, a school of foraging glass eyes swims through the Red Sea. Even if a predator threatens, the fish stay in a tight bunch rather than scattering, coordinating their movements as they try to escape. This is a selfish response – each fish is trying to put others between itself and the approaching danger.*

ALL FOR ONE AND ONE FOR ALL

Since most lone animals are in constant danger, many value the safety of numbers and the advantage of having someone on watch.

Circles of safety to protect the weak

Adult male African elephants lead largely solitary lives. Elephant society therefore revolves mainly round the females. They live in permanent groups made up of related individuals together with their offspring. These small herds present a formidable front against most forms of threat. The sheer size of adult elephants makes them practically invulnerable to attacks by lions and other large carnivores, unless they are sick or old. Only the youngest calves are at risk, and

even then lions only stand a real chance of killing a healthy young elephant if they manage to separate it from the main group.

In the face of danger, elephants usually form a defensive half-circle with the youngest calves secure between the adult females. At other times, however, they will charge furiously and instantly at a glimpse or scent of a lion. On such occasions, a single elephant has been known to chase several lions up a tree, trampling to death any cubs unable to make their escape.

Looking after each other

Whalers of the last century had many tales of their quarry helping one another in moments of danger. For example, how sperm whales,

instead of attempting to escape, snapped the lines holding those already harpooned, before turning on their aggressors. There were stories, too, of herd leaders that sacrificed themselves to allow the rest of the herd to get away.

There may be truth in such yarns. Sperm whales are highly sociable, travelling in herds of about 40 cows and their offspring, that are joined during the mating season by males. If one is injured, the herd gathers around in a protective ring, even helping the victim to the surface to breathe. This behaviour was well known to whaling captains who would harpoon an individual, then close in upon the herd as they rallied round to help.

Fortress that walks *Though given a wide berth by most predators, an elephant herd instinctively bunches together for security in open grassland (below). Calves on the move (left) will be safe from lions if they stay beneath their mothers' bellies.*

Teamwork tactics to ward off predators

The musk ox is found in one of the least promising of all the world's habitats – the tundra of Greenland, northern Canada and Alaska. But its layered, heavy coat is well able to protect it from the searing cold of an Arctic winter. The animals live in herds made up of one or more adult males and several females and their offspring. They range far in search of the tundra's sparse grazing.

Their only natural predators are wolves which, hunting in packs, might pull down an old or sick musk ox. But the wolves' more usual technique is to snatch a calf while they dodge the retaliatory sweeps of the adults' horns.

The approach of a wolf pack sends the musk oxen into a tight, defensive huddle that is known as a phalanx from its resemblance to the battle formation of ancient Macedonian infantry. Keeping the calves at their centre, and with massive horns lowered, the adults face outwards. Each consisting of up to 700 lb (320 kg) of solid bone and muscle, they make formidable opponents, and the only way the wolves can obtain a calf is to goad the musk oxen into breaking the circle. Occasionally they succeed, but the risk is high. When a musk ox does move out of the circle, it is often to throw a wolf over its back to be trampled by the herd.

Fending off greedy gulls

The common guillemot breeding colony on Funk Island, 40 miles (64 km) off Newfoundland, gathers together about half a million pairs each year. After spending autumn and early winter out at sea, the

Safety in numbers *Alaskan musk oxen calves are protected from wolves and blizzards by a defensive ring of adults (above). Nesting guillemots on St Paul Island in the Bering Sea (right) huddle together and keep robber gulls at bay.*

guillemots start to collect in late January about the cliffs on which they will nest. In spring, when they are ready to breed, they take up positions on ledges facing the sea.

Although the birds are quite large, the space that each pair occupies is surprisingly small. As many as 76 pairs have been observed huddled together in an area roughly equal to that of an armchair. But though space is limited on the island, the guillemots have a more important reason for packing so closely together.

High density breeding protects eggs and fledglings from the large gulls that try to feed on them. As long as the guillemots retain their dense formation the gulls are unable to penetrate the forest of upward-pointing beaks.

A guillemot that makes the mistake of breeding alone is an easy target. Those breeding without the protection of the colony are rarely successful parents. But in the safety of the dense nesting groups as many as 90 per cent of the pairs manage to hatch their single egg and fledge the chick.

A united front helps to promote longevity

Though they hardly pose much of a threat as individuals, a group of banded mongooses is treated with caution by even quite large predators. The mongooses live in highly organised tribes, up to 40 strong, in the grasslands of central and southern Africa.

Some adults act as baby sitters, keeping watch over the youngsters while others search for the insects, small rodents and fruit that make up their diet. Each mongoose pack occupies a home territory of some 6 sq miles (15 km²).

The close family ties ensure a usefully united front. A jackal may occasionally take a lone mongoose, but a pack will advance purposefully on the larger animal in a tight-knit group, and invariably put it to flight. They will even go to the rescue of an individual.

On one such occasion, a martial eagle swept a mongoose up in its talons and carried it to a nearby tree. At once the pack, led by the dominant male, stormed the tree in a coordinated attack upon the bird. The surprised eagle dropped its captive, which then escaped, uninjured, to safety.

Banded brothers *A group of banded mongooses sunbathe together in the morning sun secure in the knowledge that, if one of the pack is attacked, the others will hasten to the rescue.*

STAYING OFF THE MENU

Some animals depend on the vigilance of sentries, others place hope in sheer weight of numbers and still others push a neighbour towards the threatening predator.

Meerkats rely on the neighbourhood watch

From its lookout post on top of a tree, bush or rock, a small, alert meerkat scans the skies and surrounding landscape of southern Africa's Kalahari Desert – straining on its hind legs as it watches for the first sign of a predator.

Only when they undertake this very important role are meerkats ever seen alone. Relatives of the mongoose, they are highly sociable and live in well-organised groups of ten or more. So great is their interdependence that it is doubtful if one on its own could survive.

Most group members take a turn at sentinel duty. While the lookout is on guard the rest relax. They play and groom one another, or track down scorpions and other snacks, putting their trust in the sentry's vigilance. On glimpsing an eagle or other predator, the lookout gives the alarm in plenty of time for the group to run for cover.

Defending group territory

The sentinel also keeps an eye open for intruding meerkats. The animals are very territorial – a group defends its patch fiercely, inflicting wounds on outsiders.

Individual meerkats assume specific roles within the group. Only the dominant pair breeds; the others give them support until the time comes – if they live long enough – for them to take their turn as breeders. While they wait, they assist the sexually active pair in such tasks as baby sitting. So dedicated do some female helpers become to their baby-minding role that they have been known to produce milk and feed their charges.

Who goes there? *From his lofty vantage point, this meerkat sentry can spot any animal approaching across the flat Kalahari. A diligent lookout is essential to the clan's safety and continuance.*

Safety and success lie at the colony's centre

Among bluegill sunfish, raising the young is an entirely male preserve. Between 50 and 100 build their nests close together on the floors of North American lakes and wait for females. The largest males take the central positions where the females prefer to lay their eggs – with good reason, for these areas are least likely to be preyed on by bullheads and catfish.

The males nesting on the edge of the group shield the older males in the centre, not through choice but because the alternative is to nest alone, so reducing still further their ability to protect whatever eggs a female might lay for them.

Even males on the colony's periphery have a better chance of success than the loners. These benefit from the anti-predator chases of the bigger males, and increase their chances of survival to the next season. By then they should be larger and better able to find a more secure nesting place nearer the centre of the colony.

Feasting and death in 'duffer's fortnight'

The last few days in the life of a mayfly is a climactic period for many creatures other than itself. Birds, fish and fishermen all benefit from the flurry of waterways activity that takes place in the loveliest late spring weather, and brings the brief careers of millions of mayflies to a close.

Most of a mayfly's two or three year lifespan is spent in the water as a whiskered larva, living underneath stones in fast flowing rivers. Then one May morning it floats to the surface and undergoes a first moult into the dull, immature, weak-winged flying insect known to fishermen as a 'dun'. But within a very short time – minutes or, at the most, hours – the dun moults again into a true adult, about 2 in (50 mm) long, with a triple-haired tail and beautiful wings that look like tiny leaded windows.

Male mayflies swarm into the air in a dense, living cloud. Females fly among them in order to mate, then return to the water

A cast of millions *The final scene in the brief drama of mayfly existence (above) sees huge numbers of males and females fluttering over streams and rivers, much to the delight of birds and fish. Death comes swiftly after mating and egg-laying, leaving the area thickly carpeted with their fragile bodies (right).*

to lay their eggs and die – all in the space of a crowded day.

Birds – sparrows, wagtails, swallows and blackbirds – and fish in the streams come crowding to this feeding bonanza. Mayflies are not strong fliers. They are vulnerable during their brief emergence. Trout find their fluttering attempts to leave the water irresistible, and rise to the surface, snapping at anything that moves, to the joy of

fishermen, who call this brief spell 'duffer's fortnight' because even an incompetent angler is guaranteed a good catch.

The dice seem heavily loaded against mayflies, but in fact there is safety in numbers for them – by changing from larvae to adults in such bewildering profusion, far more survive than if they emerged only a few hundred at a time to be picked off by predators.

Confusion of numbers helps penguin security

Life is not by any means easy for Adélie penguins. Even by Antarctic standards, they have so much stacked against them – from the brown skuas, the large sea

birds that attack their eggs and young on shore, to the swift and terrible leopard seals that await them in the sea.

Their chances of survival are bound up with how they group on land and the manner in which they put to sea. Both survival gambits depend on the one thing penguins

have in abundance – numbers. The Adélies breed in huge colonies, within which are subgroups, each slightly withdrawn from the next.

Breeding in a group is definitely better than breeding alone, since a group affords warmth and some protection from attacks by skuas. Skuas are reluctant to enter the centre of a breeding colony to raid nests for eggs or chicks, so by far the best breeding place is at the centre of a group. The larger groups are generally the most successful because the exposed outer fringe of

Stepping warily *In some trepidation, Adélie penguins take the plunge into Antarctic seas, well aware that a leopard seal killer may be lurking beneath an icy ledge. Keeping together in a high-speed group gives them their best chance of safety.*

each group is smaller in relation to the number of birds that are protected by it. Being part of a large group also contributes to survival when it comes to feeding. Penguins must go to sea in order to feed and, as they are only too aware of the patrolling leopard seals that await them offshore, they always depart from the colony in a crowd.

Nervously the penguins congregate on the ice at the edge of the water, anxiously examining each wave trough and crest for the sleek form of a leopard seal. Even a suggestion of a dark head bobbing in the water will send them all back up the beach in a panic, to regroup and approach again.

As soon as one has jumped – or been pushed – the rest follow in rapid succession, swimming as fast as they can beyond the leopard seal's area of activity. The more penguins there are entering the water at any one time, the smaller an individual penguin's chance of becoming the next victim.

SUCCESSFUL TOGETHERNESS

Making a living in the natural world is a tough business, but some plants and animals have found that chances are much improved by taking in a partner.

Mutual protection and domestic harmony

Like a blind man and his guide dog, the South Pacific blind shrimp and Luther's goby, a small fish, live together in mutual dependence. Each takes on tasks suited to its abilities. With its dexterous limbs and claws, the shrimp digs a den, and in return the goby acts as the shrimp's guide, taking it out to find food. The two creatures travel side by side, and the shrimp, so as not to lose touch with its partner, uses its long antennae to keep in contact with the goby's tail. At the end of the expedition, they return to their burrow.

This unusual but highly practical relationship has yet a further

Partners in living *A Luther's goby and a blind shrimp share chores in the sea off Papua New Guinea. The shrimp digs a home and the goby finds their food.*

benefit in that if the goby sees any possible danger when the pair of them are out looking for food, it signals its misgivings to the shrimp by wagging its tail, and the two dart back to the safety of the den together.

Guards and gardeners of the ant world

Aspen sunflowers grow in the Rocky Mountains of Colorado, where they provide a nuptial couch for picture-winged flies. Having mated, the females lay their eggs on the buds and flowerheads, to ensure that when they hatch, the larvae have a plentiful supply of food. In fact, they eventually eat their way through the flower's entire reproductive system, devouring its seeds and effectively sterilising the plant.

However, the aspen sunflower is not entirely helpless. With luck, it attracts and recruits a team of some 25 ants to act as guards. Though the ants cannot catch the flies, they deter them from landing. In return, the plant secretes a rich nectar to feed its sentinels.

Similarly, many acacia species have evolved complex relationships with ants. Among them is the Central American bull-horn acacia, which provides both food and shelter for its protective insect army.

The ants patrol the tree, attacking any intruding insect that ventures into their domain and carrying off its remains to feed their young. An even more unusual aspect of the relationship is the manner in which the ants tend

Ants provide food in return for a home

Growing from the top of a tree in Australia, the vivid green leaves of an ant-house plant positively glow with health. And this despite the fact that the plant's bare roots tap no food source and serve only to anchor the plant in its eyrie.

The ant-house plant owes its robust condition entirely to its relationship with ants. It has somehow evolved a ready-made ants' nest in its swollen stem, complete with nesting chambers, ventilation shafts and walkways.

On its outer surface, the plant stem is covered in spines that provide easy footholds for the ants and protect them from predators.

Even the entrances to the network of protected tunnels are ant-sized, inaccessible to larger creatures and easy to defend.

Although the ants guard their home against leaf-eating and other pests, it is not their most important contribution to the plant's welfare. When the ants feed insects to their larvae, they deposit the remains of their kills and their own faecal wastes neatly in refuse chambers, where an assortment of microbes breaks the material down into a rich compost.

An ant-house plant absorbs this nutritious food through warty structures on the inner surface of the chamber. It is entirely due to this rich supply of fertiliser that these plants manage to survive in their difficult environment.

Compatibility *The swollen stem of an ant-house plant in Australia provides a ready-made home for ants (above and right). In exchange, the ants guard against pests and deposit their waste for the plant to employ as food.*

their home trees. They clear away any seedlings that germinate around the base, and keep the soil beneath the tree free from weeds that might compete for moisture and nutrients. Vines that reach across to the branches from other trees are also severed.

By doing this, they cut the bridges that might be used in an assault by marauding leaf-cutter ants. Only one route remains for these invaders to take – that of straight up the main trunk of the bull-horn acacia. Such a frontal assault is a good deal easier for the acacia ants to repel than would be a flank attack via the vines.

Free board and lodging

The ants are repaid for their work with food and shelter. They live in the acacia's large, hollow thorns, which they enter by chewing into a weak spot near the tip. In one of them a home is established for the brood and queen.

The acacia yields nectar from its flowers for the adult ants and a special food for the larvae, which is collected by the worker ants from the tips of its leaflets. This takes the form of tiny, brightly coloured structures called Beltian bodies, which are rich in fats and proteins and provide the larvae with a valuable dietary supplement.

Another denizen of Central America that attracts a particular species of ant is the giant piper plant. This also offers shelter and tiny food packages rich in protein and fat. The ants live in the hollow curled leaf blades but are too small to provide a defence against leaf-eating insects. So they serve the plant instead by picking off fungal spores from the leaves and stems.

The relationship between the piper plant and this single species of ant has developed so far that the plant will not produce food bodies when its leaf blades are unoccupied. This is, however, a relationship that one species of beetle has learned to exploit, for the beetle larvae are able to mimic the ants' secretions so convincingly that the piper plant responds by producing the food packages for them. But in this case, the plant gains nothing in exchange, because the beetles neither tend it nor guard it.

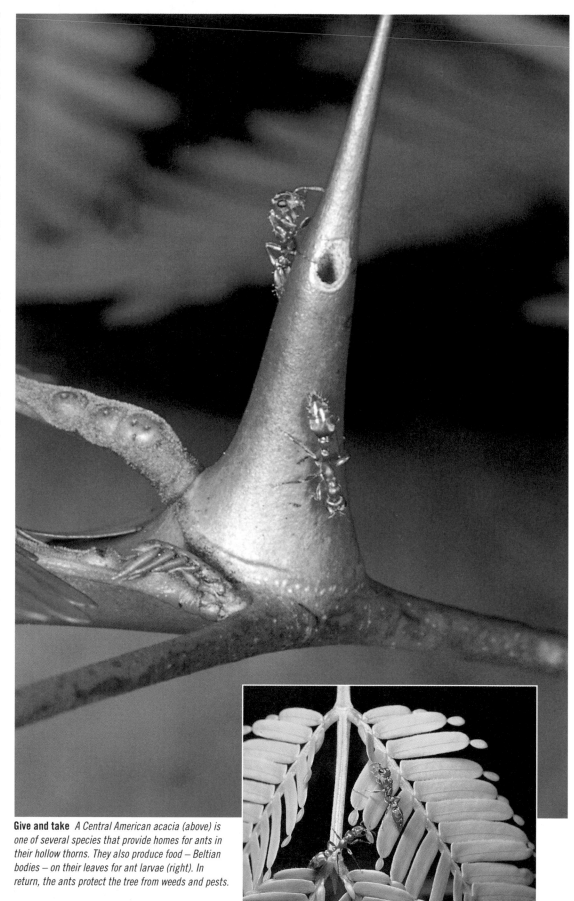

Give and take *A Central American acacia (above) is one of several species that provide homes for ants in their hollow thorns. They also produce food – Beltian bodies – on their leaves for ant larvae (right). In return, the ants protect the tree from weeds and pests.*

LIVING IN ISOLATION

The lonely life has its own rewards – cutting down competition from members of the same species for food, breeding partners and shelter.

A lifetime's work *A male Australian brush turkey devotes all his energy to building and caring for his nest and tending the eggs laid in it by passing females.*

Why polar bears prefer to hunt alone

Still and silent, flat on the ice with front legs outstretched, a polar bear watches a seal approach a breathing hole in the ice. In the split second before the seal breaks the surface and spots the danger, the bear smashes down with a powerful, double-pawed blow. A swift, scooping movement with its long sharp claws, and the unconscious seal's limp, bloody body is lying on the ice. The polar bear's long, patient wait beside the seals' breathing hole has paid off.

Polar bears are supremely independent. During the Arctic winter they prey mainly on seals, hunting them on the sea ice. To get close enough for a kill, the bears rely on a silent, stealthy approach – best done alone. So they wander the icy wastes unaccompanied, avoiding one another as far as possible.

Fights between polar bears are rare, but can be vicious between males in dispute over a female. Mating time is one of the few times that bears seek company. Females with cubs are particularly wary of males, which can easily deliver a fatal blow to a youngster.

Food is where you find it

Polar bears are opportunists, taking food where they can find it. They have a remarkable sense of smell, and Arctic zoologists say the best way to see a polar bear is to fry some bacon. Attracted by the smell, bears will come running!

Bears will converge on any food source, whether it is a town rubbish dump or the carcass of a stranded whale. At such times they give the impression of being social animals, but in reality they are merely tolerating one another. Once the food has gone they pad off to continue their solitary lives.

Cold and lonely wait *A polar bear stretches out and prepares for a long wait by a seal's breathing hole in the Arctic sea ice. It keeps low so that the seal will not see it until it is too late.*

Lonely brush turkey gets no thanksgiving

The loneliest father in the bird world may be the Australian brush turkey. This bird spends his adult life building, tending and defending a huge mound of vegetation and soil. It may take him weeks or even months to scrape together from two to four tons of material, and he can lose up to 20 per cent of his body weight during this mammoth construction task.

It is a lonely life, but if the turkey is lucky females will visit the mound and lay eggs for him. Once he has a clutch he toils to keep the mound at the right temperature, constantly adjusting it by removing or adding vegetation.

Each male defends a large territory, probably to reduce the risk of caring for eggs fertilised by other males. But because the females do wander and mate with any number of males, there is a good chance that not all the eggs in a male's huge incubator will be his own. After weeks of slavish care by their father (or foster father) the chicks break out of their eggs, struggle out of the mound and run off to start their own independent lives.

The wild cats that walk by themselves

Tense and alert, a puma crouches in the undergrowth of a North American mountain forest. A mule deer nibbling the grass is drawing closer, on the lookout for danger but oblivious of the lurking threat. When the deer is about 20 ft (6 m) away, the cat shoots out from the shadows, knocking it to the floor and delivering a fatal neck bite.

The puma – America's largest cat – hunts alone, like the majority of wild cats. It stalks small mammals in all kinds of terrain, from Canada to Patagonia. Its strategy, that of staying hidden until it is close enough to rush its victim, works best alone. Pumas shun the company of their own kind.

Each cat has its own territory, marked with 'Keep Out' signals of

Refreshment time *A puma (also known as a cougar or mountain lion) takes a drink from a mountain pool in its home range. It knows its patch well – all the best places to hunt, drink and sleep.*

urine, droppings, scratch marks and secretions from the anal gland sprayed onto trees. Although the size of the home range varies, it is always an area extensive enough to provide the cat with food and shelter. A puma's summer range, for example, may cover as much as 115 sq miles (300 km²).

Where prey is plentiful, individual ranges may overlap, sometimes completely. Cats sharing a range avoid one another, preferring not to fight because each one relies on physical fitness for its livelihood.

At mating time meetings are necessary, however, and the signs used to warn off other cats can also advertise a female's reproductive status to males in the area. When she is receptive to mating, therefore, a female puma's 'Keep Out' signals may actually lead to a brief spell of 'sociality'.

Lions are the exception to the solitary rule of wild cats. They live in prides on the African grasslands, helping one another to raise young and cooperating to bring down the very large game, such as buffaloes, found in abundance on the plains.

How caribou avoid the insect onslaught

Every summer in North America caribou (reindeer) find themselves in a dilemma – whether to face attack by wolves or by millions of swarming, biting flies?

Wolves are the main danger for caribou in the far north, but flies of various kinds are also a serious pest. Various species of mosquito, blackfly, gadfly and biting midge emerge one after the other during the summer months. In wave after wave, millions of flies plague the caribou and other mammals. The only real defence against the flies is to hide from them.

The flies find the caribou by sensing carbon dioxide in their breath. By flying towards increasing carbon dioxide concentration, the flies finally come upon their victims and feed on their blood.

They attack a caribou's belly and legs – places where the skin is thinnest and the blood vessels

are easiest to get at. For young or weak caribou the onslaught of the flies can be debilitating.

For caribou on the open tundra, the best way to avoid wolves and flies is to form groups. Each tries to get into the middle of a group where its legs and belly are less vulnerable. In the forest, however, the best strategy is to go it alone or within a small group, because trees break up the carbon dioxide trail. But wolves are more likely

to attack an animal that is on its own. The larger male caribou are better able to defend themselves from wolf attacks, so the risk of staying alone is worth taking. The females seem to prefer the relative safety from wolves that living in a small group affords them.

Respite from flies *Caribou herds on their annual summer migration in Alaska break up into small groups to rest on patches of ice, taking a break from the attentions of flies hungry for their blood.*

HATING THEIR NEIGHBOUR

In the struggle for survival, some animals treat others of their own species in a manner that seems to us to be either vindictive or cruel.

All's fair. . . *Hoping to entice a female to his own mating bower, a male satin bowerbird destroys that of a rival male (above). Once the destruction is achieved, he steals the sticks to use in his own bower (left). When his bower is completed (below) and his ornaments displayed, the male struts around in front of it to attract a female.*

Bowerbirds steal and destroy to win a mate

Vandalism and theft are common occurrences among male satin bowerbirds in the rain forests of New Guinea and eastern Australia during the mating season. The highly decorated bowers, or mating sites, that the starling-sized glossy black males build become places of intense rivalry as the birds compete to attract female partners. Because the quality of a bower and its adornments determine mating success, rival males attempt to destroy each other's bowers and steal the best decorations.

Colour conscious

A variety of bower decorations is used by different species of bowerbird. Ornaments displayed range from natural objects such as snail shells, pebbles, feathers, bits of bone and insect parts to man-made objects such as coloured glass, coins, buttons and bottletops.

Satin bowerbirds use mainly blue ornaments, or sometimes grey or greenish ones. Those most popular are blue feathers. Quantity as well as quality is important. Up to 100 objects may be laid out for display – the greater the number of feathers in a bower, the greater the mating success of the bower builder. But because blue feathers are rare, they are difficult to come by, so bowerbirds often steal them

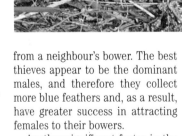

from a neighbour's bower. The best thieves appear to be the dominant males, and therefore they collect more blue feathers and, as a result, have greater success in attracting females to their bowers.

Another significant factor in the quest for a mate is the quality of construction of the bower. This can

be about 3 ft (1 m) long and 2½ ft (76 cm) high, having two parallel walls of twigs built on a platform of tightly woven sticks. A bird smears his completed bower with a mixture of charcoal and saliva, and arranges display objects in front of it. A neat, well-built bower with symmetrical walls, densely packed

sticks and an extremely sculptured appearance is the one most likely to attract females.

A bower is also a sign of a male's strength and perseverance. Each bird attempts to destroy the work of competing males, so the owner of a well-kept bower is a bird that is well able to fight off marauders.

Safety measure *Anis, which are members of the cuckoo family, lay their almost round eggs (above) in the safety of communal nests. They nest (right) in marshland reeds or in trees on the pasturelands of the Americas.*

Ani nests are breeding grounds of animosity

As many as four breeding pairs of groove-billed anis may share one nest, although each remains with its own partner. These black, parrot-like cuckoos of Central and South America live in groups, with the females laying their eggs in the group nest and all the adults working together to incubate the eggs and to feed the chicks.

But this apparently harmonious social grouping hides an undercurrent of antisocial behaviour among the pairs – with the dominant pair producing the most chicks. The dominant female begins laying her eggs only after the subordinates have already started. In this way she can throw out some of the eggs of her colleagues – any egg that is in the nest before she starts to lay is likely to be ejected.

The subordinates retaliate by laying a few more eggs after she has finished. Or they may start to incubate before her, effectively forcing her to stop laying to avoid her offspring hatching too late. Despite this, the dominant female ends up with most of her eggs hatching, whereas the subordinates have to be satisfied with only about half of their eggs hatching.

The dominant female also does less than her share of incubation and chick rearing. She leaves her subordinates to do it for her, a task they accept because the communal nest affords their eggs greater protection from predators than they would have in a lone nest.

Macaque revenge leads to family vendettas

Vindictiveness is not exclusive to human beings, for Japanese macaques seem to show it at times. If a macaque loses an aggressive encounter with a more dominant individual in the troop, it takes out its frustration on a smaller and weaker animal. But the choice of victim is not random. Invariably it is a young and vulnerable relative of the aggressor that is attacked.

Group retaliation
Striking a dominant animal's less powerful relatives is a risky form of retaliation, however – it may result in escalated aggression from the original animal.

A macaque bent on revenge, therefore, usually enlists the aid of its family group. They make sure the dominant animal is watching when the revenge attack occurs, so that it is knows why the attack is taking place.

This type of retaliation could be a subtle form of manipulation of the powerful by the weak, with the hope that, in subsequent encounters, the dominant macaque will be less aggressive towards them.

Slave-maker ants seize young recruits

Charles Darwin, the 19th-century naturalist, abhorred the slavery of human beings yet was intrigued to find similar behaviour among ants. The slave-making behaviour of certain species of ants was first discovered in 1810.

European blood-red slave-maker ants are aggressive and highly territorial. Two or three times in late summer, after their reproductive individuals have left the nest on their nuptial flights, these ants make raids on nearby colonies of black ants to obtain slaves.

A large group of slave-maker workers sets out from the nest and heads for the target nest. On their arrival, the ants linger round the entrance for a few minutes, then enter, one after the other. The occupants of the nest attempt to escape, carrying eggs, larvae and pupae with them. Only if they try

Prize slave *Holding aloft a captured ant pupa, two raiding slave-maker ants set off back to their nest, brushing aside a desperate defender.*

to repel the intruders are they attacked. The raiders seize as many pupae as they can carry back to their own nest. In time, the captured pupae emerge as ants and spend the rest of their lives as slaves in their captors' colony.

A colony of blood-red slave-maker ants can, in fact, function without slaves – its own workers performing all the normal duties of foraging and tending the eggs. But Amazon ants – which are found worldwide, and named after their warrior queens rather than where they live – are completely dependent upon their slaves. These hatch from pupae pillaged from other ant species.

Amazon workers never excavate their own nests or care for their young. Their only task is to raid other ants' nests and so increase the colony's supply of slaves.

THE SEARCH FOR FOOD

'*H*E WAS A VERY SMALL FROG WITH WIDE, DULL EYES.
AND JUST AS I LOOKED AT HIM, HE SLOWLY CRUMPLED AND
BEGAN TO SAG. THE SPIRIT VANISHED FROM HIS EYES AS IF SNUFFED.
HIS SKIN EMPTIED AND DROOPED; HIS VERY SKULL SEEMED
TO COLLAPSE AND SETTLE LIKE A KICKED TENT.'
≈ ANNIE DILLARD, *PILGRIM AT TINKER CREEK,* 1975.

Choosing only the best
Grasses form the bulk of a warthog's carefully chosen diet. It nips off growing tips with its teeth or lips, and digs up roots from the soil with the tough upper edge of its snout.

The American nature writer Annie Dillard watched, appalled, as a frog was eaten by a giant water bug. After immobilising its prey with its bite, the bug injects digestive juices that turn bones and muscles to liquid, which the bug then sucks from the victim's body. The way in which animals find their food and eat it may seem horrific to us, though they are doing no more than obtaining the nutrients that they need in order to survive. The fierce competition between individuals for the often limited food resources available to them may stimulate increasingly cunning strategies for obtaining these nutrients, and for processing and storing them to consume later in times of scarcity. As well as poisons, the weapons that animals have developed to achieve these aims include traps and lures, specialised beaks, teeth and claws, and even rudimentary tools.

Underwater hunter
A giant water bug subdues its prey with a poison that is more potent than the same volume of rattlesnake venom. A fly trapped on the water's surface is attacked from below and its body tissues liquefied and sucked out.

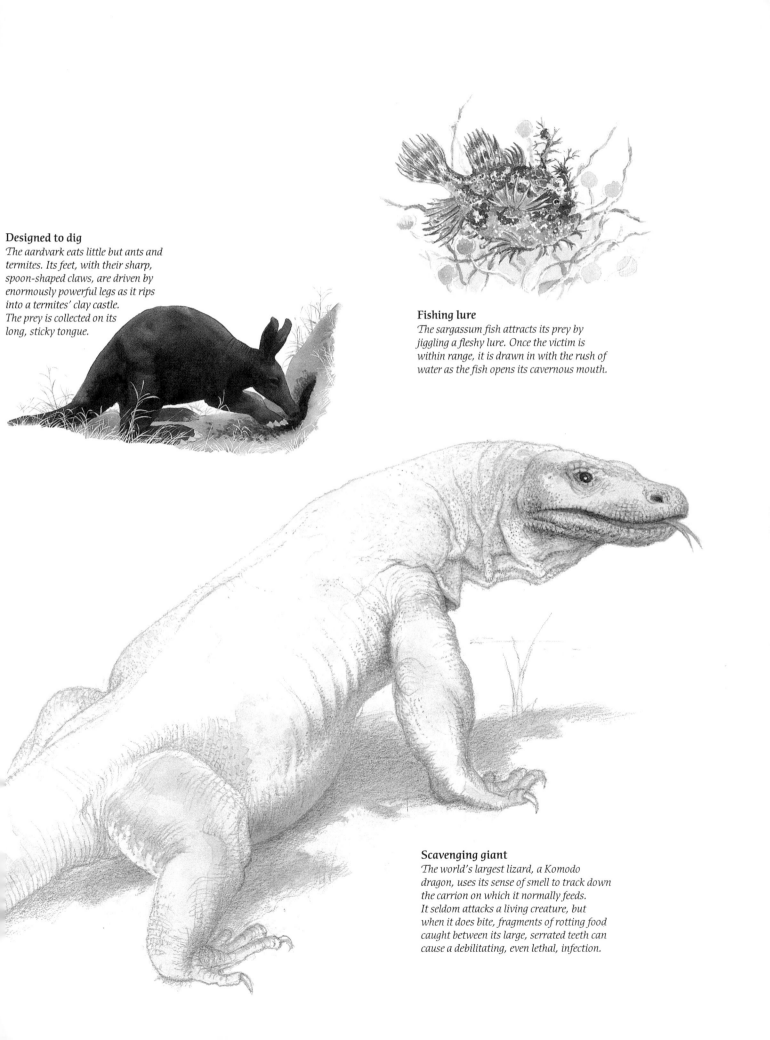

Designed to dig
The aardvark eats little but ants and
termites. Its feet, with their sharp,
spoon-shaped claws, are driven by
enormously powerful legs as it rips
into a termites' clay castle.
The prey is collected on its
long, sticky tongue.

Fishing lure
The sargassum fish attracts its prey by
jiggling a fleshy lure. Once the victim is
within range, it is drawn in with the rush of
water as the fish opens its cavernous mouth.

Scavenging giant
The world's largest lizard, a Komodo
dragon, uses its sense of smell to track down
the carrion on which it normally feeds.
It seldom attacks a living creature, but
when it does bite, fragments of rotting food
caught between its large, serrated teeth can
cause a debilitating, even lethal, infection.

HUNTING TOGETHER IN A PACK

Working as a team allows hunters to kill bigger animals than they could manage individually, giving them a wider choice of prey.

Hunting for food *As dawn glows, a pack of African wild dogs, or Cape hunting dogs, sets off across a Kenyan plain (above) in search of food. The dogs live in family groups led by a dominant male and female, and as they have large litters – up to 12 – packs may number 15-40 animals. Youngsters do not fend for themselves until about 14 months old. A group of yearlings awaiting food (above inset) shelters in a hollow from a rainstorm. A dog team (right), loping tirelessly in pursuit of its victim, runs for hours. The dogs can maintain speeds of 37 mph (60 km/h) for about 3 miles (5 km).*

End of the chase *After running their wildebeest prey to exhaustion, a dog pack closes in for the kill, led by the dominant male and female. The dogs work together to head off the victim's attempts to escape.*

Wild dogs use team tactics to catch prey

African wild dogs, or Cape hunting dogs, are sometimes also known as painted wolves because of their pack habits and the mixture of earthy colours on their coats. Their cooperation in hunting down prey is supreme.

Together these marathon runners work as a relay team to chase large prey such as a gazelle, a wildebeest or an antelope, until it drops from exhaustion. The dogs owe their stamina to characteristics that have evolved through the centuries – deep chests, slim legs that are easy to lift, and short coats that allow quick loss of the heat generated by tireless muscles.

Although wild dogs do not care if prey detects them, they do lower their heads and flatten their large, rounded ears on approaching a grazing herd, perhaps until they have picked a victim – generally a young or weak animal. On the African plains, both predator and prey do have some communication. When they see wild dogs in the offing, Thomson's gazelles 'stot', or bounce stiff-leggedly. The better a gazelle's condition, the higher it stots – perhaps telling the dogs they would be better off choosing another, less fleet-footed victim.

During the chase, dogs may take the lead in turn while the others ease off or sometimes change route to intercept if the victim swerves. The dominant pair play the main role in the kill, attacking the defenceless animal's belly and flanks.

Food for all *A pack of wild dogs demolishes its powerless wildebeest prey (below). A wildebeest weighing 400 lb (180 kg) or so is a fairly substantial meal – equivalent to the weight of about eight wild dogs. The pack shares the kill, the dogs allowing pups (right) to take their fill first. Pups can travel with the pack from about three months old – where there are younger pups, the dogs return to the den and regurgitate meat for them.*

TEAM TACTICS SUPPLEMENT MUSCLE

For lone hunters, the advantage is not having to share the kill. But skilled teamwork can sometimes produce bigger and better meals for all concerned.

Aerial fishers *A flock of blue-footed boobies (above) dive together for fish on the flight leader's signal. Great white pelicans (top left) swim in V-formation to drive fish forwards so they can scoop them up with ease. The brown pelican (bottom left) is the only pelican to dive for food, opening its throat pouch under water like a fishing net.*

Formation fishing brings a bigger catch

Several bird species, those that fish in particular, cooperate in the hunt for food. For example, the great white pelicans of Africa, Asia and southern Europe form groups numbering from 5 to 500 to catch fish. The birds advance in a U or V-formation, herding the fish in front of them. As they move forwards, the pelicans raise their wings and plunge their heads under water together, scooping up fish in their net-like bills. Only one pelican, the brown pelican of North America, fishes by diving headlong into the water. Although these pelicans catch fish independently, they dive as a loose group.

Diving by signal

Blue-footed boobies, which live along the Pacific coast of Central America, are members of the gannet family. Gannets dive for fish and squid, often in large groups, but only the blue-footed boobies seem to work together. They fly in a circle 100 ft (30 m) or so above the ocean surface, then, when one of their number gives the signal, all dive together on to a school of fish.

Great white pelicans and blue-footed boobies are not the only birds that fish in groups. Several species of cormorants, including the double-crested cormorant and the blue-eyed shag, also hunt together in huge flocks.

Double-crested cormorants may fish in groups of up to 2000 birds. Moving forwards together in a line, the cormorants splash vigorously with their wings and feet and drive fish shorewards in front of them. When the fish are trapped between the line of birds and the shore, the cormorants break ranks and dive down on a fishing spree.

Birds are not the only fish herders – predatory fish such as the bluefish and the striped marlin do the same. The 4 ft (1.2 m) long bluefish is speedy and voracious, and the striped marlin, which is nearly four times as long as the bluefish, can work up to a sprint of 50 mph (80 km/h). Both these fish are warm water hunters of the open ocean, and work in well coordinated groups, shepherding a shoal of smaller fish into a dense and panicky crowd that easily provides a feast for all.

Shares are not always fair in baboon society

Game is plentiful in the steamy swamps of the Okavango in Botswana, so chacma, or savannah, baboons supplement their usual diet of insects and fruit with meat. This is usually something small, such as a very young impala or a vervet monkey. The high-ranking males of a troop generally hunt alone, but those of equal status may coordinate their efforts.

However, baboons are not good at sharing their spoils. A dominant male always has first pickings no matter who made a kill but a large carcass may be shared by as many as 18 baboons. However, squabbles over the portions are bitter.

Mandrills are predatory West African baboons that are much

Foraging for food *A troop of chacma baboons (above) lopes across a grassy plain in the Okavango area of Botswana, where they may forage for insects, fruit or grain. In areas rich in game, some may work together to catch small animals.*

more cooperative than the chacma baboons, and hunt together in packs of 50-100. Females and young males run screaming through the rain forest, terrorising the small game and flushing it from cover. The panicked animals are driven in confusion into an advancing line of dominant baboon males, which kill as many as they can. Only when the area has been cleared is the hunt called off, and the troop gets together to feed.

First for food *A male chacma baboon feasts on a small impala. Many high-ranking males hunt alone, but even when a whole troop makes the kill, it is always the dominant male who eats first.*

Team hunters *Desert-living Harris's hawks are birds of prey that cooperate in their hunting. Team techniques are employed to flush game from its hiding place.*

Hawk families that hunt in organised squadrons

Birds of prey are not naturally cooperative, yet Harris's hawks, which are found in the deserts of Central and South America, hunt together in groups of from three to six birds. A breeding female may be joined by more than one male.

Assembling at dawn, they split up into scouting groups and make short forays in search of prey – usually jack rabbits – but gather together again from time to time. Sometimes the hawks capture an unwary rabbit by diving on it from different directions, but they also

use a flush-and-ambush technique that is well suited to the rough and scrubby terrain with its abundance of cover. In this, some of the birds surround and watch the prey, ready to pounce, while others try to flush it from its hiding place.

Another method used is a relay attack in which each hawk of the team takes turns to chase and dive bomb the quarry – this demands the most energy so is the least commonly used. After the kill, the hunters divide the prey between them. A team of six birds is the most efficient in terms of energy expended, but even then each bird's average daily share is small – only just enough for its needs.

BUILT FOR SPEED

In the hard world of the hunter, it is muscle power, quick reactions, good vision and high speed in the final chase that ensure success.

A supple, speedy and sharp-eyed sprinter

When it comes to chasing prey, the supreme sprinter among land animals is the cheetah. With its slim, streamlined body, small head, long legs and supple spine, it is superbly shaped for swift bursts of speed.

The cheetah's acceleration is astonishing. Like an arrow from a bow, it shoots forward from standstill to 45 mph (70 km/h) in three seconds – nearly as fast as a Formula 1 racing car and faster than most sports cars.

A cheetah at full speed can reach 63 mph (101 km/h), though only over a short distance. If it has not caught its prey (often a gazelle) after about 20 seconds and 550 yd (500 m), it abandons the chase. Sprinting at such a pace makes heavy demands on its system and though the run was brief, the cheetah must rest and recover its breath.

The secret of the cheetah's amazing speed lies in the flexing and extending of its supple spine, which allows it to greatly increase the length of its stride – the distance between the point where its hind feet leave the ground and where they touch again. As its spine arches to an astonishing extent, its hind legs can reach a long way forwards and then, when its spine extends, it increases the forward reach of the front legs as well as adding pressure to the backward thrust of the hind legs.

This spinal flexing gives the cheetah a stride of about 23 ft (7 m) and may be worth 6 mph (10 km/h) to its speed – enough to make the difference between success and failure in the chase.

Leaping through the air

At full tilt, a cheetah is actually moving in a series of gigantic leaps, with its body unsupported in midair twice during each stride – once while it is fully extended and once while it is flexed and tensed for the next powerful spring. The big cat's tremendous acceleration is augmented by the grip of its claws; they cannot be fully retracted and act like the spikes on a runner's shoes.

It would seem impossible for the cheetah to keep its eye on its target as it bounds through the air. But like a gun on a modern battle tank, which holds its aim however rough the ride, the cheetah can keep its head steady because of the great flexibility of its shoulders. And with a narrow strip of concentrated light-sensitive cells across the retina of each eye, it can clearly distinguish its intended prey from the details of the background.

Even with all these advantages, if it is to make a kill, the cheetah must get to within about 50 yd (45 m) of its prey before it moves and startles the animal into flight.

Unlike most other cats, the cheetah hunts by day, often during the cool of dawn or dusk, first surveying the ground from a tree branch or the top of a termite mound. Regular vantage points are sprayed with urine to warn off other cheetahs, and the resident cat may travel from one point to another before finding a suitable place from which to try a strike.

How the cheetah attacks depends on the situation. If the gazelles do not seem nervous, the cheetah may casually sidle up, or if the cover is good it may stalk them. Whatever the approach, an enormous amount of energy is released in the explosive moment of take-off. The cheetah rushes forward in a straight line, anticipating the direction of its prey so as to intercept it. Then with one last burst of speed, the cheetah swipes the gazelle's hind legs from under it, straddles the struggling body and chokes the panting animal with a strong bite to the throat, suffocating it in less than two minutes.

Both hunter and hunted have reached the limit of their lung power, which explains why the lightly built cat can so quickly subdue the gazelle. Adult gazelles are generally about half or one-third the weight of a full-grown cheetah, and not quite as high at the shoulder. Even so, cheetahs tend to single out young gazelles which are lighter.

After the chase the cheetah has to rest, whether or not it has made a kill. During a dash of some 200 yd (180 m), the cat's temperature soars dangerously from 38.5°C (101.5°F) to 40°C (105°F) – a level that would cause brain damage if maintained for more than about a minute. So the cheetah just sits and pants for 15 minutes or so to cool down. When rested, it is ready to eat – or, if it has caught nothing, to start the hunt all over again.

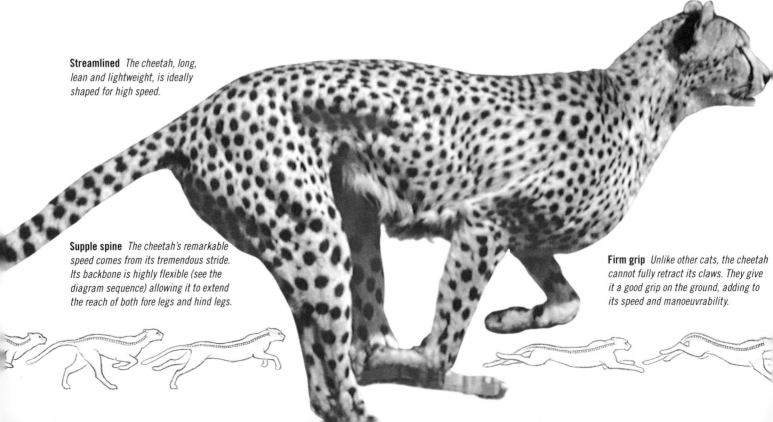

Streamlined *The cheetah, long, lean and lightweight, is ideally shaped for high speed.*

Supple spine *The cheetah's remarkable speed comes from its tremendous stride. Its backbone is highly flexible (see the diagram sequence) allowing it to extend the reach of both fore legs and hind legs.*

Firm grip *Unlike other cats, the cheetah cannot fully retract its claws. They give it a good grip on the ground, adding to its speed and manoeuvrability.*

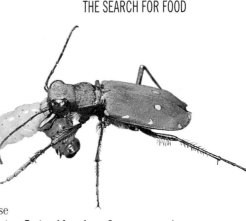

Long-legged sprinter *Its ability to run at speeds up to 25 mph (40 km/h) gives the roadrunner an edge over fast-moving prey such as lizards or snakes.*

The feathered hunter that outpaces snakes

Although it can fly, the jaunty roadrunner is also one of the most accomplished sprinters of the bird world. It uses its speed to run down such ground-hugging prey as insects, lizards and rattlesnakes. Not only is it fast, it is agile too. Using its long tail as a rudder and its slightly open wings as stabilisers, it can turn at right angles without loss of speed.

The roadrunner, a relative of the cuckoo, lives in dry, scrubby deserts of the southwest USA, where the days are hot but the nights are very cold. To conserve body heat at night, the bird slows down its bodily functions, lowers its temperature and becomes lethargic. But when dawn breaks it must warm up quickly and get on the move again. To do this, it has a built-in heat exchanger, a patch of dark skin on the back between its wings that helps to absorb the warmth of the weak morning sun. The bird roughs up its feathers to expose the patch, and then waits for its body to reach normal temperature.

The speediest killers on six long legs

Tiger beetles, which occur everywhere, must surely be the sprint champions of the insect world. Their actual speed may not be impressive – only 2 ft (60 cm) a second, or 1.5 mph (2.5 km/h). Yet if a beetle were scaled up to horse size, this would be the equivalent of 250 mph (400 km/h).

At this speed, a tiger beetle can outpace any other insect, and its large, compound eyes give it distance vision of up to 5-6 in (13-15 cm). An unwary ant, for example, that passes within a handspan of a tiger beetle, will be caught after a quick, well-timed dash, and end up as a meal in less than a quarter of a second. All in all a fearsome hunter, the beetle owes its swiftness to its six long, slender legs. No less useful are its large, sharp, four-pointed jaws — formidable weapons for catching and dismembering prey.

Fast and ferocious *Common everywhere on sandy heathland, the European green tiger beetle uses its surprising speed, excellent eyesight and savage jaws to seize and dissect its insect prey.*

Headlong flight *Thomson's gazelles graze in their thousands on East African plains. When pursued by a cheetah they rely on getting a head start, for their top speed of 45 mph (72 km/h) is roughly 18 mph (29 km/h) slower than the cat.*

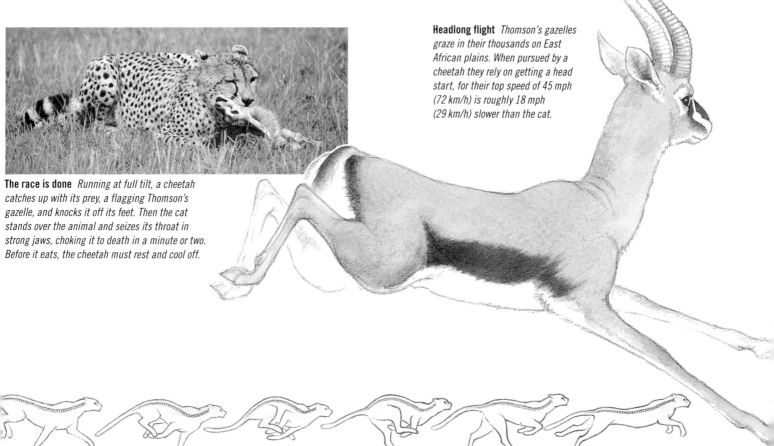

The race is done *Running at full tilt, a cheetah catches up with its prey, a flagging Thomson's gazelle, and knocks it off its feet. Then the cat stands over the animal and seizes its throat in strong jaws, choking it to death in a minute or two. Before it eats, the cheetah must rest and cool off.*

TRAPPING BY TRICKERY – THE HUNTER'S ALTERNATIVE

The fatal attraction of the irresistible worm

Chasing a meal consumes a lot of energy, so it is little wonder that some predators have evolved more subtle approaches – they tempt the prey within range instead. The bulbous-bodied angler fish, found in many oceans, is well camouflaged with trailing strands of skin that look like weeds. And on its dorsal fin, one of the stiffening fin-rays is completely separated to form a long stalk tipped with a tattered, coloured shred.

When the angler fish waves this flag-like fin on its back, small fish find it irresistible. Just as one is about to bite, the angler whisks back its fishing rod and sucks the fish into its cavernous mouth. The suction is so powerful that it has no need to advance on its prey.

Deadly twitch

A similar technique is used by the South American horned toad, but here the bait is a toe on one of its hind feet. While sitting motionless, the toad twitches the toe very slightly. Fascinated by the movement, its prospective prey – a small frog, for instance – edges closer. The toad twitches a little more vigorously, and then gulps down its bemused victim.

Some catfish lure their prey with even less effort. These fish have sensitive, whisker-like barbels round their mouths, which they use to help to locate food as they creep along the sea bottom or over rocks. Some kinds have whiskers that look like tiny worms when the catfish is resting. Fish that come to investigate within the catfish's reach meet a swift end.

Baits for fish *The angler fish lures small fish to its hungry jaws by waving a flag-like fin on its back, while the American freshwater snapping turtle (inset) uses its worm-like pink tongue.*

Deceiving by mimicry and masquerade

Pretending to be something quite different is another way of obtaining a meal. The Australian bird-dropping spider looks just like a blob of bird excrement, and also exudes a scent that closely resembles the sex pheromone of a female moth. The spider is infinitely patient, staying motionless on a leaf or twig until an unwary male moth in search of a mate obligingly flies into its waiting arms.

Not even a flower can be relied upon to be what it appears. The African devil's flower is in fact a well-disguised mantis – a carnivorous insect – hanging from a branch. Most of its body looks like a pink stalk, and its front legs are flattened and brightly coloured like petals, with the mantis's head representing the centre of the flower. Another mantis, the orchid mantis of Malaysia, has legs that are elongated and flattened to match the colour and texture of orchid petals. Insects visiting these 'flowers' for nectar do not realise the deception until it is too late.

Like Sweeney Todd, the sabre-toothed blenny fish that mimics the cleaner wrasse of the Indo-Pacific is a butcher masquerading as a barber. Not only does it look like the cleaner; it swims in the same way. But when the blenny gets close to an unsuspecting fish, it removes not just parasites but fins and flesh into the bargain, its large teeth inflicting a savage bite. However, young fish who have been bitten quickly learn to tell the difference between barber and butcher.

False colours *The bright colour and innocent appearance of the orchid mantis of Malaysia (above) lures unsuspecting nectar-seeking insects to their death. The apparent blob of dung (right) smells like a female moth, and is in fact an Australian spider lying in wait for prey such as male moths.*

Lures for the curious and the houseproud

Some herons in Japan have been known to manufacture bait to attract a meal. They fish with 'flies' fashioned from real insects, or with bread dropped by passers-by. A few even make bait from feathers and cut twigs. Fish that arrive to examine the result are neatly speared.

Tail waving is the baiting technique of the southern copperhead snake of the eastern USA. Except for its worm-like, sulphur-hued tail, the snake's colouring camouflages it among the rocky outcrops and dead leaves of its surroundings. As it slides over the ground only its waving tail is visible. Any small creature that tries to catch the 'worm' ends up in the snake.

Some assassin bugs – there are about 2500 different species – lie in wait for insects, concealing themselves beneath soil and the remains of their victims. A Costa Rican species that feeds on termites uses a termite cadaver to make an undercover approach.

The bug kills by stabbing with its dagger-like mouthparts, then sucks the victim dry. To catch another meal, the assassin bug relies on the instinct of the worker termites to remove the dead as part of their housekeeping duties. The bug picks up the carcass of its victim and marches towards the termite mound. When a busy worker attempts to take away the remains of its comrade, the assassin bug kills it too.

Attractive tail *What seems to be a luscious worm is really the tail of a southern copperhead snake in search of a meal. By waving its tail, it can entice an unsuspecting frog near enough to catch.*

Deceptive disguise *An assassin bug nymph lies in ambush covered by sand grains and fire ant carcasses. Having poisoned the ants and sucked their bodies dry, the bug uses them as bait. Fire ants coming to retrieve their dead are killed as well.*

HOW SPIDERS SET THEIR SILKEN SNARES

Poets portray the spider's web as a delicate filigree of gossamer threads. In fact, webs come in many forms and their fragile looks belie their steely strength.

Designer death traps for unwitting insects

The orb web is the most familiar form of spider architecture. A vertical spiral with linking spokes, it is equally efficient when trapping the tiny flies consumed by garden spiders or the large crickets eaten by the 3 in (75 mm) long golden orb spider of Australia.

If a bird flies into a spider's web it will come to little harm, but the spider has to reconstruct its elaborate death trap all over again, probably on an empty stomach. Some of the larger tropical spiders leave the husks of insects hanging on their webs as a signal to birds to avoid them. It was once thought that the zigzag band of thicker silk woven into the webs of some spiders served the same purpose. But it may also beckon insects by reflecting ultraviolet light in the same way as flower petals.

There are myriad variations on the orb web theme, which itself is only one of many basic web styles. The platform-web spider fashions a horizontal silken dining table and constructs a fine maze of threads above. Flying insects snared in the tangle eventually fall exhausted on to the table, where the hungry spider lies in wait.

The net-casting spider dangles from a branch on home-spun guy ropes, holding a cat's cradle of silk from its four front legs. The net it holds is spun as a rectangle, stretched out on a scaffold by silken ropes. When the spider cuts the net free, the threads retract to about one-tenth of their stretched length, producing a highly elastic web. The spider then waits for a passing insect. Its two huge eyes allow the spider to take careful aim, and flinging out its net, it hauls in the catch and proceeds to suck it dry.

Webs at work *A net-casting spider hangs, poised to throw its net over passing insects (above). An orb-web's silk grows stronger with the struggles of trapped insects, but birds can wreak havoc. So the spider leaves a scarecrow of dead insects (right) to warn them off. A platform-web spider (below) sits above its platform in the maze of threads intended to ensnare flying insects.*

Hunters' silken lifelines and lethal lassos

Comb-footed spiders lasso their prey with silken strands thrown from the combs on their hindlegs. But this is not without its hazards. One species living in the western USA feeds on harvester ants, which have a powerful sting. So the wary spider fastens its prey to the ground and bites the ant's hind leg, injecting a lethal poison. Then it simply waits for the poison to take effect before eating its catch.

Some athletic jumping spiders hunt by stalking, others lie in wait, but all capture their meals with lightning leaps which can exceed 20 times their own body length.

Acute eyesight is essential for a jumping spider to spot and focus on moving prey. Eight tubular eyes are positioned at the upper corners of its angular head to give the spider perfect all-round vision. The two main eyes at the front of the head can rotate or move from side to side independently, allowing the spider to focus and judge distance, essential for the pounce. Before it leaps, it secures itself with a silken dragline to prevent falling.

Some of the jumping spiders are spider-eaters. They craftily lure a female web-spinning spider into pouncing range by mimicking the signals of a courting male. When she responds to the signals she is jumped upon and duly eaten.

Safety first *Before making the leap to intercept a passing fly, the jumping spider (left) secures itself to a leaf with a sturdy line of silk to avoid a fall.*

Bolas spiders mix a deadly cocktail

In eastern Australia's outback, the bolas spider catches courting moths by spinning a slender silken thread with a sticky ball on the end – rather like the bolas used by gauchos, the cowboys of the South American pampas.

The spider flavours the sticky ball with a chemical cocktail that smells like a female moth. The trap set, the spider suspends itself by a silken trapeze with the bolas dangling from one leg, and settles down to wait.

When male moths, drawn by the scent, get close enough for the spider to sense the beat of their wings, it whirls its deadly lure. The moths are caught fast on the sticky ball and hauled in to be eaten. There is little chance of escape, for a strand of spider silk, 250 times finer than a human hair, is twice as strong as steel. Indeed, the United States Air Force is exploring how the qualities of spider silk might be applied to bullet-proof vests.

Once the mating season of its chosen moth species is over, the bolas spider is obliged to find other sources of food. So it changes its bait, making a new range of cocktails, each designed to attract a different species of moth.

Deadly lures *A bolas spider (right) relies on quick reactions to ensnare passing insects with a sticky globule on a string. A New Zealand glow-worm (below) uses its natural light to attract insects towards its sticky 'fishing lines'.*

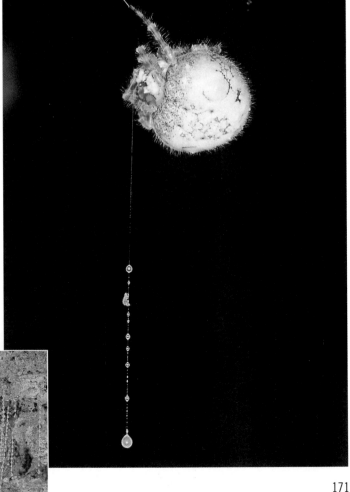

LYING IN WAIT – CAPTURE BY DECEIT

Camouflage or disguise enable predatory animals to make themselves inconspicuous. This allows them to get close enough to their prey to capture it.

Hunters that hide and wait to pounce on prey

Not all hunters chase or stalk their prey: some lie in wait. For them, being able to blend inconspicuously into the background is crucial. It gains them that vital fraction of a second in attacking prey – time that can make all the difference between a meal and an empty stomach.

The simplest way of blending into the background is through camouflage – colouring and patterning that conceals body shape. This is the method employed by the South African horned adder, a snake that lies almost invisible among the rocks as it waits for a suitable meal to come along.

Submerged in the sand
This strategy is taken to the extreme by the Namib desert adder. Not only does it match almost perfectly the colour of its surroundings, but it also buries itself in the sand with only its eyes exposed. Even so, the adder may have a long wait in this sparsely populated area. Its chances might be improved if it were able to wait in a spot that its prey found particularly attractive – a technique that is used by flower, or crab, spiders.

Flower spiders may be red, pink, purple, yellow or white. Such bright colouring is very rare among

predators that sit and wait, but as the flower spider sits on a flower that is attractive to its prey – such as butterflies and other insects in search of nectar and pollen – it is generally very difficult to see.

Invisible spiders *So effectively does this flower spider (above) match the colour of the petals behind it that an unsuspecting fly which landed on the flower has fallen victim to the ambush and become the spider's meal. Flower spiders not only match the background colour of a flower but may even appear to be part of the flower (right), as they lie in wait for pollen and nectar-seeking insects.*

Hidden death *Only the eyes of the desert adder (left) are visible as it lies in the sand of Africa's Namib Desert waiting for prey. By hiding and remaining motionless, it ensures that its victim, such as a mouse, will get close enough for it to strike.*

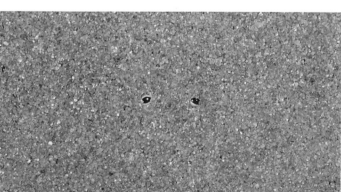

Things are not always what they seem to be

Waiting inconspicuously for a meal is a simple and effective feeding strategy, but it does have limitations. A slight movement can reveal the hunter's presence and alert the prey. Some spiders adopt a rather different approach: they mimic not the background, but another creature. One species of jumping spider that mixes with soldier ants has fang-like chelicerae, or biting tools, that resemble ants' jaws. Other tropical spiders have false eye spots on the front or rear, making them resemble ants.

It was once thought that these adaptations allowed spiders to get near ants and feed on them, but in fact ants are only a small part of their diet. The real advantage seems to be that the disguise protects them from birds and helps them to get near small flies less likely to fear ants than spiders.

False front *As weaver ants work on a leaf in Sri Lanka, another lurks beneath. But this is really a jumping spider with a false eye spot, mimicking the ants for safety and also waiting for prey.*

Dangerous mimic *Although there seem to be two ants on this leaf, the one on the right is a spider, its front 'feelers' legs.*

Unlikely partners *A coral trout swims casually among other fishes, swiftly snapping one up when it can. Drifting close beside it, a trumpet fish uses the trout as a cover until it can dart out to suck up a victim – often snatching away its partner's meal.*

Trumpet fish make an undercover approach

Tropical trumpet fish have a way of hiding from their prey. In order to get close, unseen, they approach behind another fish.

A relative of the sea horse, the trumpet fish has a long thin body and a trumpet-shaped snout. So closely does it drift beside its larger 'cover' fish that it often appears to be attached to it. If the cover fish is a predator it may lose its prey to the trumpet fish, which sometimes succeeds in snatching a meal from under its nose by sucking it in through the tiny mouth at the end of its tubular snout. Sometimes the trumpet fish hides behind a vegetarian such as a parrot fish, the easier to sneak up on unsuspecting prey.

The larvae of dragonfly-like ant lions catch prey by excavating a conical pit and then hiding at the bottom under the dry, dusty soil or sand. Small insects that fall in find it difficult to crawl up the pit's slippery, unstable sides, and the ant lion, alerted by falling particles of soil, seizes its victim in its large and deadly jaws.

Snatching a meal *Buried in the soil at the bottom of a pit, with only its eyes and jaws showing, an ant lion seizes an ant that has fallen in. The ant lion must eat enough to last it for the rest of its life – for once it becomes a winged insect it will not eat again.*

Lone hunter *An arctic wolf sits alert and surveys its surroundings in northern Canada. After scenting prey, maybe more than a mile (1.6 km) away, the wolf stands still and sniffs the air before tracking down the animal, its pale coat camouflaging it in the snow. Loners are often young animals that have left their family to start a new pack. A wolf alone hunts small prey such as beavers and hares, though wolf packs can run down moose and caribou.*

WILY HUNTERS THAT BLEND WITH THEIR BACKGROUNDS

An animal's ability to change shape and colour or to merge with and dissolve into its surroundings benefits the hunter just as much as the hunted.

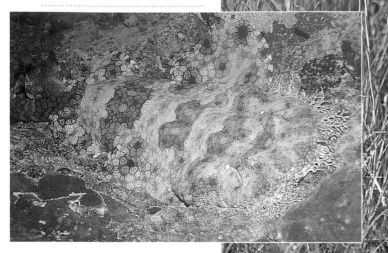

Disrupted outlines for concealment in the open

It is not just the hunted that need camouflage. Many hunters need it too, to conceal themselves until the final moment of the attack. The tiger's stripes and the leopard's spots both blur the animals' outlines and help them to blend with dappled light filtering through the forest canopy or with the shifting patterns of waving grass. Utilising their coloration, they can creep up on some unsuspecting antelope, or lie in wait until it comes near.

A different way to disrupt the outline is to evolve some unexpected and unusual appendages to the body. This is the route chosen by the Australian carpet shark, or wobbegong, which has seaweed-like fronds fringing its fleshy lips and sprouting from its head. With its flattened body and mottled patterning, the shark looks like no more than part of a coral reef or weed-covered rock while lurking in shallow water for its prey.

The angel shark, another native of Australian waters, lies on the sea bottom and snaps up fishes as they pass. Not only is the shark camouflaged by its sandy colouring, but its flattened body with its large, wing-like pectoral and pelvic

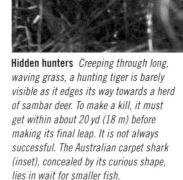

Hidden hunters *Creeping through long, waving grass, a hunting tiger is barely visible as it edges its way towards a herd of sambar deer. To make a kill, it must get within about 20 yd (18 m) before making its final leap. It is not always successful. The Australian carpet shark (inset), concealed by its curious shape, lies in wait for smaller fish.*

fins gives it more than a passing resemblance to a harmless ray.

The warty skin of the Brazilian tree frog is the same colour as its surroundings of dead leaves. As it sits in wait for passing insects, it is further disguised by three fleshy horns — one over each eye and one above its nose — that look like curled-up bits of fallen foliage.

The cheetah that has changed its spots

The news is not so much that of the leopard that changed its spots, as that of the king cheetah. Over the past century, this subspecies of cheetah, found only in eastern Zimbabwe and northern Botswana, has developed horizontal stripes of joined spots along its spine and blotches on its flanks. No one quite knows why.

One possibility is that the king cheetah's habitat has changed from grassland to a mixture of

grassland and forest, and has therefore adapted its camouflage for hunting both on plains and in woodland. This has brought it more into competition with the larger and more powerful leopard.

Although its normal spots give the cheetah disruptive camouflage when stalking in grassland, they would be less effective from a leopard's viewpoint among the branches overhead. It has been suggested that, from above, the stripes on its spine may blend with branch shadows and make the cheetah less obvious — enough, perhaps, to make a leopard hesitate to attack.

176

Changing coat fashion according to season

Colour contest *A snowshoe hare leaps for its life, pursued by an arctic fox. Both their coats have changed to white as camouflage against the winter snow.*

Some animals change the colour of their coat with the seasons. The snowshoe, or varying hare, of northern Canada, for example, is brown in summer and white in winter to ensure its year-round camouflage. The growth of new fur is triggered by certain hormones which build up in response to changes in the hours of daylight.

Thus white fur starts to grow as the days get shorter, and brown summer fur as they get longer.

But the score is kept even by those predators subject to similar variations. The arctic fox changes from a browny grey to white, while the tiny weasel of the far north has fur that turns from chestnut brown to brilliant white.

Quick-change artist *The giant cuttlefish carries sacs of pigment in its skin that allow it to effect dazzling changes of colour and pattern within a fraction of a second.*

Colour change and countershading

One of the most efficient forms of camouflage is the ability to change colour at will, in order to blend with the background while on the move. Squid-like cuttlefish are masters of this technique. Their skins are studded with nerve-controlled, elasticated sacs of pigment, called chromatophores, that can be almost instantly expanded or contracted, so changing their skin colour. Thus adult cuttlefish can float unseen in the

water, while the young can lie on the bottom, indistinguishable from surrounding pebbles.

The cuttlefish's colour change is triggered by its eyesight. Additional information about its orientation comes from the statocyst, a small, fluid-filled organ that helps to maintain balance by sensing the position of the head in relation to the pull of gravity. This signals the least change in the position of the cuttlefish's body.

Most fish use countershading to disguise their body shape. A fish with a pale belly and dark back, is difficult to see from below against

the bright surface, or against the dark seabed from above, though when it rolls there is usually a tell-tale silver flash. But when a cuttlefish turns over, it can completely reverse its countershading, lightening one flank when it turns halfway and darkening the other.

The spangled emperor fish of coral reefs has chromatophores that allow it to alter the mottled colouring of its scales. This makes it hard to see in the dappled light

among the weeds and sponges of a lagoon. Flower spiders also use chromatophores to match the hue of the petals in which they wait for prey. One of the childhood experiments of the writer Gerald Durrell was to move a flower spider from a red to a white rose and watch its red colour ebb away 'as though the change had given him anaemia, until, some two days later, he would be crouching among the white petals like a pearl'.

COPING WITH POISON IN PLANTS OR PREY

Poison is used both as a defence against being eaten and as a way of catching a meal – but it can turn into a two-edged weapon.

Seeking plant food that other creatures shun

There is an old saying 'one man's meat is another man's poison'. And some animals, too, survive on a diet of poisonous plants that others will not touch. Scarlet macaws in South America feed on about 50 kinds of seeds and fruit, including some that are poisonous.

One has seeds containing the deadly poison strychnine, but the macaws avoid these by eating only the surrounding pulp.

In the same way as people with stomachache may take Milk of Magnesia, the macaws neutralise the poisons they ingest by eating kaolin, a fine clay that is a basic ingredient of Milk of Magnesia. It binds the toxins to make them relatively harmless. Chimpanzees

have no trouble in eating all sorts of fruit without being affected by the virulent poisons locked in the seeds. Their thick, muscular lips and ridged, bony palates allow them to mash the fruit to pulp without crushing the seeds.

Desert-dwelling American wood rats slake their thirst on the fluid found in fleshy desert cacti. Though 90 per cent water, it is laced with oxalic acid, which is highly toxic in large amounts. But the rats convert the acid into harmless carbon dioxide. Chacma baboons on the fringes of Africa's

Namib Desert eat highly poisonous cactus-like spurge when water is short. In humans, it causes mania, convulsions and death, but the baboons pick off the curved thorns, peel away the thick skin, and chew the woody pith like sticks of sugar cane. No one knows how they are able to neutralise the poison.

Medicine bank *Macaws will fly up to 20 miles (32 km) from their forest homes to visit a river bank rich in kaolin (inset). This is a mineral supplement as well as an antidote to poison, for it contains the calcium and sodium, vital for health, that are lacking in a fruit-and-seed diet.*

Turning the tables with noxious toxins

Monarch butterflies have taken a step beyond mere immunity: they store and recycle poison for their own ends. These butterflies lay their eggs on the poisonous leaves of milkweed, and the caterpillars feed upon them. Not only does this assure them of a constant food supply that almost no other animal will touch, but makes them poisonous to predators too. Their stripes of black, yellow and white or blue, serve as a warning to foraging birds. When the caterpillars turn into butterflies, the poison still remains potent, protecting them as adults.

Sea slugs are masters in the use of poison. When disturbed, some species exude concentrated sulphuric acid through the skin, or when in extreme danger spit out a

large dose of the chemical. Many sea slugs that feed on jellyfishes, corals and sea anemones recycle the poisons of their prey.

Sea anemones and jellyfish kill small fishes by firing hundreds of harpoon-like threads from cells called nematocysts on their tentacles. Corals use a similar system in order to defend themselves against predators, particularly starfish. Each nematocyst contains a thread that is coiled spring-like at more than 150 times air pressure. On contact the cell explodes, and drives its barbed and venomous threads into the attacker.

Sea slugs are able to eat corals and anemones without being harmed by ingested nematocysts. Some indeed, by a process that is still not understood, end up at the tips of the fleshy tassels covering a slug's back. Even more remarkably, the slug can somehow select only the largest and most violent nematocysts to commandeer for its defences, or fire at its enemies, while digesting the rest.

Birds beware *The vividly striped caterpillar of the North American monarch butterfly eats the poisonous leaves of milkweed, rendering itself venomous. It remains so even when it has changed into an adult butterfly.*

Avoiding the results of a poisonous meal

Some animals and plants produce poison to deter predators, but these often manage to find a way round the prospective meal's defences. Some even manage to avoid the poison altogether.

American grasshopper mice and skunks, for example, both feed on a species of night-foraging darkling beetle. When molested, this beetle spurts a cocktail of assorted venoms from its rear end. The mouse, however, moves in fast to seize the beetle and push it bottom-down into the sand. As the beetle discharges its poison into the ground, the attacking mouse starts eating its head. The skunk out-manoeuvres the beetle by 'defusing' it – rolling it round with a forepaw until it has discharged all its poison.

Woolly monkeys of the Amazon rain forest tree canopy must also exercise care when seeking a meal. Many of the trees of their habitat exude poisons of different kinds, which the monkeys combat by eating young leaves in which the poison has not yet reached full

Careful consumer *Although leaves are the staple diet of this woolly monkey, they are poisonous and it has to choose them with care. Eating young leaves, in which the poison has had little time to build up, is its best safeguard.*

concentration. Although they defecate frequently, which helps to purge them before the poison is absorbed, they cannot avoid taking in some poison. When their bowels complain, they move to another species of tree whose different poison they will be able to tolerate until the build-up begins again.

EATING FOR A HEALTHY LIFE

Whether through instinct or experience, many animals supplement their diets with health-promoting minerals and even medicinal plants.

In search of salts *Elephants seek out Kitum Cave's salt-rich volcanic rocks (above). Mountain gorillas (left) eat volcanic earth to obtain the vital minerals that keep them in good health.*

Rocks and earth help to balance diets

Though animals get all of their energy from the food they eat, they may still lack vitamins and minerals which must be sought elsewhere. For some African elephants, volcanic ash provides the salts that are an essential dietary supplement.

These elephants live in a largely mountainous region on the border between Kenya and Uganda, where heavy rainfall drains minerals from the soil. To balance their diet, they visit caves in Mount Elgon, which was once an active volcano, where there is mineral-rich rock formed from ash and volcanic debris. Once inside the cave, the elephants sniff the air to detect the best seam of mineral salts. With their tusks they prise chunks from the walls, then slowly chew them.

Feeding on the soil

Mountain gorillas, which live in Africa's Virunga range, also make use of volcanic ash deposited near volcanoes on the ridges of Mount Visoke. In some places, the earth is rich in calcium and potassium, and in the dry season the gorillas dig out and eat the salt-rich soil. In very rich sites, their excavations have gone so deep that they have created caves, supported by the exposed roots of trees. The gorillas continue to dig about among these roots for health-giving minerals.

Slothful living *Not all animals select and eat particular plants entirely for their health. The Indian sloth bear apparently chews the fermented flowers of the madhuca family to get pleasantly inebriated. Unlike other bears, the sloth bear has long curved claws that it uses to hang upside-down from trees – just like a sloth.*

Genes and gender *The social status of a female howler monkey influences the gender of her young. Either way, her impulse is to ensure that as many copies of her genes as possible are passed on.*

Generally, plant-eaters have to supplement their diets because their usual food plants lack some essential nutrients. Moose in North America browse on tree and shrub leaves in deciduous forests. If this were all they ate, their diet would be seriously deficient in salt. So they usually live near water and wade into lakes and rivers to eat water plants. These, though low in calories, are high in salt content.

Australian koalas feed mostly on eucalyptus leaves, and dine on different species at different times. This is probably a way of maintaining the correct body temperature, because some trees contain oils that raise temperature, and others have oils that lower it.

Even meat-eaters feel the need to top up their diets occasionally. Dogs and cats sometimes eat grass. The reason they do so, it is believed, is because it contains folic acid – one of the B vitamins necessary for maintaining essential body-building proteins.

Not every animal sticks to a healthy diet. Whether intentionally or not, some animals eat plants out of sheer self indulgence. In India's central highlands, sloth bears become drunk through eating fermenting madhuca flowers. And in Lappland, reindeer experience a state of euphoria by nibbling certain hallucinatory mushrooms.

A birth-control mystery waiting to be solved

Choosing the gender of offspring would be a remarkable exercise in birth control. But it has been suggested that female Costa Rican howler monkeys are able to do it by eating leaves that contain a drug whose workings are, as yet, not fully understood by scientists.

Dominant females in a troop tend to give birth to dominant young males. It is in these females' interests to have sons, because a successful male can father up to 40 offspring in his lifetime and the mother's genes will be copied many times in subsequent generations.

These females always get the first choice of food as the troop moves into a new area, and they may select the specific plant with the gender-controlling drug. Lower-ranking females may be left to feed on 'normal' leaves, since they need daughters to pass on their genes as their sons are usually overlooked when it comes to mating.

Chimps know how to take their medicine

Many animals, like most humans, resort to some form of medicine when feeling ill. But chimpanzees actually seem to be able to link the eating of certain plants with relief from sickness.

It has been observed that chimpanzees occasionally eat a few leaves of *Aspilia* plants, which are rather like sunflowers, in the early morning. Unlike their usual mode of eating, they do not gulp them down. Instead, they carefully massage the leaves in their mouths for about 15 seconds without chewing, then swallow them whole. *Aspilia* leaves contain thiarubrine-A, a potent drug used in tropical Africa to combat infection from bacteria, fungi and intestinal worms. By massaging the leaves, the chimps

release the drug into their systems via their mouth tissues; if they chewed and swallowed them as they do most leaves, the drug would probably be destroyed by stomach acids. Why the chimpanzees take the drug only first thing in the morning is not known for certain. Perhaps this is when the concentration of thiarubrine is at its highest, or perhaps it stimulates waking up.

Sick chimpanzees have also been seen eating plants of the vernonia and spiderwort families. They chew vernonia shoots and suck the bitter juice, as do Africans with stomach disorders. This is an antibacterial plant that helps to boost the immune system. Commelina, the spiderwort plant eaten, grows in marshy places and is an antibiotic and anticoagulant.

In North America, the Navahos say they learnt from brown bears

how to use certain plants of the lovage family to get rid of parasites. They watched the bears chew, spit, then scratch the roots, which contain anti-parasitic compounds, into their fur.

Medicinal value *Chimpanzees swallow the stiff, hairy leaves of spiderwort plants without chewing. The milky sap is a remedy for earaches and fevers.*

UNUSUAL FISHERMEN STALK THE WATERS

Although their techniques may differ greatly, cats, birds, bats and bears all take advantage of the rich bounty of food to be found in rivers and lakes.

Fish feast *In a tree in Malawi (inset), a mallard-sized Pel's fishing owl tears into a freshly caught fish. An osprey (above) leaves the water with a big catch. These birds hit the surface hard, shattering the calm of underwater life as they seize a fish in their talons.*

Fishing birds adopt different strategies

The usual image of an owl is of a silent bird of prey swooping out of the night, its foray punctuated by the shrill cry of a mouse. But some owls have developed other methods. There are fishing owls, for instance, that inhabit wooded watersides in Africa and Asia. These feed mainly on fish and other water animals, and they are neither silent nor nocturnal. Since fish cannot hear them, they do not need to pounce quietly. And since they cannot detect the sound of a fish underwater, they do not need acute hearing.

Fishing owls rely on eyesight to catch their prey so they hunt by daylight. They perch on tall trees close to the water's edge, and after spotting a fish, swoop down and snatch it in their long, curved talons. These claws have a lower cutting edge like a knife blade, while sharp-edged spines on the

undersides of their feet help the birds to keep a firm grip on the wriggling, slippery fish. Their feet and legs are bare, since feathers would soon be fouled by fish scales.

Ospreys too, are spectacular flying fishermen. As they glide and soar 100 ft (30 m) or more above the ocean or a lake they scan the water for fish. Once a fish has been spotted the ospreys dive headlong towards the water. At the last minute before hitting the surface they swing their hooked talons forward to seize the fish. Strong legs enable them to withstand the shock of striking the water. Their momentum often carries them into the water, and occasionally even beneath the surface.

Like the fish owls, ospreys have sharp spikes on the undersides of their feet to ensure a firm grip on prey; they also turn back their outer toes to improve their hold.

Indoor fishing *An African black heron, waiting for a fish, crouches under the hood created by its wings. This bird's unusual technique has earned it the name of 'lomba comba', or 'he who fishes indoors'.*

The osprey carries its catch to a perch to eat, the fish held head forward to reduce wind resistance.

African black herons are more relaxed fishermen than owls or ospreys. Wading in the shallows of a lake, the black heron half raises its wings, curving them forward like an umbrella, and crouches with the tips of its feathers brushing the water. Cloaked by its dark

feathers, the bird waits. It is thought that the fish may be lulled into thinking the water below is shaded by a dark overhanging rock. But those seeking the shade are soon skewered and swallowed. Another explanation for the bird's behaviour is that perhaps the canopy shades its eyes from the sunlight sparkling on the surface as it peers into the water.

Catch and carry *An Indian fishing cat spots a large fish in a stream near Dudhwa, North India (far left). Without taking its eyes off its quarry, the cat jumps into the stream and pounces. After a brief, slippery struggle (left) the fish is caught and the cat carries off its meal to eat elsewhere (below). If it were not for the efficient protection of its thick, waterproof coat this cat would look rather like a drenched domestic tabby — but larger and more muscular.*

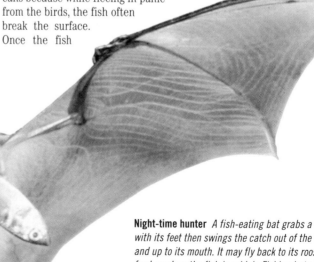

Furry fishermen pluck their food from streams

Cats do not normally like to get their feet wet, but the Indian fishing cat appears to positively relish a dip. Fish are its main food, although it will also eat crabs, frogs and snails, and it is quite happy to plunge into the rivers and pools in search of a meal.

At first glance the fishing cat might be mistaken for a rather large domestic tabby. But few domestic cats grow to the size of a cocker spaniel. Fishing cats can be 3 ft (1 m) long in the body and weigh up to 18 lb (8 kg). Their legs are well-muscled for swimming and wading and slightly webbed feet help them to swim, as well as helping to get a good grip on both rocks and fish. Another important adaption to their aquatic lifestyle is waterproofing. An outer layer of long, coarse fur stops water reaching the fishing cat's skin or its underlayer of fine, insulating fur.

North American grizzly (or brown) bears have a fishing season in July, when the sockeye salmon surge upstream to spawn in Canadian and Alaskan rivers. This is the only time that the normally solitary bears can be seen in large gatherings, tolerating each other in order to take advantage of the glut of fish. Standing on the banks or wading out to rocks the bears snatch salmon as they leap up rapids or waterfalls. Failing that, the bears scoop the resting salmon from the shallows with their paws.

Bats seize on fish that break the water surface

There are no fishing owls in the Americas, but there are fishing bats. Like other bats, the fishing bats send out sound pulses that bounce off obstacles to produce echoes. The bats read the echoes to pinpoint the shape and position of the object. However, only a small percentage of a bat's call can penetrate water, making it difficult for them to locate their prey. They do their fishing by homing in on the ripples that fish make as they break through the surface of the water.

A tiny stir on the water is sufficient to alert the bats to a fish's presence, or the merest tip of a fin just breaking the surface skin. Bats will often follow fishing pelicans because while fleeing in panic from the birds, the fish often break the surface. Once the fish have revealed their position, the bats swoop low over the water, skittering their large feet through the wavelets until they touch a victim and seize it in their sharp, tight-gripping claws.

Night-time hunter *A fish-eating bat grabs a fish with its feet then swings the catch out of the water and up to its mouth. It may fly back to its roost to feed, or chew the fish in midair. Fishing bats have long legs and large, strong feet with sharp claws for plucking their slippery prey from the water.*

FLY AND DINE

The most expert fliers have bodies designed aerodynamically, so they are fast and agile in flight. Some even eat and drink on the wing.

High precision hunters of the air

A jet fighter among birds of prey, the peregrine falcon combines precision, high-speed attack with high-class aerobatics. Classically designed for speed, it has a stocky body with pointed, tapering wings and a slim, short tail. With a bird such as a dove in its sights, the falcon starts by circling above the victim then dives almost vertically towards it, folding in its wings and closing its tail feathers as it goes to form itself into an increasingly sleek, narrow, pointed projectile. A dive such as this is known as a stoop, and with its aerodynamic drag so dramatically reduced, a stooping falcon can reach speeds of 112 mph (180 km/h) or more.

Usually, the stoop ends as the falcon strikes its prey with talons outstretched. But if the stoop fails and the falcon misses, it can chase the bird on the level at a speed of 60 mph (96 km/h). The blow from a peregrine's talons usually kills its prey instantly; its curved beak is used mostly for plucking feathers and tearing flesh.

Smaller and with shorter, more rounded wing tips and a longer tail, the sparrowhawk is designed for manoeuvrability rather than high speed. It hunts in woodland, where it needs to make tight turns among the trees and has no room for headlong dives. Sparrowhawks depend on ambush, flying out to surprise a victim such as a blue tit with a short, swift attack; but they can pursue with speed and agility if necessary, usually catching the prey in their talons before it can dive for cover.

One of the finest aerial acrobats is the hobby, a smaller relative of the peregrine falcon with scythe-shaped wings that give it both speed and manoeuvrability – it is fast enough to catch a swallow in flight, and agile enough to take a dragonfly on the wing. Courting hobbies provide breathtaking daredevil displays as they fly skywards until they all but disappear, then plummet to the earth like skydivers, opening their wings at the last moment. Male and female chase through the air together, gliding, hovering and looping, and sometimes in midair the male passes the female a tempting titbit of food. Now rare in Britain, hobbies are summer visitors only, flying south some 2500 miles (4000 km) to spend winter in the African sun, south of the Sahara.

Hot pursuit *The peregrine falcon uses sheer speed to hunt its prey in flight. A successful blow from its talons instantly breaks the neck or back of its victim, often a pigeon (above, left) or a small duck such as a teal (below) – although sometimes much heavier birds such as geese may be tackled. To achieve the greatest speeds, the peregrine folds its wings and plummets into a breathtaking 'stoop'. Falconers make the most of the bird's efficient hunting skills, taming and training peregrines to bring prey back to their masters.*

In-flight food *Three weeks after hatching, swallows are ready to fly and from that moment they rarely touch the ground. They drink on the wing, using skilful flight control to skim pools, puddles or streams. In the breeding season, parents feed their young with insects (above) which they catch in the air. Dragonflies also feed in flight (right), making the most of their exceptional eyesight and great manoeuvrability to catch smaller insects.*

Aerial acrobats that live on the wing

Swifts and swallows spend much of their lives in the air, eating, sleeping and drinking in flight – swifts even mate in the air. Both species feed primarily on insects, their short, gaping bills sieving moths, flies and aphids as they fly.

No birds spend more time in the air than swifts which, contrary to expectation, are not built solely for speed. They need to fly efficiently as well as fast, so have long wings and a low body mass in relation to wing area, and bear short, shallowly forked tails that reduce drag and increase lift. The long wings mean that less energy has to be spent on supporting the bird in the air.

The flight of a swift is about 70 per cent more efficient than that of other birds of comparable size. A thick fringe of feathers round their eyes, like eyelashes, guards against insects striking them, and their transparent eye membranes act like windscreen wipers, removing particles with each blink.

Dragonflies, too, are skilled fliers that eat, drink, fight and mate in flight. They have two pairs of wings and can reach speeds of

30 mph (48 km/h), as well as hover and fly backwards. A dragonfly's eyes have about 30 000 separate lens-like facets – more than any other insect – allowing it to see as well as most mammals. Dragonflies pluck their prey straight out of the air, catching them within a basket formed by their legs, and usually consume them as they fly.

A high-energy diet that fuels a fast lifestyle

As it darts around amongst the flowers, a hummingbird could be mistaken for an iridescent insect – some of these tiny birds from North and South America weigh less than a large moth. As they hover, they suck nectar from flowers, forming their long tongues into a tube to draw it up.

It is usual for hummingbirds to enjoy 50-60 feeds from flowers, and consume half their bodyweight in nectar every day. They must stock up on a high-energy fuel, sugar, to keep up their fast way of life. Hummingbirds are able to beat their wings more than a million times without stopping, at a rate of up to 80 flaps a second. Their hearts beat 1000 times a minute, and they take 250 breaths a minute. If human beings were to expend energy at the same rate, their bodies would heat to a temperature of 399°C (750°F) and burst into flames.

Powered by sugar, hummingbirds can reach flying speeds of up to 47 mph (75 km/h), but use more fuel in relation to their size than a jet fighter aircraft. The faster they fly, the more flowers they can visit, so the extra energy gained makes the energy expended worth while.

There is no free food, however. Plants need to be pollinated in return. For each sip of sugary solution, a hummingbird gets a fresh dusting of pollen, which it then takes to another flower, aiding the plant's chances of reproduction.

Hummingbirds have to remember which flowers they have visited and return to them in carefully timed rotation. If a bird returns too soon to a flower, the plant will not have replaced its supply of nectar and the bird will not get enough energy to compensate for its journey. On the other hand, if it does not make its visit soon enough, a rival may get there first.

Hummingbirds tend to fall into two categories: long-distance fliers and territory holders. The long-distance fliers travel between widely dispersed flowers with little nectar. They often have larger wings and expend less energy. In contrast, territory holders guard clumps of blossoms fiercely. They usually have much shorter wings and burn up more energy. They can refuel faster with less travelling to do, so can afford to expend some energy on keeping neighbours at bay.

Fast food *Rivoli's hummingbird, a native of North America, pokes its long, thin bill into a flower to extract nectar. As it hovers at around 60 wing beats a second, it takes up nectar with its long tongue at the rate of 13 draws a second.*

MAKING A LIVING OUT OF BEES

Many creatures rely on bees for their daily food, so bees' nests – with their rich stores of honey, beeswax and larvae – are prime targets for thieves.

Alliance of necessity *A black-throated honey guide perches on an African tree stump (above), next to a broken piece of honeycomb while angry bees buzz around it. These birds are able to digest wax, so eat the comb as well as the bee larvae growing inside. African honeybees nest in inaccessible places, so the honey guide cooperates with a honey badger (inset) to get at a meal. The honey badger follows the bird to the nest and uses its powerful front paws to tear it open and take the sticky honey.*

Bees make a meal for honey badgers and birds

Black-throated honey guides of Africa and Asia track down bees' nests, but rely on someone else to break into them. All the birds in this family eat beeswax and bee larvae, as well as insects taken on the wing. In Asia, the orange-rumped honey guide feasts off the exposed, hanging honeycombs built by giant honeybees. But wild African bees nest in rock crevices and hollow trees that are difficult to reach, so the African honey guides need help.

When a black-throated honey guide finds someone likely to help it open up a nest it starts to draw attention to itself, chattering noisily, like a rattling matchbox, and flicking its tail. Both humans and honey badgers have learned to read the bird's signs and to follow it to the sticky treasure.

Honey badgers live mainly on insects grubbed from under tree bark or stones, but their common name comes from their occasional raids on bees' nests. The honey guide, chirping encouragement, leads the honey badger all the way to the bees' nest. On arrival, the bird falls silent and the badger

Honey raiders *The bushmen of the Kalahari Desert in Namibia long ago learned to heed the message of the honey guide. Here they have discovered a bees' nest laden with honey in the trunk of a huge baobab tree (right and above).*

tears open the honeycomb with the large claws on its powerful front paws. To calm the bees, the badger rubs a pungent secretion round the nest from a gland beneath its tail. In any case, its tough, loose hide protects it from stings. Once the badger has had its fill, the honey guide moves in to dine, feeding on both the wax combs and the grubs inside them. Apart from certain invertebrates, these birds are the only creatures that are known to digest beeswax.

East African bee-eaters also eat bees, snapped up in midair. These aerial acrobats sometimes hitch a ride on a kori bustard, which at about 40 lb (18 kg), is the world's heaviest flying bird. As a foraging bustard walks through the grass, flushing out insects, the bee-eater sitting on its back flies off briefly and snaps them up.

It is the only recorded example of one bird hitching a ride on another in order to obtain food.

Bee breakfast *The little Australian rainbow bee-eater (right) is a skilful hunter of bees on the wing, snapping them up from below with a twist of its head, often after a zigzag pursuit. The bird carries its catch to a nearby perch, where it tears out the sting and removes the venom by rubbing the bee against the perch before swallowing it whole. Honeybees are the bee-eaters' main food, although they will also eat other insects such as wasps and dragonflies.*

GIVING A HELPING HAND

Animals are not naturally helpful but necessity produces unusual partnerships. Some creatures simply cannot live without one another.

All in a day's work *A brightly coloured shrimp appears to dice with death in the jaws of a moray eel (left). But in fact it is a welcome guest, because it feeds on parasites and damaged tissue. Crabs in the Galápagos Islands do a similar cleaning service for marine iguanas (above). A cow (right) lies in the Indian sun, allowing a cattle egret to clean her face. The bird delicately picks off parasites with the tip of its long beak.*

A cleaning job that profits both parties

For the sake of a quick meal, a cleaner wrasse fish of the Indo-Pacific coral reefs will swim into the jaws of death, or at least into the mouth of a voracious moray eel perhaps 20 times its own size. Yet the giant eel makes no attempt to eat it. In fact it seeks the wrasse's attentions. Cleaner fish and their customers have developed a working relationship for their mutual benefit – the cleaner fish gets a meal of parasites and diseased tissue, and the host gets comfort.

A cleaner wrasse advertises its services with its conspicuous white and black coloration, and by its wriggling swimming action. Often this attention-seeking can be so successful that there are queues of fish waiting for service at its cleaning station. But parasites make up only about a fifth of the wrasse's total diet. The rest is derived from the scales and body slime of the parasites' hosts.

Customers of some cleaner fish are protective towards their cleaners. Caribbean grouper fish, for example, which are serviced by small blue-and-white gobies, warn their cleaners when danger threatens. If the goby is cleaning the grouper's mouth, the grouper shuts its jaws, but leaves a big enough space for the goby to swim out. If the goby is cleaning a gill cover, the grouper flicks the cover down but lets its cleaner fish escape before fully closing it.

Some gaily coloured shrimps also operate cleaning stations and advertise their services by waving their long antennae. Rock crabs on the shores of the Galápagos Islands live in the midst of packed colonies of marine iguanas, and clean skin ticks off the reptiles. Cattle egrets, found in many of the world's warmer countries, clean ticks off grazers such as cattle or buffaloes; oxpeckers provide a similar service for animals like rhinos on the African plains.

Farmer ants and mercenary ants

Some ants earn a living by dairy farming. They protect herds of aphids against ladybirds in return for honeydew, a sugary solution which the sap-sucking aphids produce. The ants 'milk' the aphids, caressing them with their antennae to persuade them to yield up their honeydew.

Though it is usually nutritious, honeydew can be high in sugar but low in protein. So one species of Asian ant that herds mealy bugs, which also suck sap, carry the bugs in their mouths from pasture to pasture. This ensures that the creatures always feed on tender young foliage, a diet that is high in protein, and so provide the ants with a rich honeydew.

Some ant species are employed by plants to protect them from insects. South American candelabra trees, with their large leaves, provide bed and board for a private army of ants, housed in their hollow trunk and stems. Every day, the ants feed on the plant's starchy white nodules. In return, the ant army viciously attacks any insect trespassing on its plant – which is why this group is known as *Azteca* ants, after the ancient warrior race of Central America.

Scrub jay chicks benefit from an extended family

In the Florida scrub, jay parents like to keep the family at home. They need them to help raise the new brood of chicks. The jays form extended families in which the brothers, sisters and older sons and daughters of the breeding pair act as nursemaids. Because territories that provide sufficient food and nesting places are in short supply in their oak scrub and semi-desert habitat, the birds are forced to live in groups of ten or so. The younger birds simply have nowhere else to go.

Even though most of the family helpers will not be able to produce their own chicks, they are doing the next best thing – feeding and protecting their relations, who share the same genes. To begin with, anyway, the younger helpers are not very efficient at gathering food. But the practice they get while helping out will be useful should they eventually have their own brood. If the male jay dies, his eldest son inherits the territory and brings up a brood of his own, still with the help of his relations.

Family feeding *The older sister of these scrub jay chicks arrives at the nest with a tasty morsel for them. In extended scrub jay families, everyone helps to feed the new arrivals.*

FEEDING BY THEFT

Flamingos on Lake Nakuru in East Africa's Great Rift Valley provide a plentiful supply of food for hunters and scavengers alike.

On the hunt *The approach of a marabou stork looking for an easy meal sends clouds of pink flamingos flapping into the air in panic. A sick or injured bird that cannot escape fast enough falls prey to a stab of the stork's sharp beak.*

Alternative eating *As well as the marabou storks, young fish eagles — denied space in their overcrowded hunting territories — prey on Lake Nakuru's pink flamingos. Nakuru, a soda lake, has few sizable fish, so the eagles are forced to take flamingos for food. Swooping down to grab a flamingo in its talons (above top), a fish eagle carries its catch (above) to the shore for a hurried meal (right). It must eat quickly as the marabou storks watching the feast are ready to steal the kill if and when an opportunity occurs.*

190

Fighting for food *Menacing marabou storks succeed in depriving a young fish eagle of its meal (left). But not even a marabou (below), which kills by stabbing its victim and pushing it under water, can rely on keeping its meal to itself for long. Others will soon come along to steal what they can.*

STEALING A MEAL FROM SOMEONE ELSE

Not all animals hunt or forage for food, some take what they need from other animals – by drinking their blood, taking bites of their flesh, or else stealing their eggs or the food they have caught.

Liquid lunch *Vampire finches of the Galápagos Islands have bloodthirsty tastes. These small birds peck at the base of the feathers of masked boobies, usually near the elbow of the folded wing, and drink the blood.*

Taking a pint of blood or a pound of flesh

Vampire bats almost, but not quite, justify their reputation. Colonies of these mouse-sized bats are found in Central and South America. They have razor-sharp teeth to sink into their prey but, although they are not averse to attacking human beings, they feed mainly from livestock.

These bats make their long, fine-grooved tongues into tubes to lap up blood from the wound, and have an anticoagulant in their saliva to prevent the blood clotting. It works not for just the half-hour or so it takes them to drink their fill, but for up to eight hours.

Blood is high in protein, but contains few calories, so bats need to consume about three-fifths of their own 1 oz (28 g) body weight at a sitting to sustain their high-energy flight. If a bat goes without a meal for two days, it dies. A female bat who has not found a victim, and is in dire need of a drink, will be fed a meal of regurgitated blood by more fortunate fellow females.

Cookiecutter sharks, that live in the tropical waters of the Atlantic and Pacific oceans, take more than just blood; they take pieces of flesh as well. These 20 in (50 cm) long, luminous sharks have very sharp, triangular teeth – the largest, in comparison with body size, of any shark – in the lower jaw, and several rows of smaller teeth in the upper jaw. They feed by biting into the flanks and backs of whales or dolphins, twisting as they do so to

Attack after dark *The vampire bat's teeth are so sharp that it can bite into a sleeping victim at night, and suck out blood without waking the animal.*

remove a circle of meat. Cookie-cutter sharks' luminescence may be a device to lure large fish into attacking them, so that they can turn on their attackers.

How to break an egg – a consumer's guide

Eggs and insects are part of the diet of dwarf mongooses, which live in disused termite mounds in sub-Saharan Africa. The mongoose smashes an egg in a haphazard way. It grasps its newfound food

Running a risk *Ostrich eggs are a great treat for some animals. A young chacma baboon is not deterred by the risk of being hurt or killed by the parent bird.*

source with its forelegs then hurls it between its hindlegs, in the hope of dashing it against a stone.

Perhaps the neatest egg openers are African egg-eating snakes. Like most snakes, they can operate their upper and lower jaws independently, enabling them to swallow eggs wider than themselves. They have spikes on the vertebrae of their backbones that saw a slit in the shell, and the contents run into the snake's stomach. Once it is emptied, the broken shell is carefully disgorged.

Winged pirates of the oceans and islands

Some sea birds make a living by relieving birds of other species of their fishy catches. In the North Atlantic, for instance, great skuas harass cormorants, gannets and terns until they disgorge or drop their last meal or catch. And great skuas that nest on the cliffs and stacks of the Shetlands, grab hold of the wing tips of gannets, tipping them over in midair so that they cough up their catch. The skuas then catch the food and devour it before it hits the water.

Aerial piracy *A great skua harasses a common tern, forcing it to drop its catch. Skuas also harass birds much bigger than they are, such as gannets.*

Frigate birds of the tropical Indian and Pacific oceans seize the tail feathers of boobies, and shake them until they regurgitate their last meal, then swoop down to catch it in midair, as it falls. Female and juvenile frigate birds are usually the robbers, when the boobies return to feed their chicks. Red-footed boobies are the most rewarding victims, yielding their catches quite readily. The blue-footed species seem to offer more resistance, since with these the frigate birds succeed only about five times out of 100.

Noddies, members of the tern family, steal from brown pelicans. As a pelican sits on the water with a billful of fish, the noddies hover above. When the pelican opens its bill to drain off water, the pirates swoop and snatch some of the fish.

Fleas, leeches and ticks plug into a meal

Fleas dig themselves firmly into their host's skin with tiny barbs on their mouthparts, then suck blood from its bloodstream. Some fleas, like the European rabbit flea, are highly selective and feed only upon one animal species.

A rabbit's life cycle controls that of its flea parasites. When a doe rabbit becomes pregnant, hormones in her bloodstream trigger the female fleas on her body to reproduce. By the time the baby rabbits are born, about a month after mating, the fleas' eggs have hatched, developed as larvae, and matured. The new fleas leave the doe and transfer to her babies.

Despite their reputation, not all leeches feed on blood. Some eat small creatures such as worms and snails, others are fish parasites. Those that feed on warm mammal blood lie in wait in damp places, and stay on the victim only long enough to gorge themselves. Their sharp teeth make a Y-shaped bite and, like vampire bats, they have an anticoagulant in their saliva.

If a leech gets enough blood at one sitting, it can survive without food for more than a year. Blood is four-fifths water, and a leech is known to excrete water almost as fast as it sucks blood. In the past, leeches were often used for bloodletting – a popular remedy for many ailments – and are still used in certain treatments. Hirudin, an anticoagulant, is also obtained from leeches.

The first set of a tick's four pairs of legs are modified to function as cutters, enabling the creature to slice skin. It has a chemical in its saliva that dissolves tissue, so that it can embed its mouthparts in its victim's skin. The saliva also transmits diseases, including typhus.

Hanger on *Some kinds of mite live upon insects and arachnids. Here, a group are firmly attached to the legs and body of a spider-like harvestman.*

Movable feast *Ticks will feed on the blood of one host – such as a snake – for several days before they drop off. Adult ticks can live for up to five years without food. An anticoagulant in their saliva stops blood from clotting while they feed.*

Going unnoticed *A victim may not know that a leech has plugged in painlessly to its skin and is gorging on its blood.*

ARCHERS, SHOOTERS AND SLINGERS

Subduing a potential meal calls for a wide range of skills and weaponry – such as water droplets, gluey threads and minute, poison-tipped harpoons.

Meals by missile for marine marksmen

Unwary insects resting on over-hanging vegetation in the mangrove swamps of the Indo-Pacific oceans are easy targets for hunting archer fish, the sharpshooters of the underwater world. These fish bombard their prey with salvos of water droplets, and can knock an insect into the water usually from a range of up to 2ft (60cm) – but sometimes even from 10ft (3m).

Archer fish use their snouts, which are tilted upwards, like gun barrels. The fish makes a tube by pressing its tongue against a central groove in the roof of its mouth. It then forces water along the tube by contracting its gill covers suddenly. Unlike almost all other fish, archer fish have forward-facing eyes, and this helps them to judge distances. But they are not born with the ability to compensate for refraction – the bending of light as it passes between air and water, clearly seen from the apparent bend in a straw in a glass of water. Young fish shoot wildly, but their marksmanship improves with age.

Shooting parties gather under branches and aim at the same prey, so one is bound to score a hit. But the trophy does not always go to the marksman – once an insect hits the water it is anyone's prize. So sometimes, when the insect is within easy range, archer fish do not wait for the artillery barrage – they leap up from the water and grab the insect with their teeth.

Water cannon *After knocking an insect from an overhanging leaf with a salvo of water droplets, an archer fish makes certain of a meal by leaping upwards to catch the prey as it falls. Archer fish, found in both salt and fresh water, can judge the correct angle of attack for a direct hit from below the surface, then swim rapidly to the spot where the stricken prey falls in the water.*

Tropical glue-shooters and their paralysed prey

A deadly night hunter moves slowly and silently across the damp leaf litter of a forest floor in Central America. It is a type of velvet worm, *Peripatus*, that hunts small creatures such as spiders, millipedes and insects.

There are about 20 species of velvet worms, the largest reaching 6 in (15 cm) long. They each have a segmented body with many pairs of fleshy legs along the sides. Most of the legs end in little claws that are used to hold slippery prey, but two pairs have been modified – one set to form jaws with hard claws on the end, and the other pair to form a 'gun' that shoots glue.

Although the worm moves slowly, this can be an advantage, because its stealthy approach allows it to get right up to its victim unnoticed. It often sets its sights on a cricket, and unless the prey reacts quickly, it is struck by a

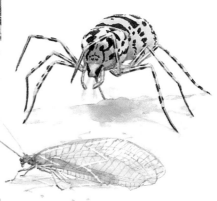

Fatal lapse *There is no escape for a cricket caught in a velvet worm's gummy threads. It failed to notice the stealthy hunter's approach in time to leap clear.*

20 in (50 cm) stream of glue. The struggling victim soon gets its legs stuck together, and if it continues to squirm, its captor stills it with more squirts of glue. The glue hardens in contact with the air, forming a sturdy rope.

With its prey subdued, the worm pierces a soft spot in the cricket's body with its claw-like jaws and injects a lethal dose of saliva, which poisons the prey and begins to predigest it. Later, it will suck out the juices. A large meal may satisfy the glue gunner for up to a fortnight, but often it has to share the feast with scavengers such as spider-like harvestmen,

the hyenas of the forest floor, who sidle up to grab a piece.

Glue is an expensive ammunition. It is manufactured in the kidney from protein, and each time the worm fires, it loses weight and energy. So it eats the rope as well as the prey, thus recovering as much of its expenditure as it can.

Glue is also used by tropical spitting spiders to capture their insect prey. They shoot out sticky streams from their jaws in a vigorous zigzag pattern, that quickly reduces the victim to a gummy lump. It is an action too fast for

Deadly deluge *Spitting spiders are common in shady places in the tropics. These spiders do not spin webs – they overcome their prey by spitting a sticky stream of glue at the victim.*

the human eye to follow – the spider simply seems to shake its head and its prey is immobilised instantly. The glue is produced in modified poison glands in very small amounts and no one, so far, has succeeded in discovering its chemical composition.

The sea anemone's barbed broadside

Its flowery name belies the sea anemone's deadly nature. Found on rocks from shallow waters and tidal zones down to the deepest parts of the ocean, it is not as

innocent as it appears, for its colourful, petal-like tentacles are capable of killing. On each one there are thousands of nematocysts, specialised cells containing tiny structures like harpoons.

When a small fish brushes up against the anemone, it triggers off a massive harpoon attack.

Each harpoon is firmly attached by a thread and has a poisoned barb that, once lodged in the prey, cannot be taken out. With its poisoned victim paralysed and secured by the thread, the anemone then devours its prey.

Lethal weapons *A heavily armed anemone (above) has just shot its poisoned harpoons into an incautious fish. Another harpoon carrier is the related Portuguese man-of-war (left), which also discharges barbed and poisonous stinging cells. It is capable of killing large fish, and can even prove fatal to human swimmers.*

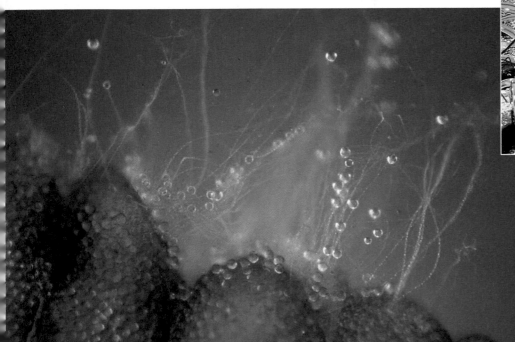

LARDERS FOR LEAN TIMES

Many animals store food against the possibility of shortage. Some of their hiding places may seem bizarre, but they are ingenious too.

Under cover *A red fox buries a newly killed hare in the snow (above). Foxes often secrete their prey, and have good memories for finding it again.*

Careful hoarders that appear to plan ahead

Perhaps the best known of all food hoarders are grey squirrels, which gather nuts in autumn and store them for winter meals, by burying them all around, in a number of different sites.

Acorn woodpeckers of North and Central America are systematic in the way they store nuts, fruit and insects. They drill holes in dead trees and place one item into each hole. An American tit, the black-capped Carolina chickadee, hoards seeds and other food to see it through the winter. The bird makes caches in autumn, when food is plentiful.

Making provision

Seed-eating giant kangaroo rats of the Californian deserts store food after rains, in readiness for future long dry periods. Having collected the seeds in their cheek pouches, the rats dry them out before burying them in small caches.

North American red, or pine, squirrels hide mushrooms, which they dry first to reduce the risk of them rotting in winter. But their principal store is of pine cones and chewed cone cores and flakes, buried in untidy middens that may cover an area the size of a small town garden.

Mountain-dwelling pikas that live above the tree-line in North America and Asia, are among the most thorough of animal hoarders. To survive the snowbound winters, the tiny pikas, which look like a cross between a mouse and a rabbit, harvest grasses and other plants and spread them on rocks to dry. Then each pika builds a small haystack, which it jealously guards from its fellows.

Arctic foxes could not survive without previously buried food stores to rely on. The icy climate keeps their caches, of birds, animals and even eggs, well refrigerated. Red foxes also bury surplus kills and eggs too, usually those of ground-nesting birds.

The fox's habit of burying surplus food may account for the apparently uncontrollable killing frenzies it indulges in when it breaks into a hen run, killing every bird in sight. The fox is probably responding to its need to obtain extra food for storage, and kills all it can, even though it cannot carry away all the birds it kills. It has been overwhelmed by the sheer number of easy kills. In the wild, no prey animals would be as readily caught as hens in a run.

Certain big cats, such as lynxes and North American mountain lions are also known to bury their surplus prey, although they do not dig holes. Instead they scrape a layer of dead leaves and twigs over the meat to keep it hidden.

Saving for the future *The acorn woodpecker (left) of American oak and pine woods prepares for winter by drilling holes in trees to store acorns. It leaves a trail of tree trunks patterned with acorn-filled holes (above). Some trees sport as many as 30 000 holes, drilled by generations of woodpeckers.*

A high table for big cats in the treetops

Leopards protect their food from hyenas and other scavengers by hauling it up into the fork of a tree. Dragging an antelope that weighs almost as much as itself some 30ft (9m) off the ground requires a considerable amount of strength. Leopards have powerful leg and neck muscles, but even so, the exertion of carrying the dead weight wears them out and they often have to rest for half an hour or so before they eat. A stored carcass may last two or three days.

Safe storage *A leopard rests next to the carcass of an impala calf, which it has dragged up onto the branch of a tree. Leopards often store their prey in this way to secure it from scavengers.*

Maintaining freshness in the store cupboard

As many as 1000 paralysed worms have been found in a mole's larder, stored there for eating in the winter when food is difficult to come by. A solitary eater of earthworms, the Eurasian common mole, like all food storers, has to prevent its food from going bad, and has devised a perfect technique for keeping its stockpile of worms fresh. It bites their heads off, which surprisingly does not kill them, then paralyses their bodies with its venomous saliva – since the worms are still alive they do not rot. The mole then seals up the victims in a cavity in its underground burrow system.

Short-tailed, or mole, shrews that live amid grass or leaf litter in eastern North America have similar habits. They prefer solitude, have venomous saliva, and also store prey such as sawflies, snails, beetles and worms in a state of paralysis.

Tropical honeypot ants have larders of a different kind – living honeypots. These extraordinary storage vessels are in fact ants, specialised types known as repletes, that are an important part of the colony. At times when sap-sucking aphids are plentiful, the worker ants force-feed the repletes with honeydew – stroked from the aphids and carried back to the nest – until they become pot-bellied and cannot move. They are hung from the roof in rows and, when food is scarce, workers stroke the bulging honeypot ants with their antennae, stimulating them into regurgitating their precious food supplies.

In autumn, beavers stockpile water plants and aspen and birch branches by the underwater doors of their lodges for winter fodder. The submarine larders keep the plants fresh. And when the water is frozen over, the beavers will still have ample food to see them through the worst of the season.

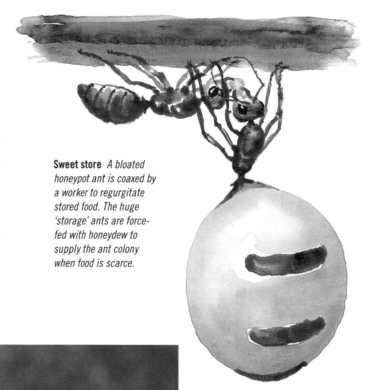

Sweet store *A bloated honeypot ant is coaxed by a worker to regurgitate stored food. The huge 'storage' ants are force-fed with honeydew to supply the ant colony when food is scarce.*

Refrigerated food *Alaskan beavers in autumn collect woody plants in preparation for winter. The stems are stored by the underwater entrance to the lodge, or at the base of the dam. The water temperature, at well-nigh freezing point, preserves the plants and maintains their nutritional value.*

MANAGING WITHOUT EATING

Many animals can go without food in times of scarcity. Survival often depends on the ability to store body fat and cut down moisture loss.

Store cupboards for easy transportation

Camels can travel long distances over several days with little or nothing to eat. They manage to do this by storing fat in their humps. The stored fat can be broken down in the body to produce energy, carbon dioxide and water.

At one time it was thought that the camel's hump acted as a chemical water reserve. However, in order to burn fat an animal needs oxygen, and to get more oxygen, it has to breathe faster. Breathing results in water loss, and rapid breathing means more water loss than usual, so in fact more water is lost than is gained. The camel's hump, therefore, is not a water barrel but a food reserve. A camel that has not had enough to eat has no hump at all, but one that is well fed carries a large hump. Thus a camel weighing 1100 lb (500 kg) can store up to 440 lb (200 kg) of fat in its hump, enough to keep it going for up to six months if it is not working hard.

Body fat is the most efficient way for an animal to store food because it contains up to 200 times more energy than other body tissue. One problem with fat, however, is its bulk – a fat animal cannot move as easily as a lean one. For a desert animal, another problem is heat retention. Most animals store fat all over their bodies, but a layer of fat under the skin prevents cooling. So in a hot desert the best place to store fat is a single receptacle such as a hump. A camel's hump allows the animal to store food for lean times and yet keep cool by losing heat freely from the rest of its body.

Tail-end storage

In a hot climate, the tail is also a convenient place for storing fat. The southern Australian dunnart resembles a mouse with a fat tail. In summer this marsupial eats vast numbers of grasshoppers and other insects, from which surplus fat builds up in its tail. This fat store keeps it going in the winter, when there are few insects about.

Fat-tailed Madagascan mouse lemurs also indulge in a frenzy of eating to build up fat stores in their tails and rumps which sustain them through the dry season. Some Australian and Asian geckos also survive hibernation and food shortage using fat stored in their tails, which swell up like balloons.

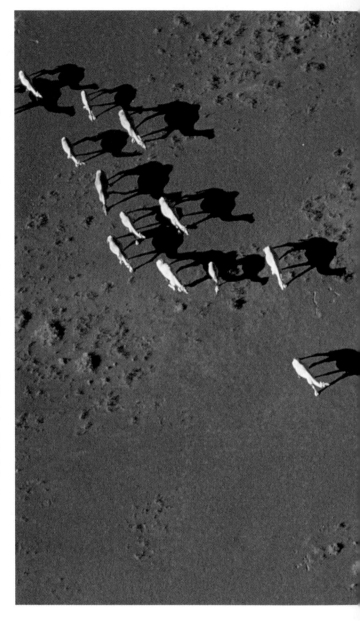

Desert crossing *A string of hardy dromedaries, one-humped camels, makes a long, hot journey across Kenya's Koroli desert. Camels cope well with dry terrain. They can go without food for weeks and manage without water for days – then drink deeply to recover.*

Dredging up a meal *Its head turned to the side, a grey whale feeds on small, bottom-dwelling ocean creatures off Vancouver Island. It may make two passes over the area – first stirring up the top 1 in (25 mm) of food-laden sediment with its snout, then scooping up mouthfuls and filtering out the nourishment.*

Building up body bulk for breeding success

Grey whales can almost double their body weight in a good feeding season. This is just as well, for during their long journey every year from the Bering Sea to their winter breeding grounds in Mexico's warmer waters, their main source of food in northern waters, shrimp-like krill, is scarce.

Along the way and at their breeding grounds, the grey whales forage for such creatures as crabs and tubeworms, but their daily

Snow baby *A three-month-old polar bear cub peers out at the world from between its mother's forelegs. In feeding and caring for her offspring, she has drawn on her body fat throughout the winter.*

when the bear family has emerged from the den and the cubs start taking solid food, their mother has to share all her catches of fish and seals with them. So by spring, she is only half the weight she was six months before, at the end of the previous summer.

From coast to sea
The life of the ancient murrelet is also austere. Named from the fringe of white feathers about its head that gives it a resemblance to an old man, this thrush-sized auk breeds on Canada's Pacific coast. The female lays two large eggs, each weighing about 25 per cent of her own weight, in a burrow close to the shore. Both parents take turns at incubating the eggs, changing shifts only at night so as not to attract the attention of predators.

To remove the chicks from any danger and take them as soon as possible to the food source, the parents lead their young to the ocean on the second night after hatching. Encouraged by parental chirps, the large-footed chicks stumble seaward over roots and rocks and finally launch themselves into the water. Although only two days old, thanks to the nourishment contained in the large eggs, they are already 15 per cent of adult weight. Much of this is in a layer of body fat that insulates them from the cold and supplies the energy needed to survive in their harsh nursery. It also cushions them against injury during the march to the ocean.

consumption is far less than their normal 1-1¼ tons. To fuel their mating and their return north, the whales rely on extra blubber carried under their skins, in their tails and round their internal organs.

Humpback whales from both Arctic and Antarctic waters stop feeding altogether during their breeding season in tropical waters, because the krill on which they fatten up in their cold-water feeding grounds are not available. The males are also more concerned with mating than feeding.

For northern fur seals as well, mating precedes feeding. These

seals go ashore to breed on the Pribilof Islands in the Bering Sea. The males arrive first and, because no female will mate with a male who has no territory, they fight to establish a patch on the beach, defending it day and night to keep rivals at bay.

The males have no time at all to snatch a meal, and rely on their body fat to sustain them through this arduous time, which may last for 30 days. How well each one manages depends on how fat he was to begin with – the fatter the male, the longer he is likely to be able to hold a territory.

Cold comfort for bear cubs and auk chicks

The polar bear mother does not eat from November until about March. During this time, holed up in the Arctic snow, she gives birth to up to four cubs and nurses them. Her youngsters are utterly dependent on her rich milk for the first three months of their lives. To supply it, and to nourish herself, the mother bear subsists on the thick layer of fat beneath her skin, built up in the summer months when food was plentiful. Even

FOOD FOR FREE – SCAVENGING

Scavenging serves to clear away the remains of carcasses left by predators and provides carrion eaters with an easily acquired meal.

Winged scavengers pick corpses clean

Eating someone else's leftovers is often less dangerous than catching your own food. Vultures are superbly designed to survive by eating the carcasses of animals killed by other hunters or animals that have died naturally.

Soaring with their long, broad wings on thermals – rising warm-air currents – vultures travel great distances with little effort. Their exceptionally keen eyesight allows them to spot the carcass of an animal such as an antelope from more than 1 mile (1.6 km) off. Different types of vulture have different tactics. In Africa, white-headed vultures and lappet-faced vultures search the ground from a fairly low level, but white-backed and Rüppell's griffon vultures soar much higher and watch for hyenas and other vultures to lead them to a kill. In the New World – where the condor is the largest vulture of all – turkey vultures use their powerful sense of smell to detect rotting meat.

Largest and most aggressive of Old World vultures, rare lappet-faced vultures are named for the flaps of red skin that hang from their faces. Weighing about 15 lb (7 kg), with a wingspan of 8 ft 6 in (2.6 m), they can drive smaller vultures from a feast until they have eaten. Their individual eating preferences allow different species of vulture to feed off the same carcass. Lappets prefer the coarser tissue and tendons, which they twist off with their powerful beaks. When dead animals are not abundant they hunt small live prey such as hares.

The white-backed and Rüppell's griffon vultures are smaller, with long, bare, snake-like necks that enable them to delve deep into a carcass in order to reach the soft, internal organs without fouling their feathers – although sometimes they will climb right inside. Backward-facing spines on their tongues help them to rasp off gobbets of flesh. Hooded and Egyptian vultures, the smallest of the Old World species, rely on the scraps.

'Vulture' bees

Another winged scavenger, a type of tropical stingless bee, is known to supplement its diet of pollen and nectar with carrion. To tackle a carcass, some workers form a circle and tear at the skin to make a small hole. Then other workers go in and work from inside. As they chew the meat, the bees partially digest it using a substance in their saliva. They then return to the nest and regurgitate the meat for the rest of the colony.

A group of 60-80 of these bees can reduce a dead frog to bare bones in three hours, and a group 1000 strong can similarly dispose of the carcass of a monkey.

Sky riders *Vultures soar on rising hot air, so cannot fly high until the ground warms up. The larger the species, the later in the day it appears in the sky. The hooded vulture of North Africa, being one of the smaller species, can lift off fairly early.*

Star-shaped scavengers of the sea floor

Starfish, which are named for the star-formation of their five 'arms', rely on their keen sense of smell to locate food – and predators such as tritons (giant sea snails). Some species feed on dead fish, or even dead starfish, but they are also voracious hunters. Starfish stalk the seabed on suckered tube-feet, and prey mainly on molluscs such as mussels. A starfish wraps itself round the mussel shell, clinging on with its suckered feet, and pulls the two halves of the shell apart with a steady tension that tires out the mussel. As soon as there is a slight gap, the starfish turns out its stomach through its mouth onto the soft body of the mussel, and begins to digest it. After it has done so, the starfish pulls its stomach back inside itself.

Normally starfish hunt or scavenge alone, producing a chemical that repels their fellows. But sometimes, after a certain amount of exposure to the chemical, they begin to find it attractive, and congregate in swarms perhaps thousands strong. Such a swarm can devastate an oyster or mussel bed.

Stomach turning *Bat, or cushion, starfish of the northern Pacific Ocean do not prey on shellfish such as mussels, but can turn out their large stomachs to dissolve the flesh of any soft-bodied creatures, including those of their own species. A starfish's digestive juices are secreted from sacs circling the upper part of its stomach.*

Undertakers of the desert and plains

All scavengers are invaluable as the undertakers of the animal world. The Sahara's blazing heat claims many casualties, because not many creatures can tolerate for very long surface temperatures that rise to 70°C (158°F).

Silver ants are the small-scale undertakers of the desert. They emerge in armies from their cool burrows under the sand when the ground temperature reaches about 46°C (115°F), towards the hottest

Power and endurance *So strong are the jaws and stomach of the spotted hyena (above) that it can devour a whole wildebeest carcass – bones, hoofs, horns and hide. These hyenas, although they are scorned for their scavenging habits and ugly looks, are also very efficient hunters. Silver ants (right) brave the hottest part of the day in Africa's Sahara Desert to feed on the dead body of a grasshopper. At this time they are less likely to fall prey to a desert lizard.*

part of the day, to gather corpses of creatures such as spiders and woodlice. Silver ants can endure much higher temperatures than any other land-living creature, but even they have to find sufficient food to eat before the ground heats up to 55°C (131°F). Once the surface temperature gets to around 50°C (122°F), they cool off by climbing up stems of dried vegetation – if they fail to find any, or do not get back to their burrow soon enough, they die.

These ants have a good reason for choosing this cruel time for their forays. At other times they are likely to be lapped up by the desert lizard, which often lives near an ant burrow. When the sun is at its hottest, the lizard is forced to retreat from the heat.

On the plains of Africa and Asia, hyenas are among

the most efficient of scavengers. Their jaw muscles are so strong they can crush bones with ease, and their stomachs can digest both skin and bones, allowing them to extract the utmost nourishment from a carcass. They regurgitate horns, hooves and hair as pellets. Hyenas have good night vision and a very keen sense of smell, and can scent carrion with ease. A hyena's nose is at least 50 times as sensitive as a human's.

Hunting for live prey

Although hyenas are well known as scavengers, they also hunt regularly, chiefly at night, tracking prey down with their keen noses. They hunt alone or in packs. In Africa south of the Sahara, spotted hyenas – which are the largest of the four species of hyena – hunt and kill more animals than they scavenge. A fully grown animal is strong enough to tackle a wildebeest about twice its own weight without any help.

TAKING THE WATERS

Water is essential to life, but some creatures make do with little of it and others find the simple act of drinking fraught with danger.

A drink on the wing *The graceful swallow spends a great deal of its time in flight, and it is adept at taking a drink while skimming low over the surface of rivers and ponds.*

Keeping a watchful eye open at the waterhole

Forever wary of predators, and justly so, many small birds have evolved specialist adaptations for the particularly vulnerable act of drinking. Woodpeckers and sparrows, for example, fill their bills with water then tilt their heads back to let it run down their throats, so casting a glance about at each tilt between dips. Pigeons and doves, on the other hand, drink fast with a pumping action, and because they are briefly unsighted as they do so, the time spent in thirst quenching is brief.

Some animals are simply not well designed for the act of drinking. The elephant overcomes this problem by sucking water up in its trunk and squirting it into its mouth. An adult elephant's trunkful amounts to rather more than

1 gallon (4.5 litres), and it needs to drink 19-24 gallons (85-110 litres) of water a day. However, the trunk technique is one that takes a while to learn, and baby elephants, until they have done so, lap water awkwardly with their tongues.

Giraffes have made other adaptations. Each time a giraffe lowers its head to drink, it has to raise it again from 7 ft (2.1 m) below its heart to 11 ft (3.4 m) above; in theory, this could cause it to pass out from the sudden loss of blood

from the brain. But the giraffe possesses an extremely fast heartbeat – 150 beats a minute – so its circulatory system is better able to withstand sudden shocks.

In addition, the blood vessels supplying the brain have elastic walls that can cope with sudden increases of blood, and valves in the neck artery stop blood rushing to or from the brain as the head moves up and down. All very necessary to an animal that must constantly look about while drinking.

Drinking styles *An elephant calf (left) now three years old, neatly places a trunkful of water in its mouth; a year earlier its aim would have been less certain. A giraffe's stance (below) leaves it vulnerable to predators.*

Where water droplets divide life from death

For animals dwelling in deserts or semi-deserts, getting sufficient moisture to support life is a constant preoccupation. One way of meeting the challenge is to avoid working up a thirst.

The koala of eastern Australia's eucalyptus forests, for example, rarely descends to the ground, where it is both clumsy and in some danger from dingoes. With little opportunity for drinking, it gets what moisture it can from its diet of leathery eucalyptus leaves, which are low in nutriment. It eats around 1 lb (450 g) of these each night, and conserves energy by sleeping for up to 18 hours a day.

Kangaroo rats have made more constructive adaptations. They live entirely without drinking in the hot, dry deserts of southwestern USA, yet have achieved a far more active way of life than the koala. Their only moisture comes from the seeds they eat, which draw a certain amount of moisture from the damp earth in the animals' underground stores.

The kangaroo rats are admirably geared for conserving body fluids. They have no sweat glands, and by passing exhaled air over cool nasal passages and absorbing the condensed moisture, they cut water loss to a minimum. Their dung is dry, and the small amount of their urine so concentrated that it has twice the salt content of sea water. They save moisture, too, by sleeping the days away in cool, humid burrows, emerging to forage only in the cool of the night.

Camels are the most renowned of water conservationists. They too minimise water loss by passing concentrated urine and dry dung; camel dung is so dry it can be used as fuel as soon as it is produced. Even in very high temperatures, a camel can survive for about a week without drinking, and up to three weeks in more moderate climes. A man who sweated away 14 per cent

Dawn drink *A Namib darkling beetle chills its rear in cool sand, then points its rear upwards to condense mist on it.*

of body weight would die of overheating as his blood became too thick to circulate properly. But a camel can tolerate losing 30-40 per cent of body weight, and make it up again in one gargantuan drinking session – it can absorb about 9 gallons (40 litres) at a time.

Many mammals maintain body heat at about 37°C (98°F), but a camel conserves body water because it does not sweat until its temperature is 40.5°C (105°F) – high fever in a human. The excess heat stored by day is dissipated in the cool night as the camel's temperature sinks to 34°C (93°F), so

Cool koala *The Australian koala keeps its temperature down simply by sitting still for most of the day. It finds what water it needs in gum leaves.*

no water loss is involved. But the most miserly of moisture retainers must be the Namib Desert's darkling beetles, which capture dawn mist on their chilled, upturned rear ends, where it condenses and trickles down to their mouths.

Animals that drink salt water to survive

Sea water is too salty for human beings to drink. 'Water, water, every where, nor any drop to drink', said the Ancient Mariner of Samuel Taylor Coleridge's poem. It is true that many land-based living things would not long thrive by imbibing salt water, but a few creatures that were originally land-based have successfully adapted to salt-water living. Both sea otters and seals have kidneys geared to excreting excess salt. Sea turtles and marine iguanas have evolved salt glands that do the same thing, as have most seabirds.

Seabirds of the 'tube-nose' group – such as giant petrels, albatrosses and fulmars, which seldom touch land except to breed – have long, tubular nostrils at the tops of their bills. These may be involved in the birds' ability to navigate by scent, but they have another use too. Excess salt from ingested sea water is transferred from the blood to large nasal glands at the bill base; these excrete a concentrated salt solution, giving the birds an air of suffering from perpetual colds. In cormorants the fluid from nasal salt glands runs down inside the bill to emerge at the tip.

A sufficiency of salt *The giant petrel of the Falklands (right) and the cavorting California sea lions (below) have both evolved mechanisms for getting rid of excess sea salt. The sea lion has specialised kidneys and the bird dribbles concentrated brine from its nostrils.*

SUPERSENSITIVE SIGHT

Birds of prey have sharp eyes for locating food from a height or in cover. Other creatures have exceptional sensitivity to heat and light.

The amazing eyesight of feathered hunters

A sharp-eyed human being is often described as 'eagle-eyed'. Yet an eagle's vision, like that of other large birds of prey, is much keener than that of any human. Its sight is so acute that from 2 miles (3 km) high, a potential meal of rabbit size is crystal-clear. The bird owes this ability to the light-sensitive cells in its eyes – they are eight times more densely packed than in a human eye, making them more sensitive to fine detail.

As with most hunters, an eagle's large eyes are situated at the front of its head, so the images received by its eyes overlap to produce a three-dimensional picture, essential for accurately judging distance when making a high-speed kill.

Hawk eyes *The eyes of the African fish eagle (left) are so sharp that it can pinpoint a fish beneath the surface of the water below and dive in to catch it. The Asian brahminy kite (right) quarters the swamps, attuned to the tiniest movements of frogs or lizards. The prey is seized in its talons and often eaten while the bird is on the wing.*

Warm prey *The simulated image (below) suggests how a viper locates a rat with the heat sensors in its snout. The boa (left) has sensors on its upper jaws.*

Pit vipers' sensors to defeat the darkness

Although rattlesnakes do not have particularly good eyesight, even in the dark they can locate a mouse up to 6 ft (1.8 m) away, and strike accurately. This is made possible by the rattlesnake's ability to 'see' heat. Like all members of the pit viper family, it has sensitive

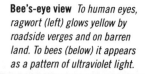

Bee's-eye view *To human eyes, ragwort (left) glows yellow by roadside verges and on barren land. To bees (below) it appears as a pattern of ultraviolet light.*

Flowers send signals to the birds and the bees

Ultraviolet light may be invisible to humans, but bees can see it and use it to their advantage. Many types of flowers – ox-eye daisies, for example, which to humans look as though they have uniform white petals – appear to bees as ultraviolet lines on a white background.

This pattern is a flower's secret signalling system. Like the runway lights at an airport, it is a direction indicator that guides flying insects to the flower's hidden nectar store, ensuring that the route taken dusts them with pollen. Bees rely on flowers for food and the flowers depend on bees to carry pollen from one flower to the other so that they can reproduce. But bees are not alone in their ability to see ultraviolet – other insects such as moths also read a flower's signals.

Unlike insects, which do not like cold, wet weather, hummingbirds fly in most weathers to collect nectar. They are guided by red light, so some plants, such as bananas, advertise their nectar stores with red and orange petals. Only long-billed hummingbirds can reach the nectar, which lies at the bottom of a long flower tube.

Scarlet gilia plants on Fern Mountain in Arizona, USA, change colour to attract a variety of pollinators. In early summer, deep red, a colour that attracts hummingbirds, dominates over white. But when the birds leave, more white than red flowers are produced. White gilias attract hawk moths, which remain all summer. When moths are the only pollinators, the white flowers set twice as much seed as do the red ones.

Flower pollinator *Bees and other insects gathering nectar inadvertently pollinate flowers. Pollen from the flower's male anther sticks to the insect's body and brushes off on the female stigma of the next flower that the insect visits.*

cells located in pits in its snout that can detect infrared light. Humans recognise infrared as the heat which emanates from all warm, living bodies. A snake uses its sensors to distinguish the temperature difference between an animal and its background, even if the difference is no more than a fraction of a degree.

The snake's heat-sensitive cells send signals to the same part of the brain as do the eyes, producing an image that is a combination of thermal and visual information. The sensors also inform the snake how far away its prey is, and in which direction it is moving.

As a rattlesnake bares its fangs to strike, its eyes and sensors no longer point at the prey, so it is blinded. But a back-up heat sensor inside its gaping mouth ensures that its fatal bite is on target.

HIGH-TECH HUNTERS

*F*inding food under water cannot be left to luck, so some animals use electrosensors to detect victims and electric charges to kill them.

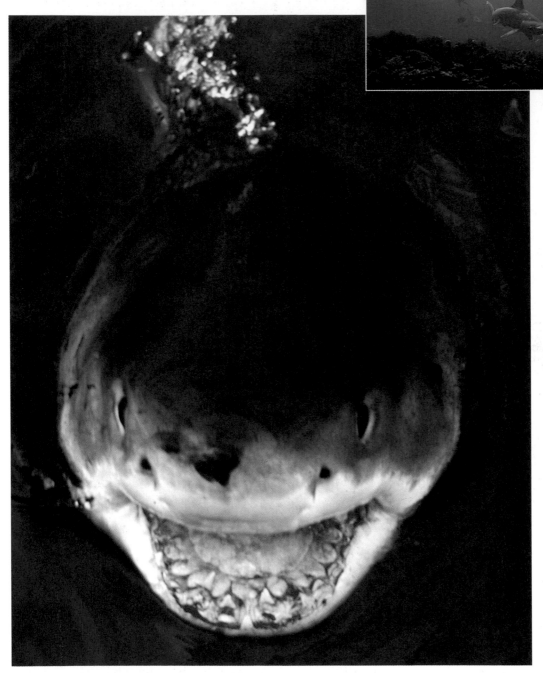

The smile of death *A great white shark (left) moves in for the attack, jaws agape and eyes sunk deep into their sockets for protection against flailing fins or claws. After a night of solitary hunting, hammerhead sharks (above) join forces at their morning meeting place, where they cruise up and down in groups of 30 to 100.*

Sharks – the perfect killing machines

The ultimate underwater hunter-killers, sharks have been in their present state of evolutionary perfection for some 63 million years.

At a distance of 1 mile (1.6 km) or more, a shark can hear and locate accurately low-frequency sounds that indicate a commotion in the water, such as a struggling fish. At about 440 yd (400 m), it can smell weak concentrations of blood or other body fluids in the water, and can then follow the smells to their source.

Using the line of detectors along each side of its body, a shark compares minute differences in the flow of the current and swims up the current to locate its victim. A shark's eyes are ten times more sensitive to dim light than a human being's. Even in near darkness it can see the movement of prey at 25 ft (8 m). If it is heading rapidly towards the surface, it can switch off its dark-adapted system and instantly function normally as it enters the brighter light. But when closing in for the attack, a shark swims virtually blind as its eyes are covered by a membrane or they sink back into protective sockets, depending on the species. At this point a remarkable sense takes over – one that can detect electrical activity. Using receptors located in its snout, the shark can detect minute electrical currents caused by contracting muscles – such as a beating heart – in its victim's body. It is the predator's ultimate attack sense, guiding it in for the last short spurt to the kill.

This may explain why sharks sometimes attack boats. They are not trying to reach the occupants inside but are attracted by the weak electrical currents produced by metal fittings immersed in sea water. In response to the stimulus, the shark behaves instinctively – it opens its jaws and attacks the source of the signals.

This electrical sensing system is also used by hammerhead sharks to detect concealed prey, such as stingrays and flatfish buried in the sand of the seabed. Its curiously shaped head carries the secret of the hammerhead's hunting success – electroreceptors are spread out across its 'hammer' forehead, and these guide the shark precisely to its hidden prey.

A sensitivity to weak electrical signals may also explain how a group of hammerheads are able to rendezvous every morning by the the same submerged reef, after hunting alone all night. It is thought that they might well locate their meeting place by adjusting to Earth's geomagnetic field.

Shocking tails and sensitive snouts

In some species of fish, locating prey, killing it, avoiding obstacles and talking to the neighbours can all involve electricity.

Skates and rays, like their near relatives the sharks, have electroreceptors on their snouts with which they can accurately detect buried food. But some fish can generate their own electricity. The torpedo rays of temperate and tropical seas, South American electric eels and African freshwater catfish have modified muscles that generate high voltages that can stun or even kill their prey.

Some species, such as elephant-trunk fish, are known as 'weak electric fish'. To find their way about in the murky waters of the lakes and rivers in which they live, they generate a weak electric field round their bodies. If the field is interrupted, they know there is an obstacle to be avoided or prey to be caught. To obtain more detailed information about the object, some species, such as South American and African knife fish, can focus their electrical sensing systems. By bending their tails round an object in the water, they can concentrate the self-generated electric field on the object and 'interrogate' it to find out more about it.

These fish can also 'talk' to each other using electrical signals. Each species has its own signal pattern that contains information about its identity, sex and age, as well as about its readiness to mate or to defend a territory. During 'electro-arguments', the electrical pulse rates of the fish rise sharply in an attack pattern. Friendly fish are known to change their broadcast wavelengths in order to avoid jamming the signals of another fish.

Electrical contact *The elephant-trunk fish (above) creates its own electrical field to help it recognise friend, foe or food in muddy waters. Stingrays (left) use electrosensors to detect buried prey, and other rays can generate charges of up to 200 volts. The electric eel (below) stuns its prey with 650 volts. Its legendary ability to kill a horse probably arose when one stunned a horse that then fell in the water and drowned.*

A worm digger down under hunts blind

When scientists in the Natural History Museum in London received the first dried skin of a platypus in 1799, they thought it was a fake. And no wonder – an animal with the tail of a beaver, the fur of a mole, the webbed feet of a frog and a beak like a duck's was unbelievable. But what they could not know was that this egg-laying mammal, or monotreme, from eastern Australia has electroreceptors and touch receptors all over its leathery beak.

As dusk falls, the platypus leaves its daytime burrow on the riverbank and slides into the water to hunt. Once under water, its eyes, ears and nose shut tightly so that it is effectively swimming blind. It then uses its beak like an electric probe as it methodically searches the riverbed for food. This includes worms, water-living insect larvae, small freshwater shrimps, immature water snails and the occasional small fish or frog swimming about in the muddy water.

Shrimp search *Electroreceptors on the beak of the platypus are sensitive enough to pick up, from a distance of about 3-4 in (75-100 mm), the electric field generated by the flick of a freshwater shrimp's tail.*

HUNTING FOR FOOD UNDER WATER

Sharp eyesight is not necessarily an advantage to animals that hunt in the sea or in a river – hearing may serve their needs instead.

Dolphins read echoes to survey the seascape

Vision under the water is often limited, particularly so when the water is clouded by debris or algae. Creatures that live under water therefore tend to depend on senses other than sight. Mammals such as toothed whales, porpoises and dolphins 'see' with sound.

As well as the high-frequency whistles used to communicate with each other, dolphins produce clicks that bounce off objects and provide information about the surrounding seascape – a process called echolocation. The returning echoes, after bouncing off a target, do not enter the dolphin's ear canal but are picked up instead by the teeth of its lower jaw. The teeth absorb the sound vibrations and transfer them to the thin bone of the jaw. From there, they travel along the jaw to the middle ear via a channel of fatty tissue.

The dolphin's clicks, some of which are too high for the human ear to detect, are produced in the complicated plumbing below the blowhole on the top of its head. They pass out through its bulbous forehead, which holds a fatty body known as the melon. This projects them into the sea ahead in a beam fanning out from the forehead at an angle, about 9° in the case of a bottlenose dolphin. If the angle were narrower and the beam any more intense, the sound energy would turn to heat. The beam enables a dolphin to find and identify small objects at great distances. A bottlenose dolphin can locate a tangerine-sized ball from 124 yd (113 m) away.

High-speed analysis

The speed with which a dolphin produces clicks – up to 700 a second – is much too fast for the analytical capability of the human ear and brain. At 20-30 clicks a second our ears fuse the sounds together, so to us the echolocation clicks that can be heard sound like the squeaks of a rusty hinge. But a dolphin can distinguish each tiny item of sound. Returning echoes inform it about the structure of the object that it is investigating and whether it is animate or inanimate. Dolphins in captivity can distinguish between plates of copper and aluminium painted the same colour, and can tell a hollow tube from a solid one.

Most of the dolphin's large and complex brain is dedicated to analysing the returning echoes. They yield detailed information about its surroundings, the movements and composition of its prey and the positions and activities of the other dolphins in the school.

Sound pursuit *As they generally feed at night, when underwater visibility is poor, dolphins like this 12 ft (3.7 m) bottlenose dolphin use sound echoes to find prey such as fish and squid. The bottlenose dolphin is the species that has been most studied by scientists.*

Seals may be 'seeing' with their whiskers

Crabeater seals spend their lives in the cold, dark waters of the Southern Ocean that surrounds Antarctica, apart from when they mount ice floes to rest or to give birth. Yet these seals successfully hunt and navigate, even under the winter ice, and are among the most numerous of sea mammals.

How the seals find their way and track down their food, mainly krill, is a question that has long puzzled scientists. It is possible that they may use echolocation, as dolphins do, but seals have no melon in the forehead to focus sounds, and their hearing appears to be inadequate under water. Seals are known to produce clicks, but they are only at low frequencies that can be heard by humans and these frequencies are not ideal for echolocation.

It is the seals' whiskers that may be the key to their agility in the dark. Each long facial whisker is set into a follicle surrounded by

fatty, connective tissue which is richly supplied with nerve fibres. Each whisker has about 1200 nerve endings attached to it – compared with 200 or fewer in most other mammals. This sensitive tissue is called the sinus membrane and

may be stimulated by sound vibrations travelling down the whiskers. Perhaps, then, seals 'see' through their whiskers, by analysing the vibrations. The theory is yet to be proved, but it may explain how seals can hunt in the dark.

Coming up for air *A crabeater seal breathes at its purpose-made hole in the Antarctic ice. A seal can submerge for about an hour because its rich blood is well supplied with oxygen-carrying red blood corpuscles. It can also slow its heartbeat and other body functions when under water so consuming less oxygen.*

River rovers *Amazon river dolphins (above), like all river dolphins, have longer snouts than their marine relatives. They find fish by echolocation, as does the Ganges dolphin (left), which gets extra information by swimming on its side and touching the river bottom with a flipper.*

Freshwater dolphins with twin scanners

There are freshwater dolphins in several of the world's largest rivers, among them the Amazon and Ganges. They are considered to be less sophisticated than their sea-going relatives, but they use echolocation in much the same way. Visibility in fresh water varies

with the place and season, but in general the clarity of the water is reflected in the degree to which a river dolphin's eyes are developed. The blind susu found in India's River Ganges, for example, where visibility is very poor in places, has eyes with no lenses and muscles that have almost disappeared.

The sound beam produced by a river dolphin fans out at an angle of about 65°, but it is believed that the animal can alter the pattern by changing the shape of its melon. This sound beam, although less intense than a sea-going dolphin's, seems to be just as sensitive.

The susu also has unique crests of bone projecting from the sides of its face which may well help sound transmission and reception in somewhat the same way as a loudhailer. It emits two sound beams – the second one projects downwards and forwards from its throat. It has a flexible neck, like all river dolphins, and when it is investigating an object, the susu nods its head, maybe to bridge the blind spot between the beams.

FOLLOW YOUR NOSE AND FIND A MEAL

Some animals win by a nose in the race to find food. A highly developed sense of smell gives them an advantage over animals that rely only on sight or sound.

It is a sense of smell that makes a dog's life

Dogs all over the world – wolves, jackals, coyotes, foxes, dholes, dingoes, African wild dogs and domestic dogs – have a highly developed sense of smell. They are at their happiest, it seems, when they are sniffing. Sight and hearing are also well developed and play an important part in a dog's life, but it is mostly smell that dominates. Inside a dog's nose there is a sensory surface area much larger than ours, with about 50 times as many smell-sensitive cells. While a human's sensory area is no larger than a postage stamp, the average dog's, if straightened from its folded structure, would be nearly as large as a postcard.

A healthy dog has a cold, wet nose, and scent particles dissolve in its nasal secretions, stimulating the production of more secretions. The nose's shape encourages air to circulate round the sensory area inside. In tests, dogs have been found to be between a thousand and a million times more sensitive to smell than humans are, which is why they are used to sniff out substances varying from edible truffles below ground to drugs and explosives hidden in luggage.

Wolves, when they are passing downwind of potential prey, stop and turn to scent upwind, then head straight for their victim. Studies have shown they can scent prey from a distance of 400 yd (365 m) or more, and a pack has been seen to detect a cow moose and her twin calves from more than 1½ miles (2.5 km) away.

Nose to the ground *The North American coyote combines an acute sense of smell with sharp eyesight and speed to catch food in even the most inhospitable terrain. It sniffs out rabbits, rodents and carrion, and when they are not available, feeds on insects and fruit.*

Kiwi question *No one knows how this hen-sized bird stops soil blocking its nostrils as it grubs about, probing the ground for beetles, spiders and worms.*

Birds that are led by the nose to their food

A kiwi could almost be accepted as an honorary mammal. It looks like a hedgehog, it feeds like a hedgehog and it has a hedgehog's sense of smell – but it is a bird.

In New Zealand, where there are no hedgehogs, the flightless, hen-sized kiwi fills the ecological niche normally occupied by small spiny mammals. The bird has all the senses and the physical make-up needed to root about in leaf litter and to dig up the earth in search of worms, slugs and other such juicy morsels. It searches for food at night, stabbing the ground with its long, sensitive bill.

Most birds that probe the soil use touch or sight to locate their food, but the kiwi relies on its sense of smell. It has nostrils at the tip of its bill and smell receptors at the base in the breathing chamber. Its smell-sensitive membrane is convoluted, like that of a dog, to increase its surface area.

Although the kiwi may appear to be unusual among the earth-probing birds, its sense of smell does not make it unique in the bird world. In North America, engineers repairing damaged gas pipelines began to notice that turkey vultures tended to gather over leaks. This simple observation not only saved them time and money, but provided further evidence that some birds have a well-developed sense of smell.

Old World vultures, such as the griffon vulture, rely on sight both to locate a carcass and to spot other vultures flying down to feed on an open plain. But New World vultures, particularly those flying over forested areas where they cannot see through the canopy of trees, must often rely on smell to detect dead and decaying animals. They have large areas in the brain devoted to the sense of smell.

African honey guides find bees' nests by smell – they have large nostrils edged with raised ridges, on their beaks – and are especially fond of the wax honeycombs as well as the larvae reared inside them. In 16th-century Africa, a Portuguese missionary found that every time he burned beeswax candles in his church, it was overrun by eager honey guides.

On the scent *Perched high on cactuses, these Mexican turkey vultures use their well-developed sense of smell to find carrion, even when it is covered up or hidden from sight in the undergrowth. They provide a useful clean-up service in the wild.*

Amazon fish sniff out seeds in a flooded forest

After the snows have melted in the South American Andes, the meltwater rushes down into the Amazon river basin and drowns huge sections of rain forest. In this strange, flooded world, tambaqui (pronounced tam-bah-key) fish swim between the trees seeking seeds of the rubber tree.

The fish has an extraordinary nose. Each of its funnel-shaped nostrils is covered by a flap that, when raised, allows more water to flow past the smell-sensitive cells inside. Each tree species produces its own unique combination of compounds such as latexes, oils and acids, and it seems likely that the tambaqui can identify trees by their smell signature.

While they are fruiting, trees will undergo distinct biochemical changes, and it is possible that a tambaqui can smell which trees are about to drop their fruits. So it swims around waiting for them to fall. Alerted by the sound of a fruit dropping into the water, the fish then uses its sense of smell to home in on it. Although each fruit has a tough outer casing, the tambaqui has no trouble crunching through it with its strong teeth and jaws to reach the seeds inside.

Risky catch *Rising to the surface to take a rubber seed it has detected by smell, a tambaqui runs the risk of being speared by fishermen who use the seeds as lures.*

211

LOCATING FOOD BY FEEL

Some hunters have a sense of touch so highly developed that they can detect vibrations made by prey on the move through water or air.

Using water ripples to track down food

When a fly falls into a pond, the pull of the surface tension may prevent it extricating itself again. As the insect flails about in panic, it creates tiny ripples, signalling to hungry pond skaters where they might find their next meal.

Supported by dense pads of hair on their legs, the skaters can move easily over the surface of the water. Though they can detect approaching predators by sight, the skaters rely on the ripples sent out by struggling insects to locate food. It is thought that receptors on the pond skater's body can sense the time lapse that occurs when a ripple hits adjacent legs. In this way, the tiny hunter can determine the whereabouts of its victim.

Pond skaters also use ripples to send each other messages and the frequency of the ripples determines their meaning. Signals transmitted at a frequency of about 90 waves a second are messages from one male to another. During their courtship displays, males strike the water at a frequency of 22 ripples a second to attract females. The insects' ability to detect vibrations is so acute that they seem to be able to distinguish individual signals 1½ ripples apart from about 2 ft (60 cm) away.

The Mexican bulldog bat uses echolocation signals to detect the telltale ripples made by the heads or fins of fish breaking the surface of a lake or river. Once the bat has located a fish, it swoops low over the water and snatches up its meal in the sharp, strong claws on its elongated hind feet.

Skating on water *Pond skaters (right) propel themselves across the water surface by 'rowing' with their middle legs. They steer with their hind legs, and use their fore legs to catch prey (above).*

Whiskers – ocean floor radar of the walrus

The walrus, whether male or female, is noted for its exceptionally fine moustache, which is in fact a vital aid in finding food. During the long Arctic winter, walruses feed in complete darkness on the floor of the ice-covered ocean.

Even in the summer, little light penetrates the murky depths, and visibility is never very good.

The walrus's main means of finding food is by touch. At the tip of its snout, it sports a moustache formed by 450-500 whiskers, each one set in an area of thin, sensitive skin. With these whiskers, the animal searches through the mud of the seabed for clams, cockles and mussels, which make up its chief food.

Once it has located a shellfish, the walrus uses a tougher ridge of hard skin on its upper jaw to dig it out. When extricating a shellfish buried in the mud, the walrus squirts powerful jets of water into its burrow. Once the shellfish has been captured, the walrus puts its versatile

A nose for food *The whiskers of walruses (above) and the fleshy tentacles of the star-nosed moles (right) are essential aids to finding food, since both animals hunt in the dark. The mole's feelers wave around constantly as it forages in its tunnels for worms.*

Tigers and tabbies alike rely on whisker sense

All cats, big and small, possess an additional sense organ. If it is too dark for the cat to see, or if its vision is obstructed as it opens its mouth wide to make a kill, its whiskers take over.

Cats have an average of 24 whiskers arranged on either side of the nose in four rows, several more above the eyes and some on the back of the front legs. They are long, thick, toughened hairs that are regularly shed and regrown.

Super sensors

Whiskers operate as feelers which a domestic cat, for example, might use to check that a gap in the fence is wide enough for it to slip through. The whiskers can be moved backwards or forwards at will, according to the task in hand. They are also employed to translate air currents, allowing the cat to detect the presence of a solid object by the minute air eddies it creates, and to react accordingly. When a cat is simply sniffing about, it keeps its whiskers out of the way, flat against its cheeks. But when it is on the move or about to pounce, it points its whiskers forward. When it is about to deliver a fatal bite, the whiskers form a net in front of its mouth permitting it to determine the shape of the prey and judge the precise placement of the bite on the back of the neck. With its prey held firmly, the cat may wrap its whiskers about the victim's body to check for any movement.

The parts of the cat's brain dealing with vision and touch are close together, therefore the two senses are closely coordinated. Combined with the cat's sensitive hearing, they give a detailed picture of the world around. The cat is a very well-equipped hunter, but damage to its whiskers can be disastrous.

Whisker to whisker *Two Siberian tigers use their whiskers to help to size each other up in preparation for a play fight. All members of the cat family use their whiskers – stiff, sensitive hairs on the face and legs – as feelers, or to detect air currents. They enable a cat to find its way, or to judge the shape and size of obstacles, when its vision is impeded.*

moustache to another use. Using its strong whiskers to hold the shellfish in position, it sucks the body from the shell.

Nosing out a meal

Measuring only 5 in (13 cm), the star-nosed mole of North America is named for its extraordinary nose, which is tipped with 22 pink, fleshy, touch-sensitive tentacles. The mole uses these tentacles to feel about for worms and other soft-bodied creatures to eat as it travels through its underground tunnels or swims about in ponds.

The golden mole of southern Africa is almost blind, and 'swims' through the soft sand of its habitat in a constant search for insects and spiders. It has large ear bones that pick up the vibrations of approaching predators, but it relies mostly on its sense of touch to find food.

LOCATING BY LISTENING

Bats are the champions of sound navigation. From the echoes of their calls, they can build up a detailed picture of their surroundings.

Hunter in the dark *As it homes in on its prey, a brown long-eared bat holds its ears well forward to receive the echoes from its own high-pitched shrieks. These bats have ears nearly as long as their bodies – hence their name.*

Bats that listen for the sound of insect wings

Some bats have such sensitive hearing that they can detect the sound of an insect's wing beats. Bats hunt at night, and most spot flying insects by echolocation – they send out high-pitched shrieks at regular intervals and listen for the echoes that bounce off an insect's body. By this means they can pinpoint its position and how far away it is.

The whirr of wings *A pallid bat from North America snatches a moth in midair, having heard the sound of its beating wings. Pallid bats use hearing more than echolocation to hunt.*

Being able to find an insect against a solid background such as a wall, however, is difficult because the wall will also return echoes. Most bats are unable to distinguish an insect against such a background. This 'blind spot' offers a feeding opportunity for any bat that is equipped to take up the challenge. This is what a group of bats known as gleaners have done.

The gleaner group includes the brown long-eared bat of Eurasia and the pallid bat of the American West, which use their particularly large ears to listen for the sound of an insect's wings beating as it prepares for flight, and swoop in for the kill. If there is sufficient light, these bats rely on eyesight to find their way about, but they also use very weak echolocation signals once it gets too dark to see.

Using echolocation to capture prey

As it homes in on a moth, a bat such as a European noctule bat may emit up to 200 shrieks per second in order to locate its insect prey. All insect-eating bats use their sensitive ears to pick up the echoes of these high-pitched shrieks, or pulses, as they bounce back off surrounding objects.

Bats other than horseshoe bats emit the sounds through their mouths. All have large and very

Bats versus moths – a battle of abilities

For millions of years, bats have been hunting moths, and moths have been trying to avoid bats. This has led to an evolutionary arms race in which one contestant constantly tries to outdo the other.

At first glance, bats appear to have a huge advantage over their prey – they are faster and more manoeuvrable on the wing. They do, however, have one disadvantage, the high-pitched shrieks by which they navigate announce their approach before they arrive.

Moths have developed senses to exploit this. Unlike most insects, they have ears, although these are simple – the ear of a noctuid moth has only two nerves, but a human ear, for instance, has 17 000. A moth can therefore detect sound well enough to know that a quiet bat is far away, a loud one too close. As a moth has an ear on each side, it can tell from which side a bat is approaching.

A tiger moth is able to pick up the echolocation calls of the North American big brown bat from about 120 ft (40 m) away, but the bat can only detect a moth-sized object from 15 ft (5 m) away. This gives a moth time to take evasive action. First it flies in large loops, trying to dodge its adversary. If this fails, the moth tries another defence. On each side of its upper body it has a plate with minute ridges on it. When this plate is distorted, the ridges make a loud pop. If the moth produces a pop just as a bat is about to snatch it, the bat may be so startled that it aborts the attack. If this does not work, the moth has one last line of defence – it folds its wings and plummets to the ground, where the bat will not be able to distinguish it against a solid background.

Flying praying mantises have also adapted in an attempt to evade bats. When a mantis hears a bat's signals it takes evasive action. First it flies upwards, then it stalls suddenly and hurtles downwards in a power dive. The bat pursues, but has to pull out of the dive before it is in danger of ploughing into the ground. The mantis lands and waits for the danger to pass.

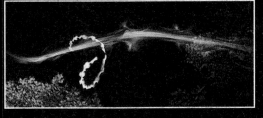

Headlong chase *A long-exposure photo shows a moth looping in a spiralling dive as it attempts to elude a pursuing bat intent on a meal.*

Horseshoe bats check the pitch to find a meal

Horseshoe bats echolocate by emitting sounds through their noses, the calls being focused into a narrow beam by a leaf of flesh round the nostrils. Unlike other types of bat, these Eurasian bats emit their calls at a constant pitch. They tend to fly low, and have broad wings for slow flight and easy turning in narrow spaces such as the caves where they hibernate.

By turning its head to scan from side to side, a hunting horseshoe bat can tell not only the position of an insect by echolocation, but also the direction in which it is flying. It can do this because of the Doppler effect, a phenomenon named after Christian Doppler, the 19th-century Austrian physicist who discovered it.

An obvious demonstration of this effect occurs to a pedestrian as a police car with siren wailing goes by. The siren's notes seem to be higher as the car approaches and lower as it speeds away. This is because, although the notes have not changed pitch, as the car gets closer the sound waves have less distance to travel, so their frequency per second increases, and as the frequency increases so does the pitch. As the car speeds away, the sound waves returning have farther to travel, so their frequency decreases as does the pitch.

A horseshoe bat compares the pitch of the echoes from a flying insect with the pitch of the constant-frequency signals it sent out. An echo of lower pitch than the signal means that the insect is moving away. An echo of higher pitch means that the insect is moving closer. In this way, the bat tracks the insect's flight path.

Last moments *Swooping in for the kill, a greater horseshoe bat makes short work of a moth. These bats get their name from the shape of their noses.*

Silent noise *As a noctule bat flies through the night, it emits location signals. The sounds are too high-pitched for human ears, but they are as loud to a bat as a pneumatic drill is to a man.*

sensitive ears so that they can pick up the echoes from their own signals. Echolocation allows them to both navigate and to spot flying insects in total darkness. A bat's echolocation shrieks are too high for a human ear to hear, but they need to be. Sound travels in waves, the length of a wave being determined by the pitch of the sound. The higher the sound, the shorter its wavelength, and therefore the smaller the objects it bounces off. The highest bat sounds can reach a frequency of 200 000 hertz (or 200 000 waves per second) and can pick up something the size of a midge from 20 yd (18 m) away.

The echoes not only reveal the presence of an object, they also tell the bat its position. Because sound always travels at the same speed in air, the bat can judge distance by the length of time an echo takes to return, and the relative intensity of the sound in each ear tells it the direction. To further aid detection, bats use sound at different pitches.

Usually, each bat call starts at a high pitch and falls rapidly, sending out a range of wavelengths. This has two advantages: the longer wavelengths penetrate farther and scan a wider area, and the shorter wavelengths bounce off tiny objects. Different wavelengths strike an object in different ways and so can give a more detailed picture. A cruising bat maps its surroundings with 10-20 pulses a second, but increases the output rapidly to get more detailed information as it gets nearer to its prey.

AVOIDING PREDATORS

'THE LIFE OF A PREY ANIMAL ALWAYS HANGS IN THE BALANCE, FOR IT
NEVER KNOWS IF IT HAS MADE A SERIOUS ERROR UNTIL A LION
HAS FLUNG ITSELF INTO THE FINAL RUSH. YET PREY IS NOT CONSTANTLY
ALERT; IT DOES NOT ANTICIPATE MOMENTARY DEATH.'
≈ GEORGE B. SCHALLER, *GOLDEN SHADOWS, FLYING HOOVES*, 1974.

Few animals are not at risk from predators at some time in their lives and sudden death is, for many, an ever-present possibility. But there is more to life than merely staying alive. Obtaining sufficient food and securing a mate and a territory also make significant demands on an animal's time. While a zebra grazes with its head down in a patch of grass, or fights with another stallion for control of a harem, it cannot be on the alert for lions.

Unable to spend all their time actively looking out for danger, potential prey animals have adopted a variety of passive defences. Some use camouflage to blend into the background; others make themselves conspicuous, warning of poisonous or dangerous qualities. Armour and defensive weaponry also play their part. Zebras, for example, seek safety in numbers and, as a herd flees in panic, the animals may also be helped by the confusion generated by their dazzling stripes.

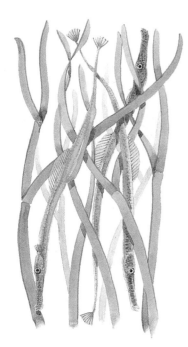

Acting the part
By stationing itself vertically in the water, the peculiarly shaped pipe-fish camouflages itself as a waving frond of seaweed.

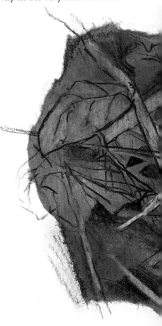

Still life
The mottled colouring of the woodcock blends so well with the leaves and earth round its nest that its best defence is to lie motionless when threatened, hoping to be overlooked, and flying up and away only at the very last moment.

Gentle giant
The sunfish has no obvious means of defence. However, its extremely thick, tough skin and 10ft (3 m) body make it a daunting prospect for predators.

Colour coded
The spotted salamander warns predators of its foul taste with bright colours. Many salamanders exude a mild poison through pores in their skin.

More than a mouthful
By inflating itself and stretching its legs, a common toad can make itself appear much larger than it really is. This is a useful defence against grass snakes that must swallow their food whole.

Racing to safety
A few moments' inattention by a feeding zebra is all a lion needs to get within striking distance. For the zebra, escape depends on speed, agility and the possibility that the lion may be confused by the dazzling pattern of its stripes as it runs with the herd.

Keeping safe *A large colony of puffins nests on Sule Skerry (right), a remote Orkney island. Parent birds find safety in the large flocks that fly back and forth daily, bringing fish to feed their young.*

SAFETY IN NUMBERS

By keeping close together, animals can significantly reduce the ability of a predator to single out an individual and attack it.

Puffins fly in flocks to evade hungry gulls

For most of the year, Atlantic puffins live at sea, diving for food such as small fish or shellfish. But when the breeding season comes round each summer they make their way to coastal cliffs to nest. Here they must share their cliff-top breeding grounds with nesting greater black-backed gulls, large and voracious predators.

To protect their eggs and chicks from attack, puffins nest underground in shallow burrows in colonies up to a million strong. A pair may dig their own burrow or take over an abandoned rabbit burrow. In it the female lays one egg. When the chick hatches, both parents feed it for about six weeks.

Within the teeming, raucous squall of sea birds wheeling about the cliffs, puffins feeding chicks fly to and fro on their stumpy wings with maybe ten or more small fish gripped in their triangular bills.

But between burrows and fishing sites the puffins have to run the gauntlet of patrols of foraging black-backed gulls, that are much larger and quite able to snatch up a puffin in flight. To cut down the risk of being caught, the puffins fly in flocks in a continual shuttle between land and sea.

The flying shuttle is not quite as haphazard as it appears – it is a continual circular procession, and when each puffin leaves its nest, it joins its fellows flying seawards until it is ready to alight on the water. The flying cluster of puffins makes it difficult for a gull to pick one out – it tends to be stragglers that get caught.

When their parents go back to sea for winter, chicks stay alone in their burrows until ready to fly at about seven weeks old. Each then leaves at night to avoid the gulls.

Baboons face attack in battle formation

Leopards are one of the baboon's main enemies. They hunt by stealth, and often spring out from cover in an attempt to make a quick snatch from the troop before battle lines can be drawn.

African plains baboons that find themselves face to face with a snarling leopard on open ground are not too proud to run away if

Frontline defence *An aggressive Asian macaque defends his troop by adopting the defensive stance typical of large monkeys. African plains baboons use similar tactics when facing a leopard.*

there is an opportunity to do so. But if there is no chance of escape, the baboons employ a 'retreat' formation of sorts.

The dominant males of the troop, about the size of large dogs, bare their fangs in a threatening grimace and position themselves between the predator and the females and young. Even powerful predators such as the leopard will flee from the muscular, flailing arms of a mature male baboon.

When crossing exposed terrain, the baboons will usually move in formation, with the females and young at the centre of the party and the strongest males around them. Lower-ranking males walk in front and bring up the rear.

Birds' alarm calls keep mongooses safe

As day dawns, hornbills gather in a group in the treetops of East Africa's tree-scattered grasslands, at the place where a group of dwarf mongooses have their den in a disused termite mound.

But these eastern yellow-billed hornbills present no threat to the dwarf mongooses. This is just the normal start of a day in the lives of the two creatures, which have an unusual relationship that works to their mutual benefit.

The rat-sized dwarf mongoose is the smallest species of mongoose, and is very vulnerable to many different predators, such as hyenas and hawks. The mongooses spend much of their time on the look-out for danger, and guard themselves by living in colonies of up to 20 animals, with sentries on termite towers. They also rely on the support of the hornbills.

Most species of mongoose hunt alone, but not dwarf mongooses, which hunt in packs. As the mongoose pack scurries through the undergrowth foraging for insects and small mammals, the hornbills fly overhead, acting as lookouts in exchange for the rich pickings of insects flushed out by the mongooses. Hornbills have sharp eyes, and their raucous alarm calls when they spot danger make an early-warning system for the mongooses. The mongoose pack has lookouts, too, which give loud alarm calls.

Airborne sentries

Both the mongooses and hornbills have predators in common, such as birds of prey, but the hornbills also warn of predators that prey only on the mongooses, and are no danger to themselves. If the mongooses have not appeared by the time the hornbills arrive in the morning, the birds call loudly to waken them. If, on the other hand, the mongooses rise early and find no sign of the birds, they wait expectantly for them. They are reluctant to set off without their airborne sentries.

Although the two creatures compete for food to some degree, the hornbills never eat young mongooses, although they are quite capable of doing so – but they are not above pushing them out of the way at mealtimes. And if the foraging patch is small, the mongooses chase off the hornbills.

Clusters of foul-tasting nymphs deter predators

Shieldbugs emit a noxious smell when they are threatened, so are also known as stinkbugs. They are believed to have an unpleasant taste, and many of the 5000 species advertise both their bad taste and repugnant smell with bright warning colours. By making sure that they can be easily identified, the bugs reduce the risk of being accidentally devoured by predators.

Newly hatched, wingless, shieldbug nymphs often congregate near their old egg shells, their sheer numbers magnifying the warning effect of their bright colouring. Nymphs of one Peruvian species even line up in a neat yellow row and wave their legs in the air to mimic a moth that is feared for its stinging spines. By staying together until they have moulted several times into winged adults, nymphs stand less chance of having eggs laid on them by a parasitic wasp, or of being eaten by a bird.

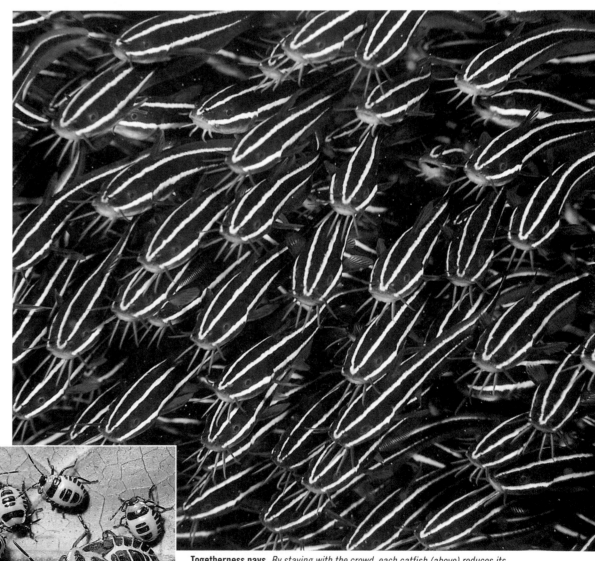

Togetherness pays *By staying with the crowd, each catfish (above) reduces its chance of being the unlucky one that gets eaten by a predator. Brazilian shieldbug nymphs (left) also stay together. Their mother may stay with them and protect them by buzzing her wings, emitting a foul odour and even kicking out at parasitic wasps.*

THE ART OF STAYING STILL

To make the most of camouflage, it is best to refrain from movement. In fact, freezing in your tracks may work even without camouflage.

Sitting tight and staying safe

No matter how close danger may come, many hunted creatures simply keep low and freeze – they know instinctively that nothing attracts attention more readily than movement. Some animals are so confident of their ability to 'disappear', that they freeze in their tracks in quite exposed positions.

The bearded dragon lizard of the Australian outback is a good example. If disturbed in the open while basking on a branch, this large lizard, which can stretch out to 2 ft (60 cm), simply holds itself rigid and points its scaly head skywards. It may not look exactly like part of the branch it is lying on, but neither does it resemble anything edible, so it is likely to be left unmolested.

The dragon lizard has a smaller relative and compatriot, Leseuer's velvet gecko, which disguises itself as a seed cone of a banksia bush, curling its tail and body to copy the cone's design.

Cold-blooded animals that need to sun themselves, even those with elaborate colouring and texture, can be betrayed by the clarity of the shadows they cast. The leaf-tailed gecko of Madagascar has irregular folds of skin hanging from its sides and legs. These alter the gecko's outline and therefore the outline of its shadow as well. Together with its uncannily accurate imitation of the colour and texture of the branches it basks on, this disguise is so effective that the gecko is confident enough to bask in the open.

Disappearing trick *Well camouflaged against a background of lichen-covered bark, a leaf-tailed gecko blends in with the tree trunk on which it is resting. The animal's camouflage is improved by the addition of a leaf-shaped tail.*

Concealing features *Neck extended and bill pointing skywards, a bittern stays motionless among the reeds to escape detection. The brown and buff stripes on its underside so closely follow the pattern of the reeds that the bird becomes almost invisible.*

In hiding against a backdrop of reeds

At breeding time in the spring, many reed beds in Europe and Asia echo to the booming call of male bitterns. These can be heard at a distance of 1 mile (1.6 km) or more, as they proclaim their presence to potential mates.

But once their eggs are laid, the bitterns cease to draw attention to themselves. Although their nests are inconspicuous platforms among the reeds, they are always at risk of being found by minks or other marshland predators.

The birds do their best not to be seen. In its creditable attempt at invisibility, the bittern stands stock-still with its beak pointed upwards. In this way it does not break the pattern of its backdrop – the vertical lines of the reeds. The bittern's eyes can swivel down so that it can see the ground while maintaining its peculiar but effective defensive stance.

Deer who keep a distant watch on their young

Contrary to the usual behaviour of mothers in the wild, the North American white-tailed doe stays away from its young for hours on end during the first weeks of its life. This is an essential part of the maternal safety strategy of many species of woodland deer, including the female white-tailed deer.

The doe behaves in this way so that she will not draw attention to her newborn. She grooms the fawn as soon as it is born, to make it as scentless as possible, and between bouts of nursing she leaves it on its own among the undergrowth. To remain close by would only attract unwelcome attention, so she walks off and watches it from a distance. The fawn remains quite motionless among the woodland debris, where its dappled back looks like a patch of sunlit leaves.

Although young deer are born frail and helpless, they have a full covering of hair, their eyes are open at birth and soon afterwards they are alert to their surroundings. The deer's highly developed senses and survival strategy cut down the risk of detection by bobcats and other foes, and the animals flourish in their forest homes.

Keeping safe by speed and stillness

The brown hare is a familiar sight on European farmland, often to be seen far off as it lopes across an open field. If it sees a fox or a dog, its initial reaction is to crouch down with ears laid back and freeze, which can be highly effective, especially in open ploughland. Only if the enemy gets too close will the hare race away.

But before expending energy on a speedy escape, the hare will always try to avoid being noticed. The decision to flee is left until the last possible moment. If its presence has not been marked in the first place, its sudden retreat can be quite startling.

An animal that has no need to freeze or move fast is the three-toed sloth of the rain forests of South and Central America. It has few natural enemies and lives one of the least active existences of any large mammal. It spends most of its time hanging in languid fashion from a limb high up in the forest canopy, out of reach and out of sight. Its disregard of personal hygiene makes the sloth even harder to see. It grooms itself so seldom, and moults so slowly, that algae (minute plants) grow in its long, greyish brown hair and turn its coat to a delicate shade of green, forming a living camouflage.

Tree-top hiding place *Slumbering in a fork of a tree, the three-toed sloth blends into the Panamanian rain forest canopy by means of minute green plants that grow in the long grooves in its hairs.*

Sheltering in the sand

Because black skimmers of the Americas build their nests along the shores of lakes and lagoons, their chicks are open to attack by gulls and other aerial predators. To survive, the chicks must look after themselves from an early age.

When danger threatens, a black skimmer chick scoops a shallow pocket in the sand and holes up until danger has passed. The chick's speckled coat blends well with its hiding place.

But when there is a suitable low-growing shore plant close by, the chick will hide there instead. It particularly favours those plants with branches growing outwards along the ground. Then the chick wedges itself in between two low branches, with its beak as close to the heart of the plant as possible. The branches obscure the chick's outline, and it virtually disappears.

Safety first *The turtleweed crab makes itself nearly invisible to enemies by virtue of its translucent green shell.*

Stay-at-home crabs of the Great Barrier Reef

Beneath the brilliant green of the turtle weed growing along eastern Australia's Great Barrier Reef live some remarkable crabs. Unlike most other swimming crabs, the turtleweed crabs have retreated from the dangers of open water. They stay within their green home, feeding upon the tiny organisms that inhabit it. Their green-tinged shells keep them safe from the sharp eyes of hungry predators.

The small coral blenny fish has a wider range. Its brown-spotted skin blends with the corals, and with this protection it can venture forth in search of food.

CLOAKS OF INVISIBILITY

Swift wings and a fleet foot are not the only means of staying safe. Camouflage and a little cunning also have roles to play.

Changing appearance to fool predators

At least since the invention of the bolt-action rifle, it has been a basic rule of the soldier to look as inconspicuous as possible. If he cannot conceal himself by digging in, then he merges with his surroundings. He wears overalls patched in different colours, camouflage netting covering face and helmet – anything to change his outline. An enemy eye seeking out the characteristic human shape passes over him; he is invisible.

A similar defence technique occurred long ago to the ostrich. As it stands up to 8 ft (2.4 m) tall and lives in sparse scrubland, concealment is not easy, and the only possibility for the bird is to try to look like something quite different. It has an ally in the heat that causes the air to shimmer over the plain. A flock of ostriches, if alarmed, will often tuck in their heads and necks, raise their tails and then fluff out their feathers. Standing immobile and seen from a distance through the shimmering light, they take on the appearance of a group of round-topped bushes growing above tall, thin stems.

But should the ploy fail, the birds can fall back on their speed. Ostriches can run at about 45 mph (72 km/h), keeping them out of the grasp of most predators.

Confusing outlines *Blurred by dust, warm air and distance, this ostrich flock might well suggest a clump of bushes. But they have other defences, too. Apart from speed, they have a disembowelling kick that even big cats are wary of.*

Matching the wardrobe to the season

From the tiger's stripes, which echo the light and shade of the forest, to the bright green of the tree frog, most animals have developed colour schemes that blend with their environment. In situations where that environment is subjected to extremes of seasonal change, however, extra and rather special adaptations are called for.

Like other birds living in landscapes that are snow covered for part of the year, the Scandinavian willow grouse regularly exchanges the tones and patterns of its brown summer plumage for winter whites. Not that the transition is abrupt; rather it is gradual, mirroring the drift of summer into autumn and then into winter. The willow grouse's life is constantly under threat. Terrestrial predators such as lynxes and wildcats share its mountain and tundra home, and eagles wheel overhead. Survival depends upon the grouse making the most of its colouring by gearing its movements to the state of its surroundings. Thus its greatest security is achieved when there is a good blanketing of snow and the bird is in full white feather.

During the long spring thaw, the landscape becomes a patchwork of snow, rock and exposed vegetation. While the grouse retains its winter colours, it will feed only against a snowy background. Not until its plumage is almost completely changed again will the bird move to snowless terrain. So important is the right camouflage to the grouse that it will even cut down its food intake rather than risk exposing itself against a contrasting background.

Still lives *The East Asian jungle nightjar (above) and the golden plover (right) both depend on mottled plumage and immobility for safe rest.*

Birds that know when to hide their beauty

For a great deal of the year the golden plover struts conspicuously among the dune grasses and heathers of its moorland breeding ground. It has striking black and white plumage on the front, and a broken, spangled pattern on a golden-brown back. But when the time comes to incubate its eggs, it cannot afford to draw attention to itself. It is then that the plumage on a female's back shows its value as camouflage.

As the hen crouches low on the nest, her back blends in with the surrounding carpet of windblown, flower-speckled grass. She is practically invisible from above and from the sides. Thus her eggs are able to hatch in safety.

A relative of the golden plover, the eye-catching blacksmith plover of tree-scattered African grassland, is so conspicuous in its black and white feathers that it would be futile for it to attempt to blend with its background. Its nesting technique, though, is of startling originality – it often lays its dark, mottled eggs in a pile of zebra dung, which is probably the last place any hungry predator would think of looking for a meal.

Another relative is the ringed plover – a wader that breeds on rocky coasts. Rejecting formal nest building, it lays its mottled eggs

straight onto the shingle, from which they are indistinguishable. The adult is similarly camouflaged, with sandy wings and black and white head. The downy chicks are equally difficult to see against the pebbles and debris of the shore.

It takes a very good disguise to enable a bird to sleep safely on the ground by day. The white-throated nightjar hunts moths at night; but at daylight, it selects a spot among the dried vegetation, where it is practically invisible. It is probably more at risk there from being trodden on than from being attacked by a predator.

Hoary bat *This North American native owes its name and protective colouring to its silver-tipped coat, which blends with the pattern of grain on conifer bark.*

Parrot hide-outs in the vegetation

Rest periods are the times when birds are at their most vulnerable and, as when incubating eggs, the times when they must be least conspicuous.

Thus the blue-crowned hanging parrot of Southeast Asia – with its bright green upper parts, scarlet throat and rump, gold nape and flanks, and bright blue crown – is at a disadvantage. Nevertheless, it has evolved a roosting posture that comes to terms with its brilliant colour scheme. Placing its feet close together and holding tightly to a branch, it presses its tail firmly against the wood, arches its body and hangs head down. Its green back is then indistinguishable from the green leaves among which it sleeps.

New Zealand is home to several unusual species, as so many breeds have developed there in isolation. Among them is the kakapo, a

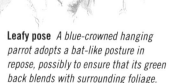

Leafy pose *A blue-crowned hanging parrot adopts a bat-like posture in repose, possibly to ensure that its green back blends with surrounding foliage.*

flightless, nocturnal parrot whose upper plumage, a handsome mixture of moss green crossed with yellow and black bars, allows it to blend almost seamlessly with its undergrowth habitat. But the kakapo's camouflage proved effective only until the introduction of rats and stoats from Europe. Now only a tiny population of the birds survives, conserved mainly on predator-free Stewart Island.

HARMLESS MIMICS

Not for every creature the proud display of the peacock. Many have elected for less hazardous but humbler guises – some of them very humble indeed.

The benefit of looking utterly repellent

Camouflage allows an animal to blend in with or resemble the prevailing background, but this is not enough for some creatures who wish to disguise the fact that they are edible. So they adopt the look of something clearly inedible, such as stones, twigs, thorns and even fresh bird-droppings.

There is little more unappealing than a fresh bird-dropping – and any creature that mimics one will avoid being eaten by all but the most desperate of predators.

The Chinese character moth, for example, which lives in hawthorn hedges, looks very much like a shiny, rather watery, bird-dropping. Making no attempt to conceal itself, the moth sits among the foliage with wings closed, ignored by even the hungriest predator.

The nymph of a species of bush cricket, or katydid, a native of Trinidad, takes the impersonation of bird-droppings even further. It

Daylight disguise *The Australian bird-dropping spider, a night hunter of moths, is named for its habit of sitting disguised as a bird-dropping by day.*

splays its hind legs so that, from above, it looks as if it has dropped from a height and splashed all over the leaf. It polishes the disguise with a realistic uric acid glint and 'dribble' effect that give the bush cricket a high degree of security.

Imitating the inedible *Rather than hiding from predators, some small animals, such as the Ecuador tree frog, have chosen to be inconspicuous. Bird-droppings are inedible and unremarkable, both excellent reasons for using this disguise.*

Animals that act their way out of danger

As well as adopting a disguise as a means of eluding predators, some creatures have enhanced their deception by the way in which they behave. Among such actors is a stick insect that lives in New Guinea. Its flattened, frayed body looks like a leaf in the last stages of insect-chewed dilapidation. It adds to this impression by suspending itself from a bush by one of its legs, and spinning in the breeze like a leaf that is about to fall off.

Another actor is a Kenyan beetle. Active at night, it spends its days among drifts of last year's seeds and is no more likely to move unaided than they are. If it does stir at all, it is only by being moved by the same breeze that is blowing the seeds about.

Some insects have assumed double disguises. There are some species of praying mantis that live in thorn bushes and look like twigs, while their offspring resemble thorns. Similarly, the tortoise beetle of Trinidad has the appearance of a seed while sitting on the

ground; but on a twig it presents another aspect of itself and looks like a thorn.

Animals that blend with their backgrounds are to some extent imprisoned by them, since they would be dangerously conspicuous elsewhere. A creature resembling a blade of grass for example, would be an easy prey if it spent much of its time sitting on a slab of concrete.

Another example is the leafy sea dragon, a form of sea horse. This astonishing fish lives among kelp beds off the coast of eastern Australia, and its trailing, weed-like appendages so resemble the surrounding plant fronds as to be practically indistinguishable from them. Outside the kelp, however, its disguise would be both conspicuous and a hazard.

Many amphibians also have to live amid the background they mimic. The casque-headed frog of Ecuador is exclusively a ground dweller that blends so closely with the forest-floor vegetation that it is virtually invisible. Horned toads are equally convincing as leaf litter – until the males' piercing calls uttered in the breeding season betray their presence.

Just part of the scenery *Blending with the background is an effective defence mechanism that is adopted by many creatures in widely differing habitats. The leafy sea dragon (above) lives in kelp beds, and the Brazilian potoo (right) gives a convincing imitation of a broken tree branch while incubating its eggs.*

Leaf litter look-alike *Like other rain forest amphibians, the horned frog of Brazil has evolved a combination of shapes and colours — plus highly realistic blotches — that make it almost indistinguishable from the countless dead leaves of the jungle floor.*

DEFENCE THROUGH DISGUISE

Some species of insects avoid predators by having developed almost uncanny resemblances to the leaves, grass or bark of their habitats.

Forest floor hideaway *Only long, thin antennae reveal the presence of a bush cricket in the rain forests of Costa Rica. Looking like a leaf on the forest floor provides perfect cover. Bush crickets are among the insect world's most accomplished mimics, capable of copying dead or decaying leaves and even reproducing delicate leaf veins.*

Gone to seed *Indistinguishable from the grass in which it lives, this grasshopper avoids predators by having a head that looks like a grass seed. This ability to blend into a particular background is a result of natural selection. Only species that avoid the attention of predators survive to pass on their genes.*

Poised to strike *By keeping stock still this mantis seems no more than an extension of the twig on which it sits. Not only does the disguise fool predators such as frogs and birds; it also helps to make the mantis one of the insect world's most efficient killers. By fitting in with its surroundings, the creature is able to surprise its prey and go some way towards satisfying its voracious appetite.*

Plant fake *By resembling a stalk, one type of looper caterpillar becomes almost invisible. It attaches itself to the plant at the same angle as the real flower stalks, and predators give it scant attention.*

Sharp practice *Looking like a thorn enables some species of treehopper to discourage even sharp-eyed birds. Sometimes the treehoppers form rows on twigs just like real thorns, creating a double bluff – that they are not only inedible, but cannot be perched on.*

Twig-like moth *The curious markings on the many types of moth that belong to the nocturnal prominent family allow them to rest by looking like bark or leaves. One species (right) has a talent for displaying itself as broken twigs.*

LOOKS THAT DECEIVE

To prevent themselves from becoming a meal, many animals copy the behaviour and warning colours of more dangerous creatures.

Pretending to be predators saves lives

A bird that is stung by a bee is impressed by the experience and avoids giving offence to another bee – or to any insect that looks like one. Thus the drone fly, a species of hover fly, manages to dupe birds because it looks very much like a honeybee. But it cannot deceive all birds. Spotted flycatchers, for example, eat drone flies and do not even try to remove the stings, as they would before eating bees.

Avoiding predation by pretending to be something dangerous is known as Batesian mimicry – a pattern of behaviour first recognised by Henry Bates, a 19th-century British naturalist. Bates first noted it in South America when studying butterflies. He need not have gone so far afield, for there are plenty of examples closer to home. Some European hover flies mimic bumblebees so well that it is hard to tell the difference. Each type of bee has its mimic; not even the smallest variation in markings goes uncopied.

Some animals not only look like a dangerous species, they also behave like one. The wasp beetle, for example, in addition to sporting a wasp's warning colours parodies its characteristically 'busy' behaviour, jerking and darting across leaves. When flying it even copies the wasp's flight patterns. Many moths imitate the markings and behaviour of wasps, even managing to buzz as they fly.

One type of cricket found in South America mimics a wasp's egg-laying tube as well as its bold, yellow-and-black colouring. It walks on only five of its legs and sticks the sixth out behind its abdomen to resemble the wasp's tube. Some stick insects use a similar technique; they arch their entire abdomens over themselves to look like belligerent scorpions.

Disguise against danger *Anyone who has ever panicked at the sight of a harmless hover fly, thinking it was a wasp, will understand how hunters are deceived by its bold disguise. Moths and hover flies (left and below) carry the distinctive yellow-and-black colouring of bees and wasps in the hope of discouraging birds that might otherwise prey on them.*

Keeping danger away *By curling over to resemble a scorpion, this Malaysian stick insect hopes to deter a hungry predator. Stick insects may also attempt to bluff a would-be attacker by keeping still, as many hunters will take only prey that moves.*

The advantage of flaunting false colours

Many snakes in Central and South America are ringed with vivid combinations of black, red and yellow. Some, like the coral snake, are highly poisonous, and some, known as false coral snakes, deliver a painful and enfeebling bite that is not, however, lethal.

Some scientists believe that the deadly coral snakes are mimicking the colours of the mildly poisonous false coral snakes. This is because an attacker, a bird of prey perhaps, that is bitten by such a creature learns to avoid snakes of that colouring. It is unlikely that the mimicry is the other way round, for the deadly coral snake either kills or is killed, and no one learns anything by the encounter.

Snakes banded in red, black and yellow, such as the Honduran milk snake, pretend to be more harmful than they are. They gain protection by mimicking the mildly poisonous false coral snake. All species overlap in range in Central America, but there are many areas with only one species. It may be that here these creatures are protected by their startling colours, rather than through any mimicry.

Harmless fish who pose as deep-sea killers

Impostors are found everywhere, even in the deepest parts of the ocean. Harmless fish are sometimes clad in the 'costumes' of their poisonous neighbours.

Harmless leatherjacket fish, for example, cruise among coral reefs in relative safety having adopted the colouring of striped and deadly tobies. The only thing that sets them apart is their dorsal, or back, fin. A toby has a short, stumpy fin set some way down its back, and a leatherjacket has a transparent fin running the length of its spine.

But the fundamental difference between them is that the leatherjacket lacks the deadly nerve poison tetraodotoxin, which makes the toby lethal to both humans and fish. As predatory fish have no way of knowing this about the leatherjackets, they keep away from them.

The leatherjackets' mimicry is effective only as long as there are fewer of them than there are tobies. If a predator encounters too many non-toxic mimics, then it is unlikely to be fooled by them.

Double deception *Even experts have been fooled by the similarities between the striped toby fish (inset) and its mimic, the harmless leatherjacket (left). The leatherjacket relies upon convincing predators that it is the lethal toby.*

Sharing bright colours *In the Costa Rican rain forest, a deadly coral snake (above) shares the vivid colouring of the mildly poisonous false coral snake (left). It is more likely that the deadly species is the mimic, since opossums and predatory birds that have received painful bites from the false coral snake learn to avoid it.*

229

YOU HAVE BEEN WARNED

Striking red, yellow or black colours on a creature indicate clearly that it is poisonous or ill-flavoured at best. So give it a wide berth.

Changing signals *Treehoppers are sap-sucking insects. The treehoppers in a Peruvian rain forest (above) have an unpleasant taste, and their coloured markings warn off predators. The newly emerged adult has a bright red dot on its back, but as it matures it will turn black with a yellow stripe. Only the creamy nymphs are unmarked.*

Red for danger *So effective is the foul-smelling, toxic liquid emitted by this South African grasshopper (left) that it has lost the ability to fly and does not even leap to avoid the attentions of hungry lizards or birds. Its red and black warning colours are generally sufficient to put them off.*

Toxic toad *Seen from above, the oriental fire-bellied toad (above) is modestly coloured and difficult to see on the rain forest floor. It is semi-aquatic and feeds on small water creatures such as shrimps, as well as insects. When the frog is threatened, it sometimes flings itself into the air, flipping belly-up and displaying (left) its gleaming red and black underside . This is not simply window-dressing – it is a warning that the toad has poison glands in its skin.*

Colour coding warns of poisonous prey

Flaunting glaring colours such as red, black and yellow is a warning that the carrier is dangerous in some way – maybe poisonous, foul-tasting or with a sting.

Warning colours work on the principle that if noxiousness is clearly advertised, encounters are more likely to be avoided. Once tried, foul-tasting prey is unlikely to be forgotten and will be left alone in future.

Some animals make use of both warning colours and camouflage to defend themselves from predators. Fire-bellied toads, for instance, have inconspicuous backs, but if threatened they show their bright red bellies, which warns potential attackers of their toxicity.

Deadly glamour *Found in the sea off Japan, the sea slug (right) displays the typically exotic 'plumage' of these seemingly defenceless creatures. Like most of its relatives, it protects its soft body with powerful poisons stored in glands just below the skin on its back.*

It pays to advertise *South American harlequin frogs (left) and arrow-poison frogs (below) advertise their deadly skin toxins with bright, garish colours. These toxins are used by Amerindians to poison the tips of blowpipe darts. The poison contains a painkiller more powerful than morphine, as well as strong antibiotics that seem to protect the frogs from many of the disease-carrying bacteria that plague other animals.*

EYESPOTS THAT FRIGHTEN

Some animals startle their attackers by displaying prominent, eye-like markings that make them resemble a much fiercer creature.

False faces that keep hearty appetites at bay

Many a hungry bird has been horribly frightened when the juicy caterpillar it is about to seize suddenly rears up from the foliage and turns itself into the terrifying head of a snake, complete with a flicking 'tongue'.

This is the defence employed by the great mormon caterpillar of tropical Asia and North Australia. It has eye markings on its rear end, which resembles the shape of a snake's head – a disguise reinforced by the bright red, forked 'tongue' positioned just below the eyespots. When agitated, the caterpillar flicks the 'tongue' and gives off a foul odour. Eye-like markings

are very effective at deterring birds and small carnivorous animals. The 'false faces', and particularly eyespots, appear to be part of the head of a much larger, more ferocious creature, and so frighten away the hunter.

The caterpillar of the European elephant hawkmoth, which grows to nearly 3 in (76 mm) long, has two pairs of large black and white eye markings that stay hidden until danger threatens. As soon as it is alarmed it withdraws its real head and raises its fake head towards the source of the disturbance.

Many butterflies have small eyespots on their hind wings, and if they fail to startle they may be the first thing that a predator attacks. An Australian ringlet's eyespots are always visible, and again are quite

Snake disguise *Many animals and birds seek to make meals out of caterpillars which need ingenious defences in order to survive. This moth caterpillar from Costa Rica (above) startles would-be assailants by displaying its rear end. This has bold eye-markings and bears more than a passing resemblance to the head of a small viper about to strike.*

Eye to eye *Emperor moths have eyespots and, like the species (above) from Ecuador, rely on the bright, round markings on their underwings to confuse predators. When these striking insignia are suddenly unveiled from beneath the moth's drab forewings, their effect is to startle an investigating bird, giving the moth time to escape.*

Two-faced *When threatened, the Indian cobra (right) rears up, hissing and spitting. It also flaunts vivid 'face' markings on the back of its neck, just where a mongoose, the most adept of its hunters, might try to bite. These marks help to protect it from the rear, where it is most vulnerable to attack.*

Ambiguous signs *The juvenile emperor angelfish (above) has a pattern of white concentric circles and wavy lines on its body, making its front and back hard to tell apart. This may confuse an enemy that seeks to attack the fish head on.*

likely to be the first thing that a determined foraging bird will peck at. The butterfly will sustain least damage in this area, and the peck may serve as a warning that gives the butterfly the chance to escape. A ringlet butterfly with pieces of its wing missing is probably the survivor of such an encounter.

Turning tails into heads

Larger fish can catch smaller ones from any angle. But the one sure way to swallow a fish whole is head first, otherwise fins, scales, spines and gills stick in the mouth. As fish usually swim forwards, this is the direction in which they can be expected to attempt to escape. It follows, therefore, that most fish have very good reason to blur the distinction between their heads and their tails. A remarkably effective method is to evolve a pair of false eyes on the tail – a feature that is common to a wide variety of successful species.

For example, a freshwater fish of South America, Oscar's cichlid, is preyed on by piranhas. It has clearly defined eye markings on the stem of its tail which give it a better chance of escape should a piranha attack from the rear.

The tail seems to be the ideal place for a fish to wear its decoy eyes, but some species have false eyes on their fins or on other parts of the body. One example is the juvenile lemonpeel angelfish that has large eyespots in the middle of its body. It could be that the eyespots have the same offputting effect as those that are found on the wings of moths.

Deceitful eyes *The butterfly fish (above) and the two-eyed coral fish (right), both found in coral reefs around the world, have eyespots at the tail end of their bodies. Their real eyes are disguised by a band of black. Predators that attack these fish from behind, aiming at what appears to be the more vulnerable head, are startled when their prey darts off in the 'wrong' direction.*

Backward look *The eyespot frog of South America (above) protects itself by turning away from its attackers and showing two huge false eyes on its rump. When faced by these great spots and an inflated body, a hungry snake cannot be sure what it is taking on. The African pearl-spotted owlet (left) also has white spots that look like eyes from a distance. These may confuse larger birds of prey.*

TO BE – YET NOT TO BE

Though unable to achieve invisibility, the ultimate form of defence, some animals have evolved illusions that come very close to it.

Bold harlequin patterns help to fool predators

Decorated with an outlandish colour scheme, the sweetlips fish of Australia's Great Barrier Reef vividly demonstrates the advantages of the harlequin effect. This is a form of natural camouflage that not only echoes the surroundings – in this case a coral reef – but by its random splashes of colour blurs the shape of the creature and confuses any would-be predators. The clown angler fish also inhabits coral reefs and its patches of red and creamy-yellow suggest clumps of coral or seaweed. The irregular shape of its body also makes it difficult to distinguish from the reefs.

Stripes for security

The tree-living white-lined bat of the Caribbean is named for the pale stripe that runs the length of its back. It could be that this would draw attention to an otherwise unremarkable animal. But when the bat clings to a silk cotton tree, a favourite perch, the line blends with those of the bark. By this means, the bat seems to melt into the trunk. To enhance their disguise, white-lined bats do not roost in a huddle, but maintain a little space between themselves.

Another striped deceiver is the elusive African okapi, not seen by Europeans until this century. The stripes on its hindquarters and across its legs blur its outline as it retreats into the undergrowth, and its paler underside adds counter-shading to its camouflage.

Several theories have been advanced to account for the zebra's highly conspicuous markings. It may be that when the animals are moving about in herds, individuals are lost in a mass of stripes rippling in the heat haze, making it difficult for a lion or other large predator to select and home in upon a single victim.

Comical killer *The shape of the clown angler fish mirrors the sponges and corals it lives among, and conceals it from predators. Its irregular shape also disguises the fish's own hunting equipment – a dorsal fin that acts as a lure-baited fishing rod to attract prey.*

Dazzling success *The stripes on the Grevy's zebras (left) may dazzle a predator into a vital second of hesitation. As each individual's pattern is in some way different, they could help promote recognition. The stripes might also aid temperature control – heat-absorbing black balancing heat-reflecting white.*

Where brightness is the key to survival

The penguin's distinctive 'dinner jacket' markings may not look much like camouflage, but they are. Viewed from beneath as it swims, the penguin's gleaming white front tones in with the brightness of the surface. And seen from above, its dark back becomes indistinguishable from the murky depths beneath.

Many creatures have evolved lighter-coloured undersides, a form of camouflage known as counter-shading. It is particularly useful to fish which, like penguins, are vulnerable to attack from below.

Seen against light coming down from the surface, the bright, silvery bellies of many fish make them practically invisible. Each scale on the fish bellies behaves like a miniature mirror, catching whatever light there is in the water or that may be reflected up from the sandy bed.

Swimming safe *It is the cool Humboldt current that enables the Galápagos penguin (left) to live at the Equator. Like its Antarctic cousins, it is preyed upon by sea lions – but its colouring helps it to escape their attentions.*

Changing shape and living longer

Few animals have come closer to achieving invisibility than the Central American glass frog. Its body is transparent in some places and dappled green and black in others. When it sits still on a leaf, its outline is so indistinct that it looks more like a small blemish on the foliage than a living creature.

This camouflage is known as splash camouflage, which blurs the frog's outlines. Nothing declares an animal's presence, nor identifies it, more readily than shape, so the ability to apparently change this is an invaluable aid to staying alive.

The skin patterns of the grey tree frog are arranged in such a way that they appear to continue across the frog and onto the branches to which it clings. Even the suction discs on its long toes are splashed with colour, and darker bands run right across its back and limbs, so that they merge into one overall shape.

Some South American tree frogs are similarly camouflaged, but can enhance their disguise by pulling their limbs into their bodies to blur their shapes even more.

See-through frogs There are about 65 species of glass frog, all of which live in trees that hang over streams in the cloud forests of the Andes. Generally they are green and flecked with bright colours, a camouflage that merges readily with their vivid surroundings. The effect is enhanced by the skin of their undersides, which is so transparent that their internal organs show through.

Dressed crab A decorator crab of Papua New Guinea masks its outline and colour with a covering of plant debris or even small animals such as sponges. These are all held in place by a coating of tiny hooks that cover its body. The decoration merges with the crab's background, and renders it almost invisible. When it moves to a new locale, it discards the old disguise for one appropriate to the new surroundings.

Marked for safety The random darker splashes on the North American grey tree frog unite body and limbs, bark and lichen, in a subtle disguise. Only when it leaps is the frog's orange-patterned underside visible.

COATS OF MANY COLOURS

Some animals can alter their appearance by adopting the colours of their background, and so can blend into a changing environment.

Octopuses - camouflage specialists of the sea

Although it is one of the fastest colour-change artistes in all the animal kingdom, an octopus does not, apparently, have colour vision. Yet it is so adept at changing its colouring to disguise itself that it can match any background in less than a second, and can even generate colour patches to blend with mottled terrain.

The secrets of an octopus's camouflage skills lie in its complex and sensitive skin and in its ability to distinguish colours by means of their different light intensities. Chromatophores, the sac-like cells in the octopus's skin, each contain either red, yellow or black pigments, and the animal alters its skin colour by adjusting the muscles surrounding them.

It can contract the muscles to enlarge a chromatophore, in order to make the colour it contains more obvious. And when it relaxes the muscles, it reduces the chromatophore to a barely visible blob of colour. This ability to expand or contract its many chromatophores means the octopus is able to flash coloured patterns across its body. But an octopus's range of disguises far outstrips the range of its chromatophores. There are no sacs of blue pigment, for example, yet the creature can appear blue. It is the small stacks of reflective plates, like tiny mirrors in its skin, that make this possible. It can use them to reflect light and thus automatically match the colour of its background.

Octopuses can also mimic the texture of the terrain they are crossing. On flat sand their skins appear smooth, but as they move on to spiky corals, muscles pull the skin into pimples and peaks.

Hidden crawler *An octopus creeps across a coral reef (right), then stops between a purple and a yellow sponge (below), changing colour so that it is barely visible. Octopuses are usually so well disguised that divers stumble upon them by accident.*

Why ptarmigans change coats for the seasons

A white-tailed ptarmigan hen, its feathers mottled in black and white, yellow and a greyish brown, crouches among the low growth on the windswept heights of the North American Rockies. Only her blinking eyes give her away.

It is the beginning of summer, and she is incubating a clutch of nine eggs laid in a scrape in the ground which is almost invisible among the lichen-covered stones.

The chicks hatch after about three weeks and are soon able to fend for themselves, although they will continue to stay fairly close to their mother. In autumn, the birds feast on cowberries and other fruits but as the season draws to an end, and as the days grow shorter, snow begins to fall.

To remain concealed from hunting ermines and eagles against this changing background, the ptarmigans must moult again. Gradually the birds replace their coloured feathers with white ones. The snow cover is more or less established once October comes, and the ptarmigans move down the mountain to lower slopes. Now they have thick coats of white feathers that serve as camouflage and insulation in the bitter winter cold. Ptarmigans burrow into the snow not only to hide but also to keep warm.

Snowshoe hares put on their winter whites

As September brings shorter days and colder weather to Alaskan and Canadian forests, snowshoe hares start to moult their grey-brown summer fur and grow white tipped hairs. During the next three months the hares turn completely white, except for the black tips on their long ears.

While the landscape is covered in snow, a snowshoe hare's white winter coat provides good camouflage. The hairs are hollow and colourless, so appear white as they reflect light. Their hollowness allows the animal not only to have a thick and lightweight coat but also provides excellent insulation as it traps air against the body.

In autumn, each hare also grows thick pads of fur on the soles of its feet – its 'snowshoes'. These insulate the animal's feet and help it to get a grip on the snow so that it can stay one jump ahead of the lynxes, foxes and coyotes that prey on it as it feeds on the buds and twigs still found above the snow.

When March comes, the snowshoe hare begins to moult its white hairs to greyish brown, changing its camouflage once more to blend with the changing colours of the surrounding landscape.

Night dress *By day (top) black-backed butterfly fish are easily recognisable members of a coral reef community, with their vibrant black, yellow and white markings. By night (bottom), their dazzling colours become muted and the reason for the name 'black-backed' becomes apparent. This darkening could serve to hide the fish while it rests.*

New outfit *Because it changes its coat in spring and autumn, the North American snowshoe hare is also known as the varying hare. As the days get shorter and the air colder, it changes to a white winter coat for camouflage in the snow. In areas where snow rarely falls, snowshoe hares do not turn white.*

FAKING DEATH IN A BID FOR LIFE

When in danger, some animals feign death to gain a few seconds, and others even sacrifice a limb in a last-ditch attempt to escape.

'Playing possum' is a game of life and death

A hungry coyote grabs hold of a cat-sized Virginia opossum and makes off into the bushes, with the victim hanging limp and seemingly lifeless in its jaws. As the coyote settles down to its meal, it relaxes its grip momentarily. Immediately, the opossum leaps up and scuttles to the safety of the nearest tree, leaving the startled coyote empty-mouthed and hungry.

The opossum is North America's only marsupial – pouched mammal – and its name is derived from the Indian word 'apasum', that means white animal. Its habit of feigning death whenever threatened is well known. At the approach of danger the opossum goes limp, droops its head and lolls its tongue from its open mouth.

Although it seems dead and does not even flinch if badly bitten, the opossum's brain remains fully engaged, ready to seize a chance of escape. How the animal achieves this apparent total shutdown of its senses is of perennial interest to zoologists. Certainly, its coolness under pressure is impressive and convincing, but 'playing possum', as such behaviour is called, is still a risky strategy.

The escape tactic of pretending to be dead (known to scientists as akinesis or thanatosis) is not confined to opossums alone. It is also employed by the chameleon, a lizard better known for changing the colour of its scaly skin than for its acting skills. But when face to face with danger it puts on an equally convincing show of lifelessness by flopping onto its side with drooping eyelids and stiffened legs.

Acting the part *The North American opossum (above), known locally as the possum, is famous for its convincing death act – it lies stock still, eyes open and a rigid grin on its face. This state can be sustained for minutes or even hours. Once the danger has passed, the animal snaps back to life instantly.*

Snakes that play the corpse for their foes

Snakes in trees often simply relax and fall to the ground out of harm's way if they are threatened, but there are snakes, such as the European grass snake and the American hognose, that are truly consummate actors. Despite the fact that a snake, dead or alive, cannot fall over, a 'dying' grass or hognose snake will lie belly-up if it is threatened.

The sagging jaw, lolling tongue and deathly expression are all quite convincing, but the effect is sometimes spoiled by the wriggling involved in staying upside-down. The snake's instinctive desire to remain belly-up is so strong that it betrays itself by writhing back into its upside-down death pose if a predator tries, out of curiosity, to roll it over.

The prize for the most impressive use of props for playing dead goes to the West Indian wood snake. When threatened, this small boa twists itself into a taut coil, mimicking the stiffness of death. Fluids coating the snake's scales give off a foul stench of decomposing flesh to add to the success of the illusion.

As a final effect, blood, released from special tiny blood vessels, flushes the eyes of the coiled 'corpse' a dull red, and trickles from its gaping mouth. Thus a predator, such as a mongoose, is led to believe that the snake is dead – and that it has been so for some time.

Unless the predator is particularly hungry, or has a taste for rotting flesh, this performance is usually enough to put it off, or to make it hesitate for long enough to give the snake a chance to make its escape.

Playing dead *The hognose snake (above) and the grass snake (right) are both fakers. They instinctively pretend to be dead when danger threatens, throwing themselves on their backs and lying with their mouths hanging open.*

Lizards sacrifice their tails to save their lives

Lizards rely on speed and agility to flee from danger. But if running does not suffice, then the lizard brings its tail into use. Most lizard species shed their tails when they are threatened, an action that not only tends to confuse the attacker but focuses its attention on the distracting tail while the lizard makes a dash for safety. So the lizard offers its tail as a snack, albeit a fairly paltry and fleshless one, for the safety of the rest of its body. Predatory monitor lizards take full advantage of this and feed almost entirely on such discarded tails.

A lizard's detachable tail has sections that can be snapped off at

New growth *Just as a lizard can grow a new tail, a starfish can regrow a limb that has been bitten off.*

will by the simple contraction of some of the lizard's muscles. In spite of the fact that the fracture occurs across the spine, the loss causes the creature little discomfort. This is because the joints at the 'crisis point' where the tail breaks off are made of cartilage rather than bone, and blood vessels and nerves are constricted to reduce the pain and blood loss.

Although a lizard's tail is not essential, it does play an important

role in balance and in breeding success. The lost tail grows again with time, although it may differ in length or pattern from the original, and the lizard may even end up with more than one tail. Victorian records, for example, tell of a lizard which had seven. But regrowing a tail takes

considerable energy. If a predator refuses to eat the snack, some skinks have been known to return to eat their own discarded tails.

The glass snake is really a lizard with no legs. It takes its name from its extraordinary ability to shatter its own body. If under stress, this 5 ft (1.5 m) long creature fractures its tail at all or most of its joints. Each piece then wriggles around on its own, while the snake itself slips away – sometimes reduced to two-thirds of its original length.

A species of gecko found in Puerto Rico also dismantles itself spectacularly when in danger. It sheds bits of skin from all over its body, or even its whole outer covering, and moves off to safety.

Loss and gain *The bright blue, expendable tail of the skink (right) is designed to attract the attention of an attacker so that the rest of the creature can escape. A tokay gecko (below) has been injured, perhaps in a tussle with a predator, and a new stub has grown from the old wound, leaving the gecko with a misshapen, two-pronged tail.*

AN ARSENAL OF CHEMICALS

When confronted by an attacker, many animals react by spraying their assailant with a harmful substance, often with an evil odour.

A spitting fulmar leaves a foul, lingering smell

Approach a nesting fulmar at your peril – it will probably spit at you. When this bird is threatened it spews amber oil, brought from the pit of its stomach, over its attacker. The noxious liquid has a repellent smell that is virtually impossible to remove from clothing, plumage or fur.

On the Scottish island of St Kilda, where fulmars were once a staple part of the inhabitants' diet and their oil a vital commodity, an islander once recalled: 'If you don't get them quickly they'll make an awful mess of you!'

Like the rest of the petrel family, the fulmar has an unusual

Lethal weapon *A fulmar on the Shetland Islands opens its beak and spits defensively. The spit can clog up the feathers of a large bird of prey, leaving it unable to fly and likely to die.*

digestive tract. Its gizzard – the part of a bird's stomach for grinding food – is small compared with that of other birds. Vast quantities of the oily digestive juices are produced by glands in the bird's stomach, which has a greatly twisted inner surface. The juices are used for preening and for feeding the fulmar chicks, as well as for defence – with dramatic effect.

Fulmar spit can be fatal for some creatures. A thick coating of the juice renders other birds flightless, which can lead to exposure and death. Fulmar spitting caused the death of a white-tailed sea eagle released on remote Fair Isle, off Scotland, as part of a programme to reintroduce the species. What at first appeared to be easy prey for the eagle proved to be a well-armed and lethal foe.

With such dangerous chemical defences, seemingly weak creatures can put up a formidable resistance to an attack without having to make physical contact.

Bad taste *The stinkbug nymph (above) is one of thousands of species of stinkbug – insects that give off putrid odours when under threat. Their unpleasant secretions can be projected 1 ft (30 cm), and the odour lingers on leaves and fruit giving them a bitter taste.*

On target *A Mozambique spitting cobra can aim its venom with remarkable accuracy at the eyes of an approaching enemy when the creature is still 10 ft (3 m) or more away. When the poison hits the victim's eyes, it produces a strong burning sensation and may even cause temporary blindness.*

The hidden weapons of a duckbilled platypus

With a jerk of its hind legs, an angry male duckbilled platypus can stab an enemy and inject a large, potent dose of poison – a dose strong enough to kill a dingo outright. The weapons used are a pair of horny spurs – one on the back of each ankle of its hind legs, hidden amid its fur.

Yet the flat-beaked, web-footed platypus, which lives by rivers in eastern Australia, has few enemies except man and dingoes. So just why a male platypus is equipped with these odd but highly effective defences is a mystery.

Men and dingoes appeared on Earth later than the platypus, so its deadly spurs may have evolved as a defence against enemies now extinct. Or perhaps they were once used for settling territorial disputes between males, and later became more useful for defence.

The last resort *As an inquisitive coyote approaches a cat-sized skunk (right), the skunk snarls and then tries to discourage the intruder by stamping its front feet, raising its tail and swaggering about stiff-legged. If and when all this fails, the skunk turns to lift its tail and emits a pungent spray of liquid (below). Finally put off by this evil-smelling odour, the coyote beats a speedy retreat. Skunks develop this ultimate and highly effective means of repelling attackers when they are less than one month old.*

The anal glands of a skunk secrete chemicals known as mercaptans, which it can fire about 16 ft (5 m). The fact that the smell can be detected 1 mile (1.6 km) away and lingers on clothing for a year or so, shows the power of the skunk's chemical defence system. A direct hit causes the recipient to retch violently and may injure its eyes. Few animals wait to put the threatening posture of a skunk to the test, and those that do so are unlikely to repeat the experience.

The horned lizard of Texas has a particularly macabre defence system. When threatened, it bursts a number of small blood vessels in its eye membranes and squirts thin jets of blood towards its attacker. A well-aimed jet can be sufficient to frighten an assailant, and may even leave it temporarily blind.

A skunk's stench puts assailants to flight

Skunks have become a byword for unpleasant smells. A skunk facing danger stands its ground and tries to warn off its assailant with stamping feet and raised tail. If this fails to work, it rises on its forelegs and, with tail raised, points its rear at the enemy's face. Then it squirts a nauseous spray.

Blood stream *To protect itself from being eaten, a Texas horned lizard fires a jet of blood from its eyes towards its attacker. This is one of several defence mechanisms on which the lizard relies.*

Explosions made by bombardier beetles

The bombardier beetle gets its name from the explosive sound it gives off when threatened, loosing up to 50 burning, chemical volleys of heat, colour and noise from a 'gun barrel' situated in the tip of its abdomen.

To take aim, the beetle swivels its abdomen from side to side and fires straight at an attacking

insect or frog. The attacker is left with a nasty taste in the mouth and even minor burns.

The beetle's body manufactures and stores the chemical ingredients needed for the volleys. When a bombardier beetle is under stress, the liquid chemicals are forced out of cavities in its body into a thick-walled, heat-resistant 'explosion chamber' in its abdomen. Here, a rapid chemical reaction takes place that turns the liquids into gases and water. As pressure builds up in the chamber, the bubbling chemicals squirt out in a series of rapid bursts.

Fiery defence *A bombardier beetle under threat can burn its attacker with an explosive chemical potion brewed in its own abdomen.*

USING CHEMICALS IN SELF-DEFENCE

A mouthful of stinging spines, a bad taste or a disorientating dose of chemicals can all play their part in confusing or repelling a predator.

Impalas use airborne warning signals

There is not much an impala can do but flee, once it is being chased at full speed across an African plain by a cheetah. But as the chase begins it can warn the rest of the antelope herd by leaping straight-legged 10 ft (3 m) high into the air and releasing scent from glands on its hindquarters.

This startling leap, the strong warning scent and the impala's zigzag course together spell out an urgent message to the rest of the 200-strong herd – run!

They follow the airborne scent trail laid by the front-runners, keeping close together – if all the impalas ran in different directions the herd would fragment, and each individual would be more vulnerable to the hunter. Should a few animals become separated from the main herd, they can follow the scent trail to find their way back.

Striking signal *A springbok leaps high on stiff legs on an African plain. Scent from a gland on its hindquarters reinforces its warning to the herd.*

South African springboks also leap straight-legged into the air – often as high as 10 ft (3 m) – and emit a distinctive scent from a gland that stretches from midback to tail base. As a threatened animal leaps up, a pouch on its back opens, revealing long, erect, white hairs that draw the herd's attention to its warning signals.

Birds and frogs share a powerful poison

The pitohui, a thrush-like bird from New Guinea, is one of the few birds that possesses any kind of chemical defence. Its feathers, skin and muscles contain a poison called homobatrachotoxin, which is also found in the arrow-poison

frogs of South America, but in much higher concentrations. How these birds and frogs produce the same toxin is uncertain, but the answer may lie in their diet. Perhaps the pitohuis acquire their predator-repelling poison from the insects or berries they eat.

People living in Papua New Guinea do not eat pitohuis because they taste and smell repellent, and their flesh numbs the mouth. Scientists believe that birds of prey or snakes that seize pitohuis may also be put off by the toxins in the bird's feathers and skin, and they also spit them out.

Numbing singer *The brilliant orange-and-black plumage and strong smell of a hooded pitohui of the New Guinea forests warn of the mouth-numbing poison its body contains.*

242

Fish that release poison to see off attackers

Stonefish, which are found on the sea bottom in warm, shallow waters, are among the most venomous of venomous fish. Like most others, such as weevers and toadfishes, they only inject their poisons in self-defence. It takes pressure from a predator – pressing down on one of the hollow spines along the stonefish's back – to release the poison, rather like a hypodermic syringe. The poisons are painful but rarely lethal.

The stonefish also defends itself by being perfectly camouflaged – as a rock. Partly buried under sand or mud, its disguise is enhanced by a covering of warty lumps that secrete a sticky substance to which small organisms become attached.

Lethal rock *Perfectly disguised as a rock, some types of stonefish produce mock strands of algae from their own tissue to fool prey and deter predators.*

Chemical confusion keeps sawflies safe

When a scouting wood ant finds a large cluster of pine sawfly caterpillars feeding in a Scots pine tree, it hurries back to its nest laying a scent trail that will guide a party of worker ants to this rich food supply. But the caterpillars are not entirely helpless – they can disable the scouting ant using gum they produce in a pouch in their guts, and so prevent an attack.

The caterpillars' gum is made of pine-needle resin mixed with a chemical very similar to the one that ants themselves emit as a danger signal. A little gum dabbed on the head and antennae of the lone wood ant scout so confuses it that it has great difficulty finding its way back to the nest.

Any scent trail the ant lays in its attempt to get home is so strongly tainted with the ants' own danger smell that other worker ants are warned off. Even if the tainted scout manages to reach the nest, the workers kill it instantly.

Bristles and spines ward off danger

As a bristly fireworm crawls along the seabed foraging for corals, it makes no attempt to avoid predatory fish because it is armed with fearsome weapons. Found in warm shallow seas off rocky coasts, these 8 in (20 cm) long worms are well protected by the dense tufts of poisoned bristles sprouting along their sides. A curious or careless fish brushing against the bristles experiences intense pain as they break off and embed themselves in its flesh. The unlucky victim is likely to steer well clear of fireworms ever after.

Hairs and bristles also provide moths, butterflies and caterpillars with an armoury of weapons. Some tiger moths retain the poisons they took in when browsing on leaves as woolly bear caterpillars. This makes them unpalatable to wolf spiders, which would otherwise pose a threat. In tropical and subtropical America, the atala hairstreak butterfly eats a certain type of palm-like cycad called coontie or comfortroot to make itself poisonous. Its eggs are also covered with poisonous, orange-red scales. The Australian cup moth caterpillar has stinging hairs.

In China, there is a spiny newt that has a flattened back with each rib sharply defined. If a shrew grabs the newt, these rapier-like ribs burst out through pores in the newt's skin, piercing enlarged poison glands on the way out and inflicting painful wounds in the mouth of an attacker.

Protective weaponry
A thick fringe of stinging hairs earns the Australian fireworm (left) a fiery reputation. The branching spines of a South American io moth caterpillar (below) sting like a nettle. The sting of one species can cause dire reactions, preventing blood clotting.

Armoured yet vulnerable *In 1840, the African traveller Sir William Cornwallis Harris described the white rhino as: 'Attaining a height of nearly seven feet at the shoulder, and carrying a cranium not very dissimilar to a nine gallon cask; he flourishes upon his square and truncated snout a formidable weapon some three and a half feet long fashioned after the method of a cobbler's awl and capable, when wielded by a warrior so unquestionable in pith and renown, of being made to force its way through any opposition . . . superadding to the almost impenetrable folds of shagreen wherein nature hath encased his ribs.' Despite these considerable advantages, the rifles of modern poachers have gone far towards threatening the creature with extinction.*

WEARING SUITS OF ARMOUR

A solid shield of body armour gives the best protection against predators large and small, however persistent they may be.

Thick-skinned *The folds of a rhinoceros's skin have long caused the animal to be described as 'armour plated'. Recent research has shown that the skin along the back and flanks of a rhinoceros does indeed act as protection against the horns of other rhinoceroses, being thicker and having tougher fibres than the skin of other mammals.*

How caterpillars deal with attacking ants

Most caterpillars are soft bodied, and as they move slowly over the leaves that they feed on, they are vulnerable to fast-moving, sharp-jawed ants. The caterpillar of the Australian moth-butterfly is an exception. Not only is it impervious to ants, but in later life it preys on their larvae.

A leathery shield covering the caterpillar's back turns it, in effect, into a tiny tank. The shield guards its soft underparts from attack and allows it to make its way to the heart of its feeding grounds – weaver ants' nests. This leathery shield fits so snugly against a leaf that ants simply cannot get under it. Neither can they see what is happening beneath it.

When the caterpillar reaches a patch of ant grubs, it lifts the edge of its shield, takes a mouthful of grubs, then clamps down on the leaf again. Protected by its overhanging armour, it sucks in the captured grubs one at a time.

The moment of transformation from heavily armoured caterpillar

Missile-proof invader *A moth-butterfly caterpillar invades a nest of weaver ants foraging for ant larvae. The sharp bites and caustic sprays of the colony's soldier ants make no impression on the caterpillar's leathery armour.*

to fragile butterfly would seem to be a good time for the ants to go on the offensive. But once again they are thwarted, for the caterpillar does not spin a cocoon. Instead it changes inside its tough covering, so protecting itself from the ants until it emerges as a butterfly.

Flying to safety

As the ants attack the apparently defenceless newly emerged adult, they come up against a new range of defences. Loose, greasy scales cover the butterfly's legs and crumpled wings, and its body is coated with fine, coiled hairs ready to come off at the first touch.

The butterfly is unaffected by the ants' attempts to get a grip on its slippery scales and loose hairs. As soon as it is strong enough, it takes off on its maiden flight, leaving the ants deprived of their anticipated meal and trying to clean the scales and hairs from their clogged mouthparts.

Why giant clams close their shells

When the shadow of an intruder passes over the light-sensitive mantle that lines the shell of a giant clam, the clam automatically starts to close its shell. As the shell can weigh 400 lb (180 kg) – and is up to about 3 ft (1 m) across – this requires a great deal of

force. This means that the clam cannot slam its shell; it can only pull it closed slowly.

Even when the shell is fully shut, the gaps between its fluted edges are so large that, if a man pushed his arm through one of them – or if a diver accidently put his foot in one – the clam would not be able to grip it. So the intruder would be able to get away safely.

Home guard *After digging themselves into the sandy seabed around coral reefs, giant clams do not move from the spot. If disturbed, they close their large shells.*

Transparent cloak *When night falls, parrot fish sometimes encase themselves in a cloak of jelly-like mucus so transparent that it would be almost invisible if it were not for the tiny grains of sand sticking to it. Why they do this is uncertain, though it may be to hide their scent from nocturnal predators, such as some eels that hunt by smell.*

Scales and shells keep slow movers safe

Armour plating, as medieval knights well knew, does have one serious disadvantage – it slows up the wearer. But for many animals the advantage of being able to enclose their soft, vulnerable bodies inside a hard, protective coat makes it worth the cost.

Instead of trying to run away from their predators, slow-moving American armadillos and African pangolins, or scaly anteaters, roll into a ball, presenting an attacker with an impenetrable surface of tough, bony plates or leathery scales. A pangolin clamps itself closed with its broad, muscular tail, and cannot be forced open.

Tortoises are well known for their slowness and since they are unable to run away they simply draw their heads and limbs into the safety of their hard shells. The African pancake tortoise, as its name suggests, has a flattened shell that allows it to crawl into crevices and under overhanging rocks when threatened.

Hinged tortoises and turtles, found worldwide, benefit from a mechanism for closing their shells completely, providing valuable defence against small predators such as army or driver ants.

Sealing the shell in this way is also an effective means of preserving body moisture. A relative of the tortoise, the Asiatic spiny turtle has an almost circular shell fringed with sharp points, causing youngsters of the species to look like tiny cogwheels. This helps to keep predators at a distance.

Body shields *If threatened, pangolins (above and right) curl up inside their tough shields of scales. Armadillos (below) also have a horny shield, though some species, unable to curl up, retract their limbs.*

247

SPINES AND SPIKES KEEP ENEMIES AT BAY

Animals' spikes signal a simple message to would-be attackers: 'Keep away!' Once pricked, an aggressor is unlikely to risk approaching the animal again.

Defensive weapons that wound and kill

A back covered with sharp quills protects the echidna, a rabbit-sized Australian mammal that is also known as the spiny anteater. Disturb an echidna while it is busy foraging and within a minute it will have dug itself into the earth, leaving only a small forest of razor-sharp spines protruding through the loosened soil. It stays buried until the intruder has left and all threat of danger has passed.

The common Eurasian hedgehog is armed with more than 5000 sharp, brown and cream spines each 1 in (20-30 mm) long. Within hours of being born, a baby hedgehog's prickles break through its skin – they develop there to protect the mother's womb during birth. When danger threatens, a hedgehog usually sits it out, raising the coat of spines that normally lies flat against its back and pulling itself into a ball with the

strong muscles ringing its back. The tighter the hedgehog curls, the more erect its spines are pulled. Some species are less passive than others, and ram their spines into an inquisitive snout, so emphasising the warning message.

But a hedgehog's prickles do more than just ward off predators. Hedgehogs appear to be enthusiastic, if inept, climbers, and their spiny coats cushion their frequent

falls. As the spines are hollow, air trapped in them may even help a hedgehog to float.

Porcupines of India, Africa and the Americas, can weigh as much as 40 lb (18 kg) and could make a good meal for any of the larger cats. Should a cat try to molest it, however, a porcupine erects the sharp quills on its back and tail.

If the sight of these is not enough to scare away the attacker,

Advance warning *An echidna digs into the earth to leave only its sharp spines protruding. Few animals will attack and risk a barrage of spines in their flesh.*

it advances, rear end first, with its quills rattling. These quills are loosely attached to the porcupine's body, but their barbs make them difficult to remove once they are embedded in some other creature's flesh, and they can cause a wound that may become fatally infected.

Tough going *Few creatures would try to swallow a grotesquely swollen porcupine fish when faced with its spiky armoury and unmanageable shape.*

Fish that swell up to protect themselves

Porcupine fish are covered with sharp spikes that ordinarily lie flat against a fish's sides. But when a fish is threatened, it gulps in water or air to distend its body until it is almost spherical. As the body balloons, the spikes become erect and stand straight out, turning the fish into a spiky ball that looks impossible to swallow.

The spiny box fish, on the other hand, wears its spines erect at all times. It, too, increases its size by gulping in water, swelling up until

it resembles a prickly pumpkin. As a result, would-be predators find it impossible to swallow.

Deceptively elegant to look at, but deadly in an encounter, is the beautiful lion fish. Its long, graceful, hollow spines contain poison and work like hypodermic syringes. Unlike the porcupine and box fish, the lion fish uses its armoury to defend itself actively rather than as a passive warning. It is a wise predator that swims away from an advancing lion fish.

In fresh water, the finger-length three-spined stickleback is protected from large, hungry trout by its spines – they stick in a trout's throat, making it painful to swallow. Experiments have shown that predators will usually eat smooth minnows in preference to spiny sticklebacks in the same tank.

Insects and reptiles in suits of armour

If ugliness alone were enough to frighten off predators, the giant weta of New Zealand would surely stay unmolested. This huge bush cricket has long been known in Maori mythology as Wetapunga, or the Ugly Thing. Its back legs are twice as long as its 4 in (100 mm)

long body, and are also covered in spikes resembling rose thorns that can painfully scratch an assailant. Most crickets call by rubbing their wings together, but the giant weta has no wings, so it probably does not make any noise at all.

Giant wetas are now protected by New Zealand law because they are threatened by rats with extinction. Rats arrived on the islands of New Zealand centuries ago with

European travellers, but the weta's spikes were not enough to protect it against the rodents.

Some types of shieldbug rely on one large hook in the middle of the back to put off hunting birds. Because of this hooked spike, the insect has to be dismantled before it can be eaten – an inconvenience that may encourage a predator to seek an easier meal.

There are many species of lizard that have evolved sharp spikes from the tough scales that make up their skin. The bearded-dragon lizard of Australia inflates the skin

of its throat, which, like its body, bristles with spikes, and spreads its ribs to make itself look much bigger and so frighten attackers. A dragon lizard will sometimes even rush at an intruder if disturbed while foraging on a roadside verge.

Armadillo lizards of Africa and Madagascar belong to a lizard family that has developed a body armour of short, spiky scales. Most of the family use the spikes on their tails to block their burrow entrances; but armadillo lizards copy their animal namesakes in times of danger.

By flipping onto its back and grasping its spiky tail in its mouth, an armadillo lizard presents only its tough, jagged surface to the world – a circle of spikes far too awkward and sharp for a hunting animal to tackle.

Barbed defences *The armadillo lizard (left) presents an attacker with a ring of sharp and inedible prickles by lying on its back and grasping its tail. The giant weta (above), a type of cricket with spiky legs, also uses barbs to defend itself.*

Painful prospect *The thorny devil, a 6 in (15 cm) long Australian lizard, has no need to adopt a threatening pose if attacked. Its strong, sharp spikes are enough to put off most predators.*

RUNNING OR JUMPING AWAY FROM DANGER

There are many ways of escaping an enemy – sprinting across water, turning somersaults or simply zigzagging away at high speed.

Lizards escape pursuit by walking on water

If a basilisk lizard feeding on the bank of a Central American river is cornered by a predator, it has an unlikely avenue of escape – the surface of the river. It jumps in and runs across the top of the water. Although it soon starts to sink, the few strides it takes are enough to put it out of reach of a predator such as a small cat. With a suitable distance between itself and its enemy, the basilisk can then swim away, dive or stay submerged for up to two minutes – a useful tactic if the pursuer is a bird of prey.

It is the basilisk's long, powerful back legs and broad feet with long, scale-fringed toes that allow it to walk on the water – a feat that has led to the lizard also being called the Jesus Cristo lizard. Buoyed up by the surface tension of the water and the spread of its own feet, the basilisk strides far enough to leave its pursuer behind on dry land.

Water runner *Spraying tiny droplets as it goes, a basilisk lizard rushes across the surface of a Central American river. The basilisk is also called 'tetetereche' – an imitation of the sound it makes as it skitters away across the water.*

The slender basilisk hunts during the day for insects, small rodents and birds. When it runs, it rears almost upright and using only its hind legs, races off at high speed. On firm ground, an adult can reach a top speed of just under 7 mph (10 km/h). At night basilisks sometimes sleep in bushes overhanging a small river, from where they can drop easily to the water's surface if danger should threaten.

Leaping to safety with a double back-somersault

One of the most outstanding of insect athletes, the springtail, performs regularly in British gardens. But because it is so small – only about $\frac{1}{5}$ in (5 mm) long – and moves so quickly when it leaps, its feats are seldom seen by humans, even though it is one of the most abundant insects, with more than 300 species living in Britain alone.

A springtail can jump some 8 in (20 cm) into the air – about 40 times its own length. It is wingless, and uses its remarkable jumping ability to escape predators.

Only when scientists managed to photograph a springtail's jump – at exposures of one ten-thousandth of a second – were its acrobatic abilities fully appreciated. When it is startled, it hurtles into the air, executing at least one, and often more, back-somersaults as it goes. Direction is unimportant, escape is

all that matters. This haphazard method of fleeing uses a great deal of energy, but has the advantage of taking an attacker by surprise.

The insect's spring results from the forked, tail-like appendage that is usually tucked away along the underside of its body, rather like a closed safety pin. When this 'tail' is released, it hits the ground with such force that the springtail is catapulted into the air, spinning round and round.

The same principle applies to the maggot of the Mediterranean fruit fly, another creature that shakes off attackers by jumping into the air. Since the maggot is a soft-bodied creature, this acrobatic manoeuvre takes a lot of energy.

Spinning into safety

At the first touch of a wasp or ant, the maggot curls up into a loop, grasping the end of its tail with small hooks in its mouth. Then it tenses the thin sheet of muscles lying just below the surface of its skin, forcing the skin across its back to stretch. When it releases the tension, the maggot is sent spinning into the air, and may land up to 5 in (13 cm) away just a quarter of a second later. When it hits the ground, it takes a moment or so to regain its balance; then it repeats the action – sometimes as many as 30 times.

So successful is this method of getting about,

that the maggot also uses it whenever it is searching for a suitable burrow in which it can make its change into an adult fruit fly.

Unlike most shellfish, queen scallops do not simply rely on their hard shells for protection. As soon as a queen scallop is aware of the approach of a predatory starfish, it claps its hinged shell vigorously and repeatedly, forcing out jets of water that propel it away from the starfish. The slow-moving starfish is unable to match this burst of speed and will go in search of a less mobile meal, such as a mussel.

Tail spring *In times of danger, a springtail catapults to safety.*

Rapid escape *Clapping the two halves of its shell together, a queen scallop shoots out of range of a starfish. The eyes along the mantle at its shell rim may not help the scallop to see the starfish, but they do help it to orient itself as it escapes.*

Outrunning an enemy by speeding or swerving

Rabbits and hares are built to run. Their long, powerful back legs give them speed, and cushions of bristly hairs between their strong toes make them sure-footed. To make sure they get a good start, they also have big ears and sharp eyes that can see a predator from afar, and although most try to avoid detection by freezing until the danger passes, they can move very fast when they have to. Some of the larger hares can reach speeds of up to 50 mph (80 km/h).

If a predator, such as a fox, is spotted while still far enough away, the rabbit or hare often stands up on its hind legs, perhaps to send the message: 'I have seen you, and I am fit and strong. Chasing me is a waste of energy.' Once a chase is on, however, the animal zigzags to throw the pursuer off-balance and prevent it from building up speed.

Jumping for life *Red kangaroos (above) can cover 42 ft (12.8 m) in a single bound when fleeing from a predatory dingo. Springboks (right) jump straight up in the air, perhaps to warn others or to show a predator it has been seen.*

In Africa, springboks, impalas and gazelles will pronk or stot – leap straight up in the air – if they see a lion or cheetah. Why they do this is still a matter of controversy among biologists. It may be to tell the predator it has been seen, so the chase will be hard, or it may be to warn relatives within the herd. Another theory is that it may allow gazelles to see over tall grass or bushes and locate other dangers, such as lions lying in ambush, before deciding which way to run. If forced to flee, these antelopes zigzag wildly to make it harder for the predator to reach top speed.

Australia's kangaroos move at speeds up to 40 mph (64 km/h) in two-footed hops on their powerful hind legs, holding their front paws up against their chests and using their big tails as counterbalances. Adults do not normally leap higher than about 5 ft (1.5 m), but can clear obstacles twice as high when being pursued by dingoes.

PARENTS MAKE A STAND TO PROTECT THEIR YOUNG

Some parents risk their own safety to guard their offspring from predators and to ensure the survival of the next generation.

Feigning injury to distract a predator

A killdeer, a common plover of the Americas, sits on the eggs she has laid in a shallow scrape on the gravel bank of a river. A fox is approaching, on the lookout for food, and the plover knows it will eat her eggs if it finds them.

As soon as the fox gets near enough to spot her, the killdeer abandons the nest and runs away across the open ground, fluttering one wing and holding it awkwardly as if it were broken. At the same time, splaying out her tail feathers to expose her bright orange rump, she screeches and makes a fuss to attract the fox's attention. Once she has been seen, the killdeer staggers away from her nest, but 'recovers' instantly when she has lured the fox away from her clutch.

Members of the plover family all nest on the ground in open, exposed places – and they, as well as several other species of bird, use the same manoeuvre. The blacksmith plover, found in Africa south of the Sahara, has even been known to feign a broken wing to distract elephants wandering too close to its nest. An elephant has no interest at all in a plover's nest, but it might accidentally crush the fragile eggs or chicks.

Attention seeking *A female killdeer staggers around with a seemingly broken wing. Her distress is a sham, however, as she is trying to draw attention away from the eggs in her nest.*

Driving danger away *A young Cape cobra joins battle with its opponents – two South African ground squirrels. A ground squirrel can easily size-up a snake above ground, and small snakes are often attacked and driven off. American ground squirrels sometimes tackle rattlesnakes underground, judging the size and condition of the snake in the dark by the sound of its rattle.*

Ground squirrels take on rattlesnakes

On the North American prairies, ground squirrels feed by day on seeds and flower heads. But if an eagle soars overhead, they soon dart for the safety of their burrows. It is in these underground homes that their litters of blind, defenceless young are born in spring, and spend the first six vulnerable weeks of their lives.

But the ground squirrels' snug, grass-lined den is by no means completely safe. Rattlesnakes hunt in the tunnels after dark and, in California, baby ground squirrels make up a large part of their diet. But even in that confined space, mother squirrels will often face the snake and put up a tough defence of her offspring.

It has been discovered that ground squirrels can tell a lot about snakes from their rattles. The sound of the rattle changes according to how warm and lively the snake is, and larger snakes have deeper rattles. If the snake sounds sluggish or small, the squirrel stands its ground and drives it fiercely from the burrow.

Defending the young against heavy odds

Every summer, the reed beds of southern England become nest-building grounds for large flocks of reed warblers from Africa. These birds are favourite victims of the cuckoo, which removes an egg from a reed warbler's clutch of 3-5 and lays one of its own in the nest. Once the cuckoo chick is hatched, it heaves the rest of the reed warbler's eggs from the nest. Then it demands the full attention of its foster parents, which instinctively respond to its constant, open-mouthed demands for food.

But reed warbler parents are not just passive victims of the cuckoo. While their own eggs remain unhatched, they keep a watchful look out for marauding cuckoos, and if they catch one in the act of egg-swapping, they will attack ferociously and drive it off — even though it is twice their size. As soon as all the chicks have hatched, however, the cuckoo will ignore the nest.

Ordinarily, reed warblers stay well away from a hunting sparrowhawk, which is three times their size. But once their eggs have hatched, the plucky parents will attempt to chivvy a sparrowhawk away from the nest before it gets a chance to snatch a chick. In spite of the fact that cuckoos and sparrowhawks look very much alike, the reed warblers can distinguish between them, and recognise that each poses a different threat to its young at different times.

Sounding the alarm

A harsh, three-note call — the cry of the redshank — rings out over the coastal salt marshes of eastern England, and hundreds of nesting lapwings 'scramble' into the air like miniature fighter planes. They are flying to meet incoming crows and gulls intent on raiding their nests. The alarm call of the redshank, dubbed 'the sentinel of the marsh', is the shore birds' early-warning system and it also alerts the wandering redshank chicks, which crouch down and freeze.

Mute swans are well known for their aggression towards intruders.

Staying together *A pair of mute swans takes their brood of cygnets with them wherever they go. Nestled securely in the soft white plumage of their mother's back, the three grey-feathered youngsters peer out, while their father swims watchfully alongside.*

When danger threatens, a mother carries her small cygnets to safety on her back within the protection of her wings. Grebes also carry their chicks on their backs, but these youngsters must hold tight as they take a ducking when the parent dives to look for a mouthful of weed. Water rails carry their chicks in their beaks, and woodcocks are even known to fly with a youngster held firmly between the thighs. And in the world's oceans, dolphins do their best to shield a calf from a killer whale attack by throwing a cordon round it.

Support group *A school of spotted dolphins swims in protective formation round a calf breathing at the surface, ready to fend off any attack by killer whales. The group is kept together by calls and the youngster swims in its mother's slipstream.*

AGAINST ALL ODDS

When threatened, some animals take on attackers far larger and stronger than themselves in a last-ditch stand for survival.

Animals fight back if flight is impossible

A cat, when cornered, reacts with bared teeth, flattened ears and fierce hisses. Back arched and hair on end, it makes itself look bigger and more ferocious than it actually is. Usually the cat will try to flee its attacker but, although it is agile and alert, there are times when it has to stand and fight. Animals less able to defend themselves still instinctively put up a fight if fleeing is impossible – the victim may even manage to inflict severe damage on its attacker.

Lions prey on a wide variety of animals, and occasionally their prey turns on them. A kick from a

On the defensive *Teeth bared, ears flattened and hairs raised, a European wildcat faces up to an attacker. All cats are ferocious if they are cornered.*

zebra stallion can knock out a lion's teeth, and a giraffe's kick will send the big cat sprawling – or even cripple it. There are reports of a gemsbok snagging a lion on its long, curved horns and tossing it over its back. An enraged herd of wildebeest has been seen to trample hunting lions to death.

Packs of yellow baboons in southern Africa attack leopards if sufficiently aroused, and even the torpid sloth of South America can be provoked into giving a vicious swipe with its arm. In Europe, badgers cornered in their setts by dogs sent to attack them turn and fight, sometimes inflicting terrible wounds on their attackers.

Seals will try to divert killer whales from their pups and, even more extraordinarily, dolphins will turn into submarine battering rams and kill a predatory shark by butting it repeatedly – and at high speed – with their blunt snouts.

Screams and hisses scare attackers away

When a Brazilian screaming frog is threatened by a predator such as an opossum, it does more than just inflate itself to avoid being eaten, as many other frogs do. It also opens its mouth wide and emits a startling scream. If the opossum is startled into even one moment's hesitation, the frog takes the initiative, jumping at its predator and biting it before making good its escape.

Sounding like a much fiercer creature may also deter unwanted intruders. The thrush-sized burrowing owl of the Americas makes a noise like a rattlesnake to deter any intruder that enters the darkness of its burrow. If cornered, an African cut-throat finch writhes and hisses like a snake, especially when it is brooding eggs or chicks.

All these responses serve to startle an attacker, relying on an animal's innate fear of sudden movements and loud noises. They

may simply make the hunter hesitate long enough for the prey to escape, or they may unnerve it so much that it goes away.

Another reason for the success of this method of defence may be that the predator is itself afraid of becoming prey. Most small hunters can quickly find themselves the hunted rather than the hunter, especially if a victim creates such a commotion that it attracts the attention of larger enemies.

Empty threats *With its mouth wide open and its ruff of neck scales spread out, an Australian frilled lizard (left) hisses defiantly at an enemy. The frill makes the 18 in (46 cm) long insect-eating lizard look far larger and fiercer than it actually is. The parrot snake of Central American rain forests (below) adopts a similar method. Although it is quite harmless, it mimics the open-mouthed threat of a viper to scare off attackers.*

The many ways of fending off aggressors

Sunstars, which are a variety of starfish, feed mainly on limpets. But limpets have a defence mechanism that often outwits them. At the first touch of a sunstar, a limpet extends the mantle under its shell so that it slides up and over the shell. The mantle's surface is so slippery that the sunstar cannot get a grip on it.

The silky anteater, a squirrel-sized inhabitant of South America, is a slow-moving creature that spends most of its days asleep in trees. If threatened by owls or harpy eagles, however, it holds its front paws in front of its face, displaying a single huge, curved claw on each paw. These claws are formidable weapons, capable of disembowelling a dog, and are certainly enough to discourage any predator.

If a house mouse is caught and toyed with by a cat, it may sit up on its haunches facing its tormentor and raise its paws in front of its upturned face as though begging for mercy. But this is far from being a pleading attitude, for it appears that the mouse is actually showing aggression towards the cat. Dormice also fight back against weasels or ferrets, showing

their sharp teeth and making a chattering cry of defiance in the hopes of unnerving the predator.

Mice do not hesitate to stand and fight if needs be, and will work as a group to drive off another mouse intruding on their territory. Even mouse 'pups' barely out of the nest have been known to help to repel an intruder.

A praying mantis, lying in wait for any small insect that comes its way, holds its powerful forelimbs beneath its head, ready to snatch up a meal with lightning reactions. But sometimes it is itself forced into a defensive position by the approach of an insect eater such

as a tree shrew. Its reaction is very dramatic. Hissing fiercely, with forelimbs held wide in a threatening pose, it opens and flashes the brilliantly coloured wings that are normally concealed beneath its wing cases. Bold markings, such as eye-spots on its wings or body, add to the startling effect, disconcerting the attacker momentarily and giving the mantis sufficient time to fly away to safety.

Deceptive appearance *Despite its sleepy nature, the silky anteater (right) can be a formidable opponent if forced to fight. When threatened, it holds its claws in front of its face ready for instant use.*

Shock tactics *A Malaccan praying mantis (right), with forelimbs spread and brightly coloured wings extended, attempts to unnerve an attacker and give itself a chance of escape.*

Safety move *As a starfish closes for the kill, a limpet (above) lifts its slippery mantle to stop its enemy getting a grip.*

COURTSHIP AND MATING

*'G*ENERALLY, THE MOST VIGOROUS MALES, THOSE WHICH ARE BEST FITTED FOR THEIR PLACES IN NATURE, WILL LEAVE MOST PROGENY. BUT IN MANY CASES VICTORY WILL DEPEND NOT ON GENERAL VIGOUR, BUT ON HAVING SPECIAL WEAPONS, CONFINED TO THE MALE SEX.' ≈ CHARLES DARWIN, *On The Origin of Species,* 1859.

Gift giving
Animals will go to whatever lengths are necessary in order to court and win a mate. Scorpion flies must usually produce a gift of some kind if they are to entice a female to mate with them – in this case, a nutritious ball of regurgitated spittle.

Darwin's book is the most influential natural history book ever published. Through years of painstaking collection and study, Darwin built up a massive body of evidence to support his theory that plants and animals produce more offspring than could possibly be supported by their habitat and that, of these, only the fittest survive. He called this process natural selection. But to explain the bizarre courtship and mating rituals he had witnessed on his travels, Darwin introduced a second theory of sexual selection. According to this, males increased their progeny by competing for mates, and females by choosing the most melodious or beautiful of the courting males. The theory has proved controversial for more than a century, but in the last few decades biologists have increasingly come to agree that here, too, Darwin was correct.

Mating game

Contrary to Darwin's expectations, stags without antlers, known as hummels, do survive. They pass on their genes, not by fighting, but by sneaking unnoticed into the harems of dominant males.

Fighting fit

Male jungle fowl fight for the chance to mate with the hens, using their spurred legs as potentially lethal weapons. This sort of contest increases the chances that a female will mate with a healthy male.

Perfumed persuasion

If a female red spotted newt is unwilling to mate and tries to escape, the determined male seduces her with an aphrodisiac, applied by rubbing his cheek glands against her snout.

Fine feathers

'He who thinks he can safely gauge the discrimination and taste of the lower animals may deny that the female argus pheasant can appreciate such refined beauty,' wrote Darwin. But he refused to accept that the extraordinary posturing and displays of courting male animals served no purpose and instead proposed his theory of sexual selection.

FIRST MOVES IN THE MATING GAME

Among courting animals, the correct signals or a handsome display are generally essential for finding a suitable partner and winning a healthy mate.

Fine feathers *There can be more than 200 feathers in a peacock's magnificent, shimmering tail (above), which he displays to attract a mate – the more eyespots, the better his chances. A courting Emperor of Germany bird of paradise (top) uses his long white flank feathers to catch a hen's eye – he raises his wings to display them.*

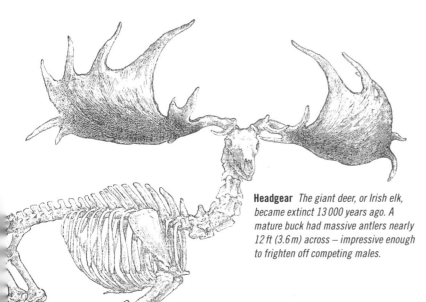

Headgear *The giant deer, or Irish elk, became extinct 13 000 years ago. A mature buck had massive antlers nearly 12 ft (3.6 m) across – impressive enough to frighten off competing males.*

Fine feathers – the sure way to win a mate

A peacock with its long, blue-green-spangled tail fully fanned out gives one of the most dazzling courtship displays seen in the bird world. Each breeding season, a male bird establishes a territory where he struts around, at one of several selected sites, displaying his fully spread tail to any female that happens to pass by, in the hope of attracting a mate.

The most successful males mate up to a dozen times, and the least successful fail to mate at all. Just who gets to mate depends on the choice of the peahens. Their selection is based entirely on the size and effect of the cock's spectacular tail – in particular the number of eyespots it carries. Presumably a long and many-eyed tail shows the strength and fitness of a particular peacock and impresses a female.

However, the extravagant tail of the peacock is also a handicap to its owner. Like the tail plumes of a bird of paradise, it is so cumbersome that it affects the peacock's ability to fly and hampers escape from predators – so decreasing the bird's chances of survival.

Even so, despite the problems it causes, the outsize tail increases the bird's chances of reproducing and leaving many descendants. This ties in with Darwin's theory of natural selection – that almost all physical features, especially among males, evolved because they were to their owners' advantage.

The importance of sticking to their own

When a canary and a goldfinch produce hybrid offspring, they are known as mules, and like mules – the offspring of a male donkey and a female horse – they are sterile. Normally offspring such as these are produced only by domestic animals. In the wild, matings between animals of two different species are extremely rare. This is because hybrids fare so poorly that natural selection has favoured individuals that respond only to the courtship signals of their own kind.

Courting in the dark

Animals usually recognise others of their own species by their looks, but those that court in the dark need to find other ways. Frogs and crickets, for instance, have their own particular calls.

Fireflies, which are nocturnal beetles, find partners by emitting flashes of light from their undersides. Different species flash at different rates. A North American black firefly male, for example, will flash every 5.7 seconds while he is airborne, seeking a mate. Then, when he is 10-14 ft (3-4 m) from a female on the ground, she flashes back exactly 2.1 seconds after him. Some male fireflies can even flash different colours – they produce orange flashes in flight and green ones when they are on the ground.

Nodding terms Bobbing up and down, exposing its vividly coloured throat and belly to attract a mate, the western fence lizard – named for its habit of sunning itself on fences – bobs quite differently when frightening off competing males.

More than one mate means healthy offspring

Females of many species seek the strongest and fittest male to mate with, so that their offspring will have a good chance in life. But females of some species cannot do this, either because they cannot distinguish between good and poor males or because they have little control over who mates with them.

Female European adders, however, seem to have found a solution to the problem. They emerge from hibernation in early spring with fully formed eggs waiting to be fertilised, and release an irresistible scent to advertise their availability to male adders. During a study of adders in southern Sweden, female

Mating ritual European adders usually mate in April, after a sensuous courtship ritual in which the light-skinned male runs his tongue along the browner female and vibrates his body against hers. Young adders, born in late summer, are about 12 in (30 cm) long.

adders were observed mating with several different males. After the offspring were born, DNA tests were used to discover the identity of the fathers. These revealed that females who had the most partners had produced the greatest number of surviving offspring.

This could have been the result of the keen competition between the various sperms in a female's reproductive tracts. This, in turn, meant that a larger proportion of her eggs had been fertilised by genetically fitter males.

Choosing a mate by the length of his tail

From a distance, male and female swallows are virtually indistinguishable. Closer scrutiny shows that a male's plumage is somewhat brighter, but the main difference is that a male has longer streamers on his forked tail. Although this is unlikely to give him any aerial advantage, it does have a purpose.

The length and symmetry of a male swallow's tail reveals what a female looking for a mate needs to know about him. Growing a long tail demands a great deal of energy, and only a strong bird can afford to do it.

So females prefer mates with long tail streamers, and they are the first males to find breeding partners in spring. Swallows that breed early have enough time in the summer to raise an additional brood of up to six. Consequently, long-tailed males tend to father more offspring than their shorter-tailed counterparts.

Fitness test *The length and symmetry of a male swallow's tail indicate how fit he is. Longer-tailed males are more likely to survive the long annual flights to winter quarters in South Africa.*

Getting the message *Upon catching the smell of a lioness's urine, a male lion lifts his head and opens his mouth with upper lip curled. This behaviour, known as flehmen, brings the scent in contact with a sensory organ in the roof of his mouth, telling him if the female is ready to mate.*

SNIFFING OUT A MATE

At certain times, many animals release scents that, when interpreted by prospective mates, convey volumes of vital sexual information.

A sexual promise that is borne on the air

It has often been observed that a male lion patrolling in the vicinity of his females will occasionally stop, sniff, and then tilt his head upwards with a backward curl of his upper lip. He closes his nostrils and breathes deeply through his mouth. He has intercepted a distant scent of female urine, and his reaction is to bring the scent into contact with the Jacobson's organ in the roof of his mouth, where it is analysed for its content of sex hormones. This action is called the flehmen response and is exhibited

Scent detector *Lifting his head and baring his teeth in the flehmen response, a North American male bighorn sheep brings a female's scent in contact with the Jacobson's organ in his mouth to determine if she is on heat.*

by a wide range of carnivores and other mammals. The Jacobson's organ gives them a more acute sense of smell than that of humans and is a particularly valuable sensory tool when sniffing out a mate.

The female lion's urine carries scent messages – pheromones – which provide information about her fertility. Deciphering these messages helps the male to target his sexual attentions where they are most likely to reap rewards. The messages are also important to females, who read the pheromones deposited by their sisters in the pride, and use these to synchronise their own fertile period, or oestrus. The chances are that if one female is on heat, then they all are. The advantage of this appears in lions' sexual behaviour.

Males mate every 25 minutes or so for several days with a single lioness. There are usually two or

Male sensitivity *Having picked up a female's scent, an East African lion curls back his lip as he analyses its message of sexual readiness.*

three adult males in one pride and if only one lioness were to achieve oestrus at a time, the males would fight with one another for the right to mate with her. Injury would result, to the detriment of the pride – which needs strong and healthy males to protect it.

By synchronising oestrus, the females ensure that all the males

are kept too busy to fight with each other, which prevents social disruption of the pride.

Women fall into step

Like lionesses, women who live in close proximity also tend to synchronise their fertile periods. It has been suggested that this tendency of women to fall into step with one another's menstrual cycle has its roots in the prehistoric development of human societies. Maybe by simultaneously signalling their period of infertility, females made it possible for males to leave the group for cooperative hunting trips, with no worry about intruders mating with their women while they were away.

As for scenting, while humans lack a Jacobson's organ, our sense of smell is perhaps rather better than we realise. Some mothers, for instance, are able to pick out the clothes of their own children, just by smell; and trained perfumiers can identify more than 10 000 separate and distinct aromas.

Scent ties the garter snake love knot

One of the wakening signs of the long-awaited Manitoban spring is the emergence of thousands of male red-sided garter snakes from hibernation pits in the rocks where they have spent the past six months. Though they have not eaten in that time, they make no effort to disperse and find a meal. Instead, they remain by the pits in anticipation of the emergence of the females.

Because the females come out singly, or in small groups, they are outnumbered by the waiting males by something like 5000 to 1. As she appears, each female exudes a scent that signals her readiness to mate. Each male within range picks up the molecules on his flickering, forked tongue, which transfers them to the receptive Jacobson's organ in the roof of the snake's mouth. This triggers the male sexual response and, in moments, a lone female can find herself at the centre of a pile of perhaps a hundred writhing males, tying themselves into a living ball, and all trying to get into position to mate with her. Only one of the suitors is successful, for when he has mated, he leaves a cement-like secretion that bars other males from penetrating the female.

At the same time, she switches off her scent signal and the males depart in search of more receptive mates. The large number of suitors guarantees that every female has been impregnated within 30 minutes of emerging from the pit. This in turn ensures that the young are born before the northern winter and the next hibernation.

Tied up in knots *Canadian red-sided garter snakes form a large mating ball in the branches of a tree. The bundle may consist of a hundred or more males, all fiercely competing for the chance to mate with a single female.*

Day and night scents to woo and confuse

The ability of moths to find each other by following a scent trail over great distances is astonishing, though a very necessary adaptation for creatures that are active at night. Usually it is the female who attracts the male by wafting her distinctive odour onto the air, to be picked up on the male's antennae. But male summer fruit tortrix moths also put out a scent, though in their case it functions differently. They release a pheromone that inhibits other males from following a trail laid by a female. So the first male to pick up the female's trail is likely to be the one that mates with her.

Being day-flying insects, butterflies do not usually need the help of a scent trail, and rely more on sight to find a mate. When a male sees a suitable female, he pursues her, making repeated dives in the direction of her head. Although they do not follow a scent trail to find females, some male butterflies, including monarchs, pierids and fritillaries, do make use of an aphrodisiac pheromone to entice the females to mate.

Male North American queen butterflies carry this aphrodisiac in fine 'hair pencil' clusters, which they push out from their abdomens when sexually aroused. These clusters then fan out into brushes that disperse the male's scent on the air. This encourages the female to stop flying and settle, enabling the male to mate with her.

Tempting smells *Most butterflies, like the eastern pale clouded yellow (right), rely on sight to find a mate. Moths depend more on scent. For example, the male snout moth (below) disperses aphrodisiacal pheromones from tufts of hair on its underside to entice females.*

FIGHTING FOR THE RIGHT TO MATE

Males that must compete for females assert their place in the mating hierarchy by engaging in fights and in violent displays of dominance.

A symbolic fight for land before mating

When the mating season begins in April, some male European adders defend their patches of ground against other males. Most of the fighting is symbolic – the adversaries rear up against one another, each striving to press the other to the ground. Once the weaker snake has been forced to yield, it will leave the scene. No biting occurs – venom is kept for the business of killing prey. Often, the sight of writhing, entwined male snakes has been mistaken for a courting ritual.

As a prelude to mating, a male adder runs his tongue along the female's back. After mating, the female stores the sperm for 60 days before fertilising her eggs. Then after about another 60 days, her 6-20 young, which are each about 7 in (18 cm) long, are born complete with fangs and venom.

Strong rivalry *Like European adders, male African black mambas compete to mate. Each tries to push its rival's head to the ground. Venomous black mambas grow to 13 ft (4 m) long and are Africa's most feared snakes.*

Heavyweight males that ward off their rivals

It is midwinter off the coast of California, and a male northern elephant seal hauls his vast bulk sluggishly onto an island shore. Apart from one or two other males the beach is deserted and the newcomer is unchallenged. But as spring approaches more and more males emerge from the sea and each new arrival roars out a challenge through his inflatable trunk. The males fight to establish a hierarchy until one among them emerges the winner and becomes the beachmaster. Only then do the females start arriving.

Mated the previous season, they drop their pups within a few days of arrival. After 28 days, when the pup is almost weaned, the females come on heat for mating again. This is what the males have waited for, but they have to give way to the top male, who has first choice. The others then wait at the fringes of his harem, watching for any unguarded moments that allow them an

Choosing a champion *Mature elephant seal bulls of up to 20 ft (6 m) long, fight each other in one of a series of fiercely contested battles held in the mating season to find an overall winner. The champion bull then has the first pick of the females.*

opportunity to mate. The most successful males are the large, older ones. But by pretending to be females, small males can sometimes sneak into the harem and mate successfully.

By the end of the season the beachmaster may have inseminated as many as 100 females. In contrast, most other males fail to mate at all. But the top male pays a high price for his achievements. The constant round of fighting

and mating, all on an empty stomach (for these males have no time to eat during the entire breeding season), wears him down. A really exceptional bull may dominate for about three seasons, but usually dies within a year or two of his most successful season.

Warning noises

Adult male African and Indian elephants usually live apart from the females, either alone or in small groups made up of other males. Young males spar together for dominance, which, once established, may last throughout life.

For two or three months a year, an adult male elephant becomes frenziedly aggressive and develops a discharge from glands on his temple as the testosterone (male sex hormone) in his blood begins to increase. This state is known as musth, and was first noticed in Indian elephants – the word comes from the Urdu for 'drunk'. A male's musth rumble, one of the loudest of the sounds made by elephants, announces his sexual state to females and warns other males to keep out of his way.

A male in musth can move up the hierarchy and win contests with bulls that would normally dominate him. However, by the end of the musth season, the male elephants have lost their energy and strength and need time in which to recuperate.

How horns help males to overcome rivals

Sharp cracks echo across the high slopes of North America's Rocky Mountains in autumn – the sound of bighorn sheep head-butting during the rut. Astonishingly, the rams seem to suffer little damage. Their curling horns are mounted on a reinforced skull that absorbs the shock. The sheep are wanderers and do not defend territories. If different-sized rams meet, the smaller one usually retreats. Fighting occurs only if two rams are evenly matched. One will try to get uphill of his rival and charge down on him.

Bighorns always try to face their opponents, since their horns are shields as well as weapons. But with Rocky Mountain goats, related to the European chamois, the opposite occurs; their needle-sharp horns and thin skulls make head-butting risky. The males use their horns to aggressively defend territories, especially in the hard months of winter. Rivals circle head to tail, and a bloody battle may occur if one fails to yield. Each tries to gore the other's flanks, and their horns may even pierce the padding that grows on a male's rump at rutting time – skin nearly 1 in (25 mm) thick.

Males of the Japanese horned beetle are more aggressive, often fighting over territory. The beetles emerge from damp, rotting wood as adults, their size depending on how much they ate as larvae. Large males may be 3 in (75 mm) long with a large head horn and a shorter horn on the thorax – the midsection of the body.

At night the hornless females, up to 2 in (50 mm) long, visit oak trees to feed on sap. Males fight for possession of these coveted sap sites. They use their horns to flick rivals off the branch. Big males tend to have disproportionately large horns and usually win, monopolising the sap sites and the females. Small males do not fight. They sometimes manage to mate by sneaking into sites before bigger males get there. But the females may mate with a big male later, which may displace all the smaller male's sperm.

Male dominance *Bighorn rams clash (above) in a ritual that may last for more than a day. Rivals rear up on their hind legs, then drop onto all fours and come together in a head-on collision. Males use their horns to dominate other rams – the bigger the horns, the more dominant the animal. They fight if neither will back down, usually when their horns are of equal size. Japanese horned beetles (below) use their horns to force rivals off their territory, usually oak tree branches, where they feed on the sap.*

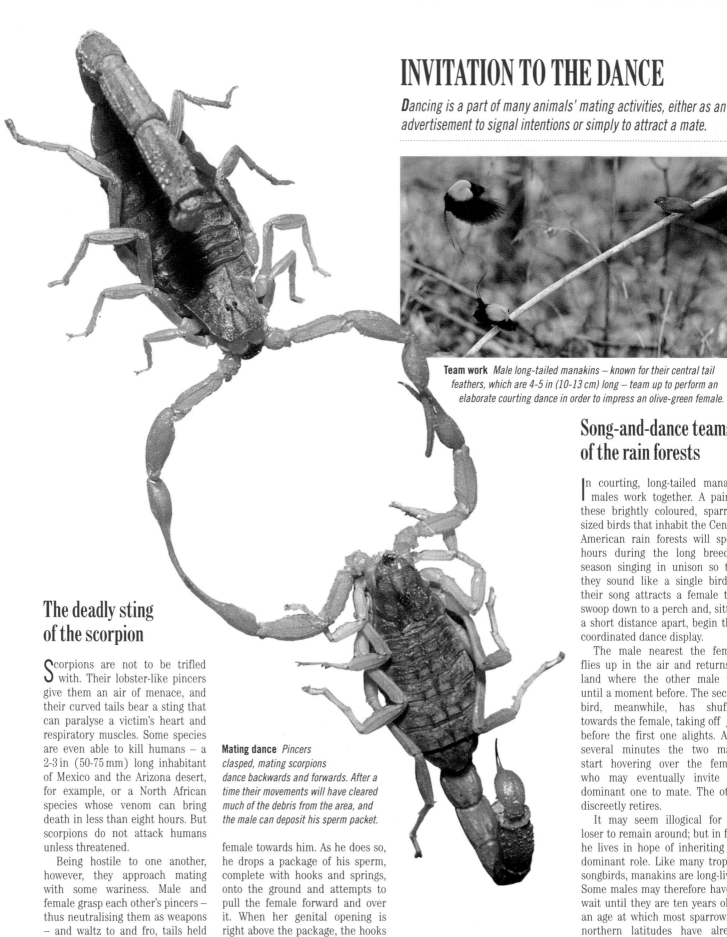

INVITATION TO THE DANCE

Dancing is a part of many animals' mating activities, either as an advertisement to signal intentions or simply to attract a mate.

Team work *Male long-tailed manakins – known for their central tail feathers, which are 4-5 in (10-13 cm) long – team up to perform an elaborate courting dance in order to impress an olive-green female.*

Song-and-dance teams of the rain forests

In courting, long-tailed manakin males work together. A pair of these brightly coloured, sparrow-sized birds that inhabit the Central American rain forests will spend hours during the long breeding season singing in unison so that they sound like a single bird. If their song attracts a female they swoop down to a perch and, sitting a short distance apart, begin their coordinated dance display.

The male nearest the female flies up in the air and returns to land where the other male was until a moment before. The second bird, meanwhile, has shuffled towards the female, taking off just before the first one alights. After several minutes the two males start hovering over the female who may eventually invite the dominant one to mate. The other discreetly retires.

It may seem illogical for the loser to remain around; but in fact he lives in hope of inheriting the dominant role. Like many tropical songbirds, manakins are long-lived. Some males may therefore have to wait until they are ten years old – an age at which most sparrows in northern latitudes have already died. This is a long wait; but in terms of producing offspring and passing on genes it is worth it.

The deadly sting of the scorpion

Scorpions are not to be trifled with. Their lobster-like pincers give them an air of menace, and their curved tails bear a sting that can paralyse a victim's heart and respiratory muscles. Some species are even able to kill humans – a 2-3 in (50-75 mm) long inhabitant of Mexico and the Arizona desert, for example, or a North African species whose venom can bring death in less than eight hours. But scorpions do not attack humans unless threatened.

Being hostile to one another, however, they approach mating with some wariness. Male and female grasp each other's pincers – thus neutralising them as weapons – and waltz to and fro, tails held up and out of the way. But this is a dance with an ulterior motive to it. After a while the male pulls the

Mating dance *Pincers clasped, mating scorpions dance backwards and forwards. After a time their movements will have cleared much of the debris from the area, and the male can deposit his sperm packet.*

female towards him. As he does so, he drops a package of his sperm, complete with hooks and springs, onto the ground and attempts to pull the female forward and over it. When her genital opening is right above the package, the hooks catch and the package is catapulted into her. Thus inseminated, she departs to lay her eggs.

Colourful courtships by birds of paradise

The most dazzling inhabitants of New Guinea's rain forests are the highly promiscuous male birds of paradise, who display their vivid feathers against the dark green forest canopy. The brilliant orange plumes of the male raggianas, or Count Raggi's birds of paradise, are seen at their best during the birds' spectacular courtship dances.

Groups of male raggianas gather at traditional courting sites in trees, each bird defending its own perch. When the brown females arrive the males begin a frenzied bout of song and dance, hopping about, flapping their wings and shaking their orange tail feathers. They then freeze into a head-down posture that shows off their tail feathers and allows their female visitors to inspect them.

If a female does not find a male she likes, she moves on to another display area. But if she does find one, she perches beside him. The male then performs a brief pre-copulatory dance, almost inverted and throwing his feathers over his head and into her face, while she plucks at his feathers. Once mated, the female flies off to lay her eggs and to raise her young on her own. The male birds, meanwhile, await the next female visitor, and then begin the whole procedure again.

On display *Male raggianas try to outshine each other in courtship displays, with one or two of the birds getting most of the matings.*

The stylish water ballet of courting grebes

In spring, the brown-and-white winter plumage of the great crested grebe is enlivened as its head feathers grow to form a black double crest, and reddish-brown ear tufts sprout on its face. Grebes have only one mate and pairing is established (or resumed after winter separation) by an elaborate water ballet. One bird dives beneath the water and swims just below the surface, towards the other. The mate adopts a position like a crouching cat as it watches the approaching ripples. When it reaches its prospective partner, the first bird rises vertically out of the water. Both then begin shaking their heads from side to side, and preening each other's wings.

This is just one in a series of displays. Most elaborate is the weed ceremony, which takes place just before nesting. The birds dive together and surface carrying bunches of waterweeds in their beaks. Swimming quickly towards each other, they rise up, treading water in an ecstatic vertical dance in which their heads sway from side to side. The actual mating takes place on platforms of vegetation built in the water.

In a species that mates for life, and where male and female rear the offspring together, partners must be carefully chosen. The complex ceremonies carried out by great crested grebes are, in part, fitness tests in which each sex checks the qualities of the other.

Quickstep *Like great crested grebes, western grebes of North America perform elaborate courtship dances. These include the rushing ceremony in which couples rise in unison from the water, holding themselves erect with only their legs under the water, and rush together for some 22-33 yd (20-30 m).*

BUILDING TO IMPRESS A MATE

A male animal's suitability as a mate is often measured by the quality of the nest or structure that he builds to impress his future partner.

Fresh nests find favour with female weaverbirds

Postcards from Africa sometimes show huge collections of nests hanging like fruit from trees. They are weaverbird nests, and one of many species that create such colonies is the sparrow-sized village weaverbird. The male builds the home, but the female rears the offspring. And while the female incubates the eggs, the male may try to attract another partner.

A male's success in getting any females at all depends on his physical fitness and the quality of the nest he constructs. Breeding takes place in the rainy season when there is plenty of new grass around for building and lots of insects for feeding the young. The male bird weaves the outer shell of a nest hanging from the tip of a branch, and whenever an unmated female visits the tree in search of a partner, he hangs from the nest by his feet, fluttering and showing off the bright colours under his wings.

If his display is adequate, and his nest is suitably fresh and green, the female may accept him. But she will refuse him, however good his display, if his nest is brown and dry. A nest turns brown in a week as the grass dries in the hot sun, so if a male does not attract a female while the nest is still green, he has to dismantle it and start again with fresh leaves. Only by insisting on a green nest can a female be certain it is newly built and strong enough to house her and her family.

The complex courtship of the stickleback

Seduction, fancy dress and even do-it-yourself all have a part to play in the courtship ritual of the three-spined stickleback, a finger-length fish of fresh and salt water. The male picks a suitable site among weeds and uses scraps of vegetation bound together with a sticky secretion to build a tube-shaped nest open at both ends.

During the breeding season he adopts vivid coloration (bright red belly and blue eyes) which he displays with zigzag movements in front of a passing female. If she is ready to spawn, she responds by swimming with her nose up and follows him back to his nest. He

Capricious male *As soon as a female three-spined stickleback has swum through a male's tunnel-shaped nest and laid her eggs, he chases her away.*

entices her to enter by thrusting his snout into the entrance. If unimpressed, she will swim away and may return to eye the nest again. When at last she does enter, the male prods the base of her tail, which stimulates her to lay eggs. As she finishes, the male swims in after her, chasing her away. He discharges his sperm over the eggs and then seeks another mate.

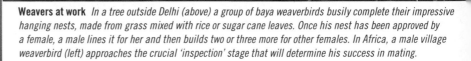

Weavers at work *In a tree outside Delhi (above) a group of baya weaverbirds busily complete their impressive hanging nests, made from grass mixed with rice or sugar cane leaves. Once his nest has been approved by a female, a male lines it for her and then builds two or three more for other females. In Africa, a male village weaverbird (left) approaches the crucial 'inspection' stage that will determine his success in mating.*

The underwater mystery of an African lake

Strange things happen in Lake Malawi, in central Africa. The waters teem with many species of cichlid fish, whose mysterious courtship rituals baffle zoologists.

In some types of cichlid, each male builds a bower or egg-mound in the sand, which he hopes will so impress a female that she will lay her eggs above it. These bowers vary in height from about 1½ in (40 mm) to 6 in (15 cm) or more, some being splendid 'sandcastles' 10 ft (3 m) across. Yet others may be crater-shaped, flat-topped or just a scrape in the sand.

Males of the same species build their bowers close together in one of the areas where courtship displays take place. This enables interested females to inspect all the bowers and select a mate.

What makes a female cichlid choose one male above all others, is still a mystery. There is no discernible pattern of behaviour, and what determines a male's success remains unknown.

Bower builder *A male cichlid patrols the water above the impressive bower he has built, which is 2 ft (60 cm) across. If it attracts a female, she will lay her eggs above it, then later swim away with her fertilised eggs in her mouth.*

The highly decorated homes of bowerbirds

Early explorers in New Guinea were intrigued to find thatched, hut-like structures about 3 ft (1 m) high in the jungles, and assumed that they were the playhouses of local children. They were amazed to learn that the structures were actually the work of bowerbirds, relatives of the birds of paradise.

So rich in fruit-bearing trees are the tropical forests of New Guinea and northern Australia that the birds can eat enough fruit in a few minutes to keep them going for the day. The rest of the time is free for courtship and mating and for developing the architectural and decorative skills found nowhere else in nature – apart from man.

Males of each of the 18 species of bowerbird construct elaborate bowers – as distinct from nests – that are intended to attract a

Flowery welcome *A great grey bowerbird (above) stands before the entrance to his bower, which is bedecked with hibiscus. He is one of the species that build bowers of avenue shape (above left). Generally, the drabber the bird the more exotic his bower.*

mate. Most decorate their bowers with natural or man-made objects, such as butterfly wings, flowers, feathers, fungi, shells, pieces of crockery, rags or bottle caps.

The simplest bowers are those of Australia's tooth-billed catbirds. A male clears a space on the forest floor and covers it with upturned leaves, their pale undersides easily

visible in the dark. As they wither, he replaces them with fresh ones. The male sings close by until a female willing to mate arrives. Afterwards she flies off to lay her eggs and rear the chicks alone.

Maypole bowers are made from twigs piled round a sapling. That of Australia's golden bowerbird is one of the most elaborate – when the pile is about 4 ft (1.2 m) high, the male repeats the operation at an adjoining tree. Then he uses a branch between the two as a perch on which to display to females. Maypole bowers are kept in good repair and used year after year.

Courting in the avenues

Male satin bowerbirds are avenue builders, arranging upright sticks in two parallel lines usually running north-south. They are reputed to paint the inside walls with a mixture of saliva and charcoal, berries or pigments, and then decorate them with bright objects.

Most females appear to favour the colour blue. As blue feathers and flowers are scarce where the birds live, a bower with plenty of blue attracts a female. Once she is tempted into the bower, the male picks up one of his decorations and prances in front of her, fanning his tail and making a whirring noise. After half an hour or so, they mate.

HOW ANIMALS SHOW THEY ARE READY TO MATE

A dramatic display of colour and movement often advertises an animal's readiness to mate, but some have good reasons for keeping their condition secret.

No mistake *A male chimpanzee examines a female (above and right) to see if she is ready to mate. When females are on heat, they become red and swollen round the genital area.*

Male chimpanzees make sure of the moment

Female chimpanzees are fertile for only a short while, at the peak of their sexual cycle. Mating at any other time is unlikely to produce offspring. When a female is on heat, the pink or red skin round her genital opening becomes swollen and enlarged, a sure signal to male chimpanzees in her troop of 15 or more animals that she is ready to mate.

As the female's cycle progresses the swelling gets bigger, and is largest and most prominent at the time of ovulation (release of the egg) – the time when she is most fertile. A female is on heat from four to six weeks and during that time mates, on average, six times a day, probably with all the males in her group. But during the final week, as she approaches ovulation, the dominant males guard her fiercely and fight to mate with her.

After ovulation, the chimp's genital swellings subside, and remain small during pregnancy. Once her baby is born, a female chimp will not be sexually receptive again for three or four years.

Among female vervet monkeys, however, such conspicuous advertising of sexual availability is unknown. They conceal their most receptive time, showing no genital swelling or changes in behaviour as they come on heat. So a male cannot be sure when the female is at her most receptive.

Like chimpanzees, vervet monkeys live in groups where there are a number of sexually active males and females. Because bouts of mating occur over a period of several months, a male is unlikely to know whether or not he is the father of any particular youngster.

Parental confusion

The coyness of female vervets may have evolved precisely because it generates confusion about parenthood among the males of a troop. In several species of primate – for example, hanuman langurs – older males sometimes behave very aggressively towards young langurs that are not their own. Some are even known to kill youngsters who are not their relatives. Naturally,

Guessing game *Among vervet monkeys, females give no clear signs that they are on heat. Males that mate with them, therefore, do not know which youngsters are theirs.*

this is something female vervets want to prevent. By confusing the issue of paternity, females may be buying security for their offspring.

The reason why chimpanzee females advertise their sexual readiness and vervet females hide it could lie in the different structure of their societies. In a troop of vervets, all the females tend to be related to one another, and the young males leave to join new groups as they reach maturity, at about five years old. So the young

monkeys in the troop they join are unlikely to be related to them.

Among chimps it is the other way round. Young males stay with the group into which they were born, and young females move to a new group as they become sexually mature at seven to ten years old. If the males in a group are related, they have nothing to gain by killing young animals because the victims could be their relatives. By killing them they would be destroying part of their own genetic stock.

Masculine appeal *A blue bird of paradise puts on a spectacular display to attract a mate. He swings upside-down from a branch (right) with his two-toned, bright blue tail fanned out.*

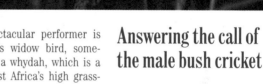

A show of fine feathers attracts female birds

When a magnificent blue bird of paradise wants to find a mate, he hangs upside-down high on a prominent branch in the New Guinea rain forest and puts on a brilliant show. His iridescent blue tail plumes are spread out in a shimmering mass above his velvety black head and breast, and his two extra-long black tail straps rise skywards in graceful curves. Once in position he swings to and fro, making strange, grating calls.

When he has caught a female's eye, the jay-sized bird relies on his spectacular plumage to encourage her to choose him to be her mate.

Another spectacular performer is the Jackson's widow bird, sometimes called a whydah, which is a native of East Africa's high grassland. The shiny black males are thrush-sized. In their prime, the birds' feathers grow to about 8 in (20 cm) long, making them easy to spot as they swoop above the tall grass in their distinctive pattern of flight.

A male widow bird that wants a mate beats out a circular arena about 4 ft (1.2 m) across at the birds' communal dancing ground in the long grass. He leaves the central column of tall grass standing, and stamps out a cup-shaped recess on each side of it. When a brown-streaked female passes by, the male throws himself with gusto into a bizarre dance. He calls as he leaps up and down with his head flung back. He thrusts forward some of his long tail feathers to touch his chest and leaves just two pointing outwards and downwards. If the female is suitably impressed by his display, she stays to mate with him.

Showing off *A Jackson's widow bird (left) launches into his energetic mating dance to impress a female and try to lead her to his nest. A long-tailed widow bird (top left) soars into a dazzling display flight above a female in the grass below, intent on catching her eye.*

Answering the call of the male bush cricket

Tremblings in her legs lead a female European bush cricket to a prospective mate. The male bush cricket advertises his position and availability with a loud mating call. Firmly grasping a stem of the bush on which he has settled, the bush cricket scrapes his forewings together to produce both his high-pitched song and also a series of low-frequency vibrations, which are transmitted through the plant. His call, picked up by other bush crickets, attracts females but also warns off other interested males.

But there is a problem. When a female nears a potential mate, she cannot identify where he is sitting because she is deafened by his loud call. So she switches her sensory systems from sound to vibration detection to locate the calling male and make her final approach.

She has, in the lower part of each leg, specialised receptors that detect vibrations in the plant. She uses these to feel the vibrations transmitted by the male, and makes her way up the plant to seek their source. Reaching a fork, she puts one leg on one stem and one on the other, to compare the intensity of the vibrations before deciding which branch to follow in order to locate her future mate.

THE HAZARDS OF MATING

So strong is the urge to reproduce that many courting animals are prepared to risk losing their lives to waiting predators, or even to cannibalistic mates.

Advertising for a mate can bring sudden death

Calls, scents or flashing lights are often used to attract a mate. An animal must make known its availability for reproduction if it is to succeed in producing young. But, as messages can be intercepted by predators, this can be dangerous.

Male tungara frogs, for example, call loudly at night to signal their availability to potential mates. But their calls not only attract amorous females – they also attract hungry bats. A fringe-lipped bat likes to feed on a tungara frog, so it homes in on the source of the sound to find and devour the calling frog.

Methods used to attract a mate are determined by the costs and benefits they entail. The benefits of calling loudly are high in that they attract a female to mate with; but the costs are too great if a predator overhears the serenade.

Like all creatures, the tungara frog has to compromise to increase its chances of survival. It is safer in a crowd, so calling males join together in a large group in the hope that it may be an unfortunate neighbour that the raider grabs.

A male who finds himself alone modifies his call. Usually a tungara frog's mating call is made up of two sounds: a 'whine' and a 'chuck'. By including only the 'whine' part of his song, a solitary male draws less attention to himself. This might make him less attractive to females, but he is also far more likely to escape the unwanted attention of nearby bats.

In for the kill *A fringe-lipped bat (above), mouth agape and fierce teeth exposed, swoops down on its prey – a defenceless tungara frog. A male tungara frog (inset) makes a tempting target as he puffs out his throat while he is calling for a mate.*

Bats are also a hazard to courting crickets that are calling loudly to find mates. But the crickets seem to have found a solution to this problem – they frequently sing in unison at exactly the right sonic frequency to 'jam' the tuning-in signals used by prowling bats.

Fighting for a mate *Horns locked in a fierce struggle for dominance, two male topi antelopes fight it out for the chance to mate with visiting females. However, they put themselves at risk from predators at their lek, or mating ground, in a Kenyan reserve.*

The risk of mating with more than one female

Topis, or tiangs, are East African antelopes. Males of the species have two ways in which to secure a mate. Some defend large territories where there is plenty of food, and can mate in reasonable safety with the relatively few females that come there to feed.

Those who are unable to win a large territory gather at a lek, a mating arena where males display their fitness and strength to visiting females. Here the males have their own small stamping grounds, which are set close together and bitterly defended by each individual. These tiny territories may be only some 27 yd (25 m) across, and have little food available.

Lekking can be spectacularly successful, however, because some of the stronger, more competitive males within the group manage to mate with several females. But the disadvantage is that frequent and prolonged fighting to defend a mating area without much food is exhausting. And there is a very high risk of injury or of being killed by a predator. Often, predators such as spotted hyenas simply sit and watch the contests. As soon as a worn-out male lies down to rest, they attack and devour him.

Female insects that feed on their mates

Cannibalism is a natural part of the reproductive behaviour of a praying mantis. After mating, the female may devour her mate, so obtaining the nutrients that help to make eggs. This enables her to produce far more eggs than she would otherwise have done.

A male mantis, guided by scent released by the flightless female, lands about 3 ft (1 m) away from her and approaches with caution. Once he has transferred his sperm, he drops from the female's back and scuttles away before she can seize him and feed on him. Most of the time, however, he escapes and is free to mate again.

As a female mantis copulates with any male that comes her way, there can be no certainty that a male she eats after they have mated has been responsible for fertilising all her eggs and so will be the father of all her offspring. In addition, the victim's body may nourish eggs fertilised by others rather than by him. His eggs will have been laid before the female assimilated his body's nutrients.

Sacrificial offering

With many species of spider, the female is threateningly large in comparison with the male, and may easily mistake him for a trapped insect and proceed to eat him. So any male wanting to mate must approach with the utmost caution. Different species of spider use different tactics. A male may frantically wave his legs or his pedipalps (the sensory appendages on his head), or he may tread carefully over the female's web using a complicated dance-like step to distinguish himself from any other insect. Alternately, he may resort to bribery and offer her an insect as a distracting snack.

Tarantulas do not have good eyesight, so they communicate by touch. When a tarantula male meets a female, he signals his presence by using his front legs to drum a tattoo on her body. She is alarmed, and raises her front legs ready to strike. It takes a lot of soothing and stroking from the male to calm her down.

At last she raises her body and opens the lethal fangs that could finish him off with a single bite. But he is not unprepared. He has hooks on his front legs specially for holding her jaws apart. Safe at last, the male inseminates the female and then makes his retreat as quickly as possible.

Fatal attraction *Mating with his much bigger mate (above) is a life-threatening activity for the male praying mantis, as afterwards he may well be eaten by the female (right).*

Into the jaws of death *Tarantula spiders (above) mate after the male has successfully secured the female's death-dealing fangs. The spurs on his front legs (below right) hold her jaws apart and keep him safe during this hazardous encounter. Normally, the mating of the two tarantulas lasts about a minute.*

MAKING SURE OF FATHERHOOD

Competition between males has led to the evolution of many bizarre techniques to get rid of a rival's sperm and so ensure paternity.

Rough wooing *Nurse shark mating, like that of other species, is a brusque business in which the male gives the female several bites before inserting a pair of claspers into her genital opening. These implant his own sperm and flush out that of any rival.*

Last in line ensures that his genes will survive

Beneath the gossamer exterior of the male damselfly lies a ruthless determination to assure the continuance of his genes.

Females will fly from one male's territory to another in order to lay eggs. But before they can lay, they have to copulate with the male occupier, even though they may be carrying the sperm from a previous encounter. No sooner has a female entered his territory than the male grasps her about the neck with claspers, set at the end of his long abdomen. Once she is secured, sperm is transferred from his testes to his penis. The female swings herself forward until the couple's genitals come into contact. But before the male implants his own sperm, he removes any sperm left by a rival during previous couplings. His penis is barbed for the purpose, and not until every trace of any earlier rival has been scraped from the female's

Staking a claim *Mating damselflies make genital contact by curving their bodies together (below). For the male, a vital part of the act is to remove a rival's sperm from the female, which he does with his barbed penis (left).*

reproductive tract will he inject his own sperm. After mating, the female is released and, if the male is lucky, she will lay eggs fertilised with his sperm before she encounters the next suitor.

Expunging a rival's sperm is crucial in the bid for fatherhood, and the male shark has his own way of achieving this. The shark's sexual organ is double-barrelled. One tube squirts a powerful jet of seawater into the female to flush out sperm from previous matings, while the second introduces his own. In this way he ensures that the offspring will carry his genes – unless, of course, another male intervenes and flushes away his sperm in turn.

Fathers-to-be who are doomed to die

Female ghost spider crabs of the Mediterranean mate with many males during each breeding cycle, but only the sperm of the last male will fertilise the eggs. He ensures this by using a mixture of sperm and natural glue.

First he deposits the glue into the female's sperm storage organs, and follows this with his sperm. Previously deposited sperm is pushed to the back of the storage area and sealed in as the glue sets, preventing it from fertilising any eggs. In this way the female's last mate ensures he is the father of all the eggs laid.

The male mosquito employs a similar system, but rather than injecting the glue first, he uses it to seal in his own sperm, so blocking off later rivals. Male apollo butterflies have evolved yet another method, by which they introduce numbers of large, headless sperm along with the normal type. The headless sperm have no other purpose than to take up space in the female's reproductive tract, leaving no room for the sperm of any later males. Her original mate creates a second safeguard by secreting a plug which temporarily seals the whole mass inside her.

For the honeybee drone, mating is fatal, since he leaves his genitalia as a plug to seal in his sperm. Genetically, the sacrifice is worth the cost, since it increases the number of eggs his sperm will fertilise. And as there is only one virgin queen to each colony, with many males in pursuit, his chances of mating again are negligible.

If a male has to die in order to procreate, it is important that his sacrifice should not be wasted. So the male insectivorous midge stays attached to his mate, who eats him alive, leaving only his genitalia as a plug to prevent other males from entering her.

The male has thus provided her with sufficient food to keep her well nourished until she has laid her eggs. This eliminates the need for her to go hunting for food, so exposing herself to the risk of being attacked by predators.

Determined fatherhood
The devices employed by male insects to ensure paternity are many and varied. The male mosquito glues his sperm into the female during mating (below), and the male Heliconius *butterfly (right) wastes no time at all – he mates with the female the moment she emerges, wings still crumpled, from the chrysalis.*

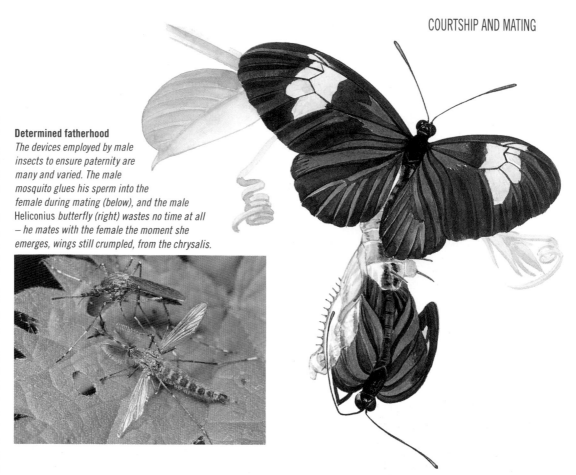

Insect suitors put rivals off the scent

The use of chemical scents, called pheromones, to attract a mate is not rare in the animal world. But some insects have evolved scents that have quite the opposite effect; they succeed in putting off other male suitors.

Mating between houseflies, for example, usually lasts for about an hour, but the sperm is transferred within the first ten minutes. Then, during the remaining 50 minutes, the male gives the female a fluid that will make her unreceptive to any other male for several hours – in the hope that it will be only his sperm that fertilises her eggs.

During mating, male *Heliconius* butterflies pass on a scent to the females that make them smell like males, so repelling other suitors. The females store these secretions for up to three months, suggesting that being unattractive may be of benefit to them. Perhaps, free from male attention, they can spend more time feeding and getting on with the business of laying eggs.

Courtship battles among the cow pats

Female yellow dung flies lay their eggs on fresh, wet cow dung. Males of this widespread species know this, and try to get there first to increase their chances of mating successfully. A male can be fairly certain that he has fertilised a particular batch of eggs if he can mate with a virgin female and then hang on to her until she lays.

However, as male dung flies have poor eyesight, they will grab at anything. If it turns out to be another male, they will release him after a brief tussle. But if it is a female, the male will keep hold of her with determination while other potential mates struggle frenziedly to snatch her

Mating ground *Drawn by the scent of a fresh cow pat, a female yellow dung fly is about to lay her eggs. The male who has mated with her guards her fiercely, fighting off other males who are anxious to mate.*

from his grasp. Here, size means everything, since a large male can successfully ward off other males and keep the female to himself.

Even females that have already been fertilised are fought over. This is because, despite the short interval between mating and fertilisation, the last male to mate before the eggs are laid will be sure of fertilising most of them.

All this fierce and frantic competition ensures that the hardiest males father the most offspring, but it does not always benefit the females. In the battle for their possession, they are often trodden into the wet dung by the eager males.

FATHERING BY FRAUD AND FORCE

Some males use disguise, force or piracy to mate with a female that is already paired, so avoiding the effort of courting or of rearing young.

Stay-at-home salmon get their reward

Both male and female salmon grow to maturity at sea. They make their way there from the streams where they were hatched, and stay for several years without breeding. The time spent at sea ranges from one to four years, depending on the species. Then the salmon put all their energies into reproductive growth and begin the arduous journey back to their home streams in order to breed.

By the time they reach the freshwater breeding grounds, both sexes have undergone remarkable changes. Males now bear a heavy hooked jaw, which they use to keep other males away from their chosen mate, and most of their internal organs are reduced in size while the testes are enlarged. Females have also changed, and they are now filled with eggs.

Once a female has found a suitable location in the gravel bed of the stream, she scoops out a nest called a redd with sweeps of her body. Then she releases her eggs into the redd as her partner sheds his sperm on them. He fathers the vast majority of the offspring – but not all. Some of the eggs are fertilised even before the female can finish laying, because lurking in the vicinity, almost invisible, are tiny male salmon. Little more than a finger-length, they may be less than one year old – young males that have not yet made their way to sea to grow to maturity.

By sneaking in while the female is laying and releasing their own sperm on her eggs, these minute males may fertilise as many as ten per cent of the eggs before the large male has a chance – a quick genetic return for very little effort.

Ten-spined stickleback males welcome as many females as they can into the nest during spawning, to get as many eggs as possible to fertilise. Some males, however, are duller coloured, resembling more the drab coloration of a female. These 'transvestite' males sneak in to a nest with the females and fertilise a clutch already in the nest, thereby cuckolding the host.

Mating game *A spawning female Atlantic salmon (below) is guarded by her hooked-jawed partner. Even so, a much smaller male may slip in and fertilise some of the female's eggs. Some eggs of a pair of ten-spined sticklebacks (right) may be fertilised by an intruding male in the guise of a female.*

Male intruders that rely on brute force

Many pairs of birds share the hard work of rearing their young. But in the race to continue their genes into the next generation, some males gain by duping other males into bringing up their young. They are thus spared all the effort and so have time to mate with more females.

Common guillemots, for example, nest in large colonies on rocky cliffs in the Northern Hemisphere. The males use a variety of tactics

Absent fathers *In common guillemot colonies, some males may succeed in fathering young without being burdened with the task of feeding them. They manage to mate with another male's partner and leave him to rear the chicks.*

to try to mate with a female paired with another. These 'extra-pair' matings occur regularly, but only if the intruder avoids the defences of the male partner.

One trick used by intruders is to wait until a male has just mounted his female, run at him at high speed, push him off and take his place. The original partner, once knocked from his cliff ledge, may take several minutes to gather his senses and return to the site. By the time he gets there, the brash intruder will have completed the mating, and the cuckolded male is left to rear any resulting offspring. The female does not seem to react at all to the change of mates.

Scientists have determined the extent of infidelity among guillemots and other species by using genetic fingerprinting, the same method used to identify criminals.

Females that pick up the wrong package

With tiger salamanders, striped, lizard-like amphibians of North America, mating requires some careful coordination. First, the female nudges the male on his tail with her nose; this is a signal that triggers him to drop a package of his sperm on the ground. He then moves forward slowly, followed by the female, who positions herself to pick up the sperm in her genital

opening. However, things do not always go according to a couple's intentions. Another male tiger salamander is drawn to a courting pair like a magnet. He rushes up and pushes himself between them. Then, copying a female's behaviour and nudging the male, the interloper induces the first male to drop his sperm package. He moves forward swiftly and puts his own package on top of it. The female picks up the top sperm package, and the first male's sperm package is left abandoned on the ground.

Guile wins the day *A courting pair of tiger salamanders may attract the attention of another male who will interfere in the proceedings and get his own sperm accepted instead.*

Double-dealing in the insect world

A Texas field cricket sings for a mate by rubbing his wings together. Females home in on the mating song, but they are not the only ones tuned into the male's frequency. Flies are also listening in, seeking a place to lay their eggs.

These flies use a calling male cricket as a nursery and a larder for their larvae. Once a fly has located such a cricket, it lays its sticky eggs on and around him. The attentions of the fly are fatal to the cricket, which always dies just after the fly's larvae pupate.

Pirates on the prowl
Some male crickets have adopted a different strategy for securing a mate – piracy. These are the satellite males, which sit quietly near a calling male and try to steal the mates he attracts. Not only do they find a mate, but by not calling, they also avoid the attentions of parasitic flies.

When a male hanging fly woos a female he presents her with a dead insect, on which she feeds while they mate. This gift is essential if the mating is to proceed smoothly. However, some hanging fly males

Stealing a gift *A male hanging fly encourages a female to mate by offering her an insect, which she eats during copulation. Some males mimic a female to rob another male of his offering, using it to attract a partner for themselves.*

adopt the tactic of transvestism. By assuming the manners and mating habits of the opposite sex they deceive other males into thinking they are females – an effective strategy in winning partners.

Mimicking the wing postures and abdominal movements of a female, a transvestite manages to rob an ordinary male of his nuptial gift. The transvestite then uses the gift to attract a female for himself. The time and energy saved by not hunting for the insect can allow the transvestite to mate more often and, at the same time, cuts down the risk of being attacked.

SAYING IT WITH PRESENTS

In many cases a male has a far better chance of mating if, when he is courting, he presents the female with a gift, preferably something she can eat.

Female insects who get a free nuptial feast

At mating time, male crickets and katydids, long-horned tropical grasshoppers, supply their partners with protein-rich food packages attached to their sperm sacs. The packages are so big that, after mating, part of the sac stays outside the female's genital tract and slowly contracts, forcing the sperm into her. If no food were provided, the female, as in many other insect species, might devour the sperm sac. But as it is, by the time she has eaten the food gift, the sperm will have been safely injected.

Almost all male animals transfer much more sperm than a female needs. But often, the more sperm a male supplies, the more likely he is to fertilise the eggs if the female takes more than one mate.

The bean weevil male inseminates a female with about 46 000 sperm. These are delivered to a large sac in the female called the bursa copulatrix. After a few minutes, sperm move towards her sperm store (spermatheca), where there is only room for 6000 of them. The first to arrive will eventually fertilise some 80 eggs, while she digests the sperm left in the bursa copulatrix – a free meal.

Parting gift *During mating (above), a male katydid transfers a high protein food parcel with his sperm package, which protrudes from the female. The bigger the food parcel the longer it will be before she mates again, so increasing the male's chances of fatherhood.*

Food gifts can distract or entice the female

A courting dance fly male offers his mate gifts of insects, then mates while she is absorbed in devouring her free meal. The bigger the gift, the more time she takes to eat it and the longer he has to mate with her.

In his search for a suitable gift, a male dance fly is quite likely to become a courtship gift for some other insect, such as a male nursery web spider. Normally, this type of spider eats the dance fly in the state in which it is caught, but when he presents it as a courtship gift, the male spider wraps it in a dense covering of fine silk.

It was originally assumed that this silk wrapping was meant to occupy the predatory female while the male inseminated her; however there are other, more probable purposes for it. One theory is that the

silk wrapping is impregnated with a type of chemical message that enables the female to identify the donor. The other is that the gift packaging is to catch the female's eye and arouse her interest.

Careful approach

The manner in which the nursery web spider presents the gift is also crucial. When he finds a likely female, he holds the gift very prominently in front of him as he approaches, and raises his long front legs and his large palps (sensory organs near his mouth) well away from the gift – body language expressing non-aggression.

This is necessary because a female nursery web spider, far from being predatory, shows signs of extreme nervousness at the approach of a male. Unless her curiosity about the shiny white gift overcomes her, she will hurry away with the male chasing after her, still waving his silk-wrapped gift.

Fully occupied *A female dance fly (right) examines a long-legged fly, while the male who gave it mates with her. The male supports the weight of all three, leaving the female free to feed.*

Present tense *A male nursery web spider (below), his silk-wrapped gift finally having been accepted by a female, is about to mate. Catching her eye and patiently overcoming her instinct to scuttle away was time well spent, as females mate many times, even close to the moment of laying their eggs.*

Air-filled presents that impress female flies

Male balloon flies try to impress potential mates with elaborate presents. They feed on nectar, and expend a lot of energy transforming it into silken threads, which are produced from an anal gland.

The male fly weaves the silk into a large, empty balloon – a useless but very effective courtship gift. Groups of male flies congregate to display, each one carrying its balloon with its feet and using it to try to attract a female. A female that is impressed and willing to mate takes a male's proffered gift and probes it all the time he is mating with her. She relinquishes it afterwards, and unless she has damaged it beyond repair, he may use it again to court another female.

The balloon has no food value at all. Therefore it may be intended as a form of advertising; an indicator, perhaps, of the male balloon fly's ability to forage.

Gift-wrapped *A balloon fly (left) sets out with his huge gift in search of a female. He has to be a competent forager to make a good balloon. It is rather like judging the size of a man's bank balance from the make of car he drives.*

Fish is the choice of the female arctic tern

A gift of fish from a male is the deciding factor in the female arctic tern's choice of mate. This is because picking a good provider can have a profound effect on her breeding success.

After spending the winter in the Antarctic, these terns fly back to cool temperate or Arctic regions to breed. A novice male flies around carrying a fish such as a sand eel or a sprat in its bill, in the hope of tempting a female. When one is attracted, she lands beside him and takes his fish. Then she waits,

Good providers *A male arctic tern (below) proffers a female an impressive gift of fish as a nuptial offering. A Texas roadrunner (right), with his gift of a lizard still dangling from his beak, mates with the female he has wooed with tail-wags, calls and, finally, with food.*

to see how many more he will bring her. A poor performance from the male prompts her to move on in search of a better provider. But if he offers plenty of fish at this stage, he will almost certainly turn out to be a good father too, bringing home enough food to feed the chicks.

These early season gifts of fish are not just a way to win a mate. The more food the female eats at this time, the more energy she has for producing eggs. An arctic tern usually lays two to three eggs, but a well-fed mother produces larger eggs of better quality, and these are more likely to hatch into strong and healthy chicks.

THE MANY WAYS OF MATING

Eggs can be fertilised either inside or outside the female's body. Successful breeding requires luck, skill, timing and sometimes even outright trickery.

A balancing act for a pair of bald eagles

A male bald eagle swoops from the sky to alight on a branch beside his perching mate. She welcomes him by leaning forward until her body is almost horizontal, opening her wings and calling. He mounts her, his sharp talons curled to avoid hurting her. She raises her tail to allow him access to her genital opening, and he presses his sperm vent against it.

Mating is the culmination of several months of elaborate aerial courtship displays. Birds cannot store sperm, so generally mate a number of times to ensure that each egg is fertilised, which must be done before the shell is formed. Regular matings increase in frequency to five or six a day just before the female lays her eggs.

Mating manoeuvres *In a flurry of feathers, a pair of North American bald eagles mate beside their huge treetop nest. Aligning their reproductive vents while keeping their balance in high winds takes skill and cooperation.*

Getting together *Encased inside its hard shell, an acorn barnacle extends its lengthy penis to fertilise its receptive neighbour. At the same time, both barnacles reach out with their feathery limbs and scavenge tiny particles of drifting food.*

Neighbourly mating and changes of role

Barnacles occur upon seashores in amazing numbers, clamped head-down onto rocks. They are hermaphrodites, both male and female in one, but do not usually fertilise themselves.

Most barnacles mate with their nearest neighbours, one performing the male role and one the female, but do not cross-fertilise one another at the same time. The one playing the female part lays eggs inside its mantle cavity after moulting, and the scent associated with egg laying attracts a response from a neighbour.

The one playing a male part produces sperm and uses its long penis – the longest relative to body size of any organism – to inject them into the female opening of the other and fertilise the eggs. Later, the fertilising barnacle will play the female role itself.

Nautilus pairing *The nautilus uses its arms for mating, like its relatives the octopus and squid. Four of the 90 or so tentacles that protrude from a male nautilus's shell are used to carry sperm into the female.*

A special arm for a mating octopus

During the breeding season, a male octopus develops a modified third right arm, called a hectocotylus. Initially he may use it to caress his mate, then after a while he reaches into his body with it and pulls out a mass of spermatophores – large sperm packages shaped like baseball bats. Each has a spring-like ejaculatory organ held by a cap at one end. In one octopus species, spermatophores may be more than 3 ft (1m) long.

Using his hectocotylus, the male pushes the sperm package into the female's body through her breathing siphon. Sometimes the arm breaks off and stays inside the female. If the male completes this manoeuvre successfully, the sperm package takes up water through a syringe-like system. The water pressure inside eventually pushes off the cap and the spring uncoils, pulling out the mass of sperm and spilling it all over her eggs.

With common squids, a female has more control. She stores the male's sperm in a cavity under her mouth until her eggs are ready for fertilisation. Then she reaches inside her own body and removes her eggs in a string. She makes sure they are fertilised by pressing them one by one against the stored package of sperm, and then she attaches them to the ocean floor in a cluster of 10-50 long strings.

In primitive insects such as the springtail, a male has to trust to luck. He leaves his sperm package on the ground hoping a receptive female will stumble across it. The moisture within her genital cavity melts the protective skin of the package, allowing the sperm to swim free and fertilise her eggs.

If a male finds another male's sperm package, he will eat it and then substitute one of his own.

Armed for the task *A male octopus uses one of his eight arms, which is specially modified for the breeding season, to deposit tubular sperm-filled packages into the female's body cavity. The sperm packages travel down a groove in the arm.*

Male artifice *In an African lake, a female mouth-brooding cichlid fish gathers into her mouth her newly laid eggs. A male fish intent on fertilising them lures her towards him with the yellow spots on his anal fin, which look just like her eggs. This brings the female's mouth close enough for the male to reach the eggs with his sperm vent.*

Keeping offspring safe in their mouths

Most fish eggs are fertilised outside the female's body, the eggs and sperm being shed into the water at the same time. This is a risky business, because sperm have a short lifespan, so bad timing or an unexpected water current can reduce the chances of the eggs being fertilised.

Some fish, though, have refined the process of fertilisation. The cichlids, for example, are a large and varied group of African fish, some of which are mouth-brooders. They keep their offspring safe from predators in their own mouths.

Some species of cichlids begin brooding their eggs almost the instant they are laid, but when the brooding parent is the female, there is a danger that she may snatch the eggs into her mouth before they have been fertilised. So in at least two species, fertilisation takes place in the relative safety of the female's mouth. As a female lays her eggs, she takes them into her mouth for safe keeping, but there are males waiting nearby, watching her. A male wants to get his sperm to the unfertilised eggs before another male can do so, and to accomplish this he appears to resort to trickery.

The pattern of bright yellow spots on a male's anal fin looks like the eggs a female has just laid, so she is lured towards him. Believing the spots to be her eggs, she tries to pick them up in her mouth. This brings her egg-filled mouth close enough to the male's sperm vent to allow him to fertilise the eggs she is already holding.

Mouth-brooding tilapia fish in Zaire's Lake Mweru behave in a similar fashion. A female is lured into collecting a male's sperm by a conspicuous tassel hanging from his sperm vent. The tassel is made from long filaments of tissue festooned with white blobs that so closely resemble a female's eggs that she tries to collect them, too.

A GOOD SENSE OF TIMING

Factors such as changes in day length can trigger animals to mate at specific times, confining some to only one or two days of the year.

Waiting for the right signal to breed

Mass spawning at sea *Both corals (top) and sea urchins (above) are triggered to release millions of sperm or egg packages by the phase of the moon. This way the males and females of each species closely synchronise their sexual activity, sometimes to just one hour on a particular night.*

During November and December, as the sea around the Great Barrier Reef off Australia's north-east coast gets warmer, the corals prepare to spawn. The minute coral polyps – the soft-bodied marine animals that secrete a hard limestone skeleton from which a coral reef is formed – each produce eggs or sperm that mature in small packages.

Then four or five nights after the December full moon, when the sea is warm enough, they release the packages. Millions of them float up from the reef, varying in colour according to the coral species. The packages burst open within a day, and eggs and sperm of the same species fuse together, then divide to create tiny larvae that float away. This mass spawning ensures that enough will survive. Over the next two weeks, the larvae settle and develop into polyps, founding new colonies. Coral polyps also reproduce non-sexually, by repeated division.

Many animals breed in summer, when there is plenty of food to feed their young. Birds are triggered to mate by the amount of daylight as

Feeding time *British great tit chicks hatch in time to catch the annual glut of winter moth caterpillars. Timing is precise because this vital food source, which feeds on oak leaves, abounds for only a few weeks.*

the days lengthen in early spring. Their chicks hatch in summer, when food is abundant. Great tits, for example, feed their chicks on winter moth caterpillars. The moth eggs hatch in spring as new oak shoots appear for the caterpillars to feed on. Just as the caterpillars reach full size, the great tits catch them for their chicks – in three weeks, a pair may feed some 8000 caterpillars to their young. In the tropics, where there is little change in day length, birds rely on other signals to breed, such as variations in rainfall.

A male mouse that dies after mating

The entire male population of Australia's jerboa-like brown antechinus, a species of broad-footed marsupial mouse, is dead before the females' eggs have even been released from their ovaries. Females may live up to three years and bear two litters, but males live for just under a year and breed only once.

At the start of the breeding season a male's body undergoes changes that will inevitably bring about his death. His testes grow until they make up about a quarter of his total body weight, and they start to produce large quantities of sperm, as well as the male sex hormone, testosterone. With so much testosterone in his bloodstream, the male develops an insatiable sexual appetite and travels great distances in search of females.

Then for periods as long as 12 hours at a time, he mates with as many females as he can find. This intense activity may be repeated every night for up to a fortnight.

Despite its invigorating effect on the marsupial mouse's mating habits, testosterone has the side effect of closing down the male's immune system, leaving his body unable to fight off infection and disease. After the exhausting mating period, it is only a matter of time until a male falls victim to some illness. The whole male population is usually dead within ten days of mating, in July or August.

For most mammals, the shelf life of sperm once it has passed to the female is little more than a day or two, but for the brown antechinus it is much longer. The female's eggs are released about two weeks after the mating frenzy. They are then fertilised by sperm that she has been storing in her reproductive tract.

A short-lived relationship *A pair of brown broad-footed marsupial mice mate inside a hollow tree in southeast Australia. At the end of the mating season, the male will die.*

Rushed and unrushed mating strategies

The time available for mating varies greatly between animals. Take frogs and toads, for example. Some species are 'explosive' breeders that congregate to breed in huge aggregations often numbering thousands, and find mates and spawn in perhaps less than a week. In other species, males sit in a pond and call for females, night after night, for extended periods.

Once a male has found a female, he grabs her from behind in a position known as amplexus, and stays there until she spawns. With explosive breeders, mating is a mad scramble as single males try desperately to separate pairs and grab females for themselves. In their frenzy, unmated males catch at anything that moves – even trying to mate with fish or sticks.

Temperature may influence the time taken in amplexus, since bodily reactions are faster where temperatures are higher. With British common frogs and toads it is usually completed within a day, but prolonged amplexus lasting several months is known among frogs living high in the cold of the South American Andes. By contrast, species living in tropical climates, arrow-poison frogs for example, tend to complete amplexus quickly.

Joined together *A pair of European common frogs (above) stay in the mating posture, the amplexus, before the female lays her spawn. A pair of common toads (right) may mate within a day or could be in amplexus for several days before the female spawns.*

HOW MANY PARTNERS?

In the mating game there seems to be room for every possible kind of partnership: role reversal, lifelong devotion and fly-by-night deception.

Faithful couple *A female mara leaves her young in the colony's nursery and returns periodically to feed them. Her watchful male partner is never far away.*

When a life partnership can be an advantage

Maras, or Patagonian hares, live on the grasslands of South America. Although hare-like with long hind legs, they have hoof-like claws and look like a cross between a hare and a small antelope. In fact they are rodents of the guinea pig family. Maras are thought to mate for life, a relationship that is rare among mammals.

When animals form life partnerships, the labour of looking after the offspring is usually shared. Most birds form monogamous relationships, and some even mate for life, quite possibly because both parents are equally capable of taking food back to the nest. Among mammals, only three per cent of species have monogamous relationships; this may be because feeding the young is solely the female's responsibility, as only she can provide milk.

Young maras are born in a burrow, with up to three in a litter. Caring for them is exclusively the mother's job, as she supplies them with milk. Their father's indirect contribution to their well-being is the care of their mother. To have enough energy to nurse babies, she must spend as much time as possible feeding on grass and plants. With her head lowered she is vulnerable to predators, so the male stands sentinel for her. But his apparent altruism is really selfishness. The female is sexually receptive twice a year, but for only a few hours at a time. Thus the male must stay close to her if he is to have a chance of mating successfully. He must also keep a lookout for single males and guard the female from their advances. She benefits from his vigilant defence because she is left free to eat in peace.

Among carnivorous mammals, some males, wolves among them, also help with providing for the young. Although only the female suckles the newborn pups, the male brings food back to the den for his mate and older pups. Once the pups are a few months old, both the male and female regurgitate meat for them.

Family holdings

Included too among mammals that mate for life are gibbons. They feed on fruit in Southeast Asian jungles, but fruit supplies are limited. It is thought that the only way males can be sure of sufficient food for their offspring is by defending territories that contain fruit trees. As the male can hold only enough territory to feed himself, his mate and offspring, he is forced to cleave to a single female.

Male gibbons stay close to their partners and youngsters to guard them from other males. Single males are always seeking a chance to steal mates and territories, and if successful they may kill the young of their predecessor.

Klipspringers are small African antelopes that live in thick bush and are also territorial in habit and monogamous. Pairs defend small territories, and the male offspring leave home when they are about a year old to find mates and establish territories of their own.

Family territory *Klipspringers (above), a species of dwarf antelope, are territorial and monogamous. In a Southeast Asian forest, a mated pair of lar gibbons (right) rests in the treetops. Males of both species defend no more territory than is essential to the support of their families.*

Birds turn breeding roles upside-down

When a female bird has more than one partner at the same time, there is often a remarkable reversal of roles in courtship and caring for the young. In most birds of this kind, the females are larger and more colourful than the males, and it is they who will compete furiously for mates. Male birds in turn take on most of the parental duties, including nest building.

Among wattled jacanas living in marshy areas of Central America, each female defends a large territory. Contained within it are the smaller individual territories of each of her three or four male partners, usually side by side. The female mates with each male in her 'harem' and lays eggs in each of their nests. The males incubate and care for the eggs and chicks, even though they are not certain which of them are their own offspring.

Every day the female does the rounds, visiting each male in turn and even helping him to defend his territory from the others, intervening first on one side of any dispute, then the other. Female wattled jacanas are always on the lookout for more males and are not averse to stealing them from their neighbours. If a female dies, another quickly takes control of her males.

When a female takes over a new male, the first thing she does is to destroy his clutch of eggs or kill his chicks. She wants him to abandon his current family and rear her offspring. This behaviour is similar to that of male lions taking over a new pride – after driving off the resident males they kill the cubs of the previous fathers, so forcing the lionesses to come on heat again and put all their energy into bearing the offspring of the new male.

Smash and grab *In a South American marsh, a female wattled jacana (on the left above) approaches a male on the nest of another female. The two display to each other (right). The female then manages to attack the eggs in the male's nest (below) and runs off with a broken eggshell in her beak. She is disposing of the eggs of his existing mate before courting him herself.*

Two-timing males get the best of the deal

Pied flycatcher males arrive in Europe from Africa in spring. The females arrive slightly later, by which time the males have established territories in woodlands.

After a male and female have paired, she builds a nest in a tree hole and lays a clutch of up to ten eggs. But once she has settled down to incubate them, the male very often flies off and begins courting a second female. Once they have mated, however, he abandons her to her nesting and returns to his original mate to help raise the first brood he fathered.

It is too late for the abandoned female to find herself another male, so she has to cope as well as she can. So although the male fathers two families, he is only saddled with the work of rearing one.

Left alone *After mating, a brown and white female pied flycatcher may be left to care for her young alone. Despite this, she is generally able to raise at least some of her family.*

CHANGING SEX OR SEXUAL ROLES

To make the most of every mating opportunity in the competitive world under water, fish may change sex or play both sexual roles.

Size determines a fish's change of gender

Among blueheaded wrasses living on western Atlantic coral reefs, there are two types of male. There is a small proportion of large and brightly coloured males that are about 6 in (15 cm) long and compete for mating sites with each other and pair up with a succession of females. There are also smaller, yellow males that spawn in groups of females.

Blueheads are a wrasse species that feeds on small marine animals and on the parasites of larger fish. The large, blueheaded breeding males actually start life as diminutive, dull-coloured females. A large male's presence suppresses the sex change of other females, but when such a male dies, the largest of the females changes both her sex and colour, developing a bright blue head and a black-and-white collar. Females may also be stimulated to change into males if the number of females in a particular community increases too greatly.

On Australia's Great Barrier Reef, thumb-length anemone clown-fish have a different strategy. They start life as males, but change to females when they are fully grown. These fish live among the sea anemones and feed on plankton – minute plants and animals.

A family group is dominated by a large female who mates with the males of her group. Her offspring all hatch as males, but some will develop into females. Individual offspring may split away from the group to join other shoals or to become rovers. When she dies, the largest male of her group changes sex and takes over.

Modes of approach *In the crowded waters of a coral reef, blueheaded wrasses fight for territory and food (above). Both fish (inset) are blueheaded wrasse males. The larger of the two competes for mates and pairs with just one female at a time. The small yellow one spawns among whole groups of females.*

Deadly nursery *The poisonous tendrils of a sea anemone provide protection for a colony of anemone clownfish and their eggs – the fish are immune to the anemone's stings. A clownfish colony contains only one large breeding female, who started life as a male.*

Stacking the odds *Slipper limpets often live in a pile of females and males. To make sure all have a chance of reproducing and that there are enough of both sexes, they change sex as they get older.*

Slipper limpets pile up to produce their young

A slipper limpet is usually to be seen as one of a pile of limpets stacked one on top of the other in shallow, muddy waters of the North Atlantic. At the base of the pile are the oldest and largest limpets, all females. Towards the top are younger limpets, all males.

The males have penises that are many times longer than their bodies, enabling them to reach a female at the bottom of the stack. Each pairing sends a host of larvae into the sea, where they float free for a brief period.

Slipper limpets, which grow up to 2 in (50 mm) long, feed on small organisms filtered from the water

and need to be attached to a firm surface. Such surfaces are scarce in the seas where they live, so once a larva has found somewhere to settle it releases a scent into the water to advertise the fact.

Other slipper limpet larvae are attracted by the odour and begin to arrive. The first one to get there settles on the oval, reddish-brown shell of the colony founder, which matures to be a female, whereas the settler becomes a male. Slipper limpets change sex from male to female as they get older.

Eventually the male on the top of the stack matures and changes to a female. This attracts another larval male to settle. So it goes on, with female limpets dying off at the bottom of the pile and new larval males joining at the top.

Slime eels keep their strange sex secrets

Hagfish live on the deep ocean floor and burrow in the mud with only their heads protruding. They are eel-like but with tail fins, and are called slime eels by fishermen because they secrete slime when handled. Hagfish are almost blind, their eyes being covered with a layer of skin. They sniff out

their food, mainly soft-bodied sea creatures or dead fish. In places where they are found, hagfish often occur in huge numbers.

The population always includes pure males and females, and some that are hermaphroditic in varying degrees, although each one develops only one sexual function. The reason for this is uncertain, but it is thought that hermaphroditism evolves mainly among species that are unable to move about much.

Mud dwellers *Eel-like hagfish are relatives of the lamprey. They grow to about 16 in (40 cm) long and burrow into the mud at very deep levels of the ocean floor. The females lay tough-skinned, yolk-filled eggs, from which miniature adults hatch after several weeks.*

Versatile fish *Hamlet fish of the Caribbean play both sexual roles when they meet, taking turns to lay eggs and fertilise them. Curving round in graceful arcs, they stimulate one another into releasing eggs and sperm.*

Taking simultaneous roles of male and female

Earthworms are hermaphrodites, each individual being both male and female at the same time. Mating earthworms lie head to tail in a parallel embrace to exchange sperm. This passes directly from the male duct of each worm into the female duct of the other.

This reciprocal embrace neatly avoids the danger of the earthworms fertilising their own eggs. Few animals do fertilise their own eggs, because by doing so they would lose the fundamental advantage of sex – the mixing of their genes with those of another individual to produce varied offspring. But there are exceptions.

Killifish, or egg-laying top minnows, are also hermaphrodites, and are one of only a handful of vertebrates (backboned animals) able to release eggs and fertilise them with their own sperm at the same time. This may be because many killifish live in tropical coastal ponds subject to floods and long droughts, and often find themselves alone. The eggs lie dormant in the mud during a drought, hatching when the pool fills.

For most hermaphrodite fish, however, the advantages of breeding with others are far greater than the short-term benefits of being self-sufficient. If fish were to play

both male and female roles at once, some of the eggs might be fertilised by sperm from the same parent as the eggs and milt mingled in the water. Hermaphroditic black hamlet fish of the Caribbean have evolved a neat solution to the problem. Pairs meet at dusk, and one fish initiates the mating sequence by pushing its nose under its partner's tail. Then it swings round so that each fish is floating with the other's tail curved over its head.

Turn and turn about
In this position, the first fish releases a few eggs, then waits for its partner to shed sperm over them. Having fulfilled its part of the bargain, the second fish now releases a few of its eggs and waits for them to be fertilised in return.

The pair continue releasing eggs and sperm a few at a time. By this means, each fish protects itself from exploitation by the other, as producing eggs takes more effort than producing sperm. If one fish released only sperm, it would be making the same contribution to its next generation of offspring for less effort, but the other would be making more effort for less gain.

OTHER STEPS TO THE NEXT GENERATION

Not all animals reproduce by male to female mating. Some lay eggs without mating and others duplicate themselves. A few lay one egg that divides into many.

Female insects that need no males

No rose grower need be told about the phenomenal rate of aphid reproduction. It may however surprise them that this is largely accomplished without male aphid intervention.

During the summer months, without benefit of mating, female aphids produce vast quantities of unfertilised eggs. These develop within the mother, who each day gives birth to 20-odd exact replicas of herself, each with their own eggs already maturing inside them. And each of these is the mother of a further generation of females.

In this way aphid populations expand rapidly. There are no males to take up food and space, and the females need not spend time mating. Every aphid reproduces and only cold weather, a predator such as a ladybird or a food shortage – or an insecticide – can stop them. Within days, the descendants of a single aphid can smother a rose bush.

In autumn, the pattern changes, and both male and female offspring are produced. This generation mates, laying fertilised eggs that spend the winter in crevices. The eggs hatch in spring, producing only females – and the cycle begins all over again.

Aphids owe their success to their dual method of reproduction. In the asexual phase, all individuals contribute to the next generation, while the sexual mode mixes and therefore refreshes the genes.

Oak gall wasps also reproduce by both methods. Having spent two winters encased in small galls, or swellings, on the roots of oak trees, wingless females surface and scramble up the trees to lay eggs in the buds. These females have not mated, and therefore reproduce asexually. The oak tree's tissues react by producing another gall that encases the eggs. By midsummer its occupants are mature and winged, and fly into the world to find a mate.

Inseminated females burrow into the soil to lay single eggs in the roots of oak trees. There again galls are formed, from each of which, two years later, a wingless female emerges to climb up the tree and restart the cycle.

Virgin births *A female aphid (above and inset) gives birth to another female able to reproduce herself. Inside each of the oak galls (right) there may be as many as 30 oak gall wasp larvae. Although they will develop into male and female wasps, they were laid by a female that has never encountered a male.*

Ways of becoming a self-contained parent

Parthenogenesis, the creation of a new generation from unfertilised eggs, is not the only way to reproduce asexually. A freshwater hydra, for example, simply buds. Miniature hydras grow from the tissues of the parent, eventually detaching to become independent individuals. Only the food supply limits the numbers.

Budding is not the only way in which hydra produce offspring. In autumn, they reproduce sexually, laying eggs. These grow a protective shell to survive the winter, and hatch the following spring.

Sponges can also reproduce both sexually and asexually. Some marine species grow stalked buds that break from the parent to drift with the currents until they find a suitable spot and begin to grow. Freshwater sponges have a more elaborate system. As they die they release small groups of cells in capsules called gemmules – like packeted, instant sponges.

In suitable surroundings, the 'ingredients' activate and become a new sponge. Sponges do not seem to have any special reproductive organs, although some are hermaphroditic – that is, each one produces both sperm and eggs.

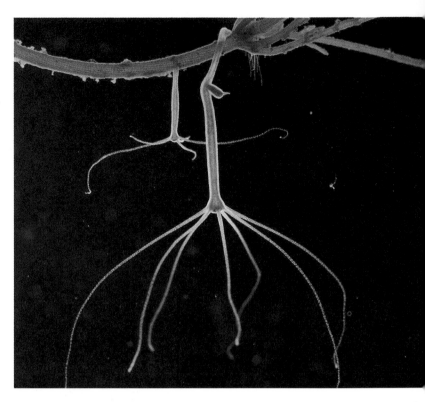

Chipped off the old block *With one of its offspring beside it and a new one beginning to emerge, this freshwater hydra is capable of reproducing itself asexually, time after time, simply by budding. Sexual reproduction takes place in autumn – eggs are laid and survive the winter, to hatch out into asexually reproducing hydras in the spring.*

The amazing world of wasps and bees

A wasp possessing no common name has an uncommon means of reproduction. Known to science as *Litomastix truncatella*, it lays a single egg beneath the skin of the silver-Y moth caterpillar. This egg provides the wasp with 30-80 identical offspring by dividing itself again and again – a method of reproduction called polyembryony. The wasp larvae hatch and eat their way through their host's tissues, finally pupating inside the now empty caterpillar skin. On achieving adulthood, they emerge and repeat the whole process.

Bees and wasps belong to the insect order Hymenoptera. Some of them lead solitary lives and others live in social groups, but all have the ability to reproduce without actually fertilising their eggs.

Reproductive females of social bees and wasps mate in summer or autumn, then store the sperm that they receive in receptacles within their bodies. Although they only mate once, the supply of sperm lasts for their entire lives – up to five years in the case of the honeybee, but little more than one in the case of the bumblebee.

Each queen has total control over her store of sperm and can decide whether or not to use it to fertilise each egg as it passes through her

Underground nursery *Busy workers in a common wasps' nest continue to feed the larvae, despite the fact that their nest has been cut open. They will repair it, using chewed up wood in a fine, papery form. Each cell will be used up to three times as the colony continues to grow through the summer.*

reproductive system. If she withholds sperm the unfertilised egg becomes a male.

The queen bumblebee spends the winter hibernating under the bark of a tree, or among dry, fallen leaves. In spring she emerges, and singlehandedly begins to build her nest of mosses and grass. Having made a cell of wax, she lays about a dozen fertilised eggs within it. The hatched offspring are female workers who help the queen to build more cells, but do not themselves lay eggs at this point.

The coming of the new queens
When the colony reaches its maximum size, at the end of summer, it begins to produce new queens which, like the workers, emerge from fertilised eggs but have been given more food at the larval stage. The existing queen then lays eggs which, despite being unfertilised, develop and hatch. All offspring from these eggs are male.

In bumblebee colonies near the end of summer, some workers also lay unfertilised eggs that hatch into males, and very occasionally, honeybees may do the same. The new bumblebee queens and males leave the nest and fly off to mate and, in the females' case, to found new colonies after hibernating.

MANY WAYS TO COMMUNICATE

'*THE LANGUAGE OF BIRDS IS VERY ANCIENT, AND LIKE OTHER ANCIENT MODES OF SPEECH, VERY ELLIPTICAL; LITTLE IS SAID, BUT MUCH IS MEANT AND UNDERSTOOD.'* ≈ GILBERT WHITE, *NATURAL HISTORY AND ANTIQUITIES OF SELBORNE*, 1789.

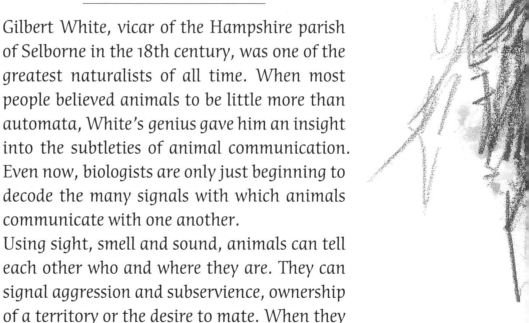

Gilbert White, vicar of the Hampshire parish of Selborne in the 18th century, was one of the greatest naturalists of all time. When most people believed animals to be little more than automata, White's genius gave him an insight into the subtleties of animal communication. Even now, biologists are only just beginning to decode the many signals with which animals communicate with one another.

Using sight, smell and sound, animals can tell each other who and where they are. They can signal aggression and subservience, ownership of a territory or the desire to mate. When they are courting, some animals can even provide information about their health, their age and the amount of time and energy they are willing and able to invest in the care of their young. There is still much to be learnt of the intricate network of animal communication, and the following examples may one day prove to be a mere foretaste of its true complexities.

Communal scents
By passing food from one adult to another, wasps spread the characteristic odour of their colony and distribute a chemical produced by the queen wasp. This reassures the workers by communicating to them that the queen is still alive, and all is well in the nest.

A foot that 'speaks'
A male blue-footed tree frog from Borneo communicates by waving one of its hind legs and spreading its toes. Living close to waterfalls, its call would be drowned out by the roar of rushing water.

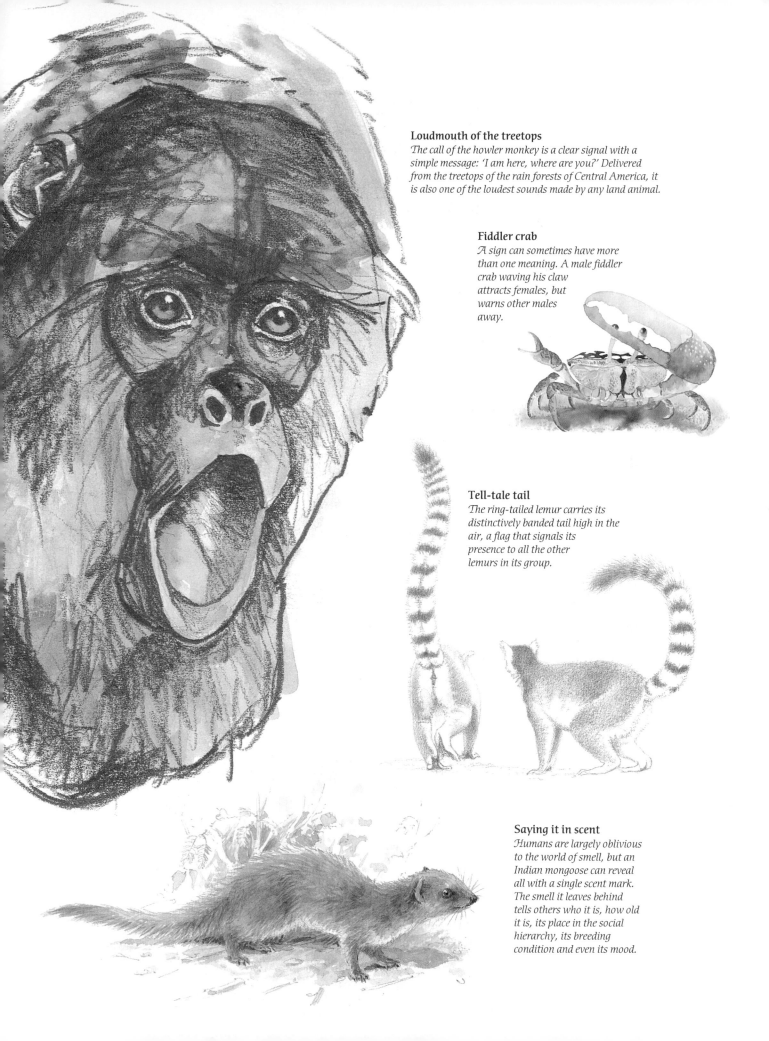

Loudmouth of the treetops
The call of the howler monkey is a clear signal with a simple message: 'I am here, where are you?' Delivered from the treetops of the rain forests of Central America, it is also one of the loudest sounds made by any land animal.

Fiddler crab
A sign can sometimes have more than one meaning. A male fiddler crab waving his claw attracts females, but warns other males away.

Tell-tale tail
The ring-tailed lemur carries its distinctively banded tail high in the air, a flag that signals its presence to all the other lemurs in its group.

Saying it in scent
Humans are largely oblivious to the world of smell, but an Indian mongoose can reveal all with a single scent mark. The smell it leaves behind tells others who it is, how old it is, its place in the social hierarchy, its breeding condition and even its mood.

Booming bass songs from the ocean depths *The largest creature ever to have lived on Earth, the 100 ft (30 m) long blue whale, makes the loudest noises in the animal kingdom. Its bass calls reverberate through the water for 30 seconds or so, and carry over vast distances. One whale was recorded giving an output of 180 decibels – a volume that would be deafening to human ears, and is even higher than the sound of heavy gunfire at close proximity. So far no one has been able to decipher the exact meaning of these stentorian songs, but they are most likely used during courtship, pairing and social gatherings.*

TENORS AND BASSES OF THE DEEP

The underwater songs of whales and dolphins allow them to communicate in a highly developed way, sometimes over huge distances of the ocean.

Largest mammals make the loudest noise

Not only are blue whales the largest living creatures on Earth, they also make the loudest noise. These ocean giants have been known to reach lengths of about 100 ft (30 m), and at the end of their feeding season can weigh up to 148 tons. Their long, low moans can carry through the water for vast distances, and may last for more than 30 seconds.

Although the repertoire of the blue whales consists mainly of a few low-frequency grunts and moans and is fairly limited, compared with that of their humpback relatives, they can also produce soprano notes using ultrasonic frequencies. These may help with echolocation – the emission of short bursts of clicks and the interpretation of the returning echoes to gain detailed information about the surroundings. But the blue whales' usual long moans are thought to be used only for communicating with each other.

Right whales also produce long, low-frequency moans for sending messages over extensive stretches of the ocean. These long-distance calls seem to serve a specific purpose – to call members of a school. When the whales congregate in fairly confined areas in mixed groups of males and females, their simple calls give way to more complex songs. The usual low-pitched sounds are interspersed with higher-frequency notes.

The most likely explanation for these swooping songs is that the males are alternately trying to attract a female with their higher-frequency notes and showing aggression towards rival males with low-pitched notes. Certainly after a bout of growling, if a male is left alone with a female, he changes his tune to more melodic, higher-pitched calls.

Tuning in *When calling to each other through the water across distances of more than 15 miles (24 km), huge southern right whales (above and right) choose the exact frequency 'window' to carry their low-frequency sounds most effectively. Like cellular telephone subscribers, they are tuned in to each other in quieter parts of the sound spectrum.*

A repertoire of sounds aids a busy social life

For more than 2000 years humans have been fascinated by the rich and varied language of the dolphin. From low-frequency whistles to high-frequency clicks, it appears to be capable of expressing a great range of ideas and emotions.

A dolphin makes noises for two purposes – to exchange messages with its companions and to gain information about its environment, in particular the availability of its fish prey. Dolphins reserve the full range of their repertoire for communication. Each individual can make about 30 different kinds of sound, including a personal whistle that, although it resembles its mother's, is unique. Other sounds include furious clicks, which are often conducted between aggressive males, and intimate chuckles, exchanged when males and females caress.

Researchers are attempting to compile a dictionary of dolphin sounds, but many still remain enigmatic to humans. They are also trying to discover exactly how dolphins manage to produce these widely differing sounds.

The Hawaiian spinner dolphin of the Pacific is a particularly social creature that lives in groups of 20-1000 or more individuals. The group size depends on the activity and the location. During the day, for instance, spinner dolphins rest inshore in small groups, safe from predators. Towards evening they begin congregating in larger numbers, indicating a willingness to set off to hunt in deeper waters. Their spinning activity begins to increase (they leap from the water and roll lengthways) and is followed by a stage of zigzagging through the water together.

By feeding in great numbers, spinner dolphins can comb large areas of the ocean more efficiently. As they hunt for fish, they may interchange between groups, but remain in close contact with one another. To coordinate these large numbers, individual dolphins constantly communicate with each other, using a wide range of sounds such as clicks, whistles and short pulses of sound.

Party animals *Bottlenose dolphins (above) and spinner dolphins (below) like to perform most of their everyday activities in groups. This serves to strengthen ties between individual members as well as aiding particular functions. Playing, caressing and feeding are common social occupations, all accompanied by characteristic songs. The whole range of a dolphin's emotions, too, is expressed in its different calls.*

SONGS FROM UNDER THE OCEAN

Whales have developed a range of different ways of communicating with each other, from the harmonious songs of the humpback whale to the high-pitched clicks of the sperm whale.

Impressive outpourings from the ocean depths

In the waters of the Pacific Ocean a male humpback whale is singing a song – a regular pattern of booming roars that are punctuated by shorter sighs and squawks. Each song may last anything from 5 to 30 minutes, with some parts repeated just like the verses and choruses in human song. The singer may decide to give performances that continue for up to 24 hours. Male humpbacks in the Atlantic Ocean sing too, but theirs is a different song from that of their Pacific cousins. The overall patterns are much the same but the component parts (the 'lyrics') are quite distinctive.

Studies of humpback songs reveal that they are constantly changing, with phrases altered or new parts inserted. The songs are long and complex, like musical epics. What is the purpose of these beautiful outpourings? Humpbacks do most of their singing when swimming in the waters where they breed. One theory is that the songs are a 'spacing'

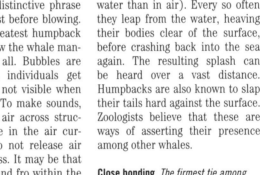

Attention seekers *Humpback whales are known to explode out of the water headfirst, then crash sideways back into the sea – an action known as breaching. As well as stunning fish shoals, it is thought to be a dramatic way of attracting the attention of other whales.*

mechanism to keep males apart in the gigantic lek – the courtship display gathering. Another is that the songs advertise how long the male can hold his breath, showing how fit he is. A distinctive phrase is always sung just before blowing.

Perhaps the greatest humpback mystery is just how the whale manages to 'sing' at all. Bubbles are seen only when individuals get angry – they are not visible when they are singing. To make sounds, humpbacks blow air across structures that vibrate in the air current, but they do not release air during this process. It may be that air is passing to and fro within the complex network of tubes and hollows inside the whale's head, which acts like a huge soundbox.

Humpbacks, along with other whales, make dramatic use of the

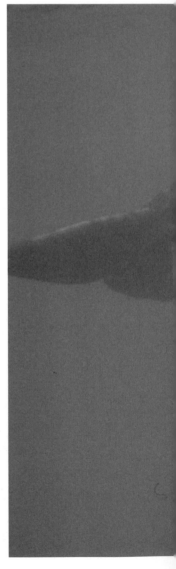

water's acoustic properties (sound travels about four times faster in water than in air). Every so often they leap from the water, heaving their bodies clear of the surface, before crashing back into the sea again. The resulting splash can be heard over a vast distance. Humpbacks are also known to slap their tails hard against the surface. Zoologists believe that these are ways of asserting their presence among other whales.

Close bonding *The firmest tie among whales is between a mother and her young. A humpback mother and calf (below) often stay together for about a year after birth. Other relationships among humpbacks are temporary, lasting only a few hours or days.*

The mysterious cry of the fin whale

There is a curious sound in the sea – almost a pure tone with a very low frequency of just 20 Hz, equal to the lowest recorded note sung by a human being. The song is heard in pulse sequences that last about 15 minutes, with 2½ minutes' silence between. For years the sound was a mystery, until it was discovered that the '20 Hz signal', as it became known, is produced by the fin whale.

With a body length of up to 85 ft (26 m), the fin whale is second in size only to the blue whale, and is the fastest of the baleen (filter-feeding) whales. Fin whales are gregarious creatures and their

Bass of the deep *The fin whale is distinguished by its unique dorsal fin, and is known for its haunting song of low, continuous pulses.*

long-distance calls, audible 500 miles (800 km) away, are thought to be the means by which relations and acquaintances keep in touch with one another.

Transocean news is told in underwater code

Not all whales are tenors or basses. For example, the largest of the toothed whales, the sperm whale, uses an impressive range of higher-pitched clicks to communicate with its own species. Each individual whale has a special combination of clicks, rather like a sound signature, that identifies it within a group.

Sperm whales congregate in family groups, normally of 10-20 animals. The group is usually composed of adult females and their offspring. Males tend to leave their family when they reach puberty, at 7-11 years old, and join a group of young males. They may go off on

their own at 18-21 years of age, going back to a group only during the mating season.

When a family returns to the surface after diving, individuals communicate with a series of clicks. These clicks are thought to regulate important social functions such as mating and feeding. They are also used by whales in distress. A harpooned sperm whale, for instance, sends out clicks to which whales far away may respond.

Big head *The sperm whale (below) has a distinctive profile, unlike that of any other species. Its rectangular head develops disproportionately to the rest of the body until it reaches about 16 ft (5 m) – a third of its adult length. Adults can stay submerged for 90 minutes, and usually signal their intention to dive by raising their tails high in the air.*

NEWS AND NEEDS IN BIRDSONG

The songs of birds are their way of communicating with each other – to warn of danger, to call a mate or simply to keep in touch.

The messages relayed in the dawn chorus

At daybreak on a May morning, the northern European woodland fills with the sounds of birdsong. First a trilling blackbird call, then perhaps a thrush song. Slowly it builds up to a climax of trills, warbles and chirps as male birds stand on their song posts and lustily sing their parts in the dawn chorus. A songster has to be awake and singing as early as possible in the morning if it is to keep hold of its hard-earned territory.

To human ears this chorus of birdsong is powerful and varied, but the voice of each individual bird is virtually impossible to pick out. In the midst of the chorus, each bird sings its own song and listens for any intruders nearby, for each species can distinguish the individuals of its own kind.

A male pigeon, with its simple two-note call, is heard and understood by other pigeons. The other males know that he is laying claim to a patch of woodland, while the females recognise his advertisement for a mate.

When starlings gather early in the evening, and again just before they part in the morning, each bird chatters until the noise level rises to a grating peak. It is not known why they do this, though it may be to coordinate the gathering and movement of the colony in and out of the roost.

Maintaining contact through calls and song

In an English woodland on a moonless night or in the tangle of lush growth in an African tropical forest, when it may be difficult for birds to see each other, song can be an effective way of keeping in touch. The familiar 'too-whit, too-whoo' of the tawny owl, often mistaken for a single call, is in fact a duet between two birds – they may be male and female, or two males – who are checking each other's whereabouts.

Black-capped chickadees of North America warn each other of a predator's presence, then set up a chorus of thin, ventriloquial notes. Confused by the disembodied chirps, the predator often gives up the hunt. These chickadees have over 350 calls, each of which carries specialised information.

The musical duets of some species of African shrikes are so fluid that they sound like a single unbroken song. The song is shared by mated pairs, sometimes equally, but at other times one will sing most of the notes, with occasional punctuation from its mate. These shrikes, which mate for life, use duetting not only as a way of keeping in touch with each other, but also to reinforce their union. They have been observed singing their duets side by side and, should one of a pair be absent, the lone bird has been known to sing both parts.

Some species of bird make use of low-frequency songs to attract a mate. The male sage grouse of North America, for example, uses an inflatable throat pouch to produce a booming call. The male capercaillie of northern Europe has an apparently insignificant call, making it difficult to understand why the female should be attracted to it. Shaking with effort, he emits a sequence of feeble pops and gurgles.

However, speeded-up recordings of the capercaillie's call reveal that much of the sound the bird produces is too low in pitch for human ears. To make such a call normally, the bird would need a windpipe as long as a church organ bass pipe. But the capercaillie has a special tube in its throat, and the deep note is produced when air passes across the open end of this tube, in the way someone might blow across the top of a bottle.

Calling for a mate *The mating call of the American sage grouse (top), performed by the male, is a loud boom audible 440 yd (400 m) away. Crimson-breasted shrikes (above) from southern Africa, sing complex duets in which each pair's calls are so interlinked they sound like one.*

Sunset chat *On autumn evenings, colonies of up to 5 million starlings gather for the night – sometimes from 30 miles (50 km) away – creating a huge noise as they do so. Once a colony has settled, the din subsides, though low chattering continues through the night. At dawn the noise crescendos once more, and then stops abruptly. A few seconds later the whole flock takes flight, dispersing for the day's foraging.*

Keeping in touch *A female American goldfinch lays her eggs in July, and takes sole responsibility for incubating them. As this involves sitting on the eggs for hours at a time, the male visits her frequently to bring her food. The birds call to each other to keep contact, using a distinctive call that helps the male to find the female. The goldfinch's attractive song has led to its being called, inaccurately, the wild canary.*

Birds that change their tune to live or love

Though many birds can be easily recognised by their calls, some are known to change their song or to use more than one. The chaffinch, for instance, has three distinctive courtship songs, each for different parts of the mating cycle, and at least three different types of alarm call, depending on the degree of danger – one call as it prepares to take flight, another when it is injured and a third, a low buzz, when it is aggressive.

Sometimes, however, birds' trills and warbles seem unrelated to any particular activity, though they do

Accent on song *Chaffinches have a loud, jangling song, which starts slowly and accelerates as it moves down the scale, usually ending with a flourish. The song varies slightly from bird to bird, and there are even regional dialects.*

tend to be uttered at specific times of the year. They may indicate aspects of bird life that have, as yet, no meaning for us.

The ability of a male American goldfinch to subtly alter his basic song shows that birds' songs are not necessarily passed on unchanged from one generation to another. The birds breed late in summer, and during the breeding season this striking yellow male finch flies off to find food for his mate while she incubates the eggs.

While he is airborne he makes his 'flight' call, a complex arrangement of notes, to which she responds.

As the season progresses, the male finch's call becomes slightly modified, imitating that made by the female. Their similar-sounding calls then identify the pair to each other throughout the breeding season. Should the female die or move away, the male can easily pick up a new female's call, allowing him to remain a successful breeder throughout his life.

CALLING FOR A MATE

A hubbub of honking, clicking or singing may be the path to success in the difficult business of attracting a mate.

A dazzling display of song attracts a mate

The male sedge warbler's song is a vocal version of the peacock's tail – an elaborately beautiful display that catches the attention of possible mates. The sedge warbler's compelling song advertises his ownership of territory as well as proclaiming his gender and his status as a willing partner.

Whereas most songbirds put together songs that last several seconds from just a few syllables, the sedge warbler is prodigiously inventive. Some individuals have a repertoire of over a hundred syllables. The male selects from five to ten of these syllables, combining and recombining them in numerous permutations so that, instead of a repetitive stereotyped song, he produces an extended, ever-changing string of variations on a theme.

An accomplished mimic, a male sedge warbler is able to incorporate the songs of other birds into his own repertoire. Analyses of tape recordings of sedge warbler songs show that the males with the most elaborate songs manage to find a mate much quicker than those with plainer songs. Such are the rewards of virtuosity.

Vocal seduction *Although his plumage is dull, the male sedge warbler's song is powerfully attractive. This small bird depends upon his voice to charm a female, because she will be drawn only by the most accomplished warbler. Some male sedge warblers stop singing once they have found a mate for the season.*

Calls to entice a partner and deter a rival

Sitting at night in the rain forests of Puerto Rico, a tree-dwelling coqui frog calls to attract a mate. His is a distinctive call, a two-note 'ko-kee' that is quite unlike the single-note croaking of most other species of frog.

Sometimes, though, the coqui frog uses only the 'ko' part of his song, particularly early in the evening. This variation is due to the fact that the two parts of the song mean quite different things: one is for mating, the other is to keep other males out of the caller's territory. 'Ko' is frog language for 'keep out', and is used to establish a male's patch. When he is sure that his evening will not be interrupted he adds 'kee' to mean 'come hither' to passing females.

The hearing systems of males and females are attuned to either one note or the other. Their brains have receptor cells that respond to the signal appropriate to their sex. Never, it seems, do coqui frogs mix their 'kos' and 'kees'.

Unmistakable message *The balloon-like vocal sac of the male tree frog enables him to shunt air from his lungs across a series of vocal chords to produce a mating call that fills the forest night.*

Sound engineers of the insect world

In his quest for a mate, the male cricket, a skilled communicator, sings three different songs: one to advertise his presence, one to court and one to ward off unwanted competitors.

First comes the calling song, a high-frequency sequence of simple chirps that is maintained for as long as it takes to attract attention. Should a female show interest by approaching, the male increases the frequency and shortens the duration of each note. This results in an excited buzz which seems to entice the female cricket.

If a male approaches, this song gives way to another, more aggressive outburst in which each chirp is drawn out in an expression of self-assertion.

Females, for their part, are well adapted to pick up these signals. They use different receptor cells in their ears and nervous systems to distinguish between the songs of competing males, and will travel right through the territory of an unwanted partner to a male that produces a more attractive song.

The male cricket produces his songs by 'stridulating' or rubbing together specially adapted areas at the base of his wings. On the underside of one wing is a row of teeth-like protrusions similar to a comb; on the edge of the other lies a tongue of toughened tissue. The tongue acts like a guitar plectrum. Each time it strikes one of the teeth it creates a sharp click. This sound is then amplified and transmitted by a resonating part of the wing called the 'harp'. The rate at which the plectrum strikes the teeth gives the songs the distinctive quality of each species.

The male grasshopper uses similar means to amplify his mating songs, but the method used to make them is different. He calls by scraping rows of tiny pegs on his back legs against a thickened vein on the forewing. Each species of grasshopper has its own call which is determined by the arrangement of pegs and the rate at which they are scraped. The number of pegs also varies from 80 to 450 per leg.

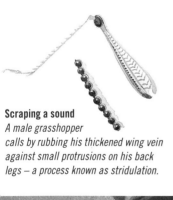

Scraping a sound
A male grasshopper calls by rubbing his thickened wing vein against small protrusions on his back legs – a process known as stridulation.

Deafening squeak *Bush crickets court over long distances. The male of one African species (above) cuts a hole in a leaf, shaped to fit his wings, to amplify the sound he makes when rubbing his wings together. A female cricket in Borneo (left) is deafened by a calling male, so switches sensory systems and tracks him down by detecting his sound vibrations with the receptors on her legs.*

Auditioning for a mate *The hammerhead bat is one of the few mammals to choose a mate at a lek – a collection of males displaying to attract a female (above). As many as 150 male bats hang from foliage, calling loudly, while a female makes repeated visits to the line before picking the grotesque-faced male (right) who sings loudest.*

The loudest honk wins the mating game

The male hammerhead bat, the largest of all African bat species, has a strangely contorted face. He sports a huge mouth and lips, with exaggerated pouches hanging from his cheeks. The female, by comparison, has a slim, pointed face. The differences are important because they give the male his ability to win a mate – not with good looks but with a strong voice.

The male's larynx is so big that it fills most of his chest. So too are the air passages within his nose. This gives him the wherewithal to produce the loud honking needed to attract a female during the twice-yearly mating seasons.

Every night, spaced out and hanging upside-down in the trees, the males flap their wings and honk several notes a second. If a female parading along the near mile-long line-up, hovers close to a particular male, he increases the frequency of his honking until each individual note blurs into one seductive call. Females are drawn to the loudest honkers in this male sonic beauty parade. But after all a male's efforts, the mating process lasts only a brief 30 seconds.

CONVERSING FISH

What seems a peaceful underwater world is really one buzzing with messages – winking lights, electrical pulses and a range of sounds.

Flickering fish *The lights under a flashlight fish's eyes – the brightest produced by any living creature – are visible from as far away as 33 yd (30 m). The Red Sea species (left) turns off its lights by rotating its light organs down into pockets, but the Indian Ocean species (above) switches off by drawing up a skin curtain, like an eyelid.*

Winking flashlight fish send luminous signals

Flashlight fish keep in touch with each other by using their own natural torches. A shoal feeding off a tropical coast on a moonless night appears as a blue-green glow. The light comes from fluid-filled pouches on the fishes' cheeks, home to colonies of minute, light-emitting bacteria – about 50 billion per teaspoonful of fluid. The fish provide these microscopic creatures with the warmth and oxygen they need to live, and in return the bacteria light the way through the dark ocean – they generate light as a by-product of living, just as we exhale carbon dioxide.

The fish can conceal their living lights, and this enables them to produce patterns of light-flashes that some scientists believe are used for communication as well as to confuse predators, to lure prey or to light the way ahead. Blinking can serve as a warning to a flashlight fish that strays into the territory of a flashlight fish pair on the reef. The defending female swims towards the interloper with her light off, then when she gets close, she flicks it back on again. This shock tactic seems to work, so that the intruder is usually driven away.

The green knife fish, found in slow-moving rivers, lakes and lagoons in South America, also has special organs for sending messages. The male 'telephones' a female by transmitting a series of rapid electrical pulses from a special organ and, if she is interested, she replies with her own electric call. Scientists have been able to make captive females spawn simply by playing recordings of male electric chirps.

Spiny lobster lovers call across the sea floor

Spiny lobsters keep in touch with each other through rasping conversations. The sound is produced when a lobster rubs a serrated pad at the base of its antennae against a projection called a rostrum that is on its shell between its eyes.

The lobster's rostrum amplifies the sound to produce a call that can carry as far as 55 yd (50 m). The disturbance these vibrations produce in the water is picked up by other lobsters through the tufts of hair upon their antennae.

The lobsters are found in large groups on the bed of the Atlantic. While they are foraging, they keep in touch with low-level rasping calls that also signal it is safe to be out and about. If danger such as a prowling shark threatens, the lobsters that spot it sound the alarm by stepping-up the rate of their rasps and the group moves into shelter under nearby rocks.

When a female spiny lobster is ready to mate, she sits on a rock and rasps away to announce her

Humming haddock *As courting haddock entwine (below), the male's excited calls to his impassive mate merge into a high pitched hum and red spots appear on his flanks.*

Haddock and toadfish sing their serenades

The male North Sea haddock sings a mating song that sounds like a motorbike engine – a stream of knocking sounds as he circles his chosen female. The excited fish's calls quicken and rise in pitch until they produce a continuous purr. He finally falls silent when the powerful sexual message in his call stimulates the female, floating silently in his embrace, to lay her 10 000 eggs.

A haddock's sound repertoire can communicate many different things. Knocks are usually calls of excitement made during courtship, or in aggressive encounters with other males. The tenser the situation, the faster the knocks. Grunts, however, are made in submission as males flee from fights.

As with many fish, these noises are produced by special muscles pulling on the haddock's heart-shaped swim bladder – an organ filled with gas that maintains buoyancy. The muscles clench the front end of the swim bladder up to 100 times a second to produce the songs, and are richly supplied with blood to stop them tiring quickly.

Bottom-dwelling toadfish also attract females with songs that they drum out on their swim bladders. The calls are also used to mark a male's territory or to sound an alarm, and may last for as long as an hour. When toadfish swim in a bay where there are houseboats, their grunting serenades are amplified by the wooden hulls, which all vibrate like sounding boards. The resulting low hum in the air can be heard as distinctly as an aircraft overhead, or the rumble of distant thunder.

Lobster chatter *Groups of 100-1000 spiny lobsters use rasping calls to communicate as they feed along Atlantic or European coasts. If one sounds the alarm, they all shelter in rock crevices.*

availability. Males that are within her calling range head towards her, fighting for the privilege of mating.

As soon as one of the males reaches the female, she stops calling and the other males instantly lose interest. The courting lobsters caress each other's antennae and the female releases a 'love potion' of chemicals into the water; this compels the male to mate with her.

Pistol shrimps send out cracks of sound

One of the loudest ocean noises is created by the snapping or pistol shrimp, which inhabits tropical coastal waters. This ferocious underwater hunter, only about 2 in (50 mm) long, stalks small fish and knocks them out with stunning 'shots' of high-intensity sound. The immobilised fish tip over and the shrimp catches and eats them.

So loud is this sound that it has been known to set off sound detectors on navy submarines. In the South Pacific, fishermen are said to use the loud cracks of pistol shrimps on a reef to guide them home. The sound is made by one of the pistol shrimp's front claws, which is almost half as big again as the creature's body, although it is carried on a leg of normal size.

To produce the noise, a shrimp strikes together two parts of this enlarged claw, used both to stun prey and to defend its burrow.

Gunfire on the reef *The shot made by a pistol shrimp is so loud that it can even shatter glass. This 'gunman' of the coastal waters is armed with an enormous front claw that it shuts with great force to produce a prey-stunning report.*

COMPREHENDING APESPEAK

Apes and monkeys are able to express aggression, submission and alarm with a rich repertoire of calls, expressions and body language.

Social climbing baboons *To gain any social status, male olive baboons must devote time to ingratiating themselves with females by grooming them (top). A male shows his weapons and signals aggression by yawning widely (above).*

Silverbacks send threatening signals *A dominant male silverback gorilla on the slopes of a volcano in Rwanda sees off an interloper. Such displays of aggression are rare in gorilla groups, where life revolves round the all-powerful silverback. The arrival of a young adult male looking for females of his own, however, provokes threatening displays from both male gorillas.*

Gorilla dramatics and lip-smacking baboons

A group of mountain gorillas is contentedly feeding and resting in patches of sun in a forest in Central Africa. They are a closely knit unit and keep in touch with low grumbles similar to stomach rumbling. Scientists studying gorillas in the wild have identified at least 16 different communication calls, from a 'wraagh' scream of alarm to disciplining grunts and to 'hoot barks' that seem to indicate curiosity. At the sound of human poachers approaching through the trees, however, the group falls into

a tense silence. The lack of sound can be a powerful signal too.

Each gorilla group is led by an enormous mature male, known as a silverback because of his silver-grey saddle of hair. The silverback is the most vocal and physically expressive member of the group and his 'hoo hoo hoo' keep-out call can often be heard nearly a mile (1.6 km) away. He can discipline a youngster or settle a quarrel in the group simply by adopting a rigid stance and glaring at the offender. However, if he has to face up to the leader of a rival group, he will put on an intimidation display of awesome dimensions – strutting, head hair erect, hooting and beating his

chest. If this fails to intimidate the opposition, the silverback thumps the ground and crashes through the foliage, ostentatiously breaking off branches. This ritual display of strength is usually sufficient to see off the unwelcome intruder.

Olive, or savannah, baboons of East Africa also use body language within their large communities of up to a hundred. But their societies are based on the hierarchy of the females. The oldest female is likely to be the most important, with her daughters enjoying higher status than the offspring of other females. Although males are bigger and stronger it is only by making friends with important females

that they gain any status. To get a social foot in the door, the males must ingratiate themselves.

A male baboon uses lots of body language to make friends. As he approaches a female he moves one of his feet backwards and keeps his tail erect while assuming a 'fear-grin' – an anxious smile. To signal that his approach is friendly he smacks his lips. Then, if she will let him, he will groom her coat.

If another male interferes while he is making his advances, the social climber yawns widely to show his vicious canine teeth. But if the intruder is too big to handle he turns round and shows his bottom in a gesture of submission.

Songs in the trees *A siamang gibbon (below) makes whooping calls to its mate through the tree canopy of the Sumatran jungle. The pileated gibbons (right) of Kampuchea make yodelling calls to each other. The calls of both species last about 18 seconds.*

The yodelling duets of gibbons and monkeys

The dawn chorus of gibbon song reverberates throughout a rain forest in Southeast Asia, filling it with meaning. From the tops of the tallest forest trees, gibbon couples sing 'whooping' songs to each other across the tree canopy.

As well as keeping the pair in touch their songs serve as a warning to other gibbons, telling them to keep out of the couple's home range. Those listening in can probably estimate the physique and standing of a singing pair from their duet. The song may also indicate how well established a pair is since a practised couple will sing a well-coordinated duet. Gibbons mate for life, and their songs are essential to strengthen and refresh the bonds between a couple.

A siamang gibbon uses its deep, resonating throat pouches to add distance to the sounds it produces. Siamang males and females sing at the same time, but in other species of gibbon the two sexes alternate their songs. The yodelling duet of pileated gibbons is a spectacular example. After a quiet opening by the female, the duettists alternate a rhythmic song that quietens down so that the female can finally give voice to her dazzling 'great call'. This is the climax of the duet, with both animals exhibiting a great deal of excitement as they swing through the upper branches of the trees.

Howler monkeys also defend their home-range with sounds that echo across the South American rain forests – in fact they produce the loudest sounds of any land animal. A howler in full voice can be heard up to 10 miles (16 km) away. These noisy residents of the upper reaches of the rain forest canopy use their calls as a kind of 'audio fence' to define the limits of their home-range. Both sexes have a loud, gruff howl, although the male's call is deeper than the female's bark-like yell. A male is particularly well equipped for producing eerie calls. His neck is thick and stubby, and he has a drooping double chin. The bones inside a male howler monkey's throat have gradually evolved into a cage shape that amplifies and accentuates his calls.

Howlers move around in groups of about 20 individuals, including males and females of all ages. As soon as two groups get near each other they begin to call, the whole group joining in to produce a deafening racket. This is how howler monkeys 'fight'. There may occasionally be some light skirmishing, but on the whole the communicative howlers prefer to avoid physical confrontation, and settle disputes with these shouting contests. Early morning and late evening are the most vocal times of the day, when troops use their calls to warn each other of their presence.

There is no idle chatter in vervet communities

Foraging in a tree-scattered area of African grassland, a vervet monkey spots an approaching leopard. It lets out a loud, barking cry of alarm and the whole of its troop takes to the trees.

Later one of them sees another dangerous predator, an eagle, hovering above. This monkey makes a different call, a kind of chuckling sound, and the troop looks up, then dives for cover in the bush. Then one discovers a python and makes a high-pitched chattering sound. All stop in their tracks, stand on their hind legs and scan the ground in search of the danger.

The vervet's alarm calls are so specific that each one sparks off a different (and appropriate) evasive action. Young vervets have to learn how to use and interpret these warnings correctly, but once they do, they have mastered key words in the language of survival.

Warning signal *A vervet monkey in Botswana screams a warning to the rest of her troop while clutching her baby to her chest. Eagles, leopards and snakes all prey on vervets, so these monkeys use three distinct alarm calls. Each tells the other troop members the kind of danger they face so they can take the right evasive action.*

FIGHTING CALLS AND BODY SIGNS

Self interest ensures that animals of the same species fight only as a last resort. More often, voice, expression and display decide the issue.

Signals that proclaim victor and vanquished

The cat from next door strays into your garden just as your own cat emerges for a stroll. The effect on both animals is electrifying: from their relaxed, tails-down, ears-erect posture they become fierce and aggressive. Hindquarters arch and tails shoot bolt upright as the cats express their displeasure with fierce hisses.

If the intruder backs down, it shows its submission by crouching low to the ground and hissing in a quiet, placatory fashion. But if it does not respond to the 'back off' message and stands its ground, then the last stage before an all-out fight is for each cat to square up with tail erect, fur standing on end and claws unsheathed. Even then, however, one cat may decide to give in and walk away.

In the back garden as in the wild, animals use both their voices and their bodies to express aggression or, just as effectively, submission. More often than not, these unmistakable signals are enough to prevent bloodshed.

Wolves, too, combine bodily and vocal expressions to convey challenge or conciliation. There is no mistaking the growling, snarling, fangs-bared, hackles-raised, ears-and-tail-erect posture of the dominant individual. But equally clear-cut, and just as important in the social structure of wolf packs, are the gestures of a less confident animal, anxious to avoid trouble. Its ears fold back, its tail squeezes between its legs and, to emphasise the point, it may lie down and gaze submissively up at its pugnacious aggressor.

The value of these signals in animal societies is that the hierarchy is established without a single bite being exchanged.

Showing the white flag

When rival male chameleons meet, they put on their fiercest expressions. They hiss, puff up their bodies, and open their mouths wide to display a red lining.

One species of chameleon, from Madagascar, has evolved a means of avoiding bodily harm. When the less aggressive of two males recognises that the moment has come to either submit or suffer possible injury, he simply changes colour – from green to a blotchy white – and then goes on his way, bowed but unbloodied.

Amphibians challenge for mates and territory

Male tree frogs in Sri Lanka vie for territory, by calling out aggressively, rather in the manner of two bidders at an auction. They begin with single, pulsed threat calls. Then each, in turn, challenges the other's call by adding ever more notes to his response. Such vocal contests last for ten minutes or more, either until one of the bidders bows out, or the two frogs meet in furious combat.

In the case of the common toad of Europe, fighting calls, body size and ultimate success are all related. When two males compete for possession of a female they emit soft, peeping sounds. Even though they may not be able to see each other, each toad can tell his opponent's size and stature from the quality of his call. Deeper-pitched callers are bigger, and the smaller contestant will often yield without ever having seen the victor.

Top wolf *Squabbles in a wolf pack are frequent, but rarely end in bloodshed. Challenges are made with laid-back ears and bared teeth, but the dominant animal soon prevails and the challenger shows submission, often by lying on its back with throat exposed. Such behaviour lessens aggression in the victor and reinforces social hierarchy.*

Clarion calls of the monarchs of the glens

Each year, as the bracken glows and the first frosts sparkle along the edges of the lochs, the roars of red deer stags ring out on the clear air of the Scottish Highlands. It is a thrilling sound, at once an assertion of supremacy and a challenge to all comers.

October is the month of the annual rut, when male red deer compete for the possession of harems of up to 20 females. If each stag's invitation to fight were accepted, casualties would be high, for their antlers can inflict terrible wounds. However, most prefer to settle their battles vocally.

In rut, the stag's voice box enlarges, giving its bellow plenty of carrying power. Both stags with harems – and those without – emit thunderous roars in a contest that may last for an hour or more. In the end, one of the two contestants generally retires exhausted before any physical contact is made.

Roaring takes a considerable toll of a stag's reserves of energy – an average performance often runs to five bellows a minute, with breaks in which to recover. The competition makes sense, for the stag that roars hardest is likely to be the stronger of the two animals. If the roaring match fails to settle the dispute, then the

Judging an opponent *Vying for a female, two Grant's gazelles gauge each other's strengths and weaknesses before finally locking horns in combat.*

Battling baboons *Ethiopian gelada baboons are well armed with long canine teeth, but are more likely to settle disputes with angry stares and noisy ground-slapping. The loser indicates submission by exposing his teeth and pink gums in a 'fear grin'.*

All-out challenge *As autumn clothes the Scottish Highlands in russet and gold, a red deer stag raises his head and roars his readiness to fight any rival for the control of a harem of females.*

stronger animal would almost certainly be the winner in a fight.

Without the sound and fury of the stags, and rather more in the manner of boxers, competing male Grant's gazelles in Africa first move cautiously round each other, showing off their strength and length of horn. Next, they toss their heads, showing their white throats and displaying the sweep of their horns in profile. Only if this last display fails to make one of them submit do the contenders commence to fight in earnest.

Stares and shouts can lead to battle

Eye contact is the first part of a gelada baboon conflict. It starts when two males eye each other balefully from a distance and begin shouting threats. Then they edge closer, still staring hard and hunching their shoulders. Calling excitedly, they reinforce these signals with resounding slaps on the ground and warning lunges at each other. If this behaviour does not intimidate one or the other, they will start to fight in earnest, tearing at each other's flesh with formidable canine teeth.

SIGNALLING THEIR CLAIMS

Many animals seek the security of occupying their own clearly defined territory, marking out its boundaries by the best means available.

There is no place like a well-defined home

For an animal, a well-stocked and stable territory means a reliable food supply, somewhere to shelter, an enticement for sexual partners or a safe breeding site. So some animal species have evolved different sound, sight and odour signals that all proclaim: 'No trespassing!'

Hippopotamuses spend the daylight hours in African rivers and feed on the banks by night. As the herd, perhaps 150 strong, emerges from the water, the animals go to their communal grazing area.

Each hippopotamus roams at will to find the best vegetation. Grazing rights are not contested, but this tolerance does not extend to mating, which often takes place in the water, with dominant male

hippopotamuses laying claim to a prime section of the river and a stretch of the bank.

On land, the hippos defecate in large piles, which act as 'signposts' to their grazing grounds. A bull approaching a territory not his own is warned off by a 'boundary' of high-smelling dung that the territory holder has scattered by whisking his tail.

Saying it with scent

Scents are better than sound signals as boundary markers. They last longer, and continue to work

even when the animals are absent. Nomadic army ants that range through the lowland tropical rain forests of South America travel in colonies 600 000 strong and forage for food on the forest floor. When the army camps, each raiding party lays down a chemical trail to beacon its path and to ensure that areas are not foraged twice over.

Other colonies of the same species of ant recognise the chemical markers of another colony and avoid them. So soldier ants warn potential competitors off patches crossed by their foraging trails.

Daytime drowsing *The hippopotamus spends its days resting in water with its companions and its nights feeding in its own separate territory in adjacent grasslands. The reason for this is the hippo's unique skin structure, which causes the animal to dehydrate more rapidly than any other mammal when it is exposed to sunlight. In the river, however, its skin absorbs water like a sponge, so that by nightfall it is ready to spend some four or five hours grazing.*

Clear warning *The throat sac of the male African common toad gives its voice a resonance that carries a long way, warning intruders to keep off the territory it has staked for itself. Because of its distinctive spotted markings, this toad is also known as the leopard toad.*

Calls that identify *Indris spend almost their entire lives in the Madagascan forest canopy, where family groups defend their territories with loud howls repeated up to seven times a day. They also have a code of warning calls that make a clear distinction between aerial predators and any danger threatening from the ground.*

Toads bellow out their territorial rights

Particular methods of fixing the boundaries of a territory are best suited to particular terrain. Territorial marking by sound can be highly effective wherever the visibility is poor and it is not easy to move from one place to another.

The male African common toad, found from West Africa to Egypt, is particularly well equipped for sound signalling. By vibrating its vocal cords, it produces deep croaks that, magnified by an inflatable air sac in its throat into resounding booms, can be heard nearly half a mile (800 m) away.

This toad is intensely territorial and is ever ready to fight with a neighbour over a boundary. What fixes the toad's range is the depth and frequency of its call – the deeper the call, the older and larger the toad, a fact quite apparent to smaller competitors who yield him the best patch of pond rather than chance a fight. Older toads also get the widest choice of females, because females find their deep calls more attractive than those of the younger males.

However, once the boundaries have been clearly established, the toad will ignore the familiar calls of neighbouring males, probably because it has become accustomed to them. It is only when it hears the croak of a stranger, that the territorial male starts bellowing out his unmistakable 'No trespassing' messages once more.

The warning power of a true and simple song

Most birds are territorial to some degree, as is apparent when watching such northern European garden regulars as the blackbird, the robin and the great tit. Observations of the great tit show that it is the most aggressively territorial males who get the best nesting holes and foraging places in which to attract a female, while the less successful are left with the less promising hedges and gardens.

It has long been assumed that within the simple 'teecher-teecher-teecher' phrase of the male great tit's song lies a warning to other birds to keep off its patch. The theory was put to the test in a 15 acre (6 ha) wood near Oxford. There, resident territory holders were removed from the copse and, in some cases, replaced by loudspeakers linked to tape recordings of their own songs.

Suburban warrior *To thrushes, robins and other small birds, gardens, parks and the seemingly decorous countryside form a jungle in which every creature must struggle for its own or go under. Here a male great tit insists vociferously upon his territorial rights to a hedgerow where it can find food and a mate.*

Other territories had a recording of a two-note phrase similar to that of the great tit, but played on a penny whistle. A third group of territories was left silent.

In less than 24 hours male newcomers were moving into the wood and singing take-over songs in the silent territories and in those with tin-whistle recordings. But it took a further 36 hours before any bird ventured into the areas that had been rigged with true great tit song recordings. Clearly, the male birds that were looking for a good patch were deterred, for a while at least, by the song's warning – even though it was only a recording.

Waving when sound signals do not work

Using display in order to lay claim to a territory has its limitations. An intruder has to be in visual contact, otherwise the signaller's efforts are wasted; also, only one spot in the boundary can be established by each display. However, visual signalling does have its uses, especially where other means of communication are not possible.

Recent studies have found eight species of frog that display by waving one foot, like a flag. Seven of these live by rain forest streams, where the constant noise of rushing water drowns all other sound including the calls that are the normal language of frogs.

When biologists first saw the frogs' foot displays they assumed that they were linked to courtship and that males were signalling to attract females. But close studies of two Australian species – the green-eyed tree frog and the torrent frog – have revealed that male frogs are definitely signalling their ownership of a particular territory to other males.

The green-eyed tree frog displays to intruders by raising its right hind leg, stretching it out and then rapidly vibrating its outstretched toes and foot. This is alternated with vigorous bouts of wrestling.

BROADCASTING FALSE INFORMATION

Colours, songs and flashing lights may all be used by animals to pretend that things are not what they are, and so confuse their predators or rivals.

Movement and mimicry can fool the enemy

Many small and normally drab insects rely on camouflage for protection. But should a hungry predator crack their disguise, they employ another visual trick: they transform their appearance with a flick of their wings, suddenly exposing vividly coloured patterns that momentarily startle the hunter, so allowing them to escape.

In Peru's rain forest, the brown, female leaf katydid (a relative of grasshoppers and crickets) flashes on and off a dazzling array of white marks, known as eyespots, on her hind wings. These are guaranteed to confuse an inquisitive predator such as a bird or lizard.

One type of Malaysian weevil with long, stiff legs continues to baffle naturalists. There appears to be no reason for an insect living in a rain forest to need such limbs. It cannot be for the same reason as an African Kalahari beetle, a desert dweller that uses its legs to keep its body off the hot sand. Perhaps the weevil's spindly legs help it to mimic the movements of certain spider-like and foul-tasting harvestmen that are avoided by predators. By aping the harvestmen, the weevils increase their chances of survival.

Colour warning
At first sight the brown female bush cricket (above) looks like a leaf. When threatened by an enemy, she flashes the brown, red and white eyespots on her hind wings (right), hoping to scare it off.

Damselfly in disguise *Females of the common blue damselfly (left) are usually a dull olive green, while males (lower left) are conspicuously blue. Some females however are disguised as males. This subterfuge confuses the males, who are eager to mate as many times as possible during their brief lives and it allows the females to get on with the vital task of egg-laying.*

Disguised females mislead a host of males

In the vast majority of animal species, males and females look different in some way. But in several species some of the females imitate the appearance of males. They are transvestites and avoid the unwanted attentions of too many males.

A damselfly's existence is short and intense. Adults live for only a few days, during which time they mate, each coupling lasting, on average, three hours. The aim of males is to find as many females as possible to carry their genes.

Females have different objectives. Once fertilised, they want to get on with laying eggs, and not waste time in repeated mating. By aping a male, a female is sending out a false signal in order to buy time. Although males will try to mate with damselflies of either sex, they are more attracted to the distinctive female colours.

Fireflies that prey on other fireflies use false sex signals to catch a meal. These insects, which are in reality beetles, fly at night, and to find a mate in the dark, they use a dramatic light show, flashing their body lights on and off. As there are so many types of firefly in the same habitat, all flashing luminescent coded signals at once, each group must recognise its own kind. So each species has its own distinct pattern or sequence, consisting of a certain number, frequency and intensity of flashes. This enables males to home in on the right species of female.

A male sends out light signals through his abdomen as he flies about 20 in (50 cm) above the ground. A female responds only if the signalling male comes within a range of 6 ft (2 m) or so – then an exchange of correctly timed flashes continues until the two are close enough to mate.

Just occasionally, however, a female firefly of a predatory type joins the throng looking for a meal. A superb mimic, she waits until she spots the telltale flashes of the male of another species and then reproduces the flash pattern of the appropriate female. A male who approaches her is promptly eaten.

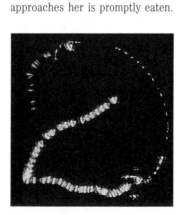

Signalling with light *A male firefly (left) blazes a trail through the night to attract a mate. He generates the light through his abdomen, where the chemical luciferin reacts with the oxygen in his body to produce energy in the form of a bright, but cold, light.*

A blackbird's songbook deceives its rivals

In P.C. Wren's novel *Beau Geste*, a sergeant in the French Foreign Legion defends a desert fort by propping the dead bodies of his men into embrasures round the ramparts to make it look as if the outpost is at full strength.

Males of the North American red-winged blackbird move round their marsh or farmland territories singing at different points along the way, and varying their songs.

Perhaps, like the sergeant's strategy, this is a charade designed to convince invaders, in this case blackbird males, that the area is already occupied by a number of birds. Quite possibly this deception enables the male blackbirds to hold larger territories than they could with a restricted song, an important factor in breeding, since males with large territories will attract the most females.

Fooling the invader *The varied songs of a male red-winged blackbird, delivered from different points around his chosen territory, may convince his rivals that the territory he is defending is occupied by many more male birds.*

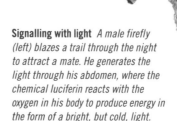

MASTER MUSICIANS' MESSAGES

Lacking voices or finding them inadequate, some animals have other highly effective ways of producing sound to communicate their needs.

Resonant rhythms of musical cicadas

In many Mediterranean lands, the high chirruping of cicadas is so familiar that it is only noticeable when it stops at night. Cicadas are the loudest of insect musicians, and usually play at top volume. The instruments they use are pairs of organs called timbals. These stiff plates lining either side of the thorax (the part of the body bearing legs and wings) are flexed and unflexed rapidly by powerful muscular contractions and relaxations, thus producing two loud clicks.

Loud pedals, soft pedals

The controlling muscles can operate at up to 600 times a second, thus giving the cicada great variation in its clicking speeds. Most of its abdomen behind the timbals is hollow, forming a resonating chamber that amplifies the sound. The cicada can also raise and lower a covering over the timbals which further increases or reduces the volume of sound. In full song, a cicada can be heard from more than 600 yd (550 m) away.

By varying intensity, speed and rhythm, a male cicada can alter his song considerably. His calls are designed to attract females who, once drawn to a particular caller, communicate their interest by producing a ticking sound with their wings. Each of the 1500 or so types

Sound broadcaster *Owner of the most complex sound system in the insect kingdom, the cicada's song can build up to an almost deafening climax.*

of cicada has its own song. And, like fireflies with their flashing coded signals, each recognises its own kind, which is vital for ensuring that each mates with its own species.

Lost voices *Larval stag beetles produce a warning noise by rubbing their hind legs together, an ability that is lost once they become adults. Male stag beetles compete for females (right) not by singing but by fighting with pincer-like jaws (below). Rivals interlock jaws and wrestle like rutting stags.*

Making things clear by sight and sound

On alighting upon its untidy nest, the first thing a western white stork does is to make it clear to its mate, already in occupation, that it comes in friendship and means no harm. The way it conveys these peaceful intentions is to clapper its beak – open and shut it rapidly and noisily – before throwing its head far back until it rests upside-down on its body. The male palm cockatoo of Australia goes one better. With its beak, it breaks off a small branch, strips off the leaves and trims it to length. Then, taking the stick in its foot, it uses it as a drumstick to beat out a tattoo on a hollow eucalyptus, all the while pirouetting to impress its female companion. It also drums to proclaim its ownership if another male tries to take its nest site.

Utilising parts of the body to make sounds is a fairly widespread form of animal communication. Passalid beetles, for example, which live underneath the bark of rotting logs, scurry about their tunnels in well-organised groups. In keeping up their cooperative way of life, both the larvae and adults communicate a great deal by means of various parts of their bodies. The larvae

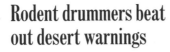

make a rasping sound to encourage adults to help them build their pupal cases (in which they change to adults). They rasp with their third pair of legs – tiny pointed limbs that they rub against ridges situated near the top of their second pair of legs. Adult passalid beetles rub the undersides of their wings against the abdomen in a number of situations: if disturbed during courtship, while mating, or when facing up to an aggressive confrontation with another beetle.

Stridulation (rubbing together parts of the body to make a noise) is common among beetles. Stag beetle larvae stridulate with their hind legs, probably to scare off predators. The burying beetle produces a buzzing sound like that of a bumble bee in order to frighten away would-be aggressors.

Rodent drummers beat out desert warnings

Banner-tailed kangaroo rats that live in the southwestern deserts of the United States drum noisily with their feet on top of the sandy mounds that contain their burrows to signal warnings and send information to neighbours. Each signal is a rapid tattoo, repeated so as to produce a recognisable sequence. Each banner-tail's signal is subtly different, varying as to the number of beats in each phrase and the number of phrases in a sequence.

Apart from conveying warnings of intruders, the rhythm will also advertise the nocturnal drummer's age and sex, because the beat rate increases from infancy onwards to a maximum in young adulthood, and shades off again as old age approaches. Throughout life, males drum faster than females.

The Indian crested porcupine is another creature that communicates by drumming. Both in alarm or in anger, it shakes its tail violently, so producing a harsh warning rattle. If further annoyed, it will stamp its feet angrily on the ground as a final warning before running backwards at the source of its irritation, brandishing its quills and preparing to thrust them into the intruder's face.

Night noises *If it chose to, the banner-tailed kangaroo rat, like other rats, could communicate by scent. But it prefers to drum with its feet, which suits its nocturnal way of life – as sound, unlike scent, does not linger in the air to attract predators.*

The right vibrations bring couples together

The tiny fruit fly's wings are most expressive – each is just ¹⁄₁₆ in (1.5 mm) long. A male fly vibrates one or both of them to make a range of low-frequency sounds that speak volumes.

These sounds are inaudible to human ears, and have a range of less than ²⁄₅ in (10 mm). But they transmit all kinds of information. The males deliver a courtship song in a series of pulses – each wing vibration being punctuated by gaps. One European species intersperses staccato bursts with a continuous humming, probably the actual courtship song. The staccato pulses may well serve as a means of identifying itself – an important part of the fruit fly's communications system – because a number of different species might be feeding and courting in close proximity. It is essential for a female to be able to determine whether another fly is one of her own kind or not. Sometimes males and females play a duet during courtship. This is another check for telling species apart, with both flies making sure that their partners are suitable.

One of the marvels of fruit fly communication is how they make sound pulses at all, given that they seem to be designed to beat their wings continuously in flight rather than in intermittent bursts.

The explanation lies in a most remarkable body mechanism that acts like a clutch in a car. In flight, the clutch is coupled to the wings. In order to sing, a male continually uncouples and then re-engages the clutch. A female picks up the call with her antennae.

Homecoming *Neck bending and beak clapping is the white stork's way of announcing to its partner: 'I'm home'. Storks mate for life, and often nest on chimney pots, whose owners welcome them as omens of good fortune.*

Signature tunes *As various species of fruit fly often eat near one another, they identify themselves by the different 'music' they make by vibrating their wings. The insects are known for living largely on rotting fruit, but this group in Kenya is seen feeding on fermenting sap.*

BODY LANGUAGE

Animals use colour, movement and posture to communicate a variety of needs, including finding a mate, scaring an enemy and luring prey.

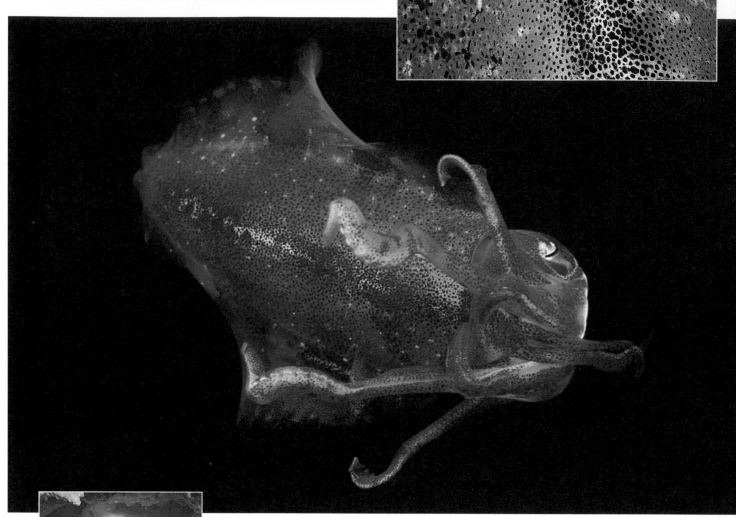

Night on the reef *While fusilier fish are feeding around the coral reef during the day, their bright colours advertise their presence, enabling them to recognise each other (top). But as they settle down for the night each fish changes into its less conspicuous night attire (above).*

The squid's varied expressions of 'emotion'

Squid are very expressive body linguists, using light, colour and form to communicate with each other and to deceive other marine creatures. In their skins they have tiny sacs of pigment known as chromatophores, which allow them to express a mood or change their appearance with eloquent pulses of shimmering colour. Deep water squid may replace chromatophores with photophores, tiny light producing organs, which create pulsating patterns of light.

While hunting, a squid can flash its body colour from white stripes to yellow flecks and to solid bars. Scientists are convinced that these mesmerising changes reflect the squid's 'emotions' – its fear, alarm, arousal and aggression – and also serve as a means of communication from one to another. The show of brilliant colour or light may also be used to lure unwitting prey, or as camouflage when a squid ambushes a victim. While the squid lies in wait, it changes colour in harmony with its surroundings, and becomes almost invisible. To change shape is another camouflage trick. The pop-eyed squid holds its two tentacles and eight arms in a neat bunch to make it look like a plant; other species wave their arms to distract and confuse their prey, producing a near-hypnotic effect for just long enough to catch, poison, paralyse and then devour their victims.

Public announcements *Close-up, the tiny spots of pigment in the skin of the Atlantic oval squid are plainly visible (top). These spots, or chromatophores, are small sacs of colour beneath the skin. They contract and expand to produce the waves of colour and pattern that suffuse the creature as it moves through the water (above). Among deep water squid, shimmering waves produced by special light organs add to the repertoire of signs and messages.*

In the oceans around the coral reefs, a profusion of flamboyantly coloured fish is constantly on the move. Their bright colours act like name badges, identifying and advertising each fish's presence, essential for finding a mate in the crowd. The colours can also send a warning saying: 'This is my patch and I will attack any trespassers.'

314

Male mallards woo their mates with fancy steps

A male mallard in his full courting plumage is a handsome sight. His shimmering green head feathers, iridescent blue wing patch and curly black tail are all intended to impress the drab brown females.

As courting mallards gather in mixed flocks, the males jostle for position, each trying to achieve the best possible side-on stance to display his magnificent presence to the onlooking females.

Once in a good position, a male performs a ritualised dance to keep the females' interest. He signals his intent to court by drawing his head down between his shoulders and raising his head feathers. This is an invitation to watch the rest of the show. If a female is watching, the male will continue with his next number, which includes some vocals as well. A successful performance will eventually persuade one of the male's female audience to mate with him.

Both sound and body language are incorporated in the mallards' range of courtship displays. In the grunt-whistle display, a male dips his bill in the water then rises up, lifting his breast clear of the water surface. At the same time, he jerks his head sideways and sends a spray of water droplets skittering towards his chosen female. This display is accompanied by a peculiar grunting call and followed by a high-pitched whistle. Neither of these sounds bears any resemblance to the usual duck 'quack'.

Some males include extra steps when they particularly want to impress. By bending the body into a U-shape with the head and tail up, a male exposes his distinctive, curly tail feathers.

At this stage, if the female is interested in the male's display, she will let him know by answering his body talk with displays of her own – nods, mock preening and 'pumping'. The pumping motion of her bill as she bobs her head up and down excites the male. He in turn responds with fervent head pumping of his own.

Now that the correct overtures have been made, rival males have been seen off and the courtship rituals are complete, the mallards can go ahead and mate.

Duck steps *Colourful male mallards use complicated dance routines to impress their drab, brown females. This male has just successfully seen off a rival.*

When the hippo's yawn means 'back-off'

Stretching and yawning when you are tired fills your lungs with air. This in turn drives the blood from your lungs into your heart and from here the re-oxygenated blood is pumped to your muscles and helps to combat fatigue. Fish, however, yawn before they get tired, in anticipation of some great effort. By opening their mouths wide, fish accelerate the flow of blood through their bodies and so prepare themselves for imminent action – usually a dash to safety or the pursuit of prey.

For other animals, yawns can not only be invigorating but also symbolic – a way of communicating with others of the same species. A yawning hippopotamus is an awesome sight. It rears up out of the water and opens its huge mouth to reveal its tusk-like canine teeth. This is a message for other hippos around, but the meaning differs, depending on who is watching. If the spectators are male then the yawn is an aggressive, territorial gesture, intended to terrify any potential competitors with its immensity. If male hippos were to fight over territory or females they could inflict terrible injuries on one another. Disputes rarely end in violence; the hippos rely mainly on yawning shows of strength to quell brewing unrest.

If a hippo opens his mouth wide in the company of a female, however, the meaning is completely different. The yawn is part of courtship play-fighting – a gesture of 'affection' from a hippo.

Male baboons also yawn to intimidate would-be opponents, displaying their dangerous canine teeth. But yawning, stretching and scratching are also an essential part of the baboons' complicated ritual of grooming, which bonds their societies together.

Grouper gape *In the Indian Ocean, a grouper opens its mouth wide to increase the flow of blood around its body, giving the fish energy for a dash from danger.*

Threat or invitation *Male hippopotamuses display their huge tusks to intimidate each other. But this vast yawn sends a quite different message to a female – it is a gesture of playfulness that leads to courtship.*

MAKING SENSE OF SCENTS

Strong-smelling signposts carry important messages for animals sharing a territory. They use scent to tell when food is near, call for help or give a 'Keep off!' signal.

Animals that send aromatic messages

To help to identify the boundaries of their territory, many animals mark them with a distinctive smell. An odour lingers in the air long after its creator has travelled on, and can be informative about the status, sex and even the mood of the animal that has left it.

Most land-living animals excrete urine and defecate, and many animals advertise their presence by depositing their excreta in conspicuous places. Animals as different as musk deer and rhinoceroses use carefully chosen latrine sites to leave their droppings – sites that are used again and again. Cheetahs spray their urine over prominent trees to mark their territory, and African bush babies and Asian lorises (tree-dwelling primates) spray their pungent urine on their own feet, so marking the branches as they move around.

To reinforce the messages left in urine and dung, many animals also utilise special scent glands. The South African klipspringer antelope has scent glands just below each eye, and it uses these glands

High marks *An Alaskan grizzly bear (left) rubs against a tree to mark its territory. Bears roll in their urine, and as they follow regular paths between dens and feeding sites they rear up and rub against trees, leaving scent and hair clumps as markers. A dwarf mongoose (below) handstands to put its scent high up and make it seem bigger than it is.*

Slow and odorous *A loris creeps along a branch to catch an insect. It marks its territory as it goes with urine sprayed on its paws.*

very daintily to mark the tips of grasses. Hamsters rub their scent on tufts of grass using glands on their flanks, and Mongolian gerbils, which produce little urine or dung, rub their belly glands onto stones and rocks as they walk over them.

Scent marks reveal a lot about the sex, health, reproductive state and mood of the animal, and may also give an idea of its size. How high up a marking post an animal places its scent indicates its size to others discovering the smell – although some try to make themselves seem much larger. A dwarf mongoose performs handstands to mark rocks and trees as high as possible with an anal scent gland.

Visible signs may also draw attention to scent marks. Squirrels tear bark from trees they are scent-marking, and tigers leave deep scratches as they rub glands between their toes against trees.

Smells speak volumes to sniffing hyenas

Hyenas rely as much on their sensitive noses as on their whines, yelps, growls and laughs to communicate with each other in their complex clan society. The convoluted surface of a hyena's nasal membranes is 50 times bigger than a human's. This gives it a sensitivity to smell that allows communication approaching the subtlety of human speech.

From a single patch of urine, a hyena can tell what type of animal secreted it, even if the patch is several hours old. And if the urine was passed by one of its own clan, it can tell which animal it was.

As the members of a clan set off to find food at night, they leave many odiferous traces of their presence. They defecate in special communal latrines, and as they reach the edges of their territory, they 'paste', or secrete, a pungent white substance from glands under their tails. Also they rub their hind quarters on the grass so that powerful scent traces are left behind. Hyenas constantly sniff the ground for scents – members of rival clans pick up and understand the information encoded in one another's smells, and act accordingly.

Hyenas also use their noses to coordinate hunting. Just as members of a sports team sometimes huddle together before a match to discuss last-minute tactics, a group of hyenas assembles at a regular meeting place before setting off to hunt. The hyenas spend some time smelling one another, perhaps to check which ones are present and to organise scent signals that play an essential part in regulating and defining their roles in the hunt.

All present *When they are about to set off on a hunt, spotted hyenas (below) stand close together, sniffing at one another's mouths, necks and heads. This may be some sort of roll call before moving off in pursuit of prey – often a young or weakened zebra or wildebeest.*

Follow your nose *Army ants on the march to find food follow chemical trails laid by their scouts. An army like this, which marches on its stomach, cannot afford to search the same area twice.*

Scents that lead to food or summon help

Living in colonies of 600 000 or so, South American army ants must constantly forage for food – they eat any small creature. The nomad ants march and bivouac through lowland tropical rain forests from Peru to Mexico. They alternate 15 days of marching with 20 days of camping while the queen lays eggs.

Foraging parties leaving the camp follow scent trails laid down by scouting soldier ants. These powerful scents also act as territory markers, and are recognised and avoided by other colonies of army ants. When out on a foraging expedition, successful scouts head back down the trail and encourage any ants they find en route to continue onwards by pummelling their antennae and offering them a blob of regurgitated food.

Scenting the alarm
An ant chancing upon an enemy sends out an alarm signal by running about in loops and trailing its abdomen over the ground. Now and again it raises its abdomen and releases a chemical signal into the air that attracts ants from as far away as 4-5 in (10-13 cm). Before coming to the rescue of the signalling ant, other ants release an alarm scent that works them up into an aggressive state.

Weaver ants also lay scent trails to food. They mark the route by rubbing secretions from an intestinal gland onto the ground, using two stiff, trailing hairs.

SENSES AND SENSING

'*B*Y CONVENTION, SWEET IS SWEET; BY CONVENTION, BITTER IS BITTER; BY CONVENTION, HOT IS HOT; BY CONVENTION, COLOUR IS COLOUR. BUT IN REALITY, THERE ARE ONLY ATOMS AND THE VOID.' ≈ DEMOCRITUS, 460-370 BC, *TETRALOGIES.*

Animal senses are not like human senses. Some animals see light that is invisible to us. Others hear sounds beyond the range of our hearing. Some are sensitive to the Earth's magnetic field or to electric current. Dolphins create a three-dimensional image of their world that may be more detailed than the image we create by sight, but they do this by sonar, listening to the echoes of their voices. The image of the 'atoms and the void' which a dolphin creates by processing echolocation signals in its brain is almost certain to be very different from the one that we create with our eyes and our brains. It may always be beyond our abilities to perceive the world as a dolphin perceives it, but by studying how animals behave, we can at least discover what stimuli they are sensitive to, and how these senses help them to survive. Democritus would be surprised at such modest progress.

Eye spy
Our knowledge of the physics of light tells us that the horsefly's eyes cannot distinguish fine detail, but since we do not understand enough about how brains work, we cannot reconstruct the image that a fly sees.

Hunting with sound
The horseshoe bat hunts by detecting the echoes of its calls as they rebound off flying insects. A single note, repeated ten times a second, locates the insect. As it closes in for the kill, it produces a glissando – blending a series of notes together – which may help to pinpoint prey.

Limited senses
With no eyes or ears, the starfish is dependent on its senses of touch and smell to find its way over the sea floor in its hunt for food.

Night sight
The huge eyes of the slender loris help it to move about in the blackness of a forest at night. Being nocturnal, lorises rely mostly on smell to find their prey, and communicate with scent messages and sounds.

Snake's sensitivities
A gaboon viper 'sees' in the dark, pinpointing small changes in temperature with the help of heat-sensitive pits on either side of its snout. Its ears are sensitive only to low-frequency vibrations. It smells by 'tasting' the air with its forked tongue.

Boned dome
The beluga whale's dome-shaped head is part of its sonar transmitting system. The 'melon', as it is called, may act as a lens, focusing sounds into a narrow beam.

SUPER SIGHT

Eyesight is designed according to an animal's needs, giving it tunnel vision for locating prey, or a wide field for keeping a lookout – or sometimes both.

Different ways to get an all-round view

So flexible is the neck of the great horned owl of the New World that it can turn its head through almost three-quarters of a circle. The bird has a highly accurate but narrow field of vision, and its neck-swivelling ability counterbalances the limited field.

As with all hunting birds, an owl's eyes sit at the front of the head, allowing its visual field to be scanned by both eyes together. This binocular system is essential for accurately judging size and distance, both crucial for predators. The problem with forward-facing eyes is that the bird must turn its head or its whole body to see what is happening behind or to the side.

Vision is further hampered since the owl cannot move its eyeballs in their sockets. Most owls hunt and defend their territory at night, so have only the moon and stars for light. They need eyes that let in as much light as possible – hence their exceptional size. The owl's eye is elongated due to a greatly enlarged cornea, pupil and lens. Though this shape restricts movement within the eye socket, it increases the amount of light that enters the eye so that a brighter image falls on the retina.

Looking out behind them

The hartebeest, an antelope of Africa's grassy plains, needs to spot danger from behind even as it lowers its head to graze. So like most hunted animals, it has an eye on both sides of its head, each giving a separate view. But both together cover almost a full circle. Because the hartebeest has only a narrow overlap area in the forward vision of each eye, it has only limited binocular vision. But its wide monocular field of view enables the animal to keep a continual all-round watch for predators.

Nocturnal hunter *Africa's milky eagle owl relies on excellent night vision to detect cane rats, hares and guinea fowl. The secret of the owl's success lies in the size and construction of its eyes, which are designed to take in as much light as possible.*

Keeping watch in two directions at once

Chameleons are among the few creatures that can move each eye independently, enabling them to look in two directions at once. These small lizards, commonest in Africa and Madagascar, have large, distinctive eyes that are covered in skin except for a small central area. The eyes are positioned one on each side of the head, and a chameleon can use one to watch for insects to feed on while the other keeps watch for approaching enemies, such as birds of prey.

A chameleon's ability to swivel

Skew-eyed *A Mediterranean chameleon balances on a slender branch, with one eye facing forwards and the other facing behind. Being able to move its eyes independently provides the chameleon with superb all-round vision that is ideal for hunting. If a meal is sighted, the chameleon turns both eyes towards it in order to get a stereoscopic image.*

its eyes instead of swinging its whole head round is a great advantage, because it spends most of its life balancing on tree branches high above the ground. Once a chameleon spots a meal, both eyes swivel round and lock on the target. In this position the fields of vision from both eyes overlap to give an accurate three-dimensional image. When the prey is in range, out shoots the chameleon's long, sticky tongue to capture it. A chameleon can extend its tongue for a distance nearly as long as its 7-10 in (17-25 cm) long body. Dwarf chameleons of southern Africa direct their tongues just ahead of the target, anticipating the victim's flight path.

An insect resting on a branch out of the chameleon's range is not necessarily safe, because the lizard remembers its position. Even if it has to make a detour and the target is out of sight temporarily, it still approaches from the right direction and catches the prey the moment it is within tongue range.

Waiting patiently for a lightning strike

Each leg of a praying mantis, a slow-moving predatory insect of tropical and sub-tropical climates, is equipped with large spikes. It sits perfectly still while it waits for a victim to come close to its powerful front legs, and when prey such as a butterfly or other small creature moves into range, the mantis reaches out to spear it in a lightning twentieth of a second.

For such action the mantis needs vision that will pinpoint its victim's position. It gets this from a pair of large, widely spaced, compound eyes located towards the front of its head. Each is made up of many closely packed cylindrical light-sensitive segments that are each topped with a hexagonal lens. They provide only a coarse mosaic image, but are particularly sensitive to any movement. If prey stirs close by, the mantis quickly angles its head towards the movement.

The pictures from each of the compound eyes then overlap to

create a three-dimensional image, and this enables the insect to determine distance. As soon as its victim is within grabbing range and focused in a particular part of its field of vision – always the same part – the mantis thrusts out its forelegs and snatches up its meal.

Eye-openers *With eight specialised eyes, a jumping spider from West Africa (below) can sense food or danger in almost any direction and judge fine detail as far away as 20 times its body length. A praying mantis from Trinidad (right) has compound eyes that are highly sensitive to movement, and so are ideal for locating prey.*

Small jumping spiders, found all over the world, also need to be able to judge distance well in order to pounce on their prey. They have four pairs of simple, strategically placed eyes called ocelli.

The two rear pairs are used as lookouts, scanning for predators

such as lizards. The two front pairs of eyes scan for prey such as flies or mosquitoes. Together, these four eyes are bigger than the spider's brain, and give it high-resolution, three-dimensional sight that allows it to focus sharply on its prey at the moment of the pounce.

SUPER SIGHT BELOW SEA LEVEL

To spot either hunters or prey clearly under water, some creatures scan with many eyes, while others rely on very high quality eyesight.

The scallop uses many eyes to detect danger

While lying feeding with its shell open, the scallop keeps its eyes skinned for danger. Each eye has two retinas – one retina is sensitive to decreases in light intensity, and the other to increases. There is also a mechanism that increases each eye's sensitivity in low light.

Why the lowly scallop possesses such complicated eyesight may be

All eyes *The great scallop (left) has up to 200 eyes that appear as two rows of blue, pinhead-size dots peering out from between the two halves of its shell.*

to do with the creature's mobility. Unlike cockles and mussels, the scallop is able to swim by squirting water from near its shell's hinge. It propels itself forward and upward in a series of jerks in the direction of the shell's opening.

Though its eyes can sense only different intensities of light and dark, that ability is sufficient for the scallop to detect a potential source of danger, in time to snap its shell shut.

If sufficiently alarmed by what it sees, the scallop can jet itself rapidly backwards, out of harm's way by opening and closing its shell repeatedly, using its eyes to help it to orient itself while fleeing.

The most sophisticated eyesight under the sea

Octopus, squid and cuttlefish have the most highly developed eyes of all invertebrates and some have eyes that are among the largest in the world. A fully grown, 60 ft (18 m) long giant squid has eyes the size of footballs.

These animals are known as cephalopods and the structure of their eyes is similar to our own, even though cephalopod and mammal eyes evolved quite independently. There is, however, one distinct difference. Unlike human eyes which change the shape of the lens to achieve fine focusing, the eyes of cephalopods do this by moving the lens backwards and forwards, more like the focusing mechanism of a slide projector.

Among most land-living animals, the cornea, a curved, transparent outer covering at the front of the eye, assists in bending incoming rays of light so that they converge on the lens. The greater the curvature of the cornea, the more the light is bent. The cornea developed to compensate for the bending of light as it passes from the air outside the eye to the liquid on the inside. Once the cornea has more or less focused the light entering

the eye, the lens then fine-tunes the image projected onto the retina, a screen of light-sensitive cells at the back of the eye.

Marine creatures, however, have no need to compensate for the bending of light as it passes from air into liquid. In octopus and squid the cornea contributes little to focusing, which is done almost entirely by the lens.

In experiments, it has been proved that an octopus is capable of recognising and remembering different sizes and shapes. For example, it can tell the difference between vertical and horizontal rectangles. A sedentary predator, the octopus ambushes crabs and

Sharp-sighted hunter *A deep-water squid can use polarised light – a rare ability which allows it to make out the shape of its quarry extremely clearly, even in low-light conditions. Combined with its speed and natural aggression, this facility makes it a highly efficient hunter.*

other small marine animals from the safety of a crevice in a rock. Its highly developed sense of touch adds to the information it is able to obtain through its eyes. The squid, however, is an open water hunter and so it relies more on sight to help it to home-in on a target. Because it is so much more dependent on its eyes, a larger area of its brain is used to process visual information.

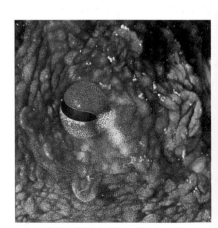

Seeing high and low *The eyes of an octopus, like those of a shark, can adapt to rapid changes in the amount of light available as it moves quickly from the depths of the ocean to near the surface.*

Sensitive sight of the great white shark

A great white shark attacks from below and behind, taking its victim by surprise. To do this it has to come up fast and keep its quarry in sight. Its eyes must react rapidly to the change in light if its hunt is to be successful.

Like all other sharks, the great white relies on its array of senses to locate prey such as seals and sea lions. But its sight is crucial to pinpointing a victim at the surface, silhouetted against the light.

Just as a human, entering a brightly lit room from the darkness outside, can be briefly dazzled and take a few seconds to adjust to the change, so a shark, rising to the surface from the murky depths, must cope with a rapid increase in light. It cannot afford to wait for its eyes to adjust – a lost second and the prey could be gone.

The secret of this ability lies in the tapetum, a layer of mirror-like plates at the back of the eyeball. It is the tapetum that eerily lights up a cat's eyes when it is caught in car headlamps at night. By reflecting light back through the retina, it effectively doubles the amount of light for the eye to use. This is essential for night hunters, like the

cat, if they are to see with clarity, especially in faint moonlight. In the day, though, too much light can be a problem. The cat copes by narrowing its pupil, the gap that lets in light, to a wafer-thin slit, using the muscles in the iris.

The great white shark's tapetum greatly enhances its vision in the murky depths, but it has no iris to protect its eyes when it surfaces rapidly. In order to compensate, it

has developed a 'curtain' of cells containing pigment. As the shark moves into bright light, these automatically expand over each tapetal plate, and then contract as it returns to the depths.

While it is swimming in shallow water, a shark needs to be able to see into the light above it and into the dark below. In this case the tapetal curtain reacts differently in each half of the eye. The lower half

Eye of a killer *While hunting deep in the ocean, a blue shark relies upon reflective plates behind its eyeballs to increase the amount of light striking the retina.*

of the tapetum, which reflects light from above, is covered to protect the retina. The upper half of the tapetum, which reflects light from below, is exposed to make the most of the light hitting the retina and so give as clear a picture as possible of the murky depths below.

How diving birds find their food under water

An eye which has been designed to work in the air is virtually useless under water. The curved, lens-like cornea which normally focuses an image onto the retina is flattened by water pressure. As a result of this distortion, the cornea is ineffective and most land animals cannot see to hunt under water. But some, such as diving birds, are able to exploit the rich supply of food that lives there.

Terns and pelicans cannot see clearly under water, but they can spot and take aim at a fish from the air diving beneath the surface to catch it. Nature has given penguins and cormorants

other solutions to the problem. The penguin's cornea is more flattened than is usual among other birds, allowing it to work just as well in water as in air. The cormorant's solution is different, but it is just as effective. The lens of this diving bird is particularly soft, so that it can

Adjusting for depth *The cormorant's eyes have special soft lenses which can be distorted easily to allow focusing at great depth below the surface.*

be stretched and squeezed easily by the eye muscles. It can be deformed so much that it actually bulges out through the disc of the iris and into the pupil. This bulging increases the curvature of the lens which allows an image to be focused on the retina, under the water. This enables the cormorant to see clearly and to chase its prey in quite deep water. Oil-rig engineers in a submersible in the North Sea have even observed a cormorant swimming at a depth of about 150 ft (45 m).

When it is at the surface, the cormorant's lens is flattened by the eye muscles so that the eye can focus accurately in air. This gives it the advantage of being able to hunt both above and below water.

COMMANDING THE BEST VIEW

Whether an animal's vision operates like a camera or a slide show, it produces images that are adapted to the creature's particular needs.

The four-eyed fish that can fool its predators

Poised on a branch overlooking a river in tropical South America, a vibrantly coloured green kingfisher spies a small fish just below and prepares to dive and snatch it up. Suddenly the water erupts with 30 fish speeding across the surface in different directions. Startled by the commotion, the bird hesitates – the moment is lost and the wily four-eyed fish have all made good their escape.

This remarkable four-eyed fish, known in Spanish as *quatro ojos*, has unusual two-tiered eyesight that enables it to keep a wary eye above the water for predators, such as kingfishers, while at the same time searching below the surface for its own food.

In fact, four-eyed fish have only two eyes, each with only one lens. Its eyes are positioned on the top of its head, and they protrude above water when the rest of its body is moving just below the surface. Each eye has an upper and a lower section with its own clear outer tissue (or cornea) and light-sensitive focusing screen (or retina). The lens is egg-shaped. When a fish is looking under water, light passes through the length of the lens to give it good near-sighted vision. When it is looking into the air, light passes through the short width of the lens, giving good distance vision.

On seeing a kingfisher hovering low overhead, a four-eyed fish will take evasive action, jumping out of the water and skipping over the surface like a flying fish. As four-eyed fish tend to swim in shoals, a lot of them jumping out at once can confuse a predator.

Conning towers *A four-eyed fish (inset) is able to see above and below water simultaneously. These fish swim in shoals (below) just under the surface with their eyes protruding above it.*

A hunter with more than a thousand eyes

Dragonflies are fast flyers that hunt on the wing near water, eating their own weight of other insects in about half an hour. A dragonfly's two large and bulging compound eyes play a major part in its hunting skill. They cover almost the whole of its head and give it complete all-round vision.

Each eye is composed of more than 1000 tiny eyes – six-sided facets each with its own lens and retina. Through these compound eyes the dragonfly sees a mass of images that together resemble a speckled newspaper photograph.

Each facet is stimulated successively by movement through its field of vision. This 'flicker vision' through many facets enables a dragonfly to spot even the smallest movement of prey. The number of facets dictates an insect's quality of vision. An ant, with only nine facets, gets a very unclear picture.

Goggle-eyed *A dragonfly's prominent compound eyes (right), seen here magnified about 20 times, are made up of thousands of individual eyes.*

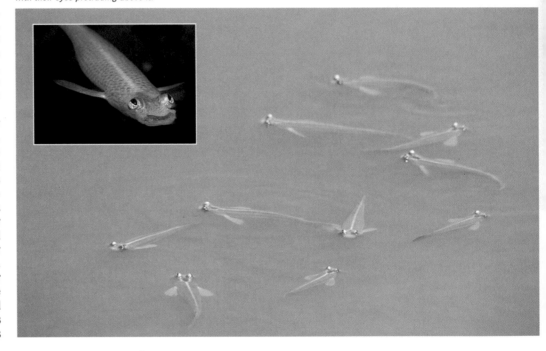

Ancient reptiles keep a third eye on the clock

Sightless eye *A third eye on top of a tuatara's head is covered with a layer of skin.*

Found only on a few islets off the New Zealand coast, the curious tuatara 'lizard' appears to have a third eye sitting just under the skin on the top of its head.

This primitive reptile, which is about 2 ft (60 cm) long, is thought of as a living fossil since it has survived more or less unchanged for about 140 million years. Similar reptiles became extinct along with the dinosaurs about 65 million years ago.

The tuatara's third eye is known as the parietal eye because it sits between the parietal bones that form the top and sides of the skull. It has all the structures found in an eye – a lens, a retina and nerves connecting it to the brain – and may function as a light receptor. The tuatara cannot see through it, however, because it does not send any images to the brain. But the eye is linked to the pineal gland, a gland that is present in all animals with backbones. In human beings the pineal gland is positioned quite deep inside the head.

The pineal gland produces a hormone known as melatonin, the output of which increases during the night, controlling the cycle of sleeping and waking. The gland is also thought to control the body clock responsible for timing such functions as mating and hibernating. This biological clock is triggered by changes in natural light which, in the case of the tuatara, may be registered by the third eye.

A frog's eyes make its everyday decisions

A common frog's life is governed by its eyesight. It has several kinds of optic nerve that pick out what is immediately crucial to it and that automatically trigger the appropriate reflex. So a frog is programmed to react automatically in the safest way – only essential information makes the journey from its eyes to its brain.

Finding food depends upon the frog's ability to detect movement. To provoke a frog into shooting out its tongue, the prey must be small and round and, above all, on the move. Much of its diet consists of small, active insects and other creatures such as spiders and ground beetles. A dead insect, or one that is standing motionless, is ignored, even though it may be perfectly good to eat. The optic nerve that detects movement and enables the frog to catch food also permits it to locate approaching danger. Its immediate reaction to movement by anything other than prey is to jump swiftly into a pond. It is sensitive to blue light, which is reflected by water, and this tells it in which direction to hop.

Finding somewhere to hide

Frogs spend much of their time on land, and are secretive creatures that hide in damp places beneath rocks or under leaf litter. This talent for concealment depends on another optic nerve that responds to very dark areas. It enables a frog to find shady spots where it can hide from predators such as birds.

Finally there is an optic nerve that identifies the shapes of boulders and bushes, allowing a frog to find its way about its territory.

Frog's-eye view *The prominent eyes of a common frog contain detectors that control many of its actions, such as catching prey, hiding from danger and getting about.*

FEELING THE WAY WITH WHISKERS, HAIRS AND SKIN

All creatures have a sense of touch, but some rely on it more than others for their protection, movement and manipulation.

Sensitive hairs are invaluable for tunnel life

Moles have touch sensors at both ends of their bodies – a logical adaptation for shuffling backwards and forwards through dark tunnels. The whiskers that fringe a mole's muzzle and tip its tail are embedded in touch-receptive cells. Any movement of these whiskers, whether by a draught or by touch, alerts the animal to approaching danger or a source of food – for example, a wriggling worm.

When a mole is on the move in its tunnel, it holds its tail upright, so that the whiskers touch the roof. It is thought that this provides the mole with information on the size and shape of its tunnel.

The naked mole rat looks more like a wrinkled sausage than either a mole or a rat. In fact it is neither. The mole rat is a small, burrowing mammal found only in Africa. It is, however, 'naked' except for stiff, touch-sensitive hairs that protrude from its pink body. These are used by the mole rat to feel its way along the dark tunnels of its home.

Blind faith in feeling *A mole rat's sightless eyes are sensitive to air currents. It uses them to find damaged tunnels by tracing the draughts caused by air entering the holes.*

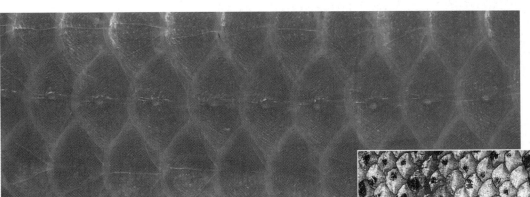

Fish sense *The lateral lines of a goldfish (left) and a salmon (below) are the outer signs of a special sensory system used by fish to detect movement of other animals in the water close by. The lines consist of canals containing cells receptive to pressure changes in the surrounding water. Any other animals nearby causing movement of the water are immediately detected by the system.*

Lateral line lets fish feel imminent danger

Fish have a 'sixth sense' that enables them to detect the presence of other aquatic animals before making any visual or physical contact. This ability relies on an organ known as the lateral line, which senses changes of pressure caused by movements in the water, up to five body lengths away.

The system consists of a row of pressure receptors (called neuromasts). These are buried at intervals in a tube running along each side of a fish's body and in a complex of canals on its head.

Each tube lies just below the skin and is open to the outside through a series of pores. Sensitive hairs extend from each pressure receptor into a jelly-like projection. Water flows freely through the pores and along the tube.

Movement in the water round the fish causes the water in the tube to move. The jelly-like projections are distorted by the water movement, bending the sensitive hairs. The strength and direction of water disturbance determines how much and in which direction the hairs bend. The message is picked up by the pressure receptors, which transfer it to the fish's central nervous system.

By this means, a fish can detect the movements of potential prey, predators or partners, and can also tell the direction of current flow.

The lateral line is of enormous importance to fish that have poor eyesight. Lungfish, for example, are practically blind to both form and movement, and respond in the main to light and dark. To compensate for this, however, they are highly sensitive to smell, pressure, vibration and touch. Lateral lines, in intricate patterns that vary from species to species, cover their heads and pick up messages in the water. African and South American lungfish are also equipped with long, spindly fins, which they wave about constantly. But the fins are not employed to propel these unusual fish through the water. Instead they serve a similar purpose to the white stick carried by a blind or poor-sighted person – they help a fish to feel its way about.

How primates rely on touch-sensitive skin

Cleaning by hand *Sensitive fingers are essential for thorough grooming. Barbary apes, like all primates, have a cluster of touch receptors in their fingertips which help with such delicate tasks.*

The skin of most animals is sensitive to touch; only hard parts such as shells or horns feel nothing. Even simple animals such as sea slugs (or nudibranchia) have particularly sensitive skins. In fact, they rely on little else for their perception of the world around them, because their hearing and vision are minimal.

An animal's touch-receptive cells are usually concentrated in those parts of the body that do the sensing – the tip of an elephant's trunk, for example. The cells are usually stimulated by hairs or whiskers embedded in them, which bend in response to an outside influence, such as a breeze.

But in primates (humans, apes and monkeys) it is the hairless hands, feet and tongues that are especially sensitive. In the tip of a human tongue, for example, there

Keeping out of trouble *A basic sense of touch alerts sea slugs, such as this Spanish shawl, to obstacles. The slugs rely on their vibrant warning colours and repulsive flavour to deter predators.*

are about 200 touch cells concentrated in an area about one-quarter the size of a postage stamp. Because of this concentration, the tongue can easily feel two sharp pencil points just a pinhead apart. But on the skin of the back, where there are fewer touch cells, the points seem to merge, even when only about 2½ in (65 mm) apart.

Primates mostly use the tips of their fingers to touch. The sensitivity of human hands, for example, has enabled man to fashion and use tools as well as to manipulate food. Despite their importance, fingertips have only half as many touch receptors as the tongue. If they were too sensitive, they could not withstand rough contact.

Some monkeys, for example the South American spider monkey, have a small, bare patch of sensitive skin on the underside of their prehensile (grasping) tails. This 'fifth limb' is as sensitive to touch as the animal's hands and feet, and can be manipulated to pick up objects as small as peanuts.

327

FINE-TUNED EARS FOR GOOD LISTENERS

Both predator and prey rely on keen hearing to survive; the predator to pinpoint its victim, the prey to get an early warning of danger.

How the barn owl hears whispers in the night

Although it has particularly good night vision, a barn owl relies mainly on its remarkable hearing when hunting for prey in the dark. It can pick up even the smallest sound and pinpoint its source with incredible accuracy.

Small nocturnal rodents such as mice, shrews and voles are the owl's main prey. It is very sensitive to small sounds such as the busy rustling of a field mouse in the undergrowth. As the owl's flight is almost noiseless, it is able to get within striking distance of its victim without being heard.

After locating its prey, the owl swoops in for the kill, following every twist and turn of its victim's path. It aligns its talons along the prey's body – a remarkable feat

Night hunter *A barn owl's heart-shaped face is sculpted to direct sounds to its ears, which are at different levels. This system enables it to pinpoint its prey, a mouse for instance, and swoop on it accurately in the dark.*

considering the zigzag course of a field mouse. Even in the dark the owl easily changes the alignment of its talons, relying entirely on the rustling of its victim's movement.

The barn owl's superior sound location system relies on two oval depressions in the tightly packed feathers on either side of its beak. Each depression funnels the sound waves from over a wide area into an earhole, in the same way that a satellite dish concentrates radio waves onto its antenna.

Comparing sounds

To pinpoint a moving target, the owl has to determine its direction. It can do this because its ears are at different levels. The right ear is higher than the left ear, and the depression round it tilts upwards to pick up sounds from above. The depression round the left ear, however, focuses downwards to receive sound from below.

The effect is that noises from different levels sound different in each ear. It is only those directly ahead and at the owl's eye level that sound similar. By comparing the sounds received in each ear, the owl can determine the position of its prey to within a whisker.

Sound scanner *As it forages in the African grasslands, a bat-eared fox periodically stands still, its huge ears tilted forwards as it listens for the sounds of insect activity under the ground. Termites are its favourite food.*

Listening for insects under the ground

Its disproportionately large ears are so sensitive that the bat-eared fox of southern and East Africa can even detect the tiny scrabbling noises of a dung beetle larva gnawing its way through a ball of dung under the ground.

Most foxes hunt mainly by scent and feed on ground-nesting birds, small rodents or carrion. A bat-eared fox hunts prey by sound and lives chiefly on termites and dung beetles. It is equipped with extra molars and has large, powerful jaw muscles that help it to eat quickly.

Bat-eared foxes are usually found in small family parties, but when foraging they spread out through the grassland and scrub, often near grazing animals such as zebras, which stir up insects.

Each fox concentrates on its own patch, nose down and ears tilted forwards as it listens for insects, its head turning from side to side to determine the precise location. Once it finds food, a fox digs it out with paws and teeth.

Males that are drawn by a humming female

The male mosquito hears by using organs called Johnston's organs, one at the base of each of its two antennae. They enable it to tune in to the sounds made by a female in search of a mate.

The incessant drone of a female mosquito, a sound rather like a distant aeroplane, is well known in tropical lands and in the Arctic. It is produced by the beating of the insect's wings at up to 600 times a second. A male's antennae

vibrate in sympathy, triggering its Johnston's organs to the same frequency. To avoid confusion, each species of mosquito beats its wings at a slightly different frequency. But things can go wrong.

Male mosquitoes have flown into the open mouths of opera singers holding a note at the crucial pitch. In New York, the insects were seen to congregate on a hotel's electric sign. This was because the hum of the transformer was at the same pitch as the wing beats of females of the species. It was this observation that alerted scientists to a mosquito's hearing abilities.

Hearing aid *The caracal (above), a cat of Africa and the Middle East, and the puma (right) from the Americas, both swivel their ears to listen for prey.*

Ears that provide an early warning system

Instead of moving the whole of the head, animals such as deer and antelope swivel the outer parts of their ears, or pinnae, to locate a sound. This enables them to spot where the sound is coming from almost immediately, and also to listen for predators sneaking up from behind while they are busy eating or drinking.

A deer that hears a rustling in the undergrowth swivels its ears until the sound is as loud as possible. If it then recognises that the sound is likely to come from a predator, the deer flees instantly. So its survival depends on the sensitivity and directability of its ears.

Surviving in the desert

Hiding places are few and far between in a desert so, for the animals that live there, an early warning system is essential to avoid being eaten. As a result, many desert animals – from the tiny kangaroo rat of North America to the large addax, a grazing antelope of the Sahara – rely on their acute hearing to warn them of danger. They also tend to have similar ear adaptations to magnify sound.

It is the size of the middle-ear cavity that determines an ear's sensitivity. The bigger the cavity, the more freely the eardrum can vibrate and the more sound can be magnified. The middle ear of a

kangaroo rat magnifies sounds 100 times and is very sensitive to low-pitched sounds. This makes it unusual among small rodents, because they normally communicate with high-pitched sounds.

But the kangaroo rat's sensitive ears enable it to hear the quietest movements of a predator on the prowl – even the almost silent wing beats of an attacking owl.

All-round hearing *Impalas amid a grazing herd in Zimbabwe (above) stand alert with ears cocked forwards to pick up a suspicious sound. In Tanzania, a Thomson's gazelle (above left) listens with ears pointing rearwards. The ability to swivel their ears gives these animals an early warning of the approach of hunters such as big cats.*

TASTING AND SMELLING

Whether airborne or waterborne, scents convey essential messages to animals. Some help them to find the right food, others tell of danger.

For snakes, taste and smell are the same

A snake smells by literally 'tasting' the air, flicking out its forked tongue to collect scents on its moist surface. Then it samples the chemicals from the air by pushing the tip of its tongue into the roof of its mouth, into the paired sensitive pits known as Jacobson's organ. The pits are lined with very fine hairs that pick up the chemical messages and send them directly to the snake's brain.

Unlike mammals, snakes do not have separate senses of taste and smell. Mammals make use of their noses to analyse the chemicals carried in the air and their tongues to analyse substances they take into their mouths. But what is clearly distinguishable to a mammal may be all the same to other animals.

For example, a strong-smelling substance such as petrol gives off chemicals that evaporate easily and are present in the air in large concentrations. On the other hand,

a substance like sugar evaporates little and gives off weak chemical signals. Humans can smell petrol but detect sugar only by taste. In some creatures taste and smell overlap, and they are so sensitive to particular chemicals that they can detect them in the air even if in minute quantities. Blowflies, for instance, are 200 times more sensitive to the presence of sugar than humans – they can scent a sugar solution without touching it.

But insects also need discriminating taste in order to identify suitable food and to detect poisons or other noxious chemicals. They often have taste-sensitive cells set round their mouthparts, but may also have sensors on their feet that enable them to identify the surface they are standing on.

Foot sensors are crucial for butterflies, which have to ensure they lay their eggs on the plant that is correct for their species. A butterfly's mouthparts are not capable of tasting and testing leaves as they are adapted for feeding on liquid nectar or juices only.

Something in the air *An Asian white-lipped pit viper (above) samples the air with its tongue to identify surrounding scents. A red admiral butterfly (right) tests the surface of a rotting apple with its foot sensors before sipping juices from it.*

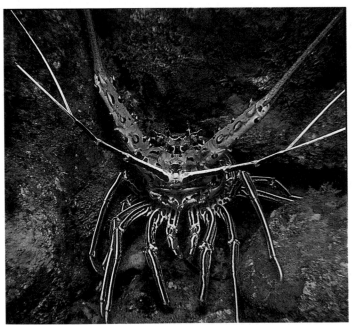

Extrasensory antennae *The painted lobster, a crayfish found on Indo-Pacific reefs, is a scavenger that uses its extremely large antennae to pick up the smell of rotting flesh. Sensitive to taste, smell and touch, its antennae supplement its eyesight.*

How fish track down a meal under water

Some fish, including freshwater carp and deep-sea rat-tails, have many taste receptors lining their mouths and throats, and even more round the lower parts of their gill arches. Each receptor is made up of a cluster of 12-20 cells, some of which have minute bristles, resembling a flower bud. Carp and rat-tails grub about for food in the bottom mud, and use their array of taste buds to sort out the edible from the inedible.

Many fish that live close to the bottom have taste-sensitive organs that complement their nostrils in the search for morsels of food. For example, catfish have poor vision and rely almost entirely on taste-sensitive, fleshy filaments that hang from their mouths. And lake-living gourami have 'fingers' lined

with taste buds hanging from their fins. Starfish living in the darkness of the oceanic abyss are quick to find the remains of dead fish that fall to the bottom of the sea. They can detect waterborne chemicals given off by rotting food, and are able to follow scent trails carried in the slow-moving currents that cross the ocean floor.

The deep-sea prawn has two whip-like antennae to help it to detect and track down food. The stiff, bottom part of each antenna is held outwards so that the thinner, more flexible part, which is twice the length of the prawn's body, trails backwards.

Of the seven varieties of sensory hair on each prawn's antennae, only two are sensitive to smell and the rest are concerned with touch. However, the taste-sensitive hairs at the bottom of an antenna can pick up waterborne odours from as far as 22 yd (20 m) away.

The secret courtship messages of moths

One day in the late 19th century, Jean Henri Fabre, a French naturalist who had been studying a female giant peacock moth in his laboratory, was surprised when his son came running excitedly to him.

'Come quickly,' his son cried, 'come and see the moths, big as birds. Your room is full of them.' It was true – the laboratory was full of male moths flapping round the cage that contained the female. Somehow she had managed to call this army of suitors to her. How male and female moths found each other had long mystified scientists. Jean Henri Fabre now began to think that the answer was a scent.

It was not until 80 years later that chemists were able to prove his theory, and identify the scent. It was found in such tiny amounts

that experimenters had to collect the secretions of half a million moths in order to amass an amount as small as 12 milligrams.

They discovered that the female moth raises her abdomen to protrude a pair of glands, and releases from them a scent known as a pheromone. She flaps her wings to waft the scent into the air, and a plume of it spreads out and trails away downwind.

The pheromone trail

The male silk moth has an exceptional sense of smell. His feathery antennae are covered with smell receptors, each of which consists of a hollow hair containing two nerve endings immersed in fluid. Scents enter the hair via pores on its surface, then pass down a small tube and make contact with the pheromone receptor cell. A male silk moth has about 60 000 sensory hairs on his antennae and three-

quarters of them are sensitive to one substance alone – bombykol, the pheromone which unmated female moths release. The merest whiff of it alerts any male moth within a range of 3 miles (5 km). His antennae are so sensitive to it that they can detect one molecule, although he does not fly upwind and search for the female until the signal is much stronger.

Flying in a zigzag pattern, the male compares the concentrations of the scent that are picked up by each antenna. If he senses that the pheromone is strengthening in one direction, he heads that way. By flying towards the increasing concentrations of pheromone, he finds his way to the waiting female moth.

Scent detectors *A male silk moth's feathery antennae spray out from his head like two large ferns. With them, he can pick up the faintest trace of a female moth's airborne message – the scent that tells him she is unmated.*

GIDDY GOATS

Aided by their extraordinary agility and sense of balance, some goat antelopes have found a remote haven in the mountains.

Natural athlete *With apparently effortless grace, a chamois (above) bounds down a treacherous mountain slope. Like many of the goat antelopes, chamois have developed their amazing agility in order to escape predators – in the chamois' case, eagles, wolves, lynxes and brown bears – by fleeing to more inaccessible places. Ibex too (left), have found sanctuary from natural enemies among the crags. Their split hoofs with soft outer edges give them excellent purchase on the rocks. Within days of being born, young ibex can follow their mothers along narrow cliff ledges, over deep crevices or down precipitous mountainsides.*

Home on the range *Although their balancing skills seem almost supernatural, the mountain goats of the Rocky Mountains in North America are not born with any special senses. Mostly, it is practice that allows them to move so easily around their mountain homes. Young goats (below) develop sure-footedness by standing on top of rocks and trying to push each other off. Mountain goats spend their entire lives above the tree line, where they are safer from pumas and wolves that would otherwise prey on them. Their agility too enables them to reach precipitous ledges (bottom) where salt leached from the rocks provides a valuable dietary supplement.*

Mountain sanctuary *In their homes among the cliffs and crags near the snow line, Alpine ibex (above) are relatively safe from predators like wolves. One hunter, however, is still able to reach them – man. Since medieval times, men have stalked ibex – the horns could be fashioned into charms, the blood was believed to remove callouses, and the heart muscle and undigested contents of the stomach were thought to be cure-alls. By the early 1800s the Alpine ibex were almost extinct. In 1854 however, a reserve was established for them in the Italian Alps. Since then, the ibex population has increased slowly, and the animals are no longer considered endangered.*

333

INNER SENSES

Hairs, nerves, feathers, gravity and compressed air all provide means for different animals to determine their position in relation to their surroundings.

Guidance systems for under water and flight

Water scorpions are not very good swimmers and spend much of the time hiding among leaf debris in muddy ponds and ditches.

To navigate when hunting, the scorpion – in reality, a water bug and not a true scorpion – uses six small, air-filled holes on its belly. Each hole has a thin membrane stretched across its opening. As the water pressure increases with depth, the air is compressed and the membrane is forced inwards. If the scorpion's head is nearer the surface than its tail, the holes nearest the head are subject to less pressure than those towards the tail, so the front membranes move less than the back ones. This tells the water scorpion that it is heading for the surface.

African clawed frogs, which wait just below the water surface for passing prey, use pit-like organs along their sides to find their way. Each organ is lined with microscopic hairs that bend with the water flow along the body, sending messages from nerves to brain. This enables a frog to measure its movement in relation to the water flow and set its course accordingly.

Flight gauges

Birds have several different types of feather, each with a different function. Long wing feathers are used for flying, and downy feathers insulate the body. The filoplumes, the tiny, hairlike feathers that are left behind when a bird is plucked, are thought to provide it with a flight-monitoring system.

Each filoplume has a long shaft with a tuft of soft barbs at the tip. It is always next to a large feather, and it is believed that it senses the movements of the larger feather and triggers nerves that send signals to the bird's brain about air speed, wind direction, buffeting

and any other air movements that might affect its flight.

A grasshopper, which leaps into the air and then uses its wings to glide, monitors flight with dome-shaped receptors in the hard outer covering of its back. These act like strain gauges, picking up distortions in its body casing as it flies. Similar receptors monitor muscle activity in its body. There are at least 148 pairs of receptors on

each side of a grasshopper's body. By detecting strain and movement, they ensure that muscle activity is evenly distributed, and keep the insect flying on an even keel.

All flying insects have similar check-and-balance systems, which are supplemented by hairs on the antennae and face. Air currents passing over the hairs are thought to stimulate and to maintain the insect's flight. Experimenting with

A sense of place *A cockchafer, like all species of beetle, has sense receptors in its muscles. These relay information about the position of the creature's body, helping it to control its movements.*

locusts suspended on string, scientists found that they flapped their wings only if a gentle breeze was blowing across their faces. If their facial hairs were painted over, the breeze did not affect them and, on release, the locusts would not fly.

When gravity indicates balance and direction

A bee can tell whether it is the right way up or upside-down by the hairs on its neck. These hairs are so arranged that when the bee is on a horizontal surface, they are in even contact with its head. As the bee's position changes, the pull of gravity on its head asserts more pressure on different areas of the hairs on its neck.

If the bee is crawling upwards its head is pulled towards its chest, which puts more pressure on the neck hairs there. If it is crawling downwards, its head is pulled away from the chest, putting pressure on the hairs on the back of the neck. The steepness of the slope determines how much pressure there is on the hairs.

Cats, renowned for their powers of balance and their ability to land on their feet if they fall, also use hairs to determine their position. As in most mammals, these hairs are in the inner ear.

Inside a cat's ear there are three U-shaped canals joined to a spiral tube called the cochlea – an organ mainly used for hearing. Within these canals there are small pads of mucus-like material, weighted by heavy granules, that rest on delicate hairs. As the cat moves its head, the mucus-like

Guided by gravity *While a southern stringray some 5 ft (1.5 m) across is swimming, a network of nerves informs it of the position of each part of its body.*

pads are tilted to and fro, bending the hairs. The hairs in turn trigger signals in the nervous system. The message varies according to the direction in which the hairs have been bent.

By acting on information from these sensory organs, the animal can alter its course and position. A falling cat rights itself from upside-down to upright by twisting its body from the head end to the tail, so that as it lands, its back is arched and all four feet are down.

This balance system is constantly at work in most backboned animals, guiding even the simplest action. Even a seemingly effortless movement such as the graceful, winged glide of a stingray through the ocean is, in fact, the result of complex and rapidly changing messages buzzing back and forth along its nervous pathways.

Nerves coordinate a complicated body

A millipede does not trip over its own legs, although it may have up to 200 of them. This miracle of coordination is possible because the nerve cells associated with muscles and joints constantly monitor stresses as the creature moves. Every animal's nervous system is central to its ability to move effectively – it has a complex network of nerves that constantly monitor the body, sending messages in the form of tiny electrical impulses.

Getting the picture

In vertebrates, those animals with a backbone, the brain and spinal column form the central nervous system. From specialised nerve cells, or sensory neurons, the central nervous system receives information from around the body about temperature, pressure on the skin, tension or posture.

Using these senses, people can create an internal picture of themselves that is quite independent of vision. For example, poor-sighted people may have to grope around for their spectacles but, once they have them, they have no trouble placing them in the right position.

Nervous reaction *Even though a giraffe's brain is roughly 16 ft (4.8 m) from its feet, the complex of nerves constantly monitoring its system allows the animal to gallop across the African grasslands without difficulty. In a similar manner, a millipede (right) can control its many legs.*

When the central nervous system receives messages, it sends out a response immediately, which is carried to the muscles by another set of nerves, the motor neurons.

Much of this work is done subconsciously, and a lot of the nerve messages never reach the brain. Instant responses are triggered by nerve complexes in the spinal column. A hand is pulled away from a hot stove plate before its owner has time to think about it.

Complex calculations, even in invertebrates, are carried out at this subconscious level. Millipedes, like human beings, do not have to concentrate on putting one foot in front of the other. The degree of flexing in one leg is automatically adjusted in relation to the other legs by clusters of nerves, each in charge of a pair of legs, positioned in its body segments. This allows the millipede's brain to apply itself to other problems.

INTELLIGENCE AND INSTINCT

'ANIMALS NEVER DEVELOP TO A POINT WHERE ANY SIGN OF THOUGHT CAN BE DETECTED IN THEM.' ≈ RENÉ DESCARTES, *IN A LETTER TO HENRY MORE*, 1649.
'NO TRUTH APPEARS TO ME MORE EVIDENT THAN THAT BEASTS ARE ENDOWED WITH THOUGHT AND REASON AS WELL AS MEN.' ≈ DAVID HUME, *A TREATISE OF HUMAN NATURE*, 1739.

The mind of the octopus
We are inclined to credit primates with the highest levels of intelligence, but there is proof that octopuses, too, are among the most intelligent of animals. Laboratory tests have shown that they are able to discern shapes, remember events and carry out certain techniques – one learned to pull the stopper out of a bottle in order to reach a shrimp. Other laboratory octopuses waited for nightfall to leave their tanks and steal fish from neighbouring tanks.

The controversy about how much animal behaviour is instinctive, and how much is rational, has endured for centuries. Biologists have made great progress in understanding how instinctive behaviours are inherited and in discovering how remarkably intelligent some animals can be. But far from resolving the argument, these discoveries have only served to intensify it. While much animal behaviour can be explained by reflexes and conditioning, there is increasing evidence to suggest that some animals are conscious and rational beings, with a clear sense of self and a subtle understanding of their relationships with others of their kind that are very similar to our own. Understanding the animal mind is one of the most difficult, challenging fields of modern biology.

Acting on instinct
Camouflaged with the remains of previous victims, an assassin bug uses the body of a termite to fish for new prey. The bug is exploiting the termite's natural impulse to recover the carcass of a former nest mate.

Satisfying stick-work
An African elephant scratches herself with a stick. Until quite recently, the use of tools in this way was thought to be behaviour unique to humans, and was regarded as evidence of our superiority to other animals.

Making it better
A mother capuchin monkey presses a mixture of leaves and mud to the wound in the head of her crying baby, to staunch the flow of blood. Capuchin monkeys are extremely intelligent and, like chimpanzees, have been observed using tools for cracking nuts.

Learning rewarded
A dwarf mongoose hurls an egg between its legs, to smash it on the rocks behind – complex behaviour which has almost certainly been learned from watching older animals gain a tasty meal in this way.

REASONING

Although much animal behaviour is instinctive, there are many examples of animals with the ability to use reason and learn from experience and each other.

Keen-minded squirrels rise to every challenge

When a nut is the prize, it seems that a squirrel is prepared to tackle practically any problem. Zoologists studying wild squirrels have sometimes set them the most complex tasks, such as negotiating more than 20 obstacles to reach food. Each of these presents a problem that must be solved, such as pulling a lever to release a gate, balancing on thin wires, working a seesaw or pulling up a string with a nut suspended from it.

But a squirrel's readiness to meet a challenge does not indicate that it is foolhardy. A squirrel that is feeding stops repeatedly to look round for danger from dogs, cats or hawks. Its caution is instinctive, but its reactions are often based on reason. The squirrel is continually assessing the risk of being caught to help it to decide whether to feed on the food scraps at its feet or take them back to the safety of the tree. It might expend more energy in taking scraps to the tree than it would gain by eating them.

Weighing the chances

In one experiment, squirrels were given biscuits, which they do not bury, and their reactions noted. It was found that if trees were near enough to provide a ready refuge, the squirrels immediately ate all the pieces thrown to them. When farther from the trees, they ate the small pieces on the spot – as these could be devoured quickly – but they took larger ones to the trees. These decisions involved weighing the risk of being caught against the benefit of eating at once.

Ever watchful *A grey squirrel has retreated to the safety of a lofty branch to eat the seeds in a pine cone. Although the squirrel found the cone on the ground, to have eaten it there would have put it at risk from predators.*

338

Helping others to find food has advantages

Sparrows often tell one another about a good food supply by making chirruping calls from a safe perch. Once a group has gathered, they all begin to feed.

There is a good reason for this unselfish behaviour, however. In Britain, the house sparrow population is thought to number about 12 million. But they have found that life around humans can be dangerous. Domestic cats pose the main threat, and the recovery of the suburban sparrowhawk population in recent years has renewed another.

By breeding and feeding in a large group, each bird cuts down its risk of being caught by a hungry predator, so it can spend less time on the lookout for trouble and more time searching for something to eat. But when the food, a piece of bread perhaps, cannot be shared easily, the sparrow reverts to its natural selfishness and secretly gorges itself.

Juvenile North American ravens also appear to help each other out. In winter they range widely for food, and often find it on an adult bird's territory. The youngsters use a special call to summon others from more than 1 mile (1.6 km) away to help them hold off the stronger adults. A young bird that is alone when it finds food will not call, however, for fear of reprisals from the older birds. It waits until there are sufficient youngsters in the vicinity to put up a defence.

Secret feast *Having found a scrap of bread that is too small to share, this sparrow keeps the knowledge to itself and enjoys a solitary banquet.*

Red ants send their fire brigade to the rescue

In the 1930s, a French researcher at a government laboratory discovered fire-fighting ants in the laboratory garden. When a lighted match was placed near their nest, the red ants of one particular colony lined up to squirt it with formic acid from their abdomens. But none of the other colonies of red ants in the garden responded to fire in this way.

It turned out that an official at the laboratory regularly dropped cigarette ends near the nest of this particular red ant colony while taking a walk round the garden. So the ants were used to fire and had learned how to deal with it.

Birds learn solutions to their problems

Marsh harriers, which frequent wetlands in many parts of the Old World, have been observed drowning waterfowl that they have caught in pools or shallow streams. They hold the victim's head under water until it stops struggling. But as these birds never try to drown fish they have caught, it must be assumed that this behaviour is learned and not instinctive.

Crows, too, are excellent problem solvers, both in the wild and in captivity. Fatty treats hung on string in gardens to attract tits, for example, are often taken by crows. They pull up the string with their beaks while holding the slack against the branch with one foot.

Cracking the problem

Foraging successfully in an uncertain world takes skill, and crows are very adaptable – in western Canada some of them take whelks from the seashore at low tide.

Experiments have shown that the crows pick up only those shells that weigh enough to contain a live whelk. They seem to know that an underweight shell is likely to contain only the shrivelled remains of a dead whelk. To get at the meal inside the shell, the crows have learned to drop them onto a rocky surface time and again. On average, it takes four drops from a height of 9-26 ft (3-8 m) to crack open a shell. Dropping it from a greater height, may be more effective in breaking the shell, but it often results in the contents being scattered or contaminated with sand, so judging the correct height is crucial and must be learned.

Many other birds have acquired the skill of breaking a shell, too. European thrushes hammer snail shells on stones until they splinter, and the bearded vulture of Africa

Death by drowning *After catching a goose in a Tunisian swamp, a powerful marsh harrier subdues it by holding it under water until it stops struggling.*

and Asia drops bones onto rocks from a height in order to break them open and allow the bird to reach the marrow inside.

WHEN INSTINCT CONQUERS SENSE

Complex behaviour in animals is not always a sign of intelligence. It may simply be the result of instinctive reactions, which can sometimes cause problems.

The compulsion to feed an ever-open mouth

Working frantically, a female reed warbler with a chick in the nest searches constantly for caterpillars with which to satisfy the chick's enormous appetite. So does her mate. But it is a cuckoo chick that occupies the warblers' nest. One of their eggs was removed by a female cuckoo when she laid her own egg in late May. The rest were pushed out by the young cuckoo soon after it hatched some 11 days later, thus giving it the undivided attention of its foster-parents.

Yet the warblers will continue to feed the chick instinctively, unable to resist the powerful stimuli of the young bird's cavernous, bright orange gape and its wheezy call. Even warblers that just happen to be passing may make a detour to answer the cuckoo's persistent call for food. Within three days of hatching, the chick is as heavy as its foster-parents, and after three weeks it is four times their weight.

Delayed departure

A young cuckoo may grow so big that its bulges over the nest edge, forcing the warblers to stand on its back to feed it. A cuckoo chick may even burst out of the domed nest of a wren, for example, and sit calling amid the wreckage. Still its foster-parents continue to feed it.

Even when a cuckoo chick is ready to leave the nest at about a month old, the foster-parents carry on looking after it for yet another two or three weeks. Finally, it takes to the air, and in August leaves to winter in Africa.

Cuckoos lay their eggs in the nests of about 50 different species of bird. They rely on the fact that birds feed their chicks by instinct, triggered by the infants' insistent calling and brightly coloured, wide-open gapes – the gape of a song thrush chick is bright yellow, for

Hearty appetite *Although dwarfed by the intruder, a tiny wren feeds a hefty young cuckoo that has left the nest but not yet flown off. To satisfy its appetite, its foster-parents hunt insects almost round the clock.*

example, and that of a young greenfinch a startling red. These are colours the parents find impossible to resist and easy to aim for.

So powerful is a parent bird's instinct to feed the gape of a chick that a North American red cardinal finch once dutifully fed a goldfish in a pond. The fish had learned to stick its mouth above water to take food from its owners. On seeing the bird's shadow, it duly gaped. The finch instinctively shoved a beakful of insects into the fish's mouth.

Mistaken identity *A laysan albatross (right) of the North Pacific sits conscientiously on an old Thermos flask washed up near its nest on the Midway atoll, 1150 miles (1850 km) northwest of Honolulu. All sorts of objects, such as fishing floats, teapots, oranges and plastic bottles, seem to trigger the incubation instincts of the albatrosses.*

The confused actions of cross-bred birds

Although the peach-faced lovebird and the Fischer's lovebird are closely related species and both belong to the African parrot family, they differ strikingly in the way they carry nest-building materials – strips of bark or leaves.

A peach-faced lovebird of southwest Africa tucks several strips at a time into her rump feathers. A Fischer's lovebird of Kenya and

Sitting pretty *Peach-faced lovebirds (left) live on the dry steppes of southwest Africa. In captivity they breed with Fischer's lovebirds of East Africa. In the wild, distance keeps them apart.*

Tanzania carries each strip, one at a time, in her beak. In the wild the two species live too far apart to interbreed. In captivity they do so readily, but the resultant offspring are sadly confused.

The hybrid females have great difficulty building nests. Strips of vegetation tucked into their rump feathers fall out. Only after some two years of continual practice do the birds learn to take their nesting material to the nest site in their beaks. Even then, they go through the motions of tucking it into the rump feathers first.

This shows how some aspects of behaviour are tightly controlled by genes – a satisfactory arrangement in Nature thrown out of gear by the artificial environment of an aviary.

Home security *After digging out a nest (left), a sand wasp masks the entrance (below) with flat stones unearthed during excavation. If the stones are removed, it will rebuild the entire nest.*

Maternal instinct *In her search for food for her larva, a female sand wasp finds and paralyses a caterpillar (above), which she then drags back to her burrow, which is sometimes as far as 85 yd (77 m) away.*

Building by instinct rather than design

Even though the very carefully constructed mud nest of a mud-dauber wasp may seem to be the result of intelligent planning, it is built entirely by instinct.

This is illustrated by the wasp's inability to adapt to changes in its environment. Jean Henri Fabre, a 19th-century French naturalist, once watched a wasp carefully build its mud nest on a shining white house wall – then work hard for several days carrying moss and twigs to camouflage the nest.

To have to build a nest purely by instinct may seem a disadvantage, but it is vital for a mud-dauber wasp to have this inborn ability because it has no opportunity to learn how from other wasps. Once a female wasp has completed her

nest, she lays her egg, hunts down food such as an insect larva and puts it next to the egg. She then seals the nest and flies off. The larval wasp is left to develop on its own. Once it has developed fully it breaks out of the nest and lives a solitary existence.

Starting all over again

Sand wasps also build nests by instinct. Each wasp goes through a series of steps, first excavating a nest chamber, then checking it before laying an egg and sealing the hole with gravel. The completed nest is then tamped down with a pebble collected from close

by. However, if anything disrupts the wasp's routine – maybe the stones sealing the nest entrance are disturbed – it starts again at the beginning of the entire building sequence. Once again it digs out and checks its nest chamber, even though there is absolutely nothing wrong with it.

Leaf-cutter bees are equally unable to adapt to changes in building routine. A female bee cuts sections from leaves and uses them to builds cells in which she lays her eggs. If she chances upon a conveniently shaped piece of leaf, however, she ignores it. Her instinct is to cut leaves to the right

shape and size and transport them back to her burrow. If she drops a piece of leaf she has cut, rather than pick it up, she goes off to cut another leaf.

Nor are insects the only ones to become trapped by instincts and routine. A weaverbird's nest, suspended from a branch, is a complex structure of strands of grass laced together. The sequence of actions for building the nest is a long one. But if a bird's routine is disrupted by the destruction of a part of the nest it has just completed, instead of simply repairing the damage it tears the whole nest to pieces and starts again.

MEMORY AND LEARNING

While memory enables some animals to find their way back to specific places, learning allows others to work and communicate with humans.

A good memory helps an animal to survive

North American nutcrackers are jackdaw-sized birds with such good memories that they can find as many as 33 000 pine-cone seeds or hazelnuts they have hidden previously. This helps them to survive the harsh winters in the Rocky Mountain pine forests where they live. Even when the ground is covered with snow, the nutcrackers can find the food caches they hid around their territories in autumn.

Being able to find places again is crucial for the survival of most animals. Some species do this by instinct – eels, for instance, that find their way back from European rivers to their mid-Atlantic breeding grounds in the Sargasso Sea. Other species, such as the nutcracker, have a strong spatial memory – the ability to find their way to a particular place. In birds, as in humans, the ability seems to relate to the size of a part of the brain known as the hippocampus.

The blenny, a fish of tidal rock pools, makes its way unerringly back to the sea at low tide by slithering or leaping from one rock pool to another, even though it has no overall view of the arrangement of the pools. It seems to learn the layout of the terrain by swimming above it when the tide sweeps in. Learning the lie of the land is essential, too, for creatures such as wasps and sand bees, which need

Safe deposit *As winter clamps down on a Rocky Mountain pine forest, a Clark's nutcracker probes for some of the many pine seeds it cached in autumn.*

to find their burrows or nests when they return from a foraging trip.

A digger wasp, for example, before it sets off from its nest hole, flies in two or three circles to learn the pattern of small stones and twigs around the nest. This was discovered by G.P. Baerends, a Dutch scientist studying animal behaviour. He put fir cones round a female digger wasp's nest hole, then moved them a short way to one side after she had left. On her return, the wasp went straight to the centre of the cone circle rather than to her nest, which she found later only after a thorough search.

Going home *A blenny makes its way across rocks at low tide on its way back to the sea. It is adept at orientating itself, even though it cannot view its overall position.*

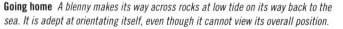

Learning a job and earning a living

During the 1880s, Jack, a chacma baboon, helped his disabled owner to run the signal box at a South African railway station. For the nine years until his death, Jack pulled the levers that set the points and changed the signals without ever having been known to make a mistake. Jack was talented but he was certainly not exceptional. Another chacma baboon, Jock, who learnt to operate the signals on a branch line outside Pretoria, was paid the princely sum of 1s 6d (7½ pence) a day.

Macaque monkeys have been used for centuries in Malaysia to harvest coconuts from tall palm trees. And in Australia, a macaque monkey named Johnnie regularly drove the tractor while his owner tossed fodder out for the sheep from the trailer behind.

More recently small South American capuchin monkeys have been trained to act as companions for disabled people. Their duties have included switching on the lights and television as well as tasks as complex as feeding and washing their charges, and even preparing drinks for them.

Elephants are used in Asia to help loggers with forestry work. An elephant can learn about 40 commands, both spoken and physical, and may be trained to push and pick up heavy logs with its trunk.

Navigation by memory *Minke whales (left) which grow to 26 ft (8 m), are found in all the world's oceans. Like other whales, they are thought to be sensitive to the Earth's magnetic field. Formations such as underwater cliffs or mountains cause slight variations in the contours of the field, and whales may memorise these and navigate by them.*

Fruit finder *Fruit, especially mangoes, figs and lychees, forms about 60 per cent of the orang-utan's diet. To locate widely dispersed fruit trees, orang-utans need a wide knowledge of their rain forest home and the changing seasons. They also watch where other fruit-eating creatures, such as hornbills, are feeding.*

Smart chimps master a human language

When animals call to each other, they are exchanging information, communicating in very much the same way that humans do. Scientists have discovered that the information is contained in the sound itself, just as in human words. Monkeys, for instance, take the same action whether the calls they hear are live or played back from a recording.

Some apes have learnt to respond to human sign languages. Several chimpanzees, beginning with the American-trained Washoe during the 1960s, and including a gorilla and an orang-utan, have been taught the American deaf-and-dumb language that is known as Ameslan. Washoe even managed to teach it to a young companion.

A chimp named Sarah mastered a form of language in which coloured shapes stood for words or concepts. In question-and-answer sessions, she became proficient at placing shapes on a magnetised board to create short sentences. Sarah could frame messages such as 'Give apple Sarah'. She was also able to differentiate between like and unlike objects, placing a plastic symbol for 'same' between like objects and a symbol for 'different' between unlike ones.

Two chimpanzees known as Sherman and Austin learnt a language that comprised shapes on a computer keyboard in a similar way. They were able to interchange simple instructions with both their keepers and each other.

Accomplished ape

But the best communicator of all must be Kanzi, a bonobo (or pygmy chimpanzee) that, at the Language Research Center near Atlanta, USA, learnt the same keyboard language as Sherman and Austin. But Kanzi also learnt the spoken English names for the computer keys used. By 1992 he could carry out verbal instructions, including those for lighting and putting out camp fires and for cooking on a stove. He could even respond, in computer-language, with requests, comments and questions of his own. Apes are not the only species to have demonstrated some kind of capacity for learning a language. Dolphins have been trained to carry out complex commands given in both words and symbols.

One of the most surprising cases of animal learning is that of an African grey parrot named Alex. In the 1980s he was taught a wide range of English words by Irene Pepperberg, an American scientist. Alex's conversational abilities seem to be as proficient as those of the chimps Washoe and Sarah, and are comparable with those of a child of two to three years old.

IMITATING SKILLS AND SOUNDS

By imitation or innovation, birds acquire the habits and calls of their species – and some even pick up the food-finding talents of others.

Looking on *After a sudden snowfall in central France, a hungry robin (below right) watches a kingfisher scan an icy pool for signs of a fish. The kingfisher (above) hovers over a hole in the ice and then plunges in to emerge (above right) with a small fish in its beak.*

The little milk thief on your doorstep

At one time milk was delivered to British doorsteps in bottles with a card disc as a stopper. In the 1920s, bluetits learned how to remove the card stoppers to get at the cream. It seems that the habit began independently in as many as three different bird populations in London. But by the 1930s, birds across much of southeast England were carrying out these doorstep raids, too.

When card tops were replaced by foil caps, the tits learned to pierce the foil. Later, many other bird species, including magpies, learned to do the same. Within a matter of decades, the ability to remove milk-bottle tops spread through the nation's tit population.

It seems likely that, rather than learning the technique from watching others, individual birds solved the problem of getting at the milk for themselves. Why they should all think of it at once is not clear. Maybe a bird removing a bottle top attracts the attention of others to the fact that food is to be had by solving a problem. Each bird then works out a solution for itself by trial and error. Just seeing the result, and not the behaviour, seems to be enough for many birds.

Sometimes individual birds feed by copying the behaviour of birds of a completely different species. Some sparrows, for instance, have learned to hover above ponds to catch damselflies as they emerge from the water, a technique possibly copied from kingfishers. They have also found out how to hang upside down from bird tables to reach food suspended below, in the manner of tits, and to hop across water lily pads pecking off insects as wagtails do. Other birds, like the

robin pictured here, have learned how to fish in winter. Wrens have taken tiny trout from hatcheries, and blackbirds have caught tadpoles in ponds.

Captive mynah birds and parrots are famous for their mimicry, but wild birds also pick up sounds. British Telecom once had to change the tone on a new range of telephones because song thrushes began to imitate the sound, causing great confusion.

French crows sound quite different to British crows. Though the 'caw' of all crows sounds alike superficially, studies show that there are distinct 'accents'. These are acquired in the same way that humans pick up regional speech patterns and pronunciations when they move to an area with a strong local dialect. Dialects develop over generations, and often newcomers are unaware of gradual changes in their pattern of speech.

Among crows, it may work both ways – a group of crows, settling into an established area, may influence its neighbours and succeed in

Joining in *The robin, deprived by ice and snow of its normal diet of worms, insects and spiders, follows the kingfisher's example. It flutters down to the hole and catches a small fish for itself (above right). Then the hardy robin, its feathers fluffed out to trap warm air round its body (right), stands on the ice, eyeing its catch.*

Following the leaders *After observing the kingfisher and the robin catching fish from a small hole in the ice, a blackbird, unable to obtain its usual meal of grubs, also tries – and succeeds.*

altering the sound or pattern of the established local accent.

In a population of European chaffinches, all the males sing variants of the same basic song. With time, this song pattern gradually changes as some notes and phrases are dropped and others are added. This means that populations in neighbouring valleys – or the same population, but at different times – may be singing songs that are recognisably different.

During the 1940s, a small population of house finches established itself on Long Island, New York. Since then, as they have expanded to occupy neighbouring islands and the mainland, distinctive variations in their song have been noted by ornithologists, who find there are now 29 recognisable dialects.

DECEIT FOR GAIN

Primates often use deception and counterdeception to get both food and mates, and some seem to tell tales out of spite. Birds play tricks on each other, too.

The battle of wits is won by deception

Among most monkeys and apes, the powerful dominant male in a troop expects to monopolise all the mating opportunities with the females on heat. The females, however, may be interested in other males. So furtive matings between a female and her preferred partner, out of sight of the dominant male, are quite common.

Females seeking an opportunity for a clandestine coupling often deliberately 'get left behind' when the troop is on the move. A young male with similar intentions may cover his erect penis with his hand so that the dominant male will not suspect his intentions.

Scientists studying behaviour have experimented with gelada baboons in captivity. They removed a dominant male from his group

Dangerous liaison *A female chimpanzee mates discreetly with a low-ranking male well out of sight of the troop's dominant male. But he may be informed of the event by treacherous witnesses and will rush angrily to the site to confront the two miscreants.*

and put him in a separate cage out of sight but not out of hearing of the others in their big compound. While he was gone, a female mated with a subordinate male. However, the pair suppressed the noisy calls normally emitted by this species of baboon at the climax of mating.

Many occurrences of seemingly deliberate deception mark daily life among monkeys and apes. In one troop, for example, an adolescent baboon was observed causing distress to a very young baboon, and was chased by a group of older baboons set upon chastising him. Suddenly, the miscreant stopped running and stood up on his hind legs, peering forwards as though

Request refused *A young chimpanzee (left) gestures with her hand to ask an adult female feeding on a juicy bulb to give her a titbit; but the older chimpanzee refuses to do so.*

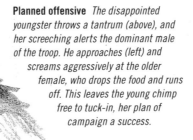

Planned offensive *The disappointed youngster throws a tantrum (above), and her screeching alerts the dominant male of the troop. He approaches (left) and screams aggressively at the older female, who drops the food and runs off. This leaves the young chimp free to tuck-in, her plan of campaign a success.*

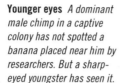

Younger eyes *A dominant male chimp in a captive colony has not spotted a banana placed near him by researchers. But a sharp-eyed youngster has seen it.*

Strategic thinking *Instead of taking the banana or drawing attention to it, the young chimpanzee sits down next to the older animal and waits there quietly and patiently, studiously ignoring the tempting fruit.*

he had spotted the approach of a predator. His attackers stopped immediately to see what he was looking at, and by the time they realised nothing was amiss, their anger had cooled.

Behaviour such as this shows up a weakness in the structured societies of primates (man, apes and monkeys). If everyone was dishonest, society would disintegrate. On the other hand, checking the truth of everything would be much too time-consuming. To assume that everyone behaves honestly saves a lot of time, but makes it possible for occasional cheats to profit at others' expense. Researchers who study primate behaviour agree that in a close-knit group based upon strong family connections, fewer deceptions seem to occur. This is true of gorillas, gibbons, tamarins and marmosets, all of which live in extended family groups.

Chimpanzees and baboons, however, live in groups that change constantly as some animals leave and others join. So the degree of familiarity between animals is likely to be lower, and individuals do not know one another well enough to be able to anticipate treachery.

Counterdeception, in which one animal guesses another's ploy and outwits it, indicates that apes and monkeys are able to see an event from another's point of view. For example, observers have seen a female baboon position herself so that a rock hid her hands and the young male she was grooming from the view of the troop's dominant male. She seemed to have worked out that all he would be able to see were her head and shoulders.

The fruits of deception *The dominant male chimpanzee, perhaps puzzled or irritated by the youngster's presence and apparently inexplicable action, gets up and strolls away (left). The young chimpanzee's careful planning has now paid off. He can take the banana and eat it without interference.*

Birds use false alarms and scare tactics

Few birds tolerate the intrusion of outsiders into their particular feeding area. Sharing with another species cuts down the amount of food available in the lean, winter months. When great tits, for example, find flocks of tree sparrows invading a supply of berries they have had to themselves, the tits shriek out alarm calls even though there is no danger in the offing. The sparrows fly away in panic, leaving the food to the tits.

Handsome and wily

Anna's hummingbird is a much-studied finger-length Californian bird; the gaudy males have green plumage and a scarlet crown and throat. In an experiment, scientists set up a mist net, commonly used for bird trapping, in the territory of a male they called Spot, who spent

some time flying over the net and then perched on it. Shortly afterwards, another male bird flew into Spot's territory and began to feed.

Usually male hummingbirds are very aggressive towards intruders, flying at them while giving their territorial call. On this occasion, however, Spot voiced no warning but flew low round the borders of

his territory until he was directly behind the invader. Only then did he give vent to his squeaky call and fly straight at the other bird – upon which the startled intruder flew right into the net.

Enough for everyone *Great tits and tree sparrows share a generous supply of nuts and seeds on a washing line. But when food is scarce, the sharing stops.*

AN APE'S HOME TOOL KIT

Though many other animals use tools to obtain food, chimpanzees are the undisputed champions – some even carry tools for future use.

Liquid refreshment *As the stream is too shallow to yield a proper drink, a thirsty chimp (below left) lifts out wet leaves one by one and licks off the moisture. Chimps usually lap water, but when they cannot get close enough to it, they use a handful of chewed-up leaves as a sponge. Giving his sponge a firm squeeze (inset), a chimp receives a refreshing draught.*

How chimpanzees use twigs to fish for food

A chimpanzee carefully selects a thin, supple twig from a branch, pulls the leaves from it and then, with great delicacy, pokes it down the narrow entrance hole of a termite mound. Very gently the chimp withdraws the twig, its stem now covered with a wriggling mass of termite soldiers, their powerful jaws gripping the 'intruder'. Deftly the chimp pulls the stem through its lips to remove the termites, and chews contentedly.

More than 30 years ago Jane Goodall, the zoologist, was amazed to discover wild chimpanzees using twigs to fish for termites. For many years the human species had identified itself as 'Man the tool maker'. The ability to use and manufacture tools had long been considered one

Snack on a stick *Crouched beside an ants' nest (left), a determined chimpanzee peels the bark off a twig and frays the end. Then with great deliberation, it inserts the probe into a hole in the nest (above). Ants bite angrily into the twig and are drawn out. With a neat movement, the chimp then wipes the twig between its lips and swallows the snack.*

of the features that set man apart from all other animal species. But ever since Jane Goodall made her momentous discovery, humans can no longer claim to be the only tool-using animal.

Since then many other examples of animals making use of tools have emerged. Wild chimpanzees have been seen using twigs as toothpicks, and leaves to wipe pus from a sore. They also chew up wads of leaves to use as sponges, which they dip into water-filled holes and suck out the moisture. To avoid being bitten by driver ants, the chimpanzees dip for them with grass stems. Researchers have even seen chimps using sticks and logs as weapons against a stuffed leopard placed in their path.

Planning in advance

In addition, the chimpanzees' tools are carefully selected and prepared. For example, a chimpanzee will smooth the twig it is going to use for termite fishing so that it will not snag as it is withdrawn from the hole and dislodge the soldier termites clinging to it.

A chimp may prepare a fishing tool before heading for a nearby termite nest, and carry the tool with it. This shows an intellect not only capable of understanding a problem and solving it, but also one able to anticipate the likely recurrence of the problem.

Captive orang-utans learn new skills

In the wild, the only occasions on which orang-utans have been observed to use tools is when individuals break off branches as weapons, or large leaves to form umbrellas during rainstorms. Yet in captivity the orang-utan is nearly as skilful at solving problems as its cousin the chimpanzee.

An orang-utan will, for example, use a twig to poke out seeds stuck in the floor of its cage. It can also solve many of the same puzzles that psychologists have put to chimpanzees.

It may be that orang-utans use tools less often than chimpanzees because their high forest home is richer in food. Life there is far less demanding than it is in the dry woodlands typically favoured by chimpanzees.

It may be, too, that chimpanzees have had to become more inventive in order to survive. Among chimpanzee populations, the more demanding the environment, the more tools they tend to use.

Keeping dry *An orang-utan (below) uses a leaf as a makeshift umbrella in the rain. Broken-off branches make effective weapons for throwing at predators prowling beneath the tree canopy of the orang-utans' forest home.*

Look and learn *A young Ivory Coast chimpanzee looks on as its mother cracks open a tasty nut. It will learn from her example how to prepare its own food.*

Teaching their offspring how to crack nuts

Chimpanzees in the Tai National Park on the Ivory Coast of West Africa use branches or stones to crack the hard shells of panda and coula nuts. The chimp places the nut on a carefully chosen rock or tree root, which serves as an anvil, and smashes the outer casing with his selected tool. To crack the nut without ruining the kernel inside, the animal must hammer with just the right amount of force. An inexperienced chimp soon learns that too much force will smash the kernel, making it inedible.

Positioning the nut in just the right place demands skill and considerable practice. Infants watch their mothers closely, and nibble at the titbits offered to them. As they grow older, their mothers allow them to practise nut-cracking for themselves, handing them the right kind of hammer and positioning their hands carefully to show them exactly how to crack the nut successfully. This is one of the few clear examples of genuine teaching in the non-human world.

When they decide to go collecting nuts, the chimpanzees pick up rock hammers for cracking open the cases on the way, often using rocks nearest to the tree from which they are about to feed. Rock hammers have to be heavy enough for the job – but must not shatter when they are used.

In many cases the chimps make their tools in anticipation of their need. They know that only certain rocks make good hammers, and often remember where they have left a suitable hammer. Studies of the chimps in the Tai National Park have shown that individuals not only remember where they last used a particular rock, but also keep track of it as other chimps make use of it at new sites.

The technique seems to have spread – very similar behaviour has been observed in chimpanzees in Guinea and Liberia.

SURPRISING TOOL-USERS

Humans and chimpanzees are not the only animals to use tools.
Many others use them to find food, frighten enemies or build homes.

Smashing shellfish and eggshells with stones

Sea otters are among the most entertaining animals to watch. They live in the coastal waters of the northeast Pacific, and seldom go ashore – not even to give birth or to sleep. Sometimes a resting otter will anchor itself with long strands of kelp to keep itself from drifting about. Fish and shellfish, such as sea urchins, are the sea

Egg smasher *Holding a stone in its beak, an Egyptian vulture stretches up to deliver the final, shattering blow to an ostrich egg. A hungry vulture will fly up to 3 miles (5 km) to find a stone and carry it back in its beak to eggs laid in a sandy area with no stones available.*

otter's main diet. But before eating an urchin, an otter has to remove the urchin's poisonous spines. To do this it wraps its dangerous meal in seaweed and then breaks off the spines beneath with its paws. Once the spines have been stripped off, the urchin is easy to consume.

Otter's anvil
Other shellfish, clams for example, have harder shells, and to get to the succulent flesh inside the otter has to be even more resourceful. It collects a stone from the seabed, and swims to the surface with the stone in a flap of skin under one armpit and the shellfish in its paw. Then, as it floats on its back, the otter puts the stone on its chest and smashes the shellfish against

Shell cracker *Floating amid kelp, this sea otter is about to crack a clam against the rock it holds on its chest. Its thickened breastbone is strong enough to take the blow.*

it. Once an otter has found a good stone, it carries it about, tucked under its armpit. If the otter loses the stone, it looks carefully for another, probably rejecting several before it finally finds one that is suitable as a food-opening tool.

Egyptian vultures are expert shell-breakers too, but they tend to

concentrate on much larger prizes. These birds break into ostrich eggs and devour the contents. To get through the egg's immensely thick shell, a vulture picks up a large stone in its beak and repeatedly drops it on the egg, until eventually the shell cracks and the bird can get at the rich feast inside.

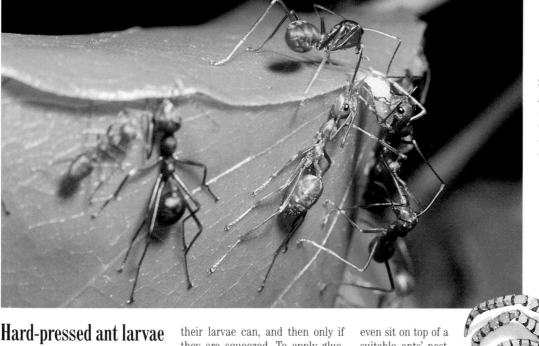

Sticky end *A weaver ant worker (left) gently squeezes the sticky silk from an unresisting larva as it helps to seal the edges of a leaf seam to make a nest. Inside the nest, other workers are squeezing larvae to create a silky lining.*

Hard-pressed ant larvae are used as living tools

Weaver ants get their name from their practice of rolling up leaves and apparently weaving them together to build nests. But a more appropriate name might be gummer ants, because the leaves that make up the nest are not woven at all, but stuck together with a gluey silk.

While some of the ants in a group hold the curled edges of two leaves together with their jaws and feet, others move along the seam applying the silk. Adult weaver ants cannot make this silk – only their larvae can, and then only if they are squeezed. To apply glue, an adult picks up a larva and squeezes its abdomen to make it produce the sticky silk. The larva appears unhurt and stays passive – seemingly unaware that it is being used as a tube of glue.

Another example of the use of living tools is the bird behaviour known as 'anting'. European starlings, for example, occasionally pick up ants in their beaks and press them against their feathers. Ants squirt formic acid as a defence, and the acid is believed to act as an insecticide, helping to keep the bird free of parasites such as feather lice. Some birds even sit on top of a suitable ants' nest with outstretched wings and their feathers fluffed up, while the disturbed ants squirt acid at them. Some 200 bird species are believed to use ants in this way. Boxer crabs use living tools too – they carry small anemones about in their claws, as live, stinging weapons.

Astonishing as the behaviour of these animals is, it is the result of millions of years of chance and natural selection rather than of innovative minds. Animals behaving in these ways survive better.

Stinging defence *A boxer crab defends itself with a sea anemone held in each of its specially adapted pincers. Because these pincers are fully occupied with the task of defence, the crab must use another pair of its walking legs, suitably modified, in order to feed itself.*

Weighed down and stored up *A double-crested cormorant (left) overcomes its natural buoyancy when diving for fish by swallowing pebbles. But this makes it more difficult for the bird to take off from the water's surface afterwards. A great grey shrike (below) uses sharp thorns or barbed-wire fencing to hold its mouse meal steady while it tears at it. Food not eaten immediately is stored on the hook, and the 'butcher' bird will use it later to feed its incubating mate or their youngsters.*

Sticks and stones can be versatile tools

Baboons have been reported to throw stones on occasions, but always in defence rather than attack. People who have disturbed baboon colonies in Africa have often been surprised to find themselves caught in a hail of stones. In most cases, however, the animals have been on hillsides above the travellers, and may simply have dislodged stones while fleeing.

In captivity, South American spectacled bears often use sticks to knock down fruits they cannot reach, or to retrieve floating pieces of bread from water. But, unlike early man, surprisingly few animals have used sticks or stones as a means of defence or attack.

351

A SENSE OF SELF IN MONKEYS

Humans are not alone in having a sense of self-awareness; some apes and monkeys seem to understand their own individuality.

Mother and child *A rhesus monkey and her youngster have a strong emotional attachment. The youngster will grow up able to recognise the relationships between members of other families of rhesus monkeys. This ability to understand that other monkeys are related suggests a sense of self similar to that of humans.*

Recognising a mirror image – or the mirror?

A sleeping chimpanzee has a dot of paint put on its forehead by an experimenting scientist. Later, after it has woken up, the captive chimpanzee passes a mirror fixed to the wall of its room. The chimp stops, peers into the mirror, then puts its hand up and picks at the paint mark on its head.

The mirror test has been used to find out if animals other than humans are aware of themselves as individuals – whether an animal is able to appreciate the difference between itself and other creatures around it. An animal is considered to be self-aware if it recognises itself in the mirror. Chimpanzees regularly pass the self-awareness test, and orang-utans and gorillas occasionally do so. But monkeys have so far failed the test. In fact they often threaten the image, apparently believing it to be a stranger. Sometimes they even try to go behind the mirror to get at the 'monkey' on the other side.

Walking through the mirror

When the same test was tried on elephants, using wall-sized mirrors, the animals simply walked through the glass. Apparently they thought it was an opening to another place, and did not appreciate that it was a solid object.

However, what is not clear from this test is whether the monkeys and elephants, by failing the test, proved that they lacked self-awareness or that they simply did not recognise a mirror for what it is.

Manipulative monkeys can fool one another

Reading the intentions of another is an activity at which monkeys and apes seem to excel. This ability enables them to deceive each other in skilful ways. But chimpanzees, which are apes, seem to be better 'mind-readers' than monkeys, and monkeys do it better than cats, dogs and birds.

Human beings appear to have a much better grasp of one another's thought processes than do other animals. Whether this is a primary distinction between Man and other animals is the subject of studies by scientists. Some indication of how monkeys and humans compare is given by the story of a male vervet monkey in Kenya's Amboseli Park.

Smooth operator *When a male black-faced vervet monkey tries to bully his way into another troop, resident males may try to drive him away by guile.*

Friends and family *After a dispute, chimps (left) make a special effort to kiss and comfort one another. Macaques (above) spend hours mutually grooming in order to cement already established close relationships with each other.*

Monkeys know who is family and who is not

A powerful test of self-awareness is to find out if an animal can recognise the similarity between its own family relationships and those of other individuals. In the complex societies of monkeys and apes, many of the more subtle interactions that make each group unique could not occur unless the animals had a good understanding of one another's relationships.

Experimenting scientists have used colour slides to test whether captive macaque monkeys could judge the relationships between the monkeys pictured. In a study conducted in 1987, two macaques were rewarded with sips of honey water if they could distinguish mothers and their offspring from pictures that included other pairs of related monkeys.

Responses were made by pressing a button, and the high number of correct responses indicated that both macaques could pick out mother and offspring pairs from other related pairs, regardless of the age of the offspring.

During studies of wild vervet monkeys in Kenya, scientists noted that if a monkey had been threatened by a more dominant member of its group, the aggrieved party would, within the next two hours, threaten a friend or relative of its attacker. It appears that, being unable to take revenge on a more powerful attacker, the offended vervet turned on the weaker members of its enemy's family.

This shows that an adult vervet monkey is certainly capable of making comparisons between sets of relationships. But as young monkeys seem unable to make this distinction, it is probably something learned through experience.

Weighing the odds

In both ape and monkey societies, alliances are important. When two animals form an alliance, they will help each other out when either one of them is attacked by another member of the group.

Sometimes, however, the odds are too heavily weighted against an allied pair, and the partner not under threat may decide on prudence rather than participation.

It has been noted that a rhesus macaque female, for example, may refuse to support an ally when it is attacked by a member of a more powerful family. The prudent macaque seems to realise that her involvement would result only in members of the attacker's family joining in to support their relative, and that then both she and her friend would be worse off.

However, failing to support a friend in a moment of need inevitably weakens the relationship. A monkey that has broken faith with its ally later goes through an elaborate process of making up – the guilty party grooms the offended friend with extra enthusiasm. Chimpanzee allies often make up with a kiss.

One day, while his group was feeding in a grove of trees, the monkey spied a strange vervet male coming towards them across the open grassland. Because a migrant male gaining entry to a group can displace a resident male, the monkey began to give leopard alarm calls.

The intruder at once fled for the safety of another grove of trees, and the two males spent the rest of the day watching each other suspiciously across the stretch of open ground between their respective groves. Every time the intruder decided to brave the open ground again, the resident male gave another series of alarm calls, and the intruder would retreat.

However, the following day the resident male gave the game away completely by giving leopard alarm calls while walking nonchalantly across the open ground. The intruder immediately realised the deceit, and that there were no leopards in the vicinity, so walked across to join the group.

Seeing through subterfuge

Although the resident male knew how to manipulate another individual's behaviour very successfully, his problem was that he could not comprehend the world from the other's point of view. He therefore could not work out how the other male would interpret actions that might reveal his subterfuge.

In much the same way, a two-year-old child may believe that it can successfully convince accusing adults that it has not eaten all the ice cream in the fridge, but cannot see that the mess of ice cream round its mouth exposes the lie.

UNDERSTANDING DEATH

Animals may mourn one another's deaths in the same way as humans do. Some certainly appear to show distress when a close relative dies.

Sorrowing for lost friends or relatives

Greyfriars Bobby, a Skye terrier, was owned by John ('Jock') Gray, a Scottish shepherd. When Jock died in 1858 on one of his weekly trips to Edinburgh, he was buried in the Greyfriars Kirk and his small dog was sent back to Jock's farm in the Pentland Hills. The faithful dog, however, made his own way back to Edinburgh and appeared beside his master's grave the day after the funeral. Fed and watered daily by locals and inquisitive sightseers, Bobby stayed by the grave for the next 14 years, until he too died in 1872.

By this time the dog's fame was so widespread that Queen Victoria herself suggested that he should be buried alongside Jock Gray in Greyfriars churchyard.

Today a statue commemorating Greyfriars Bobby stands on the street corner next to Greyfriars Kirk. Dogs are often said to grieve at the loss of their owner, but whether Bobby's story implies a genuine understanding of death or just distress at separation from a familiar situation is uncertain.

Signs of anguish

It seems likely that some apes and monkeys do genuinely understand death. Washoe was a captive chimpanzee trained in America in the 1960s to learn a sign language. She gave birth to a baby, but it became sick and died in an animal hospital. When her handlers returned, Washoe asked 'Where baby?' They replied 'Baby finished'. Washoe at once went into deep depression and sat huddled in a corner, and refused to communicate.

Even apes and monkeys in the wild show signs of distress when a close relative dies. A young mother baboon who loses her newborn baby often carries the body around for a week or so, carefully brushing away flies and grooming its fur.

The death of an animal living in a group can cause far-reaching changes in the group's organisation. Some individuals move up a step in the pecking order as they fill the gap left by the dead animal, and others lose a valuable ally.

Distressed mother *An elephant on the Amboseli Nature Reserve, Kenya, carries her lifeless, prematurely born calf with her tusks and trunk. When an elephant calf dies, its mother may carry her dead offspring around for several days, unwilling to abandon it.*

A family tragedy in the African bush

Cries of distress once drew Iain Douglas-Hamilton, a zoologist, to a tragic scene in the Manyara National Park, Tanzania. He found three young elephants of varying ages gathered round the body of their mother, who had fallen down a steep slope to her death. One youngster leaned against the lifeless mother while the youngest attempted to suck her milk and the oldest moaned and tried to move the dead cow with its tusks.

People who work with elephants can tell of instances that suggest the animals do understand death. Female and young male elephants live in close-knit family groups led by an ageing female. On Africa's Serengeti plain, observers have watched some of the family of a dying matriarch try to lift her to

Grieving family *Elephants in the Tsavo National Park (top left) try to raise a dead calf back onto its feet. Groups of elephants often stop to sniff and examine the skeletons of dead elephants (left), paying the most attention to the mouth parts and the tusks.*

her feet while others pressed grass into her mouth or stood around helplessly, shrieking and trumpeting in their distress.

Even when the cow was dead the group seemed unwilling to leave her, and returned time and time again during the next few hours. They caressed the carcass with their trunks, or gently placed them in the dead animal's mouth.

If an elephant calf is sick or hurt, its family gathers round to protect it. A mother may stay with her dead calf for some time, chasing off predators, and even carry the corpse away on her tusks.

Bones of ancestors

A group of elephants will often stop to examine and touch a long-dead elephant carcass, carrying off bones and tusks into the bushes, or just moving them about with their trunks. They pay particular attention to the bones round the mouth, perhaps because it is the part most used for greetings in life, and to the tusks, which change little with death. No one knows why elephants are so curious about the bones of their kind. Maybe this gave rise to tales of ancient graveyards where elephants go to die.

The watery graves of Antarctic penguins

South Georgia is a bleak island that lies in the South Atlantic. It is also one of the main nesting grounds for gentoo and king penguins. Scientists studying birds on the island have watched ageing and sick penguins congregating round inland pools that have been formed from melting snow. The bottoms of these same pools are covered with layer upon layer of penguin corpses.

The observations have sparked off speculations about dying penguins making their way inland to traditional graveyards. It is more likely, however, that the sick or ageing birds go there in search of fresh water to drink, and happen to die or drown in the attempt.

In hot deserts there also tend to be lots of skeletons round waterholes. This is generally thought to be because dying animals need water more than they need food, so make their way to water and stay there. What may at first appear to be a graveyard is in fact only the result of the creatures' natural instinct for survival.

MIGRATION AND TRAVEL

'ALL ANIMALS HAVE AN INSTINCTIVE PERCEPTION OF CHANGES IN
TEMPERATURE, AND JUST AS MEN SEEK SHELTER IN HOUSES IN WINTER,
OR AS MEN OF GREAT POSSESSIONS SPEND THEIR SUMMER IN COOL
PLACES AND THEIR WINTER IN SUNNY ONES, SO ALSO ALL ANIMALS
THAT CAN DO SO SHIFT THEIR HABIT AT VARIOUS SEASONS.'
≈ ARISTOTLE, 384-322 BC, *HISTORY OF ANIMALS.*

Crossing the skies
*Rising effortlessly on an updraught
of warm air, storks gain height over
Gibraltar before setting off on the
long journey south to their tropical
wintering grounds. An innate sense
of direction and the guidance of older
birds help young storks to find their
way across these great distances.*

Aristotle recognised the seasonal movements
of animals 2000 years ago, and deduced that
these migrations were in response to changes
in temperature. Yet little more than a century
ago, the explorer and naturalist Humboldt
believed that swallows hibernated each winter
in the muddy bottoms of ponds and marshes,
a belief that was commonly held by country
people until well into the present century.

Finding out how animals travel, where they
go and how they find their way, has involved
trapping and marking thousands of birds and
animals, as well as gathering data from radar
installations, radiotelemetry and laboratory
experiments. This combination of hard work
and high technology is, at last, beginning to
reveal just how a stork can find its way from
its wintering grounds south of the Sahara,
across thousands of miles of land and water,
to return to the village in which it was born.

Up and down the mountain
*The American red-bellied newt uses
a 'magnetic compass' to help it to
migrate between the valley bottoms
where it breeds and its feeding
grounds higher up in the redwood
forests.*

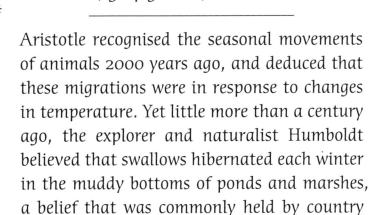

Ancient routes
Barren Grounds caribou of North America travel over 3100 miles (5000 km) in a year – the longest annual migration of any mammal. This amazing journey follows traditional routes, taking vast herds from their forested southern wintering grounds, where food is easy to find, to their summer breeding grounds in the far northern tundra where they can give birth without threat from wolves.

Going with the flow
Helped by ocean currents, many blue sharks migrate annually from the east coast of the United States to the waters off the coast of Spain, where they give birth to their pups. They are known to be sensitive to the earth's magnetic field, and it is thought that they migrate by reference to this.

DEALING WITH OVERCROWDING

Reproducing too successfully can lead to overcrowding, with the result that many animals suffer stress and starvation, and take drastic measures to escape.

Crossbills leave home when food is short

From time to time, a massive increase in an animal population, known as an irruption, results in huge numbers moving to new areas. Irruptions occur irregularly, so cannot be termed migrations. Mass movements may occur two years running, for example, and then not again for years.

Between 1800 and 1965 there were 67 irruptions in the European crossbill population, resulting in huge flocks of them leaving the northern conifer forests and heading south across the continent. Some birds were known to travel as much as 2500 miles (4000 km) to southwest Spain.

A crossbill feeds exclusively on conifer seeds. The upper part of its beak overlaps the lower part to form a double hook, which enables it to prise out seeds from the cones

of pines, spruce, larch and other coniferous trees. When food is plentiful, crossbills stay in northern conifer forests all year round, but if supplies run out they are forced to leave home and look for new feeding grounds.

Irruptions usually occur after a successful breeding season. Led by juvenile birds, masses of crossbills set off in search of new conifer forests, some going so far afield

Diet dilemma *A male crossbill feeds on the seeds of a spruce cone. Conifer seeds are by far the most important crossbill food so, when supplies run low, flocks fly in search of new conifer forests.*

that they are unable to make their way back again.

Birds that fail to find good feeding areas die, but those that are successful may breed in their new home for several years before returning to the northern forests.

Mites travel the globe by catching the wind

Spiders, mites and small insects are not strong fliers; in fact some cannot fly at all. In spite of this, they have been found as high as 16 000 ft (5000 m) in the air. Carried about by high-level winds and air currents, they are known collectively as aerial plankton.

When spiderlings emerge from their silken cocoons, they disperse by heading for the nearest vantage point, such as a grass stem or a twig. There each one raises its abdomen into the air and releases a silken thread. Once its thread is caught by the wind, a spiderling lets go of its perch and is whisked away, hanging beneath its single-strand 'parachute'.

Some other tiny creatures, bean aphids for example, fly upwards,

attracted by the sun's ultraviolet light and are caught by warm-air currents, or thermals, which carry them even higher and across vast distances. This very successful means of dispersal allows these minute creatures to cross barriers such as mountains, oceans and deserts, which would normally restrict their movement.

Taking to the air *A wolf spiderling, with its abdomen raised, prepares to release a thread of silk that will catch the wind and carry it away to a new home.*

On occasions, however, aerial plankton may be carried too far. Swarms of aphids and hoverflies have been found on the Greenland ice cap. Here, with cold temperatures and no food, they soon died.

Stay-at-home barnacles send out their larvae

All types of barnacle have one thing in common – they cannot move to another area unless they cement themselves to a whale or a ship. So to colonise new places, they send out their larvae.

At first, barnacle larvae swim weakly and feed on tiny plants, building up fat reserves. After three weeks or so they stop eating, transform into site-seeking larvae and search for a place to settle. Once a larva finds a suitable site, such as a rock, whale or boat bottom, it checks for the presence of other barnacles – all species like company – tests the surface and monitors the strength and direction of currents.

If the site is a good one, the larva cements itself in place and begins to change into an adult. But countless millions of barnacle larvae never find a home, and drift until they die or are devoured.

Locusts eat their way across North Africa

When a swarm of desert locusts is on the move, it may fill the North African sky with a cloud so thick it blots out the sun. Blown on prevailing winds, the locusts fly from one patch of greenery to the next, devouring every last leaf of natural vegetation and valuable crops. A single swarm can number more than 50 thousand million and cover 400 sq miles (1000 km²). A swarm such as this, feeding at both dawn and dusk, can eat 3000 tons of vegetation in one day.

Desert locusts do not normally live in such large groups. Solitary during dry seasons, locusts are drably coloured and well camouflaged against predators. They eat very little, and their fat reserves enable them to survive a drought.

Locust-laden *The weight of feeding locusts has bowed the branches of this Mauritanian shrub. When the swarm flies on, it will be left without a leaf, as will every patch of vegetation around it.*

When the rains come, however, the locusts mate and lay eggs. If food is plentiful, the reproduction rate is high and dramatic changes start to take place. Instead of avoiding one another, the locusts begin to gather together and, in place of their parents' discreet colouring, the new generation, at this stage wingless hoppers, has colourful stripes of orange, black and yellow.

Generations on the move

Bands of brightly coloured hoppers begin to merge, and soon huge armies of rapidly growing hoppers march across the land eating all the vegetation in their path. As they mature, the hoppers develop wings and the great swarm takes to the air, roosting in the trees during the hottest part of the day.

Eventually the swarm settles to mate and lay eggs and, if the weather remains good, another generation of hoppers takes over and continues to strip the countryside. But if drought returns, fewer and fewer hoppers emerge and the locusts gradually return to a solitary and inconspicuous way of life.

Why Norway lemmings flee from their homes

Contrary to popular myth about lemmings, they do not commit suicide by flinging themselves off Arctic cliffs. The idea of mass suicide probably arose because of the numbers of Norway lemmings that die during the mass dispersals of populations – dispersals that have made these guinea-pig-like rodents famous. About every four years or so, lemming populations get so big that their burrows are overcrowded and there is not enough food, such as roots, grass and lichens, to go round. So huge numbers of lemmings, most of them young males, go off in search of new homes.

Lemmings dispersing to look for fresh pastures cover enormous distances, even crossing lakes and glaciers. Confronted by a river or fiord, the lemmings will only swim across if they can see the opposite shore. On occasions, however, a change in the wind direction, or a

Misleading myths *In this woodcut by a 16th-century Swedish priest, lemmings are seen falling from the clouds. Lemmings were believed to form from foul matter in the air and fall to Earth in rainstorms. Terrified peasants thought that they destroyed crops and caused illness. The woodcut shows foxes attacking some of the lemming host.*

strong current, causes them to be swept away while they are trying to cross and, if they do not find any landfall, they drown. Predators such as owls, weasels and foxes also gorge on dispersing lemmings.

Mass dispersals follow the cycle of food abundance. More food and fewer predators provide the best conditions for a long breeding season, with females giving birth to large litters. Before she is a year

old, a female can have as many as six litters of up to 13 young. Such numbers from each female in a population may result in as many as 100-250 lemmings per 2½ acres (1 ha) – up to 30 times as many as found in normal years. So mass dispersals occur after high breeding

success has caused overcrowding, which also leads to fighting. But when numbers reach a peak, the breeding pattern changes. Perhaps because of a shortage of food and space, fewer youngsters are born and young lemmings take longer to mature, so the population crashes.

CREATURES THAT HARDLY MOVE AT ALL

Animals that stay in one place throughout their lives have developed unique ways of feeding themselves, finding mates and reproducing.

A waiting game for a wingless female moth

The female vapourer moth has no wings – only small stubs that are incapable of providing flight. She lives her entire adult life, lasting perhaps two weeks, in the place where she transformed from a caterpillar, which is usually on a hawthorn, sloe, hazel or fruit tree.

Once she has emerged from the silken cocoon hidden in a crevice in the tree bark, she simply sits on the empty cocoon and waits, giving off a strong scent that drifts off on the breeze. A male vapourer moth as far away as 3 miles (5 km), will pick up the enticing odour with his feathery antennae and then follow it upwind until he finds the flightless female.

After the pair have mated, the male takes to the air to look for another partner. The female lays her 300 or so eggs, usually on the cocoon, then dies. The hairy caterpillars that hatch from them feed on the tree leaves until they, too, are ready to become moths.

A sedentary life *A male and female vapourer moth (below) rest beside newly laid eggs. Even after the female has ceased to emit scent, the lingering odour will continue to attract nearby males.*

Sitting on the seashore and feeding off the tide

The seashore, washed each day by the rising and falling tide, is a good place to sit and wait for food to arrive. But the battering waves make it precarious too – sea anemones, limpets and barnacles can only stay in place by clinging to the rocks; piddocks burrow into them, while honeycomb worms, sponges and moss animals (called bryozoans) form mats on them with their own tissues. Corals simply construct their own rocks.

When it is time for these sea creatures to strike out and find new sites, they all solve the problem in the same way: their fertilised eggs hatch as free-floating larvae that drift in the ocean until they mature, then settle on rocky shores to make new colonies.

Close attachment *Sea anemones (right) anchor themselves to seashore rocks and use their petal-like tentacles to catch other marine creatures.*

Royal watchers *A termite queen (left) spends her life laying eggs, relying on her attendants to remove and tend them.*

A termite queen that never leaves her room

In the centre of a busy termite colony – within a mound, maybe 30 ft (9 m) tall – there is a special room, the royal chamber. Here lives the termite queen together with, in some species, her royal consort. The sausage-like queen is huge compared with her subjects – up to 1 in (25 mm) across and 6 in (15 cm) long. Her huge abdomen is about 1500 times larger than the rest of her body.

Neither the queen nor her consort ever leave the chamber. They are fed and cleaned by termite workers, and the queen is constantly groomed to encourage her to lay eggs. Every day she lays around 36 000 of them, which the workers then remove and place in separate brood chambers for hatching.

Once, when she was a winged princess, the queen flew briefly with a swarm of termites erupting from their parent colony. When she had found a mate, she and her attendant male dropped to the ground, shook off their wings and began building a mound for a new colony. Their first brood was raised as workers to continue the task of construction and maintenance.

Now the queen is just an egg-laying machine, and will remain so for the rest of her 50-year life.

Devil's Hole pupfishes make legal history

Once Devil's Hole, in the middle of the USA's Nevada desert, was an underground cave. In some long ago cataclysm, the roof of the cave fell in, leaving a hole about 500 sq ft (46 m²) in extent, with a pool at the bottom of it, about 60 ft (18 m) below the desert floor. This is the home of the Devil's Hole pupfish – a small fish about 1½ in (38 mm) long, that is officially listed as an endangered species.

Pupfish feed on the tiny water creatures that thrive amid mats of green algae. In Devil's Hole they grow only on a single ledge just below the surface of the water. In winter the sun is so low on the horizon that sunlight does not reach the ledge at all, so the algal mat is very slow to grow. There is therefore very little room for water creatures, and scant food for the pupfish. In spring, as sunlight reaches the ledge and tiny plants begin to grow rapidly, the fish feed

Limited existence
The Devil's Hole pupfish is confined to just one pool – the Devil's Hole in the Nevada desert. It survives off minute creatures that collect on an algae-covered ledge just below the surface of the water.

well and this is the trigger that starts their breeding season.

Should anything upset the pool's natural balance, these tiny fish would become extinct. Once they were threatened by a scheme to pump water, planned to take place some distance away. It would have lowered the water table in time, exposing the feeding ledge in the pond. Deprived of their only source of food, the pupfish would have died. But the matter was brought before the United States Supreme Court, and the pupfish made legal history. The court ruled in their favour, the pumping was stopped, and the pupfish were saved.

How mussels stay firmly fixed in turbulent seas

After starting life as free-floating larvae, young mussels, or spats, eventually settle on suitable rocks and spend the rest of their lives anchored there.

A mussel secretes from its foot a sticky substance that hardens in contact with sea water to form a thick thread made up of a mass of filaments. These threads are so strong that only the roughest of

seas can tear the mussel away from the rock.

As mussels cannot go in search of a meal, they must wait for food to come to them. So the largest mussels are found below the low-tide mark, where they are able to feed constantly. They take in up to 10 gallons (45 litres) of sea water a day, filtering out the minute plants and animals called plankton. One species, the fan mussel or pen shell, is anchored to the seabed by golden threads that were once harvested and made into cloth of gold.

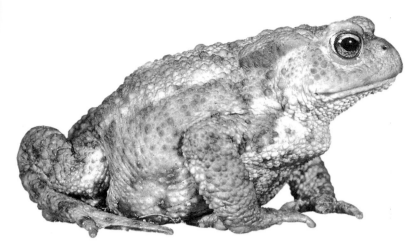

Toad migrations cause rural traffic hazards

In some parts of Britain during March and early April, special signs warn motorists that they may encounter multitudes of common toads crossing the roads.

The toads are on their way to breed in the ponds where they were spawned. Each spring they leave their hibernation places in the surrounding countryside and follow the same migration routes across fields, through hedgerows and sometimes over busy roads. Most of the toads return at night when poor visibility puts them at

Testing time for toads *Driven by an irresistible urge to breed, European toads migrate in their hundreds back to the ponds and streams where they were born, risking life and limb to get there.*

risk. Enthusiastic volunteers turn out to gather them in buckets and carry them safely across the roads.

Even when they are not spurred by the desire to breed, toads show powerful homing instincts. One female is known to have returned every spring for 36 years to the same spot under some steps leading into an English garden. Some toads have been captured, tagged for identification and released far from home, only to make their way back with remarkable speed.

EPIC JOURNEYS FOR NEW LIFE

To find the right place to breed, give birth or lay eggs, some animals find it necessary to travel great distances and take huge risks.

Harem master *A burly male northern fur seal guards his harem on a beach on one of the Pribilof Islands. Ever vigilant, he stays on his territory and guards his cows from other bulls. As a result, he may not go to sea to feed again for at least two months.*

Fur seals swim north to give birth on icy islands

By the time northern fur seal cows from the North Pacific arrive at their breeding grounds on the Pribilof Islands in the Bering Sea, the bull seals are already there. They have staked out their territories and are waiting to establish their harems, some of which may number 50 cows.

A few days after they arrive the females give birth to pups from last year's mating, and stay with them for about seven days. Then they mate again, and leave their

pups for brief feeding trips to the sea, returning again to suckle them. The islands are ideal breeding sites for the seals, being free of predators such as polar bears.

In late September and early October, the newly mated cows leave the islands and head some 3000 miles (5000 km) south to spend winter off the Californian coast. The bulls and youngsters leave in November, and make a shorter journey to spend the winter in the Gulf of Alaska. As winter ends, the cows begin the long journey back to the Bering Sea, arriving at the end of June in time to give birth again.

Crossing the icy wastes *Adélie penguins (left) set out in the early Antarctic spring on their annual journey to breeding grounds some 60 miles (100 km) inland and a week's walk from the coast. Once the eggs are laid, the males incubate them while the females head back to the sea to feed. If his mate does not return within three weeks, the hungry male bird may abandon his eggs and set off for the sea to feed. A solitary polar bear (below left) covers great distances as he patrols the icy Arctic wastes in a never-ending hunt for food and, in the mating season, for females without cubs. Females will not mate again until their cubs are quite independent.*

The European eel – a partly solved mystery

Wild stories that European eels spring from mud, dew or horse hairs dropped in rivers are now part of folklore. Not until the end of the 19th century did naturalists find out that eels hatch somewhere at sea, and not until the beginning of the 20th century did they discover exactly where.

Adult common eels travel some 4000 miles (6400 km) to breed, setting off from lakes, rivers and ponds in Europe. Some wriggle across damp fields and ditches to reach streams and rivers flowing down to the Atlantic Ocean.

The eels swim at such great depths that scientists have been unable to locate them. The only proof that they have made the journey is their offspring – found in the Sargasso Sea in the North Atlantic off the coast of Florida. Its calm, slow-moving waters offer the conditions that suit eel larvae. Warm water at a temperature of about 20°C (68°F) reaches to depths of some 1500 ft (460 m), and it is here that the adults spawn and then die.

Eel larvae look so unlike their parents that it was many years before researchers realised what they were. The larvae look like flat, transparent willow leaves and are just under ½ in (13 mm) long. In their first summer, the larvae rise to about 600 ft (180 m) below the sea surface and begin to drift in the Gulf Stream. This is the start of their three year journey to Europe, during which they will grow to a length of 3 in (75 mm).

Arriving at the European coast in early winter, the young eels gather in estuaries and change into miniature grey or black adults, known as elvers. Filled with the urge for fresh water, they start to swim upriver. The males stop in the lower reaches, but the females migrate farther, dispersing into the waterways in which they will live for the next five to eight years. One autumn, they feel the need to seek salt water again and to mate. This sends them struggling to the coast, to embark on their final journey back to the Sargasso Sea.

How eel larvae find their way to Europe remains a mystery. They seek fresh water although they have no experience of it. Maybe they simply follow the flow of the currents sweeping clockwise round the Atlantic, or perhaps they navigate by the Earth's magnetic field. The answers are still unknown.

Return journey *An adult European eel, driven by the urge to breed, crosses a muddy estuary at the start of its long journey back to the Sargasso Sea.*

Easy riders *Carried along in front of a wave, two dolphins give an impression of effortless grace and speed. Dolphins surf on waves at any opportunity, as it allows them to maintain speeds of up to 35 mph (56 km/h) using virtually no energy. They will also ride the waves made by ships, cruising alongside vessels for long periods.*

HITCHING A RIDE

When free-riders attach themselves to another animal, they may be saving energy, choosing a mate, finding food or just having fun.

Fast and easy *Hourglass dolphins surf on breakers in the Indian Ocean, saving energy while gaining speed.*

Common dolphins take a long boat trip

Boat passengers in many warm or temperate seas may watch common dolphins surfing along on the vessel's bow waves, hitching a ride of maybe 70 miles (110 km). Sometimes the bow-riders can be heard squealing, which suggests to observers that the 8 ft (2.5 m) long animals are there just for pleasure. But it is more likely that they are taking an energy-saving free ride.

Many kinds of dolphin – such as the bottlenose, common, spinner, dusky and white-sided – ride the bow waves of boats for hours on end. Even killer whales, false killer whales and pygmy sperm whales have been known to do it.

The wave rider turns its body in various ways to take advantage of a wave, allowing it to sweep through the water without so much as a flick of the tail. But sometimes, they turn their tail flukes downwards to increase propulsion. Hitchhiking dolphins may also body surf on the waves breaking in a vessel's wake.

Why dolphins behave in this way, and how they developed the habit, is still a mystery. There is some speculation, however, that they began the practice by riding the bow waves of large whales and then extended it to boats.

Remoras hang on for a ride on the wild side

It takes a brave fish to approach and attach itself to one of the most feared killers of the deep. But convenience, more than bravery, is the key when a remora fish hitches a ride on a shark. Whales, manta rays, other large fish and turtles also often have one or two free-riding remora fish firmly attached to their bodies.

Remora fish, which may be up to 3 ft (90 cm) long, fix themselves to a host by means of a flat, oval sucker on the top of the head, so they are also known as suckerfish or sharksuckers. A remora presses its head sucker onto a host before pulling the centre of the cup away to create a vacuum. In this way it clings to the top or underside of a host's body, or to the inside of its mouth or gills. This method of travel has many benefits for the remora. The host's body becomes a platform for a free ride. It is also an effective shield from predators and a hiding place from which the remora can dart out after prey.

The host transports the remora to new feeding sites, as well as providing it with scraps of food that fall from its mouth. Sharks are particularly messy eaters, so there are always plenty of titbits for their travelling companions. Some remoras swim close to the host

Fellow travellers *Using the flat, oval sucker (inset) on its head, a remora attaches itself to a whale shark in the waters off Western Australia.*

without actually attaching themselves to its body, but they follow the creature's every twist and turn.

Remoras do not like to travel unaccompanied. Their need for a host appears to be so strong that, in the Caribbean, fishermen once attached lines to remoras and used them to catch turtles.

If no host is available, remoras sometimes swim round in circles, stacked like dinner plates one above the other – the smallest at the bottom and largest at the top. They swim round in this way until a suitable host comes along.

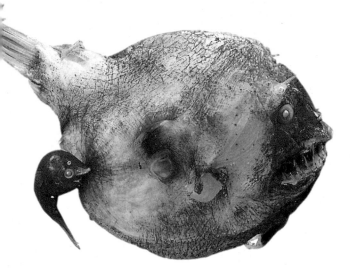

At home in the fur *The 2 ft (60 cm) long three-toed sloth (above) spends much of its life hanging from branches, holding on with its long, hooked claws. Colonies of sloth moths (above right) live in its fur, as do tiny plants, which give it its greenish tinge.*

Sloth moths opt for life in the slow lane

Moths fly much faster than sloths can move, yet they still use sloths as a form of transport. A single three-toed sloth, or ai – an animal quite incapable of moving faster than 1 mph (1.6 km/h) – may have as many as 100 moths hiding in its coat. They are not there to feed, lay eggs or for any sinister reason. They have merely climbed aboard for the ride.

Sloths spend most of their time hanging upside-down from trees in the forests of Central and South America, where they feed on leaves and fruit. It is seldom that they move, except to visit their latrines on the forest floor, for instance.

The moths lay their eggs in sloth dung, and their caterpillars hatch, feed and transform into adults on the dung heap. When adult moths are ready to leave the area, they fly into the tree canopy to seek a sloth – they do not climb aboard one visiting a latrine. It is believed that male moths find females when the sloths themselves meet at breeding grounds.

Togetherness is a pair of angler fish

A male deep-sea angler fish is only about one-thousandth of the weight of a female This is just as well, since he attaches himself to her with a bite and then stays there for the rest of his life, totally dependent upon her for food and oxygen. Eventually even his blood supply fuses with hers, making him little more than a parasite.

The female angler fish accepts this seemingly one-sided state of affairs because it is to her advantage. The chances of her finding a mate in the dark expanses of their

Close couple *With her mate attached firmly below her tail, a female angler fish (above) swims in the inky waters of the ocean depths. There is no specific joining place; a male may fasten on to his mate's side, belly or back.*

ocean home are extremely small. Once a female – she can be 4 ft (1.2 m) long – has found a partner, it makes sense to carry him about with her. Drawn to her by a scent she gives off into the water, several males may attach themselves to one female, and all become part of her life system.

The female angler fish has a luminous 'fishing rod' on her back – a long spine with a light organ at the tip. With it, she lures shrimps and fish into snatching range.

Riding on the wind *Albatrosses are built for gliding rather than flapping flight and fly long distances across southern oceans with hardly a beat of their long wings. The bird builds up speed as it dives downwind, turning into the wind when it nears the water. This gives it lift and it glides upwards until it begins to slow, then dives once again.*

BY THE LEFT, QUICK MARCH

Animals travelling in formation may gain in mobility or defence; sometimes, though, it may be for no more than company.

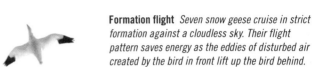

Formation flying has hidden advantages

The sight of a flock of geese flying overhead in the familiar V-shape formation often pleases observers on the ground, but there is more to this formation flying than just its beauty. Some birds, such as geese and cranes, migrate over vast distances. Rare Siberian cranes, for example, fly from their wintering grounds in India and China to their breeding grounds in Siberia and back again each year. By flying in a V-shape the birds save

Formation flight *Seven snow geese cruise in strict formation against a cloudless sky. Their flight pattern saves energy as the eddies of disturbed air created by the bird in front lift up the bird behind.*

energy, as each receives a boost from the bird in front. Flapping wings produce small eddies of air at their tips. These swirls of turbulence are a nuisance to the bird producing them as they act as a drag on flight. But they help a bird following a little way behind, because the upwash of air provides extra lift, so the bird does not have to work so hard to stay airborne. The best effect is achieved if the birds fly with wing tips overlapping, but there is still some benefit in loose V-formations.

Snow geese will often fly slightly behind and above the bird in front, with the head adjacent to the

neighbour's wing tip. This configuration gives each bird a better view of where it is going. By flying in a V-formation, the birds in front help the ones behind to save energy and therefore the group can fly farther for the same amount of 'fuel'. The leading bird receives no help, so every now and then it drops back and another takes the lead.

Single file *Long lines of spiny lobsters (above) move to deep water in an orderly migration each autumn. Equally orderly, elephants (right) join trunk to tail as they file along a well-worn path to their watering hole.*

speed of about 18 ft (5 m) per minute. Several files may weave across the sandy bottom at once.

The lobsters keep in touch on their journey through their long, spiky and sensitive antennae. They seem to play follow-my-leader, the shorter antennae (antennules) of one lobster touching the tail of the one in front. Sometimes the train is coupled, as each lobster hooks its front legs around the tail of the one in front. In this way, they march for up to 50 miles (80 km) in a week, heading south across an underwater plateau of the Great Bahama Bank.

The lobsters' body temperature drops and their metabolism slows down once they are in the deeper, cooler water. And with less food available, they simply 'shut down' until spring. The lobsters then return to the coast when the sea is calmer and food is more abundant.

Spiny lobsters play follow-my-leader

Hurricanes and powerful storms hit the Bahamas and Florida each autumn, by which time the spiny lobsters that have been breeding and feeding amongst the coral reefs have moved out to avoid being battered by the turbulence of

the sea. Towards the end of their summer on the reef, the lobsters become restless. They emerge from their communal dens under rocks and coral and form up in files of up to 70 individuals. Once the files are complete, the exodus begins and the lobsters strike out for deeper water. Heading away from shore, they walk across the ocean floor, through both day and night, at a

Endless night marches for the Arabian oryx

Searching for scarce food in the desolate, sandy landscape of central Arabia is a tough test of endurance for herds of Arabian oryx. Well-equipped with splayed, shovel-like hooves, they survive in these dauntingly harsh conditions. Summer temperatures reach 50°C (122°F) in the shade, but in winter they plunge to 6°C (43°F). Rain is rare. In some areas, droughts have lasted many years.

The search for pockets of vegetation never ends. Travelling in the cool, dark hours, an oryx herd can cover up to 20 miles (32 km) a night. Ruminating as they travel in a single file, the second-rank male leads and the dominant bull walks at the rear. The first and last oryx are generally about 100 yd (90 m) apart. When the herd reaches a feeding site, the animals disperse to enjoy the much needed nourishment, but they always keep an eye on the whereabouts of the other members of the herd.

The females tend to influence the direction in which the feeding herd moves. One female heads off in a new direction, hesitates for a moment or two, looking over her shoulder at the rest of the herd – and the others eventually follow. When the food supply is exhausted the group lines up once more and heads out, one behind the other, into the night.

Travelling the desert sands *Gemsbok, relatives of the Arabian oryx, trek ceaselessly through the Namibian desert in search of grazing. The group is led by the second most important male, with the dominant bull bringing up the rear. Their hooves are splayed and flat to stop them sinking in the soft sand.*

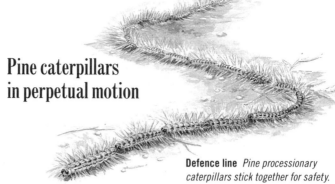

Pine caterpillars in perpetual motion

Defence line *Pine processionary caterpillars stick together for safety. If a bird eats one member of the line, it finds the toxic hairs so vile in taste that it leaves the other caterpillars alone.*

Pine processionary caterpillars of the southern European forests will follow each other almost for ever. Their days are spent safely in a tent of silk, but each evening they venture out in search of food. They file out of their nest, 100 or so at a time, and amble along branches, head to tail. They follow the scent trail left by the one in front and lay down a silk thread to guide them home. Their instinct to follow is so strong that if the lead caterpillar is tricked into joining on behind the last in line, the procession will walk in a circle for hours, until it is exhausted.

The caterpillars are covered in foul-tasting, poisonous hairs which repel most birds. Only the hoopoe bird seems able to stomach these insects, and picks them off, one by one, as they file past.

MIGRATING BETWEEN HEIGHTS AND DEPTHS

Many creatures make seasonal epic journeys over land and sea in search of pastures new. But for some, vertical migration is sufficient for their needs.

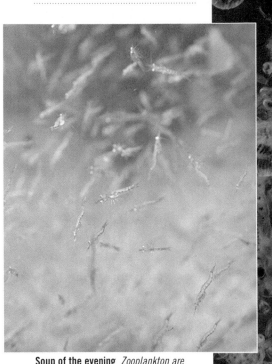

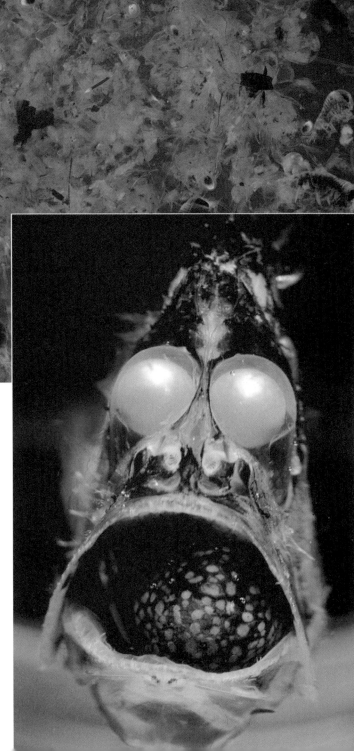

Soup of the evening *Zooplankton are minute sea animals of many different species, among them jewel-like mysids (above), crustacean larvae and round-shelled copepods (above right). Rising to the surface at night, they have many predators, including luminous, deep-sea hatchet fish (right).*

The ups and downs of planktonic existence

Tides and currents run the wide world over, in an endless journey from ocean to ocean. With them they carry zooplankton – minute sea animals near the bottom of the oceanic food chain. Although these organisms are too feeble to swim against currents, they nevertheless need to travel vertically through currents to the surface in search of their food, the tiny plants called phytoplankton.

Thus the zooplankton travel up to the surface and down to the depths through several current flows. The direction of the ocean currents varies at different depths, somewhat in the manner of a sandwich, in which the surface 'bread' flows, say, from east to west and the 'filling' flows from west to east. Zooplankton migrate up to the surface layer at night to feed upon the microscopic plant life then, during the day, sink to the deeper layer, so maintaining a roughly constant position in the ocean.

Dinoflagellates, which are the tiny organisms responsible for 'red' tides, are also vertically mobile, having a swimming hair to push them through the water. They have a light-receptive spot that draws them by day to the surface, from which they descend after dark. Some travel about 150 ft (45 m) in 24 hours, the equivalent of a man swimming 2000 miles (3200 km).

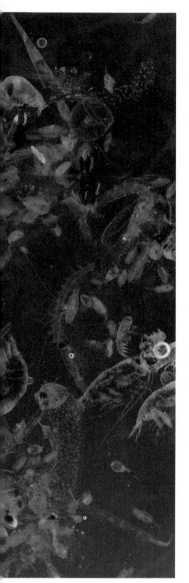

The summer odyssey of the bogong moth

In Australia, during June, July and August, areas of lush winter grassland in northern New South Wales and southern Queensland feed uncountable hordes of bogong moth caterpillars. In spring the caterpillars pupate – transform into adults inside a cocoon.

They emerge as moths in summer to a different world. The weather is hot and dry and the plains are a sea of brown stubble. So instead of immediately beginning an intense period of courting and mating, they head for higher altitudes, migrating south to cooler parts, flying at night and resting beneath logs and bushes by day.

During the journey, the migrating moth hordes blot out street lights, swarm into open windows and clog machinery and air ducts.

Eventually they reach their destination, the Australian Alps, where billions of them fold their wings, crowd into every cave and crevice, or cover rocks like living sheets. There the moths stay, not eating and scarcely breathing, for five months. Then in autumn, the plains begin to cool and the rain clouds gather. As new vegetation grows, the moths stir and then fly down from their mountain retreat, back to where they started. There they mate, lay their eggs and die.

Clinging cool *Millions of bogong moths take refuge from the Australian summer in caves and crannies 7000 ft (2100 m) high in the Australian Alps.*

Coming down the mountain *Unlike most upland birds in summer, the American blue grouse exchanges its highland habitat for rich lowland meadows.*

Grouse reverse trend in mountain migration

The usual seasonal pattern for dwellers in mountainous areas, human as well as animal, is to spend the summer months in the higher altitudes, taking advantage of the new verdure, then descend to the valleys in autumn, in anticipation of the winter to come.

There are, however, a few creatures that do the opposite. The blue grouse of North America, for example, overwinter in high mountain pine forests. Then, with the arrival of spring, they descend about 1000 ft (300 m), moving still lower as summer progresses. This downward migration accords with their food requirements.

In spring, deciduous trees on the middle slopes put out flowers and young leaves, providing early nourishment for their breeding season. Then, when the weather warms up, the parent birds usher their offspring all the way down to the bottom valleys, there to take advantage of a late-summer harvest of insects and berries. Late in the year the grouse all return to the high pine forests that will shelter them from winter blizzards.

In Europe, red grouse make a similar migration. Although they tend to avoid the moorland tops when snow begins to fall, they may return there when high winds pile it into drifts and scour it off exposed places, so uncovering the heather on which they feed.

The upwardly mobile feast of the sea

Every night, as countless billions of tiny sea animals (zooplankton) migrate upwards to feed upon minute surface-dwelling plants (phytoplankton), their journey is attended by larger creatures that swallow them in their millions.

The zooplankton include hard-shelled copepods the size of match heads, crab and shrimp larvae and many other creatures, all rising up to 350 ft (106 m) to their grazing grounds. Their predators are in turn fed upon by still larger ones. The whole parade of the devouring and the devoured, creatures like the jellyfish, arrow worms, prawns, shrimps, squid and fish of many kinds – take their allotted places in the movable nightly feast.

In the darkness of the middle and lower depths, which are both relatively poorly populated, finding food is a hit-and-miss affair. Many inhabitants, therefore, follow the trend and make the nightly ascent to the rich pickings to be found in the upper layers.

Large deep-sea prawns, for example, rise 1200 ft (360 m) from the depths. Deep-sea fish of nightmarish aspect, though not much longer than a finger, may make a double journey of 1000 ft (300 m) or more between dusk and dawn, adapting to alterations in water pressure of as much as 50 atmospheres and temperature changes of up to 20°C (36°F). Many of these deep-sea predators have luminescent organs. Some, like viper fish and angler fish, have brightly glowing lures at the tips of modified fins to entice prey within range of their dagger teeth. Others, including lantern fish that ascend from maybe 6000 ft (1800 m), have rows of lights like gleaming portholes along their flanks.

The glowing shoals of prey and predators congregating at the surface can be enormous. A British weather ship once took five hours to pass through just one. But by dawn, many of the migrants have already returned to the deep. They anticipate the light, descending rapidly to get back to their dark realms before the sun rises.

VAGABONDS AND COMMUTERS

Some animals spend their entire lives on the move. Others live in one place but leave home every day to search for food.

Dall sheep travel to fertile grazing land

For most of the year male Dall mountain sheep (relatives of the bighorn) band together, leaving the herds of ewes with their young on the greener pastures. The males roam the mountainsides of far northern Canada and Alaska, moving from one grazing patch to another along routes established by their ancestors over centuries.

Good grazing patches may be as much as 40 miles (60 km) apart, but the older rams know the age-old routes through the valleys to these fertile areas, having been taught in their youth. Young rams who have yet to learn the way tag along, following their elders.

Sociable behaviour *Male Dall sheep rest in a mountainside grazing area. To avoid conflict with older rams in these all-male groups, the young rams behave submissively, like female Dall sheep.*

Nomadic life *Herds of saiga antelope (above) constantly travel in search of food. Their huge noses (left) moisten and warm the air they breathe.*

The endless journey of the saiga antelope

The saiga is a curious antelope, short-bodied and heavily built, with a swollen-looking muzzle and large, limpid eyes. Males look more bizarre at rutting time, when their muzzles puff up even larger.

At one time saigas nearly died out, because their heavily ringed horns were prized as medicine in China. Now, however, numbers have increased, and the nomadic saigas wander the steppes and semi-desert lands of central Asia in herds of thousands, searching for fresh pastures. Being always on the move, saigas have no settled place for feeding, rutting or giving birth.

In spring, the herds trek north in the wake of the melting snow. They move at a leisurely rate and feed on the newly-uncovered grass shoots and various herbs and shrubs. Courtship and mating take place on the route north. The males fight for the right to hold harems of 5-15 females and have little time to feed. Defending a harem can be so tiring that, when winter snows come, many males succumb to the cold, and fail to make the return journey south.

Sahara navigators *Desert ants leave their nests to find food several times a day. In search of insect corpses they may travel more than 200 yd (180 m) from their nests, but they use the sun and landmarks, such as bushes, to find their way home again.*

Desert ants 'map read' their way home

For most insects and other small creatures in the Sahara Desert, the blazing midday sun, which sends surface temperatures of the sand soaring to more than 70°C (158°F), means certain death if they are caught in the open. Desert ants limit their exposure to the fierce sun by nesting underground and making short excursions above ground five to ten times a day in search of food.

A foraging ant zigzags across the sand, stopping every now and then to turn its head from side to side. When an ant finds food such as an insect corpse, it runs back to its nest with it, heading there by the most direct route. Unlike other ants, it does not follow its own twisting scent trail home.

But the burning sun is of help to the desert ant, which uses it to navigate. Its compound eyes are able to recognise polarised light – light in which all the sun's rays oscillate in the same direction, the angle depending on the sun's position. When a foraging ant stops to turn its head from side to side, it is locking into this map of the sky, checking its position regularly so that it can work out the return direction. If it could not do this accurately, the ant would be lost and would very soon die.

Rush hour *Navigating the darkness of its cave, a dusky leaf-nosed bat (above) heads for the entrance, where the scrummage of bats and swiftlets (top) is aggravated by the falcons that swoop in to grab a meal.*

Bats and birds in aerial traffic jams

At both dawn and dusk, apparent chaos reigns at the entrances to certain huge caves in Southeast Asia. They are the scene of a traffic jam caused by the inward and outward movements of birds and bats.

At dusk, as the night shift of bats leaves to hunt for insects in the surrounding forest, the day shift of cave swiftlets is returning from the hunt – they also feed on insects. The swiftlets head for their nests on overhanging cave walls. These cup-shaped homes are built from their own saliva and are much prized by the Chinese as the main ingredient of bird's-nest

Home sharers *Horsefield's leaf-nosed bats (far left) spend their days suspended from the roofs of their caves. At night cave swiftlets (left) return to their nests along the walls.*

soup. The birds find their way in the dark with the help of echolocation. They produce low-frequency clicks with their tongues and listen for the echoes that bounce off obstacles in their path.

The outgoing bats streaming from the entrances, tens of thousands of them, have spent the day roosting in the deepest parts of the caves. Like the cave swiftlets, they also navigate by echolocation but use high-frequency squeaks. Both

incoming birds and outgoing bats have to run the gauntlet of birds of prey such as peregrine falcons and bat hawks that hunt in the twilight of dawn and dusk for the twice-daily food bonanza available in the traffic jam. The hawks swoop down at an angle across the entrances to the caves, tearing through the flocks and grabbing bird or bat in their talons. Pandemonium reigns as the dense flocks sweep and swirl to avoid the hawks. In fact,

the swiftlets spiral down to their caves from great heights in an attempt to avoid the predators.

If it were not for these daily migrations of birds and bats to and from the caves, the other cave-dwelling creatures – giant cave crickets, blind hunting spiders and long-legged guano crabs among others – would not survive. They never venture outside, but the food debris dropped by birds and bats, and their guano, or excreta, and dead bodies provide a constant supply of nutrients for the scavengers living below. So concentrated is this food supply that there are probably more creatures living on the floor of one of these caves than there are living in a similar area of the forest floor outside.

FOLLOWING THE SEASONS

Thousands of caribou trail across North America's icy landscape twice every year – south in autumn and north in spring.

Sound and motion *As a caribou herd numbering thousands (left) follows the traditional migration route, the tendons in their feet make a pronounced clicking sound when their hoofs strike the hard ground of the tundra. A group on the way south to the winter range (above) crosses the Kobuk River in northwest Alaska.*

Caribou herds carve a path north and south

In some parts of North America's Arctic regions, rocks have been worn down at least 2 ft (60 cm) by the splayed hoofs of the countless generations of caribou that follow these routes on their twice-yearly migrations. The caribou, close relatives of European reindeer, move south to winter in the coniferous forests of Canada and Alaska.

Here they dig through the loose snow to graze on sedges, mosses and lichens – each animal eating about 12 lb (5 kg) a day. In early spring, however, the caribou herds move slowly north again, following established routes, to reach the Arctic tundra. A single herd may number thousands of animals and be strung out in a long column, with 150 miles (240 km) separating the leading females from the males bringing up the rear. It may take several weeks for the entire herd to cross an ice-cold river.

The short summer in the tundra provides the herds with succulent grazing – and fewer bears, wolves and eagles to prey on them. Soon after arrival, when their young will be relatively safe and well fed, the pregnant females give birth.

By midsummer, the calves have been weaned and the huge herds disperse across the tundra to feed on new growth. At the end of the autumn rut, the caribou herds set off once again on their long trek to the south for the winter.

Travel aids *Hollow outer hairs on a caribou's coat insulate its body and aid buoyancy. Spread hoofs make crossing snow, bogs and rocky streams easier.*

375

TRAVELLING TO NEW PASTURES

For many animals, the seasonal urge to migrate is so strong that it overrides the danger and discomfort that may be involved.

Globetrotting terns' long yearly flight

Of all the birds that migrate each year to follow the summer sun, Arctic terns fly the farthest. Some fly from the Arctic Circle to feeding sites, 8000 miles (13 000 km) away or more, round the Southern Ocean. Birds that nest farthest north go the farthest south. During their lifetime, which can stretch to 30 years, some birds may travel 650 000 miles (1 million km).

Each autumn, terns which have bred in Canada and Greenland ride westerly winds across the Atlantic Ocean before heading south along the western coasts of Europe and Africa. A few stop in South Africa, but others fly onwards to islands around Antarctica. Here they will moult and feed off the rich supplies of fish in the icy waters. In February, mature birds begin the long return journey north, but the one-year-old birds fly anticlockwise around the South Pole to spend the summer in the South Pacific. How these young birds find their way to an area they have not seen before is a mystery. Only in their third spring, when they are ready to breed, will they set off with the mature birds for the far northern breeding grounds, finding their way unerringly to breeding sites they left two or three years before.

The swift's airborne life

Within hours of leaving its nest, a young swift sets its course from Europe on a non-stop journey of more than 6000 miles (9600 km) to southeast Africa. Even on reaching its destination, the swift does not land; it feeds and sleeps on the wing until it goes back to Europe to breed. When it lands to inspect a nest site, the bird will have been in the air for more than 22 months.

Wildebeest trek south to improve their milk

In spring each year, the wildebeest of Kenya's Masai Mara Reserve join zebras and gazelles in great mixed herds, some up to half a million strong, to travel more than 120 miles (200 km) southeast to Tanzania's Serengeti Plains, where the females give birth. Along the route, lions, hyenas and crocodiles prey on the herds and, each year, about 42 000 wildebeest die during the migration.

The Masai Mara has sufficient food all year for the wildebeests' energy needs, so why do they make this hazardous yearly journey? The answer is in Serengeti's grass. It grows on soil rich in phosphorus, a mineral vital to the formation of strong bones in the calves. When they are born, in the middle of the wet season, the grass is rich and lush, enriching the mothers' milk and giving the calves a better start than they would have had on the Masai Mara. In the dry season, the grass dies and the herds return to the northern woodlands.

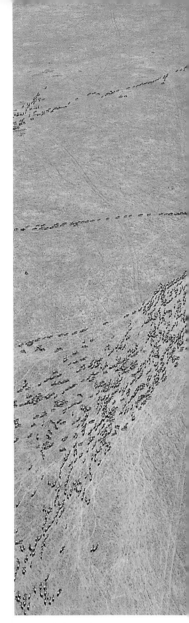

Wildebeest trek *Huge herds leave the Masai Mara. Though its food supplies are adequate, the animals migrate to richer grasslands that will benefit their young.*

Massed migrators *Arctic terns rest or dive for small fish and shellfish as they travel along the Namibian coast on their way to Antarctic islands for the southern summer. Westerly winds carry them past this coast again on their way to breed in Canada, Greenland or northern Europe.*

Winter visitors *These whooper swans wintering in Scotland have flown some 500 miles (800 km) non-stop from Iceland. Many others will migrate from northern Europe and Russia to spend winter round the Mediterranean and Caspian seas. The swans fly very high in V-formations, using fast-flowing jet streams to carry them along. One group was seen at 27 000 ft (8300 m).*

Monarchs and their mysterious flights

How monarch butterflies manage to find their way, in their millions, across North America every year is a mystery. Not one of them has made the journey before – no butterfly lives long enough to fly the 2000 miles (3200 km) journey there and back. Monarchs hatch as caterpillars during spring or early summer, and feed on milkweed in scattered parts of northern USA and southern Canada. But in late summer, now transformed into butterflies, they gather in

Natural pathfinders *Monarch butterflies (right) inherit the ability to find their way to traditional 'butterfly trees' (below) that they have never visited before.*

huge flocks and head towards the south. Resting at night in trees, the monarchs fly by day at altitudes of up to 350 ft (110 m), usually covering about 80 miles (130 km) a day. They stop to drink flower nectar sometimes, but they also draw on their own body fat, which allows some of them to fly non-stop for 100 hours or more.

On arrival in California, Mexico or Florida, the butterflies settle on certain trees that are used year after year. Throughout the winter they stay here, in a state of semi-hibernation, hiding the branches and trunks of the 'butterfly trees' under a mass of orange-and-black wings. It is not clear how they find the trees – maybe the scent of the butterflies is retained by trees, and this attracts following generations.

In spring the monarchs head north. Females lay eggs along the route before dying, and up to three generations may hatch and then arrive in Canada in the autumn.

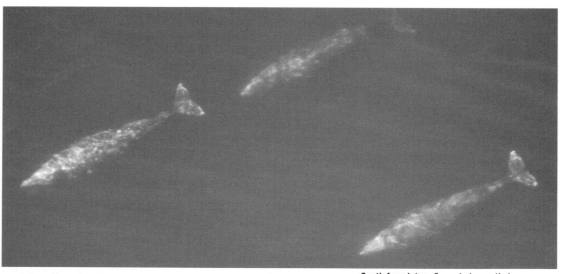

South for winter *Grey whales on their way south swim close to the Californian shore. Their twice-yearly migration is a source of pleasure for whale-watchers.*

Grey whales move to California to breed

Grey whales of the Pacific Ocean spend half the year travelling. It takes them three months to wend their way from summer feeding grounds in the icy Arctic seas to semi-tropical breeding sites off Baja California in Mexico. Another three months are spent on the return journey – a round trip of about 12 500 miles (20 000 km).

Pregnant female grey whales start the move south each October. Immature females and adult males follow, with immature males bringing up the rear. By December the first whales have reached Mexico, where they give birth in the warm, sheltered lagoons. The youngsters, suckled on their mothers' rich milk, rapidly develop the blubber they need before they head for northern waters again in March. Newly mated females lead the return – they will give birth in just over a year. Following them are 45 ft (14 m) long adult males and non-breeding females, then immature whales and finally mothers with their young. They often swim close to the shore, where the thick kelp forests provide hiding places from sharks and killer whales – the only known predators of grey whales, apart from humans.

In late May the whales reach their feeding grounds in the Bering Sea. Here, they spend the next three months feeding on the rich supply of shrimp-like crustaceans, worms and molluscs such as small shellfish, before migrating south to warmer waters once more.

377

FINDING THE WAY

Many birds live in perpetual summer by flying vast distances each year. How they navigate is only just beginning to be understood.

Navigation databanks of migrating birds

Each year, as the days shorten and the food supply dwindles, many bird species prepare themselves for a long flight to warmer, more fruitful climes. Not a few are youngsters hatched in the spring. Until the great adventure begins, these hatchlings have probably made only exploratory flights to familiarise themselves with local landmarks, and have seldom been out of sight of their birthplace.

Then one day, driven by deep ancestral urges, they set out for unknown destinations, perhaps a continent away. The swallows of northern Europe, for example, may fly 6800 miles (11 000 km) or so to their African wintering grounds. Swallows migrate in large flocks and can probably draw on the expertise of older birds, but some birds, like cuckoos, must find the way for themselves.

Like a sailor out of sight of land, a migrating bird makes use of navigational aids. It can set a course by sun or stars, and even call upon a kind of internal magnetic compass.

Magnetic map
Many birds that migrate may be sensitive to variations that occur in the Earth's magnetic field, a series of lines of force that rise at angles to the Earth's surface – they are almost vertical at the poles but parallel to the ground at the equator. Instead of discerning north and south directly, as a compass does, birds sense their position from the angle at which the magnetic field intercepts the ground.

Night-flying migrants also establish their position from the stars. This is no easy feat, because the star pattern varies with longitude and season. But in the northern hemisphere at least, there is one fixed, constant star – the Pole Star – and during the course of the night the rest of the stars appear to rotate round it. Somehow birds can relate to this movement and use the position of the Pole Star to

orientate themselves. During the day, if the sun is visible, birds use it as a direction-finder. Although the sun's position changes as the day passes, birds such as starlings are able to navigate by checking its position in the sky against their biological clocks.

Even when the sun is obscured by cloud, birds nevertheless know where it is. Light entering the Earth's atmosphere oscillates at all angles, but as it continues through the atmosphere it may become polarised, so that all rays oscillate in the same direction. The extent and angle of polarisation depends on the sun's position in the sky. Birds and insects use the pattern of polarised light – which humans cannot perceive – as a navigational aid to determine where the sun is, even when they can see no more than a tiny patch of blue sky.

Polarised light is also used by night-flying migrants when, in the evening, they begin the next leg of their journey. With its help, they can ensure that they head off in

the right direction even though the sun has already sunk below the western horizon. As the sun sets, a band of maximum polarisation runs across the sky from north to south. This, provided that the sky is clear, is the most dependable guide available. In spring in the northern hemisphere, birds head north by flying parallel to this band, using some form of biological clock and the position of the sun to orientate themselves.

Just why birds are tuned into quite so many navigational aids is something of a mystery. It might be thought that creatures able to use the Earth's magnetic field would

Scheduled flight *Each year, Canada geese fly to the southern USA following with other migrants, one of four regular routes, or flyways. One route follows the Atlantic coast, and the others the Mississippi, the Rockies and the Pacific.*

need no other system, but birds may use the different systems as back-ups – if one fails them they rely on another. Occasional irregularities in the Earth's magnetic field may be sufficiently insistent to interfere with the birds' navigational instincts. Or, perhaps, using the magnetic lines of force to maintain course is more difficult than using the stars and the sun.

Homeward urge *Silhouetted against the western sky on the Welsh island of Skomer is a crowd of Manx shearwaters. These birds are famous navigators. One shearwater was transported across the Atlantic from its nest burrow on neighbouring Skokholm Island to Boston, Massachusetts, and then set free. After 12 days the bird had returned to base, having beaten by 12 hours the letter informing Skokholm of its release.*

Harbingers of spring *At winter's end, American robins, which are members of the thrush family, migrate northwards in large numbers from Mexico and southwest USA. As they go, the flocks break up into smaller groups, all bound for their home territories, in some cases as far distant as Alaska and Labrador.*

Homing pigeons provide clue to bird migration

The homing instinct of pigeons is proverbial, and for centuries it has been exploited by mankind. Just how they carry out their considerable feats of navigation is a perennial puzzle, and has been the subject of much scientific enquiry. During one series of tests, it emerged that pigeons may be able to hear very low-frequency sounds, known as infrasound.

Infrasound is below the hearing range of human beings, though it is often 'felt' as vibrations. Wind and tyre noise in cars, and the sound of the wind humming around tall buildings, have very low-frequency components, and characteristically induce sleepiness in humans.

What use pigeons may make of this hearing ability is unclear. It has been suggested, quite recently, that it is an ability that is shared with other bird species. Scientists have speculated that migrating birds can pick out the infrasound signature of landmarks on their route. Noises such as wind blowing through canyons, or waves crashing on shore, contain elements of low-frequency sound that travel for enormous distances.

Put together, these infrasound messages reaching migrants could create a vast sound map – not a very precise map, perhaps, but one that would provide a reassuring back-up for other sensory systems.

Succour for the weary In autumn, flocks of swallows and other birds make their way from northern Europe down to Africa, many of them taking the arduous route over the Alps. Often they are overtaken by early snowstorms, and unless they find shelter, many die. High in the mountains is St Bernard's Monastery, whose monks have for centuries cared for alpine travellers – including birds, which they shelter until they are fit enough to continue their journey. Among other havens for exhausted migrants are lighthouses and ships at sea, whose decks are sometimes covered with birds in a state of collapse.

UNUSUAL AERIAL TRAVELLERS OF THE ANIMAL WORLD

Gliding swiftly through the air is a stunt mastered by some wingless animals to make foraging easier and to escape from predators.

Free fall for snakes, frogs and lizards

Not only birds and insects take to the air to move about, so too do some snakes, lizards, opossums, frogs, and colugos, even some fish.

Perched precariously upon a branch, the Costa Rican flying frog shoots out its powerful back legs and takes off into the air. By spreading its limbs wide, shaping its body like an upturned saucer, and stretching the webbed skin between its elongated fingers and toes to form four parachutes, it is able to glide up to 50 yd (45 m) to the next tree. This skill enables the frog to escape predators when pursued and enlarge its feeding range without having to descend from one tree, cross the forest floor, then laboriously climb up into the next.

At one time, stories of flying snakes were considered to be far-fetched travellers' tales, but these extraordinary aviators do exist. There are several species, all generally called golden tree snakes.

Flying snakes climb up rough bark in search of their prey – mostly lizards – by gripping the surface with the broad scales on the undersides of their bodies. When a snake wants to change trees, it speeds along a branch and launches itself into the air.

As it begins to fall, the snake shapes its rounded body into a channel, like an upside-down water gutter, and then undulates it in a series of S-shaped coils. It can glide in this way, although without much control. But by wriggling, it can change its flight path sufficiently to enable it to land close to its target.

Amongst the lizards preyed on by tree snakes are geckos. One of them, the flying gecko, also glides – not only to escape snakes but to hunt its own prey. The gecko glides using a skirt of skin that runs along each side of its body and by spreading its large, webbed toes.

Lizards of another group, the flying dragons, each have a fold of skin stretched across movable and much-elongated ribs. This opens like a fan and gives a flying dragon much greater control over its glide.

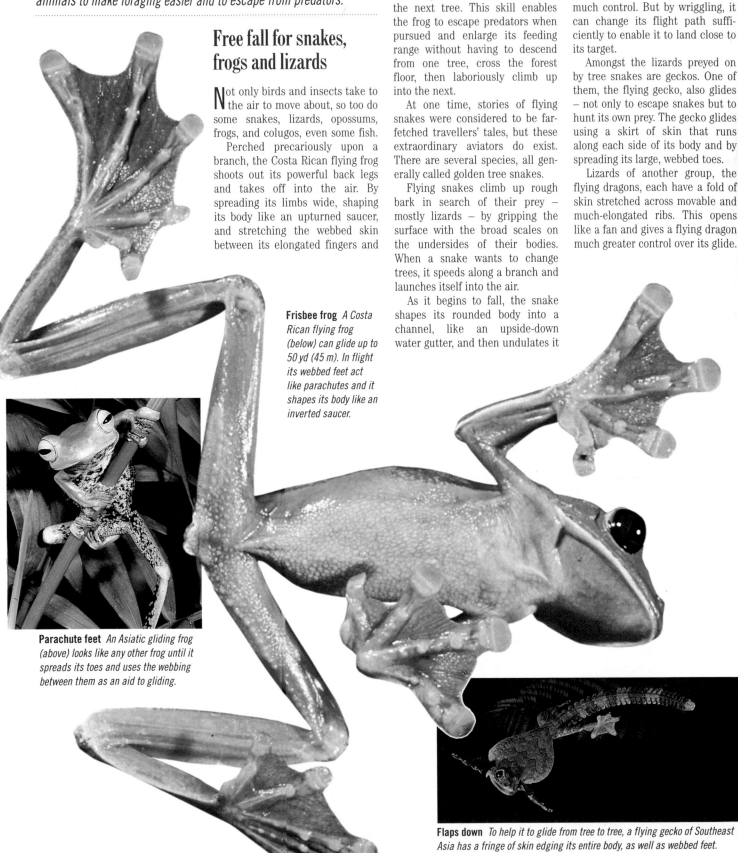

Frisbee frog *A Costa Rican flying frog (below) can glide up to 50 yd (45 m). In flight its webbed feet act like parachutes and it shapes its body like an inverted saucer.*

Parachute feet *An Asiatic gliding frog (above) looks like any other frog until it spreads its toes and uses the webbing between them as an aid to gliding.*

Flaps down *To help it to glide from tree to tree, a flying gecko of Southeast Asia has a fringe of skin edging its entire body, as well as webbed feet.*

Gliding hunters that live among the trees

The art of being airborne allows some mammals to extend their feeding ranges and to avoid hunters on the ground. Marsupial gliders, or flying opossums, for example, glide from branch to branch in the open forests of northern Australia and New Guinea to feed upon fruit, leaves, blossoms and insects. There are several species – such as the lesser and greater gliding opossums – the largest of which is about 20 in (50 cm) long, with a tail of about the same size.

As it glides with legs outspread, a marsupial glider looks rather like a rectangular kite, with a thin, furred membrane on each side of its body stretching from front to back legs. Using its tapered, furry tail as a rudder, a glider can cover up to 100 yd (90 m) at a time. Larger opossums, because of their weight, tend to fall steeply with little control, but smaller species can manoeuvre to avoid obstacles.

At the end of its glide, the animal swoops upwards to a tree trunk, landing there with an audible plop. Slow-motion photography shows the landing to be unsophisticated, the glider actually colliding violently with the tree. But to prevent bouncing back on impact, it hangs on tight with the extra-large claws on its fourth and fifth toes.

Often incorrectly called a flying lemur, the colugo of Malaysia and the Philippines also glides by means of furred membranes on each side of its body, but they stretch from its neck to its front toe tips then continue to the tip of its tail. Colugo glides average more than 120 yd (110 m), and one was seen to glide 150 yd (137 m) and lose no more than 40 ft (12 m) in altitude.

Cat-sized colugos feed at night. It is due to their nocturnal habits and lemur-like heads that they are called flying lemurs. In fact, their closest relatives are probably hedgehogs and shrews.

Flying kite *A yellow-bellied glider, a nocturnal forager for leaves and insects, controls its flight from branch to branch with its long, tapered, rudder-like tail. The glider's arm and leg bones are slightly elongated to give it as big a wing area as possible when its limbs are fully extended.*

Hang glider *A colugo (above) stretches its limbs wide and spreads out the large folds of skin that help it to fly from tree to tree to feed on leaves.*

Flying fish take to the air to elude predators

With a hungry hunter in hot pursuit, a flying fish surges to the sea surface with its side fins folded flat against its body at a speed of 15-20 mph (24-32 km/h). As the fish rockets out of the water, it spreads its large side fins to give it lift and, beating its tail vigorously, sculls across the surface. Once it has built up enough speed, the fish takes to the air, maybe spreading its pelvic fins as well, and glides at a height of 4-5 ft (1.2-1.5 m) above the water at up to 40 mph (65 km/h). After 300 yd (275 m) at most, it loses speed and glides down to the surface before rising in another leap.

Long, thin needlefish, which are sharp-beaked, fast-swimming relatives of flying fish, also take to the air to avoid pursuers, breaking the surface at tremendous speed and shooting 16 ft (5 m) into the air like tiny javelins to cover distances of 25 yd (23 m). Flying gurnards, which are not related to flying fish, are bottom-dwelling fish that are also able to leap out of the water for short distances.

Fins for wings *A flying gurnard, a fish up to 20 in (50 cm) long found in warm waters, has huge side fins divided into large and small 'wings' that enable it to glide above the sea for short distances.*

NATURE'S CHANGING FACE

'*These* hay meadow days were the Arcadian days for marsh dwellers. Man and beast, plant and soil lived on and with each other in mutual toleration, to the mutual benefit of all. The marsh might have kept on producing hay and prairie chickens, deer and muskrats, crane-music and cranberries for ever.'
≈ Aldo Leopold, *Sketches Here and There*, 1949.

Natural cure
The delicate pink flowers of the rosy periwinkle growing on the floor of a tropical rain forest give no clue to the plant's value to man. The plant has long been used by tribal peoples as an oral medicine. Western scientists have discovered that it produces chemicals which are remarkably effective in curing certain forms of leukaemia.

The marshes and water meadows of Wisconsin to which Aldo Leopold referred have now been drained and much of their wildlife has gone. Throughout the world, once-common animals and birds have been driven to extinction.

Plants and animals have always provided humans with a plentiful source of food and medicines, building materials and clothing. In return, man cleared forests and ploughed up grasslands, creating a patchwork of habitats that often increased the number and variety of plants. But in the past few hundred years, the blink of an eye in evolutionary time, 'mutual toleration' and 'mutual benefit' have been replaced steadily by our ever more destructive attempts to manipulate our environment. We humans depend for our daily survival on the intricate web of life that is the natural world, and we damage it at our peril.

No more passengers

In the early 19th century, passenger pigeons in 2 billion-bird flocks, 3-4 miles (5-6 km) wide and 300 miles (500 km) long, could be seen passing over southern USA on their migration flights. Their passage could darken the sky for hours, and sometimes days, at a time. Despite their numbers, they were unable to withstand the onslaught of man, and the last of this pretty, delicate species died in Cincinnati Zoo in 1914.

Mixed blessings

The cane toad was introduced into eastern Australia where it was hoped it would control pests in sugar cane plantations. The toads have voracious and undiscriminating appetites and attack a wide range of insects and small mammals – including several beneficial and rare native species. As the toads are poisonous to eat, they also endanger the native carnivores that prey on them. In this case, the cure was worse than the ailment.

Fatal fur

Beautiful and mysterious predator of the high mountain slopes of eastern Asia, the snow leopard has been hunted almost to extinction for its pelt. Even where it survives, its habitat is being destroyed as farmers graze their flocks ever higher on the mountain slopes.

CHOOSING THE URBAN LIFE

When rural habitats deteriorate or are built over, some species succumb. But others adapt to towns and live surprisingly well.

Ousted starlings opt for big city comforts

At the end of the working day in cities across Europe, North America and Canada, the streets are full of jostling commuters leaving their work places for home. High above the tall buildings they have just vacated, huge flocks of starlings tumble and swoop like clouds of giant midges, bound for their overnight roosting sites on building ledges, office roofs and tree tops. Moving against the commuter tide, the birds are bound for city centres from the suburban gardens and surrounding countryside, where they feed during the day.

Noisily they descend on their sleeping quarters, jockeying for the safest and warmest positions at the centre of the flock. Their squealing

Chattering class *A shrieking crowd of starlings, ragamuffins of the bird world, darkens the evening sky and whitens the buildings in London's Trafalgar Square.*

chorus, drowning the traffic's roar, has become the voice of sunset in many cities where flocks of many thousands of birds have abandoned rural habitats for urban ones. No respecters of architecture, some starlings even build nests inside the crowns and laurel wreaths of heroic statuary.

Unlike sparrows and pigeons, which have long dwelt in cities, starlings are relative newcomers to urban living. Not until the last summers of the 19th century were the first roosting flocks noted in inner city parks. Then some birds discovered the chief benefit of urban living – the 3°C (5.4°F) or more temperature rise from country to town that emanates from poorly insulated, centrally heated buildings – and the news spread.

Then, too, the steady outward sprawl of cities overwhelmed some of the starlings' traditional roosting sites. Undismayed, these adaptable birds exchanged woods and cliffs for buildings in a warmer and more comfortable environment.

Secrets of Reynard's streetwise success

A red fox sits, in broad daylight, in the shade of a parked car in a British city, alert but resting. This is a streetwise fox, born and bred in the city and skilled at exploiting it for board and lodging. It knows every nook and cranny in its territory, takes over space beneath a garden shed or warehouse as an earth for its cubs, and feeds on the great variety of natural and 'leftover' foods available.

Foxes have been spotted near London's Tower Bridge and walking along a car assembly line in Oxford. In Bristol it is estimated that there are 21 adult foxes to 1 sq mile (2.6 km²). Observations

of urban foxes suggest that they prefer the greener parts of towns and cities – suburban gardens, golf courses, playing fields, patches of wasteland. The small mammals and birds they catch there account for about a third of their total diet, supplemented by earthworms and other invertebrates. The rest is made up of human leftovers, scavenged from compost heaps and rubbish bins, where the foxes compete with domestic dogs and cats. In late summer and autumn they

top up with windfallen fruit and blackberries eaten from the bush.

Towns and cities offer rich menus to creatures prepared to sample most things. Silver foil, paper, elastic bands and string have all been found in urban fox droppings. Some naturalists think the foxes' drift into towns began in the 1930s, with its phenomenal growth in suburban development. Its generous accompaniment of back gardens certainly presented a new environment profitable to

New cub on the block *Having lost none of its proverbial cunning, a young urban fox rests on a greenhouse shelf and contemplates a world of plentiful pickings where foxhounds have no part.*

wildlife. Other naturalists put it later, attributing it to epidemics of myxomatosis that began in the 1950s and wiped out 95 per cent of the country's rabbits. Deprived of their most important prey, hungry foxes gravitated to towns where many remained, although the rabbit population is again increasing.

Monkey business spoils the town's laundry

The tropical forests that run from Afghanistan to the Chang Jiang (Yangtze river) in China, are the home of most of the world's rhesus macaque monkeys. There, without too much effort, they live on fruits, insects, plants and small animals. Some rhesus macaques in India, however, have swapped the forest for the town where finding a meal is rather more complex.

In the northeastern Indian town of Varanasi, for example, they have taken to extortion. When they see clothes spread out on a rooftop to dry, they leap up and seize a garment, preferably one that has plenty of buttons. Then they sit down and start to bite the buttons off, one by one. Experience tells the owner that chasing a monkey will result only in its departure with the clothes. So some food is thrown to it instead, whereupon the macaque releases the garment, takes the food and runs.

In some temples dedicated to the monkey god Hanuman, the macaques do not have to look for food for they are reverently fed by priests. But in others they have become skilled thieves, leaping out from behind a pillar to ambush an unsuspecting worshipper who is bringing an edible offering, a cake or chapatti, for the god. Knocking the offering out of the worshipper's hand, the macaque stuffs its cheeks with whatever fragments it can grab before it is chased away. The wily macaques usually single out women or children, presumably because they are easier to rob.

Whom the gods love *Respected for their association with the Hindu monkey god Hanuman, rhesus macaques have long been inhabitants of Indian towns and villages, where they have become more cunning than their wild cousins, and more aggressive too.*

Dextrous front paws aid raccoon city slickers

Animal garbage raiders – from the hyenas of India to the possums of Australia and the coyotes of North America – share a common philosophy: if it is at all edible, eat it. Gleanings from rubbish bins, or indeed kitchens, provide not only a supplement to their normal diets but in times of scarcity keep them alive where other, more fastidious animals would starve.

As well as having the omnivorous appetite of a scavenger, the raccoon has dextrous front paws and an agile frame, which help to make it the master of garbage raiding and burglary in many a North American town. Having long come to disregard street lighting, traffic noises and the myriad activities of a city at night, they nimbly climb fences and walls en route to the citizens' dustbins. Briskly, they lift the lids off with their front paws, push the inedible aside, and locate the discarded sandwich or hamburger – sometimes overturning a bin in the process.

Although naturally shy, some bolder individuals have been known to take advantage of an open back door to make a raid on the kitchen, rifling cupboards and refrigerators and tearing off packaging to get at the food inside. Some have even learned the art of unscrewing jars and removing stoppers from opened wine bottles.

Most urban raccoons rest during the day, in a hollow tree, in a chimney or in a seldom-visited attic in a house. When they emerge at dusk they choose routes where they are least likely to encounter people – strips of parkland, back gardens, streams and back alleys. Storm water drains are extremely popular as they shield the raccoons from the hazards of crossing busy roads.

Researchers in Washington D.C. have discovered that if young urban raccoons survive their first winter, they can be expected to live considerably longer than their country cousins. The resources available in a city will, it seems, support about three raccoons to an acre (0.4 ha), while a single rural raccoon needs a territory of about 50 acres (20 ha) in order to survive.

Capital opportunists *Raccoons have successfully invaded backyard North America, nowhere in greater numbers than in Washington D.C., where they plunder dustbins nightly. Some have even discovered how to unstopper opened wine bottles and then get drunk on the contents.*

CHANGING LIFESTYLES

Man's takeover of the planet has destroyed many natural habitats, although for some adaptable species he has provided a bonanza.

Urban scavengers *Many gulls, like the lesser black-backed (inset) have adapted to the rooftop nesting sites and plentiful food offered by cities, in whose tips they raucously squabble for titbits.*

Swapping cold cliff tops for warm city roofs

What do gulls eat? Where do they nest? Where do they spend the winter? The answers to these questions have changed radically in the past 20 years or so for at least one species of European gull. Before the 1970s, the lesser black-backed gull and the similar-sized herring gull were coast-living birds that trawled the seas for fish and scraps and gathered together on cliff tops at the beginning of the breeding season to build their nests. Herring gulls usually spent the winter in northern Europe but lesser black-backed gulls departed to more southerly winter quarters in Spain, Portugal and North Africa.

After the Second World War, the gull populations started to grow as urban development increased with a corresponding rise in the number of municipal rubbish tips and landfill sites. In the 1950s, Clean Air laws were passed forbidding the burning of rubbish in these places. The gulls that had already begun to forage at these sites now had a regular and undisturbed supply of edible waste.

This bonanza resulted in a dramatic rise in gull numbers and overcrowding in coastal nurseries. So it was not long before emigrant birds were looking for nesting sites closer to the new feeding grounds. Rooftops and ledges of office blocks and other buildings much resembled cliffs with added advantages. They offered nesting birds shelter and warmth, good visibility and seclusion. Best of all, the parent birds did not have to travel far to find a meal for their chicks.

However, herring gulls have begun to pay for their addiction to garbage. Ever-increasing numbers

Pollution no problem to a camouflaged moth

Like chameleons, some insects can change colour (usually during pupation or moulting), either to deceive predators or to help them absorb and retain body heat. But one British species, the peppered moth, has gone one step further and undergone a complete and long-lasting change of colour.

Originally a pale creature with a dusting of small, dark markings, it was practically invisible against lichen-covered, light-coloured tree trunks on which it rested during the day. By the middle of the 19th century, however, the lichens in the industrial regions of Britain had been killed off by the sooty deposits which then coated the trunks, branches and leaves of the

Before and after *The pale peppered moth (above) took on a darker coloration (left) to blend protectively in with the dirt and grime resulting from 19th-century industrial growth.*

trees. The pale peppered moths were highly conspicuous against the dark bark and became easy prey for hungry birds.

A dark form of the peppered moth, probably a genetic mutation, was first noticed near Manchester in 1848. In the ensuing decades, however, the dark insect, with its superior camouflaging, became the dominant form. Indeed, by the turn of the century, almost all peppered moths found in or downwind of industrial areas were black.

There is a fascinating postscript to this example of the process of natural selection at work: since the introduction of smokeless zones in the 1950s – and the consequent reduction in industrial emissions – there are signs that the dark form of the peppered moth is on the decline, and that the original, light-coloured form is, in fact, making a comeback.

Harmless seed-eater turns crop-killer

It was farming improvements that gave rise to the million-strong flocks of red-winged blackbirds that devastate agricultural land across North America. Originally a bird that bred among freshwater marshes and foraged for seeds in thick grasses and woodland edges, the red-winged blackbird had no trouble in switching to cereals when much of its habitat was drained and converted to farmland. As more and more land was put under the plough, so the bird population grew and increased its range, feeding on an ever more plentiful supply of corn, rice, oats and barley, to the anger of farmers. The bird is now a serious pest. Wandering the land like a plague, one vast blackbird flock can devastate the crops of an entire county.

Birds of plunder *The red-winged blackbird, probably the most numerous of North American land birds, is dreaded for its wholesale devastation of crops.*

of the birds are affected by avian botulism, a condition brought on by the bacteria that flourish in plastic rubbish bags. Without treatment, the condition is fatal.

Lesser black-backed gulls, by comparison, seem to have chosen a more balanced diet, supplementing their diet of garbage with worms and insects. As a result, thousands of these city-bred gulls no longer bother to migrate in winter, and have changed their status from summer visitors to residents.

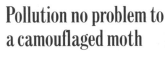

CHANGING THEIR WORLD

Most animals have to adapt to their environment to survive, but some animals simply adapt their surroundings to suit themselves.

Elephants strip trees and mine salt

Weighing up to ten tons and with a pair of tusks that serve as shovels, an elephant can change its environment as effectively as a human with a mechanical digger. If an elephant wants to eat bark from the top of an acacia tree, it simply pushes the tree over. A group of elephants, confined to a limited area, can change it from fertile grassland to barren desert, by eating all the vegetation and stripping bark from trees.

In caves in Mount Elgon in East Africa, there is an enormous salt-lick where elephants chisel off lumps of the hard, salt-rich rock with their tusks. Generations of elephants chiselling over centuries may have dug out the caves.

Digging for a drink *In the dry season, elephants keep water holes open (left) by kicking away soil and digging with their tusks. They also enlarge holes (below) when they wallow, carrying away large amounts of mud on their bodies.*

Beavers turn forests into meadows

A beaver couple searching for a place to live will select a spot on a stream or small river, where they can build a dam to make a lake or pond. Within the lake they build a dome-shaped lodge for the family. Up to 15 animals may eventually live there – the breeding pair and their kits and youngsters from last season. A beaver family's dam-building activities can in time change a forested valley with a stream running through it into a broad, fertile, open meadow.

The beavers' lake has to be deep enough for all the lodge entrances to be under water, and so inaccessible to predators such as coyotes, bears and lynxes. The dam walls are built up from the stream bed with small trees, branches, stones and mud until they protrude some 4 ft (1.2 m) above the water. As they build the dam, beavers clear all the small trees from the river banks. If felled trees are too far from the river to fall or be dragged into it, the beavers dig channels from the bank to float them down.

Beavers are well equipped for felling trees, having sharp teeth that can cut through trunks up to 20 in (50 cm) across. Their dexterous front paws enable them to dig and grasp, and their webbed hind feet and oar-like tails aid manoeuvring in the water. They can seal off the backs of their throats, allowing them to gnaw wood without choking and to carry sticks in their mouths under water without drowning. Flaps of skin can be closed behind their sharp front teeth to keep water out.

Although beavers destroy trees, their building process does have its

benefits. Digging up mud from the river bed to seal dams uncovers tiny animals, which provide food for fish. The digging also scatters water-plant seeds, creating new areas of plant growth. These in turn provide nursery areas where young fish can hide from predators. Beavers tend to be unpopular with farmers, however, because flooding upstream of their dams drowns trees and can affect nearby land. But beaver dams can also be an asset to the countryside – they regulate the flow of the river or stream, thus reducing drought, seasonal flooding and soil erosion.

Eventually, however, silt builds up on the bed of the beavers' lake and the family has to leave. The lake becomes a swamp where plants and grasses take root, and finally a green meadow – the kind on which many of North America's early settlers built their homes.

Artificial lake *A beaver trims a sapling (above) to be added to its dam (right). The animals continually repair and enlarge their dam until, where a small stream once ran through the forest, there is a large lake.*

Getting the best grass by careful grazing

The short grasses of salt marshes and offshore islands are ideal winter feeding grounds for short-billed birds such as barnacle geese. Long grass is difficult for them to eat, as well as being less nutritious and less palatable.

Every November, more than 3000 barnacle geese arrive on the Dutch island of Schiermonnikoog, and spend a couple of months there foraging on farmland. In late February they all move to a nearby salt marsh, where they spend the next seven weeks grazing on red fescue grass. Although the marsh,

which covers just under 3 sq miles (7.5 km²), is generously carpeted with red fescue, the geese carefully choose sites with the best quality grass, grazing heavily before transferring to another site. After a few days the geese return to the original site, where the grass has grown again and is long enough for them to crop it once more.

Why do the geese return to areas they have already grazed instead of spreading right across the marsh? The answer is that barnacle geese, like other birds that nest in the Arctic, need to build up their reserves of protein before they fly north. Normally, they arrive at their breeding grounds before the northern grasses have

Dutch treat *Barnacle geese arrive in the Netherlands in autumn, having flown from their breeding grounds in northern Russia. Here they feed on grass planted on newly reclaimed land.*

germinated. This means they will have to depend on their own protein reserves to survive the first few weeks – the time when they will be hatching and incubating their eggs. By grazing their chosen sites in strict rotation and regularly cropping the same grass, the geese are ensuring a constant supply of new and fine-leaved, fast-growing grass. Young grass leaves are richer in protein than older ones, so the geese are providing themselves with the maximum possible amount of protein.

HARNESSING NATURE'S PREDATORS

Introducing one animal to control another is a natural but not always acceptable solution to pest problems. It can be a two-edged sword.

When a useful guest becomes a resident pest

Estate owners in the West Indies battled with the problem of rat control throughout the 18th and 19th centuries. The alien black rat, which probably disembarked from a visiting merchant ship in the 17th century, had become a serious pest, devouring vast quantities of the sugar-cane crop annually. The settlers introduced a variety of predators – such as domestic cats – in the vain hope of reducing the rat population.

Then, in 1872, nine Indian mongooses were released on an estate in Jamaica and within months the newcomers had made noticeable inroads on the resident rat community. Other sugar-cane planters, including some on Pacific islands, impressed by this success, followed suit. By the turn of the century there were thriving populations of mongooses on most of the West Indian and Hawaiian islands and farmers were enjoying virtually damage-free harvests. With almost no natural predators to limit their numbers, and a plentiful supply of

food, mongoose populations began to increase rapidly.

However, their insatiable and indiscriminate appetites, as well as their expertise at raiding the nests of ground-dwelling animals, led to the mongoose itself becoming a pest. Indigenous birds and reptiles, with little or no skill in defending themselves or their young against the intruder's persistent attacks, were killed in great numbers.

The destruction was relentless. On certain islands entire species were wiped out: the dark-rumped petrel and Newell's shearwater on the Hawaiian island of Molokai; the burrowing owl of Antigua; the mountain dove on St Vincent; iguanas on Jamaica and neighbouring Goat Island; and eight different species of land-dwelling lizard on islands in the West Indies chain. The mongoose itself seems able to resist any sort of control, despite attempts by islanders using hunting dogs and poison.

Stop thief! *The small Indian mongoose is an agile and enthusiastic raider of birds' nests but is equally willing to take on more dangerous prey such as snakes, scorpions and wasps.*

Mosquito control *Disease-spreading mosquito larvae, with their breathing tubes at the water's surface, are about to be eaten up by voracious mosquito fish. This species, native to the southeast USA, is one of the world's most widespread freshwater fish.*

Fish with a taste for mosquito larvae

In the muddy rivers of tropical America live shoals of aggressive mosquito fish. These predators are only 2 in (50 mm) long, but will attack other fish many times their own size. They also devour huge quantities of aquatic insect larvae, such as mosquitoes. When naturalists discovered the fish's voracious appetite for insects, its frequent breeding and its ability to survive in water temperatures ranging from a few degrees above freezing to almost 38°C (100°F), they saw its potential as a mosquito control.

Introduced into many mosquito infested areas, the fish devoured large quantities of mosquito larvae, greatly reducing the risk to local

people of contracting malaria or yellow fever. By these means of control, the fish played their part in the successful completion of the Panama Canal and the settlement of the surrounding lands.

There are times, however, when mosquito fish are not effective in controlling mosquitoes. If the water has a surface layer of tangled vegetation, the fish cannot get at the surface-dwelling mosquito larvae. Or if the water is teeming with other small aquatic creatures, they can be tempted away from gorging on mosquitoes.

There is always a risk in introducing any carnivorous creature to a new area. When mosquito fish were let loose in Australian rivers as a precaution against malaria, several native fish were edged out by the fast-breeding newcomers.

Cactus killer *The larvae of the cactus moth (above) feed on the prickly pear cactus (right). Earlier this century, the moths were used to control prickly pear forests that overran Australian pastures.*

Moths blast Australian cactus plague

Deliberately introducing a new species into a country where it has no natural predators can have dire consequences for the local people and wildlife; the numbers of the new species are likely to swell beyond control. Australian farmers have had to cope with problems such as these on several occasions, usually resolving them by bringing in predators from elsewhere.

The prickly pear cactus, native to the Americas, was introduced to Australia in the 19th century, and grown as an ornamental plant and as a natural fence for livestock. In the absence of its normal predator, the cactus moth, it flourished and by the 1920s had smothered great tracts of grazing land.

The remedy involved importing cactus moths from Argentina and establishing a colony in Australia. The moths were released into the cactus fields in 1925, and as moth larvae burrowed into the succulent cactuses, the plants wilted and died. By 1929, the major infestations were under control and some 60 million acres (24 million ha) of grazing land had been reclaimed.

Australia found another natural solution for the problem caused by the importation of cattle for large-scale farming. Cow dung began to accumulate in large amounts since local insect scavengers were not able to process it – they were used to the smaller pellets of kangaroos. Pasture grasses died under the cow-dung carpet. This encouraged the growth of weeds that cattle did not eat, and which became breeding grounds for biting flies and midges. African dung beetles were introduced in 1968 to break down the dung, and the natural balance of grasses was gradually restored.

Dangerous task *Imported into Australia to dispose of cow dung, the African dung beetle is at risk from cane toads, which are also an introduced species. The toads assemble nightly round fresh pats to wait for beetles. Each toad can eat 80 beetles a night.*

SHARING MAN'S HOME

Human homes are a source of food and warmth, so some animals have forsaken the wild and moved in – welcome or not.

Kitchen scavenger *The food on a kitchen knife makes a good meal for a cockroach mother-to-be. These insects are attracted into houses by warmth and food. Immunity to pesticides, armour-plated bodies and quick reactions make them almost impossible to get rid of.*

High-speed scuttlers with lightning reactions

Armed with a tough, shiny shell and mouthparts well adapted for chewing, the cockroach is one of Nature's most efficient waste disposers. Cockroaches have been munching their way through living or dead organic matter, with little change in their design, for more than 300 million years. Like the house mouse, they did not take long to discover that wherever people set up home there is a steady supply of discarded food.

Making good use of its flattened body to crawl under floorboards or between narrow cracks, the cockroach has taken up residence in human dwellings and has journeyed around the globe with mankind. Where people live there is food and artificial warmth in plenty, providing ideal conditions for a cockroach colony to thrive. The cockroach has other advantages that contribute to its success as a house dweller: it will eat almost anything, including papers and bookbindings; lightning reactions make it almost impossible to catch. The insect is long-lived and breeds prolifically – a female American cockroach can live for up to four years and lay more than 1000 eggs in her lifetime.

Although cockroaches do not have sharp eyesight, their acute sensitivity to changes in light and to sound waves, which they detect by means of sensory hairs on a pair of protruding organs at the tail, causes them to scuttle out of sight at high speed. They are equally alert to the slightest ground vibration. Cockroaches can detect a movement that is only a fraction of a hair's-breadth – less than one millionth of a millimetre.

Lizards that hunt in the house

A gecko, a small lizard, clings to the sun-baked walls of a house on the Canary Islands. This is a common sight in many warm countries, even though the gecko may be one of a species that originated in another part of the world. The common gecko of the Canary Islands comes from North Africa's rocky scrubland, and a species that occurs in South America was first found on the Red Sea and Mediterranean coasts.

What drew the first house geckos to change their peaceful natural surroundings for the hustle and bustle of human dwellings? Undoubtedly it was the countless small insects – caterpillars, ants, flies, bugs, beetles and mosquitoes – already resident in or near these buildings. Artificial stone is a perfectly acceptable resting place or hunting ground when there is a plentiful supply of food. Tiny cells shaped like hooks upon the toe pads of some geckos will seize on any slight irregularity on a wall or ceiling, enabling the animal to stare down from a vantage point, scanning

Earning its keep *The feet of a house gecko can cling to the smoothest surface, so the sheer walls of human homes present no problems to the little lizard as it hunts for insects. It can even hunt upside-down on the ceiling.*

the surroundings for prey. Once it spots an insect it will race along the ceiling or windowpane to snatch it. At night, house geckos often stay close to an electric light bulb to take advantage of the constant stream of night-flying insects drawn to and subsequently confused by the radiating beams of the artificial light.

House geckos are usually welcomed by humans. Even the large and noisy Asian tokay, which keeps in touch with other gecko members of its species by means of a loud, dog-like bark, is tolerated in homes because it is such an efficient alternative to insecticides.

Stowaway mice travel the world with men

When people first started to sow and reap cereals in the fertile plains of the Middle East about 10 000 years ago, wild mice quickly seized on this new and plentiful food source and moved into the farmers' fields and grain stores. As human communities expanded, mice took up residence in their dwellings, sharing their food and benefiting from the shelter of their walls and roofs.

So the wild mouse became the familiar house mouse, following humans wherever they set up home and adapting to various new surroundings, from polar climes to coalmine shafts. Hidden in packing cases, personal belongings or food stores, the mice were transported across Europe and from there on trading ships to the rest of the world. The house mouse is a fast and prolific breeder and where the climate is mild and food plentiful, it can rapidly reach plague proportions: in the USA during 1941-2, biologists recorded some 82 000 house mice per acre (0.4 ha).

Over the years, some groups of modern house mice have developed special characteristics that help them to survive in their new environments. Long-term residents of refrigerated cold stores, for example, have grown much thicker fur to protect themselves against the permanently freezing temperatures of their homes.

Caught in the act *A house mouse peers from a sack of grain. For centuries these creatures have been munching through human food stores, from larder to barn.*

Millions of mites are sharing your bed

Inside any average mattress there is a thriving community of microscopic, crawling dust mites. Each one is about the size of a full stop on this page.

These eight-legged lodgers eat, rest, excrete, mate and reproduce beneath our sheets. All that they need to live out their lives is a regular supply of human skin cells and excretions such as sweat. Feasting on the particles of dead skin our bodies shed as we shift and turn in our sleep, the dust mites below us can complete their whole life cycle beneath a single mattress stud.

For most of us, sleeping on an unseen colony of dust mites – they average about 2 million in a double bed – is not a problem. But for people who are allergic to dust, the presence of mites can trigger off asthma attacks. The mites' copious droppings, combined with a constantly replenished pile of mite bodies and discarded skins, creates a layer of debris which is disturbed whenever sheets are changed or the bed is made. It is this snowstorm of mite dust that induces asthma attacks.

Invisible bedfellows *Powerful electron microscopes have made it possible to photograph tiny dust mites. This false-colour picture shows a mite, magnified 500 times, foraging among skin scales, cat fur and fibres in a vacuum cleaner. Dust mites are found almost everywhere in houses, but they are most at home in mattresses and damp places.*

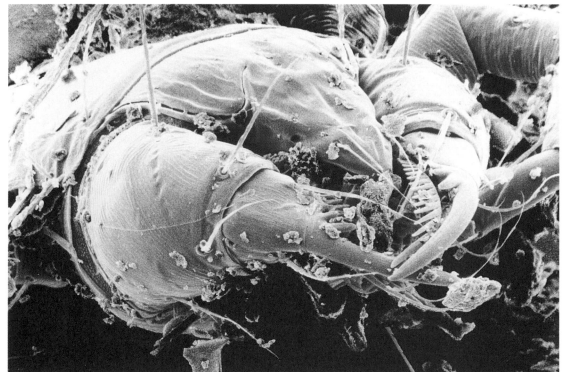

NATURE COMES TO THE RESCUE

Scientists involved with cleaning up oil pollution are testing natural remedies such as oil-eating bacteria and absorbent milkweed.

Bacteria that make a meal out of crude oil

Among the challenges that face conservationists is to find a way of dealing with oil spills that can be applied in all weathers and that is not harmful to the environment. Of the many techniques available now for cleaning up oil spillages, dispersants such as detergent are among the most effective. Marine

Black seas *The* Braer *oil spill off the Shetland Islands in 1993 (above) and the 1989* Exxon Valdez *disaster in Alaska (right), together released more than 170 000 tons of crude oil into the sea.*

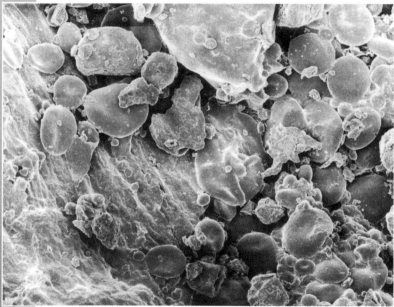

Greasy food *Round and oblong oil-eating microbes (above) cling to dried rice bran in a magnified photograph. Scientists are now experimenting with bacteria that consume oil. In this process, known as bioremediation, mixtures of these bacteria and nutrients for them to feed on are sprayed onto oil slicks. The microbes convert hydrocarbons in the oil into carbon dioxide which is then absorbed by the sea.*

Oil and water *An oil slick (left), viewed from space, moves in a swirl from the Arabian Sea towards the Gulf of Oman. An oil spill can spread 200 miles (320 km) from its source and contaminate the food chain for as long as ten years. To solve the problem of oil pollution, scientists are investigating natural materials such as absorbent milkweed and cotton rather than using harmful dispersants.*

biologists, however, say that these can be more toxic to marine life than the oil itself. Mechanical skimmers are less harmful to the environment, but they can be used only in favourable weather.

A much better method involves using one of the world's oldest pollution controllers – oil-eating marine bacteria. This system is known as bioremediation and is showing impressive results. Oil-consuming bacteria and nutrients to nourish them are mixed with inorganic clay and sprayed on the surface of the oil from boats or low-flying aircraft.

The clay breaks up the oil into solid 'cakes', allowing the bacteria to breathe and helping to keep them in contact with the oil and nutrients. The bacteria dispose of the oil by turning hydrocarbons, organic substances of which it is made, into the gas carbon dioxide, which dissolves in sea water.

An all-weather solution

The bioremediation system offers many advantages over the existing alternatives as it works on all types of oil and can be used in all kinds of weather and sea conditions.

Furthermore, bioremediation is welcomed by marine biologists because it does not cause any harm to animals and plants living in the water. It is of particular value in sensitive areas where the movements of large clean-up crews would cause considerable damage to the habitat, such as in marshes or sand dunes along the coast.

The mopping-up properties of American milkweed are also being studied by scientists. The soft, pale fibres that surround a milkweed plant's seeds are more absorbent than the man-made fibres that are currently used to soak up crude oil. Not only can floating milkweed fibres support more than 30 times their own weight but, because they are so waxy, they repel water and attract oil. They are biodegradable, and can also be squeezed out and used again. In all, they appear to be more beneficial to the environment than man-made fibres.

Cotton is also being tested as a material for absorbing oil, although up to now tests have shown it to be less effective than milkweed.

HOW ANIMALS BENEFIT MAN

Contact with animals, both wild and tame, has long been beneficial to man. But his response is often far from generous.

Birds help to monitor the health of rivers

A sturdy, white-bibbed bird about the size of a thrush, the dipper provides scientists with an accurate indication of the general health of the rivers and streams of Eurasia and North America.

Dippers patrol the beds of shallow, fast-flowing streams in search of insect larvae, fish fry, freshwater shrimps and molluscs such as water snails. They walk along the bottom, sometimes completely submerged, and manage to stay under water by holding their wings at an angle and clinging to pebbles with their toes. The nature of their diet makes dippers very sensitive to pollutants in the water.

As chimneys on factories and power stations grow ever higher, sulphur dioxide, nitrogen oxides and other emissions are wafted across greater areas and remain in the atmosphere for longer. They return to earth as part of acid rain, polluting trees and hillsides, and are eventually washed into waterways. Here, algae are the first to be affected, then the creatures that feed on them. If the water is polluted, it will eventually kill all the resident animal life, including the large fish. The dipper population, an integral part of this food chain, decreases, then disappears.

Scotland receives high levels of acid rain, and its underlying rocks, hard and lime free, do not buffer lakes and rivers against the acidity. A study conducted there found that pairs of dippers breeding along polluted streams produced fewer and lighter eggs, and these later in the breeding season. They fed their chicks less often than usual and, as a result, the chicks had a slimmer chance of surviving.

In normal circumstances, dippers can lay two clutches of eggs a year but these parents only managed one. Moreover, it was discovered that the dipper's breeding success has a precise cut-off point – it breeds best if the water is clean and the level of acidity measures 6.5 or above (pure water has a level of 7). But it does not breed successfully if the water is so acidic that the level is below 6.5.

Fish supper *A dipper emerges from a successful walk along a shallow riverbed in search of food. These birds have also been filmed using their wings to swim under water, with their feet tucked up under them for better streamlining.*

Dolphins are partners in the fish catch

Brazilian fishermen stand in the shallow, murky Atlantic waters off Laguna, a coastal town that lies south of Rio de Janeiro, watching the bottle-nosed dolphins that are their fishing partners. Because of the muddiness of the water, the fishermen are unable to see the red mullet they hope to catch with their circular throw-nets, so they rely on the one or two dolphins swimming a little distance out.

At last one of the dolphins submerges, a signal to the fishermen that it has located a shoal and is about to start herding the fish towards them. Nets at the ready, they wait for the dolphin to surface and swim shorewards until, suddenly, it stops and, with a rolling dive, disappears. This is the signal for the fishermen to cast their nets. While they haul in their catch of mullet, the dolphin eats some of those that have escaped the nets. It seems this is the only reward the dolphin seeks. The fishermen, in turn, benefit too – they get regular catches with a minimum length of time spent in the water.

Gratitude not guaranteed

The Laguna dolphins are known worldwide for being able and willing to herd fish towards fishermen waiting on shore or in boats with spears or nets. This habit appears to have been passed down through generations of dolphins, for town records confirm that local fishermen have enjoyed this association with dolphins since the mid 19th century. But not all the dolphins in the area appear to understand the technique – researchers estimate that there is a hard core of 25-30 'specialists' out of a resident population of some 200. But those that do aid fishermen are remarkably hard-working, hunting and herding for an hour or so before giving way to another dolphin.

Cooperation between dolphins and fishermen has been chronicled for centuries – ancient Greek and Roman poets told of torchlit fishing expeditions aided by dolphins. The dolphins seem to have enjoyed the work and been well rewarded.

However, modern commercial tuna fishing in the Pacific Ocean from California to Chile, poses a threat to spinner and bridled dolphins. Traditionally, they associate with yellowfin tuna, who swim in large schools beneath the dolphins. The tuna benefit from the dolphins' ability to find prey by echolocation, and the dolphins monitor any panic moves that the tuna make at the approach of sharks.

When the dolphins come to the surface to breathe, they give away the tuna's position to fishing boats. Both dolphins and tuna are netted, and although attempts are made to free the trapped dolphins, many of them die by drowning. In spite of recent improvements to the nets, many dolphins are still being lost.

The healing power of pets and wild animals

Captive dolphins in Florida play and communicate with autistic and handicapped children, who emerge from the water calmer and happier than before their swim. Wild dolphins, too, are playing a healing role for many people all over the world. At certain places along the coasts of Britain and Ireland, wild dolphins have taken up residence in the shallows and will regularly swim and play with humans, leaping over boats and nudging swimmers.

Dolphins are also reported to have helped to heal people suffering from deep depression. Many dolphin researchers are convinced that dolphins have a special therapeutic influence on the human mind and spirit. Contact with dolphins has produced a powerful emotional effect in some mentally ill patients, who claim that swimming with dolphins has had a far more uplifting effect on them than anti-depressant drugs.

Pets are also being used to help emotionally shocked patients, particularly children, who are difficult to reach during psychotherapy. The calming effect of stroking a pet or talking to it in affectionate tones seems to lower blood pressure and reduce stress levels in most pet owners. Even the sight of a bowl full of fish can be soothing. Patients awaiting surgery at a dental school with an aquarium were observed to be more relaxed before their operations than those in a control group who had no fish to watch while they waited.

Scientists are not sure exactly how the body is affected, but think that the feeling of unconditional love and acceptance that people experience from being with their pets, or animals such as dolphins, triggers the production of interferon – a protein that boosts the immune system. It is also a fact that being intensely happy stimulates the body to produce natural painkilling substances known as endorphins, which affect the whole body. A study of people who had suffered severe coronary heart disease showed that, one year after their release from hospital, those who owned pets achieved a much better survival rate than those who had had no animal companionship.

Pet therapy is being used more and more to draw out or reach people who are mentally disturbed. Certain prisons in the United States have active pet-therapy programmes in which violent and unstable prisoners are brought into regular contact with various pets. The animals provide prisoners with non-threatening relationships that allow them to express their affection and stimulate their potential for caring without fear of rejection.

Looking after a creature that is weaker than themselves, and that trusts and is dependent on them, provides the prisoners with a purpose in life. In many cases it also builds up their self esteem, which is something that other therapies have failed to do. Scottish prisons in which pet therapy has been introduced report fewer disturbances and improved relationships between prisoners and staff.

Young and old *The way in which animals can help humans is graphically shown by the autistic American boy (below) who, by holding onto a dolphin, gains the confidence to relax and exercise in the water. The elderly, like the Welsh centenarian (right) with his terrier, Tim, also benefit therapeutically.*

LONG-STANDING PARTNERSHIPS

Man domesticated animals by making shrewd use of their natural instincts. But the bargains struck were not entirely one-sided.

The wolf cub that came in from the cold

Looking at some of today's more specialised breeds of dog, it is difficult to imagine any common ancestry. Yet all 400 or so officially recognised breeds, from the Great Dane to the chihuahua, are indirectly descended from the wolf. The wolf's partnership with man began in prehistoric times, probably with an orphaned cub taken in as a plaything. When the cub, genetically primed to belong to a pack, readily bonded with its new foster parents, it was transferring its dependence on the pack leader to its new human owner. This dependence, an integral part of the wolf's social structure, is the key to the dog's domestication.

Initially, dogs accompanied men on their hunting expeditions, using their wolf-pack skills to harry and corner the quarry until their masters arrived. Their reward was a share when the hunters divided up the carcass. Human pack leaders began to favour certain characteristics – cubs that were particularly intelligent, brave or attractive. By 2000 BC the Egyptians were breeding three distinct types of dog – a guard dog, a hunting dog and a decorative, friendly one.

The Romans concentrated on fighting dogs for the circus and mastiffs from Britain were sought after. Medieval barons delighted in new hound strains and, as time went by, dog breeds became ever more specialised. A bulldog's flattened nose meant it could breathe while still retaining its grip on a baited bull, and the West Highland terrier's white coat distinguished it from fox or otter against a dark or heathery background.

Among later breeds is the one developed by Louis Dobermann, a German night watchman and dog pound keeper who, in the 1890s, wanted a guard dog to protect him on his rounds. Drawing upon his charges, which included a Great Dane, an English greyhound and a Rottweiler, he came up with a new breed, the Doberman pinscher, or terrier, that swiftly became famous for its courage and intelligence.

One man and his dog *A 17th-century woodcut depicts a hunter and his dog setting out for a day's sport – a scene enacted ever since man and canine first met. As always on such occasions, the dog's stance is a mingling of submission to its leader and eager expectation.*

Mutual dependence ensures desert survival

One-humped dromedary camels were first put to work in southern Arabia about 5000 years ago. Soon after, they were being used in Palestine and Syria, and in the 7th century AD they bore the Moslem conquerors into Egypt. It was the dromedary that made human existence in the desert viable. Laden, it can trek for days on end on its broad, splayed feet, living on the water stored in its stomach and the fat in its hump. It also has an uncanny ability to scent water and a powerful homing instinct. All these traits combine to make the dromedary the perfect desert survival machine.

Nomads and merchants long ago learned how to turn a herd of camels into an orderly caravan. In the wild, the breeding male controls the females by herding them from behind. So in a caravan, the

dominant male is placed at the rear and his intermittent calls keep the group well disciplined.

Men and dromedaries are mutually dependent. Camels can find water but rely on people to draw it from the wells. Drovers feed them when plants are scarce, and supply the salt essential to their health. It is said that it was salt fish that first lured camels into domesticity. Only domesticated and feral dromedaries now remain – wild ones may have been hunted to extinction.

Travelling folk *Afghan nomads pursue their endless journey, driving their flocks from one grazing ground to the next. Camels are vital to their way of life, an economical, tireless form of transport, whose young are also a source of wealth. In a treeless land, even the camels' dung is valued and collected for fuel.*

Man and guinea pig in domestic experiment

The first Europeans to enter the Inca houses of South America must surely have been intrigued to see scores of shaggy brown, white and piebald rodents running about the occupants' feet or huddling close to the cooking fire. Not only were these cavies, or guinea pigs, tolerated, they were positively encouraged, both as pets and as an important food source.

Cavies are still sharing Peruvian houses and though they are eventually killed for the table, they are respected for their reputation as weather prophets. They are also credited with the ability to deflect thunderstorms with their calls. They are members of the *Caviidae* family, that have colonised grasslands, deserts and rocky outcrops throughout South America. But the cavy is the only species that has elected to move in with people.

Presumably, like the house mouse, it was originally drawn by the free food to be found in early farmers' grain stores. Then, when the settlers discovered that these appealing rodents both tasted good and bred prolifically, they were encouraged to remain.

Cupboard love *Though treated with affection, cavies in Peruvian kitchens can rarely postpone for more than a year their turn in the family cooking pot.*

Arranging where sheep may safely graze

One of man's earliest encounters with sheep was probably in the Middle East, when the first farmers drove hungry mouflon (wild sheep) off their carefully nurtured crops. Eventually, though, some genius considered the possibility of a regular supply of meat, and so some 10 000 years ago the first shepherds set up in business.

Their charges took readily to domestication. Shepherds found them good grazing and protected them from predators. And though it was alien to sheep nature to be confined to a particular area, they soon adapted to being herded as their natural instinct was to follow a single, dominant leader.

In some parts of Europe, it was even the custom for shepherds to train a castrated ram to lead the rest of the flock. The early flocks were chosen for their docility and managed for their meat and skins. Later it was for their milk and wool that they were valued. Gradually, however, sheep began to be bred mostly for the quality of their wool. In certain parts of the world, flocks of sheep were bred to produce fine wool which became the basis of the medieval wool industry.

In the wild, when a herd of sheep is threatened or attacked, their natural reaction is to scatter – a device that gives each individual a chance of survival. This instinct has been bred out of many of today's herds, but on the Orkney island of North Ronaldsay the sheep, though domesticated, still retain the defensive tactics of their ancestors. Sheepdogs have to be trained to hunt rather than to herd in order to pull in the strays.

Follow my leader *Nose to tail, a flock of sheep takes the ancient drovers' route from Italy into Austria – over glaciers and shunning frontiers. The shepherds' task is made easy by their charges' instinct to follow a dominant leader.*

PESTS HAVE FEW PROBLEMS

Parasites or no, some of the creatures that we call pests are among the best adapted and least destructible on the planet.

Tiny bloodsucker brings death and disease

Whatever our reservations about them, it cannot be denied that fleas are superbly designed. Their tough bodies have flattened sides that are well suited to tunnelling through a host's hairs to reach the skin and blood that lies beneath.

Comb-like bristles and claws give them a good grip, and a network of fine sensory organs at the back of the abdomen enables them to detect the slightest change in body heat or smell. Fleas are powered by extra-large coxae (upper segments of the leg) and leap with astounding acceleration from rest to the body of a passing host, or from host to host. The human flea can clear 120 times its own height, spinning through the air to land, hooked claws at the ready, on flesh.

It is their method of feeding that makes fleas a serious hazard for, like the mosquito, they pierce the skin and inject their anticoagulant saliva into the blood to keep it flowing. In this way they pass on microorganisms from one creature to another and so spread disease. When human beings are forced to live in cramped and unhygienic conditions the effects may be devastating. By transmitting bubonic plague from rats to humans, the oriental rat flea was responsible for many epidemics, of which the most devastating was the Black Death during the 14th century that wiped out more than a quarter of the population of Europe.

The human flea, which lays its eggs in carpets and furnishings, can, in larval form, survive for years without food. It simply waits until a new host arrives, then rapidly completes the final stage of its development into adulthood and emerges to feast upon the blood of the newcomer.

The levellers
Disease carrying fleas, like the male above and female below, altered the destinies of nations.

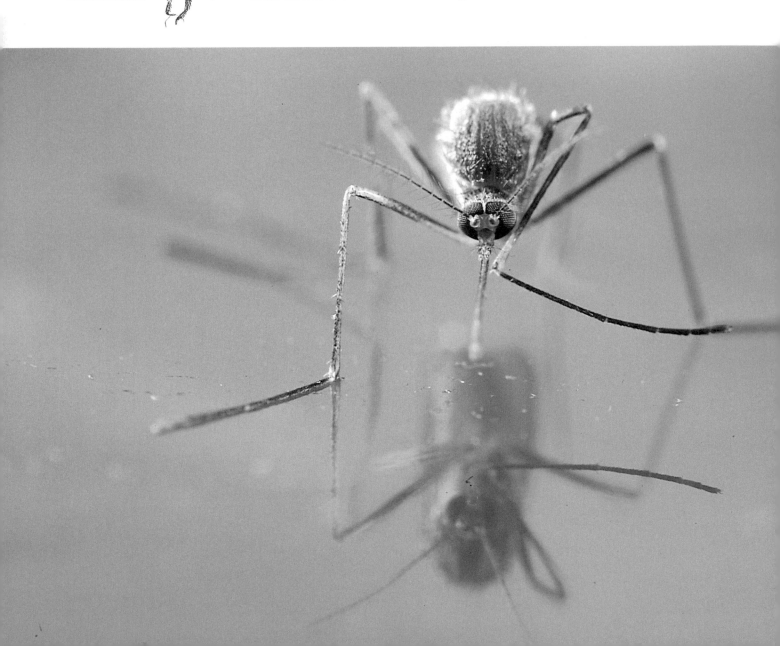

Red-billed scourge of the African plains

The red-billed quelea is a weaver bird that forages for wild grass seeds in the tree-scattered plains of central and southern Africa. A sociable feeder, it hops along the ground in company with birds of its own species, gleaning fallen seeds.

This natural food accounts for at least 80 per cent of the bird's intake, and yet the quelea, which weighs a mere ¾ oz (20 g), is the worst bird pest in the world. It is

World record *The red-billed queleas of Africa have become one of the world's worst bird pests. It is estimated that there are about 1500 million of them.*

super-abundant – recent estimates put the total number of quelea at 1500 million, undoubtedly making it the most numerous bird in the world. It is also highly gregarious, feeding, breeding and roosting in 100 000-strong flocks.

This does not matter until the birds move into the farmlands in the valleys at the start of the rainy season, when the few remaining wild seeds germinate and the crops

begin to ripen. With each quelea consuming an average ⅛ oz (3 g) of seeds each day, a huge flock of quelea descending on a field of millet or wheat is a terrifying sight for a subsistence farmer, who may lose his entire crop.

Although aerial poisoning has been used against these birds, it is difficult to control their numbers because they breed mainly in the remote parts of the plains.

An ornamental vine grows out of control

The kudzu vine, with its lush green leaves and reddish purple flowers, originated in the Far East. Imported into Philadelphia, USA, as an ornamental climber in 1876, it was soon being recommended as a natural antidote to soil erosion.

The kudzu took off, sprawling across the countryside, growing up to 75 ft (23 m) in a season. Now out of control in many parts of the US southeast, it is checked from spreading farther north by cold winters. Goats may be the answer, according to recent research – four of them can kill 1 acre (0.4 ha) of kudzu in about two years.

Cover plan *A mat of kudzu vines begins to blanket an old house in North Carolina. The plant overwhelms trees, telephone wires and all else in its path.*

Deadly embrace of the female mosquito

The seven-sectioned proboscis of the female mosquito is responsible for the spread of two of the world's greatest scourges – malaria and yellow fever. Having located a human being by following the exhaled carbon dioxide, the insect lands unnoticed on a patch of skin.

Selecting a soft spot, it pushes in the tip of its proboscis. This works like a two-way hypodermic syringe, one tube pumping in anti-coagulant saliva while a second

Killer line *This newly hatched* Anopheles *mosquito is a carrier of malaria. Its ancestors spread the disease, which closed Africa to explorers for centuries and played a part in the fall of Rome.*

one sucks up the freely flowing blood. Infection occurs when the mosquito is carrying either malaria parasites or the microorganisms of yellow fever.

The two diseases are transmitted by different types of mosquito. There are more than 200 species of *Anopheles* mosquitoes that can harbour and pass on malaria but only *Aedes* species carry yellow fever. It was the *Aedes* species that was responsible for the epidemics that killed thousands of people in tropical Africa and South America before the infector was identified.

With both diseases, however, it is the female who is the cause – she needs blood before she can reproduce. The male's mouthparts are too weak to make the jab, and he feeds solely on plant juices. Mosquito eggs develop only in

water. Even the eggs of species that live in dry areas stay dormant until rain eventually falls, then speedily complete their life cycles before drought returns. Once this need for water in the mosquito's larval and pupal stages was discovered, efforts were made to control the malaria-carrying mosquitoes either by draining large stretches of water or by pouring oil on them to suffocate the larvae.

Yellow-fever mosquitoes are far more difficult to deal with as they breed in tiny areas of water such as roof gutters, rainwater tanks or even water-filled coconut shells. They are harder to detect indoors, too – they fly silently and lurk behind curtains and furnishings. A vaccine against yellow fever has been developed, but the disease is still far from eradicated.

MAN THE DESTROYER

Animals pay a high price for sharing the planet with man. Some die to feed him, some for sport; more are brushed aside to extinction.

Endangered passengers in an emptying ark

That very symbol of extinction, the last dodo, went to its rest, or rather into the cooking pot, on the island of Mauritius in 1681. It was, however, not the 17th century but the 19th and 20th centuries that witnessed the worst examples of man's inhumanity to beast. In 1900 the North American bison was on the brink of annihilation, having numbered 30-40 million just a few decades earlier. There were several reasons for the slaughter, one of which was to deprive the Plains Indians of their livelihood.

Big-game hunting became one of the favourite sports of the rich during the 19th century, and the demands of fashion helped to put other species – rhinos, crocodiles elephants and tigers – at risk.

High-tech slaughter

Creatures of the deep were no safer. Whalers discarded the old hand-held harpoons for an explosive version fired from a cannon. Their high-tech methods were so successful that by the late 1960s only about 1000 blue whales, Earth's largest mammals, survived. Man's success has been at the expense of many other species, indirectly by changing or destroying habitats, and directly with gun and trap. Early peoples, like later tribesmen, were hunters, dependent on animals for both food and

clothing. But because they were few in number and their weapons unsophisticated, the slaughter was limited. Many hunted species were able to maintain their numbers.

Most primitive hunters regarded themselves at one with the creatures around them. Not until they became farmers were other species seen as rivals. Farmers needed grazing for cattle, protection from carnivores for flocks, and land for growing food. As humans increased in number and their tools became more efficient, wild animals were left with fewer and fewer habitats.

Large animals are especially vulnerable. Because of their size they are easy targets, and their slow reproduction rate means that the recovery of populations is precarious. The hunting of some threatened species is forbidden, and protective measures are taken, but they have come too late for such animals as the Great Plains wolf, the Balinese tiger, the Caribbean monk seal and Steller's sea cow.

Silent reproach *Chiefly known for being dead, the flightless dodo of Mauritius is an early example of species extinction by man. The last was eaten by sailors in 1681.*

The sad parable of the frogs of Calcutta

Over-exploitation of a species can have dire effects that reach even beyond the creature's extinction. Consider, for example, the warning implied in the harvesting of frogs from the marshes about Calcutta, India. In attempting to

satisfy a large demand for frogs' legs from European markets, some Indian entrepreneurs encouraged local farmers to catch as many of the amphibians as they could.

By the late 1980s, the area had become completely frogless. In the absence of their natural predators, mosquitoes flourished, as did small crabs that feast on rice plants. The pesticides needed to control these population explosions cost farmers far more than the profits gained from the sale of frogs.

A dainty dish *A cartoonist's version of a European delicacy that led to the demise of Indian frogs.*

The destruction of Florida's grassy waters

It was a widely held view in mid 19th-century America that the wilderness was waste and waste was immoral. Hence the Swamp Land Acts, which encouraged the nation's citizens to drain marshlands for agriculture. That the Acts were also a death warrant for a large number of unique wetland creatures was not a consideration that aroused much sympathy in that period, nor for some time to come. Wetlands continued to be drained well into the 20th century, and nowhere were the effects more dramatic and far-reaching than in the Everglades, the 'grassy water' marshlands of Florida.

Originally they covered most of southeast Florida – a vast, watery wilderness resting on a spongy bed of limestone, its waving, insect-rich saw grasses punctuated by tree-clad islands and inhabited by alligators, wading birds and snapping turtles. Agriculture ordered the first invasion, creating a huge network of canals, dams and locks to obliterate the swamp and replace it with citrus trees. Then roads were built, towns were developed,

They tried to adjust *This was the epitaph passed upon wood storks (right) in the Everglades of Florida, where man-made changes in the water flow had disastrous effects on their nesting habits. Now only 500 birds remain in the swamplands of the Everglades (above).*

and hotels and holiday apartments built in their thousands all along the coast. In 1934 the nation woke up to its loss and declared the Everglades a national park. But by then Florida had lost 60 per cent of its original wetlands.

The problems of the remainder were not solved by the new status. Each resident of the urban corridor to the east uses fresh water at a rate of 200 gallons (910 litres) a day and during any drought period the water requirements of the fruit and sugar plantations take priority over those of the park.

In addition, the chemical runoff from nearby farms encourages a strong invasive growth of cat-tail plants that shade out the oxygen-producing algae that form the base of the Everglades food chain. The ecosystem is fragile and this constant attack is having dire results. The number of nesting waders has fallen drastically – from 300 000 sixty years ago to about 15 000 today. The endangered wood stork

has not been able to adapt to the changes in water flow and there are now only some 500 birds left. Even more hopeless is the case of the dusky seaside sparrow. It is now believed to be extinct, its last

coastal marsh home having been drained to construct the NASA Space Center at Cape Canaveral.

Not only do wetlands provide rich breeding grounds for shellfish, freshwater gamefish and birds, but

they harbour many endangered plants and animals, too. They also absorb and filter pollutants that would otherwise enter the drinking water supplies. They deserve to be conserved before it is too late.

BACK FROM THE BRINK

Although many species have been destroyed by man's foolishness, others have been retrieved from the edge of extinction.

The fight to save the Hawaiian nene goose

Had it not been bred in captivity, Hawaii's wild goose, or nene (pronounced naynay), would most certainly have become extinct in its native islands. In 1949, when Hawaiian naturalists organised a recovery programme for this black, grey and buff goose, they could find only about 30 or so struggling to survive high up on the volcanic

Symbol of survival *The nene goose is the national symbol of Hawaii, but its mournful cry was almost silenced by the threat of extinction. Non-migratory and not good swimmers, these geese have adapted to life on volcanic slopes.*

slopes of some islands, yet during the 18th century there were some 25 000 throughout the islands.

Loss of habitat, and therefore food and breeding sites, seems to have been the main cause of the nenes' decline, and humans the chief culprits. Introduced plants such as gorse and brambles grew rampantly, smothering many of the native plants on which the nene thrived. The mongoose, an alien imported to deal with a plague of rats, raided their nests. Land was taken over for agriculture, tourist centres and ranching, and in addition, this unusually tame goose was hunted for the table.

Fortunately, there were nenes breeding successfully in Hawaiian and UK sanctuaries. The first captive birds were released in 1960, and since then more than 2000 captive-reared geese have been settled in Hawaii. But that is not where the nene's story concludes,

for although the goose has been reintroduced to its original home, the wild population numbers only about 500. Until this population becomes truly self-sustaining and no longer needs captive birds in order to maintain its numbers, the nene rescue operation can be considered only partially successful.

Knotty problems

The fate of the nene highlights the difficulties of releasing a creature reared in captivity into the wild. Experts are currently trying to establish the reasons for the nenes' poor survival and to remedy them, if possible. So far they have found that hand-reared birds are not as vigilant or skilled at avoiding predators as wild geese reared by their parents, and many have been killed because of this.

Many of the problems that caused the original decline still exist. Where vegetation is poor, female geese are forced to leave their broods while they search for nourishing food. Mongooses and feral cats and dogs destroy their eggs. The wild geese may also be suffering from diseases that originated in an infected captive flock.

Fish and fowl return to London's river

So polluted was the tidal stretch of London's River Thames – the 43 miles (69 km) from Gravesend to Teddington Lock – in 1957 when it was sampled by scientists, that not a single species of fish could live in it. Yet in earlier centuries the Thames had been a thriving fishing ground, from the estuary where salt-water fish abounded to the upper reaches where salmon spawned in the shallows.

As the city expanded, so did its rubbish, much of which was dumped into the river. But serious pollution started in the 1800s, when water closets became generally used. Before that, most of the city's sewage had been stored in cesspits and then spread on suburban market gardens.

Once it could be flushed away, untreated sewage accumulated in the river, encouraging the growth of bacteria that gradually depleted the water of the oxygen essential

Rare deer found by a French missionary

In 1865, when Père Armand David, a French missionary, discovered a herd of rare deer in the Chinese Emperor's hunting park, they were already extinct in the wild and had been so for probably several centuries. The priest had skins sent back to Europe for identification, and in 1898 the 11th Duke of Bedford bought a breeding pair for Woburn Abbey. This was fortunate, as the entire Chinese herd was eaten by hungry soldiers during the Boxer Rebellion in 1900.

Now there are more than 500 of the animals, known as Père David's deer, in zoos round the world. Their broad feet, fondness for water plants and ability to swim

indicate that they were once probably swamp-dwellers.

The stags have unusual antlers, with a forked front prong and a straight and slender rear prong, and two sets may be grown in one year. One pair is shed in November and the second pair, always smaller, is hard by January but drops within a few weeks.

Inspired intervention *Père David's deer (left) owe the survival of their species to the timely removal of breeding stock from China before the Boxer Rebellion (above), when all were killed.*

White hunter *Polar bears are agile hunters on land or in the waters of their icy homeland. But polar bears were themselves almost hunted to extinction.*

Arctic sanctuaries for polar bears

For generations of Inuit families, hunting polar bears among the Arctic wastes off Greenland and Canada meant tracking them with dogs and killing them with stone-headed spears. A few polar bears were killed for food and skins each year, but the population as a whole did not suffer.

But the 20th century brought wealthy, high-tech trophy hunters into the Arctic, bent on killing as many bears as they could. A hunting expedition might use two aeroplanes to locate a bear. Then one plane landed on the ice and left a marksman with a snowmobile and a powerful gun close to the bear, while the other plane drove the animal towards him. In this way hundreds of bears were killed each year, and their skinned carcasses were abandoned on the ice.

In 1965 Russian conservationists estimated that there were only about 10 000 polar bears left. An international forum accepted that more than 1400 were killed yearly but could not agree to a total ban on killing because the sport had become a lucrative business. Also, Norwegian seal hunters considered the bears troublesome predators.

Widespread refuge

Leading Arctic specialists continued to press for protection for polar bears, and in 1975 finally convinced the five nations in which the bears are found (USA, Canada, Greenland, Norway and Russia) to ban hunting, except by local people using their traditional methods. Sanctuaries where bears can roam, feed and give birth undisturbed were established in Canada, Greenland, Norway and Russia. As a result, not only have polar bears been rescued from extinction, but various other Arctic species, such as snow geese, foxes and caribou, have also benefited from these ice-bound havens.

A city's shame *A Punch cartoon of 1858 (left), captioned 'Father Thames introduces his offspring to the fair City of London', depicts his children as cholera, diphtheria and scrofula.*

industries. With this, fish began returning to the river, and by 1973 roach, bream, salmon and Dover sole were found among the 72 fish species counted. Once again eels could be caught in the heart of the city, and herons became a familiar sight at the power-station filters. Flocks of wild duck found green plants to feed on, and waders and cormorants once more patrolled at the water's edge.

Though the success of the river clean-up is undisputed, vigilant conservationists are still pressing for further improvements, such as banning the use of weedkillers, improving the quality of the water released from sewage treatment works so that the river is fit to bathe in, and controlling industrial discharges and the run-off from roads – both of which still deposit toxic chemicals in the river.

to plant and fish life. By the middle of the 19th century, the stench was so appalling that the House of Commons, situated beside the Thames, was hung with curtains soaked in disinfectant. Massive sewage works were built north and south of the city to try to contain the problem, but with the increase in housing and the proliferation of

gas and chemical works, which pumped effluents directly into the river, the pollution grew worse. Power stations that were churning heated water into the river further depleted its oxygen levels.

In the early 1960s there was a major conservation effort to modernise London's sewage treatment plants as well as to clean up its

NATURE'S MEDICINE CHEST

There are animals and plants both on land and in the seas that are a rich source of remedies, painkillers and health supplements.

Killer venoms can ease pain and save life

Snakes, scorpions, frogs, jellyfish and ants, which are the stingers poisoners and paralysers of the animal world, produce a range of venoms and secretions powerful enough to kill or immobilise their prey. Many of these poisons, scientists have now discovered, contain chemical compounds that can be used in medical treatments.

Pit viper venom, for example, is used in a number of drugs. The venom of the Brazilian pit viper, which induces the constriction of blood vessels and increases blood pressure, has been used to develop a drug for treating people with high blood pressure. Russell's viper of India and Southeast Asia has venom used for a drug that controls bleeding in haemophiliacs, and the vital ingredient of a drug for treating thrombosis comes from Malayan pit vipers. And from the venom of Africa's mambas, which

Kill or cure *One species of South American pit viper, the yellow beard (above), is responsible for about 600 human deaths a year. But pit viper venom is also used in medicinal drugs.*

include the deadly 14 ft (4.3 m) long black mamba, scientists have isolated proteins that can help in the treatment of brain diseases.

Painkillers from poisons

Natural substances that effectively block pain have been found in the skin secretions of frogs. The skin toxins from some of the brightly coloured arrow-poison frogs of Central America, for example, have been made into a painkiller said to be more effective than morphine.

Scientists have also investigated the toxins used by certain spiders to immobilise their prey for up to three weeks without impairing the victim's vital functions. These secretions may be useful for the production of new drugs that could sedate patients for long periods without ill effect, perhaps during lengthy operations.

Local remedies from the Australian rain forest

In the 1870s, Joseph and Thomas Bancroft of Brisbane, Australia, a father-and-son team of doctors, heard of a narcotic brew made by Aborigines. They decided to investigate the medicinal potential of this brew, made from water stored in the bark of a small tree of the eastern Australian rain forest.

Experiments with extracts from the tree, a *Duboisia* known locally as a corkwood, resulted in the production of a highly effective dilator for use in eye surgery. Other doctors used the brew to treat inflammations and fevers. Before long it was being exported to Europe.

But with the move towards synthetic medicines at the beginning of the 20th century, *Duboisia* and many other local remedies fell out of favour. Not until the Second World War, when synthetic drugs

Remedial tree *The leaves of the Duboisia (right) yield various substances that are used in medicines. Although discovered and first processed in Australia, Duboisia is now grown in India, Indonesia and Japan.*

were in exceedingly short supply, did Australian researchers begin to look once more to the rain forest as a source of natural medicines. Testing plants at random, the researchers discovered almost 500 alkaloids – potent poisons made by certain plants to protect themselves against animals that strip them of their leaves.

They found, too, that there are more poisonous plants growing in tropical rain forests than in temperate forests. This is because tropical forests have a far greater number of animals competing for food, so tropical plants need much better defences against animals.

Duboisia leaves were found to contain several alkaloids – one of

Healing and health food from the ocean

Wounds that are kept moist heal faster and better than those kept dry under traditional gauze bandages. Armed with this knowledge, scientists in the 1960s set out to find a substance that would provide this moist environment. They found it in brown seaweed growing off Scotland's west coast.

A chemical extracted from the brown seaweed, calcium alginate, is used in a fibrous dressing that is twice as absorbent as cotton gauze. When its fibres are placed on a wound, they absorb the discharges and form a flexible gel that creates a warm, moist environment.

Not only is the natural healing process encouraged by this non-woven bandage but when dressings have to be changed the gel can be washed off with a saline solution without disturbing the regenerating tissues. Seaweed bandages, patented by a UK company, are particularly successful on post-operative wounds or long-standing wounds such as burns and sores.

Green-lipped mussels, found in New Zealand's relatively pollution-free waters, contain a substance that reduces inflammation. This is being tested on people suffering from rheumatoid arthritis

Sea balm *Green-lipped mussels (left) from New Zealand contain an extract that reduces inflammation. Cod-liver oil (below) has long been known for its beneficial qualities.*

and osteoarthritis, and although it has not produced a cure it has, in many cases, decreased the pain and increased the mobility of those who suffer from these ailments.

Helping the heart

Rheumatoid arthritis, diabetes and hypertension are almost unknown to Inuits and Eskimos. Scientists think that this is possibly because of the amount of oily fish they eat.

Fish oils are two to five times more effective than vegetable oils at lowering the level of cholesterol in blood. High cholesterol levels are a major cause of heart disease, as deposits thicken artery walls and restrict blood flow. The intake of fish oils may make blood thinner and slower to clot. They are also thought to alleviate inflammatory conditions such as arthritis.

Fish-liver oils are high in vitamins A and D, essential for healthy eyes, skin, teeth and bones. The flesh of fish is high in B vitamins, especially niacin and B_6, which help the body make use of protein and are important in warding off disorders of the skin and nervous system.

which, hyoscine, is a highly effective treatment for motion sickness, shell shock and stomach disorders, as well as the side effects resulting from cancer therapy. This led to the cultivation of *Duboisia* once again becoming a commercial proposition. Now the hyoscine-rich leaves of a hybrid of two *Duboisia* species are exported in powdered form to pharmaceutical companies in many parts of the world.

Healing growth *Aborigines have long known of the medicines to be found in Australia's rain forests. They once used the seeds of palm-like cycads to combat infection, and a type of sword bean was used to treat burns and to soothe aches and pains caused by rheumatism, broken bones and even leprosy. Recently, Western science has noted the medicinal potential of the rain forests. Duboisia (or corkwood) trees and kangaroo apples are already much in use, and research on plants such as the Moreton Bay chestnut may yield a cure for some cancers.*

NATURE GOT THERE FIRST

To make life easier, mankind has invented scissors for shearing, rods for fishing, pliers for gripping, sieves for filtering, pots for storing, hypodermic syringes for injecting, nutcrackers for opening shells. But in these, as in so many matters, other forms of life had found similar solutions ages before.

SECRET WEAPONS AND ARMOUR

Man has perhaps devoted more ingenuity to means of attack and defence than to any other activity. But over thousands of years animals too have evolved weapons that far surpass the basic tooth and claw.

Beyond conventional weaponry The navies of the Byzantine Empire used Greek fire, a blazing concoction possibly of petroleum and phosphorus, to incinerate their opponents, and Renaissance tyrants despatched their foes with a range of poisons. But over the centuries mankind has made only limited use of chemical weapons – at least until the release of mustard, chlorine and phosgene gases over the trenches in the First World War. But the animal world has for thousands of years had the ability to call upon a vast arsenal of gases, poisons, syringes, fluids, burning essences and appalling smells. The bombardier beetle, when provoked, fires a caustic cocktail at its attacker. It does so by means of a swivelling 'gun turret' in its abdomen that throws out 50 jets of irritant vapour, each with an explosive click, and at boiling point.

Whip scorpions shoot acid vapour

Explosions and vapour are created in a thick-walled chamber in the abdomen. Darkling beetles squirt a foul-smelling liquid from their abdomens; but they are not as quick on the draw as the bombardier beetle and often get eaten before they can open fire. Lubber grasshoppers, when alarmed, ooze phenol and quinones, both insect repellents, and whip scorpions emit an acid vapour akin to tear gas. Giant millipedes have made an even more effective adaptation by spraying cyanide from pores along the sides of their bodies. Swallowtail caterpillars have the ability to exude a repellent smell if attacked; they carry this defence into their adult form and, when a number of swallowtail butterflies are together, in times of danger they can put out a powerful chemical miasma to protect the group.

Best avoided The variety of animal poisons are all designed to serve similar purposes – subduing a meal to the point where it can be eaten without a struggle, or warning off enemies. On land, poisons are mostly the weapons of reptiles, amphibians and insects, though a number of moles and shrews inject paralytic saliva into their worm prey as they sink their teeth into it.

Generally, animal poisons are effective against the size of prey that is most useful to the poisoner. A cobra or viper, for example, will strike at a small mammal, administering a mixture of blood and nerve poisons, then pull back to await results. Collapse and unconsciousness are swift, and the snake can then swallow its prey. To strike at a human, therefore, is a waste of time and venom – the size slows down the action of the poison, and even if it works, the victim cannot be eaten. So a snake avoids such an encounter if possible.

Similarly, there is little point in a warning poison being too deadly – the recipient will not live to learn the lesson or pass it on to others, and the striker will still be threatened. Toads, for instance, ooze from their warts a poison that instantly afflicts any attacker, especially a dog, with acute nausea and vomiting. An animal so warned will not attack a toad again.

On the other hand, the brilliantly hued arrow-poison frog of South America exudes from its skin a venom so deadly that as little as 1 oz (28 g) of it could wipe out the population of a fair-sized city. A single milking of poison from the Australian fierce snake, which grows to about 8 ft (2.4 m) long, may be capable of killing 250 000 mice. But the fierce snake has never been known to kill a human. Not so, however, the funnel-web spiders that have killed a number of people in Australian cities. Their venom contains a puzzling ingredient, atraxotoxin, which has little effect on most creatures but is deadly to monkeys and humans. Certain wolf spiders cause not only intense pain to humans, but afflict them with ulcers that rot both skin and flesh.

The armour bearers An early sophistication in human warfare was the development of means of self-preservation while inflicting damage upon the enemy. Hence helmets, then chain mail, then plate armour. Whatever chain mail's advantages in lightness, a well-delivered mace or sword blow could painfully drive its component links into the flesh of the wearer. Plate armour, however, deflected such blows even if its weight made retaliation difficult.

The problems that beset armourers occurred to insects at least 500 million years ago. In most cases, they came up with more efficient answers. Like the man-at-arms, all insects consist of a soft interior within a hard shell – in their case an outer skeleton, or exoskeleton, made of a cellulose-like substance called chitin, formed in layers like plywood. This in turn is covered with sclerotin, a hardening agent that turns the chitin into the heavy body armour of beetles and has evolved too into sharp-edged cutting tools or weapons.

As with armour, the exoskeleton is made up of cylinders inflexible themselves, but able to bend where they join. The limbs, too, are armoured, with joints controlled by muscles within the exoskeleton. An exoskeleton has the disadvantage that it will not grow with the insect. It is therefore shed periodically, exposing a soft, elastic layer beneath; this permits a day or two of rapid growth before it, too, hardens.

Armoured advantage The tank had its first success at the First World War Battle of Cambrai in 1917, where its ponderous advance, wreathed in noise and exhaust fumes, and its indifference to small-arms fire, trenches and barbed wire, helped the British to make a spectacular breakthrough.

Among its distant ancestors were siege towers whose sides were protected by hides as they were trundled up to the enemy's walls, and a Roman infantry manoeuvre in which legionaries locked shields above and about the flanks of an advancing formation. This tactic was known as the testudo, or tortoise: however, since it married all round protection with manoeuvrability it is perhaps more reminiscent of a creature the Romans never encountered, the armadillo.

A native of South America and the southern USA, the armadillo is one of the few mammals that has evolved its own armoured defence. It consists of overlapping plates of bone covered with scales and joined by leathery skin into a near-impenetrable shell that extends over both head and tail. With its powerful limbs and tough claws, it is also a notable burrower, able to tunnel to depths of 5 ft (1.5 m) or more. If attacked in its burrow, an armadillo braces its scaled plates against the ceiling and its feet against the floor, making it difficult to budge, while presenting an armoured stern to its adversary. Despite its weighty protection, the armadillo is a fine swimmer, though it has to swallow air to give it buoyancy – in principle, not so very different from that of the amphibious tanks that clambered up the D-Day beaches in June, 1944.

Seaside detractions During the Second World War, many nations were forced to contemplate the possibility of seaborne invasion, devoting considerable ingenuity

to devices for preventing enemy troops gaining a foothold on their beaches, while at the same time preparing to make similar assaults on enemy beaches. Training was given a highly authentic flavour, to the point of causing real casualties.

In one series of exercises that took place in Northern Queensland, Australia, in the summer of 1943-4, hundreds of soldiers and sailors were injured and a number were killed. But the cause of the casualties had nothing to do with the defence. Men writhed in agony on the sand, scarred with purple weals, or collapsed unconscious and drowning in the shallows.

The perpetrator was a mystery, and remained so until 1955, when it was positively identified as *Chironex fleckeri*, a transparent and almost invisible box jellyfish that has probably been responsible for more deaths in tropical Australian waters than crocodiles and sharks together. It trails bunches of tentacles that, if laid end to end, would stretch 100 yd (90 m) or more, and which are covered with minute stings, amounting to millions in all. It has

In armour clad *The tankman's wise practice of battening down hatches under attack was preceded by the armadillo which rolls into a stony ball. It is a measure that baffles most enemies, but in both cases leaves the practitioner conspicuously vulnerable to superior force.*

been estimated that the stings contained in only 3-8 yd (3-7 m) of the tentacles can easily lead to death through paralysis of the breathing muscles, while lesser stings inflict serious burns and scarring.

Chironex is not the only hazard to be found in the shallows of warmer seas. There is also the tiny blue-ringed octopus whose bite can lead to respiratory failure within 90 minutes. It feeds upon crabs, which it paralyses by poisoning the water about them. A particularly unpleasant hazard for walkers in the shallows is the stonefish, a rock-like creature that lies half-buried in sand rather like an antipersonnel mine. If it feels a disturbance in the water, it erects 13 sheathed spines along its back. An unwary foot placed upon one will, by its own weight, strip the sheath and drive the spine deep in. At the same time, it crushes a poison gland at the base of the spine and floods the wound with venom. The pain is so excruciating that the victim becomes irrational. Delirium and hours of agony follow, but patients generally recover.

More deadly are some of the cone shellfish, whose prettily patterned shells are much prized by collectors. They are better left alone, however, for they make an endless supply of barbed darts like tiny harpoons. When disturbed they fill the darts with venom and plunge them into the attacker. Human victims feel little pain, but may lapse into unconsciousness within an hour and die of toxaemia shortly after.

Borrowed plumage A sea slug's brilliant coloration warns divers to give it a wide berth, and most other creatures treat it with respect, too. Yet it possesses no obvious weapons or armour – no claws, shell or snapping teeth. The secret of its seclusion lies in the waving, fern-like growths that cover its body, many of which shoot a barbed, poisonous thread into anything that touches them.

The odd thing is that the sea slug does not produce these venom cells itself. It gets them instead from its diet of sea anemones, eating and digesting the entire anemone except for the stinging cells in its tentacles. They pass through the slug's body to the ends of its 'fronds', turning them into a highly efficient defensive overcoat.

Sonic bombardiers Submarine-seeking underwater microphones of the Second World War first revealed that beneath the waves there existed not the silent world that had been supposed, but a cacophony of whistles, shrieks, clicks, howls and groans that are the voices of the inhabitants. Particularly vociferous are the whales and dolphins which communicate with each other by sound. They navigate by it, too, through measuring the interval between a click and its echo as it bounces off some distant object, in much the same way as a ship takes echo soundings.

It is now also thought that whales may use sound as a weapon. In a sperm whale's skull, the organs produce air pressures that, translated into sound, could reach an intensity of 265 decibels – at least 150 decibels higher than can be comfortably absorbed by the human ear. Fish and squid exposed to such a level would be killed by it,

or at least rendered helpless, as would humans subjected to the explosion of a stun grenade. Dolphins, too, produce short, intense bursts of sound that they fire into shoals of small fish, causing them to scatter. This enables a dolphin to set its 'sights' on a single fish and track it down.

TRANSPORT AND NAVIGATION
Of all the technological advances made in the last century or so, few are more striking than improvements made in ways of getting from one place to another. Yet many of these methods, from jet propulsion to direction finding, had been discovered by animals long ago.

The wheel Man invented the wheel some 5000 years ago – but it is not true that, as popularly believed, Nature never got round to it. Some minute bacteria swim with the aid of their flagella – hairlike structures that thrash behind their bodies, driving them along. Each flagellum is attached at its base to a body within the cell wall that acts like a rotary motor. These motors drive the bacterium, enabling it to swim through liquids or skim across solid surfaces.

Although Nature solved the engineering problems of a rotating axle on a microscopic level, she has never got around to producing a large wheel for her creatures. This may be because the wheel is, in the last analysis, a poor means of locomotion – it is efficient on smooth, tarmac roads but next to useless

where there are boulders, tree stumps or boggy ground. As most animals have to contend with uneven terrain daily, it may well be that walking on legs is universally the most efficient means of locomotion. Engineers designing robots that have to move over uneven ground are now abandoning the wheel and looking instead at six-legged, insect-like structures.

Ladybird

Keeping in touch Great ingenuity and millions of man hours have been invested in developing the different parts of the information system in a modern aircraft. There are the Pitot-static tubes to provide data on air speed, the aerial for the Instrument Landing System, the Angle of Attack probe that shows the angle of wing to airflow, aerials for radar and identifying friend or foe, the ultra-high frequency communications radio, and a good deal more besides. All these require still more computers to feed everything into a data system for the pilot. It is remarkable that so much knowledge, memory and information can be crammed into so small a space.

Few insects, though, would be much impressed. They already receive similar information, together with many other messages essential to their well-being, via a pair of hair-like feelers, or antennae, on the head. The antennae carry tens of thousands of sensitive cells for direction finding, scenting, testing temperature and humidity and many other tasks, according to the needs of particular species. Some of these receptors are geared to distinguish between

Honeybee

Concord of wings Some
of the most sophisticated methods
of high-speed aircraft navigation and
control were anticipated aeons ago by insects.

a whole library of smells, others to reject all others and home-in on only one or two. Female silk moths, for instance, emit a scent that a male can pick up from miles away if the wind is favourable. Bees combine scent and colour sensitivity to identify a profitable food source. They will fly past almost any other blossoms upon sensing the odour and brilliance of a field of oilseed rape.

Honeybees' antennae are also alert to the atmosphere of the hive. If the temperature rises above a desirable level, the workers simultaneously fan their wings, and some go out in search of water to cool it. Species of ant that protect sap-sucking aphids for the sake of the syrup they secrete use their antennae to induce them to part with it; they tap signals on the aphids' backs.

Another parallel between flying insects and aircraft instrumentation is instanced by the Johnston's organ, a mechanism at the base of the antennae that reacts to air currents. The stronger the current, the more impulses the organ conveys to the insect's muscular system, causing its wings to beat harder. Thus flight speeds are kept constant. The organ also helps the insect to maintain course with one wing injured. One antenna directs more muscle power to the damaged member, while the other throttles back the whole wing to synchronise movement.

Beaming in The alacrity of dung beetles in tracking down a cow pat is remarkable. The technique is, in fact, not unlike that used by German aircrews on night-bombing missions during the Second World War and known as *Knickbein* (Crooked leg). In this, a powerful transmitter directed two slightly overlapping radio beams at the target. While the pilot flew along them, he heard a continuous note in his headphones, but if he diverged to right or left, he heard bursts of dots or dashes until he corrected his course. Finally, a signal directed across the beams indicated that the target had been reached. A dung beetle, lacking outside aid, flies a figure-of-eight course across and against the wind until its antennae pick up the odour of a cow pat. The beetle flies across the odour

trail to establish both outer limits, then flies on a zigzag course between the two until the scent suddenly ceases. At this point it drops down, usually right on target.

Easy floaters Jellyfish are supremely well adapted to their environment in the sunlit upper waters of the ocean. Negatively buoyant, like a submarine with its saddle tanks flooded, a jellyfish rides just beneath the surface trailing a mass of stinging tentacles that kill and enmesh any small fishes or crustaceans, such as shrimps, they touch before guiding them under the central bell to its mouth. Being 96 per cent water, jellyfish float with little effort, propelling themselves with a gentle, pulsating movement not unlike the rhythmic opening and closing of an umbrella. The bell-like body expands, filling with water, then the outer rim contracts, driving it forth again.

Stamp and go One of the better adapted denizens of the soft floors of shallow seas is the razor shell bivalve. For much of its life, most of its body, which is 8 in (20 cm) long, is buried, the shell protecting it from mud and grit. Two siphons suck in water, from which it extracts food and oxygen.

Despite its sedentary existence, a razor shell is capable of an impressive display of burrowing speed. About half its mantle is occupied by a muscular foot that extends to haul the shell down. At the same time, the bivalve expels two powerful jets of water from its siphons, rather like the air hoses used to blow away sand in underwater archaeology. These blast a hole in the sediment and help to thrust it ever deeper.

Fluid movement Many animals, among them worms and slugs, depend on hydraulics to get about. They move not by the working of muscles on joints but by the interaction of muscles and fluid pressures. An earthworm, for instance, is a muscular, fluid-filled tube. As the fluids cannot be compressed, contracting its muscles causes a worm to stretch and push its sharp end into the soil. When the muscles are relaxed, the worm gets shorter and fatter

Door beetle

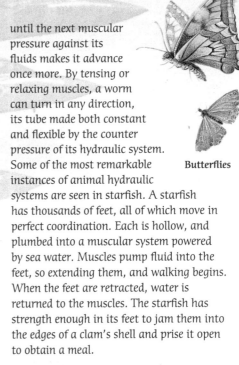
Butterflies

until the next muscular pressure against its fluids makes it advance once more. By tensing or relaxing muscles, a worm can turn in any direction, its tube made both constant and flexible by the counter pressure of its hydraulic system. Some of the most remarkable instances of animal hydraulic systems are seen in starfish. A starfish has thousands of feet, all of which move in perfect coordination. Each is hollow, and plumbed into a muscular system powered by sea water. Muscles pump fluid into the feet, so extending them, and walking begins. When the feet are retracted, water is returned to the muscles. The starfish has strength enough in its feet to jam them into the edges of a clam's shell and prise it open to obtain a meal.

Jetfoil progress Fossil-seekers along the cliffs of Dorset in southern England derive great satisfaction from the large spirals of ammonite remains dating from 400 million years ago. The monumental appearance of these ammonites might suggest that they could have pursued only ponderous paths across the floors of prehistoric seas. So it is surprising to learn that their closest living descendant is the streamlined squid, one of the swifter sprinters of the sea.

Longhorn beetle

An ammonite fossil with its outer face eroded away reveals that, despite its massive appearance, the shell enclosed air chambers that would have enabled the creature to float. Its squid descendants shed their shells and translated the air chambers into a propelling mechanism. A squid draws water into its mantle and expels it through a funnel – jet propulsion so powerful that it sometimes rockets the creature above the surface. Generally, a squid moves backwards, but it can instantly change direction by changing that of its funnel, rather as a vertical take-off aircraft alters the direction of its jets. Side fins like the planes of a submarine adjust the angles of ascent and descent. With its swift reactions, huge camera-lens eyes and an armament of ten sucker-bearing tentacles and a powerful beak, the squid is among the best-equipped of ocean predators and, like its ammonite ancestors, shows little restraint as to size. There are perfectly successful finger-length squids, and a 50 ft (15 m) long specimen was washed up on a New Zealand beach. Portions of tentacle found in the stomachs of whales suggest that there may be squid in the oceanic abysses that would make the New Zealand specimen look like a minnow.

Other marine employers of jet propulsion include scallops. To move themselves over sand and rocks they snap their valves, or shells, shut by means of powerful hinge muscles, sharply expelling a gout of water. The technique is probably more important as a means of keeping the scallop upright on the seabed than for moving it any distance,

Firefighters Protected by an asbestos safety suit, a fireman can withstand, at least for a short time, the high temperatures of a waste-oil fire. Similarly, the seeds of the protea flower (inset) are covered by bracts of tough, asbestos-like fibre, enabling them to survive the passage of a bush fire. In this way the plant steals a march in recolonising the landscape.

but even so, a jet-propelled leap, however brief, is useful when avoiding such slow-moving predators as starfish.

PLANT DEFENCES
Though seemingly vulnerable, plants have long been able to ensure their continuance. Some methods have human parallels, others are more subtle and advanced.

Fire insurance Asbestos cloth, used as a blanket to smother kitchen flare-ups or to make protective clothing for firemen, is a fairly recent development. But Nature has long had its own means of fighting fire. Once the seeds of South Africa's national flower, the sugarbush, *Protea cynaroides*, have been fertilised, they become covered by bracts of tough, asbestos-like fibre. These bracts will not reopen until after a bush fire has scorched them and passed on. Then the seeds emerge to colonise the fire-cleared land.

Peter Pan elixir One of mankind's most wistful yearnings, often reflected in legend and story, has been to discover the elixir of perpetual youth. It seems that certain plants may have achieved it but, as in the story of Faust, it has a bitter aftertaste. The balsam fir tree for example discourages insect damage by secreting a hormone that prevents their larvae

from maturing, and therefore from reproducing. The hormone will work even when the tree has become newsprint. By way of contrast, the garden flower ageratum produces a hormone that speeds an insect larva's development to an adult state, but renders it dwarfed and sterile.

Borgias of the plant world Tansy, milkweed and dogbane are plants that defend themselves from grazing animals with a bitter taste, and all are poisonous. Milkweed contains a heart poison that kills many insects, though caterpillars of the monarch butterfly thrive upon the plant and also secrete the poison to make themselves distasteful to insect-eating birds.

Defence by injection The nettle hair works like a hypodermic syringe. The slightest brush against it causes it to push into the skin, whereupon a bulb at the root squeezes a mixture of histamine – a source of human allergies – and a poison akin to wasp venom, into the unwary victim. Defence is made the more effective by the leaves on the edge of a clump dealing a more painful sting than those in the centre. The reason may be that the centre contains older plants.

TAKING TO THE WATERS
Essentially landlubbers, humans have been slow to exploit the watery world. And even in some of their best techniques, insects have long preceded them.

High-speed skaters In this overcrowded planet there can be few niches that, over aeons, some creature has failed to evolve a means of occupying. Long before skaters discovered the joy of gliding over the smooth surface of a frozen lake, several genera of insects, generally called pond skaters or water striders, had learned to move across the water surface with considerable speed and agility, exploiting the surface tension, the force that holds water together as a film.

An insect that falls in the water has to lift several times its own weight to get out, and generally finds it impossible. Pond skaters have long, very thin legs that spread their weight and allow them to skitter across the surface with each thrust of their middle legs while steering with their hind legs. They are fierce hunters, preying on insects that fall into the water. Other insects that make use of the surface tension are rove beetles of the genus *Stenus*. When alarmed, they can release a chemical that lessens the drag of the surface film on their rear legs, helping them to pull forwards in a swift, controlled slide across the water.

Breathing tube Towards the end of the Second World War, some German U-boats were fitted with a retractable tubular vent that could be raised above the surface to take in air, enabling the craft to run on diesel engines while submerged, and at the same time recharge its electric motors.

The air-vent, or snorkel, enabled U-boats to remain operational yet relatively safe from the watchful eyes of Allied destroyers. Ingenious though it was, it was scarcely new, not by a million years or so. The water scorpion is one of several insects that make use of a similar device and for similar reasons – to be both operational and invisible. Its long tail, which gives it a passing resemblance to the land scorpion, is in fact a breathing tube that the creature thrusts above the surface of a pond edge or ditch while its front end clings to a weed stalk under water, watching for prey.

An even more advanced adaptation has been made by rat-tailed maggots, the larvae of drone flies that live in ponds. The maggot can extend its tail upwards as much as 6 in (15 cm) to reach the surface. It is a true snorkel in that it supplies oxygen to gills in the maggot's rear end.

Spider under water The story goes that at Toledo in Spain in 1538, the Emperor Charles V and his court were invited to witness two Greeks climb inside an upturned cauldron holding a lighted candle between them. The vessel was then lowered into the river. When it was raised again a few minutes later, the assembled company was astonished to see that the men's clothing was still perfectly dry and that the candle still burned brightly. And so the diving bell was born. But not until the 18th century was a practical diving bell developed, to

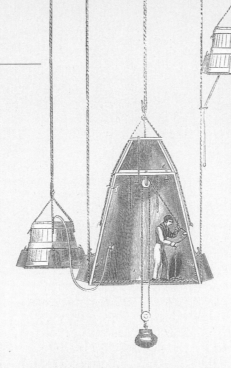

which air was sent down in weighted casks, to enable men to work under water within it for several hours.

A small brown spider whose behaviour closely mirrors the diving bell principle is the water spider *Argyroneta aquatica*, which is found in ponds and still waters across most of the temperate parts of Europe and Asia. Though not physically different from many species of land-based spiders, it spends most of its life under water, where it builds a silken platform anchored between reeds or pondweed stalks. When this is completed, the spider goes to the surface several times, each time returning with a bubble of air trapped between its back legs and abdomen, which it releases below the platform, causing the silk to bulge upwards and form a perfect, air-filled diving bell.

There the spider awaits passing prey, revisiting the surface from time to time to replenish its air supply. Females also build diving bells with sealed nursery chambers for their eggs in the upper part. When the spiderlings hatch, they chew their way into the main chamber where they remain and grow for a few weeks before venturing into the pond. Most of them climb to the bank, stretch a silken sail to the wind and blow away in search of a new patch of water.

Beetle divers For insects, as for humans, diving bells have their limitations. For true underwater freedom of movement, the most efficient method so far discovered is the

Subaqua club Successful early diving bells were open-bottomed and made of wooden staves bound with iron. Air was sent down in weighted casks and drawn up inside to replenish the supply. Far less ponderous is the silken bell (below), the home of a water spider. Its owner keeps it well provided with air, brought down from the surface in bubbles trapped between its legs.

20th-century aqualung, worn strapped to a diver's back. This method was in fact evolved aeons ago by the great diving water beetle, a creature of weed-filled ponds and the still shallows of lakes. It renews its air supply by pushing its rear end just above the surface and slightly lifting its wing cases to draw air into two breathing pores, or spiracles. Air is also trapped under the wing cases and forms a bubble round the fine hairs at the end of the abdomen. These air supplies together are sufficient for an hour or so of underwater hunting. The beetles are ferocious predators, with massive jaws that can disembowel a tadpole with one bite.

Upside-down world Another creature that carries an air supply about with it is the backswimmer, or water boatman. Its long hind legs are used in unison, like a pair of oars, giving it a fair turn of speed across a pond – or rather, across the undersurface of a pond. The backswimmer hangs downwards from the underside of the water surface. It does not possess gills, and must constantly renew the air bubble trapped in a channel between lines of hair on its abdomen and in direct contact with the insect's spiracles or respiratory tubes, enabling it to breathe under water.

This curious upside-down stance appears to be a hunting adaptation – the insect preys on mosquito larvae, which it detects by means of sensitive hairs on its rear legs, and stalks them unseen from beneath.

Lifejacket support Weddell seals inhabit the shores of Antarctica, remaining there feeding on fish and squid even when the seas freeze over. To find fish such as cod they have to go deep. Weddell seals with depth gauges strapped to them have been recorded as reaching 1600 ft (490 m), making them among the deepest-diving seals.

The seals sleep at breathing holes with their snouts pushed through into the air while their bodies hang straight down. They keep themselves in position by inflating their throats with air – an ability they share with other seals – so that it pushes them up to the surface in much the same way as a lifejacket supports a person in the water and enables him to breathe.

Inviting light Curving trails of coloured light (below) help to entice customers into a fairground. The female glow-worm (right) has a similar plan as she swings her bright tail to attract a mate out of the night. The difference is that the fairground requires a generator and energy consumption to produce its effect, while the glow-worm achieves it chemically and without effort.

MAKING LIGHT

Fire apart, instant illumination was impossible for humans until batteries were invented. Yet for aeons, many creatures have been efficient light producers.

Elfin lights Various species of fireflies, those glowing sprites of tropical nights, occur in India, Southeast Asia, South America and the warmer parts of Europe and the USA, where they are sometimes known as lightning bugs. They are actually

beetles that flash light from their abdominal organs. Displays vary from isolated sparkles to the breathtaking orchestrations of large groups that are a feature of moonless nights in Burma. In one South American species, the female on her own displays 11 pairs of green lights and a ruby-red glow at her head. In all species, the light is produced by a chemical known as luciferin, stored behind areas of transparent cuticle backed by dense tissue that probably acts as a reflector.

The 'fire' of the fireflies is a misnomer, for the light they produce is cold and, in energy terms, remarkably efficient. Whereas most electric bulbs waste 97 per cent of their energy in heat, a firefly concentrates 90 per cent of its effort into light. The glow emerging from so tiny an animal, though scarcely dazzling, is sufficient to read a printed page. Poor Japanese students, it is said, used fireflies to illuminate their nocturnal studies, and in parts of South America the flies were enclosed in perforated gourds for domestic lighting.

As far as the insects are concerned, their main reason for glowing in the dark is to advertise their readiness to mate. The males perform aerobatics, making light patterns that are answered by the females, each species producing its own characteristic recognition signals. Like naval night signals, these are remarkably precise. A male emits pulses of light that, after an exact interval, are answered by a female of the same species. Only if the timing and response are correct will a male fly over to visit a female. The females of one large predatory North American species, however, have learned to mimic the female signals of a smaller species. When the eager males arrive, they are quickly eaten.

Green for stop Most glow-worms, too, are in fact beetles – the wingless females or larvae of certain species of firefly. The common European glow-worm of damp hedgerows and meadows is most active in June and July, when the wingless females ascend tall grass stems and hang head down, twisting their bodies to expose the greenish lanterns under their rear ends. The winged males can home-in on this tiny signal from at least 100 yd (90 m) away,

though it seems that, if alarmed, the female can douse the light at will.

Glow-worm larvae, by contrast, emit an intense green light if they are disturbed, suggesting that their glow is intended to frighten off predators. If so, it is not always successful – it is not unusual to see frogs lit from within by a meal of glow-worm larvae.

Aglow in the deep Creatures that dwell in the ocean's uttermost depths have only rudimentary eyes, or none at all. Any form of light would therefore have little place in the Stygian blackness of their world. However, in the twilight zone that exists 1000-8000 ft (300-2440 m) below the surface, many crustaceans, squids and fish produce bioluminescence, or 'living light', for either attack or defence. Most light up by means of luciferin, the same substance used by fireflies and glow-worms. Others, however, support luminous bacteria that live in pouches distributed about their bodies. From this arrangement the host gets light and the bacteria get nourishment.

Most bioluminescence in sea creatures is blue-green, but gold, red and orange lights also occur. The illuminations are arranged in various ways – in patterns and whorls, in double or treble rows like lighted portholes, as lights on head or belly, or as glowing fleshy growths hanging beneath the chin. Such adaptations would certainly help the males and females of various species to find and identify one another in the gloom, but might also make them conspicuous to predators. Not necessarily, say some marine biologists – the lights scattered about a body may well resemble faint motes of sunlight or moonlight filtering down from above, and so camouflage its outline.

Lights out Bioluminescence from luciferin has the advantage of being controllable by its producer, but it is not easy for creatures using luminous bacteria to switch off the light. Some hosts achieve control by pumping oxygenated blood to or from their guests. Others simply cover them with a thicker layer of skin when necessary. The flashlight fish has a large, bacteria-filled light pouch under each eye. It cannot switch these off but it can swivel them inwards,

which has the same effect and plays a major role in its defensive repertoire. When pursued, these fish swim briefly in a straight line with lights ablaze, then abruptly douse them while changing direction.

Compleat anglers For centuries, fishermen have used lights to entice fish, and it seems certain that some species of the twilight zone use bioluminescence in the same way. Hatchet fish, for instance, have lights on their undersides, and appear to descend on their prey in the manner of a helicopter making a night landing.

The numerous species of angler fish wave a luminous bait on a 'fishing rod' above their open jaws. Over millions of years, the first spine of the dorsal, or back, fin has separated from the others, moved forwards and lengthened into a rod – sometimes short, sometimes long and slender – that can be waved about by muscular contractions. All rods have a luminous lure on the end, and are cast ahead in the way a fly fisherman does. When some curious fish closes in to investigate, the lure is drawn gently back towards the angler's mouth. Its lower jaw suddenly drops down and the gill covers expand, exposing a cavity easily able to engulf prey that is actually larger than the angler itself. The victim is swept in, the jaws clamp down, spearing it on the inward-curving teeth that draw it down whole into the expandable stomach.

As well as having a luminous tip on the end of its long dorsal fin, a viperfish has rows of lights along its sides and 300 more light organs inside its mouth. Its snake-like body gives it a fine turn of speed and it rushes upon its victims with jaws agape. Bemused by the glare of lights the victims stay immobile long enough to be impaled on the viperfish's forward-pointing fangs.

Lights of love Some biologists speculate that, as breeding time approaches, it is possible that the pattern and colour of a deep-sea creature's luminosity may intensify. Male lantern fish, for instance, have large bright lights over their tails, and the tail lights of females are smaller and borne on the underside, serving to distinguish the sexes; different species are

identified by the number of light rows along the flanks. It may be that, in the same way as fireflies, underwater animals also use lights to indicate their readiness to mate.

PLANTS AS BUILDERS AND ENGINEERS

Long before the rules of hydraulics were formulated, or the mechanics of building structures understood, plants had ironed out the problems. Some of their solutions indeed pointed out the ways that human craftsmen should go.

Pumping power A manufactured suction pump can raise water no more than 33 ft (10 m) before the weight of the water counteracts the atmospheric pressure, so breaking the lift. But a tree can raise water to ten times this height. The tree's 'pump' is powered by the sun – as water evaporates from the leaves, so more is drawn up to take its place through myriad tiny tubes in trunk and branches. These tubes are very thin, which prevents the rising column from breaking, and the chemicals taken up on the way adds to its cohesion. In this way, a medium-sized oak may draw up as much as 140 gallons (637 litres) of water in a day.

By contrast, the aerial roots of some orchids, in contact with neither soil nor water, are covered in a thick tissue called velamen. When dry, this is white and easily compressed. But, like blotting paper, it absorbs the slightest touch of damp, and in the rain it darkens and fills to capacity, channelling moisture to the aerial roots.

Cool domes Dwellers in hot countries have long been aware of the advantages of the sphere as the body with the smallest surface area in proportion to its content, thereby reducing evaporation and heat absorption. Hence domes were built. But many desert plants preceded mankind in this. One such is *Euphorbia obesa*, a spurge of the South African deserts, half of whose global shape, like the Earth itself, is always in shade.

Climbing gear A rattan palm in tropical rain forest can grow to about 650 ft (200 m) long, clawing its way through the tree canopy by means of fishhook-like barbs at the tips of its leaves – reminiscent of the pitons or ringed spikes, used by mountain climbers. A rattan's hollow stems, which when dried are strong and enduring enough to be made into garden furniture, carry water along the length of the plant.

Botanic architecture The rib structure of the huge leaves – 7 ft (2 m) across – of the giant South American water lily, *Victoria amazonica,* can support the weight of a child. These leaves were Joseph Paxton's inspiration for the pattern of the cast-iron ribs of the Crystal Palace, built for the Great Exhibition of 1851 in London. Further models may be found in the many tall trees that grow in the shallow soils of the rain forests. These push out

Lily power Sir Joseph Paxton, gardener and builder, was the first in Europe to coerce the Victoria amazonica water lily (above) into flower. Later, impressed by the load-bearing capabilities of the leaf's ribs (right), he translated them into cast iron to make the framework of the Crystal Palace that housed the Great Exhibition of 1851 (below).

aerial roots from their trunks for additional anchorage and support, giving them the appearance of the flying buttresses that embrace many Gothic churches and cathedrals. These arched stone props that rise from piers to support upper walls and towers are added to prevent the soaring structure from collapsing outwards under the weight of a vaulted roof.

Building to last Reinforced concrete is perhaps the most characteristic component of modern building. Yet this invention was not the work of an architect or engineer, but of a French gardener, Joseph Monier, who in 1867, having studied the skeletal structure of plants, converted some of their patterns into steel. The skeleton of a dead saguaro cactus, for example, closely resembles the reinforcing cage of a ferro-concrete column. This cactus also has a pleated outer skin, which marvellously expands to store water against periods of drought. The fibrous material of many other plant skeletons also share the same steely characteristics of elasticity and resilience. It is these for instance that enable a corn stalk, standing 5 ft (1.5 m) high though less than ½ in (13 mm) thick, to bear the weight of the plant's head while it whips back and forth at the behest of the wind.

Liquid engineering In the human world, hydraulic-fluid power offers competition to both electrical and mechanical power. Fluids are used in vehicle braking and

transmission systems, in mass-production units, and even structurally, as in large rockets, whose thin skins are given more 'body' by internal fluid pressure.

But, as so often, Nature got there first. The structural role of fluids can be seen in a cut flower, which droops if left without water. This is because its stem is composed of highly flexible cellulose fibres stressed by the internal pressure of sap. When this dries out, the pressure lessens and the flower wilts. The same effect can be seen on the foliage of trees after prolonged drought.

Natural windows Modern skyscrapers seem to be constructions solely of concrete and glass. Windows provide the maximum of light for the minimum of weight, and modern developments such as tinted glass diffuse the light to acceptable levels. But plants had learned the benefit of windows long before the days of office blocks.

Fenestaria, a plant of the South African desert, grows mostly underground with only a small window of translucent cells on the surface. The cells are of two types – those that block harmful ultraviolet rays, and those that diffuse the light to a workable level for the green photosynthetic tissue, the part that uses sunlight to produce food.

Sauna plants Rather like a Nordic health enthusiast, the alpine snowbell generates sufficient heat to melt a hole in snow, so permitting it to flower in early spring. So does the skunk cabbage of North American marshes. It respires rapidly and generates enough heat to melt the snow early in the year, creating an atmosphere around it that may be 35°C (63°F) higher than the air temperature. Insects are tempted out to forage in its warmth, and so pollinate it.

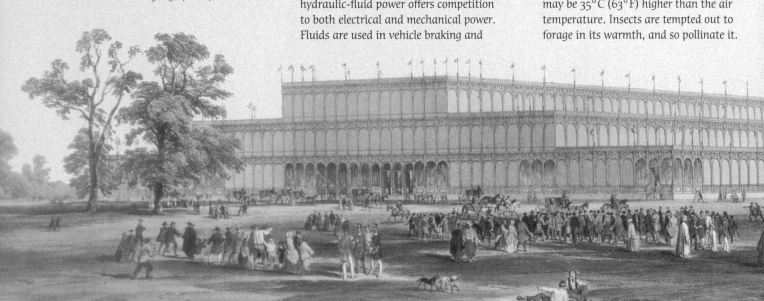

ANIMALS AS CRAFTSMEN

Anticipating human pioneers, many animal species have improved their lot by skilful use of the materials about them.

Builders in water Out of the rough, raw materials of the planet Earth mankind has fashioned mighty cities, towering pyramids, exquisite tapestries, translucent porcelains and ships of hardened steel. But predating the advent of humans, there were animal builders whose works were mightier and certainly more cost-effective.

Take, for example, those of the tiny sea creatures known as Foraminifera, which extract minerals from water and turn them into protective casings for themselves. They multiply by division, breaking up into many small parts that quit the original shell and then begin to make new coverings of their own. A pinch of beach sand might contain 50 000 abandoned shells, but over the ages the animals who made them have created limestone rocks and contributed not a little to the fabric of cities.

Other persistent builders in limestone are the coral polyps of tropical seas. Growing in colonies of uncountable billions, they create delicate abstract statuary, rainbow-hued underwater gardens of waving tentacles, tropical islets of breathtaking beauty and long coastal breakwaters that can rip the heart out of the weightiest storm-driven wave. They flourish only in sunlit waters, because they share their stony cells with algae that produce food by trapping sunlight and absorbing carbon dioxide from the water – which also helps the polyps to build their skeletons.

Yet some coral reefs plunge down to regions of perpetual darkness. This is because, over a long period, the seabed has gradually subsided, taking the coral upon it down into the twilight. The polyps died, but their skeletons provided a strong platform for the next layers of coral to grow upon. And so it went on, generation upon generation, the topmost one bathed in sunlight not far below the surface. In some cases coral ancestry is venerable indeed. Borings into some reefs have shown that the lowest coral layers were formed at least as much as 80 million years ago.

Quickset cement The swiftlets of southern Asia and Indonesia are creatures of the air, awkward on the ground but total masters of aerobatics. Even their nesting places have an aerial quality, often being no more than the sheer wall of a cave without benefit of ledge or cranny. Not that they require them, for unlike other birds, they neither collect nor use building material, but produce it entirely by themselves.

Both parents take part in the building and, as mating time approaches, their salivary glands swell greatly. Having chosen a suitable rock face, the birds fly to it, taking turns to dab it with saliva, tracing the outline of the base of the nest. Their saliva is sticky and thread forming. Each layer quickly dries and, as it does so, another layer is dabbed on top, gradually building up to form a white translucent cup shaped into the curve of the rock.

Wattle and daub Combining clay, twigs, straw, animal hair and dung into a material for building houses is common practice from Kenya to Kent to Clonkilty. The craft was perfected around 2000 years ago in the Bronze Age and continues still. But mankind may have been anticipated by another species, the ovenbirds of South America, which build domed mud nests, some the size of cannonballs, that bear a remarkably close resemblance to the bakers' ovens of yesteryear.

Both parents share the work, which begins when a tropical downpour gives them sufficient mud to work with. An estimated 2000 beakfuls of clay are needed for a nest, not counting leaf stalks, grasses and animal dung. The entrance hole is small, and the brooding chamber has an even smaller entrance hole, reached by an inner corridor. With this defence and the stoutness of the sun-baked walls, the little fortress is virtually impregnable.

Paper chase It has been suggested that humans got the idea of papermaking from the wasp's normal building material, though the end product is more akin to papier-mâché than, say, to newsprint.

All the same, the manufacturing processes have a good deal in common. Just as the paper mill makes wood pulp and mixes it with a binding agent, so the wasp chews up old dry wood and mingles it with saliva to make pellets. Each pellet is carried to the nesting site and stretched into a strip that is added to the walls or interior. Though the finished structure may appear light and fragile, it does in fact have considerable strength due to the wood fibres in the pulp all being laid longitudinally. The grey colour of wasps' nests is due to the insects' preference for obtaining their raw material from weather-bleached fence posts, boards, gates and the like.

Certain species of tropical wasps make another, and somewhat curious, use of their saliva. They place small, hardened 'panes' of the substance in the outer shells of nests to make windows. The puzzling aspect of this

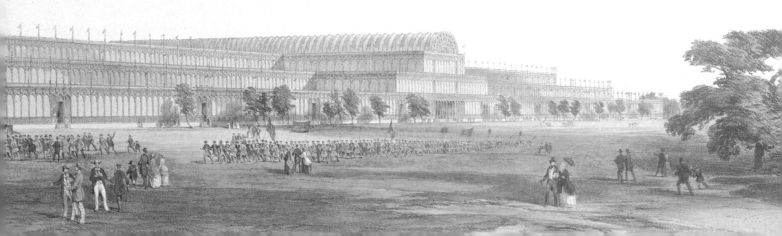

is why these particular species should want the interior of their homes illuminated, A possible explanation is that the 'windows' are in fact more of a camouflage device to break up the surface of the nest and blend it with its background.

Pottery lessons Instead of manufacturing nests from papery material, certain species of wasp opted long ago to use clay. The solitary female potter wasp, for example, collects fragments of the material, mixes it with water brought for the purpose, and carves it into strips with her forelegs.

When she has enough strips, she joins them together to make a round container like an old-fashioned wine flask, with a tall narrow neck and a small hole in the top – a form that is believed to have influenced the development of primitive pottery. Her task completed, the wasp drops in a few caterpillars stung into paralysis, lays an egg on top and stoppers the bottle with a plug of clay. When the egg hatches, the grub feeds on the caterpillars until it reaches the adult stage and breaks out of its clay cell.

Ever sharp Tooth enamel is one of the hardest of natural ceramic-like materials, but as many humans know, it wears thin in the end. Yet rodents – from husk-nibbling harvest mice to cable-gnawing rats to tree-felling beavers – inflict far more wear and tear upon their teeth than humans do and without loss or injury. Their teeth remain sharp because a one-sided sharpening action, rather like that of a man sharpening a plane or chisel blade, takes place. As the animal nibbles with its incisors, the softer bone at the back wears down at a faster rate than the enamel-covered front, so maintaining a permanently sharp edge.

Silken contradiction The lightness and apparent fragility of a spider's web is famed. But in fact the material from which it is made is, weight for weight, stronger than steel, more elastic than rubber and tougher than the stuffing of bullet-proof waistcoats. Recent developments in the synthetic production of spider silk have opened new vistas in surgery, space technology, as well as in the manufacture of such things as

rip-proof parachutes and tow-ropes.

Even garden spiders can manufacture a repertoire of threads, each with a different purpose. They use five pairs of glands in the abdomen, each of which operates independently of the other. One pair provides the workaday dry thread on which the spider moves round its web, or unravels to shin up and down. Another makes the sticky threads that interlace the web for trapping prey and a third produces the mass of fine filaments that are wrapped about an entrapped insect to secure it until the spider is ready to eat it. Then there is the gland for making the glue that anchors the dry thread, the gland for manufacturing the soft covering for the egg cocoon, and the spinnerets that roll out whatever type of silk is required. Finally, there are the delicate claws on the feet that haul the threads into position on the web, correct tension and feel for the telltale quiver that announces the arrival and entanglement of prey.

Bee varnish The chief material used in the interior furnishing of a beehive is wax. This the honeybees make themselves, but also important is another substance called propolis, a form of resin that has to be obtained from outside. It is scraped from the sticky buds and secretions of certain trees and used to plug gaps and crevices in the hive to maintain the temperature. It is also mixed with wax to make it go further, or to raise its melting point in hot weather.

Propolis also has an emergency application. If a large creature, such as a mouse, enters the hive, the bees sting it to

death. But as they cannot move the carcass, they cover it with an airtight layer of propolis, so embalming it. Legend also has it that propolis obtained from bees was one of the ingredients in the secret recipe for the lacquer used by the great Italian violin makers, like Amati and Stradivari, to enhance the resonance of their instruments.

GO FORTH AND MULTIPLY
Distribution is essential to the continuance of plant species, and nowhere has evolution shown more ingenuity than in matching methods to environments. Some natural devices have anticipated means of human transport by thousands of years; others have directly inspired human invention.

Borne on the wind Dandelion parachutes provide more subtle services than a random distribution of seed. The plant has a built-in barometer, ensuring that seeds are released on a dry, warm day, and on a steady, rather than a gusting, breeze so that they will be scattered as far as possible. Like the 'chutes of paratroops, those of the dandelion are designed to deliver their burdens gently, and in upright stance.

A Norway maple seed has a wing stretched over ribs, giving them a twist like the aerofoil of an autogiro. When released in a light breeze, the wings revolve in a circle, carrying the seed 100 yd (90 m) or more from its 30 ft (9 m) parent tree.

The gourd-like fruit of the tropical liana *Zanonia macrocarpa* opens to release

Taking to the breeze High-speed photography reveals that dandelion seed dispersal and a mass parachute drop have much in common. Both take advantage of weather and wind conditions – the dandelion preferring a steady breeze to ensure wide distribution. Like the paratrooper, the seed is intended to arrive upright; hence its elongated shape and the barbs at its upper end to anchor it in a suitable berth on landing.

squadrons of winged seeds neatly stacked one on top of the other. The most aerodynamically efficient of all seed wings, they circle gracefully in gently rocking flight. In a light wind they glide like gulls, spilling air from their wing edges.

At the beginning of the 20th century, the seed's efficiency was brought to the notice of the pioneer aviators Ignatius and Igo Etrich of Bohemia (now in the Czech Republic), who modelled a number of successful gliders upon it. In gratitude and acknowledgment, the first of them was christened Zanonia.

A kite-like structure is the model chosen as a seed box by the Chinese lantern, or winter cherry, *Physalis alkekengii*. It consists of a rounded, lightweight skeleton over which is stretched a light, orange-red, papery skin. Once detached from its stalk, a boisterous breeze will carry it over considerable distances, together with the inner berry containing its seeds.

In fine summer weather, aircraft may encounter clouds of dust-like pollen and spores at heights of up to about 20000 ft (6000 m). From here, in still conditions, it takes the lighter spores – those of some fungi, for instance – perhaps as much as a month to descend to the ground. At this height, even a light wind will carry them for prodigious distances, on pioneering voyages of world-wide discovery and colonisation.

To sea in a husk For much of his early history, Man was deterred from long voyages and colonising distant lands by his inability to make

seaworthy craft and the difficulty of carrying sufficient supplies for the journey.

The coconut palm, *Cocos nucifera*, solved both these problems aeons ago by developing fruit encased in a hard shell that provides it with a light, triple-hulled, almost unsinkable craft that can wander the oceans until cast up on some faraway shore. After germination, the seedling has, within the beached shell, its own food store to live upon until it becomes established – nourishing fruit pulp with rich, fatty oils, and even a supply of liquid in the form of coconut milk.

Velcro transport The seeds of the burdock plant are encased in burrs that consist of hundreds of tiny hooks. These engage themselves with the fur or clothes of passers-by in very much the same manner as Velcro fastenings. Even more affectionate are the burrs of the burr marigold, which, when seen through a magnifying glass closely resemble the barbed fishing harpoons used by the Eskimo and Inuit peoples.

Plant ballistics Long before armies devised means of hurling projectiles at one another, plants had already devised catapults, guns and other mechanisms to help them disperse seed.

One such is the seed capsule of sphagnum moss, which, as it ripens, contracts to about a quarter of its size, and compresses the air within it to about double the pressure of a car tyre. Towards the end of the contraction, the lid blows off and the spores within are fired out with a pop, as though by an air gun, 1 ft (30 cm) or so into the air – no mean achievement for a 2 mm gun.

The Mediterranean squirting cucumber, *Ecbellium elaterium*, is recorded as shooting forth a stream of juice and seeds under pressure to a range of 12 yd (11 m) at a muzzle velocity of 20 mph (32 km/h) or more. A rather different method has been adopted by an American form of pumpkin, *Cyclanthera explodens*. Its fruit consists of two shells clamped together about a curved lever, held down under pressures that are at least ten times greater than that within a car tyre. When ripe, the shells spring apart and the lever flies out like a sling, projecting the seeds up to 3 yd (2.7 m).

Avoiding predators *Painted sweetlips are found on the Great Barrier Reef, Australia, where they live in the lagoon channels between the corals. There is little cover there to hide from predators so the fish find safety in numbers by forming tightly packed shoals. Unlike the fishes of the corals, they are conservatively coloured and do not rely on bright hues for camouflage.*

Index

Page references in roman type denote a text entry. Numbers in *italics* refer to a picture caption.

A

Acknowledgments

The sources of the photographs are listed below. The following short forms have been used; FLPA Frank Lane Picture Agency, OSF Oxford Scientific Films, PEP Planet Earth Pictures. Abbreviations: T=top; TL=top left; TC=top centre; TR=top right; C=centre; CL=centre left; CR=centre right; B=bottom; BL=bottom left; BC=bottom centre; BR=bottom right.

(SPINE) Bruce Coleman Ltd/Stephen J Krasemann (COVER) David Hall **1** NHPA/Peter Johnson **2** Minden Pictures/Jim Brandenburg **5** NHPA/Kevin Schafer **6** OSF/Michele Hall **10-11** Bruce Coleman Ltd/Jeff Foott **11** TR Bruce Coleman Inc/Jeff Foott **12** T Survival Anglia/Jeff Foott C Bruce Coleman Inc B DRK/Fred Bruemmer **12-13** T Telegraph Colour Library **13** TR Auscape/Jan Aldenhoven BL NHPA/Peter Johnson **14** T Michael and Patricia Fogden C Bruce Coleman Ltd/ Jane Burton CR Bruce Coleman Inc/Michael Fogden B Bruce Coleman Ltd/David Hughes **15** TL Ardea, London/P Morris C Bruce Coleman Ltd/Frans Lanting BR Minden Pictures/Frans Lanting **16** TR Science Photo Library/Sinclair Stammers B OSF/J A L Cooke **17** TL Auscape/Anne & Jacques Six TR OSF/J A L Cooke CL NHPA/Stephen Dalton **18-19** Science Photo Library/ Dr Jeremy Burgess **20** TR PEP/William M Smithey Jr **21** TR FLPA/R Tidman B Bruce Coleman Inc/Alan Blank **22** Bruce Coleman Inc/Kim Taylor **23** CL Bruce Coleman Inc/Jeff Foott CR Photo Researchers Inc/Nuridsany et Perennou **24** TL Bruce Coleman Ltd/Gunter Ziesler B Ardea, London/Liz Bomford **25** TR Chris Mattison **25** CR OSF/Fred Bavendam **26** TR OSF/Rudie H Kuiter C Bruce Coleman Ltd/Jane Burton **26-27** B Bruce Coleman Inc/Alan Blank **28-29** B OSF/Doug Allan **29** TR Bruce Coleman Ltd/Jose Luis Gonzalez Grande C DRK/D Cavagnaro **30-31** T Bruce Coleman Inc/Simon Trevor/D B **31** TL OSF/Carol Farneti CR NHPA/Karl Switak **32** TL Biofotos/ Heather Angel BR Bruce Coleman Ltd/Kim Taylor **33** TR Bruce Coleman Ltd/Dennis Green CL Animals Animals/Zig Leszczynski BC NHPA/Karen Clanelli **34** TR Photo Researchers Inc/ Steinhart Aquarium/Tom McHugh CR OSF/Mark Hamnlin **34-35** B Auscape/Mark Newman **35** CR NHPA/Roger Tidman **36** TL Nature Photographers/Ian Wyllie B Nature Production/ Toshiyuki Yoshino **36-37** T Bruce Coleman Inc/Roger Wilmshurst **37** TL NHPA/E A Janes TL Natural Science Photos/Kennan Ward TR BC ©Nature Photographers/Ian Wyllie **38** C Cichlid Press/Ad Konings B Ardea, London/P Morris **39** TR Biofotos/Jeremy Thomas CL OSF/Tony Allen BR Chris Catton (Green Films) **40** TL TR Bruce Coleman Ltd/Frans Lanting BR Bruce Coleman Ltd/ David Hughes **40-41** T Survival Anglia/Annie Price **41** TR Bruce Coleman Ltd/Antonio Manzanares BL OSF/G I Bernard **42** TL OSF/Martyn Colbeck TR Bat Conservation International/Merlin D Tuttle CL OSF/Martyn Colbeck **42-43** B OSF/Martyn Colbeck **43** T PEP/James D Watt B OSF/Rafi Ben-Shahar **44** TR Neil Rettig Productions BC Bruce Coleman Ltd/Hans Reinhard BR Auscape/ Jean-Paul Ferrero **45** TL Auscape/Kathie Atkinson C Bruce Coleman Inc/Jen & Des Bartlett BR NHPA/A.N.T. B Bruce Coleman Ltd/John Cancalosi **46** C © Jeff Rotman BR Nature Production/Atsushi Sakurai **47** T (BOTH) Animals Animals/Joe McDonald CR Bruce Coleman Inc/Kim Taylor **48** BR Bruce Coleman Inc/Rod Borland **48-49** T Bruce Coleman Ltd/Jack Dermid **49** CL Bruce Coleman Inc/E R Degginger BR Bruce Coleman Inc/Bob & Clara Calhoun **52** T Bruce Coleman Ltd/Christian Zuber BC Bruce Coleman Ltd/Jen & Des Bartlett **53** TR Survival Anglia/Rick Price CR OSF/Ben Osborne BR Survival Anglia/Jen & Des Bartlett B Photo Researchers Inc/Wiliam & Marcia Levy **54** TR Bruce Coleman Inc/© David Madison 1989 B Ardea, London/Y Arthus-Bertrand **55** T Nature Photographers/Hugo Van Lawick BR Bruce Coleman Ltd/Jose Luis Gonzalez Grande B Animals Animals/© Charles Palek 1981 **56** C BR Dr Rudolf Diesel **57** T NHPA/Anthony Bannister TL Photo Researchers Inc/Pat & Tom Leeson BR Ardea, London/John Mason **58** TC TR CR Dr Rudolf Diesel BL Animals Animals/Donald Specker **59** BR Bruce Coleman Ltd/Hans Reinhard **60** L Bruce Coleman Inc/Laura Riley BC Bruce Coleman Inc/Jen & Des Bartlett BR Minden Pictures/Frans Lanting **61** TL TC National Museum, Blomfontein/Mr L H du Preez BR OSF/Roger Brown **62** TL CL B Survival Anglia/Deeble/Stone **63** TR Bruce Coleman Ltd/Gunter Ziesler C PEP/ M Ogilvie CR Bruce Coleman Ltd/C B Frith **64** TR Neil Bromhall C Nature Production/Satoshi Kuribayashi **65** TC Colin Monteath Hedgehog House, NZ Tui de Roy TR Minden Pictures/Michio Hoshino CR PEP/A & M Shah B PEP/Jonathan Scott **66** BL NHPA/Manfred Danegger BR Bruce Coleman Inc/M P Kahl **67** TL Nature Production/Fumitoshi Mori BR Bruce Coleman Inc/Erwin & Peggy Bauer **68-69** OSF/Richard Packwood **70** C Bruce Coleman Ltd/Stephen J Krasemann BL Universite de Lausanne/© Michio Hoshino 1993 **70-71** T PEP/Jonathan Scott **71** TR Edward S Ross **72** T Survival Anglia/Matthews/Purdy TR PEP/Jonathan Scott BL Jeff Foott **73** TL Bruce Coleman Inc/Des & Jen Bartlett CR Auscape/Jean-Paul Ferrero BR NHPA/Manfred Danegger **74** Hugo van Lawick **75** T TR Auscape/Jean-Paul Ferrero CR Ardea, London/Francois Gohier BR Minden Pictures/Frans Lanting **76** T TR OSF/Norbert Rosing **77** TL Biofotos/Heather Angel CR Jeff Foott BR Bruce Coleman Inc/Erwin & Peggy Bauer **78** R DRK/John Cancalosi BL Auscape/ C A Henley **79** TL PEP/Anup & Manoj Shah C NHPA/Stephen Dalton CR Anthony Bannister Photo Library/Richard du Toit/ABPL BL Universite de Lausanne/Michel Genoud **80** T OSF/Konrad Wothe **80-81** B Bruce Coleman Inc/K & K Ammann **81** C OSF/David MacDonald BR Bat Conservation International/Merlin D Tuttle **82** CR © Jeffrey L Rotman B Minden Pictures/Jim Brandenburg **83** TL Photo Researchers Inc/Len Rue Jr **83** C Bruce Coleman Ltd/Erwin & Peggy Bauer BR DRK/ Stanley Breeden **86-87** B Bruce Coleman Inc/Jeff Foott **87** TR NHPA/Laurie Campbell C Bruce Coleman Ltd/Jen & Des Bartlett **88** T Michael and Patricia Fogden BR NHPA/Anthony Bannister **89** C Survival Anglia/Des & Jen Bartlett BL Minden Pictures/Frans Lanting BR Animals Animals/ Hans & Judy Beste **90** C Animals Animals/Charles Paler **90** BR Photo Researchers Inc/Zig Leszczynski B Photo Researchers Inc/© J H Robinson 1977 **91** TR PEP/Marc Webber BL Biofotos/Heather Angel BR PEP/Robert Franz **92** TL **92-93** T Bruce Coleman Inc/Jen & Des Bartlett **93** T DRK/C Allan Morgan CR Photo Researchers Inc/Craig K Lorenz BL Survival Anglia/Andrew Anderson BC Bruce Coleman Inc/Wayne Lankinen BR Survival Anglia/Claude Steelman **94** TL DRK/Dwight R Kuhn BR Bruce Coleman Inc/Jeff Foott **94-95** T DRK/Peter Pickford **95** BR OSF/Mike Birkhead **96** TR Auscape/D Parer & E Parer-Cook C OSF/J L A Cooke CR Auscape/Hans & Judy Beste **97** T Auscape/M P Kahl **98** BL Auscape/D Parer & E Parer-Cook **98-99** T NHPA/David Woodfall **99** CR DRK/Wayne Lynch **100** TL DRK/Tom Bean C DRK/Wayne Lankinen **101** TL OSF **102** T Michael and Patricia Fogden C Photo Researchers Inc/© Scott Camazine 1991 B Photo Researchers Inc/Toni Angermayer DGPh **103** T Bruce Coleman Ltd/C B & D W Frith C Bruce Coleman Inc/P Ward CR Minden Pictures/Frans Lanting **104-5** Bruce Coleman Ltd/Jan Taylor **106** TL TC Nature Production/Hiroshi Ogawa BL PEP/Steve Nicholls **106-7** T Michael and Patricia Fogden **107** TR Ardea, London/Peter Steyn **108** TL Premaphotos CL Photo Researchers Inc/Noble Proctor C Bruce Coleman Ltd/Marie Read BL Photo Researchers Inc/Fletcher & Baylis BC Nature Production/Hiroshi Ogawa **109** T Bruce Coleman Ltd/Kim Taylor **110** T DRK/Belinda Wright TL NHPA/Peter Johnson BR Minden Pictures/Frans Lanting **111** TR CR NHPA/George Gainsburgh BL Bruce Coleman Ltd/Gunter Ziesler **112** R Nature Production/Yozo Nakagawa **113** TL Bruce Coleman Inc/Michael Gallagher TR Bruce Coleman Inc/Keith Gunnar BC Michael and Patricia Fogden BR Animals Animals/Doug Wechsler **114** TR PEP/Richard Matthews BR NHPA/Alan Williams B Auscape/Francois Gohier **115** C NHPA/A.N.T. BR PEP/Richard Coomber **116** CL DRK/ Jeff Foott B NHPA/Alan Williams **117** TL PEP/Richard Coomber TR Minden Pictures Jim Brandenburg 1980 **118** CL Bruce Coleman Ltd/Jen & Des Bartlett BC Auscape/Beste/Young **118-19** T Nature Production/Tadashi Shimada **119** CR NHPA/G I Bernard BR Survival Anglia/Mike Linley **120** TR FLPA/T S de Zylva **120-1** B Bruce Coleman Inc/Pat Lanza Field **121** TL Animals Animals/John Trott BR Survival Anglia/Dennis Green **122** TL Bruce Coleman Ltd/Jane Burton BL PEP/Peter Scoones **122-3** T NHPA/Otto Rogge **123** TC PEP/Philip Chapman TR PEP/Hans C Heap CR Bruce Coleman Ltd/Dr Frieder Sauer **124** TL Nature Production/Hiroya Minakuchi TC Ardea, London/Francois Gohier CR Michael and Patricia Fogden BR Ardea, London/John Clegg **124-5** T Auscape/Christine Deacon **128** TL OSF/Peter Parks **128-9** T NHPA Peter Parks **129** TC OSF/Scott Camazine TR NHPA/Stephen Dalton C Photo Researchers Inc/Scott Camazine **130** T Dr Glenn D Prestwich BR Anne & Jacques Six **131** T Michael and Patricia Fogden CL Nature Production/Kazuo Unno BL BC Anne & Jacques Six **132** Karl Ammann **133** TR Minden Pictures/ Jim Brandenburg CL DRK/Belinda Wright **134** TR Bruce Coleman Inc/K & K Ammann C Anthony Bannister Photo Library/Joan Ryder **135** TL Hugo van Lawick TR Nature Production/Jyuichi Yamagiwa CR PEP/Jonathan Scott **136** T Bruce Coleman Inc/Hans Reinhard BL OSF/Stan Osolinski **137** CL Anthony Bannister Photo Library/Lorna Stanton B © Jeffrey L Rotman/Paul Humann **138** TR NHPA/Henry Ausloos B Bruce Coleman Ltd/Leonard Lee Rue **139** T OSF/Owen Newman TR OSF/Richard Packwood BL OSF/Stan Osolinski **140** T Bruce Coleman Ltd/Mr Felix Labhardt B Ardea, London/M D England **140-1** T Photo Researchers Inc/Tom & Pat Leeson **142** TL CL BL Minden Pictures/Michio Hoshino **142-3** T Minden Pictures/Michio Hoshino **143** TR CR BR Minden Pictures/Michio Hoshino **144** TL CL CR DRK/Stephen J Krasemann **145** TL Norbert Wu C Nature Production/Hiroya Minakuchi **146-7** PEP/K Ammann **148** TL NHPA/Nigel Dennis BR Norbert Wu **148-9** T PEP/Kurt Amsler **149** CR Bruce Coleman Inc/ David Madison B Bruce Coleman Inc/Ron & Valerie Taylor **150** CL Anthony Bannister Photo Library/Clem Haagner B Anthony Bannister Photo Library/Robert C Nunnington **151** T Photo Researchers Inc/Jeff Lepore CR Photo Researchers Inc/© Kenneth W Fink 1982 BR Bruce Coleman Inc/Clem Haagner **152** R Ardea, London/Clem Haagner **153** TR Photo Researchers Inc/ J H Robinson CR Bruce Coleman Ltd/Dr Frieder Sauer BL Auscape/Michael Whitehead **154** TL PEP/Gary Bell C Auscape/Reg Morrison BR Auscape/Hans & Judy Beste **155** R Nature Production/Kazuo Unno BR DRK/Michael Fogden **156** T Auscape/Jan Aldenhoven **156-7** BC DRK/Stephen J Krasemann **157** TL Auscape/Erwin & Peggy Bauer BR Ardea, London/ S Roberts **158** TL TR Dr Jan Aldenhoven B Auscape/Esther Beaton **159** TL TR Sandra Vehrencamp BR Edward S Ross **162** TL PEP/Jonathan Scott C NHPA/John Shaw **162-3** T **163** CR Ardea, London/ D Parer & E Parer-Cook B PEP/Jonathan Scott **164** TL Bruce Coleman Ltd/Dr Frieder Sauer CL Auscape/Tui De Roy **164-5** T Auscape/D Parer & E Parer-Cook **165** T Bruce Coleman Inc/ M Borland CR Nature Production/Taro Takagi **166** B PEP/Anup Shah **167** TL Wyman P Meinzer TR NHPA/Stephen Dalton CL PEP/Jonathan Scott **168** L PEP/Peter David BC Bruce Coleman Inc/Alan Blank **169** TL Nature Production/Mitsuhiko Imamori CL OSF/Rudie Kuiter CR OSF/ Z Leszczynski B Bruce Coleman Ltd/Peter Ward **170** T OSF/Mantis Wildlife Films BC Nature Production/Satoshi Kuribayashi BR Nature Production/Mitsuhiko Imamori **171** TL National Geographic Society/Mark Moffett BC NHPA/A.N.T. BR OSF/Mantis Wildlife Films **172** T Ardea, London/Peter Steyn BL Bruce Coleman Ltd/Austin James Stevens BR Nature Production/Hiroshi Ogawa **173** T CR Minden Pictures/Mark Moffett BL Ardea, London/Valerie Taylor BC Nature Production/Hiroshi Ogawa **174-5** Minden Pictures/Jim Brandenburg **176** CL Biofotos/Soames Summerhays **176-7** C Bruce Coleman Ltd/Jean-Pierre Zwaenepoel **177** TR Bruce Coleman Inc/Tom Brakefield BR OSF/Fred Bavendam **178-9** B Andre Bartschi **179** TC OSF/Michael Fogden CR Loren McIntyre BR Michael and Patricia Fogden **180** L Bruce Coleman Inc/Nicholas Devore III TR Ian Redmond **181** TL Bruce Coleman Ltd/Gunter Ziesler BR The Jane Goodall Institute/Professor Kenji Kawanata **182** T Survival Anglia/L Campbell TL Survival Anglia/Tony & Liz Bomford **183** TL DRK/Belinda Wright TC DRK/Stanley Breeden R DRK/Belinda Wright B Bat Conservation International/Merlin D Tuttle **184** TL Auscape/Nicholas N Birks TR Nature Production/Masaru Kumagai **185** TL Ardea, London/John Daniels BR Bruce Coleman Ltd/Bob & Clara Calhoun **186** TR NHPA/Anthony Bannister C NHPA/Nigel Dennis **187** TL C Anthony Bannister Photo Library BR NHPA/A.N.T. **188** David & Anne Doubilet **189** TL DRK/M Cavagnaro C Bruce Coleman Ltd/Dr Frieder Sauer **192** TL Survival Anglia/Dr F Koster TR Michael and Patricia Fogden BL Tom Stack & Associates/W Garst **193** CR OSF/Raymond A Mendez/Animals Animals BC OSF/ P & W Ward **194** NHPA/G I Bernard **195** T Auscape/Kim Atkinson BR Nature Production/Shinji Kusano B OSF/Peter Parks **196** L Nature Production/Mitsuyoshi Tate Matsu TR Bruce Coleman Inc/Tom Brakefield BL OSF/Jim Clare **197** TL PEP/Jonathan Scott B Bruce Coleman Ltd/John Shaw **198** BL Minden Pictures/Flip Nicklin **198-9** T Comstock Photofile Limited **199** TR PEP/Nikita Ovsyanikov **200-1** T Bruce Coleman Ltd/Gordon Lansbury B OSF/Nortert Wu **201** T OSF/David Cayless CR OSF/P & W Ward **202** TR NHPA/Stephen Dalton CL PEP/Richard Coomber B Gerald Cubitt **203** TR NHPA/Rich Kirchner CR NHPA/Peter Johnson B OSF/Tui De Roy **204** CL NHPA/Steve Robinson BL PEP/Andre Bartschi BC PEP/John Downer **204-5** NHPA/Ralph & Daphne Keller **205** TC Bruce Coleman Ltd/W G Blake TR Bruce Coleman Ltd/Adrian Davies BR NHPA/John Shaw **206** TR © Jeffrey L Rotman/Paul Humann CL Ardea, London/V Taylor **207** TR Ardea, London/J M Labat CL PEP/Georgette Douwma CR Photo Researchers Inc/Steinhart

Aquarium/Tom McHugh BR Dr Giuseppe Mazza 208 B Auscape/Ben Cropp 209 T PEP/David Rootes C Ardea, London/Andrea Florence 210 R PEP/D Robert Franz 211 TL Bruce Coleman Ltd/Jen & Des Bartlett TC NHPA/A.N.T. BR OSF/Michael Goulding 212 C Aquila Photographics/Bill Coster BL Bruce Coleman Ltd/Rinie Van Meurs BC FLPA/Dembinsky 212-13 Science Photo Library/Claude Nuridsany & Maria Perenndu 213 BR Bruce Coleman Ltd/Rob Williams 214 TC NHPA/Stephen Dalton BL Bat Conservation International/Merlin D Tuttle 214-15 B Bruce Coleman Ltd/Frank Greenaway 215 TR NHPA/Stephen Dalton CL F A Webster/courtesy Professor D Pye 218 TL Ardea, London/David & Katie Urry TR Ardea, London/E Mickleburgh BL PEP/Hans Christian Heap 219 C Rudie Kuiter BR Premaphotos 220 BL NHPA/Eric Soder 220-1 T Nature Production/ Mitsuhiko Imamori 221 T Photo Researchers Inc/Pat & Tom Leeson CL Michael and Patricia Fogden CR PEP/Bill Wood 222 B Bruce Coleman Inc/K & K Ammann 223 TL Nature Production/ Norio Yamagata TR FLPA/E & D Hosking BC Edward S Ross 224 T Nature Production/Yukio Nanba BL Edward S Ross 225 T Rudie Kuiter BL Michael and Patricia Fogden BR PEP/Richard Matthews 226 TL PEP/Geoff du Feu B Michael and Patricia Fogden 226-7 T OSF/M P L Fogden 227 TR Nature Production/Satoshi Kuribayashi BL Michael and Patricia Fogden BR Animals Animals/Breck P Kent 228 CL Michael and Patricia Fogden CR PEP/P Losse B Nature Production/ Kazuo Unno 229 (INSERT) Nature Production/Johji Ohkata TL Nature Production BL BR Michael and Patricia Fogden 230 TL NHPA/Anthony Bannister TR Michael and Patricia Fogden BL DRK/Wayne Lynch BR OSF/Alastair Shay 231 T Nature Production/Katsutoshi Itoh BL Bruce Coleman Ltd/Jane Burton BR Nature Production/Mitsuhiko Imamori 232 TL Bruce Coleman Ltd/Stephen J Krasemann BL Edward S Ross BR Ardea, London/Jean-Paul Ferrero 233 TL Rudie Kuiter TR Auscape/Jean-Paul Ferrero CR Rudie Kuiter BC Ardea, London/Peter Steyn BR Animals Animals/Zig Leszczynski 234 TR Rudie Kuiter C Photo Researchers Inc/Tim Davis BL Auscape/ D Parer & E Parer-Cook 235 TR OSF/Michael Fogden BL Chris Mattison BC Ardea, London/Ron & Valerie Taylor 236 CR B Doug Perrine 237 TL OSF/Tom Ulrich TC Animals Animals/Ray Richardson CL Rudie Kuiter CR PEP/D Robert Franz BL Rudie Kuiter 238 TR Bruce Coleman Inc/ Joe & Carol McDonald BL Animals Animals/Zig Leszczynski B Bruce Coleman Ltd/George McCarthy 239 T Nature Production/Katsutoshi Itoh CR Edward S Ross B Photo Researchers Inc/Tom McHugh/Steinhart Aquarium 240 TL Gunter Ziesler CL Animals Animals/C W Perkins BC Anthony Bannister Photo Library/Rod Patterson 241 TR Bruce Coleman Inc/Jen & Des Bartlett BR Animals Animals/Raymond A Mendez 242 T NHPA/Peter Pickford 243 TR Auscape/Bill & Peter Boyle C Auscape/Kathie Atkinson BR Edward S Ross 244-5 Daryl Balfour 246 TL Mantis Wildlife/Densey Clyne TR Robert Harding Picture Library/Karachi Museum BR NHPA/A.N.T. 247 T PEP/Chris Huxley CR Ardea, London/Keith & Liz Laidler BR Comstock Photofile Limited 248 T DRK/M P Kahl BL Animals Animals/W Gregory Brown 249 CL Anthony Bannister Photo Library/Rod Patterson C Photo Researchers Inc/O S Pettingill B Auscape/Jean-Paul Ferrero 250 BL OSF/G I Bernard 250-1 T NHPA/Stephen Dalton 251 C Ardea, London/Jean-Paul Ferrero CR Photo Researchers Inc/Gregory G Dimijian 252 TR Animals Animals/E R Degginger BL OSF/Richard Packwood 253 TR FLPA/Philip Perry BR Doug Perrine 254 TL Bruce Coleman Ltd/Hans Reinhard C BR Michael and Patricia Fogden 255 TR Michael and Patricia Fogden BL NHPA/Norbert Wu BR Nature Production/Mitsuhiko Imamori 258 TR Bruce Coleman Ltd/ C B & D W Frith C Minden Pictures/Frans Lanting BL The Mansell Collection 259 TC Ardea, London/R J C Blewitt BR Bruce Coleman Inc/Leonard Lee Rue III 260-1 Hugo van Lawick 262 T OSF/Frank Schneidermeyer B OSF/Tom Ulrich 263 TL DRK/Fred Bruemmer BR Nature Production/Ryukichi Kameda B Science Photo Library/George Bernard 264 TR Nature Production/ Masahiro Iijima BL Ardea, London/Adrian Warren 265 T Animals Animals/Stouffer Productions BR Nature Production/Mitsuhiko Imamori 266 TR Bruce Coleman Ltd/K Wothe C Bruce Coleman Ltd/Frieder Sauer 267 TR The Bridgeman Art Library/Trustees of the British Museum (Natural History) B Animals Animals/Don Enger 268 BL Photo Researchers Inc/Nigel Dennis B DRK/ Stanley Breeden 269 T Bruce Coleman Ltd/Anthony Healy TR Ardea, London/Hans & Judy Beste BL Nature Production/Satoshi Okabe 270 T TL Bruce Coleman Inc/K Ammann CR PEP/Cameron Read 271 T TL Bruce Coleman Ltd/Brian J Coates C Ardea, London/C Clem Haagner BL PEP/ Jonathan Scott 272 T Bat Conservation International/Merlin D Tuttle TR OSF/Mills Tandy 273 TL OSF/Stan Osolinski CR OSF/J A L Cooke BL B Jacana 274 TR Doug Perrine/Norine Rouse CL Chris Catton (Green Films) B Jacana/Michel Casino 275 C Premaphotos/K G Preston-Mafham BR PEP/P Losse 276 CR Bruce Coleman Ltd/Jan Van De Kam B National Geographic Society/Bianca Lavies 277 TL Photo Researchers Inc/Lee F Snyder CR Nature Production/Mitsuhiko Imamori 278 T Michael and Patricia Fogden CR BR Premaphotos/K G Preston-Mafham 279 CR OSF/ J A L Cooke B Bruce Coleman Ltd/Jan van de Kam 280 T Bruce Coleman Ltd/Dr Scott Nielsen BL Biofotos/Heather Angel 281 TL OSF/Douglas Faulkner/Photo Researchers TR PEP/Peter Scoones BL Bruce Coleman Ltd/Jane Burton 282 T Doug Perrine C Jacana/Philippe Summ BR OSF/Neil Bromhall 283 TR Auscape/C A Henley BL Bruce Coleman Ltd/Jane Burton 284 TL PEP/Jonathan Scott TR Bruce Coleman Ltd/Francisco J Erize BC Ardea, London/Norman Tomalin 285 TL CL C Natalie J Demong 286 TR C Al Grotell © 1989 B © Jeffrey L Rotman 287 TR Biofotos/Ian Took BL PEP/Ken Lucas 288 (INSERT) R Bruce Coleman Ltd/Kim Taylor BR NHPA/E A Janes 289 TR Bruce Coleman Ltd/Kim Taylor TR Survival Anglia/Jeff Foott BL Bruce Coleman Ltd/Frank Greenaway 292-3 Minden Pictures/Flip Nicklin 294 T OSF/Doug Allan CR Minden Pictures/Flip Nicklin 294-5 B Animals Animals/R Kolar 295 TR Minden Pictures/Flip Nicklin 296 TC TC Biotica/Mark Carwardine BL Minden Pictures/Flip Nicklin 296-7 B Minden Pictures/ Flip Nicklin 298 CR DRK/Wayne Lankinen B Photo Researchers Inc/Mitch Reardon 298-9 T Jacana/ Manfred Danegger 299 CR Photo Researchers Inc/Ron Austing 300 TL Bruce Coleman Ltd/Mike McKavett BR Photo Researchers Inc/Fran Hall 301 C Michael and Patricia Fogden CR Jacana/Alain Devez BL Premaphotos/K G Preston-Mafham 302 TL PEP/Norbert Wu CL PEP/Christian Petron 302-3 C Rick Frehsee Productions 303 TL Press-tige Pictures Ltd/David Hall 304 TR Jacana/ Michel Denis-Huot CL OSF/Andrew Plumptre CR Minden Pictures/Frans Lanting 305 CL Nature Production/Mitsuyoshi Tatematsu BR OSF/Rafi Ben-Shahar 306 B Photo Researchers Inc/James R Fisher 307 T Photo Researchers Inc/Tom McHugh CL Photo Researchers Inc/R D Estes CR NHPA/Manfred Danegger BL Photo Researchers Inc/R D Estes 308 BL Survival Anglia/Bruce Davidson B Survival Anglia/Bob Campbell 309 TL Bruce Coleman Ltd/Jane Burton TC OSF/Doug Allan 311 T TL CL Bruce Coleman Ltd/G Dore R Michael and Patricia Fogden BC Biofotos/P J Herring

BR DRK/S Nielsen 312 TL Auscape/Hans & Judy Beste 312-13 C Bruce Coleman Ltd/Uwe Walz 313 BR Premaphotos/K G Preston-Mafham 314 TR CL Doug Perrine BR (BOTH) Ardea, London/ Valerie Taylor 315 T Bruce Coleman Ltd/Uwe Walz CR PEP/Christian Petron 316 L Kennan Ward BR PEP/Jonathan Scott 317 TR Edward S Ross B Nature Photographers/Hugo Van Lawick 320 R PEP/Jonathan Scott 321 TL NHPA/Stephan Dalton BC Bruce Coleman Ltd/Dr Frieder Sauer BR OSF/J A L Cooke 322 TL OSF/Paul Kay C PEP/Peter David BR NHPA/Burt Jones & Maurine Shimlock 323 TR Ardea, London/Valerie Taylor 324 (INSERT) FLPA/F Lane CR Bruce Coleman Ltd/Frans Lanting 325 T Bruce Coleman Ltd/Kim Taylor BR Bruce Coleman Ltd/Leonard Lee Rue III 326 TR Animals Animals/Raymond Mendez CL NHPA/George Gainsburgh BR NHPA/George Bernard 327 T Ardea, London/J P Ferrero BL Bruce Coleman Ltd/Jeff Foott Productions 328 TR Bruce Coleman Ltd/Jen & Des Bartlett BL Nature Photographers/E K Thompson 329 TL OSF/Renee Lynn TR FLPA/E Van Nostrand BC PEP/Jonathan Scott BR PEP/Nick Greaves 330 CR Bruce Coleman Ltd/Kim Taylor BL Bruce Coleman Ltd/Allan Power 330-1 T NHPA/Daniel Heuclin 331 B Nature Production/Mitsuhiko Imamori 332 T NHPA/Manfred Danegger B Jacana/ Jacques Blanc 333 CL Survival Anglia/Jeff Foott R Jacana/Philippe Verzier BL Jeff Foott 334 R Bruce Coleman Ltd/Kim Taylor 335 CL PEP/Georgette Douwma CR Swift Picture Library/Thomas Dressler 338 R Tom Stack & Associates/Thomas Kitchin 339 BR NHPA/Hellio & Van Ingen 340 TR Survival Anglia/Maurice Tibbles BR Bruce Coleman Ltd/Frans Lanting 341 TL NHPA/Peter Pickford CL C Photo Researchers Inc/John Mitchell CR Bruce Coleman Ltd/Kim Taylor 342 TC PEP/Mary Clay BL Bruce Coleman Ltd/Dr John Mackinnon 342-3 T OSF/Ben Osborne 343 CR Auscape/Wayne Lawler 344 TL TR 344-5 B 345 TR C BR NHPA/Hellio van Ingen 346 T Survival Anglia/Jackie Le Fevre 347 BR Ardea, London/Ake Lindau 348 T Photo Researchers Inc/Tom McHugh TL Ardea, London/Adrian Warren BL Bruce Coleman Ltd/Peter Davey BR Bruce Coleman Ltd/Peter Davey 349 TR Magnum/Nichols/Boesche 350 TR Jeff Foott B Jacana/A Gandolfi 351 TL Premaphotos/Ken Preston-Mafham BL NHPA/Henry Ausloos BC Bruce Coleman Ltd/Gunter Ziesler 352 T Bruce Coleman Inc/Norman O Tomalin BR Bruce Coleman Inc/Peter Davey 353 TL NHPA/S Robinson TR NHPA/K Ghani 354 TR Survival Anglia/Joan Root C Survival Anglia/Lee Lyon 355 TL OSF/ Cynthia Moss 358 TC FLPA/Steve Maslowski BC Premaphotos/R A Preston-Mafham 358-9 T Survival Anglia/David Shale 359 BR The Bodleian Library, Oxford/MS Douce M 723 p.617 360 CR NHPA/Anthony Bannister BL Ardea, London/John Mason 360-1 T PEP/Leo Collier 361 C Photo Researchers Inc/Steinhart Aquarium/Tom McHugh 362 T Bruce Coleman Ltd/ W G Blake BL Bruce Coleman Ltd/Dr Eckart Pott 362-3 C Bruce Coleman Ltd/Francisco Erize 363 T PEP/Jim Brandenburg B Nature Photographers/Paul Sterry 364-5 Ardea, London Francois Gohier 366 TL Colin Monteath Hedgehog House, NZ/Paul Ensor TR Auscape/Kev Deacon (INSERT) Norbert Wu 367 T L Michael and Patricia Fogden CL Norbert Wu BR Nature Production/Hiroshi Hasegawa 368 T Rick Frehsee Productions C Natural Science Photos/M Harvey 368-9 B Anthony Bannister Photo Library/Robert C Nunnington 369 TR ZEFA/Frans Lanting 370 TL Ardea, London/P Morris BR Norbert Wu 370-1 T PEP/Peter David 371 TR PEP/Richard Coomber C Auscape/Kerrie Ruth 372 TR Bruce Coleman Ltd/B & C Calhoun CL OSF/Martyn Colbeck C Zoologisches Institut der Universitat Zurich/Professor Rudiger Wehner BL Bruce Coleman Ltd/Jane Burton 373 TL NHPA/Morten Strange C Auscape/Jean-Paul Ferrero CR Bruce Coleman Ltd/Mr Jens Rydell 374-5 375 T B Minden Pictures/Michio Hoshino 376 CL Anthony Bannister Photo Library BR Aquila Photographics/Bill Coster 376-7 T Auscape/Ferrero/Labat 377 TR NHPA/ Stephen Dalton C Ardea, London/Jean-Paul Ferrero B Minden Pictures/Frans Lanting 378 BC Bruce Coleman Inc/Laura Riley 378-9 B Ardea, London/Liz Bomford 379 TL VIREO/A Morris B Mary Evans Picture Library 380 CL Animals Animals/Zig Leszczynski C Biofotos/Heather Angel BR Photo Researchers Inc/Tom McHugh 381 T Auscape/Jean-Paul Ferrero CL NHPA/Ivan Polunin BL OSF/ Peter Parks 384 TL Survival Anglia/M Wilding C NHPA/Roger Tidman 385 T DRK/Belinda Wright 386 T Ardea, London/Tony Bomford 386-7 C Network/H Silvester/Rapho 387 CL Natural Science Photos/P H Ward C PEP/Wayne Harris B Photo Researchers Inc/Pat & Tom Leeson 388 CL Ardea, London/Clem Haagner 388-9 B Minden Pictures/Frans Lanting 389 TC Photo Researchers Inc/Gregory K Scott C Aquila Photographics/Hans Gebuis 390 TR Steven Lee Montgomery BL Photo Researchers Inc/Robert Noonan 391 T Biophoto Associates TR NHPA/ C & S Pollitt 392 L Ardea, London/I R Beames B Science Photo Library/Martin Dohrn 393 T Nature Production/Paul Sterry BR Science Photo Library/Dr Jeremy Burgess 394-5 Science Photo Library/NASA 395 TL Science Photo Library/Simon Fraser C Survival Anglia/Joel Bennett BL Marine Systems/Thomas F Worthington 396 TR Nature Photographers/Colin Carver 397 C Magnum/David Hurn B Black Star, New York/© Cindy Karp 1992 398 TR Mary Evans Picture Library BR Ardea, London/Bob Gibbons 399 C South America Pictures B Italo Bertolasi 400 TL Ardea, London/John Clegg 400-1 B NHPA/Stephen Dalton 401 C Photo Researchers Inc/Gregory G Dimijian CR Photo Researchers Inc/Jack Dermid 402 C The Mansell Collection BL Punch 402-3 T 403 R Farrell Grehan 404 TL Minden Pictures/Frans Lanting BC Ardea, London/ Kenneth W Fink 404-5 T NHPA/Gerard Lacz 405 CL The Mansell Collection 406-7 T NHPA/ Stephen Dalton 407 C Bruce Coleman Ltd/John Murray BL Tony Wood BC BR Robert Opie 408-9 Auscape/Jean-Paul Ferrero 410-11 (BACKGROUND) Robert Harding Picture Library/Malcolm Robertson 411 C Mary Evans Picture Library 412 TR (BEE) The Bridgeman Art Library/Fitzwilliam Museum, Cambridge 412-13 British Aerospace Military Aircraft Division/G Lee 413 TR ET Archive/V & A Museum CR BC The Bridgeman Art Library/Fitzwilliam Museum, Cambridge 414 (INSERT) Biofotos BL Science Photo Library/A De Menil 415 TC The Mansell Collection TR OSF/John Cooke 416 C Bruce Coleman Ltd/Kim Taylor BL Aviation Picture Library 418 CL OSF/Deni Bown C Trustees of the British Museum (Natural History) 418-19 The Bridgeman Art Library 420 TC TR Science Photo Library/Jonathan Watts 420-1 (BACKGROUND) TRH Pictures/ E Nevill 421 TL Science Photo Library/Jonathan Watts TC Science Photo Library/Jonathan Scott 422 TC PEP/Gary Bell

TYPESETTING Elite Computersetting, Southampton, England
SEPARATIONS David Bruce Graphics Ltd, London, England
PAPER Nimrod Cartridge, UK Paper, Sittingbourne, England
PRINTING AND BINDING Fabrieken Brepols NV, Turnhout, Belgium

40-229-1A